ISSUES
IN EDUCATION /

An Anthology
of Controversy

ISSUES

IN EDUCATION

Edited by

With an Introduction by

An Anthology of Controversy

BERNARD JOHNSTON

Van Cleve Morris · RUTGERS UNIVERSITY

Houghton Mifflin Company · *Boston*

INTRODUCTION

SOCRATES DOUBTED his own wisdom. But he knew one thing with certainty: dialectic has a way of educing those ideas which lie at the heart of our perplexities. Somehow, the mind of man carries on the enterprise of thought most effectively when, like an ax, it is grinding against an object somewhat but not entirely like itself, i.e., another mind. If sparks fly, as they sometimes do, their flickering light is at least a symptom that we may be getting near the cutting edge of things.

Controversy is a special instance of dialectic, and although sometimes lacking in precision and focus, it is what we more ordinary mortals resort to, without a real Socrates among us, to plumb the source of our disagreements. The trick is to engage in controversy as nearly like dialectic as possible, thus to accentuate the positive gains that linguistic intercourse can be made to yield.

In the field of education this is never easy. There is hardly an area of human concern in which discussion more easily slips the harness of disciplined thought and rigorous insight. We are badgered and beset by a raucous counterpoint of views; and genuine controversy, at the outset so hopeful of harmonious issue or at least reasoned concord of mutual understanding, slides to the next lower level of discourse — mean argument.

One may reasonably ask, then, what fool would dare suppose that a book could be put together in which this retrogression is reversed so as to set us once again on the road of the higher polemics. If he asks, I offer him this book.

Bernard Johnston has dared, and won. He knows the dialectic temper and how it works, and he knows who can and who cannot carry educational controversy up to that platform of disciplined reflection where meanness is left behind in the continuing search for truth.

He has gathered in this place a symposium of articulate giants, men big with ideas and big with the words to say them. And he has put them to work discussing the big issues in the continuing educational debate. It is a round table of the most engaging character, a consortium of free minds wheeling their way to some of the finest expressions of the content and meaning of a truly human education. It is a conversation at once entertaining, discerning, and illuminating. The reader is invited to page one to listen.

VAN CLEVE MORRIS

Rutgers University
New Brunswick, New Jersey

v

PREFACE

THERE IS CERTAINLY NO DEARTH OF LITERATURE ostensibly designed to acquaint the prospective teacher with the demands of his profession. Histories of educational theory abound. Journals, yearbooks, statistical abstracts, and conference summaries abound. Smug formula books that promise facile salvation from the real or imagined ills of formal education bristle from library shelves. Moreover, the literature of education is glutted with texts that are either paeans to some wallowing platitude or busy tributes to the minutiae of school operation.

We need our histories, of course. And there is intrinsic justification for the studies offered by our more scholarly educators. Even educational evangelism, be it informed or spurious, propagated by retired military heroes, disenchanted taxpayers, or political extremists, has modest value in that it may excite public scrutiny of education — the traditionally neglected American enterprise.

However copious and diffuse the literature of education, as a teacher I have long felt the need for a textbook presenting educational issues in a format composed of historical and topical selections, a textbook that by exploiting the contributions of scientists, men of letters, philosophers, and educators ignores the modern fetish for self-consciously ingrown scholarship. *Issues in Education: An Anthology of Controversy* is, hopefully, a fulfillment of that need.

The anthology is ordered by the following assumptions: first, prospective teachers must be introduced to the atmosphere of controversy pervading their profession, an atmosphere frequently absent from the decorous classroom; second, potential teachers must examine contributions by philosophers, writers, and social critics who exhibit scholarship and conscience rather than soporific allegiance to doctrine; third, prospective teachers must be aware of historical arguments which define, nourish, and interpret modern debates in education. Admittedly, the objectives implicit in these assumptions cannot be fulfilled in one collection of readings. But a beginning is necessary. Consequently, this anthology is primarily conceived as an introductory text, although it should also prove relevant to advanced courses in the history and philosophy of education.

Each section of the text contains contemporary and historical readings pertinent to specific areas of debate. Part One, "Teaching as a Profession —

Past and Present Discontents," is devoted to the exacerbating paradoxes and disenchantments frequently experienced by the young and unwary teacher. Part Two, "Academic Freedom — A Problem in Definition," is composed of selections reflecting disparate attitudes and conclusions about a most volatile freedom. Part Three, "Traditionalism, Progressivism, and the Pendulum," and Part Four, "The Curricular Debate," present essays which define, in varying degrees of specificity, the broad and chronic controversy over *how* curricula should be constituted and taught in elementary, secondary, and collegiate institutions. Part Five, "Education and the Autonomous Ideal," contains essays reflecting comprehensive (and perhaps utopian) visions of educational reform. Broad in implication, the essays in Part Five consistently relate to themes and sub-themes encountered in earlier sections.

Obviously, the selections in this anthology do not represent all stations of argument encircling each controversy. Space does not permit a more comprehensive content. Moreover, I have used my nervous prerogative as editor when confronted with having to choose between "fair coverage" and the unexpendable. All opinions in controversy are not equal. An editor who places "equality" above excellence may enjoy a bland virtue of sorts, but little respect for his reader's patience and discernment is thereby shown. In the selection of material, only readings inherently complete or sufficiently developed were considered, so as to circumvent those molestations of meaning common to the anthology of dabs — to which, alas, many students are now subjected.

Of great assistance with many stages of research and compilation was Professor Van Cleve Morris of Rutgers University. Particularly valuable were his suggestions concerning basic format and his sedulous reading of manuscript.

I am grateful to Judith Ann Findlay and Helen Kochor for their surgery with the blue pencil and their cavalier acceptance of eyestrain over proofs.

Finally, if it were appropriate for an anthology to carry a dedication, Matthew Evans would be its recipient. He is not a sly tutor. He bestows his gifts helplessly. He is a teacher.

Point Richmond, California   BERNARD JOHNSTON
July, 1963

CONTENTS

ix

Part Three

TRADITIONALISM, PROGRESSIVISM, AND THE PENDULUM

Page 159

Part Four

THE CURRICULAR DEBATE

Page 259

I. *Liberal Education*

II. *Specialization*

III. *Humanities and Sciences: The Scholastic Schism*

Part Five
EDUCATION AND THE AUTONOMOUS IDEAL
Page 353

ISSUES
IN EDUCATION /

An Anthology
of Controversy

PART ONE

Teaching as a Profession —
Past and Present Discontents

READERS OF *Candide*, Voltaire's masterful satire, recall with disdainful
delight the antics of Dr. Pangloss, the jargon-spouting pundit who revels
in the admonition that "All is for the best in this best of all possible
worlds." With irritating frequency the pedant turns to his young student, Candide, and with eyebrows arched and body tensed exclaims the
joys of his shallow optimism. Candide, energetic and naïve, listens with
reverence; and the reader may curse impatiently for respite from the
interminable, self-congratulatory sermons of the good Doctor. But there
is no respite. Pangloss and his student stroll with a collecton of bizarre
companions through a series of calamitous adventures, events that
should discourage even the most stalwart believer in the Good, the True,
and the Beautiful. Finally, when Candide is about to matriculate with
honors for his obsequious allegiance to the self-styled optimism of Pangloss, Voltaire allows for his maturity. With his fellow sufferers, Candide avers that "We must cultivate our gardens," that men must eschew

3

abstract theories of optimism and tend to the weeds and brambles of their lives. Confronted with this rebellion, Dr. Pangloss confesses that he, too, had felt the dishonesty of his philosophy but had lacked the courage to shun its comfortable influence.

Voltaire's hatred of the sanguine optimist might well be resurrected and leveled at many spokesmen for education today. Cheery platitudes about the "joys of teaching" are too numerous to be tolerable. Conference speakers, gorged with gratuitous dinners, warm to their pleasant duties: we hear them extol the happy factories of education which are manned by rosy pedagogues, policed by beaming administrators, guided by knowledgeable school boards, and financed by a generous public sympathy. Our speakers comfortably refer to serious deficiencies in education as "problem areas." The euphemism is pleasantly, if not abrasively, challenging; and between conferences our educational gardens remain unkempt. The fervor for Panglossian deception survives.

Granting the appeal of educational optimism, it would be false to assume that it escapes competition. The optimists may actually be outnumbered by the pessimists, those critics who annually forecast the ruin of society by pointing to real or imagined failures in the American public school system. If an uncritical atmosphere encourages bland optimism, a misconceived criticism, extreme and raucous in its application, breeds new fear, uncertainty, and ignorance. An example is found in the arguments of those evangelists who have ventured forth since the recent technological advancements of Soviet Russia. Their erratic protests embody the evils of hasty criticism. They glory in glibly comparing our schools to a system we have never tried to emulate. Freely deploring communist ideology, these critics, with contradictory zeal, urge us to adopt educational assumptions which are derived from Marxian philosophy. Such self-appointed Messiahs yearn to measure our educational progress solely by the number of successful orbits etched in our skies. A cynicism supports their fads of reform.

Between the extremes of pallid optimism and faithless pessimism there exists a tempered climate of criticism nourished by men who possess not only knowledge but a sense of history as well. Their voices are heard with impatience by the extremists of joy and despair. Although tolerated, given room for their grief, at times even heeded, the advocates of meliorism rarely escape the charge of "uncooperativeness" lobbed at them by the optimists. Nor do they elude the pessimist's conviction that they are dupes of that suspiciously vague philosophy, "egghead idealism." In his notable work *Reconstruction in Philosophy*,

John Dewey[1] succinctly defines the destructive pressures created by such rancor:

> . . . Pessimism is a paralyzing doctrine. In declaring that the world is evil wholesale, it makes futile all efforts to discover the remediable causes of specific evils and thereby destroys at the root every attempt to make the world better and happier. Wholesale optimism, which has been the consequence of the attempt to explain evil away, is, however, equally an incubus.
>
> After all, the optimism that says that the world is already the best possible of all worlds might be regarded as the most cynical of pessimisms. If this is the best possible, what would a world which was fundamentally bad be like? Meliorism is the belief that the specific conditions which exist at one moment, be they comparatively bad or comparatively good, in any event may be bettered. It encourages intelligence to study the positive means of good and the obstructions to their realization, and to put forth endeavor for the improvement of conditions. It arouses confidence and a reasonable hopefulness as optimism does not. For the latter in declaring that good is already realized in ultimate reality tends to make us gloss over the evils that concretely exist. It becomes too readily the creed of those who live at ease, in comfort, of those who have been successful in obtaining this world's rewards. Too readily optimism makes the men who hold it callous and blind to the sufferings of the less fortunate, or ready to find the cause of troubles of others in their personal viciousness. It thus cooperates with pessimism, in spite of the extreme nominal differences between the two, benumbing sympathetic insight and intelligent effort in reform. . . .

Perhaps the most valuable contribution of the melioristic critic is exacted from his willingness to examine the chronic discontents of teachers, issues often ignored by the optimists and pessimists. Let us make a distinction here: A *discontent* is an educational deficiency which surpasses in stamina the strength of a mere *problem*. Although a problem may inhibit a teacher's efficacy, a discontent undermines his morale — the actual source of energy and motivation. A problem may hinder. A discontent may immobilize. Thousands of competent, even gifted, teachers have left the profession not because of any unwillingness to grapple with specific difficulties in their classrooms but because they suffered a fatigue of morale produced by the habitual and seemingly incurable evils that haunted the offices, halls, and classrooms of their schools.

[1] (Boston: Beacon Press, 1948), pp. 178–179. Original Edition, Copyright 1920, by Henry Holt and Co. Enlarged Edition, Copyright 1948 by the Beacon Press. Reprinted by permission of the Beacon Press and Holt, Rinehart, and Winston, Inc.

Each writer in Part One examines a particular area of discontent within his total vision of education, a vision which may reflect his capacities as a teacher, artist, or scholar. Certainly the essays in this first section do not compose a happy literature; nor do they constitute a despairing attitude. The praised joys of teaching are left to the reader's conscience, for to extol these valid pleasures is not to insure their existence. And no teacher worthy of his task need be taught the benefits of his calling.

Charles Dickens

Charles Dickens (1812–1870), the most popular English novelist of the nineteenth century, may well have created a universal character in Mr. Gradgrind. The following extract from Hard Times, *a novel published in 1854, vividly satirizes the stern and strident atmosphere characteristic of many British schools of the period. Dickens' attack on the pedant's fetish for fact anticipates Alfred North Whitehead's complaint that a merely well-informed man is the most useless bore on God's earth. To Dickens, a proper education stresses the uses of imagination as a weapon to be employed against social injustice. The captive children in the following scene acutely symbolize modern suffering as it is spread by the Gradgrinds active in American schools today.*

1

M'CHOAKUMCHILD'S SCHOOLROOM

I

"Now, what I want is, Facts. Teach these boys and girls nothing but Facts. Facts alone are wanted in life. Plant nothing else, and root out everything else. You can only form the minds of reasoning animals upon Facts: nothing else will ever be of any service to them. This is the principle on which I bring up my own children, and this is the principle on which I bring up these children. Stick to Facts, sir!"

The scene was a plain, bare, monotonous vault of a schoolroom, and the speaker's square forefinger emphasised his observations by underscoring every sentence with a line on the schoolmaster's sleeve. The emphasis was helped by the speaker's square wall of a forehead, which had his eyebrows for its base, while his eyes found commodious cellarage in two dark caves, overshadowed by the wall. The emphasis was helped by the speaker's mouth, which was wide, thin, and hard set. The emphasis was helped by the speaker's voice, which was inflexible, dry, and dictatorial. The emphasis was helped by the speaker's hair, which bristled on the skirts of his bald head, a plantation of firs to keep the wind from its shining surface, all covered with knobs, like the crust of a plum pie, as if the head had scarcely warehouse-room for the hard facts stored inside. The speaker's obstinate carriage, square coat, square legs, square shoulders, — nay, his very neckcloth, trained to take him by the throat with an unaccommodating grasp, like a stubborn fact, as it was, — all helped the emphasis.

"In this life, we want nothing but Facts, sir; nothing but Facts!"

The speaker, and the schoolmaster, and the third grown person present, all backed a little, and swept with their eyes the inclined plane of little vessels then and there arranged in order, ready to have imperial gallons of facts poured into them until they were full to the brim.

II

Thomas Gradgrind, sir. A man of realities. A man of facts and calculations. A man who proceeds upon the principle that two and two are four, and nothing over, and who is not to be talked into allowing for anything over. Thomas Gradgrind, sir — peremptorily Thomas — Thomas Gradgrind. With a rule and a pair of scales, and the multiplication table always in his pocket, sir, ready to weigh and measure any parcel of human nature, and tell you exactly what it comes to. It is a mere question of figures, a case of simple arithmetic. You might hope to get some other nonsensical belief into the head of George Gradgrind, or Augustus Gradgrind, or John Gradgrind, or Joseph Gradgrind (all supposititious, nonexistent persons), but into the head of Thomas Gradgrind — no, sir!

In such terms Mr. Gradgrind always mentally introduced himself, whether to his private circle of acquaintance, or to the public in general. In such terms, no doubt, substituting the words "boys and girls," for "sir," Thomas Gradgrind now presented Thomas Gradgrind to the little pitchers before him, who were to be filled so full of facts.

Indeed, as he eagerly sparkled at them from the cellarage before mentioned, he seemed a kind of cannon loaded to the muzzle with facts, and prepared to blow them clean out of the regions of childhood at one discharge. He seemed a galvanizing apparatus, too, charged with a grim mechanical substitute for the tender young imaginations that were to be stormed away.

"Girl number twenty," said Gradgrind, squarely pointing with his square forefinger, "I don't know that girl. Who is that girl?"

"Sissy Jupe, sir," explained number twenty, blushing, standing up, and curtseying.

"Sissy is not a name," said Mr. Gradgrind. "Don't call yourself Sissy. Call yourself Cecilia."

"It's father as calls me Sissy, sir," returned the young girl in a trembling voice, and with another curtsey.

"Then he has no business to do it," said Mr. Gradgrind. "Tell him he mustn't. Cecilia Jupe. Let me see. What is your father?"

"He belongs to the horse-riding, if you please, sir."

Mr. Gradgrind frowned, and waved off the objectionable calling with his hand.

"We don't want to know anything about that, here. You mustn't tell us about that, here. Your father breaks horses, don't he?"

"If you please, sir, when they can get any to break, they do break horses in the ring, sir."

"You mustn't tell us about the ring, here. Very well, then. Describe your father as a horsebreaker. He doctors sick horses, I dare say?"

"Oh yes, sir."

"Very well, then. He is a veterinary surgeon, a farrier, and horsebreaker. Give me your definition of a horse."

(Sissy Jupe thrown into the greatest alarm by this demand.)

"Girl number twenty unable to define a horse!" said Mr. Gradgrind, for the general behoof of all the little pitchers. "Girl number twenty possessed of no facts, in reference to one of the commonest of animals! Some boy's definition of a horse. Bitzer, yours."

The square finger, moving here and there, lighted suddenly on Bitzer, perhaps because he chanced to sit in the same ray of sunlight which, darting in at one of the bare windows of the intensely whitewashed room, irradiated Sissy. For, the boys and girls sat on the face of the inclined plane in two compact bodies, divided up the centre by a narrow interval; and Sissy, being at the corner of a row on the sunny side, came in for the beginning of a sunbeam, of which Bitzer, being at the corner of a row on the other side, a few rows in advance, caught the end. But, whereas the girl was so dark-eyed and dark-haired, that she seemed to receive a deeper and more lustrous colour from the sun, when it shone upon her, the boy was so light-eyed and light-haired that the self-same rays appeared to draw out of him what little colour he ever possessed. His cold eyes would hardly have been eyes, but for the short ends of lashes which, by bringing them into immediate contrast with something paler than themselves, expressed their form. His short-cropped hair might have been a mere continuation of the sandy freckles on his forehead and face. His skin was so unwholesomely deficient in the natural tinge, that he looked as though, if he were cut, he would bleed white.

"Bitzer," said Thomas Gradgrind. "Yoor definition of a horse."

"Quadruped. Graminivorous. Forty teeth, namely twenty-four grinders, four eye-teeth, and twelve incisive. Sheds coat in the spring; in marshy countries, sheds hoofs, too. Hoofs hard, but requiring to be shod with iron. Age known by marks in mouth." Thus (and much more) Bitzer.

"Now girl number twenty," said Mr. Gradgrind. "You know what a horse is."

She curtseyed again, and would have blushed deeper, if she could have blushed deeper than she had blushed all this time. Bitzer, after rapidly blinking at Thomas Gradgrind with both eyes at once, and so catching the light upon his quivering ends of lashes that they looked like the antennae of busy insects, put his knuckles to his freckled forehead, and sat down again.

The third gentleman now stepped forth. A mighty man at cutting and drying, he was; a government officer; in his way (and in most other people's too), a professed pugilist; always in training, always with a system to force down the general throat like a bolus, always to be heard of at the bar of his little Public-office, ready to fight all England. To continue in fistic phraseology, he had a genius for coming up to the scratch, wherever and whatever it was, and proving himself an ugly customer. He would go in and damage any subject whatever with his right, follow up with his left, stop, exchange, counter, bore his opponent (he always fought All England) to the ropes, and fall upon him neatly. He was certain to knock the wind out of common sense, and render that unlucky adversary deaf to the call of time. And he had it in charge from high authority to bring about the great public-office Millennium, when Commissioners should reign upon earth.

"Very well," said this gentleman, briskly smiling, and folding his arms. "That's a horse. Now, let me ask you girls and boys, Would you paper a room with representations of horses?"

After a pause, one half of the children cried in chorus, "Yes, sir!" Upon which the other half, seeing in the gentleman's face that Yes was wrong, cried out in chorus, "No, sir!" — as the custom is, in these examinations.

"Of course, No. Why wouldn't you?"

A pause. One corpulent slow boy, with a wheezy manner of breathing, ventured the answer, Because he wouldn't paper a room at all, but would paint it.

"You *must* paper it," said the gentleman, rather warmly.

"You must paper it," said Thomas Gradgrind, "whether you like it or not. Don't tell *us* you wouldn't paper it. What do you mean, boy?"

"I'll explain to you, then," said the gentleman, after another and a dismal pause, "why you wouldn't paper a room with representations of horses. Do you ever see horses walking up and down the sides of rooms in reality — in fact? Do you?"

"Yes, sir!" from one half. "No, sir!" from the other.

"Of course, No," said the gentleman, with an indignant look at the wrong half. "Why, then, you are not to see anywhere, what you don't see in fact; you are not to have anywhere, what you don't have in fact. What is called Taste, is only another name for Fact."

Thomas Gradgrind nodded his approbation.

"This is a new principle, a discovery, a great discovery," said the gentleman. "Now, I'll try you again. Suppose you were going to carpet a room. Would you use a carpet having a representation of flowers upon it?"

There being a general conviction by this time that "No, sir!" was always the right answer to this gentleman, the chorus of No was very strong. Only a few feeble stragglers said Yes: among them Sissy Jupe.

"Girl number twenty," said the gentleman, smiling in the calm strength of knowledge.

Sissy blushed, and stood up.

"So you would carpet your room — or your husband's room, if you were a grown woman, and had a husband — with representations of flowers, would you?" said the gentleman. "Why would you?"

"If you please, sir, I am very fond of flowers," returned the girl.

"And is that why you would put tables and chairs upon them, and have people walking over them with heavy boots?"

"It wouldn't hurt them, sir. They wouldn't crush and wither, if you please, sir. They would be the pictures of what was very pretty and pleasant, and I would fancy ———"

"Ay, ay, ay! But you mustn't fancy," cried the gentleman, quite elated by coming so happily to his point. "That's it! You are never to fancy."

"You are not, Cecilia Jupe," Thomas Gradgrind solemnly repeated, "to do anything of that kind."

"Fact, fact, fact!" said the gentleman. And "Fact, fact, fact!" repeated Thomas Gradgrind.

"You are to be in all things regulated and governed," said the gentleman, "by fact. We hope to have, before long, a board of fact, composed of commissioners of fact, who will force the people to be a people of fact, and of nothing but fact. You must discard the word Fancy altogether. You have nothing to do with it. You are not to have, in any object of use or ornament, what would be a contradiction in fact. You don't walk upon flowers in fact; you cannot be allowed to walk upon flowers in carpets. You don't find that foreign birds and butterflies come and perch upon your crockery; you cannot be permitted to paint foreign birds and butterflies upon your crockery. You never meet with quadrupeds going up and down walls; you must not have quadrupeds represented upon walls. You must use," said the gentleman, "for all these purposes, combinations and modifications (in primary colours) of mathematical figures which are susceptible of proof and demonstration. This is the new discovery. This is fact. This is taste."

The girl curtseyed, and sat down. She was very young, and she looked as if she were frightened by the matter of fact prospect the world afforded.

"Now, if Mr. M'Choakumchild," said the gentleman, "will proceed to give his first lesson here, Mr. Gradgrind, I shall be happy, at your request, to observe his mode of procedure."

Mr. Gradgrind was much obliged. "Mr. M'Choakumchild, we only wait for you."

So, Mr. M'Choakumchild began in his best manner. He and some one hundred and forty other schoolmasters had been lately turned at the same time, in the same factory, on the same principles, like so many pianoforte legs. He had been put through an immense variety of paces, and had answered volumes of head-breaking questions. Orthography, etymology, syntax, and prosody, biography, astronomy, geography, and general cosmography, the sciences of compound proportion, algebra, land-surveying and levelling, vocal music, and drawing from models, were all at the ends of his ten chilled fingers.

He had worked his stony way into Her Majesty's most Honourable Privy Council's Schedule B, and had taken the bloom off the higher branches of mathematics and physical science, French, German, Latin, and Greek. He knew all about all the Water Sheds of all the world (whatever they are), and all the histories of all the peoples, and all the names of all the rivers and mountains, and all the productions, manners, and customs of all the countries, and all their boundaries and bearings on the two and thirty points of the compass. Ah, rather overdone, M'Choakumchild. If he had only learnt a little less, how infinitely better he might have taught much more!

He went to work in this preparatory lesson, not unlike Morgiana in the Forty Thieves: looking into all the vessels ranged before him, one after another, to see what they contained. Say, good M'Choakumchild. When from thy boiling store, thou shalt fill each jar brim full by-and-by, dost thou think that thou wilt always kill outright the robber Fancy lurking within — or sometimes only maim him and distort him!

Charles Lamb

A British master of the essay form, Charles Lamb (1775–1834) wrote his Essays of Elia *between 1820 and 1825, from which "The Old and the New Schoolmaster" is taken. This informal contrast of teachers predates more systematic debate concerning proper method and content in teaching. A social image of the teacher is also conjured here; and Lamb's question, "Why are we never quite at our ease in the presence of a schoolmaster?" is disturbingly relevant to the current isolation often experienced by the American teacher, although one may not necessarily agree with Lamb's reasons for such alienation.*

Though eager to poke fun at the "new" schoolmaster, Lamb modestly lists his private intellectual shortcomings at the beginning of the essay. One is never sure, however, just how sincere the author is in his self-abasement,

In collaboration with his sister, Lamb also wrote a popular children's book entitled Tales from Shakespeare, *published in 1807.*

2

THE OLD AND THE NEW SCHOOLMASTER

My reading has been lamentably desultory and immethodical. Odd, out of the way, old English plays, and treatises, have supplied me with most of my notions, and ways of feeling. In everything that relates to *science*, I am a whole Encyclopaedia behind the rest of the world. I should have scarcely cut a figure among the franklins, or country gentlemen, in King John's days. I know less geography than a school-boy of six weeks' standing. To me a map of old Ortelius is as authentic as Arrowsmith. I do not know whereabout Africa merges into Asia; whether Ethiopia lie in one or other of these great divisions; nor can form the remotest conjecture of the position of New South Wales, or Van Diemen's Land. Yet do I hold a correspondence with a very dear friend in the first-named of these two Terrae Incognitae. I have no astronomy. I do not know where to look for the Bear, or Charles's Wain; the place of any star; or the name of any of them at sight. I guess at Venus only by her brightness — and if the sun on some portentous morn were to make his first appearance in the West, I verily believe, that, while all the world were gasping in apprehension about me, I alone should stand unterrified, from sheer incuriosity and want of observation. Of history and chronology I possess some vague points, such as one cannot help picking up in the course of miscellaneous study; but I never deliberately sat down to a chronicle, even of my own country. I have most dim apprehensions of the four great monarchies; and sometimes the Assyrian, sometimes the Persian, floats as *first*, in my fancy. I make the widest conjectures concerning Egypt and her shepherd kings. My friend M., with great painstaking, got me to think I understood the first proposition in Euclid, but gave me over in despair at the second. I am entirely unacquainted with the modern languages; and, like a better man than myself, have "small Latin and less Greek." I am a stranger to the shapes and texture of the commonest trees, herbs, flowers — not from the circumstance of my being town-born — for I should have brought the same inobservant spirit into the world with me, had I first seen it "on Devon's leafy shores," — and am no less at a loss among purely town-objects, tools, engines, mechanic processes. — Not that I affect ignorance — but my head has not many mansions, nor spacious; and I have been obliged to fill it with such cabinet curiosities as it can hold without aching. I sometimes wonder, how I have passed my probation with so little discredit in the world, as I have done, upon so meagre a stock. But the fact is, a man may do very well with a very little knowledge, and scarce be found out, in mixed company; everybody is so much more ready to produce his own, than to call for a display of your acquisitions. But in a *tête-à-tête* there is no shuffling. The truth will out. There is nothing which I dread so much, as the being left alone for a quarter of an hour with a sensible, well-informed man, that does not know me. I lately got into a dilemma of this sort. —

In one of my daily jaunts between Bishopsgate and Shacklewell, the coach stopped to take up a staid-looking gentleman, about the wrong side of thirty, who was giving his parting directions (while the steps were adjusting), in a tone of mild authority, to a tall youth, who seemed to be neither his clerk, his son, nor his servant, but something partaking of all three. The youth was dismissed, and we drove on. As we were the sole passengers, he naturally enough addressed his conversation to me; and we discussed the merits of the fare, the civility and punctuality of the driver; the circumstance of an opposition coach having been lately set up, with the probabilities of its success — to all which I was enabled to return pretty satisfactory answers, having been drilled into this kind of etiquette by some years' daily practice of riding to and fro in the stage aforesaid — when he suddenly alarmed me by a startling question, whether I had seen the show of prize cattle that morning in Smithfield? Now, as I had not seen it, and do not greatly care for such sort of exhibitions, I was obliged to return a cold negative. He seemed a little mortified, as well as astonished, at my declaration, as (it appeared) he was just come fresh from the sight, and doubtless had hoped to compare notes on the subject. However, he assured me that I had lost a fine treat, as it far exceeded the show of last year. We were now approaching Norton Folgate, when the sight of some shop-goods *ticketed* freshened him up into a dissertation upon the cheapness of cottons this spring. I was now a little in heart, as the nature of my morning avocations had brought me into some sort of familiarity with the raw material; and I was surprised to find how eloquent I was becoming on the state of the India market — when, presently, he dashed my incipient vanity to the earth at once, by inquiring whether I had ever made any calculations as to the value of the rental of all the retail shops in London. Had he asked of me, what song the Syrens sang, or what name Achilles assumed when he hid himself among women, I might, with Sir Thomas Browne, have hazarded a "wide solution."[1] My companion saw my embarrassment, and, the almshouses beyond Shoreditch just coming in view, with great good-nature and dexterity shifted his conversation to the subject of public charities; which led to the comparative merits of provisions for the poor in past and present times, with observations on the old monastic institutions, and charitable orders; but, finding me rather dimly impressed with some glimmering notions from old poetic associations, than strongly fortified with any speculations reducible to calculation on the subject, he gave the matter

---

[1] An approximate answer.

up; and, the country beginning to open more and more upon us, as we approached the turnpike at Kingsland (the destined termination of his journey), he put a home thrust upon me, in the most unfortunate position he could have chosen, by advancing some queries relative to the North Pole Expedition. While I was muttering out something about the Panorama of those strange regions (which I had actually seen), by way of parrying the question, the coach stopping relieved me from any further apprehensions. My companion getting out, left me in the comfortable possession of my ignorance; and I heard him, as he went off, putting questions to an outside passenger, who had alighted with him, regarding an epidemic disorder, that had been rife about Dalston, and which my friend assured him had gone through five or six schools in that neighbourhood. The truth now flashed upon me, that my companion was a schoolmaster; and that the youth, whom he had parted from at our first acquaintance, must have been one of the bigger boys, or the usher. — He was evidently a kind-hearted man, who did not seem so much desirous of provoking discussion by the questions which he put, as of obtaining information at any rate. It did not appear that he took any interest, either, in such kind of inquiries, for their own sake; but that he was in some way bound to seek for knowledge. A greenish-coloured coat, which he had on, forbade me to surmise that he was a clergyman. The adventure gave birth to some reflections on the difference between persons of his profession in past and present times.

Rest to the souls of those fine old Pedagogues; the breed, long since extinct, of the Lilys, and the Linacres: who believing that all learning was contained in the languages which they taught, and despising every other acquirement as superficial and useless, came to their task as to a sport! Passing from infancy to age, they dreamed away all their days as in a grammar-school. Revolving in a perpetual cycle of declensions, conjugations, syntaxes, and prosodies; renewing constantly the occupations which had charmed their studious childhood; rehearsing continually the part of the past; life must have slipped from them at last like one day. They were always in their first garden, reaping harvests of their golden time, among their *Flori* and their *Spici-legia*; in Arcadia still, but kings; the ferule of their sway not much harsher, but of like dignity with that mild sceptre attributed to king Basileus; the Greek and Latin, their stately Pamela and their Philoclea; with the occasional duncery of some untoward tyro, serving for a refreshing interlude of a Mopsa, or a clown Damoetas!

With what a savour doth the Preface to Colet's, or (as it is sometimes called) Paul's Accidence, set forth! "To exhort every man to the learning of grammar, that intendeth to attain the understanding of the tongues, wherein is contained a great treasury of wisdom and knowledge, it would seem but vain and lost labour; for so much as it is known, that nothing can surely be ended, whose beginning is either feeble or faulty; and no building be perfect whereas the foundation and groundwork is ready to fall, and unable to uphold the burden of the frame." How well doth this stately preamble (comparable to those which Milton commendeth as "having been the usage to prefix to

some solemn law, then first promulgated by Solon or Lycurgus") correspond
with and illustrate that pious zeal for conformity, expressed in a succeeding
clause, which would fence about grammar-rules with the severity of faith-
articles! — "as for the diversity of grammars, it is well profitably taken away by
the king majesties wisdom, who foreseeing the inconvenience, and favourably
providing the remedie, caused one kind of grammar by sundry learned men to
be diligently drawn, and so to be set out, only everywhere to be taught for the
use of learners, and for the hurt in changing of schoolmaisters." What a
gusto in that which follows: "wherein it is profitable that he [the pupil] can
orderly decline his noun and his verb." *His* noun!

The fine dream is fading away fast; and the least concern of a teacher in
the present day is to inculcate grammar-rules.

The modern schoolmaster is expected to know a little of everything, because
his pupil is required not to be entirely ignorant of anything. He must be
superficially, if I may so say, omniscient. He is to know something of pneu-
matics; of chemistry; of whatever is curious or proper to excite the attention
of the youthful mind; an insight into mechanics is desirable, with a touch
of statistics; the quality of soils, etc., botany, the constitution of his country,
cum multis aliis. You may get a notion of some part of his expected duties
by consulting the famous Tractate on Education, addressed to Mr. Hartlib.

All these things — these, or the desire of them — he is expected to instil,
not by set lessons from professors, which he may charge in the bill, but at
school intervals, as he walks the streets, or saunters through green fields (those
natural instructors), with his pupils. The least part of what is expected from
him is to be done in school-hours. He must insinuate knowledge at the *mollia
tempora fandi.* He must seize every occasion — the season of the year — the
time of the day — a passing cloud — a rainbow — a waggon of hay — a regiment of soldiers going by — to inculcate something useful. He can receive
no pleasure from a casual glimpse of Nature, but must catch at it as an object
of instruction. He must interpret beauty into the picturesque. He cannot
relish a beggar-man, or a gipsy, for thinking of the suitable improvement.
Nothing comes to him not spoiled by the sophisticating medium of moral
uses. The Universe — that Great Book, as it has been called — is to him,
indeed, to all intents and purposes, a book out of which he is doomed to
read tedious homilies to distasting schoolboys. — Vacations themselves are
none to him, he is only rather worse off than before; for commonly he has
some intrusive upper-boy fastened upon him at such times; some cadet of a
great family; some neglected lump of nobility, or gentry; that he must drag
after him to the play, to the Panorama, to Mr. Bartley's Orrery, to the Pan-
opticon, or into the country, to a friend's house, or his favourite watering-
place. Wherever he goes this uneasy shadow attends him. A boy is at his
board, and in his path, and in all his movements. He is boy-rid, sick of perpetual boy.

Boys are capital fellows in their own way, among their mates; but they are
unwholesome companions for grown people. The restraint is felt no less on

the one side than on the other. — Even a child, that "plaything for an hour," tires *always*. The noises of children, playing their own fancies — as I now hearken to them, by fits, sporting on the green before my window, while I am engaged in these grave speculations at my neat surburban retreat at Shackle-well — by distance made more sweet — inexpressibly take from the labour of my task. It is like writing to music. They seem to modulate my periods. They ought at least to do so — for in the voice of that tender age there is a kind of poetry, far unlike the harsh prose-accents of man's conversation. — I should but spoil their sport, and diminish my own sympathy for them, by mingling in their pastime.

I would not be domesticated all my days with a person of very superior capacity to my own — not, if I know myself at all, from any considerations of jealousy or self-comparison, for the occasional communion with such minds has constituted the fortune and felicity of my life — but the habit of too constant intercourse with spirits above you, instead of raising you, keeps you down. Too frequent doses of original thinking from others, restrain what lesser portion of that faculty you may possess of your own. You get entangled in another man's mind, even as you lose yourself in another man's grounds. You are walking with a tall varlet, whose strides out-pace yours to lassitude. The constant operation of such potent agency would reduce me, I am convinced, to imbecility. You may derive thoughts from others; your way of thinking, the mould in which your thoughts are cast, must be your own. Intellect may be imparted, but not each man's intellectual frame. —

As little as I should wish to be always thus dragged upwards, as little (or rather still less) is it desirable to be stunted downwards by your associates. The trumpet does not more stun you by its loudness, than a whisper teases you by its provoking inaudibility.

Why are we never quite at our ease in the presence of a schoolmaster? — because we are conscious that he is not quite at his ease in ours. He is awkward, and out of place, in the society of his equals. He comes like Gulliver from among his little people, and he cannot fit the stature of his understanding to yours. He cannot meet you on the square. He wants a point given him, like an indifferent whist-player. He is so used to teaching, that he wants to be teaching *you*. One of these professors, upon my complaining that these little sketches of mine were anything but methodical, and that I was unable to make them otherwise, kindly offered to instruct me in the method by which young gentlemen in *his* seminary were taught to compose English themes. The jests of a schoolmaster are coarse, or thin. They do not *tell* out of school. He is under the restraint of a formal or didactive hypocrisy in company, as a clergyman is under a moral one. He can no more let his intellect loose in society than the other can his inclinations. — He is forlorn among his coevals; his juniors cannot be his friends.

"I take blame to myself," said a sensible man of this profession, writing to a friend respecting a youth who had quitted his school abruptly, "that your nephew was not more attached to me. But persons in my situation are more to be pitied than can well be imagined. We are surrounded by young, and, consequently, ardently affectionate hearts, but *we* can never hope to share an atom of their affections. The relation of master and scholar forbids this. *How pleasing this must be to you, how I envy your feelings!* my friends will sometimes say to me, when they see young men whom I have educated return after some years' absence from school, their eyes shinging with pleasure, while they shake hands with their old master, bringing a present of game to me, or a toy to my wife, and thanking me in the warmest terms for my care of their education. A holiday is begged for the boys; the house is a scene of happiness; I, only, am sad at heart. — This fine-spirited and warm-hearted youth, who fancies he repays his master with gratitude for the care of his boyish years — this young man — in the eight long years I watched over him with a parent's anxiety, never could repay me with one look of genuine feeling. He was proud, when I praised; he was submissive, when I reproved him; but he did never *love* me — and what he now mistakes for gratitude and kindness for me, is but the pleasant sensation which all persons feel at revisiting the scenes of their boyish hopes and fears; and the seeing on equal terms the man they were accustomed to look up to with reverence. My wife, too," this interesting correspondent goes on to say, "my once darling Anna, is the wife of a schoolmaster. — When I married her — knowing that the wife of a schoolmaster ought to be a busy notable creature, and fearing that my gentle Anna would ill supply the loss of my dear bustling mother, just then dead, who never sat still, was in every part of the house in a moment, and whom I was obliged sometimes to threaten to fasten down in a chair, to save her from fatiguing herself to death — I expressed my fears that I was bringing her into a way of life unsuitable to her; and she, who loved me tenderly, promised for my sake to exert herself to perform the duties of her situation. She promised, and she has kept her word. What wonders will not woman's love perform? — My house is managed with a propriety and decorum unknown in other schools; my boys are well fed, look healthy, and have every proper accommodation; and all this performed with a careful economy, that never descends to meanness. But I have lost my gentle *helpless* Anna! When we sit down to enjoy an hour of repose after the fatigue of the day, I am compelled to listen to what have been her useful (and they are really useful) employments through the day, and what she proposes for her tomorrow's task. Her heart and her features are changed by the duties of her situation. To the boys, she never appears other than the *master's wife*, and looks up to me as the *boys' master*; to whom all show of love and affection would be highly improper, and unbecoming the dignity of her situation and mine. Yet *this* my gratitude forbids me to hint to her. For my sake she submitted to be this altered creature, and can I reproach her for it?" — For the communication of this letter I am indebted to my cousin Bridget.

Gilbert Highet

In his book The Art of Teaching, *Gilbert Highet, the noted scholar and critic, examines with a broad and ranging view various methods of teaching. This section from his study reveals an often shunned problem in education — the incorrigible student. Not stopping to sentimentalize over the loss of mediocre minds to incorrigibility, Highet declares, ". . . the important problem is why really talented people with the best of teaching should turn out fatally, damnably bad: like Nero, like Judas."*

Of particular value is Highet's ability to interpret a current educational dilemma by using traditional figures such as Socrates, Christ, and Hamlet, characters rich in symbolic and literal meanings.

3

GOOD TEACHERS AND BAD PUPILS*

One of Jesus' twelve chosen pupils was Judas Iscariot, who helped the Jewish authorities to carry out his arrest. Jesus knew it, too. At the Passover supper he spoke of it without mentioning the name of the traitor: although we do not hear that he said or knew anything of it until the last few hours.

This is a memorable case of one of the most important and difficult questions in teaching. Why does a good teacher have bad pupils? Jesus was one of the best teachers, and he had one of the worst pupils. Why?

It was not that Judas simply fell short of the best in Jesus. He did not try to understand the teaching of Jesus and then fail in all good will, as the others sometimes did. He did not break down in a crisis, like Peter. He turned his back and went the other way, resolutely and effectively. To prove this, think of the method he chose to single Jesus out for the police. His master's chief lesson was that all men should love and trust one another. So Judas, instead

* Reprinted from *The Art of Teaching* by Gilbert Highet, by permission of Alfred A. Knopf, Inc. Copyright 1950 by Gilbert Highet.

19

of pointing to him with his hand or standing beside him, went up and kissed him.

Spectacular as the Judas case is, it is only one of many. Socrates had a number of outstandingly bad pupils. The best known is the most brilliant — Alcibiades, who loved Socrates dearly and admired him fervently, and who also betrayed his country, went over to its enemies the Spartans and then betrayed them, returned to Athens and left it once more, and was killed after a career which included such other exploits as the seduction of the Spartan queen and blasphemy against his country's religion. But there were others — such as Critias, who became one of the Thirty Tyrants put in by Sparta after the defeat of Athens and who tortured and murdered hundreds of his fellow-citizens in a savage attempt to crush out the rule of the people. The real impetus behind the condemnation of Socrates was the people's hatred for the men he had taught to hate democracy. He had other pupils, certainly, but the revolutionaries were among the most brilliant. We cannot be quite sure how Socrates himself regarded them. Plato tells us that he thought they were potentially good young men who had been misled by other influences; and of course once they were fully embarked on their bad careers, he had little to do with them. But he seems to have been closely associated with them for a long time. Why did they go so very far wrong? Was he the best teacher in Greece, as Plato and others believed, or was he a man who, as the accusation read, corrupted the young?

The history of education is dotted with such terrible failures, as the chart of a difficult channel is starred with wrecks. Move on into the Roman empire and you will find others. Nero is one. He was the son of a princess who managed to get him adopted by her second husband, the reigning emperor, Claudius. As an heir to the throne, he was educated with great care. He was handed over to Seneca, a brilliantly clever talker and writer and an experienced courtier, who was also a philosopher attached to Stoicism — which means that he upheld a stern moral code based on the primacy of Duty, but was not unrealistically rigid about it. Seneca, assisted by an experienced soldier and administrator, worked over the young prince for years, with all the care and subtlety he could command. He gave him a thorough grounding in moral philosophy, and a considerable knowledge of literature and art. It was not all hard work and ethical principles either. After the old emporer died, Seneca wrote an outrageously funny skit about his trying to get into heaven and being kicked out, which was apparently meant to be read at Nero's coronation party; and he wrote nine blood-and-thunder tragedies which (according to one theory) were specially designed for the stage-struck young emperor to produce in his private theater, with himself as a star. The results of all this care were very good, to begin with. The first five years of Nero's reign were universally admired. Social justice, sensible financing, big public works, and much else were due to Nero's own enthusiasm and the guidance of his advisers. Then he began to deteriorate. From the age of twenty-two or so he got worse every year. He retired his tutor Seneca. He divorced, and then executed, his wife.

He executed, or murdered, his mother. He started a career of absurd and foul debaucheries. He threw off every good influence, neglected his duties, ruined the empire, provoked it to revolt against him, and even then had scarcely the courage to commit suicide. And Seneca, his tutor? Several years earlier, Nero had condemned Seneca to death, like everyone else who had ever benefited him.

But why did he go wrong? Was it simply that the limitless power of an emperor was too much for anyone to bear? No, because others used it sanely. Or did it come too suddenly upon him? No, because he had been carefully trained for it by experts for years. Or was he badly trained — did Seneca perhaps encourage him to loose living so that he would be easier to handle? No, we do not hear that he did. On the contrary, all the evidence is that Nero was well educated, on a high moral standard.

There are many more like him in history, on a smaller scale: hundreds; thousands; tens of thousands of young men and women who had talent, and health, and security, who were trained by teachers who understood them, who were surrounded by people who loved them, and who threw the whole thing away. The mediocrities do not matter so much — the expensively educated girls who turned out to be bumpkins or bridge-fiends, the privately tutored and hand-tailored youths who went on the Grand Tour and returned without an idea in their sleek narrow heads. Chesterfield's son is a good example of that sort of unimportant failure. They are simply bald patches, thin and sandy gardens, depressed areas. No, the important problem is why really talented people with the best of teaching should turn out fatally, damnably bad: like Nero, like Judas.

This is a very hard problem for teachers, and for parents. To solve a question so tough as this, there are two devices that we can use. One is to find out what answers have already been suggested, and to think them over, comparing them together and filling up one by the help of others. The second is to ask whether the same problem appears in any other shape, to see what answers are given to it then, and to apply them.

Not many useful answers are given to our question. Why did Judas betray Jesus? Why did Nero kill his own teacher? Why did Alcibiades destroy so much that Socrates admired — integrity, purity, patriotism? Judas himself did not know. After he had finished, he knew he had done wrong. He knew it could not be put right; and he knew it had nothing much to do with the bribe he was paid; but he could not tell why he had done it.

As for Nero, he said Seneca was mixed up in a plot against him, but did he believe it in his heart? When he forced Seneca into retirement and disgrace, was he only safeguarding himself against assassination — against a plot made by the old man who could have killed him at any time for years?

Alcibiades has left no record except his acts. But his fellow-pupil Plato gives a valuable explanation of the problem, evidently written with him in mind. He says in effect that all sorts of pupils go wrong, including many mediocrities. But, he adds, philosophy is an exceptionally difficult type of education. It takes unusual talent to be a good pupil of Socrates. Therefore, when such a pupil goes wrong, he goes spectacularly wrong, by applying his unusual gifts to bad purposes. Remember that Plato was not thinking only of brain-power, but also of the other strengths that make up an exceptional personality — physical and spiritual energy, rapid and strong will-power, social adaptability and charm, bodily dexterity and beauty. When a young man or woman so richly endowed goes wrong, he or she goes very far wrong.

Plato adds another solution, which is certainly true in part. It is, he says, fearfully difficult to teach such a gifted pupil efficiently, because evil influences compete much harder for his attention. This is certainly true, so far as it goes. Obviously if Seneca had been able to train Nero under laboratory conditions he would have made a better thing of it. But he could not watch the young prince all the time. Even if he could, it would have been ill-advised to do so. And how can you teach self-control when every pretty slave-girl in the palace contrives to catch the master's eye and brush against his hand? How can you repress his extravagance when the rooms are full of courtiers anxious to sell everything they possess and procure whatever the master fancies? Can anyone learn clemency, even from Seneca, when vile whisperers slander every decent man at court, suggest confiscations of great wealth, describe the pleasures of inflicting torture?

True in part . . . but is this the only explanation? Is it all the truth? Do we feel that it explains everything?

No, we do not. We feel that men like Judas and Nero who turn against their teachers are not merely led aside by other influences. They do not simply wander off the path. They turn right round and go in the direction opposite to their guides. They do not merely drop their teachers, forget lessons and personalities. They deliberately attack their teachers, trying to annihilate them and all they stand for. And the problem we have to solve is: why does this so often happen to teachers of exceptional brilliance and goodness?

*   *   *

Perhaps we can solve it by asking if it appears in any other shape. As soon as we consider it, we find that it does.

We have already noticed the peculiar fact that the best schools, with the oldest and noblest traditions, produce some of the most complete scoundrels. This is the same pattern. They do not simply turn out stupid and mediocre, these failures. Instead, they turn out brilliant but bad. Usually they retain something of what their school taught them. It may be only a set of intonations, a social technique, a haircut and a style of dress; it may be a whole intellectual attitude as complex as that which the Jesuits gave to their pupil Voltaire. But in everything else they are rebels. All that the school tries to teach, they deny and pervert. Sometimes they hold it up to ridicule by caricaturing its customs and personalities with a plenitude of detail which is positively boring for outsiders though evidently necessary for themselves. Sometimes, when they cannot write, they try to shock and disgrace the school in other ways. All their conduct is marked by a compulsive reference to the school, a strong emotional link which, it seems, they both love and hate, like a dog playing with and worrying the chain he cannot break.

This begins to look like a problem which is rooted somewhere below the level of ordinary rational behavior. Lots of people dislike their old schools and school-teachers. When they remember their school adventures, perhaps once or twice a year, they think: "Well, thank heaven that's over." But they do not go on and on having dreams about Public School 97, remembering what Frog-eyes said in P.S. 97 after the incident with the ink, writing poetry based on the slang of P.S. 97, becoming a dervish in order to wipe P.S. 97 out of their souls, going specially to live in Tierra del Fuego or the slums of Naples because these are the extreme reverse of P.S. 97, or planning new social systems in which there will be nothing like P.S. 97 and all the schools will be its exact 180° opposite. They just forget the whole thing. It does not alter their way of living from day to day. But to suffer such an extreme and powerful set of obsessions as seems to afflict the bad or rebellious sons of certain schools and colleges — that is a kind of spiritual illness. Does it appear in any other form?

We have seen it in two forms: the pupil revolts against the good teacher, the student rebels against the ancient school. Now, are these not minor variations of a much more difficult and fundamental conflict, the revolt of the son against the father? Surely it would be wrong to discuss them without also discussing the many cases in which a boy, well brought up by a wise and good father, has wasted his life in trying to bring disgrace on himself and his family, trying hard and repeatedly, again and again committing actions which are perfectly ridiculous in themselves and can be explained only as expressions of the wish to belittle his father and destroy him. That also is a problem of education. It is not the most serious, but it is certainly the most painful, because it is one of the hardest to understand.

If it were only revolt against authority, it would be simple. All the young hate authority. They feel it as tyranny. If it actually is tyrannical, they often take action to escape it. If the father is a proud cruel domineering man who believes his son should be his slave or his carbon copy, his son will either become slavish and imitative, or else break out violently, kick over the traces, leave home, knock the stick out of the father's hand and thrash him with it. Such a father deserves what he gets.

But the sad cases are much more complex and difficult. In these, the father is not cruel and tyrannous. He is gentle and considerate. He does not try to impose his will on his son. He tries to guide him, rather than to drive him. He wants his son to be happy and successful — not necessarily in the same line as himself, but in any line the boy can usefully follow. When there is a conflict of wills, the father does not always win. Often he wins only half the arguments. More often there are no real conflicts, above the surface. The family atmosphere is not tense with constant dueling. Usually it is calm and reasonable, and, from the outside, charming. And yet now and then such a family has a son who, apparently without provocation, without even a semblance of reason, chooses to make a career of thwarting and disgracing his parents. That becomes his aim in life. Other young men may go wrong because they cannot get accustomed to hard work or monotonous duty, because they like women or gambling. This youth has no such simple guiding principle. He merely wanders through life wrecking his prospects and himself. The débris looks as ridiculous and pathetic as a chapel or a schoolroom after a gang of naughty children has invaded it, breaking up the seats, throwing ink at the walls, turning everything movable upside down, and staining everything else. The wreck appears to have no design whatever. But it has. It has a purpose. And the apparently random, unreasonable, and even unenjoyable aberrations of the young man are not meant to shape a life for himself, but to wreck his father's life, or the life which he shares with his father. Usually the boy does not understand what is happening to him. The father almost never does. They both suffer, that is all. Their talents and their lives are wasted.

Shakespeare, who thought a great deal about the relations of fathers and children, makes this problem the subject of several of his best plays. He shows us a father who, with vast dexterity and energy, has won himself a great position. The father loves his son, and hopes that he will share the rewards and responsibilities of power. The son is talented and charming, brave and energetic. It would be easy, one would think, and pleasant for him to join his father. There is no compulsion. He can do whatever he likes. He may sit at home playing shove-ha'penny if he chooses; or hunt all week during the season; or waste time harmlessly in other ways. But he chooses to become a gangster. He is only an amateur, but he is on the fringe of the professional crooks. His best friend is a broken-down old ruffian who has drunk almost all his gifts away and is living by the remainder of his wits. He sees far more of Falstaff than he does of his father, King Henry IV. He makes Falstaff into a sort of substitute father, laughing with him as he cannot with his father, tricking and befooling him as he would like to belittle his father. As the play goes on, it is harder and harder to understand what is wrong with Hal. Why should he throw away his chances? Why does he want to hurt his father? He *says* he is doing it so that he can get more praise for reforming later; but that is not the real reason, and it never comes up after his reform takes place. The real reason appears when his father is in genuine danger and when Hal himself is challenged by a rival of his own age. Then he rushes to help the king's cause, and kills his challenger, Hotspur. Immediately afterwards, when his father is gravely ill, Hal goes in to see him, finds him unconscious, and — as though he were already dead — picks up his crown and puts it on. That is what he could not do before. That is what he has always wanted. In default of that, he has done the extreme opposite. In order to *be* something, he has had to be something totally unlike his father: for he could not be his father while his father was still alive. The moment King Henry IV dies, Hal becomes king. He is a model king, strong, chivalrous, wise, energetic. And he rejects Falstaff, his substitute father, the false staff he had used to prop him for a while: doing so with such coldness and cruelty that the old man dies of it. Now both Hal's fathers are dead, and he can be himself.

Yet we are left to feel that he might never have reformed. If his father had lived another ten or fifteen years, if no war emergency had arisen, would Hal have broken with his bad life and his dissolute companions? Would he not have been in danger of becoming a perpetual wastrel? He would have grown older, more set in his silly protest, until it grew into an end in itself enjoyable for its own sake. Or, even worse, he might have decided to make the protest more pointed, to do something which would hurt his father more grievously, overthrow him or destroy him. *Henry IV* and *Henry V* are happy plays. But often in life this conflict ends tragically. After these dramas, Shakespeare wrote *Hamlet* and *King Lear*.

*   *   *

We have suggested, then, that the revolt of some pupils against good teachers and of some students against good schools rises from the same conflict which is expressed in the revolt of some sons against good fathers. If so, it is a permanent conflict, rooted very deep in the human soul. Freud, who named it the Oedipus complex, described it as based on the sexual competition between son and father for the undivided love of the mother-wife. But it looks as though Freud had, here as elsewhere, exaggerated the importance and pervasiveness of sexual drives. Many subtle observers of the human soul have traced the same conflict between sons and fathers (or father-substitutes such as teachers) without discovering any sexual basis for it. Some, like Shakespeare, have seen the conflict sometimes as emphatically sexual (in *Hamlet*) and sometimes as quite divorced from sex (in *Henry IV*). Certainly in the revolt of pupils against schools and teachers there are some sexual overtones, but the main emphasis is elsewhere.

Although we have tried to describe the conflict, it is still difficult to understand. And it is terribly hard to see it as a frequent, almost inevitable conflict in which neither side is to blame. We see only the grieving father; we can scarcely spare a glance for the son. We read of the painful death of Seneca, and spurn Nero as a monster. Jesus was betrayed and executed. Who thinks of Judas except with hatred? Yet the clash is a disaster in which both sides lose. If we are to understand it, we must be sorry for both. Jesus was crucified, and the world weeps at his agony. But we should spare a tear for Judas, mad with remorse and hopeless regret, hanging alone on a tree in the field of blood.

If the conflict is no one's fault, what causes it? Is it merely a misfortune for the father and son, as when the boy is born blind? Does it strike by chance, like death in a traffic accident? Or is it regular but governed by laws still undiscovered, like the incidence of Mongoloid births? Or are both father and son, teacher and pupil, partly responsible?

We do not know. Psychologists have their hypotheses, but none of them has yet been accepted as a law. Teachers can only guess, and their guesses are irregular and unreliable. In fact, there are some eminent teachers who have had loyal pupils and disloyal children. Parents never know. There are some fathers who have had four or five sons, all of whom turned out well, and one other who, with the same treatment, turned out a coward, a liar, a traitor, a sponger, anything that would hurt most. They have done their best with all. They cannot see why they failed with only one. No one knows. All we can do at present is to try to understand what goes on in the mind of the rebellious pupil and the bad son.

He is trying to be himself. He does not know what that is. Like all the young, he has hardly any idea of his own powers and weaknesses. His spiritual growth is even more mysterious to him than his physical development, and far more erratic. He feels as though he were driving a car very fast, without knowing which are the brakes, where the steering-wheel is, and whether the road-signs are telling the truth. He knows he must keep going, but he does not know where. He knows he must grow, but into what?

Now, if he has an unusually good and admirable father, or a teacher who seems to have no weaknesses, he is led to believe that he must follow his father or his teacher. He must copy them in everything. He must try to *become* them. Yet he feels that if he does so, he will have lost something, he will not be himself. And he also feels that he *cannot* become them, because they are so much better. The boy of eighteen cannot reproduce the calm wisdom and self-control of the man of forty-five. The hot young emperor can never be as poised as an elderly Stoic. Therefore, rather than be a weak and inferior copy, he decides to be a bold original. My father is king? Good. Rather than be an imitation kinglet, I shall be king of the rascals, the prince of the underworld. Some Christian theologians say that the first sin ever committed was the same action, when the creature rebelled against the creator, when the prince of angels made himself the king of devils, saying:

Better to reign in hell than serve in heaven.

But usually the revolt is less systematic. The young man wanders about doing disgraceful things with the maximum of publicity, so that they will make him as real as his father and as important. Meanwhile, he wastes his substance. Sometimes he kills himself, or undertakes a symbolic suicide. Even then he is both punishing himself for being unworthy and killing the image of his father.

In this conflict, as in all conflicts between father and son, or between teacher and pupil, more weight of responsibility rests on the father and the teacher. He knows more, and can plan better. But it is very hard for them both.

One method of minimizing the conflict is for him to allow his son, or pupil, to differ from him. He should encourage him to differ. He should suggest new paths along which the boy can move freely without treading in his father's footsteps. Even then there will be a danger. The boy may be torn between the desire to be his father's image and the need to be something different. It is the father's duty to try to help the two parts of his son's personality to harmonize and grow together.

Another method, which is even more difficult, is to diminish the distance between father and son, and to make the boy understand that achievement is quite possible. Tell him the mistakes you made. Describe your early struggles and conflicts, not as titanic battles which only a superman could have won, but as anxious skirmishes similar to his own. If you beat him hollow in some areas of competition, allow him to beat you in others, and praise his wins. When he emerges successfully from some trial you have never faced, make much of it and show him how it has strengthened him. It is awful for a young man to feel his father or teacher has no human weaknesses. To show him yours will actually help him in conquering his own.

This conflict is not altogether suffering and loss. Its other aspect is growth. For a conflict challenges both parties to show the best in them. The pupil who questions and criticizes every statement made by his teacher learns far more than the nestling who absorbs everything with a gaping mouth. The son who knows that it will be difficult to rival his father will, if he thinks he can succeed, put out energies he never knew he could command. Therefore, the wise father and the good teacher will challenge their sons and pupils to equal them, and help them, where it is wise, to differ and even to excel. The best proof of the educational genius of the Jesuits is that many of their best pupils were not Jesuits. The best proof of Plato's genius as a teacher is that Aristotle worked with him for twenty years, and then founded a mighty school of his own, based partly on his criticism and refutations of Platonic doctrine. The aim of good teaching is summed up in Aristotle's own remark about these differences: "Though both truth and Plato are dear to me, it is right to prefer truth."

John Ciardi

An accomplished poet, John Ciardi also is known for his pungent column in the Saturday Review, *"Manner of Speaking," from which the following essays are taken. A Fellow of the American Academy of Arts and Sciences, he has won the Harriet Monroe Memorial Award*

and the Prix de Rome. *Regarded as a talented teacher, Ciardi has provided students beyond range of his lectures with virile translations
of Dante's* Inferno *and* Purgatorio *and with a compelling introduction
to poetry,* How Does a Poem Mean?

*With sly impudence Ciardi reveals his disdain for the powers of
administrators, a disdain echoed today with new candor by teachers
active in elementary and secondary education. That the authority of
administrators, whether rightly or wrongly assumed, is a major source of
controversy can no longer be disguised by weak oaths of solidarity, by
those habitual messages of good will infesting administrational press
releases and the cautious minutes of the teachers' meeting. The question, belatedly, is upon us: Is the administrator's ultimate responsibility
one of administering to the needs of his teachers, or one of creating and
enforcing educational policies beyond their jurisdiction?*

4

TO THE DAMNATION OF DEANS

(A PREJUDICE) *

I leaned on my first lectern in January of 1940 as a new-minted instructor
at the University of Kansas City. After a shade under four years with the
Army Air Corps, beginning in 1942, I taught for seven years at Harvard as
an instructor and then for eight years more at Rutgers, ending up as a full-
chicken professor of English, a post and tenure I resigned last June.

These are not notes for a *curriculum vitae* but credentials in faith, as
testimony that I have served a fair stint of campus time, and that if I cannot
assemble facts and figures to do my lying for me, I have at least invested a
lot of years in the prejudices I take away from the ivy.

Nothing has fueled my prejudices as richly as has the discovery that the
college at which I dreamed of teaching does not, to my knowledge, exist.
Harvard is the one possible exception I know of, and if it shines both by
comparison and its own merit, its splendor is yet marked to some extent by
the fungi of that administrative blight that has marked the face of all

* From the *Saturday Review*, March 24, 1962. Reprinted by permission of John Ciardi
and the *Saturday Review*.

American colleges, a blight whose simple disaster is the fact that college policy has passed almost entirely from the hands of the faculty into those of the administration.

I make no effort to be impartial on this point. Education is too important a business to be left to deans. The deanly condition is the condition of ignorance camouflaged by secretaries, charts, IBM cards, and statistics, but ignorance none the less. That ignorance is occupational. Let a good man be trapped into a dean's swivel chair and his inhumane ignorance grows upon him as a condition of his employment. The only real difference between the arrogant and the apologetic deans is that the apologetic ones know to what extent their work drains them of mentality. How can one leave educational decision to men who lack the time to read a book?

My nostalgic notion of the true college was of an absolute and self-determining body of scholar-teachers. They are the faculty. They are appointed for their distinction and responsibility. And they, by discussion and vote, set the college policy, which is then passed on as formulated to a variety of clerk known as a dean. The duty of such clerks is to count the paper clips and add up the totals as instructed, leaving the faculty free for the important business of gathering information, of thinking about it, and of transmitting the information, the thought, and the method of thinking to students.

But if that is the ideal college, the ideal world is a cloud. Far from being clerks, those deans, sub-deans, over-deans (and the janitors) have become executives who outrank the faculty in pay, power, and persuasion. I have known distinguished professors to go into a reasonable approximation of a tizzy when a dean raised his voice. I have known a dean to walk into a departmental meeting called to elect a new chairman, and to announce to the department that no matter how they voted, only so-and-so would be acceptable to the administration. I have known presidents to convene the full faculty for a discussion of academic policy, and within a few days announce a policy exactly opposite that voted by the faculty.

Now and then a professor has rebelled, but professors are poor rebels. They have, in fact, largely abdicated their responsibilities as members of the ideal faculty, probably for the same shabbily genteel reasons that have made them shy away from anything so sordid as the discussion of pay and working conditions. They have shown less professional character in making themselves respected than have plumbers and steamfitters.

There are times, in fact, when my then profession made me ashamed for it. As a former president of the National College English Association, I attended a number of meetings between teachers of liberal arts and corporation executives. I happen to believe, let me say more than parenthetically, that most academics begin by making a central decision about money and the competitive life. I myself made such a decision until I found that planned poverty among sheep bored me. It can be a good decision. In essence, a faculty member decides to live on about one-third the life income (if that much) that he might have earned in business. He is buying time for the life of the mind. His decision is both honorable and self-dignifying. Or so I thought, with occasional lapses into doubt, until that meeting.

The meeting took place at Corning, and a number of high-ticketed executives took the floor to say the liberal arts colleges were important to them, that they sought liberal arts graduates for employment, and that they would continue to support the colleges as a sound investment so long as the colleges turned out men they could use. In fact they loved us.

The last gold-plated executive was hardly seated when my colleagues were up all over the floor begging to know what they could do to turn out a better-suited product. The sheep! Had they elected the life of the mind only to nibble at the feet of the first golden tower they came upon? It was a pleasure to tell them they had disgraced themselves and to remind them that they had no duty to provide raw material for Republic Steel or Standard of New Jersey; that their one function was to lead students to the disciplined life of the mind for its own sake; that if corporations could then make use of men so humanized, let that fact be to the credit of the corporations; but that the faculty destroyed all it stood for when it thought of mechanizing students for readier passage through the employment office.

That abdication of responsibility, whether to corporate lures or to front office directive, has gone too far, and it has done so needlessly. An unreasonable dean can always be put in his place by a responsible faculty member.

Some years ago I received a reasonably standard nasty letter from a dean. "You will explain at once," it began. And then it went on to say that "to not keep adequate records is a grave matter."

I sent the letter back with a note saying its tone was unacceptable, that his request for information would have to be rewritten in a form acceptable to the consensus of a full faculty meeting, and that while he was rewriting, I should prefer that he not split infinitives.

The point was not bravado. I have had to write several such letters in my time and they were always written conscientiously. The point is that the dean always becomes a dear good fellow when he writes again. He is always sure that I must have misunderstood his intention, that certainly there is no need to burden the agenda of the faculty meeting, and that he is, of course, delighted to extend all due apologies.

And the point behind the point is the fact that our faculties, in all but the most depraved institutions, still have the power — if they will demand it and exercise it. Our colleges will be measurably better the day deans become the clerical servants of the faculty. A faculty incapable of self-determination is incapable of governing a classroom dedicated to the discipline of mind in good order.

5

MORE DEANS, MORE DEANERIES*

In my remarks awhile back about college administrators I was not, as various letter writers would have it, courageous (thanks for the medals), nor striking-a-blow-for (I have no worlds to save), nor probing to the core of the problem (has it a core?). Neither was I, as others would have had me be, exhaustive, omniscient, nor dispassionate. Neither was I entirely fair. Why waste fairness on deans? I was simply enough — and as labeled — declaring a prejudice. To state a simple fact, deans have, in general, grown to be officers of higher rank than the faculty, and I see no good in that fact.

That it is a fact is beyond dispute. Two years ago I lectured at the Air Force Academy (Sky Blue U or Aluminum U, as the boys call it), and there the matter of relative rank was left in no doubt: the classroom teachers hold various ranks up to Light Colonel, department heads are Full Chicken Colonels, the dean I saw listed was a Brigadier, and what corresponds to the university president is (or was then) a Two-Star Splendor.

What the Air Force has made dog-plain in its table of organization is not left in much doubt in the civilian colleges. The deans have become higher brass, the faculty is at best made up of field-grade subalterns, and the books, I suppose, are rapidly reaching the point where they can be scanned by IBM machines with no real need to distract the G.I. student-body from its extra-curricular patrols.

Yes — to reply to some of the busier letter writers — I happen to know some civilized deans. I even know a few who are learned men, or who were on their way to being learned men before their careers in intellect were interrupted by their careers in administration. And yes, I think I know a few administrative people I should guess to be superior to anybody on their faculties. The fact remains that deans as a whole are an over-busy lot much too far from the bookshelves and not to be entrusted with educational policy. Let them take care of building and maintenance, of the details of classroom utilization, of student discipline, of the parking problem and dormitory as-signments, of medical care, record-keeping, food-services, alumni relations, and admissions — the last under careful directives from the faculty. But if our colleges are to be colleges and not social clubs or employment offices, only the faculty can be trusted to decide curriculum and degree requirements,

* From the *Saturday Review*, May 19, 1962. Reprinted by permission of John Ciardi and the *Saturday Review.*

admissions policy (as distant from the clerical procedures of admission), scholastic standards, and the academic goals of the college.

Such policies cannot be determined by inferior officers. In taking over the province of academic decision the administration has made itself the higher brass. Certainly the deans can offer good reasons for their way of going: there are always good reasons. Perhaps by Judgment Day it will have become clear that every man-made catastrophe began in the good reasons of some committee, congress, praesidium, or board of directors.

Since literally dozens of deans have written in to demand equal time in which to state their side of things, let their side be stated. The following is a report by Dave Morris, Staff Writer of the Albany *Times-Union,* under the headline "College Officials Outline Policies" and appearing in the *Times-Union* for April 6, 1962. I append all of the direct substance of his report, omitting only a further list of panelists not quoted. The parentheses are mine:

> While college and university professors should have a voice in determining the policy of the institutions at which they teach (that's generous of you, boys), it is the administrative heads who are rightly (hear! hear!) responsible for those policies.
>
> This, in effect, was the opinion of the heads of various area educational (?) institutions and organizations, who met yesterday at Renssalaer Polytechnic Institute to discuss how much participation faculty members should be allowed (by gracious permission?) in university government. The meeting was called by the Renssalaer chapter of the American Association of University Professors.
>
> Addressing the group of area educators, Dr. Bertram Davis, one of the panelists and editor of the AAUP Bulletin, Washington, D.C., said, "Faculty participation helps to insure that the purposes of a college are adequately fulfilled." (I knew there was some reason for having that faculty around.)
>
> Dr. Davis said, however, that the purposes of the educational institution could not be fulfilled by the faculty alone. "It needs deans as well," he said. Dr. Davis added that professors "should know what is happening at their respective schools (the deans will tell them, I assume), but that they must put their faith (Faith, say you? As in, for example, the Trinity?) in the administration."
>
> Dr. Edward A. Fox, a member of the faculty at RPI, pointed out that the principal job of professors was teaching and research. He said trustees and administrators have problems enough keeping the plant running. (That parking problem again.) "The faculty does not have this problem of running the plant," Dr. Fox contended, "and can thus view the goals of the university more clearly." (I think I'm with Dr. Fox, but I can't tell from this report which side he is on.)

There follows a list of other panel members, including Dr. Evan R. Collins, president of Albany State University College, and Dr. Richard G. Folsom, president of RPI, who are then quoted as follows:

Dr. Collins said that while faculty members were involved in the day-to-day problems of the university (books, for example?), it was the job of the board of trustees "to develop long-range plans" (while sitting around the luncheon table, for example?).

Dr. Folsom pointed out that deans become secretaries (assuming they know how to type) when they must listen to the dictates of the faculty (nasty word). He emphasized the importance of the dean's work, and said that the effectiveness of his office depends on the responsibility of the people in charge (a state of affairs that could not, of course, apply to the responsibility of the faculty in charge).

Even a good reporter — and I take Mr. Morris to be a good one — may in some part miss the particular emphasis a speaker intended. It may be that any one of the gentlemen here quoted would want to amend or expand the remarks by which he is represented. But, in general, no man can miss the fact that this is the official sound of the deanly mind. "We have this plant to run," it says, "and, of course, we are going to let you people in the faculty stay around to watch us run it, but making education work is really our job you know, and if you don't know, we're telling you, so pipe down and have faith in us, because we know all about how it has to be done, and if we had to listen to you we'd become mere secretaries."

. . . Something like that. Followed, of course, by reasons; a lot of them, and all of them good.

Followed by the final debauchery of our educational system into a diploma-mill in which the mere matter of ideas is relegated to faculty clerks, while the decisions are made by chart-riding administrative brass in the golden swivel chairs.

Arthur Bestor

Arthur Bestor, former president of the Illinois State Historical Society, is currently Professor of History at the University of Washington. Two of his widely discussed works are Educational Wastelands (1953) *and* The Restoration of Learning (1955). *Mr. Bestor has long been critical of professional educators, and some of his early theories of educational reform are being realized in practice today. In the following selection, Bestor presents his justification for claiming that educators are significantly responsible for the shabby professional standing of elementary and high school teachers. His attack is cogent, disciplined, and pro-*

vocative. Implicit in Bestor's argument is his definition of a "profes-sional man," a definition which invites debate from those who would disagree with him about the talents and prerogatives of teachers. Dis-couragingly enough, several of Bestor's opponents have been known to dismiss his attack by claiming that he is an "academician," not an "educator," as if the manipulation of frivolous jargon could disqualify a man from owning truth.

6

THE PROFESSIONAL STANDING OF
CLASSROOM TEACHERS*

Educationists are morbidly self-conscious about the standing of their pro-fession. They exhort one another to be "professional-minded," and each one feels his pulse from time to time to make sure it has the right professional beat. Beneath it all, however, lies a frightened uncertainty concerning the exact nature of a profession, and a desperate longing for palpable tokens of salvation. To be prompt and faithful in attending teachers' meetings, to prefer pedagogical journals to the *Atlantic* and *The New Yorker,* and to join the National Education Association (preferably as a life member) become crucial signs to distinguish a teacher with proper "professional attitude" from her benighted colleagues. And the hero of the profession, inevitably, is the teacher who goes each summer to a college of education until the pedagogical credits run off the bottom of her official transcript.

Dues payments, committee work, estival self-flagellation, and well-meaning bustle do not make a profession. Until some sense of reality enters this quest for professional status, there is not the slightest chance that public-school teaching will rise to the level of a true profession or that teachers as a group will enjoy the public esteem to which so many of them as individuals are entitled.

There is no particular mystery about the nature of a profession. A pro-fessional man — whether lawyer, physician, engineer, historian, or member of any other well-organized profession — is expected to possess three distinctive kinds of qualifications.

* Reprinted from *The Restoration of Learning* by Arthur Bestor, by permission of Alfred A. Knopf, Inc. Copyright © 1955 by Arthur Bestor.

First of all, he is expected to possess an extensive body of knowledge and a command of certain intellectual processes, both of which are defined in fairly objective terms and are, generally speaking, susceptible of objective measurement by examinations and similar means. He is supposed, as the phrase goes, to "know his stuff."

In the second place, he must obviously possess the ability to apply this knowledge to the practical purposes of the profession. If he is a lawyer he must be able to try cases. If he is an engineer he must be able to apply the mathematics he knows to engineering problems. If he is a professor of history he must be able to make history intelligible and interesting to students. This is the "know-how" of the profession and is not to be confused with the fund of basic knowledge upon which the whole profession rests.

In the third place, a professional man, if he is to be successful, must possess qualities of character and personality that will make him respected, admired, and, if possible, warmly liked by those with whom he deals.

All three qualifications are indispensable. The lack of any one effectually destroys the possibility of professional success. This, however, is not the same as saying that professional standing may be measured in terms of any one of these qualifications just as well as any other. In point of fact, only the first qualification of the three furnishes a criterion that is appropriate and meaningful. A physician may have a charming bedside manner and yet enjoy no particular eminence in the medical profession. A lawyer may be exceedingly sharp in the courtroom and yet rank in the lowest fringes of the bar. Personality and know-how are *prerequisite* to professional activity, like two legs to a runner. But professional *attainment* must be measured in quite other terms.

The paramount importance of knowledge and intellectual command in defining a profession and measuring the attainment of its members arises from the very nature of things. The personal qualities that a professional man requires are the same as the personal qualities that make any human being, in any walk of life, decent, likable, and effective. No profession can claim a special pre-eminence over the rest of mankind in the possession of these qualities. Consequently no profession can possibly be defined or measured in these terms. Similarly, every occupation whatsoever depends upon some sort of specialized know-how. Moreover, the mere know-how of a profession is not necessarily more complicated or harder to learn than that of any other occupation — indeed, it is normally far less demanding than that required by many skilled crafts. What differentiates a profession from a skilled occupation is the fact that the former presupposes and draws upon a vast reservoir of organized knowledge, theoretical reasoning, and developed intellectual power, which each member of the profession individually must command.

One cannot convert a vocation into a profession simply by labeling its particular know-how a "science" and creating pretentious instructional programs therein. Such, however, is precisely the educationists' plan. Courses in pedagogy — the mere know-how of teaching — are multiplied, expanded, subdivided, amplified, protracted, inflated, spun out, and padded. The real service that one or two such courses might perform for the prospective teacher is completely lost sight of in the frantic effort to make each petty detail of teaching into a separate course. Absurd though the process may be, it is not purposeless. Only thus can pedagogy command ever more of the time of undergraduates, and only thus can it be piled, layers thick, upon the helpless teachers who return, year after year, to suffocate in summer schools of education. The prize in this endurance test is an advanced degree in pedagogy and a vague promise of "professional" standing.

Classroom teachers have a right to professional standing and to the prestige that goes with it. They will never attain it by plodding along in the educationists' treadmill. Many teachers enjoy high respect, which they have earned as individuals. For teaching itself to be esteemed as a profession, however, instead of a simple occupation, it will have to establish high standards of knowledge — and not standards of mere pedagogical know-how — for those who are to be recognized as full-fledged members.

However lamentable the fact may appear to the educationists, the public will always judge the teaching profession by what its members know about the subjects they profess to teach. Citizens at large do not have an extravagantly high opinion of college professors (I, for one, prefer this mild skepticism to the excessive deference that is shown in some countries), but there is no question that professors are recognized as men of professional standing. On matters pertaining to their own fields they are listened to, and generally with reasonable respect, because of what they are presumed to know. This is all that professional standing really means or ought to mean. If a particular man's views carry more weight than this, it is not because of his profession but because of his own individual eminence.

Knowledge is what the public respects in any professional man. For a teacher it is the *sine qua non* of public esteem. A teacher who presents herself to the community not as knowing anything in particular but merely as possessing a certain adeptness at handling children in school is never going to be looked upon as anything but a glorified baby-sitter. She may use long words and boast of the "professional" courses she has taken, but ordinary citizens refuse to be impressed. After all, they have done considerable baby-sitting themselves, and they have carried on a good deal of "life-adjustment" education with their own children. They may not have done it particularly well, as they are usually quite ready to admit. But they are justifiably skeptical of the notion that a youngster fresh out of normal school, or a graying spinster back from a summer session in pedagogy, can hand out the definitive answers in these matters. And if these allegedly "professional" teachers have less interest in literature than the parents themselves, if they know less history than the neighboring newspaperman, if they are less skillful at mathematics than the corner grocer, then the public is bound to smile at the absurdity of calling them members of a learned profession. Citizens, we must remember, have daily contact with genuine professions.

Sadder even than the loss of public esteem is the loss of personal and intellectual independence which teachers suffer through following this falsely blazed trail to professional standing.

One of the most significant marks of a true profession is the fact that the professional judgment of an individual member is not subject to the control of those who happen to be his employers. Every professional man, of course, is dependent financially upon those who pay his fees or his salary. But his professional *judgment* is not for sale. It must be independent if his services are to be worth paying for. A doctor's judgment on medical questions is not dictated by his patients, nor would his patients wish it to be. A lawyer is not instructed by his client concerning the proper way to present his case; a man goes to a lawyer precisely because he wishes the latter's best judgment to be employed in his behalf. A professor in a reputable university is not told by his administrative superiors what philosophy of education he is to subscribe to, how he shall plan and teach his course, what particular qualities of mind he shall try to develop in his students, what he shall look for in grading his examinations. Because he is a professional man, he is expected to assume responsibility for determining these things for himself. If he is incompetent he can be fired. But so long as he is retained and recognized by those who have ultimate authority, he has a professional right — indeed, a duty — to resist their encroachment upon the sphere within which his professional judgment is to be exercised.

When classroom teachers are treated in this way, then and only then can public-school teaching be regarded as a true profession. The last thing in the world, however, that the advanced wing of professional educationists and curriculum-makers desire is a body of teachers possessing a professional outlook like this. They want teachers who will not resist being switched "from French to a course in human relations, or from trigonometry to consumer education."[1] The point of view expressed in this quotation is outrageous to every instinct of professional responsibility. Yet "life-adjustment" education and the other new curriculum are utterly dependent upon finding teachers who will accept such a "switch" without demur and without any stirrings of professional conscience. To carry out the new programs a bogus professional ideal for teachers must be substituted for a genuine one — allegiance to pedagogy instead of allegiance to learning.

Teachers who pursue this will-o'-the-wisp are not moving toward the solid ground of professional independence. As they are lured across the bogs, they are bound to sink ever deeper in the mire of occupational subserviency. Possessed of no standing in the community save that which his superiors may bestow upon him, unable to appeal to any objective measure of his personal intellectual competence, a classroom teacher is bound to be treated simply as an employee. Having blindly accepted the educationists' standards, he finds in the end that he possesses merely an occupational skill to be made use of, not a professional judgment to be consulted.

[1] Richard A. Mumma: "The Real Barrier to a More Realistic Curriculum: the Teacher," *Educational Administration and Supervision,* XXXVI (January, 1950), 39–44.

As far back as 1895 a school superintendent, addressing the National Education Association, summed up the *Führer-prinzip* that has come to characterize public-school administration: "The whole law in a nutshell should be: Every teacher responsible to the superintendent alone; the superintendent, and he alone, responsible for the schools."[2] Such a conception of a well-run school system can mean only one thing: teachers are hired to do their jobs as their superiors tell them to. When curriculum revision is under way, classroom teachers may be called in to work out the details, but it is not for them to question the general principles laid down by professors of education and by the public-school bureaucracy. Occasionally a professional educationist on the defensive will assert that "every teacher, either as an individual or as a member of curriculum committees, is a curriculum maker."[3] This is sheer mythology, true only in the sense that every laborer who spikes down the track is a railroad-builder.

Educational policy in institutions of higher learning is formulated according to theories of academic responsibility utterly at variance with those of the public schools. Even the practice, despite certain encroachments by college administrators, is markedly different. In colleges and universities administrative officers derive authority from the board of trustees only in supposedly non-academic spheres. Control of educational policy is vested in the teaching staff according to the statutes of most universities, and in such matters the administrative officers are, theoretically, mere agents of the faculty. Practice is not too far removed from theory, so far at least as course offerings are concerned, for professors, departments, and colleges are rarely subjected to administrative pressure in these matters. Faculty committees, on paper at least, determine the policy of the university with respect to larger questions like admissions and requirements for degrees. It would be unrealistic to deny that administrators exercise considerable influence upon these decisions. Even so, no competent president or dean of a college of reputable standing would think of imposing new and far-reaching academic policies upon his institution without consulting his faculty and getting its approval. "Stoutism" at the University of Nevada is the notorious exception that proves the rule, and "Stoutism" represented the irruption into higher education of an administrative mentality that had been developed within a secondary school — a school, moreover, under the direct control of a faculty of educationists.

In opposing the encroachments of administrative authority upon the field of educational policy, the faculty of a college or university derives its strength from many sources. College administrators are drawn ordinarily from the ranks of the faculty. Chairmen of departments are always regular faculty members, still active in teaching and research, and their tour of administra-

[2] Orville T. Bright: "Changes — Wise and Unwise — in Grammar and High Schools," National Education Association *Journal of Proceedings and Addresses*, XXXIV (1895), 277.

[3] Edwin H. Reeder: "The Quarrel between Professors of Academic Subjects and Professors of Education: an Analysis," American Association of University Professors *Bulletin*, XXXVII (Autumn 1951), 520.

tive duty, more often than not, is for a limited period. Deans likewise are customarily appointed from among regular members of the faculty, and they frequently continue to carry a partial teaching load. In the top levels of the administrative hierarchy, it is true, there are a few administrators whose previous participation in the intellectual life of a university has been exceedingly limited. There is likewise an alarming tendency for college administration to be viewed in certain quarters as a career in itself, distinct from college teaching and scholarly research. But at their very worst these deleterious tendencies are not likely to produce in the near future a self-conscious caste of professional administrators comparable to those who domineer over many public schools.

College faculties derive strength also from the active participation of individual professors in the learned societies pertaining to their respective fields. A scholar's true standing in his profession depends far more upon the judgment of his colleagues in the same discipline, as represented in such associations, than upon the recognition he may gain, deservedly or undeservedly, from a local college administrator. Consequently the existence of strong ties among scholars through their learned societies is an important bulwark against the lowering of college standards through administrative influence and encroachment. In the affairs of the learned societies themselves, it should be noted, university administrators as such play a completely negligible role.

Finally, the support that the faculty of one university can secure from outside in a legitimate battle over educational policy is a genuine source of strength. In part this results from an *esprit de corps* and a public opinion which recognize that the standing of the university itself is jeopardized if the faculty fails to maintain its authority over educational policy. To support their position, scholars and scientists as a group have their own organization devoted to the protection of academic standards, the American Association of University Professors. One of its functions is to investigate, and if necessary censure, the administrative officers and the governing board of an institution that fails to observe "the generally recognized principles of academic freedom and tenure." Furthermore, unlike the organizations in the field of public-school education, the Association relegates to associate membership any active member "whose work becomes primarily administrative."[4]

This elaborate structure of checks and balances is what gives the college professor the intellectual independence that entitles him to recognition as a professional man. In turn, the professional independence of the scholar or scientist on a university faculty constitutes the greatest of all guarantees of the integrity and standards of higher education. The scholar has a personal and inalienable responsibility for those standards because he is a professional man and not a mere employee. He is responsible to the institution, of course, but he is also responsible to his profession and to the community. The denial to public-school teachers of genuine professional independence and responsi-

[4] American Association of University Professors *Bulletin*, XXXVIII (Winter 1952–3), 645, 646–7.

bility is injurious not merely to them but to the nation, for it leaves the intellectual integrity of the schools without real guardians.

The greatest source of independence, both personal and intellectual, to any teacher is his consciousness of belonging to a recognized profession that includes all those working in his field, the most eminent as well as the most obscure, and of belonging to an organization that is run by the active members of the profession, not by those who may happen to be their employers. No educational association or teachers' organization of the usual sort meets these vital tests. In the meetings of societies like these, the high-school teacher does not associate with the college professor in the same field, though both, after all, are teachers of one discipline. In other words, he does not make the acquaintance of those who are dealing with the same problems on a different level and in a different context. He gains none of the intellectual stimulus and none of the sense of belonging to a mature profession that would come to him through participation in the work of a genuine learned society. Instead he finds himself, in a teachers' association, classified merely as a member of an occupational group facing common vocational problems, not as a member of a profession united by common intellectual interests. He discovers, finally, that his administrative superiors, far from being relegated to a back seat, are parading their authority as on every other day of the year.

Professional educationists are adepts in the technique of "divide and rule." They have learned to rule the lower schools by dividing them from higher learning. They have learned to rule the classroom teachers by dividing them from their colleagues in the same academic fields. As a consequence few classroom teachers enjoy the personal and intellectual independence that is the right of any self-respecting member of a profession.

The natural allies of a serious and competent teacher in the high school are his colleagues in the same discipline on university and college faculties. The educationists have worked with vast ingenuity and almost complete success to prevent such an alliance from coming into being. A chemist or a historian, for example, who teaches in the public schools is discouraged from thinking of himself in the terms I have just used. He must be careful to describe himself as a science teacher or a social-studies teacher — better still, as a high-school teacher, pure and simple — lest he be considered lukewarm in his devotion to "education." His administrative superiors give him to understand that his proper affiliation is with the National Education Association, not the American Chemical Society or the American Historical Association. He is expected to improve his mind by devising new pedagogical procedures, not by performing experiments or investigating historical problems. If he is found too often in the company of professional chemists or historians, or if he seeks publication in the pages of scientific or historical journals, he is liable to the charge of being that pedagogical pariah, a "subject-matter specialist."

Such anti-intellectual pressures upon the classroom teacher constitute a direct challenge to the scientists and scholars of the nation. They must act, and act vigorously, to protect the teacher whose devotion to learning exposes him to discrimination and retaliation. They must, through their own organizations, accord him the recognition that is denied him by the educational bureaucracy. They must provide direct incentives to public-school teachers to devote their advanced study to solid work in the intellectual disciplines. They must encourage teachers to march down the highroad of learning instead of wandering off into the dead-end streets of the educationists. The scientific and scholarly societies of the country can, I believe, give valuable assistance to serious classroom teachers in making their calling a genuine profession.

An immediate and practicable step, as I see it, would be for each of the learned societies to offer a secondary-school teaching diploma in its own field. The plans for these diplomas might well be co-ordinated through such an interdisciplinary body as the Permanent Scientific and Scholarly Commission on Secondary Education which I have suggested. There should be at least two grades of such diplomas, standard and advanced, possession of the former being prerequisite to candidacy for the latter. Each diploma would be awarded primarily on the basis of rigorous comprehensive examinations in the subject. To begin with, the diplomas should probably be open only to teachers already in possession of a state teaching certificate and with a specified number of years of classroom experience to their credit. No more than a routine check of the record on these matters would be called for, and ultimately the examinations might be opened to candidates for secondary-school teaching as well as to experienced teachers.

The examinations would presumably be offered once or twice a year, perhaps on the campuses of selected universities. Their content would, of course, be different from that of examinations designed to test the competence of a research scholar. The teachers' examinations would call for greater immediate proficiency in the matters covered in high-school courses than an advanced worker might have reason to possess. At the same time, the examinations should be comprehensive, requiring command of the subject as a whole, above and beyond the topics that would be put to direct classroom use. They would test the student's command of the bibliography of the subject, less in terms of materials necessary for advanced research than in terms of the crucial conflicts of interpretation that currently exist in the discipline and the relative weight of scholarly opinion thereon. Rigorous standards of grading must be maintained. Only the names of those passing the examinations should be announced, and an unsuccessful candidate might try the examination again after a reasonable interval of time.

To work out such a program would be, I know, a time-consuming, expensive, and delicate task. The committee charged with responsibility by the learned society in question should be composed primarily of recognized scholars in the field. It should work very closely with agencies experienced in tests and measurements, and the actual administration of the examinations might be delegated to such agencies on a contractual basis, with full power over policy retained by the committee. The latter should co-ordinate its work with that of other learned societies doing the same job, and it should seek advice from the groups who administer bar examinations and who issue advanced certificates in other professional fields.

Extensive publicity should be given to the program once it is inaugurated, so that teachers who earned the diploma would be assured of widespread public and professional recognition. Teaching diplomas in the various sciences and mathematics might well be inaugurated before those in the languages and history, because of the shortage of teachers in the former fields and the greater prestige and resources of the scientific societies. Rigorous standards of achievement could thus be set at the very beginning, and these standards could be more easily maintained as diplomas began to be offered in other fields.

What cumulative effects upon teaching might be expected from the inauguration, let us say, of a Secondary-School Teaching Diploma in History, issued under the joint authority of the American Historical Association and the Permanent Scientific and Scholarly Commission on Secondary Education? Doubtless the enterprise would be damned with faint praise by professors of education. Neither the public at large nor the actual school administrators would be likely to follow their lead in this. The prestige of a school system would be enhanced in proportion to the number of diploma-holders on its faculty. Superintendents, principals, and school boards would be well aware of this. Gradually the attitude toward advanced training would change in administrative circles. Able teachers would be urged not to pile up more credits in pedagogy but to prepare themselves to become candidates for the diplomas in their own fields. Once the state-imposed certification requirements have been met by their teachers, school administrators are under no real compulsion to require additional pedagogical course-work from their staff members. They have tended in recent years to follow the line of least resistance and thus to let the pedagogues determine what teachers should do to demonstrate "professional growth." So long as educationists alone were bestowing accolades upon particular school systems and their heads, cooperation with their demands was prudent and rewarding. Under the new conditions, however, school administrators would have good reason to back up their teachers in resisting the demand that they spend their summers playing pedagogical blindman's buff, whenever this meant the diversion of time from disciplined study in candidacy for a diploma. Obviously nothing should prevent a principal from urging upon a teacher who was manifestly deficient in pedagogical skill such courses in education as he felt reasonably sure would help her. And he might well desire to have on his staff certain teachers whose professional field would be psychology rather than one of the disciplines actually taught in the school. But with the new stimuli, superintendents and principals would be as anxious as the teachers themselves for every bit of advanced study to mean something.

Within the colleges and universities the effects would be profound and salutary. A teacher preparing for a diploma in his chosen discipline would seek guidance in his advanced studies from the recognized scholars in the field, and would be relatively immune to the pressures from the faculty of pedagogy. Even the educational bureaucracy in charge of state certification would have to respond eventually to the combined pressure of teachers and the public. By establishing diplomas of their own, the learned societies can hasten the coming of official state certificates in the various fields. . . . Once the latter are established by state certifying authorities, the standards for the diplomas of the learned societies should be raised even higher, so that they would continue to represent truly outstanding and exceptional achievement.

To the teacher himself the possession of a diploma would mean assured professional status, both in the school system and in the community. He could no longer be pushed around, "from French to a course in human relations, or from trigonometry to consumer education." His views on the curriculum would count for something. He would no longer have to take responsibility before his own community for the antics of the educationists, because his own independent position would enable him clearly to dissociate himself from policies of which he disapproved. Eventually teachers' associations might come to be controlled by teachers themselves instead of existing to control them.

Even in an economic sense, the position of the able classroom teacher would become far stronger. The holders of teaching diplomas would be the recognized leaders of their profession and the supply would always be smaller than the demand. A higher salary scale for the genuinely professional members of teaching staffs would not be long in coming. Entrance into this group would require serious effort and devotion, not the mere accumulation of the cheap credits and the cheap degrees that now flood the pedagogical market. Teaching will always have its high proportion of drifters and temporary workers. There is no reason why it should not have a central core of truly professional teachers, dedicated to learning and well aware of the difference between knowledge and know-how. The public will not accord professional recognition to faddists and the riders on band-wagons. Once it is given the means to distinguish the independent, responsible, scholarly teacher from the mass, I have no doubt that it will support his professional position and give him the financial security to which he is entitled.

Martin Mayer

After thirty months of research, Martin Mayer began to write The Schools, *a study which prompted Richardson Wood to state, "This book shows teachers and pupils of all kinds in action. Strengthened by such evidence, the author twists the tails of a whole herd of sacred cows, from brindled educational theorists to complacent authors of textbooks. The bellows of dismay should be loud and long. . . ." The bellows have indeed been loud and long, particularly in regard to Mayer's examination of teacher education. His criticism of current practices derives not only from theoretical reservations but also from what Mayer absorbed by direct observation of teacher-training classes. With no a priori ax to grind, with the reporter's eye, Mayer captures atmosphere and mood as well as fact, ending his presentation with the disturbing and logical conclusion that teacher training must become "intellectually respectable before teachers as a group receive community respect."*

Detailed and scholarly complements to Mayer's description of teacher education may be found in two recent books with ironically contrasting titles, The Education of American Teachers *by James Conant and* The Miseducation of American Teachers *by James D. Koerner.*

7

TEACHER TRAINING*

The children come to school, and are placed immediately in the hands of a teacher, a person licensed by the state to teach, on the basis of special academic preparation for the job.

I

"I want to do two things with you today," said Professor Louis Forsdale to the forty-odd students in "English 261RR — Teaching of English in secondary schools: roles and responsibilities." The class ranges from recent college graduates reading Kerouac's *On the Road* to large ladies in their fifties who keep their hats on. The classroom itself is antique, with tile halfway up the walls, but the lighting fixtures are more recent. Forsdale is a small, round man with a round face and a receding hair line; his typical expression is a bland smile. The course is described in the Teachers College catalogue as follows:

> A coordinating seminar for pre-service teachers of English in junior and senior high schools, public and private, bringing together comprehensive reading in professional literature and scholarship in the fields of linguistics, literature and communication arts and skills; systematic study of established and experimental methods of instruction with particular attention to materials, units of study, and processes of evaluation appropriate to the interests and abilities of adolescents and young adults.

"The first thing I want to do," Forsdale continued, "is to tell you about the convention of the National Council of Teachers of English in Denver. Not very much — just enough to tell you about the status of your professional organization this year.

"I hope that many of you will want to become closely associated with the National Council . . . and I am making this report in the interests of your future career. The first point I want to make is that your Council now has fifty-six thousand members — more, unless I am misled, than any other such group. Its size means primarily to you that more and more teachers of English are becoming affiliated with their national organization, and thus will have more to say about national policy. They will have more influence at local school boards. When the Executive Council votes, as it did, to do something to reduce the extracurricular load of teachers of English, the school boards will have to pay attention.

"Second, your Council is building a new headquarters at Champaign, Illinois. . . . Third, the names of the outgoing and incoming presidents . . . Fourth, the question of what are the channels of advancement in the teaching of English.

"That is, if you are interested in professional advancement. If you want to stay, your voice unheard outside the confines of a Rye, New York, classroom, then you won't be interested. But if you are looking forward to a career, to a chance to look backward on twenty years of professional leadership, not followership, let me give you a strategy for advancement.

"First, get your job and do well at it for the first two years. Don't push too much at first; you can look naïve. While you're in your job, continue to read about your profession. Read the *Times* and the *Herald Tribune,* and learn about the pressures which are being brought against teachers of English and teachers in general. You may find yourself one of five teachers in a school of one hundred who *are* informed.

"Read your professional journal, *The English Journal.* And then, begin to write. Something unusual has happened in your classroom, some unusual unit has been very successful. Begin to write. Don't worry about whether anyone is interested. Begin to write. Writing stimulates your own imagination. And the editor may wish to publish what you send in. It marks you as someone who is moving ahead.

"Begin to attend meetings of your local association — it may be an association of local English teachers or just a faculty association. And volunteer for work, on committees. You will become known, to regional committees, state committees.

"What good is becoming known? It moves you forward in every way — including financially.

"Go to the National Council meetings, become acquainted with the people who make policy. Report back to your local association, report to your school board. You become marked as the person in the system who *knows* about English.

"It costs money — especially if you go to the national conventions. But it costs a doctor money, too, to get started, or a lawyer.

"And your school board may pay for it. In Denver there were two young teachers who had been in this course two years ago. They came from Long Island. Their school board sent them — because they asked. The school board said, 'Why not? When do you want your money? Now or later?'

"Go back to school. Get your doctorate — because, as you probably know, you can advance only so far without it.

"If you decide to go to Chicago, to the next convention, or to one of these other meetings, drop us a card here at Teachers College and we'll see you get acquainted. There were twenty-five Teachers College people at Denver, and except for the very young ones they were all moving ahead . . . professionally. . . ."

II

"I'll make a rash statement," said F. C. Rosecranze, dean of the College of Education at Wayne State University in Detroit. "I'll say that I think teacher education now is where medical education was in 1910, before the Flexner Report. . . ."

III

The idea of a special education for teachers predates by some generations the idea of university education for any large fraction of the community. The problem confronting Horace Mann in the 1830's and Francis Parker in the 1890's was that of the elementary-school teacher who had no more than an elementary education herself. Moreover, once the Lancasterian system had been discredited, there was no way to set up a true apprenticeship scheme in teaching. Though principals might supervise her work in varying degrees, the new teacher essentially had to begin with the full classroom responsibilities of the experienced journeyman; unlike the lawyer or the accountant or the carpenter, the teacher could not learn her job by working under the direct and steady supervision of a practitioner. Normal schools, therefore, were established to improve the teacher's general education and to substitute special training for apprenticeship. Essentially, they gave secondary and remedial-elementary rather than university education.

These conditions persisted well into this century. When Paul Mort of Teachers College was graduated from eighth grade in 1907 he received a diploma ("largest diploma I ever got, with the fanciest handwriting") specifically entitling him to entry to the state university at Lansing, Michigan, for teacher training. In France, even today, a large proportion of elementary-school teachers (or *instituteurs*) never see the inside of a *lycée*. They go from elementary school to a *cours complémentaire* and thence to an *école normale* from which they emerge, at eighteen or nineteen, with a special *Baccalauréat* which carries an official national government guarantee of a teaching job. In Britain, the teaching community is now recruited almost exclusively from the ranks of those who are chosen for grammar schools, and the selection system for grammar-school entrance (to give the Devil his due) has probably been responsible for the striking rise in intelligence of the average British elementary-school teacher since the war. But future elementary teachers still go from a grammar school to a teacher-training college, and they go, typically, at age sixteen, without the experience of the sixth form. Until 1960 these colleges offered only a two-year program, so that the elementary teacher emerged from training just as her more fortunate fellows were entering a university.

Secondary-school teachers, on the other hand, were traditionally college graduates, in all countries. Normal schools and teachers colleges were not regarded as equipped to train people who would be dealing with the more developed content of secondary education. At the same time, most authorities held that anyone who had mastered an academic discipline on the college level was automatically equipped to teach it on the secondary level, and required no special training in education. Even today, in Britain, any university graduate is entitled to teach, though he may not teach a second year unless his work has been approved by the principal of his school and the local representative of the corps of Her Majesty's Inspectors. Nevertheless — significantly — nearly all better British secondary schools, private or state-supported, when they have to hire inexperienced personnel, give priority to candidates who have taken an additional year of teacher training after receiving their degree (a "fourth year" in the British system, where the university program is only three years long).

Compulsory education forced a semblance of order onto the chaos of teacher training in the United States. If the state insisted that the child go to school, the state also had to insist that the teacher in whose hands the child would be placed possessed at least a minimal level of competence. State "certification" of teachers was a political and ethical necessity, not a power play run by ambitious normal-school professors. But it operated, inevitably, to strengthen the hand of those whose work was the training of future teachers.

Teaching is not the only field in which practitioners require a state license: doctors, lawyers, architects, barbers, accountants and others must also meet certain minimum conditions before they can go to work. But the state is more intimately involved with teachers than it is with any other group of licensees. By and large, in other fields, state governments have been willing to delegate to professional bodies the authority to award and withdraw licenses, subject to judicial review. The certification of teachers, however, remains a governmental function; indeed, as Myron Lieberman points out in his book *Education as a Profession,* most states insist that the members of the board which passes on teacher qualifications must *not* be teachers.

Perhaps for this reason, it has been extraordinarily difficult to set logical standards of competence or training for qualification as a teacher. "Many standards which applicants must meet," William Frederick of the Council of State Governments told a meeting of the Council on Co-operation in Teacher Education, "have little apparent relationship to the ability to practice." Generally speaking, state departments of education make no effort to determine the competence of applicants for teacher certificates. Instead, they prescribe in general or detailed terms the "courses" which a prospective teacher must take before licensing, and they award their certificates entirely on a transcript of grades and the recommendation of the school at which the candidate took the required "courses." Other licensing bodies have developed examinations to test asserted competence; departments of education have not. It is fair to say that teachers, who insist on the importance of examinations for their students, have been unwilling to submit their claims of professional competence to an examination procedure in order to secure their certificates. Many larger cities, however, among them New York, hire and promote personnel on the basis of competitive examinations.

Usually, external examinations produce an undesirable rigidity in curriculum and are therefore to be avoided. Where a requirement of "course credits" is substituted for examinations, however, an even more undesirable artificiality may be introduced. "Let us now be very honest with ourselves," said Stephen Freeman of Middlebury College to the Council on Co-operation in Teacher Education, "and admit that certification on the basis of a prescribed number of credits, semester or quarter-hours, of exposure to subject in college may be next to meaningless. Time spent sitting in a class, or even the feat of passing a final examination in a course does not necessarily indicate that the student is ready to interpret this information to others. . . . It is impossible to raise standards simply by increasing the number of credit hours required for a certificate. Too often, the thirty postgraduate hours that are increasingly required are so much wasted motion, as far as improving the quality of the instruction is concerned."

Most students of the subject would agree that existing certification laws work to restrict entry to teaching without necessarily restricting it to competent personnel. Attention is commonly called to the scandal of 100,000 or so "substitutes" in the schools — teachers who have not won certificates but have been given teaching jobs because there are not enough licensed teachers to go around. It is an even worse scandal that many of these "substitutes" have been teaching for five years or even longer, to the complete satisfaction of their superiors, but must continue to bear the stigma of an inferior label (and to receive an inferior salary) simply because they have not taken required "courses." Any system which refuses to accept experience or proved ability as criteria is demonstrably unreasonable and unjust.

Examples of stupidity in the application of arbitrary certification laws can be found in almost any school system, but perhaps the most striking of all is the case of William Cornog, superintendent of New Trier High School. A product of Philadelphia's selective Central High School thirty-odd years ago ("Talk about European schools — I had eleven marks on my card in the 1920's"), Cornog went on to a Ph.D. in English and medieval Latin and a teaching job at Northwestern University. He remained, however, a faithful and interested alumnus of Central High; and one day in 1943, the Philadelphia school system came to him and asked him if he would resign his professorship at Northwestern to take over as principal at Central High. "I was as innocent as a babe about certification," Cornog recalls; he did not even look into the question of the "course credits" he might need to qualify as a principal. Eventually he had to take summer courses in visual education and American history to qualify for his certificate.

Cornog was principal of Central High for twelve years, during the course of which he picked up a nationwide reputation among working educators for intelligence, judgment and administrative ability. When New Trier found itself in need of a new top man, the board went to Cornog. By now his original innocence had been corrupted, and he was sure he couldn't qualify — each state licenses independently, and the Illinois Department of Education is one of the most insistent in the nation on "course credit" requirements for teaching. He was told, in effect, that New Trier Township could take care of such matters; and, indeed, on representations from the New Trier Board, the state granted him a certificate. Cornog took the job, which is perhaps the most attractive position in American education — a very large secondary school in a wealthy community which cares about education, paying a superintendent's salary for the more interesting work of actually running a school.

Cornog's early months at New Trier were untroubled, until the North Central Association of Schools and Colleges came around in the shape of its Illinois Committee. The Association, an unofficial body of educators, "recognizes" schools on the basis of their staff, physical plant, program and so forth, and can withdraw its recognition at any time. On the whole, this association and its peers in the other regions have undoubtedly been a force in pushing schools to higher standards of teaching as well as facilities; but like most professional bodies these organizations suffer moments of doctrinaire paralysis. A particularly severe seizure crippled the committee which investigated New Trier. Despite the manifest excellence of the school, the North Central Association placed New Trier on its "warning list" and threatened to withdraw recognition, on the grounds that the head of the school lacked eighteen credit hours in education to qualify for his job. Cornog, still a trifle naïve, asked the Committee, "Don't you give me any credit for twelve years of running a school in Philadelphia?" The answer came back: "No."

Cornog carried the message to his Board, which was annoyed but not troubled, taking the position that the prestige of New Trier was higher than the prestige of the North Central Association. The Association complained to the Illinois Department of Education, which made its own investigation, and under pressure from both directions compromised with a pronouncement that Cornog lacked *eight* credit hours in education. "They counted as education courses some of the work I'd done at college," Cornog remembers. "I never found out why." With this finding of fact, the Department notified New Trier that unless its head took eight credit hours of education courses, the school would lose state accreditation. The Board was now incensed at the proceedings, but loss of accreditation would deprive New Trier of the right to send its graduates to the University of Illinois without an entrance examination; and some of the New Trier students who wish to go to the University of Illinois probably could not pass an entrance examination. Cornog offered to resign. The University of Chicago had asked him to consider a professorship of education, and while he liked the New Trier job he felt it would be simpler for everyone if he moved on.

The New Trier Board would not hear of a resignation. "They thought I showed promise despite my lack of training," Cornog says. Not without a certain bitterness, Cornog took the only possible path out of what looked like an impasse which might damage the students at his school. He went voluntarily to the University of Chicago, where he was sought after for a professorship of educational administration, and enrolled in two courses in educational administration. As he finished moving down the registration line the first day, the girl at the last table noted from his application blank that he held a Ph.D. "Is your doctorate in education?" she asked.

"No," said Cornog.

"That's too bad," the girl said. "If it was in education, you could take these courses without charge."

"If my doctorate was in education," said Cornog rather sweetly (a good principal learns quickly to control his temper), "I don't think I'd be taking these courses at all."

The girl said, "Oh."

IV

"I find," said George Kneller, UCLA's rather suave professor of educational philosophy, "that only one in a hundred of my students has had any philosophy."

His visitor was amazed. UCLA, like many other state universities, requires two years of "liberal education" before a student can opt for education courses. Hadn't more of these kids taken at least one philosophy course?

"They may have had a course in philosophy, but it hasn't done anything for them. Mike," Kneller said, calling to his young assistant at the other desk, "wouldn't you say that?"

"It was a course," Mike said.

Didn't they take anything out of it at all?

"Take anything *out* of it?" Mike said in amazement. "Look. It was a course *in* philosophy. They took the course. If they took anything *out* of it, that wouldn't be fair to later generations. . . ."

V

The courses which people must take if they wish to be licensed to teach break into three broad categories. First in the sequence are the "foundation" courses, in the history, philosophy, psychology and sociology of education. "As much a part of general education as any course in history or psychology," says Erling Hunt of Teachers College, "though of course our critics would deny it." Next come the courses in "general methods," which may range from general titles like "Methods of Secondary School Teaching" or "Curriculum Construction" to rarefied subjects like "Film Strips in Early Childhood Education." Finally there are "special methods" courses, which claim to give instruction in the techniques of teaching specific subjects — though in fact the degree of specialization is never great. The course is always in "Reading," or at best "Reading in the Intermediate Grades," rather than "Fourth-Grade Reading"; "Social Studies in the Secondary School" rather than "Teaching of History" or geography or civics. Some universities run "demonstration schools" where students can watch master teachers at work as part of their training in general or special methods, and where the professors of the education department can practice what they preach, if they so desire.

By common consent, the most important single "course" in the program is "Practice Teaching" or "Student Teaching." This course, which comes at the end of the program, requires the student to work in an actual classroom, with real children, under the supervision of an experienced teacher. The work is undoubtedly valuable for all concerned: the student gets a necessary taste of blood, the supervising teacher gets a free assistant and sometimes a little money from the school of education for instructing and reporting on her ward, the children have the fun of helping or bedeviling an inexperienced young adult. The student teacher works in the same classroom throughout the course, either two or three mornings a week for the length of a college term or four to six weeks straight through, every morning. Once a week, she meets with her professor and the other student teachers to discuss her experiences and profit from those of others. (In France, student teachers work in teams of three and criticize each other's performance.) What the new teacher receives from her student teaching depends, inevitably, on the quality of the supervising teacher and her interest in doing this sort of work. Even at best, when the regular teacher is willing to subordinate the smooth running of her class to the interest of training someone new, the apprenticeship is less than ideal. The range of problems which arise is inevitably rather narrow. By the nature of the arrangement, the student must work along whatever lines the supervising teacher has established and cannot try out her own ideas (or those of the professors of education back home). And, as Judson Shaplin of Harvard writes, "Basic classroom control is established and maintained by the master teacher even when he is absent." Though student teaching is indispensable, it is not in itself a solution to the problems of teacher training: it often knocks the initiative and self-reliance out of the aspiring teacher without giving her the acceptable substitute of professional security.

Until quite recently, state departments of education typically offered a number of different licenses (California had more than fifty of them), and set down specific requirements for each in terms of the titles of the courses which the candidate had to take. On the secondary level, even now, many departments license secondary-school teachers for specific subjects, traditionally their college "major" and "minor," reinforced by "special methods" courses in the teaching of each. The trend, however, is toward a general certificate in "elementary education" or "secondary education." (Even where special licenses are given on the secondary level, many teachers work "out of license," teaching subjects other than those they were originally proclaimed qualified to teach. A history teacher teaching physics is not a "substitute" and is not penalized in title or salary for failure of academic preparation.) Where general licenses are given, the state department will usually allow the teacher-training institution to arrange at least the bulk of the student's program, and will issue a license on receipt of a transcript of grades and a recommendation.

The licensing requirements of the state departments usually demand course-credits in education totaling slightly more than a quarter of a full four-year college program for elementary teachers, slightly less for secondary teachers. Sometimes the university or teacher-training school asks much more than the state minimum. Recently, to cure teacher shortages and meet agitation by the Fund for the Advancement of Education, many universities have begun a "fifth-year" program in which a liberal arts graduate can win a master's degree and a teaching license via a summer session plus a year's study. The State of Connecticut will allow liberal arts graduates to begin teaching on a provisional license after only a summer session of work in education, though such teachers must make up the rest of the required courses within five years or lose their license.

Though the states set minimum "credit hour" requirements in education courses, they did not until recently take any interest in what the applicant had studied other than education (and, of course, the major field for the secondary teacher). Teachers colleges, which specialized in training elementary teachers, ran parallel to music conservatories: they offered a few relatively low-level courses in English, history, science and so forth, but put the weight of their effort on education courses, which often made up more than half the students' program. During the last decades, however, the teachers colleges have been expanding their offerings in academic disciplines, often to the point where they become full-fledged affiliates of a general state university. In the meantime, the universities, especially those with state support, have taken over the bulk of the job of training future teachers. Today, nearly two-thirds of all new teachers receive their degrees from universities rather than from teachers colleges.

The shift of locale has made future teachers more conscious of the existence of an intellectual world with which they had previously made no contact whatever. Four years at a university, even a mediocre university, is a very different experience from four years in the pale surroundings of a teachers college. Few universities, moreover, will allow prospective teachers to "major" in education from the moment of entrance. Most of them require all students to take roughly similar programs for the first two years, and do not permit future teachers to start their training courses until junior year. Many require an academic "major" other than education even for future elementary teachers, though the results of this requirement are often disappointing. "Most of our elementary teachers," says Alonzo Grace, dean of the school of education at Illinois and former Commissioner of Education in Connecticut, "major in child development, which I regard as a pain in the neck. They'd be much better teachers if they majored in mathematics and took their education and child-development courses on the side."

Theoretically, the shift of teacher training to the universities should also have given professors of academic disciplines a new interest in and insight into the problems of teacher training, which university professors had always ignored in the past. But the professors would not be stirred. They transferred their former contempt for teachers colleges to the departments of education in their own universities, creating open warfare within their own faculty clubs and common rooms. The routine joke at Teachers College holds that 120th Street, which separates TC from the rest of Columbia University, "is the widest street in the world." In a book examining their own graduate schools, the faculty of Columbia brushed aside TC with the observation that the question of its continued affiliation with the University should be carefully considered. George Bereday of TC recently told Jacques Barzun, provost of Columbia, that he and his Young Turk colleagues would within five years make Teachers College a place the University could be proud of. "In five years," Barzun replied contemptuously, "you'll be lost there in the miasma with the rest of them." In many universities, there is little if any contact between the members of the department of education and the members of the other departments in the school.

In part, the war between the academic professors and the professors of education is simply a trade-union dispute in which outsiders need take no interest. The introduction of any new subject into universities — from physics in the mid-nineteenth century to sociology in the 1930's — has provoked howls of outrage from established professors who see their own fields and personal positions enfeebled. The student who takes a course in education cannot take a course in romance philology which meets at the same hour, and the romance language department cannot avoid the feeling that philology would be better for him. Such political and economic disputes, however, could not in themselves create the bitterness that can be seen on almost any university campus. The problem, which must be faced, is more personal and more legitimate.

There are men of great personal and intellectual distinction teaching education. Any faculty in any field of study would be proud to number among its members men like Lawrence Cremin and George Bereday of Teachers College, Alan Griffin of Ohio State, Edwin Hirschi of Utah, UCLA's George Kneller and Evan Kieslar, Harvard's Robert Ulich, John Carroll, Israel Scheffler and Judson Shaplin, NYU's William Brickman and Louis Raths, and many others. And there are men of little quality teaching academic disciplines in every university. On the average, however, it is true to say that the academic professors, with many exceptions in the applied sciences and some in the social sciences, are educated men, and the professors of education are not. From the opposite point of view, Hugh Spier, dean of the school of education at Kansas City University, says that "professors of education are usually practical people, while academic professors are idealists."

"Jim Conant is a good friend of mine," said Paul Mort of Teachers College shortly before his retirement, "and he's one of the greatest men I've ever met. There's nothing like a liberal education — I know that. But what these people have to face up to is that you can't make Romans out of all the Gauls. On most people, a liberal education doesn't take. *It didn't take on me.*" With all respect to Paul Mort, who was and is one of the most useful people in American education, university professors are not likely to feel a deep academic fellowship for men who make such admissions.

During the 1950's, the university professors took their case to the public in books and magazine articles, complaining about the quality of the courses offered in the field of education. Education courses, they said, were "how-to" courses, which taught students nothing but a collection of techniques useless in themselves, without the "content" of an academic discipline. To the "how-to" or "methods" course which was alleged to be the specialty of the professor of education, the academic professors opposed the great tradition of the liberal arts, from Aristotle through Mortimer Adler. Rhetoric filled the air, and great beatings of wings and breasts could be heard from within the universities. After all, the liberal arts, as the wise Greeks said so long ago, were by definition the studies "appropriate to free men." There could be no substitute for the beauty and strength of a liberal arts "foundation." The argument flew into realms of poetry, and the outside observer was left to wonder, in great puzzlement, when the average liberal arts course had suddenly got so good.

This argument now appears to be subsiding. Though it rested on enough truth to keep it afloat for some years — most education courses are *not* intellectually respectable, because their teachers and the textbooks employed are not intellectually respectable — the theoretical basis of the discussion was always nonsense. "I am impressed," says Judson Shaplin, associate dean of the Graduate School of Education at Harvard, "with the difficulty of teaching." So is almost everyone else who has looked at the matter seriously. There is no logical basis for an argument that the practice of law requires a specialized training, while teaching does not. If a course in torts can be related to the practice of law, surely a course in "The Teaching of Reading" can be related to the work of teaching. There exists in education — still at large, not yet caught and codified — a body of techniques more valuable and difficult to master than the techniques taught in business schools or journalism schools; and probably as valuable and difficult as the techniques taught in law schools and medical schools. Nobody would deny that there are bad courses given every year in business, journalism, law, medicine, liberal arts and education. Surely the time has come for everyone to admit that there are at least *some* good courses given in education, too; and to study the elements which distinguish the good course from the bad one.

VI

The new Education Building of the University of Utah, a modest, rather barracks-like structure, stood in a sea of mud halfway up the hill toward the old U.S. Army fort which kept its guns trained on Brigham Young's Salt Lake City house through the second half of the nineteenth century. Down on the basement level, Wanda Robertson was meeting with a class of about thirty prospective elementary-school teachers, who were ranged about five tables in the room, deep in conversation with each other. "This is my nursery class, as I call it," Dr. Robertson said. "They've just done their first week of student teaching, and I've asked them to prepare questions about what bothers them, to see if we can't answer them as the year goes on." She turned to the group. "Are you ready yet?" She is a strong personality, Dr. Robertson, an unfashionable lady of indeterminate age with an inborn hatred of hypocrisy strengthened during the war by supervision of the concentration-camp schools at which American democracy "re-educated" the children of Japanese Americans exiled from their California homes. The experience drove her out of teaching briefly, and she worked with Hilda Taba at Teachers College on questions of "intercultural education," which she decided was worthless. When Hollis Caswell of TC saw her book, he said to her, "Do you really want to stick your neck out this far?" and she replied, "That's why my neck's so long." The publication made her *persona non grata* around Teachers College, and she returned to her native Utah, not unhappily. "Today, though," she says, "nobody believes in 'intercultural units' any more, except textbook salesmen."

The class is now ready with its questions, and Table One is called. A pretty girl rises somewhat uncertainly with a sheaf of notes in her hand. "Our first problem is," the girl says, "Can you teach a lesson on two levels?"

Dr. Robertson nods. "Go on."

"How much correcting should you do on a child's problems?

"How do you cope with children who are continually clinging and hanging on your side?"

Dr. Robertson says, "That depends on how old the child is, doesn't it?"

"What do you do with a negative child, who tells dirty jokes to the others?"

Dr. Robertson laughs with the class and says, "What do you mean by that?"

"Well, she tells them things they aren't ready for."

Dr. Robertson says, "She's getting them ready. Go on. No more? Next table."

An almost equally pretty girl at Table Two rises and begins reading her questions:

"When the teacher doesn't want to use phonics, how can you teach that there are other ways of spelling besides using the word in context?

"Is there such a thing as a nonreader?

"How do you individualize reading when the teacher has broken the class into groups?

"What do you do with children who read fast and teacher doesn't want them to read ahead — and when you give them library books they say there are too many words they can't understand?

"Should teachers try to find out specific children who are having trouble?

"How do you maintain discipline and make friends with the children?

"What do you do with the flighty child who gets his work done fast and doesn't do it well?

"What do you do if the children become noisy when the student teacher takes over?"

Table Three moves in:

"How do you give a child help without seeming to single him out?

"How do you make spelling more accurate without making it mechanical?

"How do you teach children to be selective in the books they read for reports?

"What kind of ultimatum can you give a child in a discipline problem? . . ."

"The leadership of the classroom teacher," said a little lady in a sack dress, speaking in a nasal, penetrating voice to a class of about thirty-five future elementary-school teachers at the University of Arizona, "is based on self-improvement. We know that it is an essential thing to be able to print with accuracy and speed. When we get into the language arts area we will talk about the influence you will have on boys and girls in guiding them to experiences in writing and handwriting. But today we wish to talk about handwriting.

"Handwriting as I see it, as your teacher, is a tool, like fingering on the piano. A fine pianist does not have to think, 'I'm hitting the middle-C with my thumb, now with what do I hit the B-flat?' Handwriting is not writing. Writing is the true thinking that comes to you creatively or passes through your brain from having read it in some book.

"But in the business world, they tell me, more money is lost through bad handwriting than through any other cause. If you don't struggle with your handwriting, the person who sees it may struggle, and make mistakes. It might be a mistake that affects the whole world. *Misunderstanding*. . . .

"Whatever we do in the education profession we should know what we're doing and why. Key questions are the crux of teaching. You can find out what a child is thinking. Or, if he isn't thinking, he'll say, 'I don't know,' and you can nudge him. So if I ever just tell you what to do, you ask me, 'Why?' If I can't tell you why, I have no right to tell you to do it. . . .

"Now, your first-grade paper must be nine by twelve inches in size, and the lines must run the *length* of the page. Some school systems use eight by ten-and-a-half paper, but I think that's a bad mistake. Before that, you use a crayon. Now, why do *you* think you use a crayon?"

She looked around the class, which was seated in a semicircle around three walls of the room. A girl timidly raised her hand, and said, "Well, I don't know, I always found it easier to write with crayon — it's smoother than a pencil."

The professor said, "That's right, you're thinking! Now, the primary pencil is a large pencil with a large lead on account of the children have difficulty with the fine muscular movements of controlling small things. Would you use line or unlined paper with a crayon?" She looked around the class again and received no volunteers. She said, "Crayon is to be used *only — only —* on unlined paper. You do not use a crayon on lined paper because the line is too wide.

"Now, what would you say to them after they've written one word with a crayon?"

A boy at the back of the semicircle, one of the few males in the room, offers, "Turn the paper around?"

"That's right — but you ask *them*, to see that they're thinking. They use the readiness crayon if your principal and the people in positions of leadership give you such materials. Then you move on to pencil. This —" she showed the class a black pencil — "is called the primary pencil. I'll give you more specifics later. There are three primary pencils with different circumferences. This is the middle one. There's one even larger than this. They use primary pencils as long as they are needing to improve their handwriting. . . ."

"If you're talking about courses in teaching methods," said Howard Wilson, dean of the school of education at UCLA, "courses in what to teach, how to organize it and present it and so forth — we don't have any."

"I'd like *you* to tell *me*," said a professor of education at NYU to the next-to-last meeting of his class in the teaching of arithmetic, "what you think the objectives of this course were, why you wanted to take it."

"I'd hoped," said a girl, "to learn how to do a lesson plan, one lesson right through."

"A lesson or a unit?" the professor asked.

"Either one. I'm not sure I know what a lesson plan is."

"Some of us," said the next girl, "came here hoping to learn devices we could use in a classroom."

"Actually," said the professor rather thoughtfully, "we did not talk about a particular lesson plan. We talked in terms of planning for objectives."

Despite all the literature denouncing "how-to" courses in schools of education, the startling fact about teacher training in the United States is the virtual absence of courses which actually deal with the specific techniques of teaching specific material. The titles in the university catalogues describe "special methods" courses freighted with case studies and analyses of the use of teaching tools. But the real content of these courses typically turns out to be a study of ends rather than means, "objectives" of teaching rather than teaching itself.

"What," asks a subhead in Grossnickle and Brueckner's textbook on the teaching of arithmetic, "what are the mental health aspects of arithmetic teaching?" What, indeed? In every area, hour after dreary hour of course time is given to the "values" of teaching with this attitude or that. Because these values, at the level of abstraction on which the courses exist, are virtually identical in every subject-matter field, the teacher-training program quickly becomes highly repetitive. Medical training would be more like teacher training if two-thirds of the time were devoted to rephrasing and discussing the Hippocratic Oath. With noble exceptions, the teacher-training institutions are engaged in communicating mystiques rather than techniques.

Generally speaking, teacher-training programs have divorced in a most artificial manner the study of how to teach a subject from the study of the nature and implications of the materials to be taught. "You're not teaching arithmetic," runs the slogan, "you're teaching children." But nobody is actually arguing, anywhere, that a teacher can teach something she doesn't know herself. Unfortunately, it is almost universally assumed at schools of education that the teacher has already picked up, via "academic" courses, all she needs to know of the subjects she is to teach. Where there is some doubt on this score, the teacher-training institution offers a "professional content" course which is remedial work pure and simple, and has nothing to do with the methods program. Meanwhile, the academic professors assume that more advanced courses in mathematics or history will by themselves improve a teacher's efficacy in presenting elementary or secondary material.

Both assumptions are false. The "special methods" course which looks at the teaching of reading and writing in terms of mental health and leadership to one side, and crayons versus primary pencils on the other, will not help teachers to handle the very profound difficulties children face in relating themselves to written language. The English department's course in Restoration comedy may be in itself an excellent course, but its potency in preparing excellent teachers is at best dubious.

What future teachers need, and cannot now find, is the course which attempts to explore the profound aspects of the deceptively simple material they are going to teach, which analyzes case by case the types of difficulty that children find in approaching such material, which suggests tools and techniques and methods of presentation that may help children overcome the difficulties. The elementary teacher, for example, needs a solid grounding in linguistics and number theory *as they relate to the teaching of reading and writing and arithmetic.* The foreign-language teacher needs a knowledge of phonetics and the physiology of sound production, and a technique for creating questions which force children to make up their own answers in the language they are studying. The history teacher needs close acquaintance with the different ways of organizing the study of specific events and the shadows they cast, plus bibliographies, textbook analyses, devices which seem to help children organize for themselves the grand pattern in which to place the events they study. The physics teacher must know the history of his subject, the processes of discovery, which aspects of secondary-school science study are pregnant with possibilities and which are mere background matter. . . .

Only after such work has been done is the teacher ready to move to that higher level of effectiveness where she teaches children, not subjects: to that confidence of quality which enables her to be silent in class and let the children get their work done. Her task (and few people, even in the teaching community, fully realize its difficulty) is to provoke, to understand and to answer the questions of children. Surely her training should be directed toward the accomplishment of that task. Until the difficulties of the work in the teacher-training program begin to approach the difficulty of teaching itself, there can be little hope for substantial improvement in the schools.

It is the understanding of the true challenge and difficulty of teaching, not the propaganda about national needs and public service, which will draw first-class people to the trade and convince the community that the schools are worth the money first-class people cost. Teacher training must become intellectually respectable before teachers as a group receive community respect.

G. W. Foster, Jr.

G. W. Foster, Jr., Professor of Law at the University of Wisconsin, concentrates in this article upon an often overlooked aspect of the American racial dilemma. Enduring a daily barrage of press releases from Southern cities, the Northerner is in danger of minimizing the racial problems of his own area. Until recently, tensions in the North and West were not sharply defined; polemical outbursts by integrationists and their enemies were erratic. Although Negro protest marches are now common events in such cities as Chicago and Los Angeles, segregationist opposition is equivocal, difficult to define in contrast to the stark violence of Southern unrest. Still, such cities as Oakland, California, after years of sleepy indolence, are struggling today to gain perspective as racial problems find space on the once routine agendas of school board meetings.

Foster's survey discloses how deep and broad the furrows of racial difficulty run. If public education assumes new obligations in the province of civil rights, the classroom teacher shall bear the intimate burdens of the new freedom, as he has borne the torment of the old inequity.

8

THE NORTH AND WEST
HAVE PROBLEMS, TOO*

By the beginning of 1963, the attack on public school segregation had become nationwide. In more than sixty communities of the North and West there were active and organized pressures for desegregation programs.

The drive in the North and West differs in many respects from the efforts

* From the *Saturday Review*, April 20, 1963. Reprinted by permission of G. W. Foster, Jr., and the *Saturday Review*.

which continue in the South. The problems are different. So are the tactics, the demands, and — inevitably — the legal issues raised when conflict ripens into court action.

In the years after the 1954 Supreme Court decision in the school segregation cases national attention focused largely upon the South. There the attack was against a whole legal structure which compelled segregation. Negroes, insisting that state officials must be colorblind, sought removal of racial classifications and demanded reorganization of schools without regard to race.

By the 1960's a drive developed against what is called "de facto" segregation in the public schools of the North and West. De facto segregation does not result from any formal, legal classifications based on race. Rather, it arises from the effect of residential segregation upon patterns of neighborhood school attendance districts.

The problems raised by de facto segregation are more sophisticated and more subtle, and they stem from complex causes. The Negro fortunate enough to find housing in predominantly white neighborhoods usually has little difficulty in obtaining access to schools that serve those areas. Most Negroes in the North and West, however, live in crowded urban slum areas that racially are almost or entirely homogeneous. Even those with resources adequate to acquire housing elsewhere encounter private discrimination that discourages and often prevents their escape from segregated neighborhoods. Still more Negroes, caught by discrimination in employment and having few developed skills, simply lack the resources to escape.

School officials, accused of being responsible for de facto segregation in the school, usually counter by insisting that residential patterns and not racial bias on their part produced the result. An attorney representing Negroes who commenced judicial action against Philadelphia school officials gave his answer to that position:

> The position of the board is that it does not consider race at all in the operation of the school system, either in setting boundaries or in administrative practices. This is not enough. The board cannot be color-blind. It is the affirmative responsibility of the board to work toward integration. Every choice which may arise in making decisions about school matters must be made in such a way as to accomplish results leading to the integration goal.

This concept of color-consciousness marks a sharp break, tactically and legally, with the thrust of school desegregation efforts in the South. It poses for many educators troublesome questions in attempting to provide adequate education for academically and culturally handicapped children in slum schools. And finally, the demand for color-consciousness raises some serious legal questions of Constitutional proportion.

Assignment by race was of course the historic basis for the dual school systems of the South. Outside the South, school assignment is typically based on geography. The school system is divided into a single set of zones and each child is initially assigned to the school in his zone of residence. Frequently some provision exists for attending school outside the zone of residence, either by permitting transfer under specified conditions or by allowing a free choice of any uncrowded school in the system. A few communities do little or no zoning and simply permit a choice among all or some of the schools in the district.

The predominant pattern, however, involves geographic zoning with rather stringent restrictions against transfer or attendance outside the zone of residence. Often this is referred to as a "neighborhood" school pattern, although there is much variation in defining the characteristics of a neighborhood. The school in a particular "neighborhood" may be large or small and it may be located near the center, or close to the edge, of the area it serves.

The neighborhood school is particularly characteristic of the organization of elementary schools in urban areas. There, with younger children involved, concern is felt for having the schools close at hand and available along safe routes which avoid major traffic problems. In more sparsely populated areas the neighborhood concept tends to break down. Buses are then provided to bring children in from greater distances, and convenience in fixing bus routes may be a major factor in determining the attendance area of a school.

At the level of secondary schools the neighborhood concept tends to be somewhat less important. These schools are generally larger and serve more extensive geographic areas. Where a high school does not offer a comprehensive curriculum, but instead is specialized and offers either a vocational or college preparatory curriculum, it may serve quite a large area of the community. In communities with two or more high schools the student populations in each are derived from a group of "feeder" elementary schools and thus a high school acquires the population characteristics of the "feeder" schools.

A neighborhood school — however defined — reflects the economic, social, cultural, and racial characteristics of the area served. Since most Negroes in the North and West live in densely populated, racially homogeneous slum areas, the schools available to them are largely or entirely segregated. Negro discontent, then, grows largely out of the problems of these slum schools.

Slum schools have traditionally had their problems. Poverty, squalid and congested housing, and social and economic discrimination combine to produce higher rates of adult crime, juvenile delinquency, general disorder, and disease. Yet the successive waves of white immigrants who once filled the slums in time found ways to escape into the white mainstream of America. The fact that escape was possible supplied motivation for many who finally succeeded in getting away.

A great fraction of the slum dwellers in the 1960's, however, are not white and they face additional handicaps which stem from their race and the peculiar problems of their cultural isolation from the whites. Oriental minorities, principally on the West Coast, with more stable family organization, higher levels of motivation, and tighter self-discipline, are steadily finding it easier to become assimilated into the community at large. But the Spanish-speaking Puerto Ricans and Mexicans and the English-speaking American Negroes, burdened after centuries of slavery and peonage with far greater rates of family disorganization and illegitimacy, and lower levels of motivation and discipline, are still finding it difficult to escape.

Many Negroes in the North and West are recent immigrants from the South and they bring with them the inherited educational and social handicaps of their rural Southern background. Hoped-for employment does not always materialize and the combination of job discrimination and their own limited skills relegate them generally to the lowest-paying jobs or, worse yet, to chronic unemployment.

Other school problems grow out of housing. Population densities in areas occupied by Negroes in the cities of the North and West rise sharply above the levels in the same neighborhoods when earlier occupied by whites. Schools become overcrowded and in many instances operate on double shifts, providing each child with only a half-day of education. Elsewhere in the community, school populations drop in older white neighborhoods because the children have grown up and left. The result is that there are often empty classrooms and smaller classes in many white sections of a city and overcrowded and sometimes double-shift classes in others which are all or largely Negro.

Still other difficulties grow out of employment barriers faced by minority groups. Racial discrimination, particularly by many of the skilled craft unions, seriously affects vocational training programs. Pupils, seeing few prospects for employment after being specially trained for it, shun vocational programs. And job discrimination generally contributes to higher rates of dropping school altogether since there is little incentive to acquire an education when it cannot be gainfully used.

The problem of obtaining an adequate supply of interested and competent teachers for the overcrowded slum schools also haunts school administrators. A Baltimore school official admitted the use of some 1,100 uncertified elementary teachers, largely in the slum schools, during the 1961–62 school year. On Manhattan in the same year more than one-third of the teachers newly appointed to the schools rejected their assignments and looked for jobs elsewhere.

The hesitation of many teachers to serve in slum schools grows out of a variety of causes. Most teachers, middle-class in aspiration if not in fact, are under many pressures which direct them away from teaching in culturally disadvantaged schools. Schools of education generally train teachers on the assumption that "a child is a child" — and use the middle-class white child as the model to be taught. As a result many teachers are but little equipped to deal with the distinctive problems of communication barriers, economic deprivation, and social and cultural disadvantages of children in depressed-area schools. This, and factors of teacher aspiration to work in the "better" schools close to where the teacher lives, create attitudes which minimize the desire or willingness to teach in the slum schools.

Physical facilities in the slum school, too, are often inferior. Many buildings tend to be old and the pressures from excessive enrollments add further burdens on the physical plant and the educational program. Major programs to rehabilitate and enlarge facilities in crowded slum areas are to be found in most large cities today. Too often, however, it has remained true that the demands for additional classrooms have continued to outrun the rising supply.

The slum schools, then, are handicapped in many serious ways and protests on behalf of those forced to attend them can commonly be grounded on objections that they furnish inadequate educational opportunities. Since the troubles are often linked with segregation as well, many of the protests take the form of demands for increased integration.

The demands for school integration in the North and West have taken a variety of forms depending upon the particular situation on which attention focused. Understandably, some of the demands have been inconsistent with one another. At New Rochelle, for example, Negroes won a court order permitting free transfer from a largely Negro elementary school to predominantly white schools elsewhere in the city. A year later, groups at Philadelphia were opposing a free transfer policy on the ground that it permitted too many whites to run away from schools in which Negroes were enrolled.

Protests against segregation in schools around the periphery of Negro neighborhoods generally suggested one or more of three alternatives:

1. *Rezoning of attendance areas.* In some instances, it has been possible to show that school officials have apparently zoned schools to "contain" Negroes once they moved into a particular neighborhood. In other instances, zone lines remained unchanged from the days that whites occupied the entire area. In both these situations it is occasionally possible to show that existing zone lines may reasonably be changed to promote integration. Thus, it has been insisted that school authorities have a duty to rezone whether the resulting segregation has been the product of intentional board policy or merely a refusal to deal with the changing character of the neighborhoods involved.

2. *The Princeton Plan.* Another suggestion, taken from a plan installed at Princeton, New Jersey, in 1948, calls for reclassification of schools to handle fewer grades and thus serve larger geographic areas. This is accomplished by pairing two adjacent schools both of which cover grades from, say, kindergarten through the sixth. On reclassification, one of the "sister" schools handles all pupils in both attendance areas from kindergarten through third grade and the other school serves both areas for grades four through six. By doubling the geographic area of each school it is occasionally possible to promote integration around the edges of segregated neighborhoods.

3. *Location of new school facilities.* The location of new facilities, either to replace over-age buildings or to handle the needs of increased enrollments, has frequently provoked much controversy. Obviously, the location of facili-

ties can have substantial short-run effects upon the racial composition of a school.

These suggestions for promoting integration along boundaries between segregated neighborhoods often have only temporary effect. Boundaries between racial groups tend to be unstable, holding only where freeways, rivers, or railroad tracks block expansion. Elsewhere the segregated areas expand, sometimes abetted by "blockbusting" techniques of unscrupulous realtors who panic whites into moving out as Negroes begin to move in. Integrated schools in these areas frequently become segregated again in relatively brief periods of time.

For schools deeper within segregated neighborhoods, other plans are suggested. Rezoning or reclassification of schools in these cases produces no change because of the homogeneous neighborhood patterns. In such situations the proposals involve moving some of the children out to uncrowded, predominantly white schools elsewhere in the city. Occasionally, protests have led to complete abandonment of a school, with resulting reassignment of all pupils to less segregated schools in other areas. The demands for transfers out of segregated areas are frequently coupled with insistence that bus service be provided without charge.

These open enrollment and free transfer policies merely scratch the surface. They provide means of escape for relatively small numbers of minority-group children who are strongly enough motivated to seek transfer. Most children, however, are left behind in congested, segregated schools.

To alleviate congestion, the urban school systems are busy with vast programs of new construction. Because of the high cost of acquiring additional land, much of this is going on at the sites of existing schools. Some systems — Chicago and Philadelphia are examples — are also using so-called mobile-unit classrooms, carried to a site on a trailer. These units are attractive and air-conditioned, but in Chicago particularly many Negroes regard them as symbols of a settled intent on the part of school officials to preserve segregation. And indeed, new school construction in segregated areas is increasingly coming under fire everywhere because of its failure to mitigate the effects of residential segregation.

There is broad agreement among educators that a policy of providing integrated experience for all children is a desirable objective if equality of educational opportunity is to be achieved. From this point on, however, there is real dispute among them over how much weight integration should be given in shaping school organization and educational practices.

Even in desegregated schools there are wide differences in classroom organization and teaching methods. These grow primarily out of the problem of dealing with differences in motivation, ability, and achievement among children at the same grade level. Most school systems make some efforts to group children according to one or more of these characteristics. In some instances, achievement grouping occurs within the classroom, with the teacher devoting attention to each group in turn. In other instances, achievement groups are isolated in separate classrooms. Less frequently, no achievement grouping is attempted and the entire class is considered as a heterogeneous unit.

The cultural deficiencies and poorer educational backgrounds among minority-group children tend to separate them at one end of the grouping scale. This means that many wind up in the "slow" group within the classroom or off in a separate classroom by themselves. There is much disagreement over the extent of damage which this kind of isolation does to social adjustment and ability to learn.

Some, placing greatest weight on the damage done by isolation, argue that properly trained teachers can handle heterogeneous classes without grouping. Others disagree, laying stress on the need to expand the horizons of the gifted child and to protect slow learners from situations in which the goals are beyond their reach.

The same sorts of differences grow out of discussing what to do about children in segregated schools. Those who strongly support policies of open enrollment and free transfer stress the value of an integrated education. They are met, however, by others who argue on behalf of strengthening the neighborhood school. The case for the neighborhood school is supported by a wide range of arguments.

Experimental programs in a number of school systems have produced striking results in upgrading the performance levels of disadvantaged children. A feature common to many of these is a concern for the child not only during the school day but in his neighborhood and his home. Social workers, school psychologists, and teachers deal with families and others with whom the child associates. Special efforts are made to enlist those around the child to encourage and support him in seeking an education. The child himself is placed in situations designed to expand his horizons and motivate him to set his own sights higher. The Banneker Group program at St. Louis and the Higher Horizons project in New York are notable examples of such endeavors. The "Great Cities" project sponsored by the Fund for the Advancement of Education has also launched experimental programs in a number of cities designed to improve educational opportunities for deprived children.

An interesting program at Hunter College in New York attacks the problems of segregated and culturally deprived schools on another front, that of training teachers for the job. This, a voluntary program open to education majors while still at the undergraduate levels, places them in slum schools for their practice teaching.

Attacks are being made on still other fronts, among them on the kind of teaching materials furnished children in depressed-area schools. Beginning with the "Look, look, look. See, see, see" elementary readers, the conventional teaching materials describe a white, middle-class world which is as foreign to that of the slum child as the back of the moon. He never sees himself in that world except incidentally as a servant or some other distantly viewed figure. He does not understand that world and cannot see himself becoming part of it. In a few places, Detroit and New York among them, efforts are being made to create teaching materials that give the disadvantaged child a chance to identify himself and see a way to goals beyond anything he or his family ever experienced.

The disagreements among educators suggest that there is much to be learned before any specific program can be imposed with much more than a hunch that it would be better than some competing alternative. Whether or not open enrollment or free transfer programs are adopted, most children will remain in their neighborhood schools. And the neighborhood schools in depressed areas will require much more understanding and attention before many of the children in them can acquire the skills, confidence, and motivation that will be needed to move into middle-class status.

Indeed, programs to increase integration by siphoning off some small fraction of these children through open enrollment and free transfer mechanisms create other problems. Placing the child in a school far removed from his home environment makes it virtually impossible for the school to work closely with his family and neighborhood problems. Again, as happened in New Rochelle during the 1961–62 school year, if the child is too far out of step with the motivation and achievement of the other children in the school to which he transfers, the result can be a humiliating failure for the disadvantaged youngster and a hardening of attitudes against him among those who make the grade and see him fail.

There are questions, too, about the effects of open enrollment on the children who remain behind in the neighborhood schools. The children who transfer are likely to be the more strongly motivated, better achievers. Their absence only makes it more difficult to create good neighborhood schools with a wide range of goals to spur everyone along more rapidly.

The concept that public officials should become conscious of race — provided they do so benignly — represents a substantial departure from the position long asserted by and on behalf of Negroes in their fight against racial restrictions. They have fought for, and won in a number of states, legislation that prohibits keeping public records by race. They have insisted that colleges and universities not require photographs as a condition to admission and that job application forms contain no reference to race.

Indeed, the principal argument advanced in the Supreme Court in the cases which led to the school segregation decision of 1954 was that classifications based on race have no place in public education. "That the Constitution is color-blind is our dedicated belief," read a key sentence in the brief submitted to the court on behalf of the Negro plaintiffs in the school segregation cases.

Yet the basic issue before the Supreme Court in 1954 was quite different from the question whether state officials could take racial considerations benignly into account. The question at that time was whether states could require separation of public schools by race in view of the obligation under the Fourteenth Amendment to provide all persons "equal protection of the laws." The court's answer was that public school segregation could not be required. "Separate educational facilities are inherently unequal," the court held. Neither then nor later did the court speak specifically to the question whether the Constitution required public officials to be color-blind, although the concept of color blindness was implied in a series of cryptic decisions which the court handed down thereafter that invalidated laws requiring segregation of parks, buses, restaurants, and the like.

Many questions remain to be decided in determining how far and in what manner state authority may — or perhaps must — constitutionally take race into account in shaping public policy.

It was abundantly clear by the beginning of 1963 that the process of doing away with the dual school systems in the South has endlessly taken racial considerations into account. Everyone involved in the process has done so — the community at large, school officials, even the courts. The patterns and practices of school operation have to be understood before solutions can be worked out. In this respect the actions of public authority are not color-blind.

It is also reasonably clear that, while racial considerations can be taken into account, they cannot be used invidiously against any racial group. Thus, school zone lines cannot be gerrymandered to contain Negroes. And even with racial considerations not in the picture, substantial questions of equal protection are raised by claims of serious overcrowding or that schools are badly deficient in physical plant, quality of teaching, or curricular offerings. Where any such questions develop, the Constitution probably affords a basis for judicial relief.

Other questions, however, are more difficult. As long as private discrimination produces residential segregation, it will affect the racial composition of the schools themselves. The state, whether it likes it or not, must take the community as it finds it. Since segregation cannot under any circumstances be erased, racial considerations must be taken into account. What is needed, it seems, is some flexibility of choice among reasonable educational alternatives to avoid placing any group at a disadvantage because of its race.

Where it can be shown that the practices of school authorities operate purposely to place Negroes at a racial disadvantage, judicial relief can be expected. There are, however, difficult and delicate problems in fixing the Constitutional line that measures the extent to which judicial relief may be forthcoming. Several illustrations suffice to make the point. San Francisco closed down a junior high school after protests that its student population would be 60 per cent Negro. Was this a "separate" — or "segregated" — and hence "unequal" school in the sense that the Constitution would require judicial action to put it out of business or to require alteration of its racial composition? Or was the action merely one which the political processes of the community are free to take — or not take? Again, it has been suggested that Negroes may be entitled to compensatory educational benefits because of damage done by past practices of racial segregation. It hardly seems constitutionally possible that the state can establish a compensatory program exclusively for Negroes and bar similarly handicapped whites who attend the same school.

Yet the controversy over de facto segregation in the schools of the North and West is reaching the federal courts under a wide range of claimed Constitutional deprivations. The most celebrated case thus far came out of New Rochelle, New York, where the court found that school board practices more than a decade earlier caused the development of a segregated elementary school. This produced a court order permitting pupils in that school to transfer to any uncrowded school in the district. Cases like this one, which produce findings of intentional segregation practices, manifestly demonstrate a need for some corrective action. The far harder question is that of determining what kind of relief is appropriate; a number of Negro children in New Rochelle suffered serious setbacks when they transferred to classes maintaining higher academic standards.

For wholly understandable reasons, Negroes continue to insist that school authorities have the duty to mitigate the effects of residential segregation. The farthest reach of judicial language on this point came from the case in Hempstead, Long Island, in April 1962. The school board moved to dismiss the case before trial on the ground that residential patterns, not school board practices, produced the school segregation. The court denied the motion to dismiss, indicating the board had an obligation to mitigate the effects of segregation, whatever its cause. The board's obligation, the court said, could be discharged either by doing something to relieve segregation or by "a conclusive demonstration that no circumstantially possible effort can effect any significant mitigation." Thus, where the Hempstead case departed from earlier cases was in the court's insistence that the state, in operating its schools, has a Constitutional obligation to mitigate the effects of private discrimination.

So far as the drive against school segregation in the North and West insists that school authorities become benignly color-conscious, it raises many questions still to be resolved. In a great many situations public authority is not, and cannot be, color-blind. The earlier insistence by Negroes that the Constitution required the state to be color-blind seems clearly inconsistent with the minimum need of the state at least to be sufficiently color-conscious to make sure that invidious racial discrimination is not being practiced in its name.

The courts, too, in passing on claims of racial discrimination, have to take race into account. That the Fourteenth Amendment requires judicial relief against intentional segregation of public schools has been settled. Whether the courts are required by the Constitution to insist upon maximum integration where segregation is attributable to private discrimination is another question. Particularly is it another question in light of the deep differences among educators about methods for overcoming social, cultural, and educational disadvantages suffered by those isolated from the mainstream of American life.

Merely that judicial action may not be available to compel maximum integration, however, does not suggest that the state cannot experiment with such educational programs. Nor does it suggest any impropriety in having Negroes and others make political demands for these things. It does suggest that there are certain questions which must be addressed to the political processes of the community and state rather than to the courts. And where state legislation requires affirmative integration programs, courts could be looked to for enforcement of the statutes; but judicial action in such cases would flow from legislation rather than from the federal Constitution.

Manifestly, public education has a great burden to discharge in helping disadvantaged children develop their abilities to the fullest extent possible. But public education seems hardly equipped to carry the whole load of mitigating and ending all the disadvantages minority groups suffer from private discrimination. Other efforts, both public and private, must continue on many fronts if America is to make good on its Constitutional commitment to equality for all its people. Fortunately, more and more Americans are aware of this. And while much more effort is still required, significant changes are taking place in lessening job discrimination, in breaking up patterns of housing discrimination, and in generally providing more and more reasons for hope among the nation's minority groups that they can share our democratic ideals on equal terms.

James Agee

James Agee (1910–1955) was born in Knoxville, Tennessee, and his early life there is reflected in two novels, The Morning Watch *(1951) and* A Death in the Family, *the latter receiving the Pulitzer Prize when published posthumously. After graduation from Harvard, Agee published a book of verse,* Permit Me Voyage, *and in 1932 he went to work for* Fortune *magazine, transferring to* Time *magazine in 1939.*

The selection that follows is part of Let Us Now Praise Famous Men *(1942), a study of the rural South accomplished in collaboration with Walker Evans, a photographer. After admitting that his research on the Alabama public schools was "thin, indirect, and deductive," he presents an account of what he directly saw and felt. Particulars nourish his discontent. But his grief is for the universal failures brought to concretion in the shacks and schools of the depressed South. Without charts he allows us still to see; without statistics he allows us still to forage for a prophecy; without bitterness or chauvinism he leads us through a time within our age, into a land within our country. He warns us, too. More desperate than surface flaws, a nation's fall resides in her ability to wither, like Ophelia, incapable of her own distress.*

9

EDUCATION*

In every child who is born, under no matter what circumstances, and of no matter what parents, the potentiality of the human race is born again: and in him, too, once more, and of each of us, our terrific responsibility towards human life; towards the utmost idea of goodness, of the horror of error, and of God.

Every breath his senses shall draw, every act and every shadow and thing in all creation, is a mortal poison, or is a drug, or is a signal or symptom, or is a teacher, or is a liberator, or is liberty itself, depending entirely upon his understanding: and understanding,[1] and action proceeding from understanding and guided by it, is the one weapon against the world's bombardment, the one medicine, the one instrument by which liberty, health, and joy may be shaped or shaped towards, in the individual, and in the race.

This is no place to dare all questions that must be asked, far less to advance our tentatives in this murderous air, nor even to qualify so much as a little the little which thus far has been suggested, nor even either to question or to try to support my qualifications to speak of it at all: we are too near one of the deepest intersections of pity, terror, doubt, and guilt; and I feel that I can say only that "education," whose function is at the crisis of this appalling responsibility, does not seem to me to be all, or even anything, that it might be, but seems indeed the very property of the world's misunderstanding, the sharpest of its spearheads in every brain: and that since it could not be

[1] Active "understanding" is only one form, and there are suggestions of "perfection" which could be called "understanding" by definitions so broad as to include diametric reversals. The peace of God surpasses all understanding; Mrs. Ricketts and her youngest child do, too; "understanding" can be its own, and hope's, most dangerous enemy.

* From *Let Us Now Praise Famous Men* by James Agee and Walker Evans (Boston: Houghton Mifflin Company, 1960), pp. 289–301. Used by permission of Houghton Mifflin Company, Boston.

otherwise without destroying the world's machine, the world is unlikely to permit it to be otherwise.

In fact, and ignorant though I am, nothing, not even law, nor property, nor sexual ethics, nor fear, nor doubtlessness, nor even authority itself, all of which it is the business of education to cleanse the brain of, can so nearly annihilate me with fury and with horror; as the spectacle of innocence, of defenselessness, of all human hope, brought steadily in each year by the millions into the machineries of the teachings of the world, in which the man who would conceive of and who would dare attempt even the beginnings of what "teaching" must be could not exist two months clear of a penitentiary: presuming even that his own perceptions, and the courage of his perceptions, were not a poison as deadly at least as those poisons he would presume to drive out: or the very least of whose achievements, supposing he cared truly not only to hear himself speak but to be understood, would be a broken heart.[2]

For these and other reasons it would seem to me mistaken to decry the Alabama public schools, or even to say that they are "worse" or "less good" than schools elsewhere: or to be particularly wholehearted in the regret that these tenants are subjected only to a few years of this education: for they would be at a disadvantage if they had more of it, and at a disadvantage if they had none, and they are at a disadvantage in the little they have; and it would be hard and perhaps impossible to say in which way their disadvantage would be greatest.

School was not in session while I was there. My research on this subject was thin, indirect, and deductive. By one way of thinking it will seem for these reasons worthless: by another, which I happen to trust more, it may be sufficient.

I saw, for instance, no teachers: yet I am quite sure it is safe to assume that they are local at very least to the state and quite probably to the county; that most of them are women to whom teaching is either an incident of their youth or a poor solution for their spinsterhood; that if they were of much intelligence or courage they could not have survived their training in the State Normal or would never have undertaken it in the first place; that they are saturated in every belief and ignorance which is basic in their country and community; that any modification of this must be very mild indeed if they are to survive as teachers; that even if, in spite of all these screenings, there are superior persons among them, they are still again limited to texts and to a system of requirements officially imposed on them; and are caught between the pressures of class, of the state, of the churches, and of the parents, and are confronted by minds already so deeply formed that to liberate them would involve uncommon and as yet perhaps undiscovered philosophic and surgical skill. I have only sketched a few among dozens of the facts and

---

[2] It may be that the only fit teachers never teach but are artists, and artists of the kind most blankly masked and least didactic.

forces which limit them; and even so I feel at liberty to suggest that even the best of these, the kindly, or the intuitive, the so-called natural teachers, are exceedingly more likely than not to be impossibly handicapped both from without and within themselves, and are at best the servants of unconscious murder; and of the others, the general run, that if murder of the mind and spirit were statutory crimes, the law, in its customary eagerness to punish the wrong person,[3] might spend all its ingenuity in the invention of deaths by delayed torture and never sufficiently expiate the enormities which through them not by their own fault, have been committed.

Or again on the curriculum: it was unnecessary to make even such search into this as I made to know that there is no setting before the students of "economic" or "social" or "political" "facts" and of their situation within these "facts," no attempt made to clarify or even slightly to relieve the situation between the white and negro races, far less to explain the sources, no attempt to clarify psychological situations in the individual, in his family, or in his world, no attempt to get beneath and to revise those "ethical" and "social" pressures and beliefs in which even a young child is trapped, no attempt, beyond the most nominal, to interest a child in using or in discovering his senses and judgment, no attempt to counteract the paralytic quality inherent in "authority," no attempt beyond the most nominal and stifling to awaken, to protect, or to "guide" the sense of investigation, the sense of joy, the sense of beauty, no attempt to clarify spoken and written words whose power of deceit even at the simplest is vertiginous, no attempt, or very little, and ill taught, to teach even the earliest techniques of improvement in occupation ("scientific farming," diet and cooking, skilled trades), nor to "teach" a child in terms of his environment, no attempt, beyond the most suffocated, to awaken a student either to "religion" or to "irreligion," no attempt to develop in him either "skepticism" or "faith," nor "wonder," nor mental "honesty" nor mental "courage," nor any understanding of or delicateness in "the emotions" and in any of the uses and pleasures of the body save the athletic; no attempt either to relieve him of fear and of poison in sex or to release in him a free beginning of pleasure in it, nor to open within him the illimitable potentials of grief, of danger, and of goodness in sex and in sexual love, nor to give him the beginnings at very least a knowledge, and of an attitude, whereby he may hope to guard and increase himself and those whom he touches, no indication of the damages which society, money, law, fear and quick belief have set upon these matters and upon all things in human life, nor of their causes, nor of the alternate ignorances and possibilities of ruin or of joy, no fear of doubtlessness, no fear of the illusions of knowledge, no fear of compromise: — and here again I have scarcely begun, and am confronted immediately with a serious problem: that is: by my naming of the lack of such teaching, I can appear too easily to recommend it, to imply, perhaps, that if these things were "taught," all would be "solved":

---

[3] This is not to suggest there is a "right person" or that punishment can ever be better than an enhancement of error.

and this I do not believe: but insist rather that in the teaching of these things, infinitely worse damage could and probably would result than in the teaching of those subjects which in fact do compose the curriculum: and that those who would most insist upon one or another of them can be among the deadliest enemies of education: for if the guiding hand is ill qualified, an instrument is murderous in proportion to its sharpness. Nothing I have mentioned but is at the mercy of misuse; and one may be sure a thousand to one it will be misused; and that its misuse will block any more "proper" use even more solidly than unuse and discrediting could. It could be said, that we must learn a certitude and correlation in every "value" before it will be possible to "teach" and not to murder; but that is far too optimistic. We would do better to examine, far beyond their present examination, the extensions within ourselves of doubt, responsibility, and conditioned faith and the possibilities of their more profitable union, to a degree at least of true and constant terror in even our tentatives, and if (for instance) we should dare to be "teaching" what Marx began to open, that we should do so only in the light of the terrible researches of Kafka and in the opposed identities of Blake and Céline.

All I have managed here, and it is more than I intended, is to give a confused statement of an intention which presumes itself to be good: the mere attempt to examine my own confusion would consume volumes. But let what I have tried to suggest amount to this alone: that not only within present reach of human intelligence, but even within reach of mine as it stands today, it would be possible that young human beings should rise onto their feet a great deal less dreadfully crippled than they are, a great deal more nearly capable of living well, a great deal more nearly aware, each of them, of their own dignity in existence, a great deal better qualified, each within his limits, to live and to take part toward the creation of a world in which good living will be possible without guilt toward every neighbor: and that teaching at present, such as it is, is almost entirely either irrelevant to these possibilities or destructive of them, and is, indeed, all but entirely unsuccessful even within its own "scales" of "value."

Within the world as it stands, however, the world they must live in, a certain form of education is available to these tenant children; and the extent to which they can avail themselves of it is of considerable importance in all their future living.

A few first points about it:

They are about as poorly equipped for self-education as human beings can be. Their whole environment is such that the use of the intelligence, of the intellect, and of the emotions is atrophied, and is all but entirely irrelevant to the pressures and needs which involve almost every instant of a tenant's conscious living: and indeed if these faculties were not thus reduced or killed at birth they would result in a great deal of pain, not to say danger. They learn the work they will spend their lives doing, chiefly of their parents, and from their parents and from the immediate world they take their conduct, their morality, and their mental and emotional and spiritual key. One could hardly say that any further knowledge or consciousness is at all to their use or advantage, since there is nothing to read, no reason to write, and no recourse against being cheated even if one is able to do sums; yet these forms of literacy are in general held to be desirable: a man or woman feels a certain sort of extra helplessness who lacks them: a truly serious or ambitious parent hopes for even more, for a promising child; though what "more" may be is, inevitably, only dimly understood.

School opens in middle or late September and closes the first of May. The country children, with their lunches, are picked up by buses at around seven-thirty in the morning and are dropped off again towards the early winter darkness. In spite of the bus the children of these three families have a walk to take. In dry weather it is shortened a good deal; the bus comes up the branch road as far as the group of negro houses at the bottom of the second hill and the Ricketts children walk half a mile to meet it and the Gudger children walk three quarters. In wet weather the bus can't risk leaving the highway and the Ricketts walk two miles and the Gudgers a mile and a half in clay which in stretches is knee-deep on a child.

There was talk during the summer of graveling the road, though most of the fathers are over forty-five, beyond road-age. They can hardly afford the time to do such work for nothing, and they and their negro neighbors are in no position to pay taxes. Nothing had come of it within three weeks of the start of school, and there was no prospect of free time before cold weather.

Southern winters are sickeningly wet, and wet clay is perhaps the hardest of all walking. "Attendance" suffers by this cause, and by others. Junior Gudger, for instance, was absent sixty-five and Louise fifty-three days out of a possible hundred-and-fifty-odd, and these absences were "unexcused" eleven and nine times respectively, twenty-three of Junior's and a proportionate number of Louise's absences fell in March and April, which are full of work at home as well as wetness. Late in her second year in school Louise was needed at home and missed several consecutive school days, including the final examinations. Her "marks" had been among the best in her class and she had not known of the examination date, but no chance was given her to make up the examinations and she had to take the whole year over. The Ricketts children have much worse attendance records and Pearl does not attend at all.

School does not begin until the children shall have helped two weeks to a month in the most urgent part of the picking season, and ends in time for them to be at work on the cotton-chopping.

The bus system which is now a routine of country schools is helpful, but not particularly to those who live at any distance from tax-maintained roads.

The walking, and the waiting in the cold and wetness, one day after another, to school in the morning, and home from schools in the shriveling daylight, is arduous and unpleasant.

Schooling, here as elsewhere, is identified with the dullest and most meager months of the year, and, in this class and country, with the least and worst food and a cold noonday lunch: and could be set only worse at a disadvantage if it absorbed the pleasanter half of the year.

The "attendance problem" is evidently taken for granted and, judging by the low number of unexcused absences, is "leniently" dealt with: the fact remains, though, that the children lose between a third to half of each school year, and must with this handicap keep up their lessons and "compete" with town children in a contest in which competition is stressed and success in it valued and rewarded.

The schoolhouse itself is in Cookstown; a recently built, windowy, "healthful" red brick and white-trimmed structure which perfectly exemplifies the American genius[4] for sterility, unimagination, and general gutlessness in meeting any opportunity for "reform" or "improvement." It is the sort of building a town such as Cookstown is proud of, and a brief explanation of its existence in such country will be worth while. Of late years Alabama has "come awake" to "education," illiteracy has been reduced; texts have been modernized; a good many old schools have been replaced by new ones. For this latter purpose the counties have received appropriations in proportion to the size of their school population. The school population of this county is five black to one white, and since not a cent of the money has gone into negro schools, such buildings as this are possible: for white children. The negro children, meanwhile, continue to sardine themselves, a hundred and a hundred and twenty strong, into stove-heated one-room pine shacks which might comfortably accommodate a fifth of their number if the walls, roof, and windows were tight.[5] But then, as one prominent landlord said and as many more would agree: "I don't object to nigrah education, not up through foath a fift grade maybe, but not furdern dat: I'm too strong a believah in white syewpremcy."

This bus service and this building the (white) children are schooled in, even including the long and muddy walk, are of course effete as compared to what their parents had.[6] The schooling itself is a different matter, too: much more "modern." The boys and girls alike are subjected to "art" and to "music," and the girls learn the first elements of tap dancing. Textbooks are so cheap almost anyone can afford them: that is, almost anyone who can afford anything at all; which means that they are a stiff problem in any year to almost any tenant. I want now to list and suggest the contents of a few textbooks which were at the Gudger house, remembering, first, that they imply the far reaches of the book-knowledge of any average adult tenant.

[4] So well shown forth in "low-cost" housing.

[5] Aside from discomfort, and unhealthfulness, and the difficulty of concentrating, this means of course that several "grades" are in one room, reciting and studying by rotation, each using only a fraction of each day's time. It means hopeless boredom and waste for the children, and exhaustion for the teacher.

[6] Their parents would have walked to one-room wooden schoolhouses. I'm not sure, but think it more likely than not, that many of the white children still do today.

The Open Door Language Series: First Book: Language Stories and Games.

Trips to Take. Among the contents are poems by Vachel Lindsay, Elizabeth Madox Roberts, Robert Louis Stevenson, etc. Also a story titled "Brother Rabbit's Cool Air Swing," and subheaded: "Old Southern Tale."

Outdoor Visits: Book Two of Nature and Science Readers. (Book One is *Hunting*.) Book Two opens: "Dear Boys and Girls: in this book you will read how Nan and Don visited animals and plants that live outdoors."

Real Life Readers: New Stories and Old: A Third Reader. Illustrated with color photographs.

The Trabue-Stevens Speller. Just another speller.

Champion Arithmetic. Five hundred and ten pages: a champion psychological inducement to an interest in numbers. The final problem: "Janet bought 1¼ lbs. of salted peanuts and ½ lb. of salted almonds. Altogether she bought ? lbs. of nuts?"

Dear Boys and Girls indeed!

Such a listing is rich as a poem; twisted full of contents, symptoms, and betrayals, and these, as in a poem, are only reduced and diluted by any attempt to explain them or even by hinting. Personally I see enough there to furnish me with bile for a month: yet I know that any effort to make clear in detail what is there, and why it seems to me so fatal, must fail.

Even so, see only a little and only for a moment.

These are books written by "adults." They must win the approval and acceptance of still other "adults," members of school "boards"; and they will be "taught" with by still other "adults" who have been more or less "trained" as teachers. The intention is, or should be, to engage, excite, preserve, or develop the "independence" of, and furnish with "guidance," "illumination," "method," and "information," the curiosities of children.

Now merely re-examine a few words, phrases and facts:

The Open Door: open to whom? That metaphor is supposed to engage the interest of children.

Series: First Book. Series. Of course The Bobbsey Twins is a series; so is The Rover Boys. *Series* perhaps has some pleasure associations to those who have children's books, which no tenant children have: but even so it is better than canceled by the fact that this is so obviously not a pleasure book but a schoolbook, not even well disguised. An undisguised textbook is only a little less pleasing than a sneaking and disguised one, though. *First Book:* there entirely for the convenience of adults; it's only grim to a child.

Language: it appears to be a *modern* substitution for the word "English." I don't doubt the latter word has been murdered; the question is, whether the new one has any life whatever to a taught child or, for that matter, to a teacher.

Stories and Games: both, modified by a school word, and in a school context. Most children prefer pleasure to boredom, lacking our intelligence to reverse this preference: but you must use your imagination or memory to recognize how any game can be poisoned by being "conducted": and few adults have either.

Trips to Take. Trips indeed, for children who will never again travel as much as in their daily bus trips to and from school. Children like figures of speech or are, if you like, natural symbolists and poets: being so, they see through frauds such as this so much the more readily. No poem is a "trip," whatever else it may be, and suffers by being lied about.

The verse. I can readily imagine that 'educators' are well pleased with themselves in that they have got rid of the Bivouac of the Dead and are using much more nearly contemporary verse. I am quite as sure, knowing their kind of "knowledge" of poetry, that the pleasure is all theirs.

These children, both of town and country, are saturated southerners, speaking dialects not very different from those of negroes. *Brother* Rabbit! *Old Southern Tale!*

Outdoor Visits. Nature and Science. Book One: *Hunting.* Dear Boys and Girls. In this you will read (oh, I will, will I?). Nan and Don. Visit. Animals and Plants that Live Outdoors. Outdoors. You will pay formal calls on Plants. They live outdoors. "Nature." "Science." Hunting. Dear Boys and Girls. Outdoor Visits.

Real Life. "Real" "Life" "Readers." Illustrated by *color* photographs.

Or back into the old generation, a plainer title: *The Trabue-Stevens Speller.* Or the *Champion Arithmetic,* weight eighteen pounds, an attempt at ingratiation in the word champion, so broad of any mark I am surprised it is not spelled *Champeen.* . . .

I give up. Relative to my memory of my own grade-schooling, I recognize all kinds of "progressive" modifications: Real Life, color photographs, Trips to Take (rather than Journey, to Make), games, post-kindergarten, "Language," Nan and Don, "Nature and Science," Untermeyer-vintage poetry, "dear boys and girls"; and I am sure of only one thing: that it is prepared by adults for their own self-flattery and satisfaction, and is to children merely the old set retouched, of afflictions, bafflements, and half-legible insults more or less apathetically submitted to.

Something there is that doesn't love a wall. . . .
ROBERT FROST

PART TWO

Academic Freedom: A Problem in Definition

THE MODERN CONFUSION concerning the nature of academic freedom has prompted Professor Sidney Hook to complain that "there is more sloppy rhetoric poured out per page about academic freedom both by those who believe that they are supporting, and those intent on criticizing it, than on any other theme with the possible exception of democracy." Mr. Hook's irritation is well founded, but the contemporary chaos surrounding this freedom is not an exclusive creation of twentieth-century unrest. Throughout the history of Western civilization, except for brief and isolated interludes, the evolution of intellectual freedom has languished in a state of tragic ambiguity. Striving to maintain the sovereignty of human intelligence, the inevitable martyrs have drunk their hemlock, marched to their scaffolds, and paced their dungeons; but the result of their sacrifices is equivocal. Socrates and Galileo are not forgotten, and from our belated perspective they emerge as exemplary heroes of a cyclic tragedy. We scrutinize the lessons of their action, but we fail, it seems, to learn from them. John Milton's protest in the seventeenth century is painfully accurate today: "Truth like a bastard comes into the world never without ill fame to him who gives her birth."

Always historically frail, the abstract ideals of academic freedom enjoy an ironic and unprecedented popularity today. Our zealous agreement as to their worth is matched by our disagreement over their meaning and application. Leaders in education, regardless of their political and philosophical beliefs, realize that academic freedom is something to aver; but their interpretational conflicts have produced a chaotic maze of tangled definitions. The confusion of history survives in the verbosity of today.

Recently in California a dramatic example of the dilemma of definition occurred when the superintendent of a junior college district publicly commended the John Birch Society. Concurrent with his praise for this group was his admission that certain textbooks possessing a "socialistic" slant were being removed from the school libraries under his jurisdiction. Following these announcements, the governing board of the school district was deluged with protests from private citizens, teachers, labor officials, and liberal political groups. Shortly thereafter, the faculty of Contra Costa College voted by a heavy majority for the superintendent's dismissal. At Diablo Valley College, the district's second campus, a vote of "no confidence" in the superintendent was proclaimed by the teachers. The protesters generally contended that the administrator was attempting to stifle freedom of inquiry, that he was supporting a movement clearly antagonistic to democratic principles of education, and that he had adopted the techniques of suppression common to his ostensible enemy, the Communist party. The superintendent's supporters, on the other hand, claimed that he was insuring the freedom of students *not* to be indoctrinated with philosophies obviously alien to American values. They argued that as an officer in public education he was committed to protect his students from any propaganda detrimental to "traditional" American capitalism. In commending the ultraconservative movement, the superintendent, they protested, was merely exercising his freedom of speech, a right guaranteed to all Americans. It soon became obvious that each faction had assumed the burden of preserving what to it *was* academic freedom.

Although many complaints had been circulated within the faculties over a period of years which pointed to the superintendent's general incompetence, academic freedom, however defined, emerged as the central issue when the governing board began a series of public hearings to determine a solution to the controversy. For months the board ingested evidence, opinion, turgid rhetoric, and evangelical sermons. Testimony streamed in from all factions of the community. The American Federation of Teachers, which had led an attack on the super-intendent, was eventually assisted by a study conducted by the California Association of School Administrators and the California Teachers Association. The board ultimately decided to dismiss the administrator, basing its decision on his cumulative record. All disputants realized, however, that academic freedom had been the acute issue of the controversy. Implicit in the board's action was the possibility that a fresh definition of academic freedom had been embraced. But the verdict of the board, though favorable to the faculty, failed to identify lucidly the limitations and prerogatives of the teachers. Six months of turmoil had resulted in the firing of one administrator, but the maze of definition remained. Presumably the instructors in this district were to enter their classrooms with the vague assurance that academic freedom was indeed a virtue. But an astute definition, to be used as a foundation for school policy, had not congealed from the controversy.

The implications of this single case are cogent, if not unique. To what extent is a teacher obligated to promote in his classroom what is already conventional in the surrounding community? How obliquely may he deviate from conventional methods of teaching to produce an atmosphere of provocative inquiry? Is a school library to be a crucible of accepted cant, harboring only a token selection of unpopular books? How much control may an administrator assume over the content and methods employed by his faculty? Should educational freedom, by whatever description, be parceled out in equal shares to all levels of formal education? If not, what restrictions should be imposed — and by whom? And, finally, is academic freedom to be construed as a teacher's *privilege* or as a teacher's *responsibility*?

Granting the vertiginous complexities of the preceding questions, several descriptions of academic freedom, varying in lucidity, have emerged since the advent of American public education early in the nineteenth century. One such description characterizes academic freedom as that freedom which allows the public to legislate school policy for the institutions it supports. Antagonistic to this view is the position that defines the school as being an island of inquiry, necessarily existing apart from, and immune to, the sanctions and whims of the taxpayer. Many state-supported colleges and universities attempt to embrace this theory. Still another definition calls for the teacher to negotiate, through his administrator, with the public to foster an integral atmosphere of "cooperation" between classroom and community. Most high school and elementary districts subscribe, at least nominally, to this procedure.

A fourth definition strives to characterize academic freedom as being simply an extension of those basic freedoms contained in the federal constitution. This seemingly reasonable view has proved to be unwieldy when applied to specific educational controversies, for the embattled parties quickly discover the semantic flexibility of the constitutional mandates. Ironically, but not surprisingly, both advocates and enemies of the California superintendent quoted copiously from the Bill of Rights.

From the foregoing theories three rather specific policies have emerged regarding the presentation of controversy in the classroom. The first policy quite simply disallows examination of contentious issues, the argument being that the teacher is commissioned only to convey that content which enjoys broad acceptance in the community. The second policy permits the use of controversial material if the instructor presents all sides with equanimity and fairness, thereby allowing his students to form independent opinions. The slogan "Teach students *how* to think but not *what* to think" embodies this view. Still another code permits the teacher to express his private convictions after he has first given fair coverage to all positions in a given controversy. Proponents of this policy argue that a frank admission of opinion obviates any suspicion that the teacher is attempting to influence his students through a slanted presentation of material. Obviously, each policy suggests an entirely different conception of the instructor's role.

While it is clear that the political turmoil of our time has produced a difficult environment for any freedom — be it academic, social, or religious — the American teacher's vulnerability to harassment and to blatant acts of suppression is without parallel among the professions. In the 1920's teachers were cautiously viewing the debate which raged between fundamental religionists and the proponents of Darwinian evolution. A decade later the teacher who revealed a predilection for liberal or New Deal philosophy was susceptible to attacks from the "Red Scare" exponents. The years following the end of World War II have yielded new tensions produced by our hot and cold competitions with communism; again the loyalty of teachers is under assiduous surveillance. The tawdry spectacle of the McCarthy era threatens to rival the excesses of classical and medieval suppression, if only through the irony of its occurrence in a presumably enlightened culture.

Although there may be no imminent possibility of our escape from the maze of definition, it would appear that a teacher's first duty, regardless of his discipline or teaching level, is to struggle independently with the enigmas which attend his calling. Well-meaning administrators, P.T.A. followers, politicians, and boardmembers will continue to set before him their respective blueprints, but ultimately he must employ his own intelligence and integrity; he must with scholarship and patience weigh past theory against current speculation. He must self-ishly examine the delicate history of intellectual freedom — its order, its confusion, its affinity to the present.

The reader is urged, therefore, to compare and contrast the modern arguments in Part Two with the positions advanced by Socrates and John Milton. Of special interest is the implicit debate weaving through the selections by Robert Hutchins, Sidney Hook, and Russell Kirk. To be sure, each man's performance is his own. Collectively, however, their views encourage the asking of intelligent questions, the acquisition of final answers being the lonely obligation of each teacher.

Plato

In 399 B.C. Socrates went on trial charged with impiety and with corrupting the youth of Athens. In the "Apology" the philosopher attempts to prove that his accusers, Meletos, Anytus, and Lycon, have trumped up false charges in their zeal to silence him. Although we do not hear the prosecution's "evidence," the defense which Socrates provides for himself exposes the major issues of the trial. The jury was composed of 501 citizens, chosen by lot; and when they returned an eventual verdict of guilt, Socrates (as was the custom in major trials) proposed his own penalty — the paying of a fine. This offer was unacceptable. The seventy-year-old teacher then implies in his last speech that he has forced the court to accept the decree of death by hemlock, the penalty advanced by Anytus. Socrates cannot, in effect, beg to be forgiven for crimes he has not committed. He must surrender his life rather than dignify his accusers by expressing a nominal contrition.

To Socrates, the philosopher's mission was a ceaseless search, never to be interrupted or curtailed by majority sentiment. By so arguing, Socrates became the first recorded martyr for intellectual freedom, an archetypal rebel indicted for what have become traditional crimes.

Although the "Apology" is not to be taken as an exact record of the trial, it is generally assumed that Plato (c. 428–347 B.C.) attended most of the proceedings. Written by the student, the "Apology," "Crito," and "Phaedo" constitute a vivid and reasonably accurate drama of the teacher's final days.

10

APOLOGY*

How you, O Athenians, have been affected by my accusers, I cannot tell; but I know that they almost made me forget who I was — so persuasively did

* From *The Dialogues of Plato* (Oxford: The Clarendon Press, 1875), translated by Benjamin Jowett. Used by permission of The Clarendon Press, Oxford.

they speak; and yet they have hardly uttered a word of truth. But of the many falsehoods told by them, there was one which quite amazed me; — I mean when they said that you should be upon your guard and not allow yourselves to be deceived by the force of my eloquence. To say this, when they were certain to be detected as soon as I opened my lips and proved myself to be anything but a great speaker, did indeed appear to me most shameless — unless by the force of eloquence they mean the force of truth; for if such is their meaning, I admit that I am eloquent. But in how different a way from theirs! Well, as I was saying, they have scarcely spoken the truth at all; but from me you shall hear the whole truth: not, however, delivered after their manner in a set oration duly ornamented with words and phrases. No, by heaven! but I shall use the words and arguments which occur to me at the moment; for I am confident in the justice of my cause:[1] at my time of life I ought not to be appearing before you, O men of Athens, in the character of a juvenile orator — let no one expect it of me. And I must beg of you to grant me a favour: — If I defend myself in my accustomed manner, and you hear me using the words which I have been in the habit of using in the agora, at the tables of the money-changers, or anywhere else, I would ask you not to be surprised, and not to interrupt me on this account. For I am more than seventy years of age, and appearing now for the first time in a court of law, I am quite a stranger to the language of the place; and therefore I would have you regard me as if I were really a stranger, whom you would excuse if he spoke in his native tongue, and after the fashion of his country: — Am I making an unfair request of you? Never mind the manner, which may or may not be good; but think only of the truth of my words, and give heed to that: let the speaker speak truly and the judge decide justly.

And first, I have to reply to the older charges and to my first accusers, and then I will go on to the later ones. For of old I have had many accusers, who have accused me falsely to you during many years; and I am more afraid of them than of Anytus and his associates, who are dangerous, too, in their own way. But far more dangerous are the others, who began when you were children, and took possession of your minds with their falsehoods, telling of one Socrates, a wise man, who speculated about the heaven above, and searched into the earth beneath, and made the worse appear the better cause. The disseminators of this tale are the accusers whom I dread; for their hearers are apt to fancy that such enquirers do not believe in the existence of the gods. And they are many, and their charges against me are of ancient date, and they were made by them in the days when you were more impressible than you are now — in childhood, or it may have been in youth — and the cause when heard went by default, for there was none to answer. And hardest of all, I do not know and cannot tell the names of my accusers; unless in the chance case of a Comic poet. All who from envy and malice have persuaded you — some of them having convinced themselves — all this class of men are most difficult to deal with; for I cannot have them up here, and cross-

[1] Or, I am certain that I am right in taking this course.

examine them, and therefore I must simply fight with shadows in my own defence, and argue when there is no one who answers. I will ask you then to assume with me, as I was saying, that my opponents are of two kinds; one recent, the other ancient: and I hope that you will see the propriety of my answering the latter first, for these accusations you heard long before the others, and much oftener.

Well, then, I must make my defence, and endeavour to clear away in a short time, a slander which has lasted a long time. May I succeed, if to succeed be for my good and yours, or likely to avail me in my cause! The task is not an easy one; I quite understand the nature of it. And so leaving the event with God, in obedience to the law I will now make my defence.

I will begin at the beginning, and ask what is the accusation which has given rise to the slander of me, and in fact has encouraged Meletus to prefer this charge against me. Well, what do the slanderers say? They shall be my prosecutors, and I will sum up their words in an affidavit: "Socrates is an evil-doer, and a curious person, who searches into things under the earth and in heaven, and he makes the worse appear the better cause; and he teaches the aforesaid doctrines to others." Such is the nature of the accusation: it is just what you have yourselves seen in the comedy of Aristophanes,[2] who has introduced a man whom he calls Socrates, going about and saying that he walks in air, and talking a deal of nonsense concerning matters of which I do not pretend to know either much or little — not that I mean to speak disparagingly of any one who is a student of natural philosophy. I should be very sorry if Meletus could bring so grave a charge against me. But the simple truth is, O Athenians, that I have nothing to do with physical speculations. Very many of those here present are witnesses to the truth of this, and to them I appeal. Speak then, you who have heard me, and tell your neighbours whether any of you have ever known me hold forth in few words or in many upon such matters. . . . You hear their answer. And from what they say of this part of the charge you will be able to judge of the truth of the rest.

As little foundation is there for the report that I am a teacher, and take money; this accusation has no more truth in it than the other. Although, if a man were really able to instruct mankind, to receive money for giving instruction would, in my opinion, be an honour to him. There is Gorgias of Leontium, and Prodicus of Ceos, and Hippias of Elis, who go the round of the cities, and are able to persuade the young men to leave their own citizens by whom they might be taught for nothing, and come to them whom they not only pay, but are thankful if they may be allowed to pay them. There is at this time a Parian philosopher residing in Athens, of whom I have heard; and I came to hear of him in this way: — I came across a man who has spent a world of money on the Sophists, Callias, the son of Hipponicus, and knowing that he had sons, I asked him: "Callias," I said, "if your two sons were foals or calves, there would be no difficulty in finding some one to put over them; we should hire a trainer of horses, or a farmer probably, who would

2 Aristoph., The Clouds.

improve and perfect them in their own proper virtue and excellence; but as they are human beings, whom are you thinking of placing over them? Is there any one who understands human and political virtue? You must have thought about the matter, for you have sons; is there any one?" "There is," he said. "Who is he?" said I; "and of what country? and what does he charge?" "Evenus the Parian," he replied; "he is the man, and his charge is five minae." Happy is Evenus, I said to myself, if he really has this wisdom, and teaches at such a moderate charge. Had I the same, I should have been very proud and conceited; but the truth is that I have no knowledge of the kind.

I dare say, Athenians, that some one among you will reply, "Yes, Socrates, but what is the origin of these accusations which are brought against you; there must have been something strange which you have been doing? All these rumours and this talk about you would never have arisen if you had been like other men: tell us, then, what is the cause of them, for we should be sorry to judge hastily of you." Now I regard this as a fair challenge, and I will endeavour to explain to you the reason why I am called wise and have such an evil fame. Please to attend then. And although some of you may think that I am joking, I declare that I will tell you the entire truth. Men of Athens, this reputation of mine has come of a certain sort of wisdom which I possess. If you ask me what kind of wisdom, I reply, wisdom such as may perhaps be attained by man, for to that extent I am inclined to believe that I am wise; whereas the persons of whom I was speaking have a super-human wisdom, which I may fail to describe, because I have it not myself; and he who says that I have, speaks falsely, and is taking away my character. And here, O men of Athens, I must beg you not to interrupt me, even if I seem to say something extravagant. For the word which I will speak is not mine. I will refer you to a witness who is worthy of credit; that witness shall be the God of Delphi — he will tell you about my wisdom, if I have any, and of what sort it is. You must have known Chaerephon; he was early a friend of mine, and also a friend of yours, for he shared in the recent exile of the people, and returned with you. Well, Chaerephon, as you know, was very impetuous in all his doings, and he went to Delphi and boldly asked the oracle to tell him whether — as I was saying, I must beg you not to interrupt — he asked the oracle to tell him whether any one was wiser than I was, and the Pythian prophetess answered, that there was no man wiser. Chaerephon is dead himself; but his brother, who is in court, will confirm the truth of what I am saying.

Why do I mention this? Because I am going to explain to you why I have such an evil name. When I heard the answer, I said to myself, What can the god mean? and what is the interpretation of his riddle? for I know that I have no wisdom, small or great. What then can he mean when he says that I am the wisest of men? And yet he is a god, and cannot lie; that would be against his nature. After long consideration, I thought of a method of trying the question. I reflected that if I could only find a man wiser than myself, then I might go to the god with a refutation in my hand. I should say to him,

"Here is a man who is wiser than I am; but you said that I was the wisest."
Accordingly I went to one who had the reputation of wisdom, and observed
him — his name I need not mention; he was a politician whom I selected for
examination — and the result was as follows: When I began to talk with him,
I could not help thinking that he was not really wise, although he was thought
wise by many, and still wiser by himself; and thereupon I tried to explain to
him that he thought himself wise, but was not really wise; and the consequence was that he hated me, and his enmity was shared by several who were
present and heard me. So I left him, saying to myself, as I went away: Well,
although I do not suppose that either of us knows anything really beautiful
and good, I am better off than he is, — for he knows nothing, and thinks that
he knows; I neither know nor think I know. In this latter particular, then,
I seem to have slightly the advantage of him. Then I went to another who
had still higher pretensions to wisdom, and my conclusion was exactly the
same. Whereupon I made another enemy of him, and of many others besides
him.

Then I went to one man after another, being not unconscious of the
enmity which I provoked, and I lamented and feared this: but necessity was
laid upon me, — the word of God, I thought, ought to be considered first.
And I said to myself, Go I must to all who appear to know, and find out the
meaning of the oracle. And I swear to you, Athenians, by the dog I swear!
— for I must tell you the truth — the result of my mission was just this: I
found that the men most in repute were all but the most foolish; and that
others less esteemed were really wiser and better. I will tell you the tale of my
wanderings and of the "Herculean" labours, as I may call them, which I
endured only to find at last the oracle irrefutable. After the politicians, I
went to the poets; tragic, dithyrambic, and all sorts. And there, I said to
myself, you will be instantly detected; now you will find out that you are
more ignorant than they are. Accordingly, I took them some of the elaborate
passages in their own writings, and asked what was the meaning of them —
thinking that they would teach me something. Will you believe me? I am
almost ashamed to confess the truth, but I must say that there is hardly a
person present who would not have talked better about their poetry than
they did themselves. Then I knew that not by wisdom do poets write poetry,
but by a sort of genius and inspiration; they are like diviners or soothsayers
who also say many fine things, but do not understand the meaning of them.
The poets appeared to me to be much in the same case; and I further observed that upon the strength of their poetry they believed themselves to be
the wisest of men in other things in which they were wise. So I departed,
conceiving myself to be superior to them for the same reason that I was
superior to the politicians.

At last I went to the artisans, for I was conscious that I knew nothing at all,
as I may say, and I was sure that they knew many fine things; and here I was
not mistaken, for they did know many things of which I was ignorant, and
in this they certainly were wiser than I was. But I observed that even the good
artisans fell into the same error as the poets; — because they were good work-

men they thought that they also knew all sorts of high matters, and this defect in them overshadowed their wisdom; and therefore I asked myself on behalf of the oracle, whether I would like to be as I was, neither having their knowledge nor their ignorance, or like them in both; and I made answer to myself and to the oracle that I was better off as I was.

This inquisition has led to my having many enemies of the worst and most dangerous kind, and has given occasion also to many calumnies. And I am called wise, for my hearers always imagine that I myself possess the wisdom which I find wanting in others: but the truth is, O men of Athens, that God only is wise; and by his answer he intends to show that the wisdom of men is worth little or nothing; he is not speaking of Socrates, he is only using my name by way of illustration, as if he said, He, O men, is the wisest, who, like Socrates, knows that his wisdom is in truth worth nothing. And so I go about the world, obedient to the god, and search and make enquiry into the wisdom of any one, whether citizen or stranger, who appears to be wise; and if he is not wise, then in vindication of the oracle I show him that he is not wise; and my occupation quite absorbs me, and I have no time to give either to any public matter of interest or to any concern of my own, but I am in utter poverty by reason of my devotion to the god.

There is another thing: — young men of the richer classes, who have not much to do, come about me of their own accord; they like to hear the pretenders examined, and they often imitate me, and proceed to examine others; there are plenty of persons, as they quickly discover, who think that they know something, but really know little or nothing; and then those who are examined by them instead of being angry with themselves are angry with me: This confounded Socrates, they say; this villainous misleader of youth! — and then if somebody asks them, Why, what evil does he practise or teach? they do not know, and cannot tell; but in order that they may not appear to be at a loss, they repeat the ready-made charges which are used against all philosophers about teaching things up in the clouds and under the earth, and having no gods, and making the worse appear the better cause; for they do not like to confess that their pretence of knowledge has been detected — which is the truth; and as they are numerous and ambitious and energetic, and are drawn up in battle array and have persuasive tongues, they have filled your ears with their loud and inveterate calumnies. And this is the reason why my three accusers, Meletus and Anytus and Lycon, have set upon me; Meletus, who has a quarrel with me on behalf of the poets; Anytus, on behalf of the craftsmen and politicians; Lycon, on behalf of the rhetoricians: and as I said at the beginning, I cannot expect to get rid of such a mass of calumny all in a moment. And this, O men of Athens, is the truth and the whole truth; I have concealed nothing, I have dissembled nothing. And yet, I know that my plainness of speech makes them hate me, and what is their hatred but a proof that I am speaking the truth? — Hence has arisen the prejudice against me; and this is the reason of it, as you will find out either in this or in any future enquiry.

I have said enough in my defence against the first class of my accusers; I turn to the second class. They are headed by Meletus, that good man and true lover of his country, as he calls himself. Against these, too, I must try to make a defence: — Let their affidavit be read: it contains something of this kind: It says that Socrates is a doer of evil, who corrupts the youth; and who does not believe in the gods of the state, but has other new divinities of his own. Such is the charge; and now let us examine the particular counts. He says that I am a doer of evil, and corrupt the youth; but I say, O men of Athens, that Meletus is a doer of evil, in that he pretends to be in earnest when he is only in jest, and is so eager to bring men to trial from a pretended zeal and interest about matters in which he really never had the smallest interest. And the truth of this I will endeavour to prove to you.

Come hither, Meletus, and let me ask a question of you. You think a great deal about the improvement of youth?

Yes, I do.

Tell the judges, then, who is their improver; for you must know, as you have taken the pains to discover their corrupter, and are citing and accusing me before them. Speak, then, and tell the judges who their improver is. — Observe, Meletus, that you are silent, and have nothing to say. But is not this rather disgraceful, and a very considerable proof of what I was saying, that you have no interest in the matter. Speak up, friend, and tell us who their improver is.

The laws.

But that, my good sir, is not my meaning. I want to know who the person is, who, in the first place, knows the laws.

The judges, Socrates, who are present in court.

What, do you mean to say, Meletus, that they are able to instruct and improve youth?

Certainly they are.

What, all of them, or some only and not others?

All of them.

By the goddess Herè, that is good news! There are plenty of improvers, then. And what do you say of the audience, — do they improve them?

Yes, they do.

And the senators?

Yes, the senators improve them.

But perhaps the members of the assembly corrupt them? — or do they too improve them?

They improve them.

Then every Athenian improves and elevates them; all with the exception of myself; and I alone am their corrupter? Is that what you affirm?

That is what I stoutly affirm.

I am very unfortunate if you are right. But suppose I ask you a question: How about horses? Does one man do them harm and all the world good? Is not the exact opposite the truth? One man is able to do them good, or at least not many; — the trainer of horses, that is to say, does them good, and others who have to do with them rather injure them? Is not that true, Meletus, of horses, or of any other animals? Most assuredly it is; whether you and Anytus say yes or no. Happy indeed would be the condition of youth if they had one corrupter only, and all the rest of the world were their improvers. But you, Meletus, have sufficiently shown that you never had a thought about the young: your carelessness is seen in your not caring about the very things which you bring against me.

And now, Meletus, I will ask you another question — by Zeus I will: Which is better, to live among bad citizens, or among good ones? Answer, friend, I say; the question is one which may be easily answered. Do not the good do their neighbours good, and the bad do them evil?

Certainly.

And is there any one who would rather be injured than benefited by those who live with him? Answer, my good friend, the law requires you to answer — does any one like to be injured?

Certainly not.

And when you accuse me of corrupting and deteriorating the youth, do you allege that I corrupt them intentionally or unintentionally?

Intentionally, I say.

But you have just admitted that the good do their neighbours good, and the evil do them evil. Now, is that a truth which your superior wisdom has recognized thus early in life, and am I, at my age, in such darkness and ignorance as not to know that if a man with whom I have to live is corrupted by me, I am very likely to be harmed by him; and yet I corrupt him, and intentionally, too — so you say, although neither I nor any other human being is ever likely to be convinced by you. But either I do not corrupt them, or I corrupt them unintentionally; and on either view of the case you lie. If my offence is unintentional, the law has no cognizance of unintentional offences: you ought to have taken me privately, and warned and admonished me; for if I had been better advised, I should have left off doing what I only did unintentionally — no doubt I should; but you would have nothing to say to me and refused to teach me. And now you bring me up in this court, which is a place not of instruction, but of punishment.

It will be very clear to you, Athenians, as I was saying, that Meletus has no care at all, great or small, about the matter. But still I should like to know, Meletus, in what I am affirmed to corrupt the young. I suppose you mean, as I infer from your indictment, that I teach them not to acknowledge the gods which the state acknowledges, but some other new divinities or spiritual agencies in their stead. These are the lessons by which I corrupt the youth, as you say.

Yes, that I say emphatically.

Then, by the gods, Meletus, of whom we are speaking, tell me and the court, in somewhat plainer terms, what you mean! for I do not as yet understand whether you affirm that I teach other men to acknowledge some gods, and therefore that I do believe in gods, and am not an entire atheist — this you do not lay to my charge, — but only you say that they are not the same gods which the city recognizes — the charge is that they are different gods. Or, do you mean that I am an atheist simply, and a teacher of atheism?

I mean the latter — that you are a complete atheist.

What an extraordinary statement! Why do you think so, Meletus? Do you mean that I do not believe in the godhead of the sun or moon, like other men?

I assure you, judges, that he does not: for he says that the sun is stone, and the moon earth.

Friend Meletus, you think that you are accusing Anaxagoras: and you have but a bad opinion of the judges, if you fancy them illiterate to such a degree as not to know that these doctrines are found in the books of Anaxagoras the Clazomenian, which are full of them. And so, forsooth, the youth are said to be taught them by Socrates, when there are not unfrequently exhibitions of them at the theatre[3] (price of admission one drachma at the most); and they might pay their money, and laugh at Socrates if he pretends to father these extraordinary views. And so, Meletus, you really think that I do not believe in any god?

I swear by Zeus that you believe absolutely in none at all.

Nobody will believe you, Meletus, and I am pretty sure that you do not believe yourself. I cannot help thinking, men of Athens, that Meletus is reckless and impudent, and that he has written this indictment in a spirit of mere wantonness and youthful bravado. Has he not compounded a riddle, thinking to try me? He said to himself: — I shall see whether the wise Socrates will discover facetious contradiction, or whether I shall be able to deceive him and the rest of them. For he certainly does appear to me to contradict himself in the indictment as much as if he said that Socrates is guilty of not believing in the gods, and yet of believing in them — but this is not like a person who is in earnest.

I should like you, O men of Athens, to join me in examining what I conceive to be his inconsistency; and do you, Meletus, answer. And I must remind the audience of my request that they would not make a disturbance if I speak in my accustomed manner:

Did ever man, Meletus, believe in the existence of human things, and not of human beings? . . . I wish, men of Athens, that he would answer, and not be always trying to get up an interruption. Did ever any man believe in horsemanship, and not in horses? or in flute-playing, and not in flute-players? No, my friend; I will answer to you and to the court, as you refuse to answer for yourself. There is no man who ever did. But now please to answer the next question: Can a man believe in spiritual and divine agencies, and not in spirits or demigods?

He cannot.

How lucky I am to have extracted that answer, by the assistance of the court! But then you swear in the indictment that I teach and believe in

---

3 Probably in allusion to Aristophanes who caricatured, and to Euripides who borrowed the notions of Anaxagoras, as well as to other dramatic poets.

divine or spiritual agencies (new or old, no matter for that); at any rate, I believe in spiritual agencies, — so you say and swear in the affidavit; and yet if I believe in divine beings, how can I help believing in spirits or demigods; — must I not? To be sure I must; and therefore I may assume that your silence gives consent. Now what are spirits or demigods? are they not either gods or the sons of gods?

Certainly they are.

But this is what I call the facetious riddle invented by you: the demigods or spirits are gods, and you say first that I do not believe in gods, and then again that I do believe in gods; that is, if I believe in demigods. For if the demigods are the illegitimate sons of gods, whether by the nymphs or by any other mothers, of whom they are said to be the sons — what human being will ever believe that there are no gods if they are the sons of gods? You might as well affirm the existence of mules, and deny that of horses and asses. Such nonsense, Meletus, could only have been intended by you to make trial of me. You have put this into the indictment because you had nothing real of which to accuse me. But no one who has a particle of understanding will ever be convinced by you that the same men can believe in divine and super-human things, and yet not believe that there are gods and demigods and heroes.

I have said enough in answer to the charge of Meletus: any elaborate defence is unnecessary; but I know only too well how many are the enmities which I have incurred, and this is what will be my destruction if I am destroyed; — not Meletus, nor yet Anytus, but the envy and detraction of the world, which has been the death of many good men, and will probably be the death of many more; there is no danger of my being the last of them.

Some one will say: And are you not ashamed, Socrates, of a course of life which is likely to bring you to an untimely end? To him I may fairly answer: There you are mistaken: a man who is good for anything ought not to cal-culate the chance of living or dying; he ought only to consider whether in doing anything he is doing right or wrong — acting the part of a good man or of a bad. Whereas, upon your view, the heroes who fell at Troy were not good for much, and the son of Thetis above all, who altogether despised danger in comparison with disgrace; and when he was so eager to slay Hector, his goddess mother said to him, that if he avenged his companion Patroclus, and slew Hector, he would die himself — "Fate," she said, in these or the like words, "waits for you next after Hector"; he, receiving this warning, utterly despised danger and death, and instead of fearing them, feared rather to live in dishonour, and not to avenge his friend. "Let me die forthwith," he replies, "and be avenged of my enemy, rather than abide here by the beaked ships, a laughing-stock and a burden of the earth." Had Achilles any thought of death and danger? For wherever a man's place is, whether the place which he has chosen or that in which he has been placed by a commander, there he ought to remain in the hour of danger; he should not think of death or of anything but of disgrace. And this, O men of Athens, is a true saying.

Strange, indeed, would be my conduct, O men of Athens, if I who, when

I was ordered by the generals whom you chose to command me at Potidaea and Amphipolis and Delium, remained where they placed me, like any other man, facing death — if now, when, as I conceive and imagine, God orders me to fulfil the philosopher's mission of searching into myself and other men, I were to desert my post through fear of death, or any other fear; that would indeed be strange, and I might justly be arraigned in court for denying the existence of the gods, if I disobeyed the oracle because I was afraid of death, fancying that I was wise when I was not wise. For the fear of death is indeed the pretence of wisdom, and not real wisdom, being a pretence of knowing the unknown; and no one knows whether death, which men in their fear apprehend to be the greatest evil, may not be the greatest good. Is not this ignorance of a disgraceful sort, the ignorance which is the conceit that a man knows what he does not know? And in this respect only I believe myself to differ from men in general, and may perhaps claim to be wiser than they are: — that whereas I know but little of the world below, I do not suppose that I know: but I do know that injustice and disobedience to a better, whether God or man, is evil and dishonourable, and I will never fear or avoid a possible good rather than a certain evil. And therefore if you let me go now, and are not convinced by Anytus, who said that since I had been prosecuted I must be put to death: (or if not that I ought never to have been prosecuted at all); and that if I escape now, your sons will all be utterly ruined by listening to my words — if you say to me, Socrates, this time we will not mind Anytus, and you shall be let off, but upon one condition, that you are not to enquire and speculate in this way any more, and that if you are caught doing so again you shall die; — if this was the condition on which you let me go, I should reply: Men of Athens, I honour and love you; but I shall obey God rather than you, and while I have life and strength I shall never cease from the practice and teaching of philosophy, exhorting any one whom I meet and saying to him after my manner: You, my friend, — a citizen of the great and mighty and wise city of Athens, — are you not ashamed of heaping up the greatest amount of money and honour and reputation, and caring so little about wisdom and truth and the greatest improvement of the soul, which you never regard or heed at all? And if the person with whom I am arguing, says: Yes, but I do care; then I do not leave him or let him go at once; but I proceed to interrogate and examine and cross-examine him, and if I think that he has no virtue in him, but only says that he has, I reproach him with undervaluing the greater, and overvaluing the less. And I shall repeat the same words to every one whom I meet, young and old, citizen and alien, but especially to the citizens inasmuch as they are my brethren. For know that this is the command of God; and I believe that no greater good has ever happened in the state than my service to the God. For I do nothing but go about persuading you all, old and young alike, not to take thought for your persons or your properties, but first and chiefly to care about the greatest improvement of the soul. I tell you that virtue is not given by money, but that from virtue comes money and every other good of man, public as well as private. This is my teaching, and if this is the doctrine which corrupts the youth, I am a mischievous person. But if any one says that this is not my teaching, he is speaking an untruth. Wherefore, O men of Athens, I say to you, do as Anytus bids or not as Anytus bids, and either acquit me or not; but whichever you do, understand that I shall never alter my ways, not even if I have to die many times.

Men of Athens, do not interrupt, but hear me; there was an understanding between us that you should hear me to the end: I have something more to say, at which you may be inclined to cry out; but I believe that to hear me will be good for you, and therefore I beg that you will not cry out. I would have you know, that if you kill such an one as I am, you will injure yourselves more than you will injure me. Nothing will injure me, not Meletus nor yet Anytus — they cannot, for a bad man is not permitted to injure a better than himself. I do not deny that Anytus may, perhaps, kill him, or drive him into exile, or deprive him of civil rights; and he may imagine, and others may imagine, that he is inflicting a great injury upon him: but there I do not agree. For the evil of doing as he is doing — the evil of unjustly taking away the life of another — is greater far.

And now, Athenians, I am not going to argue for my own sake, as you may think, but for yours, that you may· not sin against the God by condemning me, who am his gift to you. For if you kill me you will not easily find a successor to me, who, if I may use such a ludicrous figure of speech, am a sort of gadfly, given to the state by God; and the state is a great and noble steed who is tardy in his motions owing to his very size, and requires to be stirred into life. I am that gadfly which God has attached to the state, and all day long and in all places am always fastening upon you, arousing and persuading and reproaching you. You will not easily find another like me, and therefore I would advise you to spare me. I dare say that you may feel out of temper (like a person who is suddenly awakened from sleep), and you think that you might easily strike me dead as Anytus advises, and then you would sleep on for the remainder of your lives, unless God in his care of you sent you another gadfly. When I say that I am given to you by God, the proof of my mission is this: — if I had been like other men, I should not have neglected all of my own concerns or patiently seen the neglect of them during all these years, and have been doing yours, coming to you individually like a father or elder brother, exhorting you to regard virtue; such conduct, I say, would be unlike human nature. If I had gained anything, or if my exhortations had been paid, there would have been some sense in my doing so, but now, as you will perceive, not even the impudence of my accusers dares to say that I have ever exacted or sought pay of any one; of that they have no witness. And I have a sufficient witness to the truth of what I say — my poverty.

Some one may wonder why I go about in private giving advice and busying myself with the concerns of others, but do not venture to come forward in public and advise the state. I will tell you why. You have heard me speak at sundry times and in divers places of an oracle or sign which comes to me, and is the divinity which Meletus ridicules in the indictment. This sign, which is a kind of voice, first began to come to me when I was a child; it always forbids but never commands me to do anything which I am going to do. This is what deters me from being a politician. And rightly, as I think. For I am certain, O men of Athens, that if I had engaged in politics, I should have perished long ago, and done no good either to you or to myself. And do not be offended at my telling you the truth: for the truth is, that no man who goes to war with you or any other multitude, honestly striving against the many lawless and unrighteous deeds which are done in a state, will save his life; he who will fight for the right, if he would live even for a brief space, must have a private station and not a public one.

I can give you convincing evidence of what I say, not words only, but what you value far more — actions. Let me relate to you a passage of my own life which will prove to you that I should never have yielded to injustice from any fear of death, and that "as I should have refused to yield" I must have died at once. I will tell you a tale of the courts, not very interesting perhaps, but nevertheless true. The only office of state which I ever held, O men of Athens, was that of senator: the tribe Antiochis, which is my tribe, had the presidency at the trial of the generals who had not taken up the bodies of the slain after the battle of Arginusae; and you proposed to try them in a body, contrary to law, as you all thought afterwards; but at the time I was the only one of the Prytanes who was opposed to the illegality, and I gave my vote against you; and when the orators threatened to impeach and arrest me, and you called and shouted, I made up my mind that I would run the risk, having law and justice with me, rather than take part in your injustice because I feared imprisonment and death. This happened in the days of the democracy. But when the oligarchy of the Thirty was in power, they sent for me and four others into the rotunda, and bade us bring Leon the Salaminian from Salamis, as they wanted to put him to death. This was a specimen of the sort of commands which they were always giving with the view of implicating as many as possible in their crimes; and then I showed, not in word only but in deed, that, if I may be allowed to use such an expression, I cared not a straw for death, and that my great and only care was lest I should do an unrighteous or unholy thing. For the strong arm of that oppressive power did not frighten me into doing wrong; and when we came out of the rotunda the other four went to Salamis and fetched Leon, but I went quietly home. For which I might have lost my life, had not the power of the Thirty shortly afterwards come to an end. And many will witness to my words.

Now do you really imagine that I could have survived all these years, if I had led a public life, supposing that like a good man I had always maintained the right and had made justice, as I ought, the first thing? No indeed, men of Athens, neither I nor any other man. But I have been always the same in all my actions, public as well as private, and never have I yielded any base compliance to those who are slanderously termed my disciples, or to any other. Not that I have any regular disciples. But if any one likes to come and hear me while I am pursuing my mission, whether he be young or old, he is not excluded. Nor do I converse only with those who pay; but any one, whether he be rich or poor, may ask and answer me and listen to my words; and whether he turns out to be a bad man or a good one, neither result can be justly imputed to me; for I never taught or professed to teach him anything. And if any one says that he has ever learned or heard anything from me in private which all the world has not heard, let me tell you that he is lying.

But I shall be asked, Why do people delight in continually conversing with you? I have told you already, Athenians, the whole truth about this matter: they like to hear cross-examination of the pretenders to wisdom; there is amusement in it. Now this duty of cross-examining other men has been imposed upon me by God; and has been signified to me by oracles, visions, and in every way in which the will of divine power was ever intimated to any one. This is true, O Athenians; or, if not true, would be soon refuted. If I am or have been corrupting the youth, those of them who are now grown up and have become sensible that I gave them bad advice in the days of their youth should come forward as accusers, and take their revenge; or if they do not like to come themselves, some of their relatives, fathers, brothers, or other kinsmen, should say what evil their families have suffered at my hands. Now is their time. Many of them I see in the court. There is Crito, who is of the same age and of the same deme with myself, and there is Critobulus his son, whom I also see. Then again there is Lysanias of Sphettus, who is the father of Aeschines — he is present; and also there is Antiphon of Cephisus, who is the father of Epigenes; and there are the brothers of several who have associated with me. There is Nicostratus the son of Theosdotides, and the brother of Theodotus (now Theodotus himself is dead, and therefore he, at any rate, will not seek to stop him); and there is Paralus the son of Demodocus, who had a brother Theages; and Adeimantus the son of Ariston, whose brother Plato is present; and Aeantodorus, who is the brother of Apollodorus, whom I also see. I might mention a great many others, some of whom Meletus should have produced as witnesses in the source of his speech; and let him still produce them, if he has forgotten — I will make way for him. And let him say, if he has any testimony of the sort which he can produce. Nay, Athenians, the very opposite is the truth. For all these are ready to witness on behalf of the corrupter, of the injurer of their kindred, as Meletus and Anytus call me; not the corrupted youth only — there might have been a motive for that — but their uncorrupted elder relatives. Why should they too support me with their testimony? Why, indeed, except for the sake of truth and justice, and because they know that I am speaking the truth, and that Meletus is a liar.

Well, Athenians, this and the like of this is all the defence which I have to offer. Yet a word more. Perhaps there may be some one who is offended at me, when he calls to mind how he himself on a similar, or even a less serious occasion, prayed and entreated the judges with many tears, and how he produced his children in court, which was a moving spectacle, together with a host of relations and friends; whereas I, whom am probably in danger of my life, will do none of these things. The contrast may occur to his mind, and he may be set against me, and vote in anger because he is displeased at me on this account. Now if there be such a person among you, — mind, I do not say that there is, — to him I may fairly reply: My friend, I am a man, and like other men, a creature of flesh and blood, and not "of wood or stone," as Homer says; and I have a family, yes, and sons, O Athenians, three in number, one almost a man, and two others who are still young; and yet I will not bring any of them hither in order to petition you for an acquittal. And why not? Not from any self-assertion or want of respect for you. Whether I am or am not afraid of death is another question, of which I will not now speak. But, having regard to public opinion, I feel that such conduct would be discreditable to myself, and to you, and to the whole state. One who has reached my years, and who has a name for wisdom, ought not to demean himself. Whether this opinion of me be deserved or not, at any rate the world has decided that Socrates is in some way superior to other men. And if those among you who are said to be superior in wisdom and courage, and any other virtue, demean themselves in this way, how shameful is their conduct! I have seen men of reputation, when they have been condemned, behaving in the strangest manner: they seemed to fancy that they were going to suffer something dreadful if they died, and that they could be immortal if you only allowed them to live; and I think that such are a dishonour to the state, and that any stranger coming in would have said of them that the most eminent men of Athens, to whom the Athenians themselves give honour and command, are no better than women. And I say that these things ought not to be done by those of us who have a reputation; and if they are done, you ought not to permit them; you ought rather to show that you are far more disposed to condemn the man who gets up a doleful scene and makes the city ridiculous, than him who holds his peace.

But, setting aside the question of public opinion, there seems to be something wrong in asking a favour of a judge, and thus procuring an acquittal, instead of informing and convincing him. For his duty is, not to make a present of justice, but to give judgment; and he has sworn that he will judge according to the laws, and not according to his own good pleasure; and we ought not to encourage you, nor should you allow yourselves to be encouraged, in this habit of perjury — there can be no piety in that. Do not then require me to do what I consider dishonourable and impious and wrong, especially now, when I am being tried for impiety on the indictment of Meletus. For if, O men of Athens, by force of persuasion and entreaty I could overpower your oaths, then I should be teaching you to believe that there are no gods, and in defending should simply convict myself of the charge of not believing in them. But that is not so — far otherwise. For I do believe that there are gods, and in a sense higher than that in which any of my accusers believe in them. And to you and to God I commit my cause, to be determined by you as is best for you and me.

*   *   *

There are many reasons why I am not grieved, O men of Athens, at the vote of condemnation. I expected it, and am only surprised that the votes are so nearly equal; for I had thought that the majority against me would have been far larger; but now, had thirty votes gone over to the other side, I should have been acquitted. And I may say, I think, that I have escaped Meletus. I may say more; for without the assistance of Anytus and Lycon, any one may see that he would not have had a fifth part of the votes, as the law requires, in which case he would have incurred a fine of a thousand drachmae.

And so he proposes death as the penalty. And what shall I propose on my part, O men of Athens? Clearly that which is my due. And what is my due? What return shall be made to the man who has never had the wit to be idle during his whole life; but has been careless of what the many care for — wealth, and family interests, and military offices, and speaking in the assembly, and magistracies, and plots, and parties. Reflecting that I was really too honest a man to be a politician and live, I did not go where I could do no good to you or to myself; but where I could do the greatest good privately to every one of you, thither I went, and sought to persuade every man among you that he must look to himself, and seek virtue and wisdom before he looks to his private interests, and look to the state before he looks to the interests of the state; and that this should be the order which he observes in all his actions. What shall be done to such an one? Doubtless some good thing, O men of Athens, if he has his reward; and the good should be of a kind suitable to him. What would be a reward suitable to a poor man who is your benefactor, and who desires leisure that he may instruct you? There can be no reward so fitting as maintenance in the Prytaneum, O men of Athens, a reward which he deserves far more than the citizen who has won the prize at Olympia in the horse or chariot race, whether the chariots were drawn by two horses or by many. For I am in want, and he has enough; and he only gives you the appearance of happiness, and I give you the reality. And if I am to estimate the penalty fairly, I should say that maintenance in the Prytaneum is the just return.

Perhaps you think that I am braving you in what I am saying now, as in what I said before about the tears and prayers. But this is not so. I speak rather because I am convinced that I never intentionally wronged any one, although I cannot convince you — the time has been too short; if there were a law at Athens, as there is in other cities, that a capital cause should not be decided in one day, then I believe that I should have convinced you. But I cannot in a moment refute great slanders; and, as I am convinced that I never wronged another, I will assuredly not wrong myself. I will not say of myself that I deserve any evil, or propose any penalty. Why should I? Because I am afraid of the penalty of death which Meletus proposes? When I do not know whether death is a good or an evil, why should I propose a penalty which would certainly be an evil? Shall I say imprisonment? And why should I live in prison, and be the slave of the magistrates of the year — of the Eleven? Or shall the penalty be a fine, and imprisonment until the fine is paid? There is the same objection. I should have to lie in prison, for money I have none, and cannot pay. And if I say exile (and this may possibly be the penalty which you will affix), I must indeed be blinded by the love of life, if I am so irrational as to expect that when you, who are my own citizens, cannot endure my discourses and words, and have found them so grievous and odious that you will have no more of them, others are likely to endure me. No indeed, men of Athens, that is not very likely. And what a life should I lead, at my age, wandering from city to city, ever changing my place of exile, and always being driven out! For I am quite sure that wherever I go, there, as here, the young men will flock to me; and if I drive them away, their elders will drive me out at their request; and if I let them come, their fathers and friends will drive me out for their sakes.

Some one will say: Yes, Socrates, but cannot you hold your tongue, and then you may go into a foreign city, and no one will interfere with you? Now I have great difficulty in making you understand my answer to this. For if I tell you that to do as you say would be a disobedience to God, and therefore that I cannot hold my tongue, you will not believe that I am serious; and if I say again that daily to discourse about virtue, and of those things about which you hear me examining myself and others, is the greatest good of man, and that the unexamined life is not worth living, you are still less likely to believe me. Yet I say what is true, although a thing of which it is hard for me to persuade you. Also, I have never been accustomed to think that I deserve to suffer any harm. Had I money I might have estimated the offence at what I was able to pay, and not have been much the worse. But I have none, and therefore I must ask you to proportion the fine to my means. Well, perhaps I could afford a mina, and therefore I propose that penalty: Plato, Crito, Critobulus, and Apollodorus, my friends here, bid me say thirty minae, and they will be the sureties. Let thirty minae be the penalty; for which sum they will be ample security to you.

*   *   *

Not much time will be gained, O Athenians, in return for the evil name which you will get from the detractors of the city, who will say that you killed Socrates, a wise man; for they will call me wise, even although I am not wise, when they want to reproach you. If you had waited a little while, your desire would have been fulfilled in the course of nature. For I am far advanced in years, as you may perceive, and not far from death. I am speaking now not to all of you, but only to those who have condemned me to death. And I have another thing to say to them: You think that I was convicted because I had no words of the sort which would have procured my acquittal — I mean if I had thought fit to leave nothing undone or unsaid. Not so; the deficiency which led to my conviction was not of words — certainly not. But I had not the boldness or impudence or inclination to address you as you would have liked me to do, weeping and wailing and lamenting, and saying and doing many things which you have been accustomed to hear from others, and which, as I maintain, are unworthy of me. I thought at the time that I ought not to do anything common or mean when in danger: nor do I now repent of the style of my defence; I would rather die having spoken after my manner, than speak in your manner and live. For neither in war nor yet at law ought I or any man to use every way of escaping death. Often in battle there can be no doubt that if a man will throw away his arms, and fall on his knees before his pursuers, he may escape death; and in other dangers there are other ways of escaping death, if a man is willing to say and do anything. The difficulty, my friends, is not to avoid death, but to avoid unrighteousness; for that runs faster than death. I am old and move slowly, and the slower runner has overtaken me, and my accusers are keen and quick, and the faster runner, who is unrighteousness, has overtaken them. And now I depart hence condemned by you to suffer the penalty of death, — they too go their ways condemned by the truth to suffer the penalty of villainy and wrong; and I must abide by my reward — let them abide by theirs. I suppose that these things may be regarded as fated, — and I think that they are well.

And now, O men who have condemned me, I would fain prophesy to you; for I am about to die, and in the hour of death men are gifted with prophetic power. And I prophesy to you who are my murderers, that immediately after my departure punishment far heavier than you have inflicted on me will surely await you. Me you have killed because you wanted to escape the accuser, and not to give account of your lives. But that will not be as you suppose: far otherwise. For I say that there will be more accusers of you than there are now; accusers whom hitherto I have restrained: and as they are younger they will be more inconsiderate with you, and you will be more offended at them. If you think that by killing men you can prevent some one from censuring your evil lives, you are mistaken; that is not a way of escape which is either possible or honourable; the easiest and the noblest way is not to be disabling others, but to be improving yourselves. This is the prophecy which I utter before my departure to the judges who have condemned me.

Friends, who would have acquitted me, I would like also to talk with you about the thing which has come to pass, while the magistrates are busy, and before I go to the place at which I must die. Stay then a little, for we may as well talk with one another while their is time. You are my friends, and I should like to show you the meaning of this event which has happened to me. O my judges — for you I may truly call judges — I should like to tell you of a wonderful circumstance. Hitherto the divine faculty of which the internal oracle is the source has constantly been in the habit of opposing me even about trifles, if I was going to make a slip or error in any matter; and now as you see there has come upon me that which may be thought, and is generally believed to be, the last and worst evil. But the oracle made no sign of opposition, either when I was leaving my house in the morning, or when I was on my way to the court, or while I was speaking, at anything which I was going to say; and yet I have often been stopped in the middle of a speech, but now in nothing I either said or did touching the matter in hand has the oracle opposed me. What do I take to be the explanation of this silence? I will tell you. It is an intimation that what has happened to me is a good, and that those of us who think that death is an evil are in error. For the customary sign would surely have opposed me had I been going to evil and not to good.

Let us reflect in another way, and we shall see that there is great reason to hope that death is a good; for one of two things — either death is a state of nothingness and utter unconsciousness, or, as men say, there is a change and migration of the soul from this world to another. Now if you suppose that there is no consciousness, but a sleep like the sleep of him who is undisturbed even by dreams, death will be an unspeakable gain. For if a person were to select the night in which his sleep was undisturbed even by dreams, and were to compare with this the other days and nights of his life, and then were to tell us how many days and nights he had passed in the course of his life better and more pleasantly than this one, I think that any man, I will not say a private man, but even the great king will not find many such days or nights, when compared with the others. Now if death be of such a nature, I say that to die is gain; for eternity is then only a single night. But if death is the journey to another place, and there, as men say, all the dead abide, what good, O my friends and judges, can be greater than this? If indeed when the pilgrim arrives in the world below, he is delivered from the professors of justice in this world, and finds the true judges who are said to give judgment there, Minos and Rhadamanthus and Aeacus and Triptolemus, and other sons of God who were righteous in their own life, that pilgrimage will be worth making. What would not a man give if he might converse with Orpheus and Musaeus and Hesiod and Homer? Nay, if this be true, let me die again and again. I myself, too, shall have a wonderful interest in there meeting and conversing with Palamedes, and Ajax the son of Telamon, and any other ancient hero who has suffered death through an unjust judgment; and there will be no small pleasure, as I think, in comparing my own sufferings with theirs. Above all, I shall then be able to continue my search into true and false knowledge; as in this world, so also in the next; and I shall find out who is wise, and who pretends to be wise, and is not. What would not a man give, O judges, to be able to examine the leader of the great Trojan expedition; or Odysseus or Sisyphus, or numberless others, men and women too! What infinite delight would there be in conversing with them and asking them questions! In another world they do not put a man to death for asking questions: assuredly not. For besides being happier than we are, they will be immortal, if what is said is true.

Wherefore, O judges, be of good cheer about death, and know of a certainty, that no evil can happen to a good man, either in life or after death. He and his are not neglected by the gods; nor has my own approaching end happened by mere chance. But I see clearly that the time had arrived when it was better for me to die and be released from trouble; wherefore the oracle gave no sign. For which reason, also, I am not angry with my condemners, or with my accusers; they have done me no harm, although they did not mean to do me any good; and for this I may gently blame them.

Still I have a favour to ask of them. When my sons are grown up, I would ask of you, O my friends, to punish them; and I would have you trouble them, as I have troubled you, if they seem to care about riches, or anything, more than about virtue; or if they pretend to be something when they are really nothing, — then reprove them, as I have reproved you, for not caring about that for which they ought to care, and thinking that they are something when they are really nothing. And if you do this, both I and my sons will have received justice at your hands.

The hour of departure has arrived, and we go our ways — I to die, and you to live. Which is better God only knows.

John Milton

John Milton (1608–1674), one of the great English poets of the seventeenth century, is noted, too, for his polemical outbursts. Areopagitica, one such tract, appeared in November of 1644. As described by Robert M. Adams of Cornell University, the title "means 'things to be said before the Areopagus.' The Areopagus was an ancient, powerful, and much respected tribunal in Athens, before which Isocrates, in 355 B.C., delivered a famous speech. Milton's title implies a comparison between the Areopagus and the English Parliament and this comparison may be thought to validate, in some degree, the florid, oratorical tone of the tract."

Milton was angered by an ordinance for the control of printing which was passed by Parliament in June of 1643. The law forbade unlicensed printing, and although Milton thought it outrageous, the ordinance was actually a legal symptom of a printing restriction that had already been practiced by the Tudors and the Stuarts. In defiance of the order, the poet published three unlicensed pamphlets, the third being Areopagitica.

Aside from the specific circumstances of its creation, Areopagitica survives as an eloquent tribute to those freedoms of publication largely taken for granted in our time. Milton's argument recognizes the power of literature, and, at the same time, the necessity for the state to protect that power, for "Who kills a man kills a reasonable creature . . . ; but he who destroys a good book, kills reason itself. . . ."

11

From AREOPAGITICA

I deny not, but that it is of greatest concernment in the Church and Commonwealth, to have a vigilant eye how books demean themselves as well as men; and thereafter to confine, imprison, and do sharpest justice on them as malefactors. For books are not absolutely dead things, but do contain a potency of life in them to be as active as that soul was whose progeny they are; nay, they do preserve as in a vial the purest efficacy and extraction of that living intellect that bred them. I know they are as lively, and as vigorously productive, as those fabulous dragon's teeth; and being sown up and down, may chance to spring up armed men. And yet, on the other hand, unless wariness be used, as good almost kill a man as kill a good book. Who kills a man kills a reasonable creature, God's image; but he who destroys a good book, kills reason itself, kills the image of God, as it were in the eye. Many a man lives a burden to the earth; but a good book is the precious life-blood of a master spirit, embalmed and treasured up on purpose to a life beyond life. 'Tis true, no age can restore a life, whereof perhaps there is no great loss; and revolutions of ages do not oft recover the loss of a rejected truth, for the want of which whole nations fare the worse.

We should be wary therefore what persecution we raise against the living labours of public men, how we spill that seasoned life of man, preserved and stored up in books; since we see a kind of homicide may be thus committed, sometimes a martyrdom, and if it extend to the whole impression, a kind of massacre; whereof the execution ends not in the slaying of an elemental life, but strikes at that ethereal and fifth essence, the breath of reason itself, slays an immortality rather than a life. . . .

Good and evil we know in the field of this world grow up together almost inseparably; and the knowledge of good is so involved and interwoven with the knowledge of evil, and in so many cunning resemblances hardly to be discerned, that those confused seeds which were imposed upon Psyche as an incessant labour to cull out, and sort asunder, were not more intermixed. It was from out the rind of one apple tasted, that the knowledge of good and evil, as two twins cleaving together, leaped forth into the world. And perhaps this is that doom which Adam fell into of knowing good and evil, that is to say of knowing good by evil. As therefore the state of man now is; what wisdom can there be to choose, what continence to forbear without the knowledge of evil? He that can apprehend and consider vice with all her baits and seeming pleasures, and yet abstain, and yet distinguish, and yet prefer that which is truly better, he is the true warfaring Christian.

I cannot praise a fugitive and cloistered virtue, unexercised and unbreathed, that never sallies out and sees her adversary, but slinks out of the race, where that immortal garland is to be run for, not without dust and heat. Assuredly we bring not innocence into the world, we bring impurity much rather; that which purifies us is trial, and trial is by what is contrary. That virtue therefore which is but a youngling in the contemplation of evil, and knows not the utmost that vice promises to her followers, and rejects it, is but a blank virtue, not a pure; her whiteness is but an excremental whiteness. Which was the reason why our sage and serious poet Spenser, whom I dare be known to think a better teacher than Scotus or Aquinas, describing true temperance under the person of Guion, brings him in with his palmer through the cave of Mammon, and the bower of earthly bliss, that he might see and know, and yet abstain. Since therefore the knowledge and survey of vice is in this world so necessary to the constituting of human virtue, and the scanning of error to the confirmation of truth, how can we more safely, and with less danger, scout into the regions of sin and falsity than by reading all manner of tractates and hearing all manner of reason? And this is the benefit which may be had of books promiscuously read. . . .

Seeing, therefore, that those books, and those in great abundance, which are likeliest to taint both life and doctrine, cannot be suppressed without the fall of learning and of all ability in disputation, and that these books of either sort are most and soonest catching to the learned, from whom to the common people whatever is heretical or dissolute may quickly be conveyed, and that evil manners are as perfectly learnt without books a thousand other ways which cannot be stopped, and evil doctrine not with books can propagate, except a teacher guide, which he might also do without writing, and so beyond prohibiting, I am not able to unfold, how this cautelous enterprise of licensing can be exempted from the number of vain and impossible attempts. And he who were pleasantly disposed could not well avoid to liken it to the exploit of that gallant man who thought to pound up the crows by shutting his park gate.

Besides another inconvenience, if learned men be the first receivers out of books and dispreaders both of vice and error, how shall the licensers themselves be confided in, unless we can confer upon them, or they assume to themselves above all others in the land, the grace of infallibility and uncorruptedness? And again, if it be true that a wise man, like a good refiner, can gather gold out of the drossiest volume, and that a fool will be a fool with the best book, yea or without book; there is no reason that we should deprive a wise man of any advantage to his wisdom, while we seek to restrain from a fool, that which being restrained will be no hindrance to his folly. For if there should be so much exactness always used to keep that from him which is unfit for his reading, we should in the judgment of Aristotle not only, but of Solomon and of our Saviour, not vouchsafe him good precepts, and by consequence not willingly admit him to good books; as being certain that a wise man will make better use of an idle pamphlet, than a fool will do of sacred Scripture. . . .

If we think to regulate printing, thereby to rectify manners, we must regulate all recreations and pastimes, all that is delightful to man. No music must be heard, no song be set or sung, but what is grave and Doric. There must be licensing dancers, that no gesture, motion, or deportment be taught our youth but what by their allowance shall be thought honest; for such Plato was provided of. It will ask more than the work of twenty licensers to examine all the lutes, the violins, and the guitars in every house; they must not be suffered to prattle as they do, but must be licensed what they may say. And who shall silence all the airs and madrigals that whisper softness in chambers? The windows also, and the balconies must be thought on; there are shrewd books, with dangerous frontispieces, set to sale; who shall prohibit them, shall twenty licensers? The villages also must have their visitors to inquire what lectures the bagpipe and the rebeck reads, even to the ballatry and the gamut of every municipal fiddler, for these are the countryman's Arcadias, and his Monte Mayors.

Next, what more national corruption, for which England hears ill abroad, than household gluttony: who shall be the rectors of our daily rioting? And what shall be done to inhibit the multitudes that frequent those houses where drunkenness is sold and harboured? Our garments also should be referred to the licensing of some more sober workmasters to see them cut into a less wanton garb. Who shall regulate all the mixed conversation of our youth, male and female together, as is the fashion of this country? Who shall still appoint what shall be discoursed, what presumed, and no further? Lastly, who shall forbid and separate all idle resort, all evil company? These things will be, and must be; but how they shall be least hurtful, how least enticing, herein consists the grave and governing wisdom of a state.

To sequester out of the world into Atlantic and Utopian politics, which never can be drawn into use, will not mend our condition; but to ordain wisely as in this world of evil, in the midst whereof God hath placed us unavoidably. Nor is it Plato's licensing of books will do this, which necessarily pulls along with it so many other kinds of licensing, as will make us all both ridiculous and weary, and yet frustrate; but those unwritten, or at least unconstraining, laws of virtuous education, religious and civil nurture, which Plato there mentions as the bonds and ligaments of the commonwealth, the pillars and the sustainers of every written statute; these they be which will bear chief sway in such matters as these, when all licensing will be easily eluded. Impunity and remissness, for certain, are the bane of a commonwealth; but here the great art lies, to discern in what the law is to bid restraint and punishment, and in what things persuasion only is to work.

If every action, which is good or evil in man at ripe years, were to be under pittance and prescription and compulsion, what were virtue but a name, what praise could be then due to well-doing, what gramercy to be sober, just, or continent? Many there be that complain of divine Providence for suffering Adam to transgress; foolish tongues! When God gave him reason, he gave him freedom to choose, for reason is but choosing; he had been else a mere artificial Adam, such an Adam as he is in the motions. We ourselves esteem not of that obedience, or love, or gift, which is of force: God therefore left him free, set before him a provoking object, ever almost in his eyes; herein consisted his merit, herein the right of his reward, the praise of his abstinence. Wherefore did he create passions within us, pleasures round about us, but that these rightly tempered are the very ingredients of virtue?

They are not skillful considerers of human things, who imagine to remove sin by removing the matter of sin; for, besides that it is a huge heap increasing under the very act of diminishing, though some part of it may for a time be withdrawn from some persons, it cannot from all, in such a universal thing as books are; and when this is done, yet the sin remains entire. Though ye take from a covetous man all his treasure, he has yet one jewel left, ye cannot bereave him of his covetousness. Banish all objects of lust, shut up all youth in the severest discipline that can be exercised in any hermitage, ye cannot make them chaste, that came not thither so; such great care and wisdom is required to the right managing of this point. Suppose we could expel sin by this means; look how much we thus expel of sin, so much we expel of virtue: for the matter of them both is the same; remove that, and ye remove them both alike.

This justifies the high providence of God, who, though he command us temperance, justice, continence, yet pours out before us, even to a profuseness, all desirable things, and gives us minds that can wander beyond all limit and satiety. Why should we then affect a rigour contrary to the manner of God and of nature, by abridging or scanting those means, which books freely permitted are, both to the trial of virtue and the exercise of truth? It would be better done, to learn that the law must needs be frivolous, which goes to restrain things, uncertainly and yet equally working to good and to evil. And were I the chooser, a dram of well-doing should be preferred before many times as much the forcible hindrance of evil-doing. For God sure esteems the growth and completing of one virtuous person more than the restraint of ten vicious.

Robert M. Hutchins

A *former president of the University of Chicago, Robert M. Hutchins is now President of the Fund for the Republic, an organization devoted to clarifying basic questions of freedom and justice deriving from modern political and social change. The following definition of academic freedom has aroused much debate between liberals and conservatives. Even some liberals feel that Hutchins is extreme in his persistence that teachers be judged only on their professional competence, never on their philosophical convictions. Making use of J. S. Mill's classic theory, Hutchins proceeds to attack specific agencies which, to him, jeopardize the realization of Mill's theory in educational practices.*

"The Meaning and Significance of Academic Freedom" is a trenchant defense of a philosophical stance unalterably opposed by the conservative thinker, Russell Kirk, whose position is also presented in Part Two.

12

THE MEANING AND SIGNIFICANCE

OF ACADEMIC FREEDOM*

The arguments for academic freedom are the same as those for freedom of speech, and they rest on the same foundation. Here are the familiar words of John Stuart Mill:

If all mankind minus one were of one opinion, and only one person were of the contrary opinion, mankind would be no more justified in silencing

* From *The Annals of the American Academy of Political and Social Science*, July, 1955, pp. 72–78. Used by permission of the American Academy of Political and Social Science and Robert M. Hutchins.

that one person, than he, if he had the power, would be justified in silencing mankind. . . . the peculiar evil of silencing the expression of an opinion is, that it is robbing the human race; posterity as well as the existing generation; those who dissent from the opinion, still more than those who hold it. If the opinion is right, they are deprived of the opportunity of exchanging error for truth: if wrong, they lose, what is almost as great a benefit, the clearer perception and livelier impression of truth, produced by its collision with error.

Man is a learning animal. The state is an association the primary aim of which is the virtue and intelligence of the people. Men learn by discussion, through the clash of opinion. The best and most progressive society is that in which expression is freest. Mill said, "There ought to exist the fullest liberty of professing and discussing, as a matter of ethical conviction, any doctrine, however immoral it may be considered." The civilization we seek is the civilization of the dialogue, the civilization of the logos.

In such a society the intelligent man and the good citizen are identical. The educational system does not aim at indoctrination in accepted values but at the improvement of society through the production of the intelligent man and the good citizen. Education necessarily involves the critical examination of conflicting points of view; it cannot flourish in the absence of free inquiry and discussion.

In a democracy what the public needs to know about the teachers in the educational system is that they are competent. The competent teacher knows the subject he is teaching and how to communicate it to his pupils. Unlike the teacher in a totalitarian state, he is not supposed to purvey the prevailing dogma. He is supposed to encourage his students to use their own intelligence and to reach their own conclusions.

The definition of competence does not shift with every wind of prejudice, religious, political, racial, or economic. If competence had been the issue at Brown University during the free silver controversy, the President would not have been asked to resign because of his premature distaste for the Gold Standard. The modern note was struck there. What was requested of the President was "not a renunciation of his views, but a forbearance to promulgate them." And the reason was that these views were "injurious to the pecuniary interests of the University." On the other hand, the standard of competence did protect a professor at the University of Chicago who was a leading critic of Samuel Insull and the other local oligarchs of the time. He was doubtless injurious to the pecuniary interests of the university, but he and it lived through it, and he is today the senior Senator from Illinois.

WRONG QUESTIONS

We have been stifling education in this country because we have been asking the wrong questions. If you are asking the right questions, you ask about a subject of discussion whether it is important. You do not forbid students to discuss a subject, like the entry of Red China into the United Nations, on the ground that it is too important. The right question about a subject of research and the methods of investigation is whether competent scholars believe that the subject should be investigated and that this is the way to investigate it. You do not permit the Post Office Department to protect the Johns Hopkins School of Advanced International Studies from *Izvestia* and *Pravda*. The right question about a textbook is whether competent people think it can make a contribution to education. You do not ask whether incompetent people are going to be offended by passages taken out of context. The right question about a research man on unclassified work is whether he is competent to do it. You do not act like the United States Public Health Service and weaken the country by withdrawing contracts from research workers on unstated grounds that can only be grounds of loyalty.

As I have said, the right question about a teacher is whether he is competent. If we had been asking about competence we should have had quite a different atmosphere in the case of teachers who were Communists or ex-Communists, who refused to testify about themselves, or who declined to discuss the political affiliations of others. We have been so busy being sophisticated anti-Communists, detecting the shifts and devices of Communist infiltration, that we have failed to observe that our educational responsibility is to have a good educational system. We do not discharge that responsibility by invading civil liberties, reducing the number of qualified teachers available, eliminating good textbooks, and intimidating the teaching staff. The standard of competence means that there must be some relation between the charges against a teacher and the quality of his teaching. The standard of competence would have protected us against teachers following a party line or conducting propaganda. If a teacher sought to indoctrinate his pupils, which is the only circumstance under which he could be dangerous as a teacher, he would be incompetent, and should be removed as such. The standard of competence would have saved us from the excesses of the silly season, such as the refusal of the University of Washington to let Professor Oppenheimer lecture there on physics, and from the consequences of concentrating on the negative task of preventing one particular unpopular variety of infiltration. If we had used the standard of competence we should have been free to fix our minds on the positive responsibility of building an educational system, and with half the energy we have put into being scared to death we might have built a great one.

Since our guilty conscience tells us that there ought to be some connection between what a man does and the punishment visited upon him, we often try to pretend that this is the rule we are following. The Attorney General of the United States, speaking in New York three weeks ago, said that schools should not be sanctuaries or proving grounds "for subversives shaping the minds of innocent children."

This picture of subversives shaping the minds of innocent children has nothing to do with the case. The teachers who have lost their jobs in the campaign against subversives have not been charged with doing anything to the minds of any children. The case of Goldie Watson here in Philadelphia is typical: testimony about the good she had done the minds of the children in her classes was rejected as impertinent. The only evidence allowed was as to whether she had declined to answer questions about her political affiliations. She had, and she was fired. The same procedure seems to be followed everywhere, even at Harvard. When a professor there is called on the carpet, the issue is whether he is a member of something or other, or whether he has lied or refused to answer questions about such membership. The matter of his competence in his field or what he has done to the innocent minds of the Harvard students is never referred to.

FEAR OF IDEAS

We are getting so afraid of ideas that we are afraid of people who associate with people who are said to have ideas, even if they themselves have not expressed them. The State Curriculum Commission of California is now studying investigators' reports on the authors of twenty-three textbooks. Dr. C. C. Trillingham, Los Angeles County Superintendent of Schools and a member of the commission, said, "If an author is aligned with the Communists, we don't want his textbook, even if there is no Red propaganda in it."

We regard what a man says as irrelevant in determining whether we will listen to him. What a man does in his job is irrelevant in determining whether he should continue in it. This amounts to a decision that people whose ideas or whose associates' ideas we regard as dangerous cannot be permitted to earn a living or make a contribution in any capacity to the well-being of the community. The Supreme Court of California has just taken this logical next step: it has held, in effect, that a Communist can have no contractual rights that the rest of us are bound to respect.

Not long ago at a dinner of the senior members of the faculty of the University of Birmingham in England, I sat across the table from a professor who is a member of the executive committee of the Communist party of Great Britain. The British appear to be getting value out of a scholar whom none of the great American universities could appoint.

FIFTH AMENDMENT

One of the more important advances in law and government effected by the struggles of our ancestors is that proclaimed by the Fifth Amendment. Why should the government demand that a man convict himself out of his own mouth instead of requiring prosecution to make the effort to establish the charges that it has brought against him? All the Fifth Amendment means is: prove it. Injury is added to insult if there is no pretense that the questions asked must be relevant or proper. In some public school systems refusal to answer any questions by the Board of Education or any other public body is insubordination; insubordination justifies dismissal.

Surely the issue is whether the questions are legitimate. It cannot be insubordination to refuse to answer illegitimate questions. We have gone very far under the influence of one of the rollicking dicta of Mr. Justice Holmes, that there is no constitutional right to be a policeman; but not so far that public employment can be denied on the ground that has nothing to do with the duties to be performed. If the President were to refuse to employ bald-headed men in the federal establishment, the Supreme Court would find, I believe, that the bald had been deprived of their constitutional rights.

Is It Too Late?

You may say that the issue I am discussing is academic in every sense: there is no use now in talking about the right of Communists, ex-Communists, or persons who decline to answer questions about their political affiliations to teach in the United States. Milton Mayer in his forthcoming book, *They Thought They Were Free*, tells the story of the way history passed Martin Niemoeller by. When the Nazis attacked the Communists, he was a little uneasy, but he was not a Communist, and he did nothing. When they attacked the Socialists, he was uneasy, but he was not a Socialist, and he did nothing. They went after the schools, the press, and the Jews, but he was not directly affected, and he did nothing. Then they attacked the Church. Pastor Niemoeller was a churchman. He tried to do something, but it was too late.

I hope it is not too late to point out where our preoccupation with public relations and our failure of courage and intelligence may take us. The New York *Times* on March 17 and the New York *Herald Tribune* on March 19 published editorials on the question whether teachers who decline to testify about others should be dismissed. The significant thing about the editorials is this: they both, perhaps unconsciously, extend the limits of the prevailing boycott. The *Times* condemns "adherence to Communist doctrine," thus adding theoretical Marxists to those automatically disqualified. The *Herald Tribune* comes out against Communists "or any other brands of subversives," thus opening vast new unmapped areas of investigation, recrimination, and confusion.

Reece Committee

These two newspapers bitterly attacked the Reece committee, appointed in the House to investigate foundations; but they appear to have succumbed to its influence, which is another evidence that if you say something outrageous authoritatively, loudly, and often enough you will eventually find yourself quoted in the most respectable places. The Reece committee includes among the subversives almost anybody who differs with the two members of the committee who constitute the majority. Zechariah Chafee, Jr., said at the

University of Oregon last October, "The word 'subversive' has no precise definition in American law. It is as vague as 'heretical' was in the medieval trials which sent men to the stake." Leading the list of Reece committee subversives are those who do not share its philosophical prejudices. The committee condemned a philosophical doctrine, empiricism, and those who hold it as the fountainhead of the subversive tendencies now engulfing the country. If a philosophical position can be treasonable, particularly one as harmless as a preference for fact over theory, and if two politicians can make it treasonable, freedom of thought, discussion, and teaching may not be with us long.

By repetition the Reece committee is obtaining unconscious acceptance of another proposition, which, coupled with the proposition that politicians may declare a doctrine and its adherents subversive, still further imperils freedom of teaching and inquiry. This is the proposition that tax-exempt money is public money and that a tax-exempt institution is therefore subject to a special variety of public surveillance. An extension of this proposition is found in the California statute requiring all claimants of tax exemption to take a nondisloyalty oath. If carried to the logical limits hinted at in the Reece Report, this notion of the public control of private, tax-exempt corporations could deprive the independent educational institutions of this country of their autonomy, that characteristic which has given them their value in the development of the American educational system.

Tax exemption is conferred for the purpose of facilitating the performance of a public task by a private agency. A corporation that carries on education and research to that extent relieves the taxpayers of their obligation to finance such work in state-supported institutions. Tax exemption imposes no duty on colleges and universities except that of conducting teaching and research according to their best judgment of what good teaching and research are. It does not impose the duty of making sure that the teaching and research conform to the views of the majority of a legislative committee.

CALIFORNIA SENATE COMMITTEE ON UN-AMERICAN ACTIVITIES

Consider what those views might be. Richard E. Combs, Chief Counsel for the California Senate Committee on Un-American Activities, testified two years ago before a subcommittee of the United States Senate. He gave an account of how Communists reorient courses of instruction. He thought it worth while to report that the name of a course at a California university had been changed from public speaking to speech, and the books had been changed from Robert Louis Stevenson, Masefield, and Kipling to John Stuart Mill. The subversive nature of these changes may not be clear to you, but it was clear to Mr. Combs and, from all that appears, to the California committee that employs him and the committee of the United States Senate before which he testified. The appraisal of courses of study or of the performance of teachers is a professional job, not to be undertaken by the naïve and unskilled.

Consider the role of the California Senate Committee on Un-American

Activities in the administration of California institutions of higher learning. The committee claims that a chain of security officers on campuses has been welded by its efforts. If its claims are correct — and they have been disputed — professors and students at eleven institutions are being continuously spied upon for the benefit of a legislative committee. The committee has an arrangement whereby it passes on the qualifications of members and prospective members of the faculties from the standpoint of their Americanism. The reason for this is said to be that the colleges and universities are not competent to assess the Americanism of their teachers, and the committtee is. According to the committee at least a hundred members of these faculties have been forced to resign and at least one hundred prospective members have failed of appointment because of the committee's work. It is too bad that the committee has not disclosed the information that led to the interdiction of its victims. One shudders to think that it may have been enough to have been heard quoting John Stuart Mill.

BEHIND ACADEMIC FREEDOM

But the issue of legal control is not basic. Academic freedom comes and goes because of some conviction about the purpose of education on the part of those who make the decisions in society. The Kaiser gave professors freedom of research because he believed that this was one way to make Germany strong and prosperous. This freedom did not extend to professors who wanted to engage actively in politics on the wrong side, the side of the Social Democratic party. The Kaiser did not set a high value on independent criticism.

In a democratic community the question is what do the people think education is and what do they think it is for? I once asked a former Minister of Education of the Netherlands what would have happened if he had exercised his undoubted legal authority and appointed professors of whom the faculties of the Dutch universities did not approve. He said, "My government would have fallen." He meant that the people of Holland would not tolerate political interference with the universities: they understood the universities well enough to recognize interference when they saw it and felt strongly enough about it to make their wishes effective.

The public officers and businessmen who are the trustees of the provincial universities in the United Kingdom have legal control over them, but would never think of exercising it in any matter affecting education and research. They limit themselves to business. The taxpayers now meet more than half the cost of Oxford and Cambridge, but no Englishman supposes that this entitles the government to exert any influence in their academic affairs.

If the people believe that independent thought and criticism are essential to the progress of society, if they think that universities are centers of such criticism and that the rest of the educational system is intended primarily to prepare the citizen to think for himself, then academic freedom will not be a problem, it will be a fact. Under these circumstances teachers would not be second-class citizens, subject to limitations of expression and behavior that show the public thinks the teacher of today is the nursemaid of yesterday. A teacher would be appointed because he was capable of independent thought and criticism and because he could help the rising generation learn to think for itself. He would be removed only if those who appointed him proved to be mistaken in these matters. The proof of their error would have to be made to persons who could understand the issue — an out-of-hand administrative removal approved by a board of laymen without participation by academic experts is a denial of academic freedom.

ACADEMIC RESPONSIBILITY

The people of this country think that education is a perfectly splendid thing and have not the faintest idea of what it is about. The reason that they are in this condition is that educators have had no time and little inclination to explain. After all, the great desideratum of American education in the last thirty-five years has been money. If you want money, you do not talk about independent thought and criticism; you do not engage in it too obtrusively; you may even suppress it if it becomes too flagrant. To get money you must be popular. "He thinks too much" is a classical reference to an unpopular man. Or as a great industrialist once remarked to a friend of mine, "You are either a Communist or a thinker."

I have no doubt that much of the trouble of recent years about academic freedom has been the result of the cold war and our panic about it. As Professor Chaffee has said, "Freedom of speech belongs to a people which is free from fear." But the basic issue is public understanding. If public understanding had been serious and complete, the cold war could not have thrown us off our balance.

I do not deny that many eloquent statements of the purpose of American education have been made. They cannot offset the impression created by the official propaganda of educational institutions, by their fatuous efforts to please everybody, and by their emphasis on the nonintellectual and even anti-intellectual activities associated with education in this country. Freedom of teaching and research will not survive unless the people understand why it should. They will not understand if there is no relation between the freedom that is claimed and the purpose it is supposed to serve. If the teacher of today is the nursemaid of yesterday, he does not need academic freedom — at least the nursemaid never did.

Academic freedom is indispensable to the high calling of the academic profession. If the profession is true to the calling, it will deserve the freedom, and it will get it.

Sidney Hook

Sidney Hook, at present Chairman of the Department of Philosophy at New York University, would seem to fulfill the expectations of those who conceive of the philosopher as a man given as much to action as to meditation. In aggressively opposing both fascists and communists, and in organizing the Congress for Cultural Freedom, Sidney Hook has proved himself an activist.

"The Danger of Authoritarian Attitudes in Education" is a survey of those forces which Hook believes are threatening intellectual freedom on all levels of formal education in America. He is a pragmatist, affirming that the primary function of thought is to guide us in our actions and that truth is pre-eminently to be tested by the practical consequences of belief.

Books of interest by Sidney Hook are John Dewey: Philosopher of Science and Freedom, Education for Modern Man, *and* The Metaphysics of Pragmatism.

13

THE DANGER OF AUTHORITARIAN

ATTITUDES IN EDUCATION*

I

To both Thomas Jefferson and John Dewey, the cohesion of a free society rests neither on supernatural nor natural sanctions but on community of interest. But only in a perfect or angelic society are all interests, to the extent that we can speak of interests, always shared or common. Because every individual, no matter what his social origins and relations, is a unique center

* From *Heresy, Yes — Conspiracy, No*, by Sidney Hook (New York: The John Day Company, 1953), pp. 123–139. Used by permission of Sidney Hook.

of experience, because in a finite world not all desires can be gratified by all individuals at the same time, some rational principle or process of decision, which settles conflicts of interests, must be given priority over any special interest.

War, myth, custom, use and wont also serve as principles or processes of decision. But by themselves no one can regard them as rational in character. For a rational principle is one which permits every interest to find a voice and to receive a hearing, to persuade and be open to persuasion, to offer evidence for itself and to examine evidence against itself. A rational principle leads to an *informed* decision, not one determined by caprice or violence. Even if the informed decision is blocked or stopped by the brute weight of another principle of decision, that does not make it less informed.

The survival of a free society, especially in a world where its destruction is the aim of a powerful totalitarian society, makes it essential not only that the decisions of its leaders be informed but that the support or criticism such decisions receive also be informed. That is why freedom requires a principle of rational authority, recognized as primary in all its educational enterprises and embodied in active habits of inquiry.

Such authority not only differs from the spirit of authoritarianism but is opposed to it. The term "authority" and the term "authoritarian" have the same root but are widely different in meaning. "Authority" is on the whole an emotively neutral word. "Authoritarian" markedly suggests something objectionable. Every authoritarian rule is an authority but not all authority is authoritarian. And happily so, for the social life of man would be impossible without some authority.

In criticizing authoritarian attitudes, then, we shall not be criticizing authority but rather inquiring into the kind and expression of authority most necessary for the enrichment of life. Without some authority there would be perpetual conflict and disorder, but this in no way justifies the equation of authority with any kind of peace and order. The authority of freedom is obviously different from the authority of tyranny. A similar relation holds between "tradition" and "traditionalism."

In order to understand the meaning of authoritarianism in education, we must briefly indicate what the purposes and ideals of democratic education are to which authoritarianism is hostile. Among these purposes and ideals may be listed: (1) the development of intellectual and emotional maturity, (2) the readiness to meet the challenge of new experiences on the basis of relevant knowledge, (3) the acquisition of techniques and values that are themselves tested in present experience, (4) the deepening of moral awareness and responsibility, and (5) finally, the cultivation of intelligent loyalty to the underlying values of the democratic community as distinct from any particular political expression of these values. These are large terms which have to be interpreted a little differently on different educational levels. Roughly speaking, however, we may say that the pervasive ideal of democratic education — or liberal education today — is to achieve a community of persons who, on the basis of reliable knowledge about themselves and the world in which they live, can develop freely in a free society. We shall therefore call those tendencies in education authoritarian which, by blocking the roads of inquiry, prevent freedom of intelligent choice; which, by discouraging critical participation in the processes of learning, obstruct individual growth; which, by imposing dogmas of doctrine or program, blind students to relevant alternatives and encourage conformity rather than diversity; which, in short, fail to recognize that the supreme and ultimate authority, the final validating source of all other authorities in human experience is the self-critical authority of critical method — or intelligence.

II

The danger of authoritarian attitudes in teaching comes from so many quarters that one is embarrassed to decide where to begin the enumeration. For purposes of exposition I shall divide them into two classes: those that come from outside the school, and those that come from within the school.

Threats that come from outside the school may all be characterized as attempts to invade the *relative autonomy* of the school as an educational agency and to limit the freedom of the teacher as a professionally qualified educator. Such threats come from special groups which, perhaps for the most worthy and sometimes less worthy reasons, seek to pressure schools and teachers into emphasizing particular studies or into emphasizing them in a particular way to reach predetermined conclusions. Note that I used the phrase *"relative autonomy"* when I spoke of the relation of the school, teacher, and society. For it is neither possible nor desirable for the school and teacher to isolate themselves, especially in a democracy, from the great social events, movements, and problems of their community. But the main point here is this: professionally qualified educators, as individuals and as a group, are the only ones that can be entrusted with the decisions which determine what is relevant *educationally* to the needs of their charges, and what emphasis it is to receive. Otherwise the whole concept of teaching as a profession has no validity. The mere fact that the individual is a parent no more qualifies him to determine what the best *educational* regimen is for his child than what the best medical regimen is. As a parent, he is free, of course, to select the type of education he desires for his child — secular or parochial. As a citizen he is, of course, vitally concerned in the physical and psychological conditions under which his child is receiving instructions. His cooperation in helping to solve problems in these areas is most welcome. But all this is still a far cry from the assumption of educational authority or expertness.

If this is true for the parent, then *a fortiori* it is true of the businessman, the military man, the churchman, or any other man afire with zeal as to how best to save the nation and the world by reforming or revising the curriculum. To *propose* materials for instruction is one thing; to high-pressure, to denounce, or to intimidate is another. It is clear that no course of study imposed on teachers, against their better educational judgment, will be properly taught. Everyone can recall lessons endured, or taught half-heartedly, by teachers who did not see their educational significance but who had received instructions from their superiors who in turn were bowing to what they thought was the voice of the public coming from the mouths of an irate self-appointed committee, or out of the editorial pages or special feature columns of newspapers. Apparently the only thing that newspaper columnists today seem to be agreed upon is their claim to educational omniscience.

In ordinary times the relative autonomy of the educational process is commonly recognized. In extraordinary times, especially times of trouble like our own, the tendency to breach this autonomy becomes very strong — almost irresistible.

It is a commonplace that the struggle between the Communist and democratic ideologies in the next historic period will be decisive for the future of world culture. Nothing is more natural than the request by those alarmed at the prospects of Communist victory that the schools should enroll themselves in the struggle. But it is a dangerous request, if it means more than a request that the school, at the appropriate levels and courses, should critically evaluate the history, theory, and practice of communism — something that every live school system will already have been doing. And it is a dangerous request when nationalistic and ultra-patriotic organizations on the crest of a wave of justifiably angry public opinion seek to impose their own ideas on teachers as to how communism should be taught as the preconditional commitment for studying it, sometimes even for *not* studying it.

Each field has its own virtues, and the classroom in a democracy is not a field of battle. If communism, as I believe, is the greatest menace to human freedom in the world today, I believe it can be shown in the same way we show that certain growths are cancerous and not benign. If this is the truth, then we do not need more than the critical methods of inquiring into the truth to establish it. And if it is not the truth, then, since we are committed to the value of making intelligent decisions, we should be eager to discover it. Sentiment, no matter how exalted, is not a substitute for analysis. If the truth may make us free, we are not free to deny or ignore the truth wherever we find it. Not all expressions of anti-communism are prodemocratic — something we learned from Franco and Hitler — just as not all expressions of antifacism are prodemocratic — something we have learned from Stalin and his lieutenants everywhere. When it comes to understanding, patriotism is not enough. The only way to win the argument against communism in the minds of men — where ultimately it must be won if democracy is to survive — is by showing that it is condemned not merely by authority of past tradition but by the outcome of present inquiry.

This means that teachers today must make an intensive study of the ideas of communism as of fascism and other forms of totalitarianism and not permit themselves to be bullied or frightened into failing to examine these doctrines lest the study itself be misinterpreted as advocacy. No matter how ardent one may be as an adherent of democracy, if he does not, *wherever it is relevant,* consider in a scientific spirit the arguments of its opponents from any quarter, he is giving way to an authoritarian attitude. Those who come knocking at the school door with ultimatistic demands or taboos concerning what teachers *should* teach and *how* they must teach, and with ready-made formulas about the meaning of democracy and its alternatives, must be asked to show their professional qualifications as educators before they are taken seriously.

III

A second source of danger to the relative autonomy of the educational process emanates from some propaganda agencies among certain business-men and professional groups. This has come to a head in a campaign so to influence the educational curriculum of our schools as to identify, on the one hand, the free-enterprise with democracy, and, on the other hand, the welfare state with a creeping socialism which inevitably develops into the paralysis and paresis of communism. The whole subject, of course, broken down into problems of manageable proportion on the proper levels, should be an integral part of the social-science curriculum. As a *proposal* for study it is probably carrying coals to Newcastle. But as a demand that the views and sentiments described above be a *conclusion* which the study *must* reach, it is a piece of intellectual impertinence. If a free economy in the classic sense were identical with democracy, we would have less democracy in the United States than we actually do have, for the free economy of the past is certainly quite different from the economy, regulated in a thousand ways both by big government and by big industry, under which we now live. If growth in social security spells slavery, we would have less freedom, less criticism today than we ever have had in the past, which is notoriously not true. And certainly Great Britain is not behind the United States in civil freedoms even though it is far ahead of it in social-welfare legislation and socialization.

The very terms "capitalism" and "socialism" are today incurably ambiguous, more often epithets of abuse than of description. It should be one of the tasks of our social-science teachers to show how these words are often used as substitutes for clear ideas, noisy rhetorical blanks that distract us from the complex problems that resist total solutions.

There is a third source of danger to the relative autonomy of the schools which comes from very sincere individuals who are dedicated to the democratic way of life. I refer to those who maintain that this way of life is *logically* dependent upon certain religious truths which, if denied, leave democratic values hanging in the air. Consequently, in order to avoid inconsistency, they believe that the curriculum of a democracy, particularly in its higher institutions, must at some point give instruction in religion — since a non-religious school is an irreligious school and an irreligious school a necessarily non-democratic one. The argument has many variations and the proposals to implement it take many forms.

I thing it is demonstrable that neither the meaning nor the validity of moral ideas rest on supernatural foundations. But suppose for a moment they did. Introduced into the curriculum in any form — how would the study of these supernatural foundations be conducted? Like assertions made in secular disciplines for which evidence is asked and critically assessed? But a *critical* evaluation of dogmas is the last thing which many of those who believe religion has a place in schools want. It is not hard to imagine what the reaction would be of those who accept one religious dogma or another, to a critical judgment on that dogma. No, religious dogmas can be imparted only by those who have faith to others of the same faith. Whatever place they have in human experience, they have no place in the public schools.

Sometimes the argument made for the introduction of religious instruction into public schools is that it alone can provide the unifying and "living faith" which individuals need to sustain themselves in an uncertain and often tragic world. (See Canon Bell, *Life,* October 16, 1950.) It is claimed that the need and necessity of such faith is recognized even by totalitarian cultures, where it is met by fraudulent and monstrously false glorifications of men and doctrines which nonetheless are quite effective psychologically as morale builders and sustainers. It is then urged that religion in a democracy should play an analogous function.

But it is precisely in a democracy that ideas, secular or religious, cannot function like ideas in a totalitarian culture. For their hypnotic character in the latter depends upon the complete absence of critical dissent, the mobilization of all psychological techniques to insure conformity, which are foreign to the spirit of a democratic society. It is simply false to assume that faith in a functioning democracy can be of the same psychological character as faith in a totalitarian culture. We did not have to believe in democracy in the same way as fanatical Nazis believed in Nazism in order to survive Hitler's attack. Nor do we today have to indoctrinate belief in democracy in the brutalitarian way in which the Communists regiment the minds and hearts of their youth, in order to survive the Kremlin's crusade against freedom.[1]

The tendency of religious, economic, and nationalist groups to scan the curriculum and the materials of instruction in order to see whether the appropriate position is taken on some special topic creates a major obstacle to critical teaching. Professionally qualified teachers are the best judges of what texts are suitable for educational purposes and not *ad hoc* committees that regard no education as sound which challenges their private prejudices masquerading as common first principles. The best educational experience shows that, if many conflicting sources are made available to students rather

---

[1] "A democrat cannot be fanatical in the same way as a Nazi or a Stalinist, for whom an unanalyzed end justifies the use of any means. But it does not follow that because he is humane and intelligent a democrat cannot be passionate and active in his faith, that he must be a political Hamlet, irresolute before the combination of toughness and chicanery with which the enemies of democracy confront him." *Cf.* my "The Autonomy of Democratic Faith," in *Living, Reading and Thinking,* edited by Chamberlain, Pressey, and Waters, p. 654, New York, 1948.

than specially restricted material, they more readily acquire the intellectual sophistication which gives them an immunity to the tricks and semantic corruptions of totalitarian demagogy. For example, instead of barring the *Daily Worker* from the classroom, the good teacher can sometimes make as effective use of it as he can of the *New York Times*. If we are interested in exposing the logic of the total lie, I know of no better specimen material today than official Communist literature. And yet we occasionally read of committees of strong-willed, well-intentioned, but intellectually undiscriminating citizens who ransack the libraries of their schools and triumphantly flourish books and materials that may actually be helpful to the teacher in exposing communism, as evidence of subversion.

But is not the development of loyalty to our country a legitimate objective of our schools? Certainly, but nothing follows from that unless we are aware of what it is in our country and our culture which evokes our loyalties. The Loyalists of 1776 are considered differently from the Loyalists of 1861 in our history. Josiah Royce somewhere says that "true loyalty includes some element of free choice," and without making this a definition, I believe that a loyalty which depends merely on habituation, or conditioned reflexes, on the fact that there is nothing else imaginably conceivable to be loyal to, is universally regarded in the Western tradition as less worthy than a loyalty which is freely given and freely informed about alternative objects of loyalty. It is the existence of freedom and of free institutions which is the primary justification of loyalty to America. Free men cannot be loyal to slave states. That universities under nazism and communism made loyalty to their regimes a prime goal of instruction is one of the reasons we condemn them.

That American schools develop loyalties to the community of which they are a part is an indisputable fact — as indisputable as that the schools in societies less free than ours develop loyalties to their communities. What we should be concerned with then is that the loyalties American schools develop reflect the distinctively libertarian aspects of our traditions and not the chauvinism which perverts the natural piety for the sources of our being.

Let us then recognize that loyalty to America and to democracy does not mean loyalty to American*ism* or to the Democratic Party or any other party. It does not mean loyalty to any one group or class or sectional interest or to a program for free enterprise or controlled economy. It does not mean conformity; those who are not critical of the failings of democracy are less loyal than those who are.

If we interpret loyalty in this way, it is something that cannot be commanded. It cannot be sworn to. It cannot be tested by oaths. It grows slowly as the student's mind and body mature, gathers force as he understands, and tries to live up to his understanding of the democratic process, and when freedom is challenged or threatened, wells up spontaneously, fed by all the hidden springs of emotion.

Our deepest loyalties are seldom avowed. They are expressed best not in words but in actions. When the loyalty of a generation comes into question or has to be proved, there is already an acknowledgment that education and other social institutions have been remiss in their functions. The man who must be urged to say, "I love you," because his actions leave doubts, is a doubtful lover whose words mean less the more frantically they are solicited of him. If the only evidence we have of a person's loyalty is his use of a certain form of words on request, we are lost. Loyalty to American democratic traditions, processes, and values is a virtue beyond price; but if our schools do well in achieving their task of developing free and informed minds, this virtue shall be added unto them.

IV

So far I have been discussing the more overt authoritarian threats to the relative autonomy of the educational process. I wish now to consider the more subtle dangers which come from authoritarian attitudes within the school itself and which threaten not the relative autonomy of education but its quality and critical integrity. These are harder to guard against because habituation in certain traditional ways has given us a sense that they are natural and unalterable.

The first and most obvious expression of authoritarian attitude reflects the undemocratic organizational structure of many schools in various sections of the country, and even in a few metropolitan centers. Through a hierarchy of command, instructions and directives are transmitted to the classroom teacher from above without opportunity on his part to participate in their justification — if any. Where the teacher is a passive agent in executing orders, he is likely to regard the student as a passive agent in the classroom, as a living subject who must absorb nonliving subjects, conditioned to accept certain conclusions by virtue of the teacher's authority rather than the authority of evidence and method. Evidence, however, has little persuasive authority unless it is preceded by intelligent questioning and doubt. But one of the most common manifestations of totalitarian attitudes towards students is impatience with doubt, opposition, and the half-articulate bewilderments, which as often betray genuine difficulties in the subject matter being taught, as they do the personal difficulties of the learner.

Many teachers love to be asked questions but only those they can answer. There are, I fear, too few who can gracefully acknowledge that they do not know or that they were mistaken. It is a myth that the young in *intellectual* matters are naturally rebellious and it is the easiest thing in the world to silence them by ridicule, cold indifference, or the show of outraged dignity. There is a deeper courtesy than the conventionalities of outwardly polite behavior. This consists in recognizing the educational significance of the process by which the student reaches an uncoerced conclusion — or rather a conclusion coerced only by the materials he is dealing with. "It is not I who tell this," the teacher's attitude should say, "but the facts in the case" — if there are facts. There is, of course, "ancestral wisdom," but when it is invoked it must be invoked because of its wisdom, not because of its ancestry. And wisdom, whether ancestral or present, needs no external authority.

Whatever one may think of progressive education — and it must not be judged by its detractors or by the effusions of some of its mindless advocates — it places respect for the personality of any child on the same moral level as respect for the personality of our own children. Such respect emphatically does not mean that the teacher is "to let pupils do what they want to, when and how they want to do it," as progressive education is cheaply caricatured; it does mean that we have a moral obligation to let students see the *sense* behind what we ask them to do, and the when and how of it.

Authoritarianism on the part of teachers may take other forms. The teacher may follow a psychologically inoffensive course but a methodologically vicious one by indoctrinating for some special point of view which is imposed on the student because of the instructor's predetermined commitment to some faith — religious, political, economic. I do not want to discuss the general question of indoctrination here or the occasions on which indoctrination may be justified, as for example, when we induce children to take certain moral attitudes by nonrational means because they are not yet sufficiently mature to understand the rational grounds for them. I am referring specifically to indoctrination by irrational means in behalf of some controversial conclusion.

Indoctrination of this sort by the teacher is not merely authoritarian; it is dishonestly authoritarian. Instead of openly proclaiming a bias which the student can do something to nullify if he is aware of it, it conceals its bias. It abuses a position of trust and by insidious means may predispose and color the mind of a student so that he can no longer see or objectively appraise any other side than the one in which he has been indoctrinated.

If we bear in mind that we are defining authoritarian attitudes in terms of their effect on the continuous search for new modes of significant experience, new truths, and more reliable methods of inquiry, we find that just as not all who shout peace believe in peace, so not all who are professional scientists exhibit at crucial times a scientific temper. In all fields of the arts and sciences there are reigning orthodoxies. These orthodoxies are usually established on the basis of the warranted conclusions of the best available methods. But there is always an emotional wrench when some customary doctrine or theory is challenged. More often than not, the challenge is absurd or irresponsible. When this takes place there are some scientists who, not content with exposing absurdity, wish to prevent it from being uttered. In their excess of zeal for the truth they act like absolutists who forget that at best we can only reach probabilities in inquiry, that no theory can make scientific headway in a free culture unless it gets itself progressively confirmed, and that the best protection against *theoretical* error is exposure, not suppression.

Not so long ago we were confronted by the sad spectacle of scientific men evincing little faith in the logic and ethics of their own professional activity. Upon the publication of Dr. Velikovsky's book, *Worlds in Collision*, which confuses legend, myth, and warranted assertions, a campaign was undertaken by scientific men not merely to refute it, which was easy enough, but to prevent its publication, which was intellectually reprehensible. Nor is this the only instance of self-defeating and utterly unnecessary scientific orthodoxy. Here and there some administrator, happily no scientist, will vehemently oppose the presentation of the political-biology of Lysenko, overlooking the fact that the exposure of charlatanism is much more deadly to it than its proscription. I do not mean to suggest that scientists are under any necessity of examining seriously every crackpot theory that demands a hearing. They would have little time left for their own research, if they did. But I do mean to suggest that, unless they scrupulously avoid any attempt to prevent others from hearing what they may justifiably ignore, they are giving evidence of an incipient authoritarianism which, if unchecked, may become virulent. The best scientists, it should be pointed out, have a saving grace as well as a sense of humor about their most fundamental commitments.

v

I come finally to the consideration of a type of educational philosophy which would make it easier, despite its own professions of democratic allegiance, for authoritarian attitudes to develop. This is a position which is marked by basic theoretical confusion — and to be confused in these matters is much worse than being clear-headedly wrong. For a clear head can set itself right. It is held in inchoate form by different types of teachers of different social persuasions but on occasion it receives theoretical formulation. According to this school of thought an adequate philosophy of education must at the same time be a philosophy of *politics* whose task is to hatch political programs in alliance with the state. Public education becomes the ally of certain forward-looking groups in the community — and what group does not regard itself as forward-looking? — and commits itself to an advocacy of one or another social or political goal that recommends itself to the majority of educators after they have freely discussed what the goals should be.

Those who would make the schools either instruments of political conservatism or revolutionary transformation usually profess impatience with the ideals which John Dewey has made central to his educational philosophy — individual growth, participation, and the supremacy of critical intelligence. For them this is insufficient. In an amazing mixture of pedagese and poppycock, they contend that emphasis on critical method *prevents* human beings from solving problems and achieving goals. As if the methods of scientific inquiry did not recommend themselves *precisely* because they were better ways of reaching reliable solutions than other alternatives.

There is nothing new in the proposal that "education in its most comprehensive sense should become the copartner of politics . . ." (Brameld, *School and Society*, November 13, 1948). We know which partner is sure to dominate which. The proposal is in fact the hallmark of illiberalism in education — and this remains true irrespective of whether an educator wants to use public education to teach the necessity of "a thoroughly reconstituted domestic economy" or the necessity of a thoroughly stabilized *status quo* capitalist economy, whether he takes as his grand design "international world government" or rampant American chauvinism, whether it is the "old deal" or the "new deal." The schools cannot harness themselves to any political program, no matter how self-righteous or apparently benevolent, without handing over the reins, as has been the case only too often in the past, to drivers who have other goals than the development of emotional and intellectual maturity. It is not for the schools to dedicate themselves to any grand political designs. Their task is to develop the powers to recognize the grand designs which events are shaping for us, to show that they are not fated, but rather that there may be alternatives to them which our own ideas and actions may help to realize, and above all to train the faculties of critical assessment and evaluation. All this is involved in the educational effort to bring alive in students and *to keep* alive the readiness and willingness to inquire — and to act intelligently.

It is one thing to say that the schools cannot be impartial about their own commitment to the quest for truth, beauty, and integrity; it is quite another to say that they cannot be impartial in considering specific *programs* encountered in their quest.

But it is sometimes objected that it is inconsistent to oppose commitment to a specific doctrine and yet urge commitment to a method or to the ideal of the inquiring mind. This objection is completely without force with respect to the problems of education and rests on a failure to see what commitment to critical method means. Critical method is self-corrective. It is self-aware in that it can formulate alternatives to itself in the way in which Charles Peirce distinguishes four methods of fixing belief. To be committed to this method does not exclude the consideration of other methods. But to be committed to a doctrine or program, if it means anything at all different from critical analysis of hypotheses, is in practice to exclude other doctrines as species of error known in advance. For if these errors are not held to be errors in advance but only *after* inquiry, there is no more commitment involved than there is in any genuine discovery of truth. In that case we are not committed to programs but only to the *process* of finding out.

Some partisans of grand designs who urge that education commit itself to a political program are dimly aware of the dangerous alley into which it leads. For after all, if a school is committed to a political program, what shall we do with a teacher who is opposed to the program? And what will happen to the school in a community which opposes the commitment? Unless it is to impose a conformity of belief, the school must leave the processes of inquiry open. And some planners of the grand design assure us that, of course, this is what they propose to do. They do *not* advocate indoctrination but at most a kind of harmless propaganda. Well, then, if all programs are subject to critical evaluation, with the possibility of individual rejection left open, then what point is there in committing a system of education to a program *in advance* of specific inquiries? If anything is worth believing, honest pursuit of the proper method will lead to it. To beat the air with demands that the school commit itself to one program rather than another, and then blandly to deny that any indoctrination is intended, simply does not add up. Such a position, if it is not a form of spoofing or does not testify to a lack of ingenuousness, is muddled from beginning to end. *Religious* salvationists at least make no bones of the fact that they believe in indoctrination; *political* salvationists, alas, lack the courage of their confusions.

VI

I have described many varieties and sources of authoritarian attitudes in teaching. It would be absurd to assume that the danger to free teaching in a free society is equal from all of them at any one time. Wisdom here consists in keeping a sense of proportion in relation to transitory nuisances, even when acute, and the underlying massive threats which may change the whole cultural landscape. At the present time, the greatest danger to free teaching lies in the failure to distinguish carefully between the rights to heretical belief, which every freely and honestly inquiring mind has, and the practice of conspiracy, a right no one has in a democracy unless it is the moral right of an undemocratic rebel who is prepared to risk the consequences of his rebellion.

The teachers of this country do not need lessons in patriotism from anybody. Over the years I have found that the best way to meet authoritarianism, wherever it raises its head, is not to yield to it but to fight it openly. A lost battle is not a lost war. More than one dour prediction about the future of American education has been falsified in less than the liftime of the prophet.

Today we are involved in a desperate international civil war to preserve the political freedom which is the *sine qua non* of all other freedoms. If those who teach do not show wisdom and courage in their professional activity, if they permit educational leadership and initiative to pass from their hands into those that are untrained and unqualified, then educational freedom may be an unintended casualty of political victory. Here as elsewhere — the readiness is all.

Russell Kirk

As an epigraph for his book Academic Freedom, *Russell Kirk cited the following remark by Sir Thomas Browne: "Every man is not a proper champion for truth, nor fit to take up the gauntlet in the cause of verity; many, from the ignorance of these maxims, and an inconsiderate zeal unto truth, have too rashly charged the troops of error and remain as trophies unto the enemies of truth." The epigraph embodies the spirit behind Kirk's rejection of modern liberalism, a rejection which might be expressed thus: Liberalism is not evil, merely wrong; but in being wrong it abets evil by confusing the mind in its quest for good ends humanely realized. Liberalism is therefore disqualified for its capacity to retard, not for its obviously pious wish to reform.*

As an extremely articulate supporter of conservative philosophy, Kirk provides an acute contrast to the views held by Robert Hutchins and Sidney Hook, two men who represent separate shades of the liberal tradition.

Mr. Kirk is also the author of The Conservative Mind *and* A Program for Conservatives, *books which reveal in depth many of the philosophical assumptions alluded to in "Liberty and License."*

14

LIBERTY AND LICENSE*

I

"Academic freedom," says a distinguished editor, Mr. W. T. Couch, "is the principle designed to protect the teacher from hazards that tend to prevent him from meeting his obligations in the pursuit of truth." This is the best definition of the idea that I have come upon. And Mr. Couch goes further: "The obligations of the teacher are direct to truth, and the teacher

* From *Academic Freedom* by Russell Kirk (Chicago: Henry Regnery Company, 1955), pp. 1–27. Used by permission of Henry Regnery Company.

who, in order to please anybody, suppresses important information, or says things he knows are not true, or refrains from saying things that need to be said in the interests of truth, betrays his calling and renders himself unworthy to belong in the company of teachers." I subscribe to this opinion, and I may as well state here my general convictions on the important subject of academic freedom, so that the reader may make allowance for my prejudices, if he likes.

I believe that academic freedom, an idea, has reality; and, like other ideas, its reality is more important than the ephemeral reality of particular persons and circumstances. I believe that academic freedom is a peculiar kind of freedom, and peculiarly valuable. I believe that academic freedom is *not* a hoax, but an inheritance from the wisdom and the courage of our ancestors. I believe that academic freedom is gravely threatened in our time. I believe that the causes of this peril to academic freedom are imperfectly apprehended by most scholars and teachers and journalists and politicians. I believe that if we desire to preserve any institution or concept, our first necessity is to define our terms correctly, and to ascertain accurately the causes of discontent. Therefore I have written this little book, an essay in definition, hoping to assist in the endeavor to raise our discussion of academic freedom out of the pit of cant and slogan into which too many disputants have fallen in these past few years. This has not been a work wholly congenial to my cast of mind. Yet, convinced as I am that the reality of academic freedom is incalculably precious to our civilization, I have made the endeavor; and if my effort is a feeble one, I ask the reader's indulgence; for (as Newman reminds us) life is for action, and if we desire to know anything, we must make up our minds to be ignorant of much. I have done what I could, then: and I have tried to prepare myself for the undertaking by reading most of what has been written in the English language on this topic, and by conferring with people who know something of it, often by personal experience.

"Like so many of the institutional freedoms of the modern world, the roots of academic freedom lie deep in aristocratic, not to say medieval society," a sociologist of mark, Dean R. A. Nisbet, writes to me. "The university is today one of the few final enclaves that have survived (in considerable part, at least) the invasions of modern mass democracy and economism. I regard academic freedom and tenure as one of the few last and precious survivals of genuine European culture, and I am far from sanguine about our abilities to maintain it in this world of demonic fears and prejudices. If it ever dies, I think it will not be difficult to show that the pragmatic liberals with their shrill misconceptions and their worship of popular political power did a great deal to cause the death." Now I have endeavored to rise to the level of Dean Nisbet's observations on the subject, considering academic freedom in the light of recent events, it is true, but seeking to relate those events to the enduring idea of a special liberty, or body of liberties, that is attached to the academic institution, the teacher, and the scholar. Because this little work is only an essay, and not a comprehensive survey, I have decided to confine my remarks for the most part to our universities and colleges, venturing only occasionally to touch upon similar questions relative to primary and secondary instruction. But the problems are almost as pressing in the schools as they are in the colleges; and the schoolteacher, indeed, commonly enjoys far less freedom of opinion and action than does the professor. If academic freedom is to be sustained and restored, probably the energy and leadership for such an accomplishment must be discovered, initially, in the colleges and universities; therefore I have directed the greater part of my attention to those institutions.

Let us return, momentarily, to the business of tentative definition. Academic freedom is a security against hazards to the pursuit of truth by those persons whose lives are dedicated to conserving the intellectual heritage of the ages and to extending the realm of knowledge. It is the right, or group of rights, intended to make it possible for certain persons (always very few in number, in any society, when compared with the bulk of the population) to teach truthfully and to employ their reason to the full extent of their intellectual powers. We will not find these rights guaranteed by any article of the federal or state constitutions, or described in any legislative enactment, here in America; and, with some small exceptions, throughout the civilized world these liberties are the product of custom and moral prescription, rather than of positive law. Nor do these rights have any easily ascertainable sanction of force behind them. Juridical thinkers of the school of Austin, then, scarcely can admit that academic freedom is a right at all; for in the Utilitarian view of rights, a right has reality only when it is expressly asserted by the authority of the state, or when (whether through the agency of the state or of some other coherent group) it has positive force — in the final resort, *physical* force — to assert its claim. Nor is it easy to see how academic freedom can be anything more than a phrase for pragmatic thinkers, however much they may praise it; for to the pragmatist, the impulse of the present generation is everything, and what Burke called "the contract of eternal society" is nothing: in other words, rights have no origin in the laws of God or of nature, but are simply the products of social convention, to be obliterated when the experience of interest of the present generation ceases to approve them.

Academic freedom, in short, belongs to that category of rights called "natural rights," and is expressed in custom, not in statute. A great many people, nowadays, entertain a most shallow and unhistorical notion of natural right, despite the work of scholars like Professor Leo Strauss to restore a proper understanding of the concept. Natural right is not simply what Justice Holmes scoffingly called it, "a brooding omnipresence in the sky."[1] It is, rather, a moral system applied to jurisprudence: a body of belief in certain

---

[1] Justice Holmes used this phrase (in the case of Southern Pacific Company *v.* Jensen, 244 US 205, 1917) to describe a concept of the common law which he opposed; but it also represents his pragmatic contempt for the whole theory of natural law, as expounded by the Roman jurisconsults, the Schoolmen, and the English common-law writers.

rights long established by custom and prescription, and found by the test of time to accord with human nature and civil social nature. Most adherents to natural-rights theory believe that the original impulse toward these moral rights came from a source more than natural and more than human, if by "natural" and "human" is meant simple utility and private interest; but the particular forms which the search after natural law has taken are the product of human experience in history, supported by the franchises of what Chesterton calls "the democracy of the dead" — that is, the considered opinions of the innumerable good and wise men who lived before our time. These are rights which rise superior to particular governments and particular states; and if some arrogant political authority, or some presumptuous generation, ignores or tramples these rights, good men may justly obey the natural law in defiance of the ephemeral "law" that is set up in opposition to the moral traditions of the race and the historic experience of society.

Just such a right is academic freedom. Almost nowhere is academic freedom sanctioned (again in Justice Holmes' phrase) by "the articulate voice of some sovereign that can be identified." A man whose academic freedom has been infringed cannot successfully appeal to a court of law, unless, by coincidence, the violators of his freedom have happened to commit a breach of formal contract, of the same nature as a commercial contract. Nothing in the laws of our federal system, or of the several states, guarantees the enduring right of a teacher to speak the truth as he sees it, or to pursue the truth according to the light that is given him. In extreme circumstances, it is true, such a teacher might appeal to the general provisions for freedom of speech found in the federal Bill of Rights and in the state constitutions; but then he would be appealing not to *academic* freedom, but simply to the statutory freedom which is constitutionally guaranteed to all men, whatever their occupation or status. If academic freedom exists anywhere, then, it exists in the realm of natural rights and social conventions sanctioned by prescription; and if theorists deny the reality of natural law, logically they must deny the reality of academic freedom.

Far from believing that the silence of an "articulate voice of some sovereign" invalidates the idea of academic freedom, I am convinced that academic freedom is all the more real and valuable because it finds its sanction in moral belief and ancient usage. The very Decalogue, after all, is only partially and imperfectly recognized by the positive laws of modern states. Our dearest liberties and privileges are conferred upon us much more by immemorial usage and the dictates of conscience than by statutory enactment. It is not positive law which enjoins a man to honor his father and his mother, although occasionally statute may endeavor to compel him to provide for their physical subsistence. Similarly academic *rights* are more important than mere formal contracts between universities and professors, although the state will enforce the latter and not the former. I do happen to believe that a brooding omnipresence superior to human frailty implants in us, here below, a desire for justice which never can find full expression in the written enactments of a mundane sovereign; but the particular forms which that search after justice gives to human institutions are determined by many centuries of human experience, so that "academic freedom" and "just due" and "freedom of choice" are supported by historic experience and the customs of a people. I take my stand, in fine, with Thomas Aquinas and Richard Hooker and Edmund Burke; I am in opposition to the opinion of Bentham that "right" is simply what the political sovereign chooses to dispense, and in opposition to the opinion of Rousseau that "right" is whatever gratifies the undisciplined craving of the individual. It is perfectly true, I think, that every right must somewhere find an ascertainable and reasonably definite sanction; but there are sanctions more enduring, and more to be honored, than the decrees of an ephemeral master or the appetites of an ephemeral generation.

The preceding remarks may seem to constitute a digression; but if I take high ground, it is because I am convinced that academic freedom will not endure in our age unless it is defended upon sound philosophical postulates. The confusion which follows hard upon a muddy notion of "right" already is evident in the current discussion of academic freedom. A number of persons — I respect the integrity and motives of some of them — are unable to distinguish between academic freedom and the general freedoms possessed, or claimed, by everyone, in the academy or out of it. Even when endeavoring to sustain academic freedom, some such people undo the idea by confounding it with "human rights" indiscriminately applied, or with "constitutional guarantees" which make no specific provision for university and teacher, or with a vague "liberty" which considers university and teacher only so many specks in a tapioca-pudding equalitarian society. John Locke observes, in his lucid way, that often the most voluble partisans of liberty are the least effectual defenders of it. Allow me to offer a few instances of what I mean. Mrs. Agnes E. Meyer informs us that "academic freedom is only one aspect of human freedom." Colonel Robert McCormick recently inquired (an inquiry, I may be allowed to observe, is more humble than a dogmatic assertion) whether academic freedom was really something different from the freedom of all men. President Briggs of Phillips University says that "*academic* freedom is not a thing apart, nor something vague, different or peculiar, but it is *intellectual* freedom, which seems . . . to embody all the freedoms we know and cherish so well." Mr. William F. Buckley, Jr., thinks that academic freedom, at least in its modern form, is something got up as a hoax to deceive the proprietors of universities and colleges: "For in the last analysis, academic freedom must mean the freedom of men and women to supervise the educational activities and aims of the schools they oversee and support."

Now I think I understand the chain of reasoning which led each of these persons to his conclusion; and, though it is improbable that any one of these persons sympathizes heartily with any other of the four, I am inclined to sympathize, in some degree, with each position. The idea of academic freedom has been enveloped in so much rodomontade, these past four or five years, that doubt of the idea's reality or identity is excusable. Professor Sidney Hook, in *Heresy, Yes; Conspiracy, No*, declares that "there is more sloppy rhetoric poured out per page about academic freedom both by those who believe that they are supporting, and those intent on criticizing it, than on any other theme with the possible exception of democracy."[2] But for all that, I do not believe in the slogan, popular in certain quarters just now, that "liberty is not divisible." Liberty *is* divisible, unless by liberty we mean the abstract and perilous *liberté* of the Jacobins, which American and English leaders and people generally have rejected. It is in the name of that abstract liberty that crimes are committed. One of the great blessings of our political experience is that we have recognized liberty as multiple, made up of a large number of separate freedoms, varying with particular circumstances, and pertaining to particular groups and persons. There is the freedom to bear arms — under certain circumstances; there is the freedom of workingmen to organize — for certain purposes; there is the freedom of self-government — through representatives; there is the freedom of accumulating property — through lawful means. Not every man enjoys precisely the same freedoms as every other, nor should he want to. Academic freedom is not the same thing as secrecy of the ballot, or as security against the quartering of troops. And if the teacher and the scholar are constantly exhorted to throw themselves into crusades for the liberties of Indonesia, or the abolition of the poll tax, and they rally to such cries, they are going to find themselves with very little time left for teaching and scholarship. And then, in the excitement of chasing after other people's freedoms, they may find that academic freedom has ceased to be. For every right is married to an appropriate duty; and when the duty is neglected, the right shrivels.

For my part, I am convinced that academic freedom truly *is* a thing apart, different and peculiar, and that we would be foolish to confound it with the vaguer term "intellectual freedom." *Intellectual* freedom is chiefly an aspiration; it can be sought after, most of the time, only by the solitary man of contemplation. *Academic* freedom is an historical reality, with ascertainable limits and prerogatives, to be preserved and extended, often enough, by intelligent co-operative action. As with the accurate definition of words, in the accurate description of concepts and institutions we pursue the historical method: we endeavor to learn what "academic freedom" has meant to past generations, and how it has developed, if we want really to employ the phrase sensibly. And if we apply the historical method to the apprehension of the idea of academic freedom, we will not come to Mr. Buckley's conclusion that it consists in freedom simply for the masters of educational institutions to enforce their opinions upon the teachers — though we may discover, at the

---

[2] I rather think that Mr. Hook would include certain writings of mine under this head; but no matter; we must take the truth where we find it, and in this, as in much else, Professor Hook speaks plain truth. For my part, I am inclined to believe that Mr. Hook has done his share in pouring out sloppy rhetoric about democracy; and so has his adversary Mr. Robert Hutchins.

same time, that academic freedom never has meant complete autonomy for
teachers, or the licentious toleration of a bewildering congeries of private
fancies.

I propose, then, to examine somewhat summarily, in the following section
of this chapter, the historical signification of "academic freedom." The
present, when we come to seek for truth in it, is found to be no more than a
thin film — sometimes a scum — upon the deep well of the ages; and
perhaps no one does more mischief than the visionary who endeavors to guide
us by *a priori* assumptions about the unknowable future. It is only by reference to the past that we can obtain some grip upon the meaning of an
idea disputed in modern society.[3]

II

"Academic freedom is a specific kind of freedom," Mr. Sidney Hook writes.
"It is the freedom of professionally qualified persons to inquire, discover,
publish and teach the truth as they see it in their field of competence, without any control or authority except the control or authority of the rational
methods by which truth is established. Insofar as it acknowledges intellectual discipline or restraint from a community, it is only from the community
of qualified scholars which accepts the authority of rational inquiry." Now
the trouble with this definition is that no such degree of liberty for scholars
and teachers has long prevailed anywhere; Mr. Hook really is writing of his
ideal, rather than describing a tradition or defining the phrase as it has
acquired meaning from the experience of civilized society. Mr. Hook goes
on to say that academic freedom is not an absolute, but that society finds it
expedient to extend this freedom to the academy because society at large
benefits from the consequences of unhampered inquiry. If, then, the academy
either fails to accomplish its educational goals, or if it violates other moral
values more weighty than academic freedom, the community does right to
abridge academic freedom.[4] Mr. Hook, believing that such checks upon the

---

[3] We are just now beginning to recover from the effects of the anti-historical twaddle
that was popular enough in academic circles at the beginning of this century, and for a
long time thereafter. As a specimen of this infatuation, we may take this outburst of
Franz Boas, nearly half a century ago:

"The truly human ideals we find expressed where man is least restrained by historic
tradition. . . . This condition prevails particularly among the masses of the people, much
less among the segregated classes. . . . The intellectuals, who are steeped in historical
tradition, and are therefore, on the whole, little able to think clearly, belong to this group.
The rich, the nobility, the scientist, the artist, the clergyman, all belong in their great
mass to such segregated groups . . . in which the thought, couched in a catch phrase, is an
almost elemental power, stimulating man to activity without any attempt to think out
clearly what the catch phrase may mean or whether it does mean anything."

There could be no better proof than this passage that to be anti-historical is to be
anti-intellectual. The consequences of such adulation of ignorance and denial of intellectual
leadership have since been stamped upon the face of the world. The "truly humane ideals"
of revolutionary Russia and Germany, since then, have reminded us that men who ignore
the past are condemned to repeat it. No one falls a more easy prey to the catch phrase
than the man who neglects the history of catch phrases.

[4] Sidney Hook, *Heresy, Yes — Conspiracy, No*, pp. 154–161.

general principle ought to be employed only very seldom, nevertheless remarks that "the *justification* of academic freedom must lie in its fruits."

Here I begin to part company with Mr. Hook. He goes on to argue that the Academy, or university, is "a semi-public institution," a part of the community, subject in theory to the will of the community. I think he goes too far. Although rights may have a justification in their fruits, they may also have a justification in prescriptions; and although the Academy exists in part for the sake of the community, it exists also for its own sake, and more especially for the sake of private wisdom and private needs. "Its ultimate fruits are to be found not in the private, professional delight of the connoisseur of ideas, although this has merit, too, but in the public good which includes, let us hope, the multiplied private delights of others besides professors." I find in this sentence of Professor Hook's an ominous fondness for intellectual collectivism. And I believe that here Mr. Hook is unhistorical.

The first regular Academy of which we have much knowledge was the school of Plato. Now Plato's Academy did not exist in any immediate way for the benefit of the community; indeed, Plato and his pupils commonly were at odds with their community, in a political sense. The allegiance of the Academy was to something grander even than Athens: to Truth. For Truth, and in defiance of the people of Athens, Plato's master Socrates had died. Plato and his disciples were not public servants. They taught and studied for their "private, professional delight," and for the conservation and enlargement of Truth. It is true, of course, that Athens and all the civilized world benefited, in time, from their labors; but that is not the primary justification for the freedom of mind enjoyed and defended by the philosophers in the groves of the Academy. The community, indeed, often hampered them a great deal, and put the first of its great thinkers to death, and forced the second to flee to Megara and Syracuse, and compelled the third, on occasion, to take refuge in Asia. All political communities, even wisdom-loving Athens, tend to dread or despise their academies, so that to lay down the dogma of academic responsibility to the community, in Professor Hook's definition, is to run the risk of subjecting the liberties of the academy to the prejudices of the multitude, and to run the risk of subjecting the free human person to an abstract state. I do not mean to imply that philosophers have no responsibilities toward their fellow-men; indeed, the pursuit of Truth puts upon them very grave responsibilities; but they need always to remember that it is Truth they worship, not humanity, and that it is by Truth they must be judged, not Demos. If philosophers are treated as servants, even as the servants of a faceless Community, presently they will acquire the proverbial vices of servants, with few of the redeeming virtues of simple loyalty to persons.

Plato's Academy, for twenty-three centuries, has been to scholars the grand model of freedom to pursue the Truth. Although continuity of institutions is one principal evidence of prescriptive rights, it is not the only evidence. Our modern universities and colleges are not descended in a direct line, of course, from the Academy of Athens; but when, nine centuries after Plato began to teach, Justinian closed the schools of Athens, the idea of academic freedom was not extinguished. A memory may have as much power as a living thing, or more. And already the first of the great Christian universities, that of Constantinople, was nearly a century old when the end came to the Athenian philosophers. But my principal concern, just now, is this: the Academy of Athens, like the other great schools of antiquity, was not founded by the community, nor did it owe its primary allegiance to the community. It was instituted by private persons for their "private, professional delight" — or, to speak more accurately than Professor Hook does, to enable them to pursue the Truth without being servants of an evanescent community. And this idea of intellectual freedom, the freedom of the Academy, has ever since been the model for all men trained in the classical disciplines.

But modern learning owes even more to medieval institutions than it does to its classical strain; and, besides, there subsists a direct historical continuity between the medieval universities and much modern education, even in America. We ought, then, to pay close attention to academic freedom as it existed in the medieval university. Mr. Hook, no friend to the Schoolmen, nevertheless confesses that "within the framework of certain key assumptions of Christian doctrine, a considerable degree of academic freedom was enjoyed by the medieval university at a time when civil freedoms for the citizens of the community was hardly an embryonic concept."[5] Although Mr. Hook intends to be fair here, I think he has missed the point, which is this: there was freedom in the medieval universities *because* they existed within a framework of "certain key assumptions of Christian doctrine," not in despite of their Christian origin. Just as the Platonic Academy was free *because* its primary allegiance was to the Truth, and not to the community, so the medieval universities were free *because* their allegiance was to the Truth, as it was given to them to perceive it, and not to the community. Their framework of assumptions did not restrain them; it protected them. The Schoolmen, like the philosophers of the Academy, were dedicated men — dedicated to the service of Truth. The philosopher, in Greece, was a man apart, superior to many human frailties, especially the varieties of concupiscence; and he was revered accordingly. The Schoolman was a cleric, usually vowed to celibacy, and expected to lay aside, so far as he could, the vanities of the world; therefore he was privileged accordingly. These men were not servants, but masters; not the agents of the community, but seekers after divine love and wisdom. They undertook their work with a high consecration. And the academy, or the university, was a place consecrated to the apprehension of an order more than human, and a duty more than mundane.

I propose to relate these considerations, in a little while, to Professor Hook's view of academic freedom. But just now I turn to some remarks on the same subject by Dr. Robert M. Hutchins, in his *University of Utopia*:

---

[5] This generalization also verges on the unhistorical: a very considerable degree of civic freedom was enjoyed by the burghers of most of the towns in which universities came to be established. But at least Professor Hook recognizes that the freedom of the universities was not *derived* from the freedom of the general community.

The universities from which our own are descended were founded in the Middle Ages. They were either corporations of students wanting to learn, as in Italy, or of teachers wanting to teach, as in France. Corporations that had unusual legal or customary privileges for the purpose of carrying out the intentions of the incorporators were common in those days. In some Italian cities the Guelf and Ghibelline party clubs, sworn to subvert the state, were recognized corporations specially licensed to work on the project they had in view. The university corporations of the Middle Ages at the height of their power were not responsible to anybody, in the sense that they could not be brought to book by any authority.[6] They claimed, and succeeded in making their claim good, complete independence of all secular and religious control.

In asserting and establishing this claim, they had one inestimable advantage: they had no property. If any secular or religious authority sought to control them, they would simply move away. . . . All the medieval universities that amounted to anything were of the same general type. They were formed because somebody wanted to learn or somebody wanted to teach. They maintained their independence on the ground that it was necessary to their corporate function. They did not regard themselves as servants of either church or state. They thought of themselves as co-ordinate with both. . . . Although the men produced by the medieval universities became leaders in the church and in the state, they did not advertise that their function was to produce such men. Such men were a by-product of the enterprise in which they were engaged, which was singularly like the enterprise of the University of Utopia: it was the discussion of the most important questions. They would have been startled if they had been asked to justify their existence in terms of the service they performed for society, for they would have had no doubt that the discussion they were carrying on was its own justification.[7]

Here we are treated to that commingling of sound sense with imprudent generalization which characterizes much of Mr. Hutchins' writing. It is true that the medieval master and student did not consider themselves servants; and, more in jest or bravado than in sober earnest, they spoke of the three powers that govern society — Sacerdotium, Regnum, Studium. In this sense, but in this sense only, were they "not responsible to anybody": that, like other medieval guilds (which ordinarily had a churchly origin, especially in the North), they governed themselves in most matters, sometimes even in the administration of criminal justice. But self-government is not the same thing as irresponsibility. Italy excepted, throughout Christendom the universities were responsible to the church, and sometimes to the state as well. Chan-

[6] In part, this is bad history. The Guelf and Ghibelline factions, for instance, never were tolerated if their avowed intention was to overthrow the very city-state in which they existed; it was their hostility to the distant Emperor or the distant Pope which sometimes was tolerated. Some of Mr. Hutchins' generalizations on the constitution of medieval universities will not bear the scrutiny of anyone who has taken the trouble to glance through Rashdall's three volumes on the subject.

[7] Robert M. Hutchins, *The University of Utopia*, pp. 75–77.

cellor and rector, especially in the North, ordinarily were great ecclesiastics; founders and benefactors, with a few exceptions, were bishops or princes, when not popes or kings; the masters and the students were clergymen or in minor orders; and while a university ordinarily was exempt from the governance of local clergy, nevertheless it could not stand against the great prelates for any length of time. Bologna, Mr. Hutchins' favorite example, had the freest constitution of all, and, like most of the other Italian universities, is a partial exception to my remarks above; yet clerks, even there, formed a part of the student-body, and Christian doctrine permeated all the teaching, and in time Bologna and its sister universities came under the direct supervision of the Pope and the monastic orders. All this is not to say that the medieval universities were compelled to submit regularly to the inspection and direction of the officers of the state, or of the inferior clergy; on the contrary, they taught substantially what they liked, as they liked; no one presumed to set himself up for a greater scholar than a Schoolman — that seeming a manifest absurdity in medieval times, though in this enlightened age we are encouraged to take a different view. But Mr. Hutchins is confused, and confusing, when he tries to suggest that the medieval universities acknowledged no authority spiritual or temporal. Such a condition would have been as impossible as the ideal state of academic freedom suggested by Mr. Hook, or as the regime of the University of Utopia suggested by Mr. Hutchins recently. If, as Mr. Hutchins says, the American university cannot really expect to be free of the persons who supply its funds and its students, neither did the medieval university ever really expect to sever itself completely from clergy or laity. Every such university was established by a Papal bull; most had their origin in a cathedral school or some other churchly foundation; and many had royal charters, into the bargain. Substantially, the universities were parts — though autonomous parts — of the Church. (The Church also had other parts substantially autonomous, like the great orders of regular clergy.) The Schoolmen were persons dedicated to the conviction that the fear of God is the beginning of wisdom; and their students were either candidates for holy orders or else young men learning law or medicine in an atmosphere of religious veneration.

We ought not to endeavor to revise history according to our latter-day notions of what things *ought* to have been, or upon the theory that the past is simply a reflection of the present. The medieval universities did indeed enjoy academic freedom, in a larger measure, probably, than any academies before or since. But they enjoyed that freedom *because of* their status as religious institutions, not in despite of it. They did not obtain that freedom from the "community," nor as bands of enterprising secularists. Their prerogatives rarely were challenged, because everyone assumed that the universities were a natural part of the order of things here below, and because no one had presumption sufficient to sit in judgment upon the universities. When, during and after the Reformation, the universities lost their status as so many autonomous parts of a universal Church, they lost their independence correspondingly. In Protestant Europe, they came under the jurisdiction of the national churches and of the rapacious national monarchies; in Catholic Europe — although to a lesser extent — they came under the jurisdiction of the reinvigorated and consolidated Papacy, and of the sovereigns who, as in Spain and in France, made royal influence over the church establishment within their realms a condition of their support for the Roman cause. In fine, the dissolution of medieval universalism meant that learning, like nearly everything else, was forced to submit to new and more rigid dominations. With the complete or partial secularization of society which followed upon the French Revolutionary era, in nearly every country except Britain the universities were stripped of what remained of their old rights, and became little better than state corporations.

My point is this: in the Middle Ages, as in classical times, the Academy possessed freedom unknown to other bodies and persons because the philosopher, the scholar, and the student were looked upon as men consecrated to the service of Truth; and that Truth was not simply a purposeless groping after miscellaneous information, but a wisdom to be obtained, however imperfectly, from a teleological search. The community did not create these privileges of the Academy, any more than the community created wisdom; rather, the community simply recognized the justice of the Academy's claim to privilege. The community did not expect to be served, except in the sense that it might be so fortunate as to gather some crumbs that fell from the academic table. Like Socrates and like Aquinas, the learned man, the teacher, was a servant of God wholly, and of God only. His freedom was sanctioned by an authority more than human. Now and then that freedom was violated, just as anointed kings were murdered or reverend priests were robbed, on occasion; yet it scarcely occurred to anyone to attempt to regulate or to suppress the freedom of the Academy; it was regarded almost as a part of the natural and unalterable order of things. Masters and scholars, moreover, were so jealous of their rights, and so ready to band together against any infringement upon their prescriptive prerogatives, that very great power and very great boldness were required for an invasion of the universities. This unity and this spirited defiance of the vulgar came, in considerable part, from the Schoolmen's conviction that they were Guardians of the Word, fulfilling a sacred function, and so secure in the right. In medieval times, it was precisely their "framework of certain key assumptions of Christian doctrine" that gave masters and students this high confidence. Far from repressing free discussion, this framework encouraged disputation of a heat and intensity almost unknown in universities nowadays — except possibly, among us, on certain political questions. Every medieval university had its colleges and parties and factions armed cap-à-pie — sometimes literally at sword's-point, or fife and drum ecclesiastic — against one another. They were free, these Schoolmen, free from external interference and free from a stifling internal conformity, because the whole purpose of the universities was the search after an enduring truth, beside which worldly aggrandizement was as nothing. They were free because they agreed on this one thing, if on nothing else, that the fear of God is the beginning of wisdom.

III

Only faint traces remain of the medieval university, Mr. Hutchins says, in our American university. "Every American university must justify itself in terms of the visible, tangible, material benefits that it confers upon the individuals who attend it and the community that supports it." The concept of a guild of teachers and scholars is withered away almost to nothing. "To Americans universities are businesses like every other element of this business civilization. Every business consists of employers and employees. The professors are employees. They operate within the framework of the American Way of Life and are subject to punishment for deviation from the popular view of that Way like any other members of the business community. Academic freedom is, I think, generally regarded as a device by which weak-minded or vicious people in some way hang on to their jobs when all right-thinking men would agree that they ought to lose them."[8]

This is harsh; yet the truth often is very harsh, in our time. And Mr. Hutchins thinks that matters have been thus ever since the beginnings of higher education in America. "The American university was not a corporation of students wanting to learn or teachers wanting to teach. It was a corporation formed by a religious denomination or by the state for the purposes of the denomination or state. The American university in the seventeenth century was much closer to the American university today than to the medieval university." Now I think that here Mr. Hutchins ignores one element common to the medieval university and to the American college, and that the most important of all elements: the teleological view of existence, and the religious function of the higher learning. As I have suggested earlier, the medieval university was not often a mere banding together of teachers or students; its real roots were in a cathedral school, or in an endowment for chantry priests who might spend much of their time in study and teaching. And the whole of its work was suffused with the belief that the fear of God is the beginning of wisdom. In this, the early American colleges were very like the medieval universities. As Mr. Hutchins himself remarks, the education of young men for the ministry was the chief motive for the founding of Harvard, Yale, Princeton, Brown, and so many other distinguished colleges. This dedication to religious principle is still the nominal reason, at least, for the existence of hundreds of colleges and universities endowed by religious bodies in America; nor has it been utterly lacking from our state institutions. A Catholic priest, Father Gabriel Richard, had much to do with the establishment of the University of Michigan; and the first president of that university, Henry Phillip Tappan, a great educator, though very different in his

8 *Ibid.*, pp. 77–78.

theology from Newman, was quite as insistent as Newman upon the primacy of religious principle in true education:

> Man is a creature of passions and will, and therefore should be instructed in morality, and be disciplined to self-government. He is immortal, and therefore should he learn that system of religion which brings life and immortality to light.[9]

So Tappan wrote in 1851. Two years later, Newman wrote in his third discourse on University Education that the Utilitarian pedant, in ignoring the religious basis of education, leaves us all adrift: "The various busy world, spread out before our eyes, is physical, but it is more than physical; and, in making its actual system identical with his scientific analysis, such a Professor as I have imagined was betraying a want of philosophical depth, and an ignorance of what a University Teaching ought to be. He was no longer a teacher of liberal knowledge, but a narrow-minded bigot." Not merely the Catholic colleges in America, but the great majority of our institutions of higher learning, were founded upon tenets much like Tappan's and Newman's. I think that Mr. Hutchins does a disservice when he ignores this. For I believe that there is a direct connection between the concept of the scholar as the Bearer of the Word and the idea of academic freedom.

Before the Civil War, we hear little enough of academic freedom in the United States; but that does not suffice to substantiate Mr. Robert P. Ludlum's assertion that "until late in the nineteenth century there seems to have been a blithe disregard of academic freedom and tenure." The colleges — there were only two hundred and fifty, altogether, on the eve of the Civil War, and many of those were scarcely institutions of higher learning — except for the handful of state universities, were quite free of any sort of governmental interference, and so did not have much occasion for disputes in that quarter. Except for the state universities, every institution was supported by a religious denomination of well-defined views, and it was scarcely probable that a teacher would seek a position at a college hostile to his theological opinions; nor was he liable to question the right of such a college to discharge him for solitary dissent. The courses of instruction were comparatively few, and the classical languages, mathematics, and the other traditional disciplines were not calculated to provoke bitter controversy between professors and trustees. The aims of college education were generally agreed upon, and professors and students generally were drawn from families and districts tolerably similar to one another. I am inclined to think, then, that the tranquillity of a century and more was the product of a common understanding, rather than of professors' pusillanimity and trustees' intolerance. Occasionally difficulties arose, as when, in 1820, public disapproval of Thomas Cooper's skepticism made his appointment to the faculty of the

---

[9] Tappan's views are summarized succinctly in Mr. Edwin McCellan's article "The Educational Ideas of Henry Phillip Tappan," *Michigan History*, Spring, 1954.

University of Virginia impossible, despite all that Jefferson could do in his behalf; and Thomas Jefferson himself once proposed to impose a republican political orthodoxy upon professors.[10] Yet no widespread problems of this sort occurred until the increasing heat of the Slavery Question was felt in the colleges, after 1830.

Oberlin, Western Reserve, Jefferson College in Mississippi, Centre College, the University of North Carolina, the College of South Carolina, Miami University, Kenyon College, Dickinson, Franklin, Harvard, the University of Georgia, Bowdoin, the University of Iowa, and Dartmouth College all experienced the dismissal of presidents or professors, during the three decades between 1833 and 1863, for views on slavery and secession. It could hardly have been otherwise: the issues were too close to ungovernable passions, and it is improbable that any other nation engaged in such a struggle would have behaved better. During the 'seventies and 'eighties, a number of professors were discharged — though most of them soon obtained chairs at other colleges — because they had in some degree espoused Darwinianism, to the vexation of the clergymen and farmers who still made up the majority of most boards of trustees. This controversy waned, however, and toward the end of the century the chief subjects in dispute were economic — reflecting, again, the temper of the age, and also the fact that manufacturers and entrepreneurs now were replacing the clergymen and farmers as college trustees.

The powers of college presidents, almost unlimited, and the zeal of trustees, met with no effectual opposition from teachers; and now the teaching of political economy, history, and sociology afforded a field for disagreement which had scarcely existed in the earlier history of American colleges. I do not propose to discuss here in any detail the cases — estimated to number between twelve and twenty-four — of serious disagreement between the administrators and the professors. Free silver, socialism, and related matters were the principal causes of these episodes between 1884 and 1914. After 1870, the direct influence of the German universities upon American higher education increasingly drew the attention of professors to the Germanic concept of "academic freedom," a phrase scarcely heard in this country earlier; and the widening breach between teachers and trustees over questions of political economy gave the idea immediate pertinence. Just what "academic freedom" meant at the German universities, not many Americans clearly understood: it was, in fact, almost wholly an internal freedom, the right to organize the curriculum without the interference of the minister of education; and it had been developed as a last safeguard against political meddling, in the secularized universities of the new bureaucratic German Empire. It was a tolerance by the state, rather than the assertion of a pre-

10 The stormy history of academic freedom in the United States is discussed in Mr. Robert P. Ludlum's "Academic Freedom and Tenure," *Antioch Review*, Spring, 1950, and in Mr. Richard H. Shryock's "The Academic Profession in the United States," *American Association of University Professors Bulletin*, Spring, 1952. Thomas Jefferson's inconsistencies are described in Mr. Gordon E. Baker's "Thomas Jefferson on Academic Freedom," *American Association of University Professors Bulletin*, Autumn, 1953.

scriptive right or a moral tradition; but American professors took up this German concept with more good-will than clarity of apprehension.

Whatever degree of vagueness enveloped the term "academic freedom" at the end of the nineteenth century, still scholars began to display some ability to defend their rights. When President Andrews of Brown University resigned over a disagreement with the governing board over the question of the coinage of silver, in 1897, very strong protests were made by scholars; and when Professor Edward A. Ross was forced out of Stanford University, in 1900, for similar reasons, certain of his colleagues protested and were compelled to resign. This affair was too dismaying to be tolerated; the American Economic Association investigated and sustained Dr. Ross. When Professor John M. Mecklin was compelled to resign from Lafayette College, in 1913, because of his view on biological evolution, the American Philosophical Association and the American Psychological Association protested. This concern on the part of the learned societies, spreading rapidly, led in 1915 to the formation of the American Association of University Professors — or, rather, was one of the principal causes for the establishment of that organization. Ever since then, Committee A of the Association has been the most active body interested in the defense of academic freedom. The reports of this Committee on Academic Freedom and Academic Tenure, particularly its initial report in 1915, its statement of principles in 1925, and its amended statement of principles in 1940, constitute an index to the recent history of the concept in this country. The Committee has proceeded cautiously, aware that its only instrument for the defense of academic freedom is a reputation for moderation and thoroughness which may succeed in shaming violators of the principle into a reformation of their ways; and its statement of principles in 1950, drawn up by Professor W. T. Laprade of Duke University, is the best recent summary of the difficulties with which the question of academic freedom is beset at present. Although it has met with some harsh criticism, and I myself cannot agree with certain sentences in it, this statement is in general temperate and dignified, and I quote perhaps the most important passage here:

> Of the various freedoms essential if our society is to preserve itself and to promote the interests of the individuals that compose it, perhaps the most nearly absolute is that of scholars to direct their search for truth and to report the results of their findings. This freedom is immediately applicable only to a limited number of individuals, but it is profoundly important for the public at large. It safeguards the methods by which we explore the unknown and test the accepted. It may afford a key to open the way to remedies for bodily or social ills, or it may confirm our faith in the familiar. Its preservation is necessary if there is to be scholarship in any true sense of the word. The advantages accrue as much to the public as to the scholars themselves.[11]

[11] "Academic Freedom and Tenure: Report of Committee A for 1950," *American Association of University Professors Bulletin*, Spring, 1951, p. 74.

To this statement there is appended a table of cases of alleged violations of academic freedom brought to the attention of the Committee between 1945 and 1950. On January 1, 1945, seventy-four cases still were pending from previous years. During 1945, the Committee dealt with 122 cases; in 1946, with 107 cases; in 1947, with 81 cases; in 1949, with 96 cases; in 1950, with 103 cases; in 1951, with 120 cases; in 1952, with 131 cases; in 1953, with 146 cases.[12] And it ought to be understood that many cases of infringement upon academic freedom never appealed to this Committee — indeed, probably a great many more cases never are publicly discussed anywhere than the total number of those that come to the attention of the Association of University Professors. John Dewey, the first president of the Association, remarked at the first meeting of that body, in 1915, that he was confident that the topic of academic freedom "can not be more than an incident of the activities of the association in developing professional standards, standards which will be quite as scrupulous regarding the obligations imposed by freedom as jealous for freedom itself. The existence of publicly recognized and enforced standards would tend almost automatically to protect the freedom of the individual and to secure institutions against its abuse."[13] But the eleven cases brought to the attention of the committee in 1915–16 contrast sharply with the multitude of invasions of academic freedom suggested by the preceding statistics of recent years. "Professional standards" have not sufficed to guarantee the freedom of the Academy; and the report of Committee A for 1952 (also prepared by Professor Laprade) reflects this sad truth:

> Some feel that the term academic freedom has become a stereotype, that it needs restatement in different words. Members of this Committee feel rather that the meaning of the term needs to be better understood and more widely supported. The public which maintains colleges and universities will defeat the achievement for which it hopes unless scholars and teachers are left undisturbed and free to do the work for which they were appointed.[14]

I may say here that I share the opinions thus expressed by Professor Laprade and his associates. I believe that the term "academic freedom" is not outmoded, nor the idea which it expresses. I believe that the term is often badly apprehended, and that the idea is insufficiently supported by either professors or the general public. I believe that both the mind of the scholar and the tone of society will suffer gravely unless the reality of academic freedom is intelligently and courageously sustained.[15] . . .

12 *Ibid.*, p. 79; and the later tabulations in the reports for 1951, 1952, and 1953, contained in the *AAUP Bulletin*, numbers for Spring, 1952, Spring, 1953, and Spring, 1954.

13 Quoted by Mr. Robert Ludlum, *op. cit.*, p. 19.

14 Hutchins, *The University of Utopia*, p. 87.

15 A most interesting discrepancy exists between the statistics and opinions of Committee A of the Association of University Professors, and the statistics and opinions of the Commission on Academic Freedom and Academic Tenure of the Association of American Colleges. In its reports for 1951, 1952, and 1953, the latter body stated that not a single case of complaint concerning violation of the principles of academic freedom had been referred to it; and the report of March, 1952, drawn up by President Harwell G. Davis of Howard College, consisted chiefly of the following declaration (see *Association of American*

The reader who has borne with me to the end of this chapter will have gathered that I take academic freedom to be a valid idea, with both the sanction of an historically-defined meaning and the sanction of an enduring pertinence. Mr. Robert Hutchins believes that "The freedom of the modern university in a democratic society is based not on the remnants of a medieval tradition but on the proposition that societies require centers of independent thought and criticism if they are to progress or even to survive. Academic freedom means that the independence of the thought that goes on in a university is so important that a man cannot be restrained or punished by those who pay him because he holds views with which those who pay him disagree." [16] For my part, I think that academic freedom, in our time, is founded *both* upon tradition and upon our present necessities. I do not think that academic freedom deserves preservation chiefly because it "serves the community," though this incidental function is important. I think, rather, that the principal importance of academic freedom is the opportunity it affords for the highest development of private reason and imagination, the improvement of mind and heart by the apprehension of Truth, whether or not that development is of any immediate use to "democratic society." And I find it impossible to concur wholly in the almost unlimited scope accorded to academic freedom by the definitions of Mr. Hook and Mr. Hutchins (though, in subsequent remarks, these gentlemen both acknowledge some limitations). Academic freedom, like every other prescriptive right, has its boundaries and its corresponding duties. When liberty declines into license, then it must be restrained; and if it is not restrained by those who enjoy that particular liberty, then it will be checked by other persons. There are times when the persons who pay a professor would be derelict in their duty if they did not endeavor to restrain the man who violates his own privileges; and, Professor Hook notwithstanding, it is prudent and necessary that there should sometimes exist a control upon the academy besides the control of what Mr. Hook considers "the rational methods by which truth is established." That such restraints may be very seldom exercised, it is important that the scholar and the teacher, recognizing the high duties of their vocation, understand clearly the solemn, and even holy, nature of the academy and its liberties. "The public has a right to expect candor of its servants," Mr. Norman Thomas writes, "emphatically including those who, as teachers, should inspire our youth in search of truth." [17] I understand what Mr. Thomas means; yet I hold that the scholar and the teacher, before thinking of what it is to be a servant, should think of what it is to be a man.

Colleges Bulletin, March, 1952, and also the numbers for March, 1953, and March, 1954):
"Your Commission is encouraged to believe that there is an increasingly stronger conviction that the maintenance of these principles is essential not only to the integrity of our profession but also to enable us to render our most effective service to our God and our country."

Perhaps it is worth remarking that the AAUP is chiefly a body of university teachers, and the AAC chiefly a body of college and university administrators.

[16] Hutchins, *The University of Utopia,* p. 87.

[17] Norman Thomas, *The Test of Freedom,* p. 140.

AAUP Statement of Principles

In 1915 the Committee on Academic Freedom and Academic Tenure of the American Association of University Professors drafted the 1915 Declaration of Principles. In 1925 this document was revised; and in 1940, following a series of joint conferences, delegates of the AAUP and the Association of American Colleges reaffirmed the principles contained in the declaration of 1925. The 1940 Statement of Principles has been brutally attacked, devoutly supported, ignored, and celebrated. Although primarily applicable to college and university teaching, the arguments implicit in the conclusions reached by the AAUP document have been frequently used by high school teachers. Moreover, there have been erratic and unsuccessful attempts to formulate a broad and influential policy for all high school and elementary teachers; but at present the rights and responsibilities of these teachers are given various definitions by competing organizations such as the American Federation of Teachers and the National Education Association. However desirable, unanimity on this issue is still remote, all eloquent pleas for agreement notwithstanding.

15

1940 STATEMENT OF PRINCIPLES*

The purpose of this statement is to promote public understanding and support of academic freedom and tenure and agreement upon procedures to assure them in colleges and universities. Institutions of higher education are conducted for the common good and not to further the interest of either the individual teacher[1] or the institution as a whole. The common good depends upon the free search for truth and its free exposition.

* From the AAUP Bulletin, Vol. 43, No. 1 (Spring, 1957), pp. 113–115. Used by permission of the American Association of University Professors.

[1] The word "teacher" as used in this document is understood to include the investigator who is attached to an academic institution without teaching duties.

146

Academic freedom is essential to these purposes and applies to both teaching and research. Freedom in research is fundamental to the advancement of truth. Academic freedom in its teaching aspect is fundamental for the protection of the rights of the teacher in teaching and of the student to freedom in learning. It carries with it duties correlative with rights.

Tenure is a means to certain ends; specifically: (1) Freedom of teaching and research and of extramural activities, and (2) A sufficient degree of economic security to make the profession attractive to men and women of ability. Freedom and economic security, hence tenure, are indispensable to the success of an institution in fulfilling its obligations to its students and to society.

Academic Freedom

(a) The teacher is entitled to full freedom in research and in the publication of the results, subject to the adequate performance of his other academic duties; but research for pecuniary return should be based upon an understanding with the authorities of the institution.

(b) The teacher is entitled to freedom in the classroom in discussing his subject, but he should be careful not to introduce into his teaching controversial matter which has no relation to his subject. Limitations of academic freedom because of religious or other aims of the institution should be clearly stated in writing at the time of the appointment.

(c) The college or university teacher is a citizen, a member of a learned profession, and an officer of an educational institution. When he speaks or writes as a citizen, he should be free from institutional censorship or discipline, but his special position in the community imposes special obligations. As a man of learning and an educational officer, he should remember that the public may judge his profession and his institution by his utterances. Hence he should at all times be accurate, should exercise appropriate restraint, should show respect for the opinions of others, and should make every effort to indicate that he is not an institutional spokesman.

Academic Tenure

(a) After the expiration of a probationary period teachers or investigators should have permanent or continuous tenure, and their services should be terminated only for adequate cause, except in the case of retirement for age, or under extraordinary circumstances because of financial exigencies.

In the interpretation of this principle it is understood that the following represents acceptable academic practice:

(1) The precise terms and conditions of every appointment should be stated in writing and be in the possession of both institution and teacher before the appointment is consummated.

(2) Beginning with appointment to the rank of full-time instructor or a higher rank, the probationary period should not exceed seven years, including

within this period full-time service in all institutions of higher education; but subject to the proviso that when, after a term of probationary service of more than three years in one or more institutions, a teacher is called to another institution it may be agreed in writing that his new appointment is for a probationary period of not more than four years, even though thereby the person's total probationary period in the academic profession is extended beyond the normal maximum of seven years. Notice should be given at least one year prior to the expiration of the probationary period if the teacher is not to be continued in service after the expiration of that period.

(3) During the probationary period a teacher should have the academic freedom that all other members of the faculty have.

(4) Termination for cause of a continuous appointment, or the dismissal for cause of a teacher previous to the expiration of a term appointment, should, if possible, be considered by both a faculty committee and the governing board of the institution. In all cases where the facts are in dispute, the accused teacher should be informed before the hearing in writing of the charges against him and should have the opportunity to be heard in his own defense by all bodies that pass judgment upon his case. He should be permitted to have with him an adviser of his own choosing who may act as counsel. There should be a full stenographic record of the hearing available to the parties concerned. In the hearing of charges of incompetence the testimony should include that of teachers and other scholars, either from his own or from other institutions. Teachers on continuous appointment who are dismissed for reasons not involving moral turpitude should receive their salaries for at least a year from the date of notification of dismissal whether or not they are continued in their duties at the institution.

(5) Termination of a continuous appointment because of financial exigency should be demonstrably bona fide.

Jenner Committee

During the early months of 1953, a Sub-Committee of the Senate Judiciary Committee held hearings with the announced purpose of investigating the administration of the Internal Security Act and other laws relevant to "internal security." The Sub-Committee chairman was William Jenner of Indiana. Other senators on the hearing panel were Pat McCarran (Nevada), James O. Eastland (Mississippi), Willis Smith

(*North Carolina*), *Olin D. Johnston* (*South Carolina*), *John M. Butler*
(*Maryland*), *Herman Welker* (*Idaho*), *Robert C. Hendrickson* (*New
Jersey*), *and Arthur V. Watkins* (*Utah*). *Robert Morris served as Chief
Counsel.*

*Many witnesses, "friendly" and otherwise, were summoned to give
testimony relevant to alleged charges that American education was in
danger of being subverted to the ends of a communist conspiracy. The
complete record of the hearings was eventually published in bound
volumes by the U.S. Government Printing Office under the title of*
Subversive Influence in the Educational Process.

*The verbatim dialogue which follows was chosen not for any dramatic
value (Mrs. Jerome's testimony was typical of the "unfriendly" witness)
but to reveal the atmosphere of the hearings, the climate within which
many teachers and administrators were questioned. The reader, of
course, may have his own convictions concerning the worth (or worth-
lessness) of such investigations, but it is suggested that assiduous attention be paid to the type of questioning endured by Mrs. Jerome. Does
such interrogation serve either the ends of academic freedom, however
defined, or the ostensible purpose of the Sub-Committee?*

16

TESTIMONY OF MRS. ALICE JEROME, NEW YORK, N.Y., ACCOMPANIED BY DAVID REIN, ATTORNEY, WASHINGTON, D.C.*

The CHAIRMAN. You may state your full name to the committee.
Mrs. JEROME. Mrs. Alice Jerome.
The CHAIRMAN. Where do you reside, Mrs. Jerome?
Mrs. JEROME. 320 Second Avenue, New York City.
The CHAIRMAN. Let the record show that Mrs. Jerome is before the com-
mittee with counsel. Will counsel identify himself?

* From *Subversive Influence in the Educational Process* (Washington: U.S. Government
Printing Office, 1953), pp. 785–792 (Part 7). Used by permission of Mrs. Alice Jerome.

Mr. REIN. David Rein.

The CHAIRMAN. What is your address?

Mr. REIN. 711 14th Street, Washington.

The CHAIRMAN. Proceed, Mr. Morris.

Mr. MORRIS. What educational degrees do you have, Mrs. Jerome?

Mrs. JEROME. I have a bachelor of science degree.

Mr. MORRIS. Where did you obtain the bachelor of science degree?

Mrs. JEROME. The New School of Social Research in New York City.

Mr. MORRIS. In what year?

Mrs. JEROME. 1947.

Mr. MORRIS. Do you have any other degrees?

Mrs. JEROME. No.

Mr. MORRIS. In what schools have you taught during your lifetime?

Mrs. JEROME. I decline to answer that question on the grounds of the fifth amendment. I do not have to be asked to testify against myself, and also because as a teacher I would like to protest against this type of intimidation of teachers. I feel that this kind of questioning that I have just been listening to, that you have done to me this morning and that you have done to Mr. Selsam this afternoon can only serve to frighten teachers, to scare away young people from becoming teachers, to drive good teachers out of the profession, and to frighten weak teachers as a senseless kind of conformity.

Mr. MORRIS. You understand, Mrs. Jerome, that the only question put to you so far was to ask you in what schools you taught. Do you feel that that would intimidate any other teacher than you?

Mrs. JEROME. Yes, the calling of people to this kind of inquisitional investigation. I would like to read a statement which I have made, saying as follows: When the United States marshal handed me a subpena ——

Mr. MORRIS. Mr. Chairman, the witness has not submitted that statement in advance.

Mrs. JEROME. I will be glad to submit it.

Mr. MORRIS. How long is it?

Mr. REIN. It is very short.

The CHAIRMAN. Read the statement and give it to the press. That is what you are here for.

Mrs. JEROME. Yes.

When the United States marshal handed me a subpena for this hearing, I felt like the small-town German schoolteacher who was telling his children about peace and love between nations, when he heard the Nazi storm troopers marching up to his schoolroom.

This inquisition into education extends to nursery-school teachers at the very moment when the New York day-care centers are threatened with extinction by a single slash of the State budget, and thousands of working mothers will have no safe place for their tiny children. Our citizens must save these schools to safeguard the children.

Even Senator Taft agrees that teachers must be judged on their performance, not their politics. Academic freedom is a basic American right. As a nursery-school teacher, I have always taught the importance of each individual child — his right to be himself, his right to be loved, to be respected, and to have every opportunity for full flowering as a person. How can the child get this from teachers frightened or bludgeoned into conformity? It is on my record as a nursery-school teacher for the past 10 years that I wish to be judged and not by any fantastic charges cooked up in a star chamber. I want to join with all the Americans today who are answering back in ever greater numbers these native Nazis on the investigating committees who try to choke up freedom and love of people at their very source — in our children.

Mr. MORRIS. Now, Mrs. Jerome, you mentioned there that you want this committee to judge you on your record as a nursery-school teacher for the past 10 years. Would you tell us what that record has been?

Mrs. JEROME. I have worked as a nursery-school teacher in several places.

Mr. MORRIS. Will you tell us where?

Mrs. JEROME. I decline to answer on the grounds of the fifth amendment.

Mr. MORRIS. Mrs. Jerome, how can you expect this committee to judge you on your record as a nursery-school teacher when you will not even tell us what that record is?

Mrs. JEROME. I believe that my record as a teacher can be judged by my statement of my philosophy of education, how I feel about teaching. You can find out.

The CHAIRMAN. Tell us your record. Tell us where you taught.

Mrs. JEROME. I decline to answer that question.

The CHAIRMAN. Tell us what you taught.

Mrs. JEROME. I will tell you what I taught. I teach and the nursery-school curriculum includes the use of many materials by the children. It includes block building, painting, finger painting, music and rhythms, story telling, a certain amount of acceptance of routines in the nursery school, learning to live together, learning to cooperate, learning how to get along with other children through various kinds of play. I would say basically I have taught and tried to teach children first of all respect for themselves as people, because I believe that unless one has respect for himself as a person one cannot then develop respect for other people. This is a basic principle of nursery-school education, and I believe of any sound education. It is a principle which I am not sure the members of this committee have learned.

The CHAIRMAN. Now then, let me ask you, are you now a member of the Communist Party?

Mrs. JEROME. I decline to answer that question on the grounds of self-incrimination.

The CHAIRMAN. Do you think it is proper for a Communist to teach even in the nursery schools of this country when the Communist conspiracy is dedicated to the overthrow of the country?

Mrs. JEROME. I believe a teacher should be judged on her performance as a teacher.

The CHAIRMAN. Answer my question. I asked you if you thought that the Communist teacher should be permitted to teach even in the nursery schools of this Nation when communism is dedicated to the overthrow of this country. You are an intelligent lady, holding a degree. Do you brag about what a fine teacher you have been for the last 10 years, so you can answer that question?

Mrs. JEROME. I believe any teacher regardless of Communists ——

The CHAIRMAN. I say Communist teacher.

Mrs. JEROME. A Communist teacher, an Episcopalian teacher, a Catholic, a Communist, a Socialist, a Democratic teacher, any politics, any religion, if she is a good teacher, if she loves children, if she is true to the principles of good teaching and human values, has a right to teach anywhere in the United States of America, and I believe this is in accordance with the principles of our country.

The CHAIRMAN. Did you know that the Communist conspiracy is dedicated to the overthrow of this country? Do you know that as a public school teacher?

Mrs. JEROME. I don't know that.

The CHAIRMAN. By force and violence. Do you know that?

Mrs. JEROME. No.

The CHAIRMAN. If that be true, do you think they are fit to teach in the public schools or any schools in this country?

Mrs JEROME. My statement is the same as I said before, that a Communist teacher, a teacher of any political opinion, a teacher of any religious belief, a teacher of any race, has a right, as long as he or she is a good teacher and is judged on the basis of her record. I believe, Mr. Chairman, that in all of the various investigations that you have been making into teachers and into their records and into what they have done and what they have not done, that you have not yet found a single case of a teacher who was not cited and recommended and highly praised for his or her teaching work, her work as a teacher, by pupils, by parents, by fellow teachers, by principals, by other educators. This is a record that is very important.

The CHAIRMAN. I am afraid that you have not read the committee's record. I am afraid that you have not listened to all the testimony before this committee. Do you know whether or not communism is anti-God?

Mrs. JEROME. I don't know.

The CHAIRMAN. You do not know. Do you think that if communism were anti-God that that kind of a teacher should be permitted to teach the children of this Nation?

Mrs. JEROME. I will repeat that a teacher of any belief, any political or religious belief, who is a good teacher, who shows in her work she understands children, respects people and believes in teaching, and shows that she is teaching good human values in her teaching, regardless of her philosophy, politics, religion, has a right to teach in our schools.

The CHAIRMAN. Do you know that communism is a disciplinary teaching, and that no teacher can be free to teach, that she must teach what the Communists direct her to teach? Do you think that person could be free to teach in the public schools of this country?

Mrs. JEROME. I can only repeat my other statement, Mr. Chairman.

The CHAIRMAN. In what State do you teach?

Mrs. JEROME. Pardon me?

The CHAIRMAN. In what State do you teach?

Mrs. JEROME. New York State.

The CHAIRMAN. In New York State. Is that your home? Were you born in New York?

Mrs. JEROME. No, I was born in Chicago.

Senator WELKER. I have a question.

The CHAIRMAN. Senator Welker.

Senator WELKER. Do you believe that Adolf Hitler should have been permitted to teach in a nursery school in New York City?

Mrs. JEROME. I really don't know. I don't think he is qualified. I don't believe he was qualified.

Senator WELKER. How do I know that you are qualified or any other person is qualified on this long list that you have given here, Communists, Socialists, Republicans, Democrats, et cetera? You made a general statement. Now I will ask you this ——

Mrs. JEROME. No, Senator.

Senator WELKER. Would you think Adolf Hitler should teach in a nursery school in New York City?

Mrs. JEROME. The statement that I made said provided the person was a good teacher with an understanding of children and a love of children and taught these principles that I spoke of. I don't believe Adolf Hitler would qualify.

Senator WELKER. How are we to know whether they are good teachers if you sit here and hide behind the fifth amendment of the Constitution of the United States?

Mrs. JEROME. It is my understanding of the fifth amendment, Senator, that one does not have to explain the reason for invoking the fifth amendment; that the invoking of the fifth amendment does not constitute an act of self-incrimination, and I believe you are trying to make it into that.

Senator WELKER. I believe that I understand the fifth amendment just about as well as you do. You made a statement a little bit ago about this committee being "native Nazis." You made that statement, did you not?

Mrs. JEROME. I did.

Senator WELKER. What is your age?

Mrs. JEROME. 40

Senator WELKER. Did you volunteer for service in World War II?

Mrs. JEROME. No.

Senator WELKER. Did your husband serve in World War II?

Mrs. JEROME. No, he was over age.

Senator WELKER. He was over age. Well, I will inform you that on this committee composed of Senator Jenner, the chairman, and Senator Welker, the speaker, both served in World War II, and I think it is very unfair for you to come here in the public forum and class us, representatives of sovereign States, as "native Nazis."

Mrs. JEROME. I am not judging you on your war record. I am judging you on your inquisition record here.

Senator WELKER. On the inquisition record?

Mrs. JEROME. Yes.

Senator WELKER. Yes. You made a statement a moment ago that certain educators disagreed with the questions that we might ask you educators. You are also mindful of the fact that many famous, very famous educators have commended this committee and have been here before us and have helped us no end in this investigation.

Mrs. JEROME. Who are they?

Senator WELKER. Dr. Gideonse. Did you ever hear of him?

Mrs. JEROME. Yes.

Senator WELKER. Where did he come from?

Mrs. JEROME. I think he came originally from the University of Chicago. He was there when I was there.

Senator WELKER. He is a pretty good educator; is he not?

Mrs. JEROME. Well, one can have one's opinions.

Senator WELKER. J. Edgar Hoover is a pretty loyal American and he thinks the Communists should not teach in the public schools.

Mrs. JEROME. Is J. Edgar Hoover an educator?

Senator WELKER. I think he is a pretty good educator. He seems to know his subject quite well, and he has not disagreed with our efforts here; has he?

Mrs. JEROME. Undoubtedly not.

Mr. MORRIS. Mr. Chairman, when this woman was served to appear before this committee, the committee had information that she was the director of the Park Nursery School, 318 Second Avenue, New York City. When you were served with the subpena, were you the director of the Park Nursery School at 318 Second Avenue, New York City?

Mrs. JEROME. I decline to answer that question on the grounds given.

Mr. MORRIS. You feel that if you tell the committee that you were director of that nursery school you would be putting into the record evidence that would lead to your subsequent incrimination?

Mrs. JEROME. As I said before, I don't believe I am required to say why I decline to answer the question. I decline under the grounds of the fifth amendment.

Mr. MORRIS. That you would be testifying against yourself?

Mrs. JEROME. That I would not be asked to testify against myself. I believe that the fifth amendment was put there to protect people like me, innocent and honest witnesses, from people like you who are tyrannical and frightened people who happen to temporarily be in power.

Mr. Morris. Well, now, when you say "temporarily in power," do you envisage some kind of a change in the Government?

Mrs. Jerome. The Democrats might get in.

Mr. Morris. Are you presently a member of the Communist Party?

Mrs. Jerome. I decline to answer that question on the same grounds.

Mr. Morris. Have you attended secret meetings of the Communist Party?

Mrs. Jerome. I decline to answer that.

Mr. Morris. Have you attended secret meetings of the Communist Party in conjunction with your work as director of the Park Nursery School?

Mrs. Jerome. I decline to answer that question.

Mr. Morris. In connection with your work as director of the Park Nursery School have you made any efforts to recruit people into the Communist Party?

Mrs. Jerome. I decline to answer that question.

Mr. Morris. Are you the wife of V. J. Jerome?

Mrs. Jerome. Yes.

Mr. Morris. Mr. Mandel, would you put into our record who Mr. V. J. Jerome is?

Mr. Mandel. I have before me the hearings of the House Committee on Un-American Activities which show that V. J. Jerome, according to the *Daily Worker* of May 11, 1934, is identified as a member of the national agit-prop commission of the Communist Party. Further, that he is identified as the chairman or head of the cultural commission of the Communist Party by the *Daily Worker* of August 7, 1950, and the *Daily People's World* of January 24, 1951, and February 8, 1951. Further that he was a member of the national religious-political commission of the Communist Party. And finally I have here a magazine entitled *Political Affairs* which is the national theoretical organ of the Communist Party which shows V. J. Jerome is managing editor and also quotes him in a speech delivered to the meeting of the national committee of the Communist Political Association in June 1945.

Mr. Morris. Mrs. Jerome, your husband was one of the 11 Communist leaders who were indicted last January, wasn't he?

Mrs. Jerome. I decline to answer on the grounds of the fifth amendment.

Mr. Morris. You know as a matter of record, as a matter of information through reading of the newspapers, that he was one of the 11 Communist leaders?

Mrs. Jerome. If you know, you don't need to ask me. If you ask me, I decline to answer.

The Chairman. Under the fifth amendment?

Mrs. Jerome. Under the fifth amendment.

Mr. Morris. Do you have any children in school now yourself?

Mrs. Jerome. In school?

Mr. Morris. Do you have any children?

Mrs. Jerome. Yes; we have two children.

Mr. Morris. What schools do they attend?

Mrs. JEROME. Stuyvesant High School and the Downtown Community School.

Senator WELKER. Did they ever attend a nursery school conducted by you?

Mrs. JEROME. I don't believe so.

Senator WELKER. You do not believe so?

Mrs. JEROME. No.

Senator WELKER. I may not be correct word for word but you said a moment ago, as I heard your statement, that our investigating committee might scare away teachers from the profession. Is that a correct summary of what you stated?

Mrs. JEROME. Yes.

Senator WELKER. As a matter of fact, our investigation might scare away some Communists from teaching in the profession; is that not correct?

Mrs. JEROME. I read an article in the New York *Times* last week saying that there were not enough teachers, that young people were not coming into the teaching profession as they were needed, partly because teachers are not paid enough and partly because teachers are subject to this type of abuse.

Senator WELKER. Do you think that an honest, loyal, American citizen dedicated to the teaching profession would hesitate to go into his profession if he were not a member of the Communist Party?

Mrs. JEROME. Definitely.

Senator WELKER. He definitely would?

Mrs. JEROME. Yes.

Senator WELKER. Can you name me any instances of that?

Mrs. JEROME. I don't need to name people. I know many people who feel that way about teaching today.

Senator WELKER. Name one.

Mrs. JEROME. I decline to.

The CHAIRMAN. I did not hear the answer.

Mrs. JEROME. I do not know any particular names to give you, but I know that there is a good deal of feeling in the colleges where teachers are trained and among teachers, among young teachers. There is a great deal of fear today. The head of the Columbia School of Journalism stated, I think also in the New York *Times* this week, that he was not going to cooperate as fully as he had with these investigating committees in the field of education, because he felt they represented a grave danger to academic freedom.

Senator WELKER. It would be a grave danger to academic freedom, while our boys are dying in Korea, if an investigating body of the United States Senate might ask a witness whether or not she was a member of the Communist Party. Do you want us to believe that?

Mrs. JEROME. I was quoting someone, too.

Senator WELKER. Is your husband afraid of academic freedom?

Mrs. JEROME. I don't understand the "freedom."

Senator WELKER. Now, your husband has been convicted of some offense?

Mrs. JEROME. I decline to answer on the grounds of the fifth amendment.

Senator WELKER. That is a matter of public record, is it not?

Mrs. JEROME. Then you don't need to ask it.

Senator WELKER. Well, I am asking you now and you are not asking me.

Mrs. JEROME. I decline to answer.

Senator WELKER. Does your husband feel the same as you do about academic freedom?

Mrs. JEROME. I decline on the grounds of the fifth amendment.

Senator WELKER. That is all.

The CHAIRMAN. Are there any further questions?

Mr. MORRIS. I will endeavor to make further efforts to find out, Mr. Chairman, whether or not this witness is still the director of the Park Nursery School.

Have you ever attended Communist Party meetings under an assumed name?

Mrs. JEROME. I decline to answer on the grounds of the fifth amendment.

The CHAIRMAN. Does your school operate under a State license in the State of New York?

Mrs. JEROME. I decline to answer on the grounds of the fifth amendment.

Senator WELKER. How many students attend your school?

Mrs. JEROME. I decline to answer on the grounds of the fifth amendment.

Senator WELKER. One or fifty, you decline to answer?

Mrs. JEROME. I decline to answer.

Mr. MORRIS. Mr. Chairman, I have here for our record documents that have come in since preceding witnesses were on the stand. May they go into the record?

The CHAIRMAN. They may go into the record at this point.

Mr. MORRIS. There are 3 articles by Harry D. Gideonse, 1 article by William Jansen, and a statement supplied by Randolph B. Smith.

Senator JENNER. They may go into the record and be included in their proper place.

If there is nothing further, the committee will stand adjourned.

(Whereupon, at 3:25 P.M., the hearing was recessed, subject to call.)

Senator WARREN. That is a million dollars round the year.

Mr. JEROME. That is the full fact in the case.

Senator WARREN. Well I think that you answered my question, asking me the question I declare to answer.

Senator WARREN. Now, I understand, to-day, as far as you declare to answer the question.

Mr. JEROME. I decline on the ground of the Fifth amendment.

Senator WARREN. That?

The CHAIRMAN. Are these under the question?

Mr. PAGE. You will endeavor to make further inquiry to-morrow. Mr. Chairman, whether or not this witness is of the opinion of the Park money School.

Have you ever attended a Copartners' Fair meeting, under an assumed name?

Mr. JEROME. I decline to answer on the ground of the Fifth amendment.

The CHAIRMAN. Do you want a fuller answer under a Self Accusation in the State of New York.

Mr. JEROME. I decline to answer on the ground of the Self amendment.

Senator WARREN. How many dollars is attached, sir? I book it?

Mr. JEROME. I decline to answer on the ground of the Fifth amendment.

Senator WARREN. Q. Do really you decline to answer?

Mr. JEROME. I decline to answer.

Mr. CHAIRMAN. Mr. Chairman, I have here for this great amendments that have come in since preceding witness were on the stand, and they go into the record.

The CHAIRMAN. They may go into the record at this point.

Mr. SHAUGH. There are 3 articles by Mann[?]; exhibited articles by William Jenkins, and a statement applied by Edward B. Smith.

Senator. It seems their may so into the stand and be included in their series also.

There is nothing further, the committee will stand adjourned.

(Whereupon at 3:35 p.m. the hearing was recessed subject to call.)

PART THREE

Traditionalism, Progressivism, and the Pendulum

ONE OF THE MOST enduring controversies in American education is found in the debate between advocates of Traditionalism and supporters of Progressivism. This struggle has flourished on all levels of education — public, private, elementary, secondary, and collegiate — and no teacher, student, or taxpayer has escaped its impact. The combatants have borne, and continue to bear, their arms of data, theory, and presumption; and though a reader of educational journals may follow the skirmishes as they erratically appear in numerous publications of varying scholarship, the basic tenets of the warring philosophies remain obscured for lack of a systematic and *public* explication. Hopefully, such works as Lawrence A. Cremin's *The Transformation of the School* and *The Revolution in Education* by Adler and Mayer are bringing some order to the debate. Meanwhile, parents, if so disposed, watch carefully, at once puzzled by and apprehensive toward the scrim of ingrown professionalism which blurs not only the competitions among theorists but, more importantly, the concrete implications of their theories. Consequently, the Traditionalist-Progressive debate may be regarded as a healthy contest only if the opposing philosophies are clearly delineated for laymen and educators alike. But the dimensions of the controversy are not geometric. They are hybrid. They resist facile delineation.

Frequently heard, therefore, are the assertions that the once untainted factions, through crossbreeding, have evolved into philosophic mongrels, that legitimate battles (even if desired) are now impossible, and that the great rhetorical wars of the twenties and thirties have withered to inconclusive squabbles. However exaggerated these views, it is nevertheless true that some Traditionalists have embraced certain "progressive" ideals. Moreover, some Progressives have adopted opinions once considered to be "traditional." Although ambiguity has resulted from this crossbreeding, an armistice has not. Those who deny the current strength of the debate are simply oblivious to its new proportions. Certainly, the urge to create stereotypes suggests that partisans of sufficient purity exist. Rabid advocates of extreme Progressivism may characterize their enemies as red-eyed tyrants of a hickory stick barbarism. Traditionalists, on the other hand, have delighted in producing sarcastic caricatures of the Progressively influenced school by describing it as a sanitarium, manned by nursemaids, with patients rather than pupils enjoying therapy rather than instruction.

Obviously, the student of philosophy who desires to interpret clearly the hybrid issues of the debate must first understand the basic doctrines of the two positions. Second, he must learn to recognize the protean forms of argument — their relevance to actual school policy, and the pressures, direct and indirect, which they exert on teachers, students, and parents.

The heritage of Traditionalism evolved from four distinct *humanisms* implicit in the Hellenic, Roman, medieval, and Renaissance periods of Western civilization. The thoughts of Plato and Aristotle in the Hellenic age, Quintilian and Epictetus in the Roman period, John of Salisbury, St. Thomas Aquinas, and Hugh of St. Victor in the medieval world, and Erasmus, Ascham, and Montaigne in the Renaissance era were tributaries which swelled the mainstream of Western philosophy. Today, when we speak of "pure" Traditionalism we are referring to the individual *and* collaborative efforts of these thinkers to create an educational philosophy practical in its idealism, sublime in its fruits.

The assumptions of Traditionalism are astutely summarized by Mortimer Adler and Milton Mayer in "The Revolution in Education," the first selection in Part Three. The following is an excerpt from that summary:

The common practice — and the common theory — of every age preceding our own reduces, in summary, to five fundamental concepts. Upon these the institution of education rested undisturbed in Western history up to the middle of the last century.

First, the aim of education is the cultivation of the individual's capacities for mental growth and moral development. It is intended to help him acquire the intellectual techniques and aesthetic sensibilities, the knowledge, understanding, and wisdom requisite for a good human life spent publicly in political and professional action and privately in the worthiest use of leisure. As a secondary function, which it shares with other institutions, it concerns itself with the training of the body and the maturations of the emotions; this last objective (inculcated in part by rational emphasis on the "golden mean" and in part by discipline and personal concern) is viewed as a contribution to moral development. Specifically Christian education, of course, orients all these temporal objectives to the life of grace.

It was thought, in the second place, that basic schooling, given these objectives, must be "liberal" education. The corollaries of this concept were, generally, that basic schooling is the same for all who go to school, with due allowance for the varying dispositions of the normal individual; that training in the particular skills required for productive tasks is outside the area of basic schooling and is best acquired by apprenticeship; and that specialized education, after the completion of basic schooling, is to be given in only those vocations that are essentially liberal in character — namely, the learned professions.

Third, it was thought that education does not end with the completion of schooling, even of professional schooling, but, rather, that the pursuit of knowledge involves the effort of a lifetime and is one of the principal activities of those with time for leisure-work. Adult education was rarely discussed as such, partly because the stages of schooling were not so sharply defined by age level as they are now and partly, no doubt, because its pursuit, among the leisured few, was (correctly or incorrectly) assumed. But it was explicitly maintained that only the beginning of education can occur in youth because of the limitations intrinsic to immaturity and the limitations of any subject matter appropriate to immature study. To Seneca's dictum that "an old man who has still to learn his lessons is a shameful and ridiculous object; training and preparation are for the young, action for the old," Aristotle replies (three hundred years earlier!) that child prodigies may be found in mathematics and harmony, but never in morals or politics, which require the experience of life for their comprehension.

The fourth fundamental concept of education down the ages was that the profession of teaching is not only a learned profession, involving special preparation in the liberal arts and the skill of transmitting them, but also a profession of learning, in which the teacher not only practices his art but improves it by the continuous study of the subjects he teaches. The teacher is a lifelong learner.

Finally, the advancement of learning, upon which the vitality of education in any society depends, requires scholarship, or investigation and research, apart from the dissemination and acquisition of the learning already available; and scholarship is likely to flourish in a community of scholars (whether or not they are organized as the faculties of educational institutions) cooperating and communicating across the separate fields of learning which, since their common goal is truth, are implicitly related to one another.

These concepts are enumerated as five for the sake of discussion here; they might be condensed or extended. What is important is that, historically, they represent together the basic principles of educational theory and practice of every epoch preceding our own. . . . The differences and disagreements which arose in theory and in practice occurred within the general framework of these suppositions.[1]

Like many great movements, Progressivism began as a nameless, eclectic, and desultory protest against established orders. Its first measurable impact is discerned in scientific and philosophical speculations of the seventeenth century, with its specific lineage found in the works of such men as Comenius, Locke, Rousseau, Pestalozzi, and John Dewey. Lawrence A. Cremin, in *The Transformation of the School,* outlines the major concepts of the movement as they congealed in America, late in the nineteenth century:

Actually, progressive education began as part of a vast humanitarian effort to apply the promise of American life — the ideal of government by, of, and for the people — to the puzzling new urban-industrial civilization that came into being during the latter half of the nineteenth century. The word *progressive* provides the clue to what it really was: the educational phase of American Progressivism writ large. In effect, progressive education began as Progressivism in education: a many-sided effort to use the schools to improve the lives of individuals. In the minds of Progressives this meant several things.

First, it meant broadening the program and function of the school to include direct concern for health, vocation, and the quality of family and community life.

[1] Mortimer Adler and Milton Mayer, *The Revolution in Education* (Chicago: The University of Chicago Press, 1958), pp. 21–23.

Second, it meant applying in the classroom the pedagogical principles derived from new scientific research in psychology and the social sciences.

Third, it meant tailoring instruction more and more to the different kinds and classes of children who were being brought within the purview of the school. In a sense, the revolution Horace Mann had sparked a generation before — the revolution inherent in the idea that everyone ought to be educated — had created both the problem and the opportunity of the Progressives. For if everyone was to attend school, the Progressives contended, not only the methods but the very meaning of education would have to change. It was all very well for some educators to say, in effect: "We know what good education is; take it or leave it" — in much the same fashion that Henry Ford told customers they could have their cars in any color they wished so long as it was black. What happened was that youngsters in droves deserted the schools as irrelevant to the world of here and now.

Finally, Progressivism implied the radical faith that culture could be democratized without being vulgarized, the faith that everyone could share not only in the benefits of the new sciences but in the pursuit of the arts as well. Jane Addams, that noble lady who founded Hull House and led its efforts for fully forty years, once remarked: "We have learned to say that the good must be extended to all of society before it can be held secure by any one person or any one class; but we have not yet learned to add to that statement, that unless all men and all classes contribute to a good, we cannot even be sure that it is worth having." Here was the spiritual nub of progressive education. . . .[2]

Obviously, the preceding summaries do not illuminate the cross-pollinations and splinter movements particular to each philosophy. Concerning crosscurrents in Progressivism, Cremin states that "the movement was marked from the very beginning by a pluralistic, frequently contradictory, character. The reader will search . . . in vain for any capsule definition of progressive education. None exists, and none ever will; for throughout its history progressive education meant different things to different people, and these differences were only compounded by the remarkable diversity of American education." Cremin suggests a caution that should prevail, too, in one's scrutiny of Traditionalism, that sprawling movement gifted paradoxically with variations within the rigid circumference of its expectations.

In an effort to modulate the chronic discords of the Traditionalists and Progressives, David Riesman has come forth with an argument for

[2] Reprinted from *The Transformation of the School* by Lawrence A. Cremin, by permission of Alfred A. Knopf, Inc. Copyright 1961 by Alfred A. Knopf, Inc. P. viii.

countercyclical education.[3] If we grant that formal education is most valuable when it offers the student, among other experiences, an exposure to values and concepts not actively encouraged by the surrounding society, then, Riesman explains, one of the crucial functions of the school — be it an elementary, secondary, or collegiate institution — is to run *counter* to the *cycle* of societal influence. The school should be a fertile resource for comparison and contrast, not a bland factory for the duplication of values previously inculcated in the student by the natural intimidations of society. The school should act as a pendulum, swinging in an arc contrary to the familiar, to the conventional. Consequently, if the environment surrounding a particular school encourages rigorous intellectual disciplines, the school might well foster a curriculum and atmosphere conducive to the development of social skills, "citizenship," and vocational training. However, if the community atmosphere should emphasize the values implicit in progressive curricula, the school must respect that influence and work toward enforcing more traditional goals. Criticisms of Riesman's theory are inevitable, for it strives to neglect, relatively, some code of educational doctrine at any given time. But *countercyclical education* is poised, nevertheless, as a means by which we may surmount the petulance and bickering of educational antagonists; and, of greater importance, this theory defines the school as a place of inspiration and discovery, regardless of what society may manifest in its prejudice, or ignorance, or lassitude.

Writing in the nineteenth century, the American sculptor Horatio Greenough declared: "I regard . . . Fashion as the instinctive effort of the stationary to pass itself off for progress." Greenough advanced this criticism to discredit the penchant for fad so popular in the American arts of the last century. But his laconic judgment applies prophetically to the Progressive-Traditionalist struggle. Within the brief history of American education each movement has enjoyed its time of *fashion.* Each philosophy, as expected, defines its own truth as the exclusive domain of Progress. Therefore, it is incumbent upon teachers, administrators, and, hopefully, an enlightened public to grapple with the respective virtues and vices of the competing philosophies so as to separate the trappings of fad from the genuine contributions to American education. To fail this obligation is to supplant the possibility for real progress with the certainty of continued fashion — the anathema described by Greenough as the "instinctive effort of the stationary."

The historical readings in Part Three are arranged chronologically, with Hugh of St. Victor, a Traditionalist, preceding two forebears of

[3] See "Thoughts on Teachers and Schools," page 248.

Progressivism, Comenius and Rousseau. The selections by John Dewey deliver us into the twentieth century, where antagonists Bestor and Corey present their views. David Riesman ends Part Three with a half-critical, half-conciliatory appraisal of modern education in America.

Mortimer J. Adler and Milton Mayer

In "The Revolution in Education" Adler and Mayer trace the development of those principles of education which found almost universal acceptance within Western tradition until the beginning of the scientific era. The authors then examine what is properly termed the revolution in education, showing the cleavages which have resulted between past tradition and modern speculation. Of particular importance is the question revolving about the degree of obsolescence, real or imaginary, inherent in Traditional education: Can those principles and practices used to educate Aristotle and Abraham Lincoln be used today?

Mortimer Adler has taught philosophy of law at the University of Chicago and was also on the faculty at Columbia University. He served as an editor of the "Great Books of the Western World," and he has written Art and Prejudice, A Dialectic of Morals. *Recently he published a two-volume work,* The Idea of Freedom.

Milton Mayer has taught at the University of Chicago, William Penn College, and the Institute for Social Research at Frankfort University. He is the author of They Thought They Were Free, *an examination of Nazi Germany.*

17

THE REVOLUTION IN EDUCATION*

There were, in the centuries that preceded 1850, great crises in education, but there was still greater continuity. The pre-scientific, pre-industrial societies — sacred or secular — were concerned with the schooling of the few and with them alone. The polity might be a republic, an aristocracy, an oligarchy, or

* Reprinted from *The Revolution in Education* by Mortimer J. Adler and Milton Mayer by permission of The University of Chicago Press. Copyright © 1958 by the University of Chicago Press. Pp. 14–34.

even a tyranny; its basic concern was the same: to prepare the leisured few for the learned or holy vocations and, in later times, for the highest ranks of commerce and government. The pattern was no more altered by the phenomenon of the student beggars of the Continental universities at the end of the Middle Ages than it was by the English "charity schools," the pre-Revolutionary "pauper schools" in America, or the appearance of an occasional hayseed at Henry Adams' Harvard.

The two great educational crises of the ages past were not educational crises at all but religious. The first occurred with the transition from Greek and Roman antiquity to pre-medieval Christendom. The ideal function of education in the Greek city-states was defined by Plato in the *Republic* and the *Laws* and was practiced in greater or lesser degree before and after his time: the preparation of the elite few for the service of the state and its governance. The absolute supremacy of the state may have been worse abused in later ages, but it has never been better praised than it was in ancient Greece. Lycurgus, the lawgiver of Sparta, was, so Plutarch recites, "of a persuasion that children were not so much the property of their parents as of the whole commonwealth." Accordingly, "he bred up his citizens in such a way that they neither would nor could live by themselves; they were to make themselves one with the public good, and, clustering like bees around their commander, be by their zeal and public spirit carried all but out of themselves, and devoted wholly to their country." So single-minded was their education that they were not allowed to learn of governments different from their own. Some four hundred years later Aristotle was glorifying the Spartans for making education "the business of the state." "The citizen," he said, "should be molded to suit the form of government under which he lives . . . if the laws are democratic, democratically, or oligarchically, if the laws are oligarchical."

This classic doctrine had its echoes a few decades ago in the cry of "adjustment." The business of education was the adjustment of the child to his environment. But the "adjustment" school — or, at least, its slogan — passed from favor with the rise of the modern totalitarian state whose educational system adjusted the child to an environment which Americans thought abominable. Then came the Second World War and the Cold War, and Aristotle, and even Lycurgus, were heard again. "The overarching objective," says Dr. Wilbur A. Yauch, chairman of the Department of Education at Northern Illinois State Teachers College, "the objective for which schools primarily exist, is to indoctrinate for democracy."

The Spartans, the Athenians, and later the Romans espoused indoctrination of the young in the name of education partly to ward off subversive ideas and partly to secure the state, through the will and training of its citizens, against attack from without. In the face of the Communist threat the role of education in national security has come to the fore in our own time, as many of the speakers at the 1955 White House Conference on Education indicated. Citing the Soviet Union's lead in training scientists and engineers, Vice-

President Nixon told the Conference that "it is apparent that our national security has a tremendous stake in our educational system." Neil H. McElroy, then president of Proctor and Gamble Company and chairman of the President's Committee for the White House Conference (and subsequently Secretary of Defense of the United States) went further: "In this highly technical era, education has become as much a part of our system of defense as the Army, the Navy, or the Air Force. We must have good schools, not only because of our ideals, but for survival."

Another participant in the Conference was worried by the integration of education into the survival of the state. Speaking on "What Should Our Schools Accomplish?" President James R. Killian of the Massachusetts Institute of Technology said: "In Nazi and communistic societies there isn't much doubt about that question — their schools are arranged to shape youth to the needs of the state. It is of course a tradition in our own country to consider the individual paramount; we would not think of subordinating the educational desires of an individual to the needs of the state. . . . And we cling to this freedom for the individual even though it looks at times as though the welfare of the nation were suffering from it.

"For instance," President Killian went on, "we need science teachers in our schools today even more desperately than we need other kinds of teachers, but their is no way in which we can impress students into programs which would prepare them to be science teachers. . . . In an age when science is essential to our safety and our economic welfare, it might be argued that a shortage of science teachers and of scientists and engineers is a clear and present danger to the nation. I, for one, am convinced that it is just that."

Presumably, Nazi and Communist education — and Greek and Roman — would sacrifice freedom to the national danger. President Killian thinks it is not necessary: "Personal opportunities are often created by national needs — the national shortage of engineers has led to good jobs for young engineers and, as a consequence, can bring about an increase in the number of students seeking training as engineers." President Killian's hope might be realized, but what if there were a national shortage of, say, sonnet writers or saints, and the job market did not respond by raising salaries in those professions? The question has been asked before. Plato thought the state was short of philosophers, for whom personal opportunities were scarce and wages low. He offered the classical answer — which in principle seems to be the Nazi and Communist answer: Man belonged to the state, and education was to mold him to its service and survival.

The revival of the ancient doctrine under modern stress is still attacked. As long ago as 1917, with England at war, Bertrand Russell, in his *Why Men Fight*, excoriated the "molding" principle of education as the highest treason to the child: "What is considered in education is hardly ever the boy or girl, the young man or young woman, but almost always, in some form, the maintenance of the existing order. . . . Hardly anything is done to foster the inward growth of mind and spirit." And Canon Bernard Iddings Bell, in the midst of Cold War, wants the university to be "a breeding place of rebels, a sender forth of graduates who, unadjusted and unadjustable, would try to turn the world upside down"; a far and forlorn cry from the reaction to the successful launching of the Soviet Union's earth satellites in 1957, when Americans in high quarters and low called for an all-out effort by the educational system to overtake the totalitarians' lead in the production of scientists and engineers for national defense.

The aim of education remained the same throughout antiquity: to "mold" the good man and the good citizen, the two being generally held identical. The means were the inculcation of patriotism or the service of the state, the cultivation of the intellect, and (to whatever degree it might be achieved through schooling) the discipline of the passions in the direction of the classical ideal of moderation. But the school did not exist as we know it, and, until the last few centuries of Rome, it did not exist in any form. Instruction was private, or in very small groups, and peripatetic. In a world where nearly all labor was done by slaves, the students were members of that minority destined by birth or fortune (usually by both) to live a life of leisure or, in any case, of intellectual and not necessitous toil.

But Athens and Rome did not wholeheartedly follow the utopian precepts of Plato and Aristotle and make education "the business of the state." The young citizen's father directed his education and sent him with a specially designated slave, a παιδαγωγός, a "child-accompanier," from which the word "pedagogue" is derived, to hear lectures. The Romans placed more (and, in earlier periods, all) of their emphasis on the father's education of the son, directly and as supervisor of the teaching slaves (who were usually Greeks). The home was the school, and family example the primary tool of instruction. In the first century A.D., Quintilian (who kept a school of rhetoric and is sometimes called "the first public school teacher" because he was the first whose wages were paid by the emperor) grievously lamented the withering away of familial education.

Whatever adjustments were made in content and method from place to place and epoch to epoch in the ancient world, the curriculum that evolved was substantially the same. It consisted of what Cicero called "the liberal arts" of grammar (including folk literature), logic or dialectic (the art of argument), and rhetoric (the art of persuasion, which included law and law-making). These, plus geometry (including geography and natural history), astronomy, arithmetic, and music, were distinguished as the arts of liberty or the life of freedom, the political freedom of the citizens or ruling class and the economic freedom of the leisured to engage themselves in political, intellectual, or aesthetic activity. They were the arts (in contrast with the "servile" or mechanical) that freed man from the ignorance to which the slave was condemned by the conditions of economic production to perform his primitive labors.

Religion played an increasingly perfunctory role as classical culture developed, except in times of public crisis. At their height the pagan civilizations of the northern and eastern Mediterranean treated their gods ceremonially, as symbolic representations of the state and its prowess; and the symbolic representations of the state, in turn, were deified. The golden eagles of the Roman legions "were placed in a chapel in the camp," says Gibbon, "and with the other deities received the religious worship of the troops." Of course mythology — combining religion and education — was integral to the education of the child. But theology as we know it was nonexistent, and philosophy had no concern with the antics of the gods.

Far from repudiating the Greco-Roman construction of education — based on the liberal arts — the early Greek Fathers of the Church, such as Clement and Origen, regarded Christianity as a kind of ultimate philosophy. An uneducated man might be a Christian, but liberal education was the means of actually understanding the mysteries of faith. Even Augustine and Jerome advocated the liberal arts, whose ends were worldly, insisting only that they be subordinated to the Christian life, whose ends were other than worldly. It was not until the Middle Ages that the cleavage between the two objectives was sharpened into a revulsion against the intellectualism of pagan education isolated from Christian faith. But the liberal arts, preserved through the Dark Ages in the monasteries, were never rejected; with a religious foundation beneath them, they continued to dominate the medieval curriculum as they had the classical. The continuity of Western education was not interrupted by the religiously oriented schooling of medieval Christendom.

The Renaissance broke the religious pattern of the Middle Ages but not the educational continuum that began in Greece and Rome. On the contrary; re-emphasizing the secular ends of classical humanism, the Renaissance accepted the education of antiquity, rejecting only the aim of the service of the state as it rejected the medieval aim of the service of God. But the schools — such as they were — were rooted in the church, and, in spite of the progressive secularization of the university curriculum and the opening of schools under civil control in the Hanseatic towns in the fifteenth and sixteenth centuries, nearly all schooling remained in the care of the churches for another three hundred years. The churches, originally interested in augmenting the priesthood, always provided an educational opportunity for a limited number of poor boys; such a purpose in part motivated the establishment of Winchester, Eton, and St. Paul's in England between the fourteenth and sixteenth centuries. But the motivation was soon lost or submerged, and the schools became aristocratic. Education remained, from the Renaissance to the second quarter of the nineteenth century, in America no less than in Europe, the prerogative of the advantaged few, its graduates trained for the highest affairs, its basic content that of late antiquity plus religion variously emphasized in various periods.

To say that education remained substantially the same for twenty-five centuries is not to say that there was unanimity in educational philosophy. Nor does it mean that great variations, in both theory and practice, did not appear from place to place and from time to time at the level of the organization of schooling or its duration, the method of instruction, or the exact content of the curriculum. Nearly all the great contributors to educational thought and action disagreed in respect to one or another of these issues. But they agreed on the fundamental convictions which maintained the continuity, from age to age, of the insights of Greece and Rome.

There were exceptions, of course, among educational philosophers, but the marvel is that among men whose general philosophies were incompatible (men like Aristotle, Augustine, Montaigne, Erasmus, and Benjamin Franklin) there were so few dissents from the prevailing philosophy of education. The list of exceptions is pretty well exhausted by Rousseau's emphasis upon naturalism and the cultivation of the instincts and, less radically if no less prophetically, by Locke's and Spencer's advocacy of vocational training in connection with general schooling and Bacon's plans for intensive specialization at the university level. But these dissents did not seriously affect educational practice during the centuries in which they were voiced; they have appeared in general practice only during the last hundred years.

The common practice — and the common theory — of every age preceding our own reduces, in summary, to five fundamental concepts. Upon these the institution of education rested undisturbed in Western history up to the middle of the last century.

First, the aim of education is the cultivation of the individual's capacities for mental growth and moral development. It is intended to help him acquire the intellectual techniques and aesthetic sensibilities, the knowledge, understanding, and wisdom requisite for a good human life spent publicly in political and professional action and privately in the worthiest use of leisure. As a secondary function, which it shares with other institutions, it concerns itself with the training of the body and the maturation of the emotions; this last objective (inculcated in part by rational emphasis on the "golden mean" and in part by discipline and personal concern) is viewed as a contribution to moral development. Specifically Christian education, of course, orients all these temporal objectives to the life of grace.

It was thought, in the second place, that basic schooling, given these objectives, must be "liberal" education. The corollaries of this concept were, generally, that basic schooling is the same for all who go to school, with due allowance for the varying dispositions of the normal individual; that training in the particular skills required for productive tasks is outside the area of basic schooling and is best acquired by apprenticeship; and that specialized education, after the completion of basic schooling, is to be given in only those vocations that are essentially liberal in character — namely, the learned professions.

Third, it was thought that education does not end with the completion of schooling, even of professional schooling, but, rather, that the pursuit of knowledge involves the effort of a lifetime and is one of the principal activities of those with time for leisure-work. Adult education was rarely discussed as such, partly because the stages of schooling were not so sharply defined by age level as they are now and partly, no doubt, because its pursuit, among the leisured few, was (correctly or incorrectly) assumed. But it was explicitly maintained that only the beginning of education can occur in youth because of the limitations intrinsic to immaturity and the limitations of any subject matter appropriate to immature study. To Seneca's dictum that "an old man who has still to learn his lessons is a shameful and ridiculous object; training and preparation are for the young, action for the old," Aristotle replies (three hundred years earlier!) that child prodigies may be found in mathematics and harmony, but never in morals or politics, which require the experience of life for their comprehension.

The fourth fundamental concept of education down the ages was that the profession of teaching is not only a learned profession, involving special preparation in the liberal arts and the skill of transmitting them, but also a profession of learning, in which the teacher not only practices his art but improves it by the continuous study of the subject he teaches. The teacher is a lifelong learner.

Finally, the advancement of learning, upon which the vitality of education in any society depends, requires scholarship, or investigation and research, apart from the dissemination and acquisition of the learning already available; and scholarship is likely to flourish in a community of scholars (whether or not they are organized as the faculties of educational institutions) cooperating and communicating across the separate fields of learning which, since their common goal is truth, are implicitly related to one another.

These concepts are enumerated as five for the sake of discussion here; they might be condensed or extended. What is important is that, historically, they represent together the basic principles of educational theory and practice of every epoch preceding our own. They were education's answers to the questions asked of it by the social situation of twenty-five pre-scientific and pre-technological centuries, in which what was required of education was to produce a small class of educated men. The differences and disagreements which arose in theory and in practice occurred within the general framework of these suppositions.

The fact that almost all educators and educational philosophers concurred in these general principles does not establish their validity. The fact that it was Cicero or Aquinas or Kant — or all of them together — who held these views does not mean that they were right. What it does mean is that they were held, and nearly universally held, by the best minds we have known from age to age. They do not, for that reason, command our assent, but they do command, in the name of common humility, our consideration.

Anyone who undertakes to judge their validity — for their time and place — has to consider one stupendous historical fact: These are the principles upon which the men responsible for our culture were educated, generation after generation, century after century. They are the principles upon which Plato taught Aristotle in Athens and Mentor Graham taught Abraham Lincoln in Sangamon County, Illinois. For better or for worse, this is the outline of the education which (to whatever extent education civilizes) gave us our civilization.

Among these thinkers, for all their agreement, the effectiveness of education as a civilizing agency was moot, as it still is and, it seems probable, as it always will be. The question asked in the first recorded discussion of education has not been answered: "Can you tell me, Socrates, whether virtue is acquired by teaching or by practice . . . or in what other way?" Schooling, which is what we are here concerned with, is only a part of the civilizing (or educational) process; it is that part dealing formally and primarily with the cultivation of the mind and only indirectly with the formation or fortification of moral character.

The Platonic adage that "the city educates the man" sobers the enthusiast for more and better schooling. There are other forces at work — the home, the church, the organization of society and the form of government (and the government itself), the streets and the playgrounds, and in a modern society the newspapers, magazines, and books(including comic books), and the cinema, the radio, and the television screen. These, too, are educational agencies in the general sense of the term. So are the economic order and the conditions of labor, housing, diet, and medical care. So are the genes and chromosomes; we are the omnibuses, said Oliver Wendell Holmes, in which our ancestors ride, and sometimes one of them sticks his head out the window and makes a terrible fuss. The school — in a word — is just *one* contributor to the education of men.

Of this particular institution the free man is the end product. While there are certainly such men who have not been schooled, the purpose of liberal education is to contribute to the production of such a man. We may agree that moral training is central to the development of the free man, but whether such training is within the primary competence of the institution of secular education is arguable; not, however, here. What is unarguable — at least historically — is that the direct and overt objective of liberal education is the liberation of the intellect from ignorance and its cultivation as a critical instrument.

The wisest men of whom we have record agreed generally that the principles upon which education was conducted up to a century ago better fulfilled the limited objective of such education than any other principle or set of principles. Were we living today in one of the many societies in which they lived, we might follow their consensus with confidence. But we are not. We are living in a society which none of these men of imagination ever imagined.

However imperfectly the ideal of universal suffrage is realized in the United States — and it is realized more perfectly every day — its embodiment in the basic law of the land makes "every man a king," every American adult the sovereign ruler of the state, holding, like the king he is, its highest and only permanent office, that of citizen. But the king must be educated, and he must be educated to rule. A truly democratic state without compulsory education at public expense would be an anomaly. Universal education is an inescapable corollary of universal suffrage.

With the emancipation of the chattel slaves came their enfranchisement a few years later. With their enfranchisement came the desperate necessity to convert them from their condition of general illiteracy to one of adequate education. Southern demagogues — and many other men, thoroughly sincere — argued against emancipation on the ground that, even if slavery were morally indefensible, the country would not survive the ravages of uneducated freedmen at the polls, and on this point the Great Emancipator agreed with them. Nor would it have, for long; the freedman had to be given the educational opportunity of a ruler.

In 1920 almost half the adults in the United States became, for the first time, full citizens: the women. They had, of course, played a progressively freer role in society for a century, and their status was reflected in the changed character of "female education," which was steadily becoming indistinguishable from that of the adolescent male. In all ages past, women, along with slaves, had been foreclosed from liberal education. In Jefferson's time no American college admitted them. The first college for women (Wesleyan Female College, in Macon, Georgia) and the first college to become coeducational (Oberlin College, in Ohio) have the same founding date — 1837. Previously, girls of the wealthy class were instructed by private tutor or in seminaries or finishing schools in reading, writing, and ciphering for household management, in cooking, needlework, and music, and sometimes in the care of minor medical emergencies in the home. Since the adoption of the Nineteenth Amendment and the removal of the last disabled segment of our people from political ineligibility, the lines between "male" and "female" education have disappeared.

It took almost two centuries to establish in this country the principle of free education for every future citizen and almost a century more before our people agreed that schooling had to be the full-time occupation of the child and that even eight years of elementary education were sufficient for his preparation for intelligent citizenship and the blessings of private life. But then the change was rapid. In 1875 there were only 500 high schools in the United States, and in 1900 this country had a smaller proportion of its population in school than any country of western Europe except Italy. But in 1925 there were 16,000 high schools, and in 1950, 71.3 per cent of all American children between fourteen and seventeen years of age were in school. In 1900 there were about 500,000 boys and girls in all the high schools of this country, or about 10 per cent of those who were eligible. Today there are over 7,000,000 or approximately 85 per cent of all the children between fourteen and seventeen years of age. No other country attempts to give secondary schooling to more than 20 per cent of its youth.

The school-leaving age rises every year now; today almost as many high-school graduates go on to college as do not. Under conditions of advanced industrial production, the campaign for child-labor laws and a child-labor amendment to the Constitution has subsided, except in very limited areas; mechanization, which in its early stages produced the frightful torture of children in factories, mills, and mines, has finally produced, in anything like normal conditions, an adult-labor "surplus" that makes child labor unnecessary even in nonmoral terms. Automation promises to make the whole adult population "surplus labor" in increasing degree. Under present and presently projected conditions of industry, it is economically possible from a manpower standpoint for compulsory basic schooling to be lengthened to a fourteen- or even sixteen-year period; the absorption of eighteen-year-olds into the peacetime army did not retard production.

Along with the reduction of labor time, the industrial economy has vitiated the age-old distinction between a leisured class and a laboring class. With exceptions that are rapidly becoming spectacular, every adult is both a worker and a man of leisure. Not only are the idle rich disappearing, but it is not in the least uncommon, where the five-day week prevails, to find the employer working longer hours than his employees. What is more, under public and private pension systems the employer is likelier than his employee to go on working in his advanced age. The divisions of American society today — and no one supposes that the direction of change will be reversed — are no longer divisions into distinct classes. They are, rather, a division of the time of every adult into distinct activities — those of labor and those of leisure, the one devoted to wealth or the goods of subsistence, the other devoted to the creation of civilization or the goods of the human spirit.

The increase of time available for leisure activities with the shortening of the work day, the work week, and the work years has opened the possibility of continuing education to almost every adult who wants it. The adult-education movement in this country once had two primary purposes — first (still common in Europe), to provide opportunity for adults to make up for insufficient basic schooling in childhood; second, to orient non-English-speaking immigrants. With the lengthening of the period of compulsory education and the closing of mass immigration, there is less and less need for compensatory or orientation schooling for adults. Adult education tends now to become the kind of education which sustains and advances learning after adequate basic schooling has been completed in youth.

With the political, productive, and scientific revolution of the past century fully developed, the problems of education in mid-twentieth-century America can be seen by examining the realities of the present against the background of one fairly reliable assumption about the past, the assumption that the traditional principles of education (enumerated above) were valid for an undemocratic, nonindustrial, and pre-scientific society. Acceptance of this assumption leads at once to the two questions upon which the discussion of our present problems may be sharply focused: Are the traditional principles valid for a modern industrial democracy, with, of course, such adaptations as contemporary circumstances indicate? And if they are not, what is now to be the meaning of education and its fundamental aim and procedure? The serious educational controversies of the last two or three generations — the generations that have begun to feel the full impact of the great change in society — have revolved around these two questions.

If the traditional principles are valid, and by one or another means adaptable to modern conditions, certain subordinate questions are immediately raised. Do we know how to apply them so that what was once the education of the few can be made the education of all? Can the teacher, under the increased pressures of the modern profession and of modern life, be expected to go on learning? Can the community of scholars that was once thought to be an indispensable condition for the advancement of learning coexist with intense specialization in an era of science and technology?

And if the traditional principles are held to have been valid under past historical conditions, but no longer, to what criteria are we to turn for the judgment of alternative principles? What is the ideal to be substituted for the liberal education of the few who were to be free and responsible citizens, when every man and woman is to be free and responsible? What kind of men and women (in so far as education contributes to their development) do we want in order to maintain and perfect the kind of society we want, and how may education proceed to contribute to their development?

The extremist view — that the traditional principles were invalid even for their own time and irrelevant and even misleading for ours — is matched at the other extreme by the view that the traditional principles of education can be applied whole, without amendment or adaptation, to our new kind of society. This view, like its equal and opposite, is rarely advanced in contemporary discussion. In between, the two more moderate positions more or less adequately embrace those who have made a sustained and conscientious effort to think about education for our time.

Each of the two moderate positions has a different obstacle to overcome. The first, or traditionalist, position must discover and formulate the means whereby the same quality of liberal education that was once the privilege of the few can be extended to all, both in school and (given the advance of leisure) in adult life. The second, or nontraditionalist, position must redefine the aims of education to conform to the realities of an industrial democracy in an age of science, but without making it any less appropriate for all the men who are now citizens and men of leisure than the education of past ages was for the ruling few of the leisure class.

As we examine current educational controversy of an earnest — rather than a polemical — nature, we are likely to find that the two moderate positions are not wholly irreconcilable. This does not mean that there are not basic disagreements among the protagonists. It means only that their disagreements might be more manageable if they were seen in the light of their common rejection of both the extremist positions. Unfortunately, the educational literature of the last fifty years has, in bulk, tended to foist each of the appropriate extremes upon each of the moderate positions. The consequence has been more conflict than controversy. The character of the conflict has not only obscured the real issues; it has diverted attention from them, and especially the attention of each side from the difficulties of its own position. The chance of surmounting these difficulties — and of solving the problems of education in a scientific and industrial democracy — might be greater if the problems themselves could be clarified. . . .

The real differences in philosophy of education in our time are the consequence of the social revolution of 1850–1950. In the face of that revolution education could not continue in its historic forms. It could not, and it did not. The forms fell apart, or were burst by the forces generated by the democratic, industrial, and scientific revolution in America. Education went on, in any and every which way. Both of the moderate positions in the current controversy call for principled reforms in the prevalent practices of the schools, and for this reason both of them are opposed, or, rather, blindly rejected, by those (not all of whom are outside the field of education) who do not wish to be disturbed.

But they are being disturbed, willy-nilly. Parents are challenging the popular practices — or demanding to know exactly what they are and what they are for. Civic organizations are challenging them. Even pupils are, in their own often inarticulate way, challenging them by "delinquent" behavior. In the midst of the hullabaloo, harried schoolmen, who did not bargain for all the criticism the schools are getting, are heard saying plaintively that they have troubles enough without being asked, "Why?" and "What for?" The motto of all old institutions is, "Don't rock the boat." A distinguished Englishman once said that in educational reform the time is never ripe until it is rotten.

There is another, perhaps more tangible if less potent, source of opposition to both moderate positions. The traditionalists and the nontraditionalists accept the revolution of the past century and welcome it. They stand together against those who do not, against those who think either that democratic government is wrong or that the dispersion of the fruits of technology and industrial production, in the form of higher living standards and increasing leisure for the whole of our people, is deplorable. Democracy and mechanization of labor are here, and they are here together. Whatever their shortcomings in practice, they present the human race for the first time in human history with the possibility of the good life for all men and the equitable organization of human society.

The demands which modern democracy makes upon education cannot be avoided. To meet these demands in our own country — the most radically transformed of all modern societies — educational philosophers cannot bicker indefinitely. The problems are critical, and they must be faced with a view to their resolution in the best interests of our country and its people and their form of government and their aspirations. Businessmen and poets can, if they are financially independent, refine their techniques to their hearts' content before they go into production. Educators cannot; they are "producing" members of society whether or not they are ready to.

There is more, much more, at stake in educational controversy than the preservation of a point of view at any cost or the maintenance of prestige and position in an area of argument which, perhaps because educators are so often on the defensive in an activist culture, sometimes degenerates into polysyllabic fishwifery. Education needs to know what it is doing and why, and to be aggressive about it. "The keystone of the arch of our government," Jefferson called it. What the thinking of the past was able, at its best, to do for society of some, the thinking of the present must try to do for society of all.

Hugh of St. Victor

Hugh of St. Victor was a Christian mystic of the twelfth century who headed the school of the monastery of St. Victor in Paris. Under his supervision the school became a center of learning. Medieval education owed much of its philosophical foundation to Plato and Aristotle, and the following selection by the French schoolmaster embraces the Aristotelian plan of a liberal arts core that is taught to all students, regardless of their intended vocation.

Although Hugh of St. Victor was bitterly opposed to the rationalistic philosophy of Abélard, a rival teacher, his writing on education reveals respect for the notably rationalistic spirit of classical humanism. Commenting on a variety of educational problems and principles, Hugh of St. Victor has provided the modern reader with an excellent summary of traditional concepts wedded to medieval scholasticism. He died in 1141.

18

ON STUDY AND TEACHING*

There are many whom nature itself has left so deficient in intelligence that they are scarcely able to grasp intellectually even those things which are easy, and of these, it seems, there are two sorts. For there are some who, although they are not ignorant of their dullness, nevertheless strive eagerly for knowledge, with all the effort of which they are capable. And they incessantly sweat in study, so that what they might have less as a result of labour, they seem to achieve by an act of will. But there are others who, since they feel themselves unable by any means to comprehend the most difficult things, neglect the least; and as if resting secure in their own torpor, the more they avoid learning those lesser things which they can understand, the more they lose the light of truth in the greatest things. As the Psalmist says, "They do not wish to know so that they may do well." For not to know something is far different from not wanting to know something, since not to know is a weakness, but to detest knowledge is a perversion of the will.

There is another kind of men whom nature has to a great degree enriched intellectually and to whom nature has given an easy access to truth. Although intellectual power may be equal in all, yet the same virture or will has not been given to all of them to cultivate the natural intellect through exercises and learning. For there are many who, engrossed in the business and cares of the world beyond what is necessary, or abandoned to the vices and pleasures of the body, bury the talent of God in the earth, and seek from it neither the fruit of wisdom nor the profit of good work, and these indeed are most detestable men. Again, for others the lack of resources and little means lessen the possibility of learning. But we believe that it is not possible to pardon them fully for this reason, since we may see many labouring in hunger, thirst, and nakedness to attain the fruit of knowledge. It is one thing when you cannot learn, or to speak more truly, cannot *easily* learn, and another when you are able, and do not wish to know. For just as it is more glorious, with no facilities at hand, to attain wisdom by excellence alone, so it is more shameful to be vigorous in mind, to abound in riches, and to grow torpid in laziness. . . .

Philosophy is divided into the theoretical, the practical, the mechanical,

* From *Didascalicon*, C. H. Buttimer, ed. (Washington, D.C.: The Catholic University of America Press, 1939). Used by permission of The Catholic University of America Press, Washington.

and the logical. Theory is divided into theology, physics, and mathematics. Mathematics includes arithmetic, music, and geometry. Practical philosophy is divided into the solitary, the private, and the public [i.e., ethics, economics, and politics]. The mechanical arts include spinning, arms-making, navigation, agriculture, hunting, medicine, and the theatrical art. Logic includes grammar and expression; there are two kinds of expression, probable and sophistical demonstration. Probable demonstration is divided into dialectic and rhetoric. In this division, only the chief parts of philosophy are contained; there are still other subdivisions of these parts, but the parts can suffice for now. As to these, if you have regard only for number, there are twenty-one; if you wish to compute stages, you will find thirty-eight. Different authors are read in these fields of knowledge; some show how to begin the arts, others, how to advance in them, and others, how to perfect them. . . .

Among all the sciences enumerated above, however, the ancients settled on seven especially in their own studies, for the work of teaching. In these seven, they perceived that there was greater utility than in the others, so that anyone who would firmly comprehend the discipline of these would afterwards, by investigating and practising diligently more than by listening, attain a knowledge of the others. For they are, as it were, the best instruments and the best beginnings, by which the way is prepared in the mind for the full knowledge of philosophical truth. Hence they are called the *trivium* and *quadrivium*, since by these roads, so to speak, the lively mind may enter the secret places of wisdom.

In those former times, no one seemed worthy of the name of master who could not profess the knowledge of these seven. Pythagoras [of Samos, 6th century B.C.] is said to have observed this custom in his schools, that for seven years, according to the number of the seven liberal arts, none of his pupils should dare to ask the reason for anything which was said by him. But the pupil should put his trust in the master's words until he had heard everything, and thus he could then discover the reason for things by himself. Certain ones are said to have learned these seven arts with such great zeal, and kept them all so firmly in memory, that, whatever writings they then took in hand, whatever questions they proposed for solution or proof, they did not seek the pages of books, but had instantly ready by heart, one by one, rules and reasons from the liberal arts, to define whatever was in dispute. Hence it happened at that time that there were so many wise men that they wrote more books than we are able to read.

But our scholars either do not wish or are not able to observe a suitable method of learning, and for that reason we find many students, but few learned men. It seems to me, indeed, that not less care should be taken lest the student expend his labour on unprofitable studies, than lest he should remain lukewarm in a good and useful plan. It is bad to carry out a good plan negligently, it is worse to expend much labour in vain. But since not all can have enough discretion to know what is good for them, I shall briefly show the student which writings seem to me more useful, and then I shall add something also on the method of learning.

There are two kinds of writings. The first kind consists of those which are properly called arts. The second comprises those which are appendages of the arts. The arts are those which are placed under philosophy, that is, which contain definite and established material of philosophy, such as grammar, dialectic, and others of that sort. Appendages of the arts are those which only look at philosophy, that is, they are concerned with material which is outside philosophy; yet sometimes they touch, in a spotty and confused manner, on certain fragments of the arts, or, to put it simply, they prepare the way to philosophy. Of this kind are all the songs of the poets, like tragedies, comedies, satires, heroic, lyric, iambic poetry, and certain didactic works, also stories and histories, and the writings of those whom we are accustomed to call philosophers, who are wont to stretch out a little matter with long circumlocutions, and to obscure plain sense with confused phrases. They also bring together diverse things, as if to make a single picture out of many colours and shapes. Note the distinction I have made for you. The arts and the appendages of the arts are two things. It seems to me that there is as great a distance between these two as that described in the lines: "The sluggish willow yields to the pale olive, as the humble wild nard to a garden of red roses" [Virgil, *Eclog.* v.]. Thus if anyone who wishes to attain to knowledge abandons the truth and wants to entangle himself in the remnants of the arts, he will bear not only great but infinite labour, and scanty fruit.

Finally, the arts without their appendages are able to make a perfect scholar, but the appendages without the arts can confer no perfection, especially, moreover, since they possess nothing desirable in themselves which may attract the reader, unless it has been taken over and adapted from the arts, and no one will seek in them anything except what belongs to the arts. For this reason it seems to me that effort should first of all be devoted to those arts which are the foundations of all, and where pure and simple truth is revealed, especially to those seven which I have mentioned, which are the instruments of all of philosophy. Then, if there is time, the others may be read, since sometimes the playful mingled with the serious is wont to delight more, and rarity makes a good thing precious. Thus we sometimes more eagerly retain a maxim which is found in the middle of a tale. Nevertheless, the foundation of all learning is in the seven liberal arts, which beyond all others should be kept at hand, since without them philosophic discipline does not or cannot explain or define anything.

These arts indeed are so closely connected, and are each in turn so dependent on the principles of the others, that if one is lacking, the others are not able to mould the philosopher. Therefore, it seems to me that those err who, not paying attention to such coherence in the arts, select for themselves certain of these arts, and leaving the others untouched, think that they can perfect themselves in those which they have chosen.

There is again another error not much less serious than this, which is very much to be avoided. For there are some who, although they pass over nothing in their reading, yet do not know how to attribute to any art what is proper to it, but read all into each of them. In grammar they dispute concerning the meaning of syllogisms, in dialetic they investigate "case" endings, and what is more worthy of ridicule, they read almost a whole book in its title, and by the third lecture, they have scarcely got beyond the "incipit." They do not thus teach others, but they display their own learning. But would that they appeared to others as they seem to me! Look how perverse this custom would be, if indeed the more you collected superfluities, the less you would be able to hold or to retain those things which are useful.

In each art, therefore, two things especially should be discerned and distinguished by us. First, how one should practise the art itself, and second, how one should apply the principles of that art to any other matters. These are two different things: to practise an art, and to do something else by means of an art. For the sake of an example of practising an art, take grammar. He practises the art of grammar, who treats of the rules concerning the use of words, and the precepts relating to this. Everyone who speaks or writes in accordance with rules acts grammatically. It is therefore suitable only for certain writers, like Priscian, Donatus, Servius, and the like, to practise the art of grammar. But it befits everyone to speak or write grammatically.

When therefore we are occupied with any art, especially in teaching it, when everything should be restricted and confined to what is brief and easy to understand, it should suffice to explain that which we are dealing with as briefly and aptly as possible, lest, if we should multiply irrelevant ideas to excess, we should confuse rather than edify the student. Not everything should be said which we are able to say, lest those things which we should say are said less profitably. In every art, then, you should seek that which has been established as pertaining especially to that art. Then when you are lecturing on the arts and recognize something in any one of them which is appropriate for disputation and discussion, it will be permissible to apply reciprocally the principles of each, and by considering each in turn to investigate those which you have formerly understood less well. Do not multiply the byways until you have learned the highways. You will travel safely when you are not afraid of making mistakes.

Three things are necessary for study: nature, exercise, discipline. By nature is meant that what is heard is easily understood, and that which has been understood is firmly retained. By exercise is meant that the natural capacity for understanding is cultivated by labour and application. By discipline is meant that the student who lives in praiseworthy manner joins morals to knowledge. Let us touch briefly by way of introduction on each of these three. . . .

Those who are devoted to learning should be strong in both intelligence and memory; these two are so closely joined together in every study and discipline, that if one of them is lacking, the other can lead no one to perfection, just as no riches can be of use, where safekeeping is lacking. And he keeps hiding places in vain who has nothing to hide. Natural intelligence discovers, and memory safeguards wisdom. Intelligence is a certain natural power innate in the mind, and is powerful in itelf. It springs from nature, is blunted by immoderate labour, and is sharpened by temperate exercise. . . . There are two things which exercise natural capacity, reading and meditation. Reading is when we are informed by the rules and precepts in the writings which we read. There are three kinds of reading, for teaching, for learning, and reading for its own sake. For we say, "I read a book to that person," and "I read a book by that person," and, simply, "I read a book." In reading, order and method are especially to be considered.

Order means one thing in disciplines, as when I speak of grammar as more ancient than dialectic, or arithmetic as prior to music, and another in books, as when I say the Catalinarian before the Jugurthine [orations of Sallust], and another in narration which is in a continuous series, and still another in exposition. Order in disciplines is according to nature; in books, according to the character of the author, or the subject matter. In narration it is according to orderly arrangement, which is twofold: natural, that is, when a thing is related in the order in which it was done, and artificial, when that which happened later is told first, and that which happened first is told later. In exposition we consider order according to inquiry. Exposition consists in three things: the letter, the sense, and the conception. By the letter is meant the suitable arrangement of words, which we also call construction. The sense is a certain easy and evident meaning, which is manifested by the letter at first glance. The conception is a deeper meaning, which is found neither in exposition nor interpretation. In these things order consists in seeking first the letter, then the sense, and finally the conception. When this is done, the exposition is perfect.

Method in reading consists in dividing. All division begins with the finite and progresses to the infinite. Everything finite, moreover, is better known, and is comprehensible to knowledge. Learning then begins from these things which are better known, and through a knowledge of them attains a knowledge of those which are hidden. Further, we investigate by means of reason, and it properly pertains to reason to divide, when, by dividing, and by investigating the natures of individual things, we descend from universals to particulars. For every universal is better determined by its own particulars. Therefore when we learn, we ought to begin from those things which are better known and determined and comprehended, and thus, by descending little by little and distinguishing individual things by means of division, investigate the nature of those things which are related.

Meditation is frequent and planned cogitation, which prudently investigates the cause and origin, the method and usefulness, of anything. Meditation has its beginning in reading, yet it is not constrained by any rules and precepts of reading. For it is delightful to have recourse to a certain suitable distance, where a free vision is possible for the contemplation of truth, and sometimes to touch lightly now these and then those causes of things, and sometimes to penetrate into them more deeply, and to leave nothing uncertain, and nothing obscure. The beginning of learning, therefore, is in reading, its consummation is in meditation. If anyone learns to love it intimately, and wants to have time for it more often, it bestows an exceedingly pleasant life, and offers the greatest consolation in time of trouble. For that is best which removes the spirit from the clash of earthly tumults, and also makes it possible in a certain sense to taste in this life the sweetness of everlasting peace. And then through those things which have been created, one will learn to seek and to know Him who created all things; then, equally, knowledge will instruct and joy will fill the mind. And thus it is that the greatest solace is in meditation. . . .

As to memory, I think it should not at present be forgotten that just as intelligence investigates and discovers by means of division, so memory safeguards the results by bringing them together. It is necessary, then, that what we have separated in learning, we should bring together to be committed to memory. To bring together means to make a short and concise summary of those things which in writing and discussion are more prolix; this the ancients called an "epilogue," that is, a brief recapitulation of what has been said before. For every treatment of a subject has some beginning on which the whole truth of the matter and the power of judgment depends, and to this everything else is referred. To seek out and to consider this is to bring things together. There is one fount, and many rivulets; why do you follow the windings of the streams? Reach the fount, and you have it all. I say this because man's memory is sluggish, and rejoices in brevity, and if it is dispersed among many things, it does less well in particulars. We ought, then, in all learning to collect something brief and certain, which may be hidden in the secret places of the memory, whence afterward, when it is necessary, the rest may be derived. It is necessary to repeat this often, and to recall the taste from the belly of the memory to the palate, lest, by long interruption, it should fall into disuse. Therefore I beg you, reader, not to rejoice too greatly if you have read much, but if you have understood much, nor that you have understood much, but that you have been able to retain it. Otherwise it is of little profit either to read or to understand. For this reason I repeat what I have said above, that those who give labour to learning need natural capacity and memory.

When a certain wise man [Bernard of Chartres] was asked what is the method and form of learning, he replied, "A humble mind, zeal for inquiry, a quiet life, silent investigation, poverty, and a foreign land: these are wont to reveal to many what is obscure in their reading." I think that he had heard the saying, "Manners adorn knowledge," and so he joined together precepts for study and precepts for living, so that the reader may perceive both the manner of his own life and the meaning of study. Knowledge is unworthy of praise when it is strained by a shameless life. Therefore, he who seeks knowledge should take the greatest care not to neglect discipline.

Humility is the beginning of discipline, and although there are many examples of this, these three especially are important to the reader: first, that he should hold no knowledge and no writing cheap; second, that he should not be ashamed to learn from anyone; third, that when he himself will have attained knowledge, he should not scorn others. This has deceived many, who wished to seem wise prematurely. Hence they swell up with self-importance, so that now they begin to pretend to be what they are not, and to be ashamed of what they are, and thus they withdraw further from wisdom, because they wish, not to be wise, but to be considered wise. I have known many of this sort, who, while they are still lacking in the first elements, deign to interest themselves only in the most advanced, and on this account they think that they themselves have become great, if only they have read the writings, or heard the words of the great and wise. "We," they say, "have seen them; we have read their works; they often speak to us; those distinguished, those famous men know us." But would that no one recognized me, if I might know everything! You glory in having seen Plato, not in having understood him; I think then that it is not worthy of you to listen to me. I am not Plato, nor do I deserve to see Plato. It is enough for you that you have drunk at the fount of philosophy, but would that you were still thirsty! A king drinks from an earthen pot after he has drunk from a cup of gold. What are you ashamed of? You have heard Plato, you will also hear Chrysippus. As the proverb says: "What you do not know, perhaps Ofellus knows." It is given to no one to know everything, and yet there is no one who has not received from nature something peculiar to himself. The prudent scholar, therefore, hears everyone freely, reads everything, and rejects no book, no person, no doctrine. He seeks from all indifferently what he sees is lacking in himself; he considers not how much he may know, but how much he may not know. Hence the Platonic saying: "I prefer to learn modestly from another, rather than shamelessly to thrust forward my own knowledge." Why are you ashamed to learn and not ashamed to be ignorant? This is more shameful than that. Or why do you strive for the heights, when you are lying in the depths? Consider rather what your powers are strong enough to bear. He advances most suitably who proceeds in an orderly way. When some desire to make a great leap, they fall into the abyss. Do not, therefore, hasten too fast, and thus you will more quickly achieve wisdom. Learn gladly from everyone what you do not know, since humility can make that yours which nature made the possession of someone else. You will be wiser than everyone, if you will learn from everyone. Those who receive from everyone are richer than anyone. Finally, hold no knowledge cheap, since all knowledge is good. If there is time, scorn no writing, or at least read it, since if you gain nothing, you will lose nothing, especially as in my estimation there is no book which does not set forth something to be desired. If it is treated in an appropriate place and order, there is none which does not have something special, which the diligent reader has found nowhere else. The rarer it is, the more gratefully it should be enjoyed. Yet there is nothing good which is not made better.

If you cannot read everything, read that which is more useful. Even if you can read everything, the same amount of labor should not be expended on all. But some things are to be read so that they may not be unknown, and some so that they may not be unheard of, since sometimes we believe that of which we have not heard to be of greater importance, and a thing is more easily judged when its results are known. You can see now how necessary for you this humility is, that you may hold no knowledge cheap, and may learn freely from all. Likewise it behooves you not to despise others when you begin to know something. This vice of arrogance takes possession of some so that they contemplate their own knowledge too lovingly, and since they seem to themselves to be something, they think that others whom they do not know can neither be nor become such as they. Hence also these peddlers of trifles, boasting I do not know of what, accuse their ancestors of simplicity, and believe that wisdom was born with them, and will die with them. They say that in sermons the manner of speaking is so simple that it is not necessary to listen to teachers in these matters, that each of them can penetrate the secrets of truth well enough by his own intelligence. They turn up their noses and make wry mouths at the lecturers in divinity, and they do not understand that they do God an injury, whose words are simple indeed in the beauty of their expression, but they proclaim stupidities with deformed sense. I do not advise imitating such as these. For the good student should be humble and gentle, a stranger to senseless cares and the enticements of pleasure; he should be diligent and zealous, so that he may learn freely from all. He is never presumptuous about his own knowledge, he shuns the authors of perverse teaching like poison, he learns to consider a matter for a long time before he makes a judgment, he knows or seeks not how to seem learned, but to be truly learned, he loves the words of the wise when they have been understood, and he strives to keep them always before his eyes, as a mirror in front of his face. And if perchance his understanding does not have access to the more obscure things, he does not immediately burst out into vituperation, believing that nothing is good unless he himself can understand it. This is the humility of the students' discipline.

Zeal for inquiry pertains to exercise, in which the student needs encouragement more than instruction. For he who will diligently examine what the ancients achieved because of their love of wisdom, and what monuments of their power they left to be remembered by posterity, will see how inferior is his own diligence. Some spurned honours, others threw away riches, some rejoiced when they received injuries, others scorned punishments, others, abandoning the society of men and penetrating the inmost recesses and secret places of the desert, dedicated themselves solely to philosophy, in order that they might have leisure for contemplating it more freely, because they did not subject their minds to any of those desires which are wont to obstruct the path of virtue. The philosopher Parmenides is said to have sat for fifteen years on a rock in Egypt, and Prometheus is remembered because of his excessive attention to meditation while he was exposed to the vultures on Mount Caucasus. For they knew that the true good is not concealed in the opinion of men, but in a pure conscience, and that those are not really men who, clinging to transitory things, do not recognize their own good. The ancients knew also how much they differed from the others in mind and in intelligence; the very remoteness of their dwellings shows that one habitation may not hold those who are not associated in the same purpose. A certain man once said to a philosopher, "Don't you see how men mock you?" And the philosopher answered, "They mock me and the asses deride them." Think, if you can, how much he valued being praised by those whose scorn he did not fear. Again, we read of another that, after the study of all disciplines and after reaching the heights of the arts, he descended to the potter's trade. And of still another that his disciples loaded their master with praises, and did not fail to boast of his skill as a shoemaker. I would desire such diligence, then, to be in our students, that in them wisdom should never grow old.

Abishag the Shunammite alone kept the old David warm, since the love of wisdom does not desert its lover even when the body grows feeble. Almost all virtues of the body change in the old, and while wisdom alone increases, the others decline. For in the old age of those who furnish their youth with honourable arts, they become more learned, more practised, wiser in the course of time, and reap the sweetest fruits of earlier studies. Whence also it is said that after that wise man of Greece, Themistocles, had lived one hundred and seven years, he saw that he was about to die, and said that he grieved because he had to abandon life just when he had begun to be wise. Plato died after eighty-one years, and Socrates filled ninety-nine years with teaching and writing and painful labour.[1] I say nothing of the other philosophers, Pythagoras, Democritus, Xenocrates, Zeno, and Eleatus, who flourished for a long time in the studies of wisdom.

I come now to the poets, Homer, Hesiod, Simonides, Tersilochus, who, when they were very old, sang their swan songs, I know not what, but sweeter than ever at the approach of death. When Sophocles, at a very great age and because of his neglect of family affairs was accused by his own family of madness, he recited to the judge that tale of Oedipus which he had written earlier, and gave so great an example of wisdom in his broken old age, that he converted the severity of his judges into acclamation of his performance. Nor is it to be wondered at that when Cato the Censor, the most eloquent of the Romans, took up the study of Greek as an old man, he was not ashamed, nor did he despair. Certainly Homer tells us that sweeter discourse flowed from the tongue of Nestor when he was an old and decrepit man. Behold, then, how much those men loved wisdom whom not even infirm old age could keep from its pursuit. . . .

The four remaining precepts which follow are so arranged, that, in alternation, one has regard to discipline and the other to practice.

Quietness of life is either interior, that the mind is not distracted by unlawful desires, or exterior, that leisure and opportunity suffice for honourable and useful studies. Both of these pertain to discipline.

But investigation, that is, meditation, pertains to practice. It seems, how-

[1] *Editor's Note:* Historians now believe that Socrates died in 399 B.C. at the age of 70.

ever, that investigation is included under the zeal for inquiry. If this is true, it is superfluous to repeat what has been said above. But it should be known that there is this difference between the two, that the zeal for inquiry means urgency of effort, but investigation, diligence in meditation. Labour and love complete a work, but care and vigilance bring forth counsel. You act in labour, you perfect in love, you prepare with care, and you are attentive in vigilance. These are the four footmen who bear the litter of Philology, since they exercise the mind in which wisdom rules. The chair of philology is the seat of wisdom, which is said to be carried by these bearers, since it advances by exercising itself in them. Therefore, the handsome youths, Philos and Kophos, that is, Labour and Love, because of their strength are said [Martianus Capella, *De nuptiis philologiae*, bk. II] to bear the litter in front, since they complete a work externally; and behind, the two maidens, Philemia and Agrimina, that is, Care and Vigilance, since they bring forth counsel within and in secret. There are some who think that by the chair of philology is meant the human body, which is governed by the rational mind, that four servants carry the body, that is, that it is composed of four elements. Of these, two are superior, that is, fire and air, masculine in name and in fact, but two are inferior and feminine, earth and water.

Frugality also should be recommended to students, that is, not to strive after superfluities; this is especially related to discipline. For, as it is said, a fat belly does not beget a keen mind. But what can the scholars of our time reply to this, who not only scorn frugality, but also strive richer than they are? Now no one boasts of what he has learned, but of what he has spent. But perhaps they do not want to imitate their own masters, concerning whom I have not discovered what I can say worthy of them.

Finally, a foreign land has been mentioned, which in itself exercises a man. The whole world is a place of exile to those who pursue philosophy. But yet, as someone says [Ovid, *Epistulae ex Pont.*, I, iii, 35], "I do not know what sweetness of the native land alone draws us all, and does not let us be unmindful of it." It is a great beginning of virtue that the trained mind should little by little first learn to change these visible and transitory things, so that afterwards it will be able to give them up entirely. He is still weak for whom his native land is sweet, but he is strong for whom every country is a fatherland, and he is perfect for whom the whole world is a place of exile. The first confirms his love for the world, the second disperses it, and the last extinguishes it. From boyhood, I have lived in exile, and I know with what grief the spirit sometimes deserts the narrow limits of the poor man's hut, and with what a sense of freedom it afterwards despises marble halls and panelled ceilings.

John Amos Comenius

The Great Didactic is a landmark in the history of education. Practical in approach, idealistic in scope, and comprehensive in organization, this monumental work by Comenius (1592–1671) presents concepts which have strongly influenced leaders and followers of Progressivism. Before it was published Comenius wrote, ". . . after many workings and tossings of my thoughts, by reducing everything to the immovable law of nature, I lighted upon my 'Great Didactic,' which shows the art of readily and solidly teaching all men all things." The gross ambition of his fervor notwithstanding, the stature of Comenius as an educational reformer is assured.

19

From THE GREAT DIDACTIC*

1. The seeds of knowledge, of virtue, and of piety are naturally implanted in us; but the actual knowledge, virtue, and piety are not so given. These must be acquired by prayer, by education, and by action. He gave no bad definition who said that man was a "teachable animal." And indeed it is only by a proper education that he can become a man.

2. All who have been born to man's estate have been born with the same end in view, namely, that they may be men, that is to say, rational creatures, the lords of other creatures, and the images of their Creator. All, therefore, must be brought on to a point at which, being properly imbued with wisdom, virtue, and piety, they may usefully employ the present life and be worthily prepared for that to come. God himself has frequently asserted that with him there is no respect of persons, so that if, while we admit some to the culture of the intellect, we exclude others, we commit an injury not only against those who share the same nature as ourselves, but against God him-

---

* Reprinted from *The Great Didactic* by John Amos Comenius (London: Adam and Charles Black, 1896).

self, who wishes to be acknowledged, to be loved, and to be praised by all upon whom he has impressed his image. In this respect the fervor of all men will increase in proportion to the flame of knowledge that has been kindled. For our love is in direct ratio to our knowledge.

3. Nor can any sufficient reason be given why the weaker sex (to give a word of advice on this point in particular) should be altogether excluded from the pursuit of knowledge, whether in Latin or in their mother-tongue. They also are formed in the image of God, and share in his grace and in the kingdom of the world to come. They are endowed with equal sharpness of mind and capacity for knowledge (often with more than the opposite sex), and they are able to attain the highest positions, since they have often been called by God himself to rule over nations, to give sound advice to kings and princes, to the study of medicine and of other things which benefit the human race, even to the office of prophesying and of inveighing against priests and bishops. Why, therefore, should we admit them to the alphabet, and afterwards drive them away from books? Do we fear their folly? The more we occupy their thoughts, so much the less will the folly that arises from emptiness of mind find a place.

4. Things themselves, as far as they concern us, can be divided into three classes only: 1, Objects that we can observe, such as the heavens, the earth, and all that is in them; 2, Objects that we can imitate, such as the marvelous order which pervades all things, and which man ought to imitate in his actions; 3, Objects that we can enjoy, such as the grace of God and his manifold blessing here and for eternity. If man is to acquit himself creditably when brought into contact with this order of nature, he must be trained to know the things that are spread out for his observation in this marvelous amphitheatre, to do the things that it is right for him to do, and finally, to enjoy those things of which the most benign Creator, treating him as a guest in his house, has with liberal hand given him the fruition.

5. I call a school that fulfils its function perfectly, one which is a true forging-place of men; where the minds of those who learn are illuminated by the light of wisdom, so as to penetrate with ease all that is manifest and all that is secret, where the emotions and the desires are brought into harmony with virtue, and where the heart is filled with and permeated by divine love, so that all who are handed over to Christian schools to be imbued with true wisdom, may be taught to live a heavenly life on earth; in a word, where all men are taught all things thoroughly.

*   *   *

The universal requirements of teaching and of learning; that is to say, a method of teaching and of learning with such certainty that the desired result must of necessity follow.

1. Exceptionally fine is that comparison made by our Lord Jesus Christ in the gospel, "So is the kingdom of God, as if a man should cast seed upon the

earth; and should sleep and rise night and day, and the seed should spring up and grow, he knoweth not how. The earth beareth fruit of herself; first the blade, then the ear, then the full corn in the ear. But when the fruit is ripe, straightway he putteth forth the sickle, because the harvest is come." (Mark iv. 26).

2. The Savior here shows that it is God who operates in everything, and that nothing remains for man but to receive the seeds of instruction with a devout heart; the processes of growth and of ripening will then continue of themselves, unperceived by him. The duty of the teachers of the young, therefore, is none other than skilfully to scatter the seeds of instruction in their minds, and carefully to water God's plants. Increase and growth will come from above.

3. Is there any who denies that sowing and planting need skill and experience? If an unpracticed gardener plant an orchard with young trees, the greater number of them die, and the few that prosper do so rather through chance than through skill. But the trained gardener goes to work carefully, since he is well instructed, where, when, and how to act and what to leave alone, that he may meet with no failure. It is true that even an experienced man meets with failure occasionally (indeed it is scarcely possible for a man to take such careful forethought that no error can arise); but we are now discussing, not the abstract question of circumspection and chance, but the art of doing away with chance by means of circumspection.

4. Hitherto the method of instruction has been so uncertain that scarcely any one would dare to say: "In so many years I will bring this youth to such and such a point, I will educate him in such and such a way." We must therefore see if it be possible to place the art of intellectual discipline on such a firm basis that sure and certain progress may be made.

5. Since this basis can be properly laid only by assimilating the processes of art as much as possible to those of nature, we will follow the method of nature, taking as our example a bird hatching out its young; and, if we see with what good results gardeners, painters, and builders follow in the track of nature, we shall have to recognize that the educator of the young should follow in the same path.

6. If any think this course of action petty or commonplace, let him consider that from that which is of daily occurrence and universal notoriety and which takes place with good results in nature and in the arts (the teaching art excepted), we are seeking to deduce that which is less known and which is necessary for our present purpose. Indeed, if the facts from which we derive the principles that form the basis for our precepts are known, we can entertain hopes that our conclusions will be the more evident.

First Principle

7. *Nature Observes a Suitable Time.* For example: a bird that wishes to multiply its species, does not set about it in winter, when everything is stiff with cold, nor in summer when everything is parched and withered by the

heat; nor in autumn, when the vital force of all creatures declines with the sun's declining rays, and a new winter with hostile mien is approaching; but in spring, when the sun brings back life and strength to all. Again, the process consists of several steps. While it is yet cold the bird conceives the eggs and warms them inside its body, where they are protected from the cold; when the air grows warmer it lays them in its nest, but does not hatch them out until the warm season comes, that the tender chicks may grow accustomed to light and warmth by degrees.

8. *Imitation.*   In the same way the gardener takes care to do nothing out of season. He does not, therefore, plant in the winter (because the sap is then in the roots, preparing to mount and nourish the plant later on); nor in summer (when the sap is already dispersed through the branches); nor in autumn (when the sap is retiring to the roots once more); but in spring, when the moisture is beginning to rise from the roots and the upper part of the plant begins to shoot. Later on, too, it is of great importance to the little tree that the right time be chosen for the various operations that are needful, such as manuring, pruning, and cutting. Even the tree itself has its proper time for putting forth shoots and blossoms, for growing, and for coming to maturity.

In the same manner the careful builder must choose the right time for cutting timber, burning bricks, laying foundations, building and plastering walls, etc.

9. *Deviation.*   In direct opposition to this principle, a twofold error is committed in schools.

(i.) The right time for mental exercise is not chosen.

(ii.) The exercises are not properly divided, so that all advance may be made through the several stages needful, without any omission. As long as the boy is still a child he cannot be taught, because the roots of his understanding are still too deep below the surface. As soon as he becomes old, it is too late to teach him, because the intellect and the memory are then failing. In middle age it is difficult, because the forces of the intellect are dissipated over a variety of objects and are not easily concentrated. The season of youth, therefore, must be chosen. Then life and mind are fresh and gathering strength; then everything is vigorous and strikes root deeply.

10. *Rectification.*   We conclude, therefore, that

(i.) The education of men should be commenced in the springtime of life, that is to say, in boyhood (for boyhood is the equivalent of spring, youth of summer, manhood of autumn, and old age of winter).

(ii.) The morning hours are the most suitable for study (for here again the morning is the equivalent of spring, midday of summer, the evening of autumn, and the night of winter).

(iii.) All the subjects that are to be learned should be arranged so as to suit the age of the students, that nothing which is beyond their comprehension be given them to learn.

Second Principle

11. *Nature Prepares the Material, Before She Begins to Give It Form.* For example: the bird that wishes to produce a creature similar to itself first conceives the embryo from a drop of its blood; it then prepares the nest in which it is to lay the eggs, but does not begin to hatch them until the chick is formed and moves within the shell.

12. *Imitation.* In the same way the prudent builder, before he begins to erect a building, collects a quantity of wood, lime, stones, iron, and the other things needful, in order that he may not have to stop the work later on from lack of materials, nor find that its solidity has been impaired. In the same way, the painter who wishes to produce a picture, prepares the canvas, stretches it on a frame, lays the ground on it, mixes his colors, places his brushes so that they may be ready to hand, and then at last commences to paint.

In the same way the gardener, before he commences operations, tries to have the garden, the stocks, the grafts, and the tools in readiness, that he may not have to fetch the necessary appliances while at work, and so spoil the whole operation.

13. *Deviation.* Against this principle schools are offenders: firstly, because they take no care to prepare beforehand the mechanical aids such as books, maps, pictures, diagrams, etc., and to have them in readiness for general use, but at the moment that they need this or that, they make experiments, draw, dictate, copy, etc., and when this is done by an unskilled or careless teacher (and their number increases daily), the result is deplorable. It is just as if a physician, when he wishes to administer a medicine, had to wander through gardens and forests, and collect and distil herbs and roots, though medicaments to suit every case should be ready to his hand.

14. Secondly, because even in school-books, the natural order, that the matter come first and the form follow, is not observed. Everywhere the exact opposite is to be found. The classification of objects is unnaturally made to precede a knowledge of the objects themselves, although it is impossible to classify, before the matter to be classified is there.

I will demonstrate this by four examples:

15. (1) Languages are learned in schools before the sciences, since the intellect is detained for some years over the study of languages, and only then allowed to proceed to the sciences, mathematics, physics, etc. And yet things are essential, words only accidental; things are the body, words but the garment; things are the kernel, words the shells and husks. Both should therefore be presented to the intellect at the same time, but particularly the

things, since they are as much objects of the understanding as are languages.

16. (2) Even in the study of languages the proper order is reversed, since the students commence, not with some author or with a skilfully-compiled phrase-book, but with the grammar; though the authors (and in their own way the phrase-books) present the material of speech, namely, words, while the grammars on the other hand, only give the form; that is to say, the laws of the foundation, order, and combination of words.

17. (3) In the encyclopaedic compilations of human knowledge, the arts are always placed first, while the sciences follow after, though the latter teach of the things themselves, the former how to manipulate the things.

18. (4) Finally: it is the abstract rules that are first taught and then illustrated by dragging in a few examples; though it is plain that a light should precede him whom it lights.

19. *Rectification.* It follows, therefore, that in order to effect a thorough improvement in schools it is necessary:

(i.) That books and the materials necessary for teaching be held in readiness.

(ii.) That the understanding be first instructed in things, and then taught to express them in language.

(iii.) That no language be learned from a grammar, but from suitable authors.

(iv.) That the knowledge of things precede the knowledge of their combinations.

(v.) And that examples come before rules.

THIRD PRINCIPLE

20. *Nature Chooses a Fit Subject to Act Upon, or First Submits One to a Suitable Treatment in Order to Make It Fit.* For example: a bird does not place any object in the nest in which it sits, but an object of such a kind that a chicken can be hatched from it; that is to say, an egg. If a small stone or anything else falls into the nest, it throws it out as useless. But when the process of hatching takes place, it warms the material contained in the egg, and looks after it until the chicken makes its way out.

21. *Imitation.* In the same way the builder cuts down timber, of as good quality as possible, dries it, squares it, and saws it into planks. Then he chooses a spot to build on, clears it, lays a new foundation, or repairs the old one so that he can make use of it.

22. In the same way, if the canvas or the surface do not suit his colors, the painter tries to make them more suitable, and, by rubbing them and polishing them, fits them for his use.

23. The gardener too (1) chooses from a fruit-bearing stock a shoot that possesses as much vitality as possible; (2) transplants it to a garden, and places it carefully in the earth; (3) does not burden it with a new graft unless he sees that it has taken root; (4) before he inserts the new graft, removes the former shoot, and even cuts a piece away round the stock in order that none of the sap may perform any function other than that of vivifying the graft.

24. *Deviation.* Against this principle the schools are offenders; not because they include the weak of intellect (for in our opinion all the young should be admitted into the schools) but far more because:

(1) These tender plants are not transplanted into the garden, that is to say, are not entirely entrusted to the schools, so that none, who are to be trained as men, shall be allowed to leave the workshop before their training is complete.

(2) The attempt is generally made to engraft that noblest graft of knowledge, virtue and piety, too early, before the stock itself has taken root; that is to say, before the desire to learn has been excited in those who have no natural bent in that direction.

(3) The side-shoots or root-suckers are not removed before the grafting takes place; that is to say, the minds are not freed from all idle tendencies by being habituated to discipline and order.

25. *Rectification.* It is therefore desirable:

(i.) That all who enter schools persevere in their studies.

(ii.) That, before any special study is introduced, the mind of the student be prepared and made receptive of it.

(iii.) That all obstacles be removed out of the way of schools.

"For it is of no use to give precepts," says Seneca, "unless the obstacles that stand in the way be removed."

Fourth Principle

26. *Nature Is Not Confused in Its Operations, but in Its Forward Progress Advances Distinctly from One Point to Another.* For example: if a bird is being produced, its bones, veins, and nerves are formed at separate and distinct periods; at one time its flesh becomes firm, at another it receives its covering of skin or feathers, and at another it learns how to fly, etc.

27. *Imitation.* When a builder lays foundations, he does not build the walls at the same time, much less does he put on the roof, but does each of these things at the proper time and in the proper place.

28. In the same way a painter does not work at twenty or thirty pictures at once, but occupies himself with one only. For, though he may from time to time put a few touches to some others or give his attention to something else, it is on one picture and one only that he concentrates his energies.

29. In the same way the gardener does not plant several shoots at once, but plants them one after the other, that he may neither confuse himself nor spoil the operations of nature.

30. *Deviation.* Confusion has arisen in the schools through the endeavor to teach the scholars many things at one time. As, for example, Latin and Greek grammar, perhaps rhetoric and poetic as well, and a multitude of other subjects. For it is notorious that in the classical schools the subject-matter for reading and for composition is changed almost every hour throughout the day. If this be not confusion I should like to know what is. It is just as if a shoemaker wished to make six or seven new shoes at once, and took them up one by one in turn, only to lay them aside in a few minutes; or as if a baker, who wished to place various kinds of bread in his oven, were to take them out again immediately, removing one kind as he put in another. Who would commit such an act of folly? The shoemaker finishes one shoe before he begins to make another. The baker places no fresh bread in the oven until that already in it is thoroughly baked.

31. *Rectification.* Let us imitate these people and take care not to confuse scholars who are learning grammar by teaching them dialectic, or by introducing rhetoric into their studies. We should also put off the study of Greek until Latin is mastered, since it is impossible to concentrate the mind on any one thing, when it has to busy itself with several things at once.

That great man, Joseph Scaliger, was well aware of this. It is related of him that (perhaps on the advice of his father) he never occupied himself with more than one branch of knowledge at once, and concentrated all his energies on that one. It was owing to this that he was able to master not only fourteen languages, but also all the arts and sciences that lie within the province of man. He devoted himself to these one after the other with such success that in each subject his learning excelled that of men who had given their whole lives to it. And those who have tried to follow in his footsteps and imitate his method, have done so with considerable success.

32. Schools, therefore, should be organized in such a manner that the scholar shall be occupied with only one object of study at any given time.

Fifth Principle

33. *In All the Operations of Nature Development Is from Within.* For example: in the case of the bird it is not the claws, or the feathers, or the skin that is first formed, but the inner parts; the outer parts are formed later, at the proper season.

34. *Imitation.* In the same way the gardener does not insert his graft into the outer bark nor into the outside layer of wood, but making an incision right into the pith, places the graft as far in as it will go.

In this way he makes the joint so firm that the sap cannot escape, but is forced right into the shoot, and uses all its strength in vivifying it.

35. So too, a tree, that is nourished by the rain of heaven and the moisture of the earth, assimilates its nutriment, not through its outer bark, but the pores of its inmost parts. On this account the gardener waters, not the branches, but the roots. Animals also convey their food, not to their outer limbs, but to the stomach, which assimilates it and nourishes the whole body. If, therefore, the educator of the young give special attention to the roots of knowledge, the understanding, these will soon impart their vitality to the stem, that is, to the memory, and finally blossoms and fruits, that is to say, a facile use of language and practical capacity, will be produced.

36. *Deviation.* It is on this point that those teachers fall into error who, instead of thoroughly explaining the subjects of study to the boys under their charge, give them endless dictations, and make them learn their lessons off by heart. Even those who wish to explain the subject-matter do not know how to do so; that is to say, do not know how to tend the roots or how to engraft the graft of knowledge. Thus they fatigue their pupils, and resemble a man who uses a club or a mallet, instead of a knife, when he wishes to make an incision in a plant.

37. *Rectification.* It therefore follows:

(i.) That the scholar should be taught first to understand things, and then to remember them, and that no stress should be laid on the use of speech or pen, till after a training on the first two points.

(ii.) That the teacher should know all the methods by which the understanding may be sharpened, and should put them into practice skilfully.

SIXTH PRINCIPLE

38. *Nature, in Its Formative Processes, Begins with the Universal and Ends with the Particular.* For example: a bird is to be produced from an egg. It is not the head, an eye, a feather, or a claw that is first formed, but the following process takes place. The whole egg is warmed, the warmth produces movement, and this movement brings into existence a system of veins, which mark in outline the shape of the whole bird (defining the parts that are to become the head, the wings, the feet, etc.). It is not until this outline is complete that the individual parts are brought to perfection.

39. *Imitation.* The builder takes this as his model. He first makes a general plan of the building in his head, or on paper, or in wood. Then he lays the foundations, builds the walls, and lays on the roof. It is not until he has done this that he gives his attention to the small details that are necessary to complete a house, such as doors, windows, staircases, etc.; while last of all he adds ornamentation such as paintings, sculptures, and carpets.

40. An artist proceeds in the same way. He does not begin by drawing an ear, an eye, a nose, or a mouth, but first makes a charcoal sketch of the face or of the whole body. If he be satisfied that this sketch resembles the original,

he paints it with light strokes of the brush, still omitting all detail. Then, finally, he puts in the light and shade, and, using a variety of colors, finishes the several parts in detail.

41. The procedure of the sculptor is the same. When he wishes to carve a statue, he takes a block of marble and shapes it roughly. Then he sets to work more carefully and outlines the most important features. Finally, he chisels the individual parts with the greatest accuracy and colors them artistically.

42. In the same way the gardener takes the most simple and universal part of a tree, namely, a shoot. Later on, this can put forth as many branches as it possesses buds.

43. *Deviation.* From this it follows that it is a mistake to teach the several branches of science in detail before a general outline of the whole realm of knowledge has been placed before the student, and that no one should be instructed in such a way as to become proficient in any one branch of knowledge without thoroughly understanding its relation to all the rest.

44. It follows also that arts, sciences, and languages are badly taught unless a general notion of the elements be first given. I remember well that, when we began to learn dialectic, rhetoric, and metaphysics, we were, at the very beginning, overburdened with long-winded rules, with commentaries and notes on commentaries, with comparison of authors and with knotty questions. Latin grammar was taught us with all the exceptions and irregularities; Greek grammar with all its dialects, and we, poor wretches, were so confused that we scarcely understood what it was all about.

45. *Rectification.* The remedy for this want of system is as follows: At the very commencement of their studies, boys should receive instruction in the first principles of general culture, that is to say, the subjects learned should be arranged in such a manner that the studies that come later introduce nothing new, but only expand the elements of knowledge that the boy has already mastered. Just as a tree, even if it live for a hundred years, puts no new branches, but only suffers those that already exist to develop and to spread.

(i.) Each language, science, or art must be first taught in its most simple elements, that the student may obtain a general idea of it. (ii.) His knowledge may next be developed further by placing rules and examples before him. (iii.) Then he may be allowed to learn the subject systematically with the exceptions and irregularities; and (iv.), last of all, may be given a commentary, though only where it is absolutely necessary. For he who has thoroughly mastered a subject from the beginning will have little need of a commentary, but will soon be in the position to write one himself.

SEVENTH PRINCIPLE

46. *Nature Makes No Leaps, but Proceeds Step by Step.* The development of a chicken consists of certain gradual processes which cannot be omitted or deferred, until finally it breaks its shell and comes forth. When this takes

place, the mother does not allow the young bird to fly and seek its food (indeed it is unable to do so), but she feeds it herself, and by keeping it warm with her body promotes the growth of its feathers. When the chick's feathers have grown she does not thrust it forth from the nest immediately and make it fly, but teaches it first to move its wings in the nest itself or perching on its edge, then to try to fly outside the nest, though quite near it, by fluttering from branch to branch, then to fly from tree to tree, and later on from hill to hill, till finally it gains sufficient confidence to fly right out in the open. It is easy to see how necessary it is that each of these processes should take place at the right time; that not only the time should be suitable but that the processes should be graduated; and that there should be not graduation merely, but an immutable graduation.

47. *Imitation.* The builder proceeds in the same manner. He does not begin with the gables or with the walls, but with the foundations. When the foundations are laid he does not go on with the roof, but builds the walls. In a word, the order in which the several stages are combined depends on the relation that they mutually bear to one another.

48. The gardener likewise has to adopt the principle of graduation. The wild-stock must be found, dug up, transplanted, pruned, and cut; the graft must be inserted and the joint made firm, etc., and none of these processes can be omitted or taken in a different order. But, if these processes are carried out properly and in the right order, it is scarcely possible, in fact it is impossible, for the result to be unsuccessful.

49. *Deviation.* It is an evident absurdity, therefore, if teachers for their own sake and that of their pupils, do not graduate the subjects which they teach in such a way that, not only one stage may lead on directly to the next, but also that each shall be completed in a given space of time. For unless goals are set up, means provided for reaching them, and a proper system devised for the use of those means, it is easy for something to be omitted or perverted, and failure is the result.

50. *Rectification.* It follows therefore:

(i.) That all studies should be carefully graduated throughout the various classes, in such a way that those that come first may prepare the way for and throw light on those that come after.

(ii.) That the time should be carefully divided, so that each year, each month, each day, and each hour may have its appointed task.

(iii.) That the division of the time and of the subjects of study should be rigidly adhered to, that nothing may be omitted or perverted.

Eighth Principle

51. *If Nature Commences Anything, It Does Not Leave Off Until the Operation Is Completed.* If a bird, urged by the impulse of nature, begins to sit on eggs, she does not leave off until she has hatched out the chickens. If she sat on them for a few hours only, the embryo in the egg would become

cold and die. Even when the chickens are hatched she does not cease to keep them warm, but continues to do so until they have grown strong, are covered with feathers, and can endure the cold air.

52. *Imitation.* The painter, also, who has begun a picture, will produce his work best if he finish it without any interruption. For in this case the colors blend better and hold faster.

53. For this reason it is best to finish the erection of a building without any interruption; otherwise the sun, the wind, and the rain spoil the work, the later additions will not be so firm, and on every side there will be cracks, weak spots and loose joints.

54. The gardener, too, acts with wisdom, for when once he has begun to work at a graft he does not cease until the operation is completed. Since, if the sap dry in the stock or in the graft, owing to a delay in completing the process, the plant is ruined.

55. *Deviation.* It is therefore injurious if boys are sent to school for months or years continuously, but are then withdrawn for considerable periods and employed otherwise; equally so if the teacher commences now one subject, now another, and finishes nothing satisfactorily; and lastly, it is equally fatal if he does not fix a certain task for each hour, and complete it, so that in each period his pupil can make an unmistakable advance towards the desired goal. Where such a fire is wanting, everything grows cold. Not without reason does the proverb say, "Strike while the iron is hot." For if it be allowed to cool it is useless to hammer it, but it must once more be placed in the fire, and thus much time and iron are wasted. Since every time that it is heated, it loses some of its mass.

56. *Rectification.* It follows therefore:

(i.) That he who is sent to school must be kept there until he becomes well informed, virtuous, and pious.

(ii.) That the school must be situated in a quiet spot, far from noise and distractions.

(iii.) That whatever has to be done, in accordance with the scheme of study, must be done without any shirking.

(iv.) That no boys, under any pretext whatever, should be allowed to stay away or to play truant.

Ninth Principle

57. *Nature Carefully Avoids Obstacles and Things Likely to Cause Hurt.* For example, when a bird is hatching eggs it does not allow a cold wind, much less rain or hail to reach them. It also drives away snakes, birds of prey, etc.

58. *Imitation* In the same way the builder, so far as is possible, keeps dry his wood, bricks, and lime, and does not allow what he has built to be destroyed or to fall down.

59. So, too, the painter protects a newly-painted picture from wind, from violent heat, and from dust, and allows no hand but his own to touch it.

60. The gardener also protects a young plant by a railing or by hurdles, that hares or goats may not gnaw it or root it up.

61. *Deviation.* It is therefore folly to introduce a student to controversial points when he is just beginning a subject; that is to say, to allow a mind that is mastering something new to assume an attitude of doubt. What is this but to tear up a plant that is just beginning to strike root? (Rightly does Hugo say: "He who starts by investigating doubtful points will never enter into the temple of wisdom.") But this is exactly what takes place if the young are not protected from incorrect, intricate, and badly written books as well as from evil companions.

62. *Rectification.* Care should therefore be taken

(i.) That the scholars receive no books but those suitable for their classes.

(ii.) That these books be of such a kind that they can rightly be termed sources of wisdom, virtue, and piety.

(iii.) That neither in the school nor in its vicinity the scholars be allowed to mix with bad companions.

63. If all these recommendations are observed, it is scarcely possible that schools should fail to attain their object.

Jean-Jacques Rousseau

Derived from a comprehensive protest, the works of Jean-Jacques Rousseau (1712–1778) ruptured the rational composure of eighteenth-century France and placed before the Western world a radical program for philosophical, social, and aesthetic reform. The impact of his thought was abrupt and tenacious, and Goethe foresaw its consequences when he wrote, "In Voltaire we see the end of a world; in Rousseau the beginning of a new one." But the "new world," presumably so influenced by Rousseau, takes much of his accomplishment for granted. His contribution is blurred by familiarity.

Much of Rousseau's social philosophy is embodied in On the Origin of Inequality (1755) and The Social Contract (1762). In these works the French romanticist argued that man is naturally happy and virtuous until he is coerced to live in a society which denies the primacy *of emotion and imagination. Consequently, the depraved human being is the product of that social system which smothers the lessons of the heart beneath a sediment of hypocrisy and aristocratic pretension. The true nature of man, affirms Rousseau, may only flourish when the emotional life is granted supremacy over the intellectual life. Morality emerges from instinct, not from manners.*

Émile, Or Concerning Education (1762) *is divided into five books, as follows:*

Book   I. *Infancy, or education to the age of five.*
Book II. *Childhood, or education from five to twelve.*
Book III. *Boyhood, or education from twelve to fifteen.*
Book IV. *Adolescence, or education from fifteen to eighteen.*
Book V. *Youth, or education from eighteen to twenty, and the education of his future wife, Sophie.*

The selections to follow were extracted from each of the five books, tracing the idealized content and methodology of Émile's education. Writing in the nineteenth century, Johann Richter declared, "Not Rousseau's individual rules, many of which may be erroneous without injury to the whole, but the spirit of education which fills and animates the work, has shaken to their foundations and purified all the schoolrooms, and even the nurseries, in Europe. In no previous work on education was the ideal so richly and beautifully combined with actual observation as in his." Émile *survives as a fecund source from which the philosophies of Pestalozzi and John Dewey borrowed heavily.*

20

From ÉMILE, OR CONCERNING EDUCATION

Book I

All things are good as they come out of the hands of their Creator, but every thing degenerates in the hands of man. He compels one soil to nourish the productions of another, and one tree to bear the fruits of another. He blends and confounds elements, climates, and seasons: he mutilates his dogs, his horses, and his slaves: he defaces, he confounds everything: he delights in deformity and monsters. He is not content with anything in its natural state, not even with his own species. His very offspring must be trained up for him, like a horse in the ménage, and be taught to grow after his own fancy, like a tree in his garden.

Without this, matters would be still worse than they are, and our species would not be civilized but by halves. Should a man, in a state of society, be given up, from the cradle, to his own notions and conduct, he would certainly turn out the most preposterous of human beings. The influence of prejudice, authority, necessity, example, and all those social institutions in which we are immersed, would stifle in him the emotions of nature, and substitute nothing in their place. His humanity would resemble a shrub, growing by accident in the highway, which would soon be destroyed by the casual injuries it must receive from the frequent passenger.

We are born weak, we need strength; we are born destitute of all things, we need assistance; we are born stupid, we need judgment. All that we have not at our birth, and that we need when grown up, is given us by education.

This education comes to us from nature itself, or from other men, or from circumstances. The internal development of our faculties and of our organs is the education nature gives us; the use we are taught to make of this development is the education we get from other men; and what we learn, by our own experience, about things that interest us, is the education of circumstances.

In the natural order of things, all men being equal, the vocation common to all is the state of manhood; and whoever is well trained for that, cannot fulfil badly any vocation which depends upon it. Whether my pupil be destined for the army, the church, or the bar, matters little to me. Before he can think of adopting the vocation of his parents, nature calls upon him to be a man. How to live is the business I wish to teach him. On leaving my hands he will not, I admit, be a magistrate, a soldier, or a priest; first of all he will be a man. All that a man ought to be he can be, at need, as well as any one else can. Fortune will in vain alter his position, for he will always occupy his own.

Our real study is that of the state of man. He among us who best knows how to bear the good and evil fortunes of this life is, in my opinion, the best educated; whence it follows that true education consists less in precept than in practice. We begin to instruct ourselves when we begin to live; our education commences with the commencement of our life; our first teacher is our nurse. For this reason the word "education" had among the ancients another meaning which we no longer attach to it; it signified nutriment.

To live is not merely to breathe, it is to act. It is to make use of our organs, of our senses, of our faculties, of all the powers which bear witness to us of our own existence. He who has lived most is not he who has numbered the most years, but he who has been most truly conscious of what life is. A man may have himself buried at the age of a hundred years, who died from the hour of his birth. He would have gained something by going to his grave in youth, if up to that time he had only lived.

But let mothers only vouchsafe to nourish their children, and our manners will reform themselves; the feelings of nature will re-awaken in all hearts. The State will be repeopled; this chief thing, this one thing will bring all the rest into order again. The attractions of home life present the best antidote to bad morals. The bustling life of little children, considered so tiresome, becomes pleasant; it makes the father and the mother more necessary to one another, more dear to one another; it draws closer between them the conjugal tie. When the family is sprightly and animated, domestic cares form the dearest occupation of the wife and the sweetest recreation of the husband. Thus the correction of this one abuse would soon result in a general reform; nature would resume all her rights. When women are once more true mothers, men will become true fathers and husbands.

A father, when he brings his children into existence and supports them, has, in so doing, fulfilled only a third part of his task. To the human race he owes men; to society, men fitted for society; to the State, citizens. Every man who can pay this triple debt, and does not pay it is a guilty man; and if he pays it by halves, he is perhaps more guilty still. He who cannot fulfil the duties of a father has no right to be a father. Not poverty, nor severe labor, nor human respect can release him from the duty of supporting his children and of educating them himself. Readers, you may believe my words. I prophesy to any one who has natural feeling and neglects these sacred duties, — that he will long shed bitter tears over this fault, and that for those tears he will find no consolation.

The qualifications of a good tutor are very freely discussed. The first qualification I should require in him, and this one presupposes many others, is, that he shall not be capable of selling himself. There are employments so noble that we cannot fulfil them for money without showing ourselves unworthy to fulfil them. Such an employment is that of a soldier; such a one is that of a teacher. Who, then, shall educate my child? I have told you already, — yourself. I cannot! Then make for yourself a friend who can. I see no other alternative.

A teacher! what a great soul he ought to be! Truly, to form a man, one must be either himself a father, or else something more than human. And this is the office you calmly entrust to hirelings!

In this outset of life, while memory and imagination are still inactive, the child pays attention only to what actually affects his senses. The first materials of his knowledge are his sensations. If, therefore, these are presented to him in suitable order, his memory can hereafter present them to his understanding in the same order. But as he attends to his sensations only, it will at first suffice to show him very clearly the connection between these sensations, and the objects which give rise to them. He is eager to touch everything, to handle everything. Do not thwart this restless desire; it suggests to him a very necessary apprenticeship. It is thus he learns to feel the heat and coldness, hardness and softness, heaviness and lightness of bodies; to judge of their size, their shape, and all their sensible qualities, by looking, by touching, by listening; above all, by comparing the results of sight with those of touch, estimating with the eye the sensation a thing produces upon the fingers.

Book II

Far from taking care that Émile does not hurt himself, I shall be dissatisfied if he never does, and so grows up unacquainted with pain. To suffer is the first and most necessary thing for him to learn. Children are little and weak, apparently that they may learn these important lessons. If a child fall his whole length, he will not break his leg; if he strike himself with a stick, he will not break his arm; if he lay hold of an edged tool, he does not grasp it tightly, and will not cut himself very badly.

Our pedantic mania for instructing constantly leads us to teach children what they can learn far better for themselves, and to lose sight of what we alone can teach them. Is there anything more absurd than the pains we take in teaching them to walk? As if we had ever seen one, who, through his nurse's negligence, did not know how to walk when grown! On the contrary, how many people do we see moving awkwardly all their lives because they have been badly taught how to walk!

O men, be humane! it is your highest duty; be humane to all conditions of men, to every age, to everything not alien to mankind. What higher wisdom is there for you than humanity? Love childhood; encourage its sports, its pleasures, its lovable instincts. Who among us has not at times looked back with regret to the age when a smile was continually on our lips, when the soul was always at peace? Why should we rob these little innocent creatures of the enjoyment of a time so brief, so transient, of a boon so precious, which they cannot misuse? Why will you fill with bitterness and sorrow these fleeting years which can no more return to them than to you? Do you know, you fathers, the moment when death awaits your children? Do not store up for yourselves remorse, by taking from them the brief moments nature has given them. As soon as they can appreciate the delights of existence, let them enjoy it. At whatever hour God may call them, let them not die without having tasted life at all.

The surest way to make a child unhappy is to accustom him to obtain everything he wants to have. For since his wishes multiply in proportion to the ease with which they are gratified, your inability to fulfil them will sooner or later oblige you to refuse in spite of yourself, and this unwonted refusal will pain him more than withholding from him what he demands. At first he will want the cane you hold; soon he will want your watch; afterward he will want the bird he sees flying, or the star he sees shining. He will want everything he sees, and without being God himself how can you content him?

Treat your pupil as his age demands. From the first, assign him to his true place, and keep him there so effectually that he will not try to leave it. Then, without knowing what wisdom is, he will practice its most important lesson. Never, absolutely never, command him to do a thing, whatever it may be. Do not let him even imagine that you claim any authority over him. Let him know only that he is weak and you are strong: that from his condition and yours he is necessarily at your mercy. Let him know this — learn it and feel it. Let him early know that upon his haughty neck is the stern yoke nature imposes upon man, the heavy yoke of necessity, under which every finite being must toil.

In this way you will make him patient, even-tempered, resigned, gentle, even when he has not what he wants. For it is in our nature to endure patiently the decrees of fate, but not the ill will of others. "There is no more," is an answer against which no child ever rebelled unless he believed it untrue. Besides, there is no other way; either nothing at all is to be required of him, or he must from the first be accustomed to perfect obedience. The worst training of all is to leave him wavering between his own will and yours, and to dispute incessantly with him as to which shall be master. I should a hundred times prefer his being master in every case.

Reverse the common practice, and you will nearly always do well. Parents and teachers desiring to make of a child not a child, but a learned man, have never begun early enough to chide, to correct, to reprimand, to flatter, to promise, to instruct, to discourse reason to him. Do better than this: be reasonable yourself, and do not argue with your pupil, least of all, to make him approve what he dislikes. For if you persist in reasoning about disagreeable things, you make reasoning disagreeable to him, and weakens its influence beforehand in a mind as yet unfitted to understand it. Keep his organs, his senses, his physical strength, busy; but, as long as possible, keep his mind inactive. Guard against all sensations arising in advance of judgment, which estimates their true value. Keep back and check unfamiliar impressions, and be in no haste to do good for the sake of preventing evil. For the good is not real unless enlightened by reason. Regard every delay as an advantage; for much is gained if the critical period be approached without losing anything. Let childhood have its full growth. If indeed a lesson must be given, avoid it to-day, if you can without danger delay it until to-morrow.

*   *   *

We may reduce almost all the lessons of morality that have, or can be, formed for the use of children, to the following formula.

MASTER. You must not do so.

CHILD. And why must I not do so?

MASTER. Because it is naughty.

CHILD. Naughty! what is that being naughty?

MASTER. Doing what you are forbid.

CHILD. And what harm is there in doing what one is forbid?

MASTER. The harm is, you will be whipped for disobedience.
CHILD. Then I will do it so nobody shall know anything of the matter.
MASTER. Oh, but you will be watched.
CHILD. Ah! but then I will hide myself.
MASTER. Then you will be examined.
CHILD. Then I will tell a fib.
MASTER. But you must not tell fibs.
CHILD. Why must not I?
MASTER. Because it is naughty, etc.

Thus we go round the circle; and yet, if we go out of it, the child understands us no longer. Are not these very useful instructions, think you? I could be very curious to know what could be substituted in the place of this fine dialogue. Locke himself would certainly have been embarrassed had he been asked so puzzling a question. To distinguish between good and evil, to perceive the reasons on which our moral obligations are founded, is not the business, as it is not within the capacity, of a child.

Nature requires children to be children before they are men. By endeavoring to pervert this order, we produce forward fruits, that have neither maturity nor taste, and will not fail soon to wither or corrupt. Hence it is we have so many young professors and old children. Childhood hath its manner of seeing, perceiving, and thinking, peculiar to itself; nor is there anything more absurd than our being anxious to substitute our own in its stead. I would as soon require an infant to be five feet high, as a boy to have judgment at ten years of age. In fact, of what use would reason be to him at that age? Reason is given us as a check upon our power; a child has no need of such restraint.

Respect children, and be in no haste to judge their actions, good or evil. Let the exceptional cases show themselves such for some time before you adopt special methods of dealing with them. Let nature be long at work before you attempt to supplant her, lest you thwart her work. You say you know how precious time is, and do not wish to lose it. Do you not know that to employ it badly is to waste it still more, and that a child badly taught is farther from being wise than one not taught at all? You are troubled at seeing him spend his early years doing nothing. What! is it nothing to be happy? Is it nothing to skip, to play, to run about all day long? Never in all his life will he be so busy as now.

Pedagogues, who make such an imposing display of what they teach, are paid to talk in another strain than mine, but their conduct shows that they think as I do. For after all, what do they teach their pupils? Words, words, words. Among all their boasted subjects, none are selected because they are useful; such would be the sciences of things, in which these professors are unskillful. But they prefer sciences; we seem to know when we know their nomenclature, such as heraldry, geography, chronology, languages; studies so far removed from human interests, and particularly from the child, that it would be wonderful if any of them could be of the least use at any time in life.

In any study, words that represent things are nothing without the ideas of the things they represent. We, however, limit children to these signs, without ever being able to make them understand the things represented. We think we are teaching a child the description of the earth, when he is merely learning maps. We teach him the names of cities, countries, rivers; he has no idea that they exist anywhere but on the map we use in pointing them out to him. I recollect seeing somewhere a text-book on geography which began thus: "What is the world? A pasteboard globe." Precisely such is the geography of children. I will venture to say that after two years of globes and cosmography no child of ten, by rules they give him, could find the way from Paris to St. Denis. I maintain that not one of them, from a plan of his father's garden, could trace out its windings without going astray. And yet these are the knowing creatures who can tell you exactly where Pekin, Ispahan, Mexico, and all the countries of the world are.

The memory of which a child is capable is far from inactive, even without the use of books. All he sees and hears impresses him, and he remembers it. He keeps a mental register of people's sayings and doings. Everything around him is the book from which he is continually but unconsciously enriching his memory against the time his judgment can benefit by it. If we intend rightly to cultivate this chief faculty of the mind, we must choose these objects carefully, constantly acquainting him with such as he ought to understand, and keeping back those he ought not to know. In this way we should endeavor to make his mind a storehouse of knowledge, to aid in his education in youth, and to direct him at all times. This method does not, it is true, produce phenomenal children, nor does it make the reputation of their teachers; but it produces judicious, robust men, sound in body and in mind, who, although not admired in youth, will make themselves respected in manhood.

Man's first natural movements are for the purpose of comparing himself with whatever surrounds him and finding in each thing those sensible qualities likely to affect himself. His first study is, therefore, a kind of experimental physics relating to his own preservation. From this, before he has fully understood his place here on earth, he is turned aside to speculative studies. While yet his delicate and pliable organs can adapt themselves to the objects upon which they are to act, while his senses, still pure, are free from illusion, it is time to exercise both in their peculiar functions, and to learn the perceptible relations between ourselves and outward things. Since whatever enters the human understanding enters by the senses, man's primitive reason is a reason of the senses, serving as foundation for the reason of the intellect. Our first teachers in philosophy are our own feet, hands, and eyes. To substitute books for these is teaching us not to reason, but to use the reason of another; to believe a great deal, and to know nothing at all.

All children, being natural imitators, try to draw. I would have my pupil cultivate this art, not exactly for the sake of the art itself, but to render the eye true and the hand flexible. In general, it matters little whether he understands this or that exercise, provided he acquires the mental insight, and the manual skill furnished by the exercise. I should take care, therefore, not to give him a drawing-master, who would give him only copies to imitate, and would make him draw from drawings only. He shall have no teacher but nature, no models but real things. He shall have before his eyes the originals, and not the paper which represents them. He shall draw a house from a real house, a tree from a tree, a human figure from the man himself. In this way he will accustom himself to observe bodies and their appearances, and not mistake for accurate imitations those that are false and conventional.

BOOK III

In general, never show the representation of a thing unless it be impossible to show the thing itself; for the sign absorbs the child's attention, and makes him lose sight of the thing signified.

The two starting-points in his geography shall be the town in which he lives, and his father's house in the country. Afterward shall come the places lying between these two; then the neighboring rivers; lastly, the aspect of the sun, and the manner of finding out where the east is. The last is the point of union. Let him make himself a map of all these details; a very simple map, including at first only two objects, then by degrees the others, as he learns their distance and position. You see now what an advantage we have gained beforehand, by making his eyes serve him instead of a compass.

Bear in mind always that the life and soul of my system is, not to teach the child many things, but to allow only correct and clear ideas to enter his mind. I do not care if he knows nothing, so long as he is not mistaken. To guard him from errors he might learn, I furnish his mind with truths only. Reason and judgment enter slowly; prejudices crowd in; and he must be preserved from these last. Yet if you consider science in itself, you launch upon an unfathomable and boundless sea, full of unavoidable dangers. When I see a man carried away by his love for knowledge, hastening from one alluring science to another, without knowing where to stop, I think I see a child gathering shells upon the seashore. At first he loads himself with them; then, tempted by others, he throws these away, and gathers more. At last, weighed down by so many, and no longer knowing which to choose, he ends by throwing all away, and returning empty-handed.

Let the child take nothing for granted because some one says it is so. Nothing is good to him but what he feels to be good. You think it far sighted to push him beyond his understanding of things, but you are mistaken. For the sake of arming him with weapons he does not know how to use, you take from him one universal among men, common sense; you teach him to allow himself always to be led, never to be more than a machine in the hands of others. If you will have him docile while he is young, you will make him a credulous dupe when he is a man. You are continually saying to him, "All I require of you is for your own good, but you cannot understand it yet. What does it matter to me whether you do what I require or not? You are doing it entirely for your own sake." With such fine speeches you are paving the way for some kind of trickster or fool, — some visionary babbler or charlatan, — who will entrap him or persuade him to adopt his own folly.

Obliged to learn by his own effort, he employs his own reason, not that of another. Most of our mistakes arise less within ourselves than from others; so that if he is not to be ruled by opinion, he must receive nothing upon authority. Such continual exercise must invigorate the mind as labor and fatigue strengthen the body.

The mind as well as the body can bear only what its strength will allow. When the understanding fully masters a thing before entrusting it to the memory, what it afterward draws therefrom is in reality its own. But if instead we load the memory with matters the understanding has not mastered, we run the risk of never finding there anything that belongs to it.

Since we must have books, there is one which, to my mind, furnishes the finest of treatises on education according to nature. My Émile shall read this book before any other; it shall for a long time be his entire library, and shall always hold an honorable place. It shall be the text on which all our discussions of natural science shall be only commentaries. It shall be a test for all we meet during our progress toward a ripened judgment, and so long as our taste is unspoiled, we shall enjoy reading it. What wonderful book is this? Aristotle? Pliny? Buffon? No; it is *Robinson Crusoe*.

The story of this man, alone on his island, unaided by his fellow-men, without any art or its implements, and yet providing for his own preservation and subsistence, even contriving to live in what might be called comfort, is interesting to persons of all ages. It may be made delightful to children in a thousand ways. Thus we make the desert island, which I used at the outset for a comparison, a reality.

In a word, Émile has every virtue which affects himself. To have the social virtues as well, he only needs to know the relations which make them necessary; and this knowledge his mind is ready to receive. He considers himself independently of others, and is satisfied when others do not think of him at all. He exacts nothing from others, and never thinks of owing anything to them. He is alone in human society, and depends solely upon himself. He has the best right of all to be independent, for he is all that any one can be at his age. He has no errors but such as a human being must have; no vices but those from which no one can warrant himself exempt. He has a sound constitution, active limbs, a fair and unprejudiced mind, a heart free and without passions. Self-love, the first and most natural of all, has scarcely manifested itself at all. Without disturbing any one's peace of mind he has led a happy, contented life, as free as nature will allow. Do you think a youth who has thus attained his fifteenth year has lost the years that have gone before?

Book IV

Respect your species; consider that it is composed essentially of a collection of peoples; that even if all the kings and all the philosophers were taken away, they would scarcely be missed, and that things would not go worse. In a word, teach your pupil to love all men, even those who despise them; let him not belong to any class, but be at home in all. Speak before him of the human race with tenderness, even with pity, but never with contempt. Man, do not dishonor man!

When the critical age approaches, bring before young people scenes that will restrain and not excite them; give a change to their nascent imagination by objects which, far from inflaming their senses, will repress the activity of them. Remove them from great cities where the dress and immodesty of women will hasten and anticipate the lessons of nature, where everything presents to their eyes pleasures which they ought to be acquainted with only when they know how to choose them. Take them back to their first dwelling-place, where rural simplicity lets the passions of their age develop less rapidly; or if their taste for the arts still attaches them to the city, prevent in them, by this taste itself, a dangerous idleness. Carefully choose their associations, their occupations, and their pleasures; show them only touching but modest pictures, which will move without demoralizing them, and which will nourish their sensibilities without stirring their senses.

When I see that young people, at the age of greatest activity, are restricted to studies purely speculative, and that afterwards, without the slightest experience, they are suddenly thrown into society and business, I find that reason no less than nature is offended, and I am no longer surprised that so few persons know how to act. By what strange perversity of mind are we taught so many useless things, while the art of doing counts for nothing? People pretend to form us for society, and instruct us as if each one were to pass his life in thinking alone in his cell, or in treating subjects with indifference. You think you are teaching your children to live by instructing them in certain contortions of the body and in certain forms of words, which have no meaning. I too have taught my Émile to live; for I have taught him to live with himself, and besides to know how to earn his bread. But that is not enough. To live in society, we must know how to deal with men, how to recognize the means of influencing them; how to calculate the action and reaction of individual interests in civil society, and to foresee events so clearly that we are rarely deceived, or at least always take the best means to succeed.

I foresee how many of my readers will be surprised to see me let the early years of my pupil pass without speaking to him of religion. At fifteen he did not know whether he had a soul, and perhaps at eighteen it is not yet time for him to learn it; for if he learns it sooner than is necessary, he runs the risk of never knowing it.

If there is nothing of morality in the human soul, whence come those transports of admiration for heroic deeds, those raptures of love for great souls? What relation has this enthusiasm for virtue with our private interests? Why should I rather be Cato who thrusts a dagger into his heart, than Caesar with all his triumphs? Take away from our hearts this love of the beautiful, and you take away all the charm of life. He whose vile passions have stifled in his narrow soul these delightful sentiments; he who, by always centering his thoughts upon himself, comes at length to love only himself, has no more transports; his icy heart no longer palpitates with joy; a sweet tenderness never moistens his eyes; he no longer enjoys anything; the wretch no longer feels, no longer lives; he is already dead.

Be sincere and true without pride; know how to be ignorant: you will deceive neither yourself nor others. If ever your cultivated talents put you in a position to speak to men, speak to them always according to your conscience, without being embarrassed if they do not applaud. The abuse of knowledge begets incredulity. Every learned man disdains the common sentiment; each one wishes to have an opinion of his own. A proud philosophy leads to scepticism, as a blind devotion leads to fanaticism. Avoid these extremes; always remain firm in the path of truth, or of what seems to be so in the simplicity of your heart, without ever turning aside through vanity or weakness. Dare to confess God among philosophers; dare to preach humanity to the intolerant. You will be alone in your position perhaps; but you will have within yourself a testimony that will enable you to do without that of men. Whether they love you or hate you, whether they read or despise your writings, makes no difference. Speak what is true, do what is right; that which is important for man is to fulfil his duties upon the earth; and it is by forgetting one's self that one works for one's self. My child, selfish interests deceive us; it is only the hope of the just that never deceives.

Book V

On the good constitution of mothers depends that of children; on the care of woman depends the first education of men; on woman depend again their manners, their passions, their tastes, their pleasures, and even their happiness. Thus all the education of women ought to be relative to men. To please them, to be useful to them, to make themselves loved and honored by them, to bring them up when young, to care for them when grown, to counsel and console them, to render their life agreeable and sweet — these are the duties of women in every age, and what they ought to learn from their childhood. So long as we do not recognize this principle, we shall miss the end, and all the precepts we give them will be of no service either for their happiness or ours.

John Dewey

By turns idolized, misunderstood, and despised, John Dewey (1859–1952) is clearly a pivotal figure in modern education, not so much for any highly independent contribution as for the synthesis he performed with raw concepts gleaned from Comenius, Rousseau, Pestalozzi, and William James.

"My Pedagogic Creed" is a succinct summary of Dewey's major educational concerns. It was published in 1897, sounding the war cry for the gathering forces of Progressivism. Published in 1938, "Traditional vs. Progressive Education" was Dewey's attempt to clarify his position after it had become distorted through the strident efforts of overzealous supporters.

For years a revered teacher at Columbia University, Mr. Dewey's reputation is further supported by his book Reconstruction in Philosophy *(1920), a comprehensive survey of modern philosophy in evolution.*

21

MY PEDAGOGIC CREED

Article One — What Education Is

I believe that all education proceeds by the participation of the individual in the social consciousness of the race. This process begins unconsciously almost at birth, and is continually shaping the individual's powers, saturating his consciousness, forming his habits, training his ideas, and arousing his feelings and emotions. Through this unconscious education the individual gradually comes to share in the intellectual and moral resources which humanity has succeeded in getting together. He becomes an inheritor of the funded capital of civilization. The most formal and technical education in the world cannot safely depart from this general process. It can only organize it or differentiate it in some particular direction.

The only true education comes through the stimulation of the child's powers by the demands of the social situations in which he finds himself. Through these demands he is stimulated to act as a member of a unity, to emerge from his original narrowness of action and feeling, and to conceive of himself from the standpoint of the welfare of the group to which he belongs. Through the responses which others make to his own activities he comes to know what these mean in social terms. The value which they have is reflected back into them. For instance, through the response which is made to the child's instinctive babblings the child comes to know what those babblings mean; they are transformed into articulate language, and thus the child is introduced into the consolidated wealth of ideas and emotions which are now summed up in language.

This educational process has two sides — one psychological and one sociological — and neither can be subordinated to the other, or neglected, without evil results following. Of these two sides, the psychological is the basis. The child's own instincts and powers furnish the material and give the starting point for all education. Save as the efforts of the educator connect with some activity which the child is carrying on of his own initiative independent of the educator, education becomes reduced to a pressure from without. It may, indeed, give certain external results, but cannot truly be called educative. Without insight into the psychological structure and activities of the individual, the educative process will, therefore, be haphazard and arbitrary. If it chances to coincide with the child's activity it will get a leverage; if it does not, it will result in friction, or disintegration, or arrest of the child-nature.

Knowledge of social conditions, of the present state of civilization, is necessary in order properly to interpret the child's powers. The child has his own instincts and tendencies, but we do not know what these mean until we can translate them into their social equivalents. We must be able to carry them back into a social past and see them as the inheritance of previous race activities. We must also be able to project them into the future to see what their outcome and end will be. In the illustration just used, it is the ability to see in the child's babblings the promise and potency of a future social intercourse and conversation which enables one to deal in the proper way with that instinct.

The psychological and social sides are organically related, and that education cannot be regarded as a compromise between the two, or a superimposition of one upon the other. We are told the psychological definition of education is barren and formal — that it gives us only the idea of a development of all the mental powers without giving us any idea of the use to which these powers are put. On the other hand, it is urged that the social definition of education, as getting adjusted to civilization, makes of it a forced and external process, and results in subordinating the freedom of the individual to a preconceived social and political status.

Each of these objections is true when urged against one side isolated from the other. In order to know what a power really is we must know what its end, use, or function is, and this we cannot know save as we conceive of the individual as active in social relationships. But, on the other hand, the only possible adjustment which we can give to the child under existing conditions is that which arises through putting him in complete possession of all his powers. With the advent of democracy and modern industrial conditions, it is impossible to foretell definitely just what civilization will be twenty years from now. Hence it is impossible to prepare the child for any precise set of conditions. To prepare him for the future life means to give him command of himself; it means so to train him that he will have the full and ready use of all his capacities; that his eye and ear and hand may be tools ready to command, that his judgment may be capable of grasping the conditions under which it has to work, and the executive forces be trained to act economically and efficiently. It is impossible to reach this sort of adjustment save as constant regard is had to the individual's own powers, tastes, and interests — that is, as education is continually converted into psychological terms.

In sum, I believe that the individual who is to be educated is a social individual, and that society is an organic union of individuals. If we eliminate the social factor from the child we are left only with an abstraction; if we eliminate the individual factor from society, we are left only with an inert and lifeless mass. Education, therefore, must begin with a psychological insight into the child's capacities, interests, and habits. It must be controlled at every point by reference to these same considerations. These powers, interests, and habits must be continually interpreted — we must know what they mean. They must be translated into terms of their social equivalents — into terms of what they are capable of in the way of social service.

ARTICLE TWO — WHAT THE SCHOOL IS

I believe that the school is primarily a social institution. Education being a social process, the school is simply that form of community life in which all those agencies are concentrated that will be most effective in bringing the child to share in the inherited resources of the race, and to use his own powers for social ends.

Education, therefore, is a process of living and not a preparation for future living.

The school must represent life, life as real and vital to the child as that which he carries on in the home, in the neighborhood, or on the playground.

That education which does not occur through forms of life, forms that are worth living for their own sake, is always a poor substitute for the genuine reality, and tends to cramp and to deaden.

The school, as an institution, should simplify existing social life; should reduce it, as it were, to an embryonic form. Existing life is so complex that the child cannot be brought into contact with it without either confusion or distraction; he is either overwhelmed by the multiplicity of activities which are going on, so that he loses his own power of orderly reaction, or he is so stimulated by these various activities that his powers are prematurely called into play and he becomes either unduly specialized or else disintegrated.

As such simplified social life, the school should grow gradually out of the home life; it should take up and continue the activities with which the child is already familiar in the home.

It should exhibit these activities to the child, and reproduce them in such ways that the child will gradually learn the meaning of them, and be capable of playing his own part in relation to them.

This is a psychological necessity, because it is the only way of securing continuity in the child's growth, the only way of giving a background of past experience to the new ideas given in school.

It is also a social necessity because the home is the form of social life in which the child has been nurtured and in connection with which he has had his moral training. It is the business of the school to deepen and extend his sense of the values bound up in his home life.

Much of present education fails because it neglects this fundamental principle of the school as a form of community life. It conceives the school as a place where certain information is to be given, where certain lessons are to be learned, or where certain habits are to be formed. The value of these is conceived as lying largely in the remote future; the child must do these things for the sake of something else he is to do; they are mere preparations. As a result they do not become a part of the life experience of the child and so are not truly educative.

The moral education centers upon this conception of the school as a mode of social life, that the best and deepest moral training is precisely that which one gets through having to enter into proper relations with others in a unity of work and thought. The present educational systems, so far as they destroy or neglect this unity, render it difficult or impossible to get any genuine, regular moral training.

The child should be stimulated and controlled in his work through the life of the community.

Under existing conditions far too much of the stimulus and control proceeds from the teacher, because of neglect of the idea of the school as a form of social life.

The teacher's place and work in the school is to be interpreted from this same basis. The teacher is not in the school to impose certain ideas or to form certain habits in the child, but is there as a member of the community to select the influences which shall affect the child and to assist him in properly responding to these influences.

The discipline of the school should proceed from the life of the school as a whole and not directly from the teacher.

The teacher's business is simply to determine, on the basis of larger experience and riper wisdom, how the discipline of life shall come to the child.

All questions of the grading of the child and his promotion should be determined by reference to the same standard. Examinations are of use only so far as they test the child's fitness for social life and reveal the place in which he can be of the most service and where he can receive the most help.

Article Three — The Subject Matter of Education

I believe that the social life of the child is the basis of concentration, or correlation, in all his training or growth. The social life gives the unconscious unity and the background of all his efforts and of all his attainments.

The subject matter of the school curriculum should mark a gradual differentiation out of the primitive unconscious unity of social life.

We violate the child's nature and render difficult the best ethical results by introducing the child too abruptly to a number of special studies, of reading, writing, geography, etc., out of relation to this social life.

The true center of correlation on the school subjects is not science, nor literature, nor history, nor geography, but the child's own social activities.

Education cannot be unified in the study of science, or so-called nature study, because apart from human activity, nature itself is not a unity; nature in itself is a number of diverse objects in space and time, and to attempt to make it the center of work by itself is to introduce a principle of radiation rather than one of concentration.

Literature is the reflex expression and interpretation of social experience; hence it must follow upon and not precede such experience. It, therefore, cannot be made the basis, although it may be made the summary of unification.

Once more, history is of educative value insofar as it presents phases of social life and growth. It must be controlled by reference to social life. When taken simply as history it is thrown into the distant past and becomes dead and inert. Taken as the record of man's social life and progress it becomes full of meaning. I believe, however, that it cannot be so taken excepting as the child is also introduced directly into social life.

The primary basis of education is in the child's powers at work along the same general constructive lines as those which have brought civilization into being.

The only way to make the child conscious of his social heritage is to enable him to perform those fundamental types of activity which make civilization what it is.

In the so-called expressive or constructive activities is the center of correlation.

This gives the standard for the place of cooking, sewing, manual training, etc., in the school.

They are not special studies which are to be introduced over and above a lot of others in the way of relaxation or relief, or as additional accomplishments. I believe rather that they represent, as types, fundamental forms of social activity; and that it is possible and desirable that the child's introduction into the more formal subjects of the curriculum be through the medium of these constructive activities.

The study of science is educational insofar as it brings out the materials and processes which make social life what it is.

One of the greatest difficulties in the present teaching of science is that the material is presented in purely objective form, or is treated as a new peculiar kind of experience which the child can add to that which he has already had. In reality, science is of value because it gives the ability to interpret and control the experience already had. It should be introduced, not as so much new subject matter, but as showing the factors already involved in previous experience and as furnishing tools by which that experience can be more easily and effectively regulated.

At present we lose much of the value of literature and language studies because of our elimination of the social element. Language is almost always treated in the books of pedagogy simply as the expression of thought. It is true that language is a logical instrument, but it is fundamentally and primarily a social instrument. Language is the device for communication; it is the tool through which one individual comes to share the ideas and feelings of others. When treated simply as a way of getting individual information, or as a means of showing off what one has learned, it loses its social motive and end.

There is, therefore, no succession of studies in the ideal school curriculum. If education is life, all life has, from the outset, a scientific aspect, an aspect of art and culture, and an aspect of communication. It cannot, therefore, be true that the proper studies for one grade are mere reading and writing, and that at a later grade, reading, or literature, or science, may be introduced. The progress is not in the succession of studies, but in the development of new attitudes towards, and new interests in, experience.

Education must be conceived as a continuing reconstruction of experience; the process and the goal of education are one and the same thing.

To set up any end outside of education, as furnishing its goal and standard, is to deprive the educational process of much of its meaning, and tends to make us rely upon false and external stimuli in dealing with the child.

ARTICLE FOUR — THE NATURE OF METHOD

I believe that the question of method is ultimately reducible to the question of the order of development of the child's powers and interests. The law for presenting and treating material is the law implicit within the child's own nature. Because this is so I believe the following statements are of supreme importance as determining the spirit in which education is carried on.

The active side precedes the passive in the development of the child nature; expression comes before conscious impression; the muscular development precedes the sensory; movements come before conscious sensations; I believe that consciousness is essentially motor or impulsive; that conscious states tend to project themselves in action.

The neglect of this principle is the cause of a large part of the waste of time and strength in school work. The child is thrown into a passive, receptive, or absorbing attitude. The conditions are such that he is not permitted to follow the law of his nature; the result is friction and waste.

Ideas also result from action and devolve for the sake of the better control of action. What we term reason is primarily the law of order or effective action. To attempt to develop the reasoning powers, the powers of judgment, without reference to the selection and arrangement of means in action, is the fundamental fallacy in our present methods of dealing with this matter. As a result we present the child with arbitrary symbols. Symbols are a necessity in mental development, but they have their place as tools for economizing effort; presented by themselves they are a mass of meaningless and arbitrary ideas imposed from without.

The image is the great instrument of instruction. What a child gets out of any subject presented to him is simply the images which he himself forms with regard to it.

If nine-tenths of the energy at present directed towards making the child learn certain things were spent in seeing to it that the child was forming proper images, the work of instruction would be indefinitely facilitated.

Much of the time and attention now given to the preparation and presentation of lessons might be more wisely and profitably expended in training the child's power of imagery and in seeing to it that he was continually forming definite, vivid and growing images of the various subjects with which he comes in contact in his experience.

Interests are the signs and symptoms of growing power. I believe that they represent dawning capacities. Accordingly the constant and careful observation of interests is of the utmost importance for the educator.

These interests are to be observed as showing the state of development which the child has reached.

They prophesy the stage upon which he is about to enter.

Only through the continual and sympathetic observation of childhood's interests can the adult enter into the child's life and see what it is ready for, and upon what material it could work most readily and fruitfully.

These interests are neither to be humored nor repressed. To repress interest is to substitute the adult for the child, and so to weaken intellectual curiosity and alertness, to suppress initiative, and to deaden interest. To humor the interests is to substitute the transient for the permanent. The interest is always the sign of some power below; the important thing is to discover this power. To humor the interest is to fail to penetrate below the surface, and its sure result is to substitute caprice and whim for genuine interest.

The emotions are the reflex of actions.

To endeavor to stimulate or arouse the emotions apart from their corresponding activities is to introduce an unhealthy and morbid state of mind.

If we can only secure right habits of action and thought, with reference to the good, the true, and the beautiful, the emotions will for the most part take care of themselves.

Next to deadness and dullness, formalism and routine, our education is threatened with no greater evil than sentimentalism.

This sentimentalism is the necessary result of the attempt to divorce feeling from action.

ARTICLE FIVE — THE SCHOOL AND SOCIAL PROGRESS

I believe that education is the fundamental method of social progress and reform.

All reforms which rest simply upon the enactment of law, or the threatening of certain penalties, or upon changes in mechanical or outward arrangements, are transitory and futile.

Education is a regulation of the process of coming to share in the social consciousness; and the adjustment of individual activity on the basis of this social consciousness is the only sure method of social reconstruction.

This conception has due regard for both the individualistic and socialistic ideals. It is duly individual because it recognizes the formation of a certain character as the only genuine basis of right living. It is socialistic because it recognizes that this right character is not to be formed by merely individual precept, example, or exhortation, but rather by the influence of a certain form of institutional or community life upon the individual, and that the social organism through the school, as its organ, may determine ethical results.

In the ideal school we have the reconciliation of the individualistic and the institutional ideals.

The community's duty to education is, therefore, its paramount moral duty. By law and punishment, by social agitation and discussion, society can regulate and form itself in a more or less haphazard and chance way. But through education society can formulate its own purposes, can organize its own means and resources, and thus shape itself with definiteness and economy in the direction in which it wishes to move.

When society once recognizes the possibilities in this direction, and the obligations which these possibilities impose, it is impossible to conceive of the resources of time, attention, and money which will be put at the disposal of the educator.

It is the business of everyone interested in education to insist upon the school as the primary and most effective interest of social progress and reform in order that society may be awakened to realize what the school stands for, and aroused to the necessity of endowing the educator with sufficient equipment properly to perform his task.

Education thus conceived marks the most perfect and intimate union of science and art conceivable in human experience.

The art of thus giving shape to human powers and adapting them to social service is the supreme art; one calling into its service the best of artists; no insight, sympathy, tact, executive power, is too great for such service.

With the growth of psychological service, giving added insight into individual structure and laws of growth; and with growth of social science, adding to our knowledge of the right organization of individuals, all scientific resources can be utilized for the purposes of education.

When science and art thus join hands the most commanding motive for human action will be reached, the most genuine springs of human conduct aroused, and the best service that human nature is capable of guaranteed.

The teacher is engaged, not simply in the training of individuals, but in the formation of the proper social life.

Every teacher should realize the dignity of his calling; he is a social servant set apart for the maintenance of proper social order and the securing of the right social growth.

In this way the teacher always is the prophet of the true God and the usherer in of the true kingdom of God.

22

TRADITIONAL VERSUS PROGRESSIVE

EDUCATION*

Mankind likes to think in terms of extreme opposites. It is given to formulating its beliefs in terms of *Either-Ors*, between which it recognizes no intermediate possibilities. When forced to recognize that the extremes cannot be acted upon, it is still inclined to hold that they are all right in theory but that when it comes to practical matters circumstances compel us to compromise. Educational philosophy is no exception. The history of educational theory is marked by opposition between the idea that education is development from within and that it is formation from without; that it is based upon natural endowments and that education is a process of overcoming natural inclination and substituting in its place habits acquired under external pressure.

At present, the opposition, so far as practical affairs of the school are concerned, tends to take the form of contrast between traditional and progressive education. If the underlying ideas of the former are formulated broadly,

* From *Experience and Education* by John Dewey (New York: The Macmillan Company, 1938), pp. 1–13, 17–19. Reprinted by permission of Kappa Delta Pi, owners of the copyright.

without the qualifications required for accurate statement, they are found to be about as follows: The subject-matter of education consists of bodies of information and of skills that have been worked out in the past; therefore, the chief business of the school is to transmit them to the new generation. In the past, there have also been developed standards and rules of conduct; moral training consists in forming habits of action in conformity with these rules and standards. Finally, the general pattern of school organization (by which I mean the relations of pupils to one another and to the teachers) constitutes the school a kind of institution sharply marked off from other social institutions. Call up in imagination the ordinary schoolroom, its time-schedules, schemes of classification, of examination and promotion, of rules of order, and I think you will grasp what is meant by "pattern of organization." If then you contrast this scene with what goes on in the family, for example, you will appreciate what is meant by the school being a kind of institution sharply marked off from any other form of social organization.

The three characteristics just mentioned fix the aims and methods of in-struction and discipline. The main purpose or objective is to prepare the young for future responsibilities and for success in life, by means of acquisi-tion of the organized bodies of information and prepared forms of skill which comprehend the material of instruction. Since the subject-matter as well as standards of proper conduct are handed down from the past, the attitude of pupils must, upon the whole, be one of docility, receptivity, and obedience. Books, especially textbooks, are the chief representatives of the lore and wisdom of the past, while teachers are the organs through which pupils are brought into effective connection with the material. Teachers are the agents through which knowledge and skills are communicated and rules of conduct enforced.

I have not made this brief summary for the purpose of criticizing the underlying philosophy. The rise of what is called new education and progres-sive schools is of itself a product of discontent with traditional education. In effect it is a criticism of the latter. When the implied criticism is made explicit it reads somewhat as follows: The traditional scheme is, in essence, one of imposition from above and from outside. It imposes adult standards, subject-matter, and methods upon those who are only growing slowly toward maturity. The gap is so great that the required subject-matter, the methods of learning and of behaving are foreign to the existing capacities of the young. They are beyond the reach of the experience the young learners al-ready possess. Consequently, they must be imposed; even though good teach-ers will use devices of art to cover up the imposition so as to relieve it of obviously brutal features.

But the gulf between the mature or adult products and the experience and abilities of the young is so wide that the very situation forbids much active participation by pupils in the development of what is taught. Theirs is to do — and learn, as it was the part of the six hundred to do and die. Learn-ing here means acquisition of what already is incorporated in books and in the heads of the elders. Moreover, that which is taught is thought of as essentially static. It is taught as a finished product, with little regard either to the ways in which it was originally built up or to changes that will surely occur in the future. It is to a large extent the cultural product of societies that assumed the future would be much like the past, and yet it is used as educational food in a society where change is the rule, not the exception.

If one attempts to formulate the philosophy of education implicit in the practices of the newer education, we may, I think, discover certain common principles amid the variety of progressive schools now existing. To imposition from above is opposed expression and cultivation of individuality; to external discipline is opposed free activity; to learning from texts and teachers, learning through experience; to acquisition of isolated skills and techniques by drill is opposed acquisition of them as means of attaining ends which make direct vital appeal; to preparation for a more or less remote future is opposed making the most of the opportunities of present life; to static aims and materials is opposed acquaintance with a changing world.

Now, all principles by themselves are abstract. They become concrete only in the consequences which result from their application. Just because the principles set forth are so fundamental and far-reaching, everything depends upon the interpretation given them as they are put into practice in the school and the home. It is at this point that the reference made earlier to *Either-Or* philosophies becomes peculiarly pertinent. The general philosophy of the new education may be sound, and yet the difference in abstract principles will not decide the way in which the moral and intellectual preference involved shall be worked out in practice. There is always the danger in a new movement that in rejecting the aims and methods of that which it would supplant, it may develop its principles negatively rather than positively and constructively. Then it takes its clew in practice from that which is rejected instead of from the constructive development of its own philosophy.

I take it that the fundamental unity of the newer philosophy is found in the idea that there is an intimate and necessary relation between the processes of actual experience and education. If this be true, then a positive and constructive development of its own basic idea depends upon having a correct idea of experience. Take, for example, the question of organized subject-matter — which will be discussed in some detail later. The problem for progressive education is: What are the place and meaning of subject-matter and of organization *within* experience? How does subject-matter function? Is there anything inherent in experience which tends towards progressive organization of its contents? What results follow when the materials of experience are not progressively organized? A philosophy which proceeds on the basis of rejection, of sheer opposition, will neglect these questions. It will tend to suppose that because the old education was based on ready-made organization, therefore it suffices to reject the principle of organization *in toto*, instead of striving to discover what it means and how it is to be attained on the basis of experience. We might go through all the points of difference between the new and the old education and reach similar conclusions. When external control is rejected, the problem becomes that of finding the factors of control that are inherent within experience. When external authority is rejected, it does not follow that all authority should be rejected, but rather that there is need to search for a more effective source of authority. Because the older education imposed the knowledge, methods, and the rules of conduct of the mature person upon the young, it does not follow, except upon the basis of the extreme *Either-Or* philosophy, that the knowledge and skill of the mature person has no directive value for the experience of the immature. On the contrary, basing education upon personal experience may mean more multiplied and more intimate contacts between the mature and the immature than ever existed in the traditional school, and consequently more, rather than less, guidance by others. The problem, then, is: how these contacts can be established without violating the principle of learning through personal experience. The solution of this problem requires a well thought-out philosophy of the social factors that operate in the constitution of individual experience.

What is indicated in the foregoing remarks is that the general principles of the new education do not of themselves solve any of the problems of the actual or practical conduct and management of progressive schools. Rather, they set new problems which have to be worked out on the basis of a new philosophy of experience. The problems are not even recognized, to say nothing of being solved, when it is assumed that it suffices to reject the ideas and practices of the old education and then go to the opposite extreme. Yet I am sure that you will appreciate what is meant when I say that many of the newer schools tend to make little or nothing of organized subject-matter of study; to proceed as if any form of direction and guidance by adults were an invasion of individual freedom, and as if the idea that education should be concerned with the present and future meant that acquaintance with the past has little or no role to play in education. Without pressing these defects to the point of exaggeration, they at least illustrate what is meant by a theory and practice of education which proceeds negatively or by reaction against what has been current in education rather than by a positive and constructive development of purposes, methods, and subject-matter on the foundation of a theory of experience and its educational potentialities.

It is not too much to say that an educational philosophy which professes to be based on the idea of freedom may become as dogmatic as ever was the traditional education which is reacted against. For any theory and set of practices are dogmatic which are not based upon critical examination of their own underlying principles. Let us say that the new education emphasizes the freedom of the learner. Very well. A problem is now set. What does freedom mean and what are the conditions under which it is capable of realization? Let us say that the kind of external imposition which was so common in the traditional school limited rather than promoted the intellectual and moral development of the young. Again, very well. Recognition of this serious defect sets a problem. Just what is the role of the teacher and of books in promoting the educational development of the immature? Admit that traditional education employed, as the subject-matter for study, facts and ideas so bound up with the past as to give little help in dealing with the issues of the present and future. Very well. Now we have the problem of discovering the connection which actually exists *within* experience between the achievements of the past and the issues of the present. We have the problem of ascertaining how acquaintance with the past may be translated into a potent instrumentality for dealing effectively with the future. We may reject knowledge of the past as the *end* of education and thereby only emphasize its importance as a *means*. When we do that we have a problem that is new in the story of education: How shall the young become acquainted with the past in such a way that the acquaintance is a potent agent in appreciation of the living present?

In short, the point I am making is that rejection of the philosophy and practice of traditional education sets a new type of difficult educational problem for those who believe in the new type of education. We shall operate blindly and in confusion until we recognize this fact; until we thoroughly appreciate that departure from the old solves no problems. I assume that amid all uncertainties there is one permanent frame of reference: namely, the organic connection between education and personal experience; or, that the new philosophy of education is committed to some kind of empirical and experimental philosophy. But experience and experiment are not self-explanatory ideas. Rather, their meaning is part of the problem to be explored. To know the meaning of empiricism we need to understand what experience is.

A philosophy of education, like any theory, has to be stated in words, in symbols. But so far as it is more than verbal it is a plan for conducting education. Like any plan, it must be framed with reference to what is to be done and how it is to be done. The more definitely and sincerely it is held that education is a development within, by, and for experience, the more important it is that there shall be clear conceptions of what experience is. Unless experience is so conceived that the result is a plan for deciding upon subject-matter, upon methods of instruction and discipline, and upon material equipment and social organization of the school, it is wholly in the air. It is reduced to a form of words which may be emotionally stirring but for which any other set of words might equally well be substituted unless they indicate operations to be initiated and executed. Just because traditional education was a matter of routine in which the plans and programs were handed down from the past, it does not follow that progressive education is a matter of planless improvisation.

The traditional school could get along without any consistently developed philosophy of education. About all it required in that line was a set of abstract words like culture, discipline, our great cultural heritage, etc., actual guidance being derived not from them but from custom and established routines. Just because progressive schools cannot rely upon established traditions and institutional habits, they must either proceed more or less haphazardly or be directed by ideas which, when they are made articulate and coherent, form a philosophy of education. Revolt against the kind of organization characteristic of the traditional school constitutes a demand for a kind of organization based upon ideas. I think that only slight acquaintance with the history of education is needed to prove that educational reformers and innovators alone have felt the need for a philosophy of education. Those who adhered to the established system needed merely a few fine-sounding words to justify existing practices. The real work was done by habits which were so fixed as to be institutional. The lesson for progressive education is that it requires in an urgent degree, a degree more pressing than was incumbent upon former innovators, a philosophy of education based upon a philosophy of experience.

Arthur Bestor

In this essay Arthur Bestor aims his criticism at a favorite target, the professional educator who, to Bestor, suffers from a disastrously narrow perspective, one that excludes knowledge of, and respect for, traditional learning. Bestor, Professor of History at the University of Washington, defines the educational theory compounded by these men as "regressive," pointing out that much "regressive education" is the decadent residue of a once promising revolution in teaching methodology.

Although some educators have condemned Bestor for his hostility toward certain contemporary practices in education, he actually represents a moderate position — a stance encouraging maximum use of the best thought of our time, whether such thought derives from past tradition or current investigation.

For a detailed rebuttal to Bestor's charges, the reader should examine "A Scholar's Documents" by Harold C. Hand and Charles W. Sanford, which appeared in the Bulletin of the National Association of Secondary-School Principals *(April, 1953). This article was brought to the editor's attention by Dr. Hand, unfortunately too late for inclusion in Part Three.*

23

PROGRESSIVE EDUCATION VERSUS REGRESSIVE EDUCATION*

Every improvement in the technique of teaching brings closer the possibility of realizing in practice and on a universal scale the ideal of disciplined liberal education. If the tools of pedagogy are to be turned to account, however, they must be consciously directed toward ends that are in themselves defensible. Most of the shortsighted and fallacious policies discussed in preceding chapters represent the diversion of educational resources into enterprises that are shallow, trivial, and ill-considered. And this misdirection of energy has been possible because so many professors of pedagogy have insisted in recent years that their own narrow expertness ought to replace the wisdom of society and of the learned world in determining the content and aim of public education.

So long as students of pedagogy recognized the inherent limitations of what they were doing, they made important contributions to the improvement of public education. Through careful study of child psychology and through controlled experimentation in the classroom, they pointed the way to notable advances in the technique of imparting such elementary skills as reading and arithmetic; they increased the effectiveness with which such high-school subjects as history, chemistry, algebra, and foreign languages were taught; and they succeeded in so increasing the efficiency of instruction that students were prepared to undertake in the high school certain studies usually considered as belonging to the college program. In the early part of the present century these improved methods of instruction went by the name of progressive education. For that type of progressive education I have sincere respect. If educationists had concentrated their efforts upon putting these improvements into effect throughout the schools, instead of turning aside from their proper work to tamper with the curriculum itself, then educational progress over the past half century would have been an unquestionable fact.

Educational progress *was* a fact so long as progressive education meant the things I have just described. I consider myself fortunate to have received my

---

* Reprinted from *The Restoration of Learning* by Arthur Bestor, by permission of Alfred A. Knopf, Inc. Copyright © 1955 by Arthur Bestor. Pp. 139–155.

high-school training, from 1922 to 1926, in one of the most progressive schools in the country, the Lincoln School of Teachers College, Columbia University. In those years, and in that school, progressive education seems to me to have been definitely on the right track. With uninfluential exceptions the faculty of that school did not think of defining the aims of secondary education apart from the aims of liberal education generally. They believed thoroughly in the intellectual purposes that had always been central in education as a whole. They knew that the work of the secondary school must intermesh with the advanced work carried on by scientists and scholars. Adequate preparation for college was not a separate goal; it was the natural consequence of a sound secondary-school program based on the great intellectual disciplines. Mathematical instruction in the Lincoln School culminated in a senior course in the calculus, a branch of mathematics ordinarily commenced only in college. A full year was devoted to each of the sciences of chemistry, physics, and biology. The classical languages, it is true, were sacrificed to modernity — a serious mistake, I believe — but the promise that they would be replaced by sound training in the living foreign languages was honestly fulfilled. Work in English included the study of contemporary authors, but with no slighting of the great literature of the past. Composition meant a study of grammar and syntax, and in addition the practice of original writing of the sort published in Hughes Mearns's admirable *Creative Youth*.[1]

What progressive educators undertook to do, in those fruitful years, was to bring the teaching of the basic disciplines to the highest perfection possible in the light of modern pedagogy. They did so by emphasizing the relevance of knowledge and intellectual skill to the problems of practical life and citizenship. They experimented with more effective methods of instruction, and they never forgot that the good faith of an experimenter is measured by his frankness in conceding failure. Above all, they sought the ablest teachers, not the ones most fanatically devoted to newness for its own sake. The success of the Lincoln School in attracting brilliant men and women to its faculty was remarkable. To several of my teachers there I owe as much as to any of my instructors in college and graduate school, and I am proud to say that I am in correspondence with three of them more than a quarter of a century later.

Throughout the United States there are thousands of public schools in which high standards are maintained by teachers and administrators whose devotion to learning is unshaken. Where this spirit prevails, experiments with teaching methods go forward productively and safely because the ultimate aim is kept clear. If the philosophy that governs the school program as a whole is intellectually sound and responsible, wide latitude in experimentation is certainly permissible.

Typical of such responsible institutions is a large high school in the sub-

[1] Hughes Mearns: *Creative Youth: How a School Environment Set Free the Creative Spirit* (New York, 1925).

urbs of Chicago, where the problem of the slow learner is conscientiously faced without sacrifice of basic academic purpose. Sufficient sections are created in subjects with large enrollment, like English, so that students of similar ability can be grouped together. Each section proceeds at its own rate, but the same intellectual purpose animates all alike. A common stratum of content is covered by all classes; the materials and procedures employed are comparable for all but not necessarily identical. There is no thought of shunting the retarded child into a program drained of intellectual content.

The school that I am describing also imposes a definite limit on the number of purely vocational courses that can be included in any student's program. The interest of students in vocational and "practical" matters is channeled into extracurricular clubs, membership in which is possible only to those who are regularly enrolled in the standard academic courses. The announced purpose of the superintendent, moreover, is to balance every special effort made for retarded students with a comparable program for the benefit of those of exceptional ability. In line with this, a new science wing includes small laboratories in which able students can pursue more advanced work than in the standard courses, under the direction of faculty members specifically assigned to work with them.

Such a school is a responsible school — responsible both to the standards of scholarship and to the ideal of a continuously improving pedagogy. Furthermore it is responsible, in the truest sense, to its community, which created it not to be the servitor of momentary whims but to uphold for all children the ideals of liberal learning.

At bottom it is lack of responsibility that has played such havoc with American education in recent years. Experiments even more extreme than those I have mentioned would be perfectly justifiable if they were conducted as true experiments, and accepted or rejected on the basis of rigorous tests of their success in advancing the intellectual purposes of the school. No experiment is an experiment, however, if the criteria by which the results are to be measured are altered in mid-career.

Such a shift in criteria and purpose has occurred in the past twenty or thirty years, under the aegis of professional educationists. What was once progressive education — an honorable term in its day — has been replaced by what I can only describe as "regressive education," though its exponents are apt to masquerade under the old name.

The shadow of this change began to fall upon the Lincoln School even in the middle 1920's. Alongside excellent instruction in history, a course in the "social studies" was introduced. Subsequent work of my own in several of the fields supposedly embraced within this course has merely confirmed the opinion that my classmates and I entertained at the time. I remember being struck at the outset by the inferiority of this hodgepodge to the straight-forward treatment of great public issues that I had learned to expect from my instructors in history. The "social studies" purported to throw light on contemporary problems, but the course signally failed, for it offered no perspective on the issues it raised, no basis for careful analysis, no encouragement to ordered thinking. There was plenty of discussion, but it was hardly responsible discussion. Quick and superficial opinions, not balanced and critical judgments, were at a premium. Freedom to think was elbowed aside by freedom not to think, and undisguised indoctrination loomed ahead. I am surprised at how accurately we as students appraised the course. I cannot now improve on the nickname we gave it at the time: "social stew."

The course in the social studies, and the more destructive programs that ensued, marked the turning-point from progressive to regressive education. Education that called itself progressive ceased to be an effort to accomplish more effectively the purposes which citizens, scholars, and scientists had agreed were fundamental. Progressivism began to imply the substitution of new purposes. Experts in pedagogy were feeling their oats, were abandoning their proper task of improving instruction, and were brazenly undertaking to redefine the aims of education itself. By disregarding or flatly rejecting the considered educational views of the scholarly, scientific, and professional world, these new educationists succeeded in converting the division between secondary and higher education from a mere organizational fact into a momentous intellectual schism. Progressive education became regressive education, because, instead of advancing, it began to undermine the great traditions of liberal education and to substitute for them lesser aims, confused aims, or no aims at all. Intellectual training, once the unquestioned focus of every educational effort, was pushed out to the periphery of the public-school program. Into the vacuum rushed the pedagogical experts from colleges and state departments of education: the curriculum doctors, the integrators, the life-adjusters — the specialists in know-how rather than knowledge. Out of their overflowing minds they offered to furnish ready-made a philosophy to guide the entire educational system. Scientists and scholars might supply little facts to fill up the blanks, but the great schemata were to be devised by the curriculum engineers alone.

One is reminded of the spider in Swift's *Battle of the Books*, with his "many boastings of his native stock, and great genius; that he spins and spits wholly from himself, and scorns to own any obligation or assistance from without." Swift's savage rejoinder in behalf of the bee and of the ancients whom it symbolized is not without relevance to education: "Erect your schemes with as much method and skill as you please; yet if the materials be nothing but dirt, spun out of your own entrails . . . the edifice will conclude at last in a cobweb. . . . As for us the ancients . . . whatever we have got, has been by infinite labour and search, and ranging through every corner of nature; the difference is, that, instead of dirt and poison, we have rather chosen to fill our hives with honey and wax, thus furnishing mankind with the two noblest of things, which are sweetness and light."[2]

2 Jonathan Swift: *The Battle of the Books*, in his *Works*, ed. by John Hawkesworth (8 vols., London, 1755–65), I, 144–145; eighteenth-century italics disregarded.

The disastrously anti-intellectual influence that professional educationists can exert upon education when they repudiate all responsibility to the standards of scholarship is vividly illustrated by one of the studies conducted under the auspices of what is called the Illinois Secondary School Curriculum Program, sponsored by the State Superintendent of Public Instruction. The Illinois Curriculum Program (to use the shortened name that is now official) has many aspects, some of which are relatively untainted by anti-intellectualism. At the heart of the program, however, are a series of studies that are announced as "basic" to curriculum development. One of these, a so-called "Follow-Up Study," deserves careful examination, for its questionnaires and publications have been widely circulated throughout the state, and are of such a character as to affect public thinking on educational issues. The basic philosophy of the study received and apparently still receives the unqualified support of the educationists who run the Illinois Curriculum Program. And affiliation with the national movement for "life-adjustment education" is explicitly recognized in the full title which the controlling body of the Illinois Program occasionally uses on its publications: "Steering Committee of the Illinois Secondary School Curriculum Program and the Illinois Life Adjustment Education Program."[3]

The starting-point of the "Follow-Up Study" is a document entitled "Problems of High School Youth,"[4] which is described as "the list of real-life problems of youth around which the entire study centers."[5] Five separate questionnaires are based upon this list, and the answers are supposed to reveal what parents, citizens, teachers, and pupils "think is the job of the secondary school."[6] The problems are divided into eight groups, each of which consists of from three to twelve separate items. The study is to be a statistical one, and the managers of the project consistently assert that the list contains "56 real-life problems."[7] Simple arithmetic reveals that there are only 55. But simple arithmetic is not listed as a real-life problem, hence such errors are probably unavoidable in the studies that make up the new "science" of education.

The list of "Problems of High School Youth" was formulated by a single professor of education, a member of the faculty of the College of Education of the state university. He, in turn, acknowledged that his problems were derived from a list of "Basic Needs of High School Youth," which was "prepared by the Committee on the Reorientation of the Secondary School Curriculum, a subcommittee of the Curriculum Committee of the Illinois Sec-

---

[3] Illinois Secondary School Curriculum Program, Bulletin No. 9, *New College Admission Requirements Recommended* ([Springfield, Ill.]: Superintendent of Public Instruction, State of Illinois, January 1950), p. 3. The agency responsible for this series will hereafter be abbreviated ISSCP. . . .

[4] ISSCP, Bulletin No. 11, *How to Conduct the Follow-Up Study* (August 1950), pp. 30–32: "Problems of High School Youth," prepared by Harold C. Hand.

[5] *Ibid.*, p. 11.

[6] *Ibid.*, p. 33.

[7] *Ibid.*, pp. 11, 12, 13.

ondary School Principals' Association."[8] This committee (or subcommittee) of eight comprised three professors of education, two high-school principals, two representatives of the State Department of Public Instruction, and the executive director of the Illinois Association of School Boards.[9] The fundamental philosophy of the study, in other words, was determined by professional educationists, who occupied seven of the eight positions on the committee. The one other place was assigned to a citizen who was not a professional educationist, it is true, but who was closely associated with the administration of the school system. No scholar or scientist representing a basic intellectual discipline participated in the work of the committee, though the avowed purpose of the committee, embodied in its very name, was "the reorientation of the secondary school curriculum."

The first thing that strikes one on reading the list of "Problems of High School Youth" is the grotesque disproportion between the different problems presented. Trivia are elaborated beyond all reason, and substantial matters are lumped together in a very small number of separate items, thus reducing them to relative insignificance in the whole. Among the fifty-five points are such ones as these: "the problem of improving one's personal appearance," "the problem of selecting a 'family dentist' and acquiring the habit of visiting him systematically," "the problem of developing one or more 'making things,' 'making it go,' or 'tinkering' hobbies," and "the problem of developing and maintaining wholesome boy-girl relationships."[10] Scattered about in the list are a few items like the following, each of which constitutes but a single point among the fifty-five: "the problem of acquiring the ability to distinguish right from wrong and to guide one's actions accordingly," "the problem of acquiring the ability to study and help solve economic, social, and political problems," and "the problem of making one's self a well-informed and sensitive 'citizen of the world.' "[11] There is not the slightest suggestion anywhere in the entire study that these problems are any more important or any more difficult to solve than the others, or that the school should spend more than a small fraction of its time upon them.

Needless to say, the scholarly and scientific disciplines have no place among these "real-life problems." Arithmetic has sometimes been considered of practical importance, but though "athletic games," "camping," "collecting art objects," and "doing parlor stunts" are mentioned by name, each in a separate item of the list of fifty-five, not one of the branches of mathematics is even hinted at. The word "science" occurs nowhere in the list, nor any term synonymous with it or descriptive of its various branches. That history and foreign languages are absent, even by remotest implication, goes without saying. The final item on the list is "the problem of securing adequate

8 ISSCP, Bulletin No. [1], *Guide to the Study of the Curriculum in the Secondary Schools of Illinois* (August 1948), p. 15.
9 *Ibid.*, p. 42.
10 ISSCP, Bulletin No. 11, pp. 30–32, items B2, C3, E3. G1.
11 *Ibid.*, items B9, F6, F7.

preparation for successful college work. . . ."[12] One can imagine that this will prove the most difficult problem of all.

The authors apparently think that it is enough to say — in another pamphlet, not circulated with the list or questionnaires themselves — that "neither the order in which needs are given nor the amount of space devoted to each need is indicative of the relative significance of the different needs."[13] This is an insult to the citizen's intelligence. No incidental disclaimer could save me from the charge of disordered thinking if I offered the following as an inventory of my possessions: (1) saucepans, (2) library, (3) umbrella, (4) furniture, (5) fountain pen, (6) house and lot, (7) doormat, (8) automobile, (9) clothing, (10) lawnmower.

The intermingling of the trivial and the important in these lists and questionnaires is not an accident but a symptom. The arrangement of items in a list, and the attention devoted to each, do have a meaning and a very profound one. The order and emphasis of a man's writing are just as truly a part of what he says to his reader as any of his particular assertions. And what the list of "Problems of High School Youth" says to the reader is that order, balance, discrimination, and a sense of values are matters of no consequence whatever to the "life-adjustment" pedagogues who yearn to re-orient the curricula of our public schools.

In defense of the "Follow-Up Study," the author of the list of "Problems of High School Youth" and of the questionnaires based upon it has made the following statement to me:

> From studies previously conducted in other states it was believed that the principal reason that youngsters dropped out of high school was that they saw little or no relationship between the subjects they were studying and the life problems of which they were more or less acutely aware. Once the legal school-leaving age had been reached by these youngsters, it seemed apparent that they could be kept in school only if the courses they were taking were in some way or ways more convincingly related to their life problems — that if this were not done the values potential in the high school courses in literature, science, history, foreign languages, etc., would probably be lost to them by virtue of their departure from the institution. . . .
>
> When a community which has seen fit . . . to utilize the *Follow-Up Study* as a starting point for its discussions has worked out a reasonably satisfactory agreement as to what life problems (whether these problems be those included in the printed materials of the study, or others not suggested therein, or some combination of both, is not material) are to be utilized to make the courses taught in the local high school make more sense to more pupils . . . the next obvious step is that of incorporating these problems in the courses and/or extra-class activities to which they sensibly relate. There is no thought . . . that these problems are to constitute the whole of the curriculum or to replace any of the existing courses in the curriculum.

[12] *Ibid.*, item H8.
[13] ISSCP, Bulletin No. [1], p. 10.

Instead, the purpose in spotting the life problems which the community
believes to be important, and in treating these problems in the courses to
which they sensibly relate, is to make the courses make more sense to more
pupils and patrons, and thus to keep more pupils in high school in order
that they may be more fully benefited by the secondary school. It is
recognized, of course, that any school that might see fit to design some new
offering around some sensible cluster of various of these problems might
with propriety do so.[14]

This puts the matter in the best possible light, but there are many difficulties
in the way of accepting it as a valid description of the purposes and probable
consequences of the study.

Let us remember, in the first place, that the various documents of the
"Follow-Up Study" enjoyed wide public circulation and were professedly
designed to encourage discussion and action. If the object of the study were
simply to demonstrate to the public and the student the immense practical
value of the recognized scientific and scholarly disciplines, why is this clear
and admirable purpose never stated in straightforward fashion in any part of
the study? Why are references to the basic academic subjects so carefully
and completely avoided in the questionnaires? Why is there no sentence
suggesting that intellectual training can answer "real-life" problems? Pupils
are asked to say "what we should teach you,"[15] but are not permitted to
mention any of the recognized fields of knowledge. Parents are informed
that the schools "desire to teach all the children of all the people whatever
they need to know,"[16] and are asked to indicate what these things are. But
they, too, may not specify intellectual training in the basic academic subjects.
If the sponsors genuinely desired to safeguard the fundamental intellectual
disciplines and to enhance public esteem for them, they showed the most
wretched incompetence in planning their study. Every document placed in
the hands of citizens or pupils teaches the recipient to think of the schools in
utterly non-intellectual terms.

The list of "Problems of High School Youth" is not a hasty private memo-
randum. It is a formal statement of educational principles, drawn up by
those who purport to be specialists in the matter, and circulated to large
numbers of citizens under the auspices of the highest public educational
authorities of the state. It is ostensibly intended to stimulate serious thinking about "the job of the secondary school." As such it is nothing less than a
proclamation of utter educational irresponsibility.

The questionnaires not only fail to encourage serious thinking about educational problems. They do their best to prevent it. They purport to ask
parents, citizens, teachers, and pupils what they "think is the job of the
secondary school." But the persons questioned are not permitted to give the

[14] Letter from Harold C. Hand, Urbana, Ill., February 25, 1952. Quoted with the
writer's permission, the indicated elisions being authorized by him.
[15] ISSCP, Bulletin No. 11, p. 15.
[16] *Ibid.,* p. 17.

slightest indication that they believe the job of the secondary school is to give intellectual training. In the entire battery of questionnaires there is not a single blank that one may check in order to express the view that the public schools should offer sound training in mathematics, in natural science, in grammar and composition, in foreign languages, or in history. The citizen may respond in the negative to every question implying the substitution of frivolous aims, but he cannot indicate in any manner whatsoever the kind of positive program he would favor. He is not even permitted to indicate the weight he would give to the various items that are actually presented to him. Concerning each listed problem the respondent is asked to indicate whether he thinks the secondary school should help to solve it. If he answers "no," he puts himself down as a calloused enemy of social welfare. If he answers "yes," he is permitted to indicate further whether he considers it "very important," "important," or "not particularly important" for the school to give this help.[17] That is all. A parent, citizen, teacher, or pupil may think two problems "important," yet may also believe that one is a hundred times as important as the other and ought to receive a hundred times the emphasis. The questionnaires offer no means whatever of indicating this simple yet profoundly important judgment concerning relative values.

It may possibly be that American citizens do not want their children to know how to read, write, spell, and calculate. It may possibly be that they do not care whether their children know anything about history or science or foreign languages. I doubt this very much. It is quite certain, in any case, that these questionnaires do not furnish, and cannot furnish, one iota of evidence in the matter. They allow no more free expression of opinion than a Hitler plebiscite. The questionnaires are so rigged that the results are predetermined from the beginning. However overwhelming the public sentiment in favor of disciplined intellectual training may be, the professor of education who constructed the questionnaires has taken care that this sentiment shall not appear anywhere in the answers.

The "Follow-Up Study" is not an attempt to ascertain, but a deliberate effort to manipulate, public opinion. It is obviously designed to manufacture the appearance of public support for curricular changes that certain professional educationists have determined upon in advance. This purpose comes

---

[17] ISSCP, Bulletin No. 11, pp. 34 ff. In defending the "Follow-Up Study," Professor Hand denies that "the initial poll results are to be taken as a warrant for doing anything whatsoever in respect to the curriculum," and points out that instead they "are to be utilized as the beginning point for group discussions among patrons, teachers, and pupils in which choices *among the problems suggested by the Study* are to be made." Harold C. Hand and Charles W. Sanford: "A Scholar's Documents," *Bulletin of the National Association of Secondary-School Principals*, Vol. XXXVII, No. 194, p. 483 (April 1953); italics added. In view of the words I have italicized, it is difficult to see what difference this makes, unless it be a difference for the worse. My objection is that no sentiment in favor of systematic training in the basic intellectual disciplines can appear in the answers to Professor Hand's questionnaires, because none of the disciplines are mentioned in the questions. The circumstance that these answers are to be "the beginning point for group discussions" merely means that more people are going to be misled by the biased data furnished to them.

out stark and clear in the official statements explaining the questionnaires: "Given the American tradition of the local lay-control of public education, it is both necessary and desirable that a community (patrons, pupils, teachers) consensus be engineered in *understanding support* of the necessary changes before they are made."[18] I find difficulty in following some of the involved syntax of this sentence, but I have no difficulty whatever in grasping the significance of a "consensus" that is to be "engineered." We approach here the real meaning of what educationists euphemistically describe as "democracy in education." It is the democracy of the "engineered" consensus.

The "Follow-Up Study" is as great a fraud upon the teachers as upon the public. The professional educationists who planned it raised an exceedingly difficult pedagogical problem: how best to relate the subject matter of a course to the problems that are directly experienced by the students enrolled. As pedagogical experts, they might be expected to offer some answers. Instead they simply complicate and obfuscate the problem, by introducing multitudes of irrelevancies and by making grandiose promises far beyond the possibility of fulfillment. And in the end they simply dump all the problems they have created in the teacher's lap, calmly abdicating responsibility for indicating how their goals — sublime and foolish alike — are actually to be realized in the classroom.

Take, for example, "the problem of acquiring the ability to study and help solve economic, social, and political problems." All thoughtful men would agree that the school should assist the student to grapple with these questions. The great disciplines of history, economics, sociology, and political science have come into existence as the result of hundreds — indeed, thousands — of years of serious effort by able men to do precisely this in an orderly, systematic, cogent way. To dismiss these organized disciplines with the contemptuous epithet "subject-matter fields," to label them as mere academic exercises or college-preparatory work, is to reject out of hand whatever experience mankind has been able to gain in the reasoned solution of the great problems of social existence.

Responsible scholars in these fields do not offer quick and easy solutions. But they do believe, on the basis of experience and sound reason, that serious, sustained, objective, critical inquiry into these matters will equip a man with the knowledge, and develop in him the maturity of judgment, that are essential to intelligent and effective action. Only a quack will promise more than this. Responsible scholars and educators consider it their duty to do more than proclaim their ultimate objective. They feel a solemn obligation to specify clearly and publicly the means they intend to employ to reach that

---

[18] ISSCP, Bulletin No. 11, p. 10. Cf. the following: "The central purpose underlying the use of this questionnaire is precisely that of securing factual evidence which can be used to persuade a larger proportion of the pupils, teachers, and school patrons of the necessity of thus functionalizing the high school curriculum" (p. 13, repeated almost verbatim on p. 27). "The Follow-Up Study . . . is designed to yield opinion data . . . which will be helpful in 'engineering' an improved, broadly based consensus regarding what the local high school should be doing for its students." ISSCP, Bulletin No. 13, p. 14.

objective. And they are prepared to explain why they consider those means effective and appropriate. They recognize that perspective is essential, hence they advocate the disciplined study of history. They recognize that analysis and comparison are necessary, hence they propose systematic courses in political science and economics. To the "life-adjustment" educators, however, all this is sheer pedantry, just as bacteriology is so much learned nonsense to a group of happy faith healers.

Political, economic, and social problems that have taxed the intelligence of the best-educated men from antiquity to the present are to be solved, so the new educationists assure us, through a "common learnings course" in the high school wherein "materials from science, literature, history, mathematics, industrial education, homemaking, business education, art, music, and all other areas of the curriculum would be included."[19] This is the short cut to wisdom which the educationists propose as a substitute for disciplined, analytical, critical thinking. Having tied the world's problems up in this curious bundle, they consider themselves ready to pass on to other problems that seem to be of equal importance in their eyes — "the problem of acquiring the ability to select and enjoy good motion pictures," or "the problem of acquiring the social skills of dancing, playing party games, doing parlor stunts, etc."[20]

The problem of making a course relevant to the interests of the students enrolled in it is primarily a matter of intelligent and imaginative teaching. The important thing is for the teacher to know his subject and his students' problems well enough to make the connection. The elaborate polling of entire communities may add slightly to the teacher's knowledge of the latter, but it contributes nothing to his knowledge of the former. And the tendency of educationists to phrase their objectives in vague and grandiose terms actually increases the difficulties of teacher and pupil. The fallacy is the one illustrated by Dr. Johnson's famous definition of "network" as "anything reticulated or decussated at equal distances, with interstices between the intersections." I find it hard to believe, for example, that a student who is indifferent to school will recognize as a personal, compelling, "real-life" need the "problem of making one's self a well-informed and sensitive 'citizen of the world.'" If he can see no practical point in history, geography, arithmetic, and grammar, is he going to rush back to school filled with a burning desire for sensitivity and world citizenship?

The author of the list of "Problems of High School Youth" makes the categorical assertion: "There is no thought . . . that these problems are . . . to replace any of the existing courses in the curriculum." It is very difficult indeed to reconcile this statement with other assertions that appear in the literature of the Illinois Curriculum Program. Doubtless many persons have participated in the Program solely for the purpose of developing new teaching procedures within the framework of established disciplines. Nevertheless,

[19] ISSCP, Bulletin No. [1], p. 35.
[20] ISSCP, Bulletin No. 11, pp. 30–32, items E8, E10.

statements of completely opposite tenor occur too frequently and too continuously in various publications of the Program to justify giving credence to the assertion that "no thought" has ever been harbored of replacing "any of the existing courses in the curriculum."

Even the introduction to the bulletin containing the list of "Problems of High School Youth" and the questionnaires based upon it explains: "The Follow-Up Study furnishes the data which can be used to arrive at broad policies (consensus) which must be obtained before a faculty or administrator may safely embark on material changes in the scope and content of the secondary school curriculum."[21] In its very first publication the Illinois Curriculum Program announced that its goal for the curriculum was "common learnings organized in comparatively large units on [the] basis of youth and societal needs,"[22] and it relegated to the status of electives the "regular courses . . . in English, mathematics, science, foreign language, . . . and the like."[23]

By the time of its ninth bulletin the Steering Committee of the Illinois Curriculum Program had grown bolder. This publication, entitled *New College Admission Requirements Recommended*, contained the following complaint:

> The specification by the colleges of certain high school courses to be taken by all students seeking college entrance, sets definite limitations to curriculum revision. If a considerable block of courses must be retained in the high school to provide for the preparation of students who hope to go to college, the opportunity to re-examine the total high school curriculum and to replan the program in terms of the needs of all high school youth is thereby curtailed. For example, school administrators and teachers frequently mention the restrictive effect on their revision of the curriculum of the specification by some of the colleges that only high school majors and minors in English, foreign language, mathematics, science, and social studies will be counted for admission. The effect of such college entrance specifications is particularly limiting for smaller schools which comprise the great majority of Illinois high schools. The smaller schools cannot afford to provide a large number of courses; hence, when courses are specifically required for college entrance, most of them must also be the courses taken by students not going to college. . . .[24]

This statement makes the sharpest kind of distinction between programs based on "the needs of all high school youth" and education in the established intellectual disciplines. It makes it on the basis of "either . . . or." If a smaller high school wishes to offer "life-adjustment" education, it cannot afford also to offer programs in "English, foreign language, mathematics,

21 *Ibid.*, p. 9.
22 ISSCP, Bulletin No. [1], p. 6.
23 *Ibid.*, p. 35.
24 ISSCP, Bulletin No. 9, pp. 5–6.

science, and social studies." The latter are treated as nothing more than college-preparatory subjects, of value only in meeting "the specialized needs of parts of the student body."

In the larger high schools, admittedly, training in the recognized intellectual disciplines would presumably continue for segments of the student body. The bulletin uses as an example the group of students planning to go into engineering. These ought to have an opportunity to acquire some competence in mathematics, if convenient for the school to offer it. But "the Committee recognizes that smaller high schools will not always be able to provide a sufficient variety of specialized courses to meet the needs for special programs of all its graduates. In such cases, the colleges are urged to make provisions for the basic specialized work with as little handicap to the student as possible."[25] This is the end result toward which the Illinois Curriculum Program is tending. Fundamental intellectual training will continue to be offered to an élite group in a few of the larger and wealthier schools, but the graduate of the typical high school must acquire it when and how he can. And the colleges are urged to deal gently with those who come to them intellectually handicapped through no fault of their own.

It is in the light of proposals like these that we must read the jaunty prospectus published in the first bulletin of the Illinois Curriculum Program. Included was the following exhortation: "There are many ways of getting underway in a program of curriculum revision. The important thing is that we need to pry ourselves loose from the present situation. Maybe one lever will do the prying loose; perhaps, it may require several. . . . Pick your lever(s) and let's get started."[26]

Pry loose from what? The answer is implicit in any number of individual proposals. The secondary-school curriculum must be pried loose from the established disciplines of science and scholarship. It is to do so by ignoring and belittling them. The public school must be pried loose from its relationship to institutions of higher learning. The lever for doing this is to be found in the new guiding principle which the Curriculum Program advances: "Since the high school carries the responsibility for educating all youth, it, and not the college or university, has the responsibility of specifying the content of the high school curriculum."[27]

"Maybe one lever will do the prying loose; perhaps, it may require several." The metaphor is apt. The kind of lever that one uses for prying loose is sold in hardware stores under the name of wrecking-bar.

25 *Ibid.*, pp. 13–14.
26 ISSCP, Bulletin No. [1], p. 25.
27 ISSCP, Bulletin No. 9, p. 13.

Arthur F. Corey

Arthur F. Corey is Executive Secretary of the California Teachers Association, an organization affiliated with the National Education Association. The NEA is a mammoth consolidation of teachers and administrators accused frequently of fostering a sluggish and ingrown hierarchy of officers unsympathetic to realistically improving the professional lot of the classroom teacher. Corey was recently elected Chairman of the Educational Policies Commission of the NEA.

The following essay reveals Corey's answer to critics such as Arthur Bestor. It is necessary to note that many Traditionalists would disagree with Corey's self-styled definition of classical education as set forth in his "five tenets." Nevertheless, Corey's argument, ostensibly supported by "evidence" from his own commission's report, is a popular defense frequently used by educators under siege.

24

THE REAL ATTACK IS ON
EDUCATION FOR ALL THE PEOPLE*

Public education always has been an arena for controversy. First was the battle over whether we were to have free tax supported schools at all. Next came the battle over who should attend these schools, and more recently the struggle over how much such schools should cost.

Recent events indicate that we are now being engaged in a great public debate over what should be taught in the schools and how it should be taught.

Public opinion today is sharply focused on the curriculum. Any intelligent

* From *The Nation's Schools*, Vol. 62, No. 1 (July, 1958). Used by permission of Arthur F. Corey.

discussion of curricular problems depends upon philosophical considerations for its ultimate answers. This philosophical background the public and a large segment of the profession do not possess. Those who would now interpret the school program must not only know with some certainty what they believe but must be able to give convincing reasons why they believe it.

The usual defense of the status quo merely infuriates those who disagree with us. We must get below the rather futile arguments over the relative merits of various approaches to the teaching of reading — or the change in emphasis in arithmetic — or the place of grammar in the study of English — to a discussion of what we really believe the basic philosophy of education ought to be for a free society. This will require more knowledge and insight than many of us have brought to the task we face.

We need constantly to be reminded that disagreement about education is as old as education. Aristotle summed it up when he wrote: "All men do not agree in those things they would have the child learn. From the present mode of education we cannot determine with certainty to which men incline, whether to instruct a child in what will be useful to him in life, or what tends to virtue, or what is excellent, for all these things have their separate defenders."

The controversies mentioned by Aristotle were never resolved. The Greeks never found the answers to what was true, what was real, and what was important in education — and Greek culture declined.

The really important criticisms of education today are those that strike at its philosophy. These critics are striking back because they believe their own philosophy to be losing ground to the realities of life around them. They are the classicists who until recently completely dominated education in Europe and America. They see themselves being swept from the arena of educational thought and they naturally strike back. Hutchins, Griswold, Bestor and almost universally the so-called academicians are defenders of the classic thesis.

The classic thesis holds tenaciously to the following five tenets and it is important that we understand them:

1. There is a radical dichotomy between the physical and spiritual realm.

2. Mind is basically a part of the spiritual realm and cannot be understood in terms of material things.

3. The primary function of education is the development of the mind.

4. Man tends to be everywhere and always fundamentally the same. Dr. Hutchins puts this tenet in these terms: "It will be argued that this ignores the most important thing about men and that is that they are different. I do not ignore it, I deny it."

5. Values are very important and are not relative to time or place.

Now if one believes these concepts, one will believe certain things about education. Since man is everywhere the same and does not change, then education itself should change but little from age to age, and education for all men can be quite the same. To most educators these ideas seem incomprehensible, yet they are held by men who are themselves brilliant and well informed, even if not well balanced.

CLASSICISM HAS NO ANSWER

The important fact is that this classic thesis could not cope with Twentieth Century America, and it is fighting an angry rear guard engagement as it retreats. Classicism as a point of view has no tenable answer to the problems inherent in the extension of universal education through the high school. It largely ignores psychological findings and refuses seriously to consider the problem of the slow learner. He is either not admitted or dropped as quickly as possible both in educational institutions and educational discussions.

The classicists have one distinct advantage over many of us who disagree with them. They are not hypocritical. They practice what they preach. In the arena of educational theory the classicists have literally been pushed from the field, but in educational practice they still occupy a large and prominent segment of the stage.

The greatest weaknesses in the schools today are the curriculums that are most like our classical critics think they should be. Our colleges and universities (professional schools excepted) are the bulwarks of our critics and are probably themselves the least effective segment in education.

It is time we stopped assuming that public education is perfect. We ourselves must take up the cudgels of criticism. It's time the organized profession and the friends of public education began responsibly to tell the American people what is wrong with the schools.

I suggest that as beginning we might assert some certain obvious weaknesses:

1. American schools do not actually provide for the differentiated needs of pupils.

2. Educators are content to talk and dream about things as we wish they were, or as they ought to be, and dislike recognizing educational facts as they are.

3. Priority in function in education is almost entirely lacking. Schools can't do everything. What is most important?

4. American schools have accepted too much responsibility with too little resources.

*   *   *

There is no question where the American people stand in the philosophical battle over education. They are on our side. They must be made to see that the classical attack is an attack on them. It is fundamentally the rights and welfare of the people that are under attack and not the "educationists." To clarify this issue is our most immediate task. This is the imperative, immediate emphasis for public school relations.

If those who criticize the schools do so because of *their* philosophy, then we must make clear what our philosophy is, if we are effectively to interpret what the schools do for children. This, in my opinion, we have neglected to do. In this area the issues become really important. The present confusion will degenerate into chaos, unless the public has the information and philosophy upon which to base opinions.

In a recent publication, "The School and Its Program," the Commission on Educational Policy of the California Teachers Association has attempted to make a contribution by enunciating some principles it believes represent the philosophy of the educational profession. The commission believes that we have had difficulty interpreting the underlying principles upon which curriculum and method are based because no one has been able to state authoritatively what the professions believed.

You may not agree with any or all of these principles. This may be unfortunate, but certainly is not the central point at issue. If these statements are not satisfactory, then it is important that we quickly develop some others that are acceptable. Once such fundamental principles are agreed upon, they become the basic material for curricular interpretation for any school system. If the principles are understood and believed by the public, the details of subject matter and method will give us less difficulty.

The public school program is in the last analysis determined by society. The Commission's report states:

> The public school program gets its direction from the social needs which from time to time become identified in the public mind.
>
> This direction, although insistent and inescapable, is not wholly unresponsive to leadership. However, decisions are conclusive when made, being subject only to change by the long range powers of persuasion and further enlightenment. Many examples can be cited to show the effects of public pressure and decision in determining the content of education in California.
>
> Sharply rising accident rates among teen-age drivers led to mandatory legislation requiring driver-education in the high schools. The development of industrial production with necessary job specifications forced, even against the rather vigorous opposition of many educational leaders, the inclusion of specific vocational education in the high school. Widespread awareness of evils attendant upon the increased use of narcotics, alcohol, and tobacco resulted in legislation calling for instruction in these fields. Public opinion forced the elimination of German language instruction during World War I. Homemaking curriculums were added in response to public demand when changing social conditions gave rise to compulsory secondary education. National security needs brought military training, and technological advances are even now giving new emphasis to science and mathematics.
>
> The professional educator does not dictate what shall be taught in the schools. In a recent study of the history of the curriculum in California elementary schools, only two instances are recorded when revision of the school's program could be attributed to the direct influence of educators. In

scores of other instances, alteration followed the organization of public sentiment which was brought to bear upon the legislature. This is the approved, traditional American way to bring about changes in the content of education. It should remain traditional and effective as long as these changes do not mean yielding to an irresponsible minority. The manner of bringing about amendment places upon the educator the vital responsibility of serving as professional consultant and educational leader. Any profession would be vigorously condemned that did not take the public into its confidence on matters of public concern and turn to the public with proposed solutions and recommended courses of action. The public is still free to accept the proposals, or reject them, or modify them. The educator must remain free to concur in the decision or to continue to work toward a new course of action. To fail to propose is to default in a professional duty.

The point is that the public school is a servant of our changing culture. Even though language is our most generally useful instructional tool, direct experiences are commonly needed in furthering learning.

The report states:

Essential as language is for learning, it nevertheless has its limitations. Language consists of sets of symbols and it is possible to acquire the symbols without grasping the meanings they are supposed to convey. A child may memorize "six and three are nine," without understanding the words used or the relationship they are intended to embody. Similarly, a child can memorize the definition of "sentence" without being able to write a good sentence. Words become useful in thinking and in communication only as experience gives them meaning.

To be sure, language is our basic medium of communication and therefore is the most important tool in the learning process. The importance of language must not be minimized, but knowledge does not develop by memorizing words.

This necessity for experience is equally applicable to many necessary social skills. The ability to get along with others, which industrial leaders are now telling us is the single most important factor in successful business — this ability to get along with others is learned by actually doing it in a situation where one is helped to do it in the easiest possible way. A good way is in a classroom situation.

All pupils cannot be expected to achieve at the same rate or to the same degree in any learning field.

One might say that this statement is axiomatic. Yet much of the difficulty we're having in public criticism is based on the fact that the public does not yet understand that children of the same age exhibit marked differences in size, weight, strength and ability. To expect all children, regardless of their physical capacity, to jump a given distance or run at a given speed would be absurd, and even the businessman understands that. Children of a given age vary in capacity to do school work just as much. In any type of school work you might wish to mention, children of a given age vary just as much in their capacity to do it as they do in physical size or strength. In some cases more.

Intelligence itself varies as much as does height and weight in a normal fifth grade of unselected students, and when one gets to the ninth grade it's just that much worse because the further we go the more variation we have. In a normal fifth grade of unselected students one can expect to find actual variations in achievement and ability from that normally expected of a 7 year old to that normally expected of a 15 year old. And in the ninth and 10th grades this difference gets to be astronomical. So one child learns a lot faster than the other, and if the teacher does a good job and develops a situation in a classroom where everyone learns to capacity, the longer the teacher teaches the more she compounds her difficulty, because the further apart the pupils are as they progress.

Yet one still finds intelligent businessmen, intelligent laymen, operating on a philosophy of "why don't you set a standard for sixth grade arithmetic and then we'll know what everybody is supposed to do and when they do it you can pass them into the seventh grade."

How One Learns Is Important as Well as What One Learns

The attitude of the learner toward learning will ultimately determine the usefulness of that which is learned. You say, why sure this is true, or at least I hope you do say sure this is true, but the public doesn't. The most meaningful learning will be that which arises out of the purpose and interest of the learner and the most exciting learning will be that which the learner seems to discover within himself.

This creative approach of learning is even applicable to a skill like reading or to mathematics. We get into the area of creative learning when learners are taught how to discover for themselves a facility, a skill, an attitude, a bit of knowledge — rather than merely being told what the word is or what the answer is.

I saw recently in a school art exhibit in San Francisco a kindergarten boy's picture of a cow. I suspect this boy had never seen a cow, and I suspect that all his life he had been told that cows give milk, you must drink milk, milk is good for you, milk makes you healthy, milk makes you grow. And he even learned what part of the cow gives the milk, because this picture of the cow was a great big udder with a little tiny cow draped around it, and the udder had not four handles but sixteen. As far as that 5 year old was concerned that was a cow.

Then when the parents come to school and see this art exhibit they look at the picture and say: "My goodness sakes alive, that doesn't look like a cow."

This is our problem right now with the public. The public expects at any age the child to be able to do the thing like the public thinks it ought to be done. Whether it is drawing a cow at the primary level or teaching social problems in the high school, the creative approach to learning is not that the teacher gives the pattern and the child merely learns it and then gives it back, and the more nearly he gives it back like the teacher had it the better grade he gets. Of course, we still do that quite often at the college level and some of these professors are our severest critics.

In the public schools we believe it is the duty of the teacher to help the child draw his own cow; to help the child with the best information available develop his own answer. This is creative learning. But the public doesn't understand this. *The people don't understand that how one learns is just as important as what one learns.*

School Subjects Are Not Ends in Themselves, but Rather Means to the End of Producing Enlightened and Competent Citizens

The school attempts to help children learn, but the selection of what the pupil is to learn is the real issue. The school attempts to help young people learn to be or do something, not just to learn something. The pupil doesn't study subject matter just to learn subject matter. One teaches subject matter because subject matter does something to the child.

*   *   *

The traditional parental question to the teacher was: "How is Henry doing in algebra?" The proper question to ask is: "How is algebra doing in Henry?" This attitude changes the whole emphasis. The important consideration is what is going on within the child, that is, what has happened to him that makes him better able to make wise decisions as an enlightened citizen. This is the all-inclusive purpose of education.

Education Is a Process and Not a Condition

The goals of the school represent directions for personal development that are continuous throughout life. One can't give a child a test at the end of the 12th grade and find out whether he is educated. I quote again from the policy statement:

Education is a process, not a state of condition. Learning never stops; it is continuous throughout life. The adult aged 30 has quite a different conception of democracy than he had when he was 15 or will have when he is 50. Meanings should steadily become fuller and richer with the years. Interests should broaden and deepen. Values are subject to change with experience. The school is always seeking to encourage this kind of continuous development.

For this specific purpose the school establishes goals at the farthest edge of the grasp and does so with deliberate intent. It then provides learners with opportunities for personal growth toward these goals which, when extended into adult life, will produce the "enlightened" citizen. In an extreme sense these general goals of education are unattainable, for no one can hope to realize them to the full. No child or adult ever learns to read perfectly or even as well as he might, nor does he ever achieve the limit in quantitative understanding and skill. Failure to grasp this conception of education and of educational goals can only lead to a misconception of the program of the modern school.

Subjection to Reasonable Authority Is a Necessary Basis for Individual Freedom

This final principle was not included in the published statement, which has been freely quoted in this presentation. I am including it because I am firmly convinced it represents the considered opinion of the vast majority of practicing educators in America.

Freedom without authority usually develops into license. Much of the juvenile delinquency that is now so widely publicized is a natural and inevitable result of a decline in the respect and acceptance of constituted authority in American schools and American homes. The average teacher is helpless in the case of the incorrigible child who knows no authority but force when in many of our school systems teachers are prohibited from touching a child as a disciplinary measure. To permit a child to defy the teacher and get away with it is the beginning not only of crime but anarchy.

In too many classrooms the educational advantages of the great majority are being jeopardized because the teacher is required to use too much time in begging and cajoling some one child who does not respond to the influence of moral integrity, or who finds it impossible to respond to the more desirable and positive disciplinary teachings that are effective with the vast majority of pupils.

A necessary aspect of education is learning to relate oneself to reasonably constituted authority. At work, on the highway, or at play, some authority is necessary. Authority without power is a sham. There is no substitute for force with the individual who has been conditioned to respect no other influence. There is nothing here inconsistent with the principles already enunciated.

These principles may not be complete, nor is there any certainty that for any given school system they are accurate, but my thesis is still defensible. We should now determine in any school situation what our basic principles are, then set about systematically to interpret our basic philosophy to the public. If this approach is taken, the details will take care of themselves.

David Riesman

After his graduation from Harvard Law School, David Riesman was law clerk to Justice Brandeis, later becoming Deputy Assistant District Attorney of New York County. Mr. Riesman has taught at the University of Chicago, and he is at present a member of the Department of Social Relations at Harvard University.

Previously discussed in the Introduction to Part Three, Riesman's theory of counter-cyclical education attempts to reconcile to some extent the fruitful offerings of traditional and progressive sources. Riesman does not view his theory as a panacea, pointing out in his book Constraint and Variety in American Education *that counter-cyclical education could, if taken alone, become the negation of negation, "inherently relativistic and opposing new developments which appear 'excessive' although a longer perspective would show them to be fruitful. For counter-cyclical action can do no more than moderate swings of educational fashion in the avant-garde while bringing the rear guard and the home guard a bit nearer to the former. It is forced to take for granted the vested interests — the very vested existence — of the schools, and the prevailing patterns of career choice out of which teachers and scholars arise, while hoping to enlighten in small degree those interests and choices."*

Other books by David Riesman are The Lonely Crowd *(1950) and* Individualism Reconsidered *(1954).*

25

THOUGHTS ON TEACHERS AND SCHOOLS*

Progressive education in its initial American formulation (between about 1900 and 1925) was the product of highly intellectual teachers. These were men and women of marked individuality, talent, and enthusiasm, who became aware of the emotional shallowness and the rote learning of the tradi-

* From *The Anchor Review*, No. 1, 1955, pp. 40–60. Reprinted by permission of Melvin J. Lasky, Editor, and David Riesman.

tional schools, and sought to found new schools which would not only encourage the arts, the education of the emotions, and group co-operativeness, but which would do an even better intellectual job because more individualized and more closely geared to the child's developing pattern of motivations. These pioneers (being in this like other reformers whose plans have to some degree miscarried) could take for granted their own cultivation and belief in learning, as well as their own zeal, and they could go on from that foundation to try to give the children in their care — as most of us want to give our own children — the things they had missed in their own schooling. I have myself interviewed children and observed classes at several progressive private schools, and I can testify that at their best they turn out interesting and interested children, some of whom their parents and later teachers may find glib and unruly, but not stuffy or deceitful. For many children from narrow or emotionally frozen families, such a school provides an opportunity to thaw out in a milieu at once therapeutic and stimulating.

As I have remarked, the doctrinal tenets of such schools have filtered into many public schools with very mixed results. The filtering has not only been "downward" from the superior institutions (such as Teachers College at Columbia) to the junior colleges which have called themselves "teachers colleges" in the hinterland. There has also been a movement "upwards" from the nursery school model, where miracles appear to be accomplished by teachers unable to fall back on the drill of reading or writing in dealing with these preliterate tribes of fours, fives, and sixes: this demonstration of a happy school group, devoted to not much else than its being "happy" and being a "group," has influenced many primary and even high school teachers. It would not have done so to the same degree if the diffusion of progressive (and nursery model) education had not coincided with the growing emphasis on social skills in the community at large — an emphasis itself in part the product of the same social developments which freed millions to attend school and other millions to teach, transport, and feed them. As our society becomes more play-oriented and less work-oriented, more willing to admit personal sensitivity and warmth to the roster of prime virtues, more concerned with the mood of the group and perhaps less with the achievements of the individual, those goals which the original progressive educators wanted to add to traditional purposes tend in many public (and indeed some private) schools to become the only goals — goals, indeed, no longer so essential for the schools to aim at, since parents and the mass media, among many other social forces, are already active in securing them.

Listen, for instance, to a Massachusetts bread salesman describing to an interviewer what he hopes for in the high school education of one of his sons (and explaining incidentally why he is not sending the young man to college, though he is intelligent enough and the family could afford it):

> I tried to tell him where he isn't going to be a doctor or lawyer or anything like that, I told him he should learn English and learn to meet

people. Then he could go out and sell something worthwhile where a sale would amount to something for him. . . . I took typing, shorthand, bookkeeping and we had Latin, French, geometry. We had everything. But anything I would know then I've forgotten now. . . . I don't think a high school diploma is important. I mean only in so far as you might apply for a job and if you can say, "I have a diploma," it might help get the job . . .

Or listen (as recorded by William Whyte, Jr.) to a parent in Park Forest, a suburb of Chicago:

Janet is studying marketing and she's only in the sixth grade. She's studying ads and discounts, things I didn't get until college. The children are certainly getting a broad view of things.

Implicit in the attitude of both these parents is the belief that the school should prepare children for adult life by imitating that life; indeed, the same "child-centered" schools that would fear maladjustment through advancing an intellectually precocious child beyond his social age-mates often do their best to anticipate in the schoolroom the adult "here and now" of buying and selling, of parliamentary procedure and civic responsibility.

In this situation, as I have indicated, some of our teachers are fighting a losing battle in defense of the traditional intellectual values and the classical curriculum. But others (including many school superintendents) have turned necessity into virtue and favor the sort of programs that the parents I have just quoted would themselves like to see installed. Thus, Eric Baber, the high school superintendent in Park Forest, tells his teachers and parents that American education is still "far too much concentrated on the intellectual aspect of education." As he said in a teachers' workshop:

The so-called "bright student" is often one of the dumbest or least apt when he gets away from his textbooks and memory work. This is evidenced by the fact that many $20,000 to $100,000-a-year jobs in business, sales, sports, radio . . . are held by persons with I.Q.'s of less than ninety.

Baber is very proud of the "communication laboratory" his modern school plant includes; as he says, "ours is an age of group action," and one in which the children "must have actual experiences in solving problems that have meaning for *them*." No less explicit is the principal of a junior high school in Urbana, Illinois, speaking to a meeting of the National Association of Secondary-School Principals:

Through the years we've built a sort of halo around reading, writing and arithmetic. . . . The Three R's for All Children and All Children for the Three R's! That was it. We've made some progress in getting rid of that slogan. But every now and then some mother with a Phi Beta Kappa award or some employer who has hired a girl who can't spell stirs up a fuss about the schools . . . and the ground is lost. . . . When we come to the realization that not every child has to read, figure, write, and spell . . . that many of them either cannot or will not master these chores . . . then we shall be on the road to improving the junior high curriculum. Between this day and that a lot of selling must take place. But it's coming. We shall some day accept the thought that it is just as illogical to assume that every boy must be able to read as it is that each one must be able to perform on a violin, that it is no more reasonable to require that each girl shall spell well than it is that each one shall bake a good cherry pie. . . .

When adults finally realize that fact, everyone will be happier . . . and schools will be nicer places in which to live. . . .

This official may well be convinced that he is heretical and ahead of his time for, after all, he does come from the same university town as does Arthur Bestor . . . whose *Educational Wastelands* quotes this gem. This book is one of the least intemperate of a number of recent slashing attacks on just these self-styled "progressive" tendencies in secondary school teaching, some of which blame all attenuation of standards on John Dewey. We professors and intellectuals are generally inclined to trace tendencies we do not like to the ideas of other intellectuals, and this may in the long run be legitimate, but I do feel that Bestor exaggerates the autonomous role of the schools, and hence of their mentors, in fostering a mindless pragmatism and vocationalism which they often simply absorb from their constituencies.

Indeed, so strong are these constituencies that teachers and school officials are today frequently harassed beyond endurance by outsiders who have more prestige or power than they and who therefore feel free to intervene. The result is that it is hard for many in the school system to distinguish between a Barzun or a Bestor (or a Riesman) who has made some effort to understand their problems from within, and that horde of uninformed and usually reactionary "taxpayer" critics of "new-fangled" notions in the schools. The latter are apt to urge that what was good enough for grandpappy is good enough for his descendants. Since the grandchildren will face stiffer competition in terms of formal educational credentials, this penny-pinching view (sometimes abetted by local commerce and industry) simply kicks away a ladder to mobility which the new generation needs if it is to keep step with the rising educational and living standards of the country as a whole. In contrast, my own view is that grandpappy's education was not good enough for him in a day when artistic and empathic skills were seldom transmitted, but it does have certain redeeming virtues which only become evident when the rest of the society has caught up with an outlook that was rare at the turn of the century. In other words, I feel that schools can perform something of a *counter-cyclical* (or "governor") function; within the limits of their weakness, they can fall back on older traditions with very contemporary purposes in mind.

When faced with such a plea coming from a university campus, the school teacher — beleaguered, as I have said, with a multiplicity of special pleading — is apt to appear to turn a deaf ear and to use a diplomatic tongue. She knows that males are apt to be abstract, idealistic, and impractical — and patronizing. There is also the awareness that university professors, like other people, often have vested interests of their own, in discipline and in their "disciplines," to protect. Yet the very democratizing tendencies we have been discussing, which have had such unanticipated regressive consequences, compel teachers and school personnel generally to be accessible. It is hard for them to be other than defensive toward criticism, or, like all professionals faced with troublesome clients, duplicitous in finding the semantics by which all comers can be fended off.

Still, would these teachers be so vulnerable to the many competing demands now made upon them if these demands did not awaken echoes within them of unsolved problems in their own lives?

In interviews with Kansas City high school teachers, the poignant note comes up again and again of a self-confessed adolescent shyness. They feel this was bad, that they should have been "more outgoing" (perhaps they would have found a husband); some indicated that in becoming teachers they had conquered their shyness. In their relations with other teachers, they have established a coterie that they missed in school (and one that protects them to some extent from the unflattering public image of the unmarried school teacher). More important, they want very much to appear vivacious, warm, and outgoing in class. (One could make an interesting comparison here with current models of appropriate behavior in social workers and clergymen.) They want very much to be liked by the children, as well as by their colleagues, and they are perhaps more aware than before whether or not they are liked, especially as the children, good little communicators that they are, include among their social skills the ability to exploit the teachers' need for approval.

Is it true, then, that the cultivated and intellectual teacher has lost her role as a model for other teachers? Not completely. Quite a few, whatever their superintendents might sometimes prefer, do not wish to be merely "outgoing." There is the case of one high school drama teacher, the daughter of a very cosmopolitan newspaper editor; after a divorce she returned to the city of her birth and started teaching school there (political pull, of the sort now waning, helped her get a certificate). This teacher, well-traveled and sophisticated, has a remarkable gift for exciting her pupils' interest in the theatre; she is proud of "graduates on Broadway and in Hollywood." But her fellow-teachers have grave misgivings about her. They complain that she cares "too much about the drama" and "too little about the children." They complain that her productions demand too much time and effort, that the children who get so enthusiastic about putting on plays have little time for other subjects and for sociability, and they feel that the plays should involve a greater number of the children in their production, even at the cost of making the performances less professional. It would be more democratic, they say, to "give everybody a chance," and the drama, like other activities, is seen as one more way to encourage group participation rather than as a way to encourage vocations in the theatre. (The new school principal, a younger man who believes that the duty of the school is to "cultivate the total personality" of the child, has made life difficult for the drama teacher. What he wants is a good working-team of teachers, not stars on the Broadway firmament . . . nor excessive demands on the school auditorium.) I suspect, however, that these teachers would be less critical of their colleague, less articulate about her allegedly disproportionate preoccupation with the theatre, if they did not themselves in some degree aspire to cosmopolitan ways. In taking on responsibility for the child's social and emotional development, they have not wholly relinquished the older responsibility for "culture"; and it is their very ambivalence about partially contending models of school teaching that makes them so angry with those teachers, holdovers from an earlier day, who represent not only unequivocally high and secure social status but also the not entirely downgraded status of intellectual discipline and urbanity.

And it is equally true that a great many, if not all, of the "old-fashioned" teachers have been influenced and even upset by the newer pressures for a more democratic school system — democratic in its attention to the less scholarly (i.e. the non-college-preparatory) group, and to the standards set by the children and their parents. Here is an elderly English teacher at a high school which once was proud of its high academic demands (it had been modeled on the "Latin schools" of New England):

> Mr. —— believed so thoroughly in education as I really believe in it, yet I realize that it can't go on. I mean you can't go on pounding classical education into everybody's head as long as you are going to have everybody going to the same school. . . . Mr. ——, I am sure, felt that there were a lot of people who couldn't learn. . . . But he never relaxed what he thought were necessary standards . . . and if they couldn't make it they couldn't make it and that was all. . . . The older teachers who grew up with that were hard put — they like Mr. —— [the new principal], it's hard for anyone not to like him, but they just think everything is going to pot. . . . I think what he is trying to do is win over the student body to the idea that school administrators and school teachers aren't off there in another world. And then once he has their cooperation to let them make some of the rules and regulations they will be willing to abide by. . . . There have been so many educators and educators that have the theory that reading and writing and arithmetic are sort of overrated; that you must teach people how to be people. . . .

It is plain from such interviews that few teachers are so case-hardened as not to feel some ambivalence concerning the "battle of the books."

This conflict also emerges clearly in a series of group discussions with public school teachers in Chicago and Milwaukee which my colleague, Hedda Bolgar, a clinical psychologist, has been conducting. She finds that once the initial defensiveness of teachers against inquisitiveness is overcome, teachers are very eager to talk to an understanding outsider about their inner aims and external conflicts. Underneath a protective coating of cynicism and careerism these teachers frequently harbor a most grandiose and self-defeating expectation of omnicompetence in the classroom. They expect themselves to respond sympathetically to individual problem-children, even psychotic ones that would baffle an experienced psychologist. Partly aware of current mental-health emphases, they can no longer simply reject a child as "a troublemaker," or if they do they will feel guilty about it. In other words, the teachers have been exposed enough to psychiatric currents of thought to learn that children's aggressive behavior has to be explained and cannot be simply reacted to with counteraggression, but they do not often have sufficient knowledge to accept their own aggression.

Overtly, they may resist the expectation that there is no child they cannot handle, no child to whose needs they cannot minister while preventing it from dominating the group; they may say to one another, "Who does the School Board think we are, parking such little bastards with us?" Overtly, they may think they have done their job if they "keep the kids out of a messy home five hours a day," and they may, as we know, punish a teacher who does too much for the children, who is too enthusiastic — who is a scab or rate-buster in setting too high standards of performance. But underneath they seem to be demanding of themselves that they achieve therapeutic or motherly relations with all the children. Just because they no longer think of themselves as teachers of a subject but rather as teachers of an age-grade, they are at once tempted and betrayed by an ideal of omnicompetence. Though they are in fact in the position of the Old Woman Who Lived in a Shoe, they somehow accept the inner responsibility for making up in their own persons for all the deficiencies in the community. They feel badly if "their" children break windows or go to jail or drop out, no matter what the objective situation — much as many mothers feel.

I suggest that the cynicism with which many teachers talk among themselves is thus in part a defense against a still unextinguished (if often unconscious) ideal image of themselves as unruffled magnanimous individuals, at once motherly and wholly competent. If it were not for this, the teachers as a close-knit collegial group could cope somewhat better than they do with well-meant interferences by social workers, psychiatrists, superintendents, and educators, who directly and indirectly reinforce this extravagant image of what the teacher should be, pushing it always further from the traditional conception of the teacher as a subject-matter specialist, which is to say, a person of limited competence.

When it is pointed out to them that they are not, after all, psychiatrists and cannot expect themselves to cure problem-children, but only at best not to harm them, they react first with anger at the threat to their ideal of omnicompetence, but eventually with relief. And there is some evidence that they become better, less harassed teachers when they can fully realize that their function is limited — primarily, to teach a subject — and that they cannot as individuals compensate for all the ways in which our social organization now puts children in school because it doesn't want them in the labor force, or on the street corner, or because it has no other place for the disturbed child at the moment.

This relinquishment of claims, however, is easier said than done. What is a teacher to do when, as happened the other day in a Chicago elementary school, a lonely Negro girl comes to her to complain of the fact that she has "no friends in school," and that her mother will not allow her to make friends by inviting any children to her home? Is the teacher to send this twelve-year-old child back to her hopeless English lesson? What is the teacher to do as she watches a twelve-year-old boy, son of Jewish immigrant parents, develop an increasing contempt for children who have not raced through as many encyclopedias as he has in amassing an armory of unrelated facts with which, in quiz-kid style, he goes into battle? Is she to wait until the school, which needs a new building (though in general our school buildings are the cathedrals of our time) and more teachers, gets around to appointing a school psychologist? She would have to be more unequivocally devoted to learning for its own sake than are most of my university colleagues in order to be able to resist the appeal to her motherly, or clinical, sympathies. The result is that she pays less attention to the balanced and potentially gifted child who, she rationalizes, can look after himself.

In this situation, where the schools and the teachers cannot possibly meet all the demands they put on themselves, I think it would be helpful to develop a systematic theory of education as *counter-cyclical*. Just as Keynesian economics would have the government and the banks save in a time of inflation and spend in a time of depression, so teachers, in selecting among the expectations held out to them, have some modest opportunities to oppose "life" in its momentary excesses. A generation or so ago teachers were farsighted in being preoccupied with social skills, and in those many too many areas where underprivileged children still lack access to those skills, it remains important to emphasize them. In fact, to return to our theme at the beginning of the article, where the community continues to be production-minded, the schools can afford to emphasize the gentler arts of social and personal understanding; even today, the country is undoubtedly overplentifully supplied with sadistic teachers who employ their subject-matter superiorities to torment children in the Victorian manner. Increasingly, however, such settings would appear to be waning in frequency and impact; as the community becomes more consumption-minded, and as the out-of-school context helps cultivate the children's social skills, humaneness as such in the schools may on occasion be given a slightly lower priority and an emphasis on the teacher's own production-mindedness — whether with respect to French, football, or mathematics — is likely to be more beneficial and less traumatic. For in the middle-class homes of today children are listened to — they are no longer seen and not heard. The home is itself a "communication laboratory," at least in the middle class. Children can and do use the movies,

TV, comics, and magazines like *Seventeen*, as well as each other's example, to learn proper social behavior, especially since they no longer have to do many chores around the house. No one should sneer at the children's social proficiencies: if one compares American young people with their counterparts a generation ago (or in Europe today) one is struck by their poise, their understanding of themselves, each other, and adults; they can often handle touchy questions with a tact and facility our diplomats might well envy. As in the comic strip *Penny*, it is often the adults, not the adolescents, who are the awkward ones. But this very discrepancy, as I have observed, leads both parents and teachers, often conscious of their own childhood inadequacies and gaucheries, to give many children what amounts to postgraduate education in sociability when what they need, for the most part, is something very different. What they need, I suggest, is protection for those long-term intellectual and humanistic interests that are momentarily under severe pressure from so many sides.[1]

From this perspective, progressive education was undoubtedly a countercyclical force a generation ago(as it still is in many "backward" areas and for many individual children). It put pressure on conservative and conventional parents, and on their children. It involved the family in a dialectic which, if at times confusing, was frequently productive for all members — for the parents who strove to "keep up," and for the children who strove to understand and even sympathize with parents. Today, in many more prosperous suburbs, it is these children who presently are parents, and whose children are in turn attending schools that are no longer bucking the tide, are no longer experimental. No strong disagreements within the family, no tensions between family and school now require creative resolution. Yet the relaxed adjustment achieved in this way, while in some respects an undeniable advance over earlier miseries, means in terms of the life cycle less variety and less challenge.

This implies that, in many schools, where warm and outgoing teachers are present in sufficient number, effort should be directed to seeing that the children have contact with at least one teacher who cares profoundly about a subject matter like Latin or music which is at first sight remote from the concerns of everyday life. To be sure, such a teacher need not be indifferent to children. She may well come to be particularly attached to those pupils who are attached to her subject (as in Mary McCarthy's recent personal

---

[1] Counter-cyclical thinking and practice, as is evident, requires that such generalizations be perennially re-examined for accuracy and scope. My own views represent, *inter alia*, the animated revival of classical and humanistic concerns in the universities and among many businessmen. The "great books," the liberal arts, and similar activities have had the benefit of some energetic polemicists, often quite unafraid to be vulgar in attacking what they deem vulgar in secondary education and vocationalism generally. Sometimes this approach shades over into a new obscurantism which attacks the schools for any interest in the psychology of the learning process, treats John Dewey with condescending unfairness, and insists that there is only one donnish curriculum for everybody. In view of the speed with which, thanks to a resonant communications net, fashions in America change, such incipient cycles must not be overlooked even while one focuses on major national developments.

memoir). Such a person can do something to set up a competing model to the mediocrity that results from turning a school entirely over to teachers who have been shy and want to be personable and who hence care too much whether the children respond pleasantly to them and to each other; these are the teachers who have entered the profession to escape the farm or the working class and who come to be captivated by the paraphernalia of professionalism, such as "teacher talk" about classroom skills and audio-visual aids. If schools were to eliminate the difficult or eccentric teachers who present alternative models of good teaching, they would indeed become lifelike in 1955, only more so.

For truly high aims, whether they be occupational, personal, or intellectual, tend to contradict life as it is lived in any given place and time. Schools in the past, more by accident and even ignorance than design, have opened vistas to such aims (for at least a minority) by their very *un-lifelike* character. A student who, through a devoted teacher, could learn to live with Cicero or Mercutio, Joan of Arc or Jane Austen, might well succeed in discovering forms of existence transcending the observable in home or playground: transcending both the bread salesman and the idea salesman.

If children, tough and adaptable creatures that they are, can stand being confronted with a wider gamut of personal models than most public schools now make available, all I have said so far would imply that teachers — a group who reach a plateau of grown-upness early and stay on it long — are much less hardy and cannot be asked to face the personal consequences of counter-cyclical behavior. Indeed, in writing as I do I have the ironical misgiving that I, too, may only be adding to expectations for omnicompetence which, as I have contended, are already unrealistic. Just as I would not expect a banker who believed a depression was coming, and who had read Keynes, to invest his personal fortune as a way of increasing purchasing power, so I do not expect individual teachers to carry the whole system on their backs while beginning a counter-cyclical revolution. Still, I want to encourage some of them to give up trying to be psychiatrists, mothers, and moralists, to give up making citizens, democrats, and tolerant children. Could they not be persuaded to concentrate more than many now feel justified in doing on their roles as teachers of specific subjects? This is, after all, a job no one else is assigned or trained to do.

I am not arguing that the entire responsibility for counter-cyclical cultural activity must be borne by the secondary schools. The universities, the media, and the other makers of taste and opinion have a similar responsibility. Nor am I contending for a simple "middle way" between extremes, which can be discovered by a metaphorical thermostat or servo-mechanism. We lack at present the most elementary indices for telling, let us say, that the coming generation will possess "enough" social skills but not enough musical or mathematical ones.[2] I am arguing that, for the foreseeable future, no agency

---

[2] For the same reason, the Keynesian analogy is possibly misleading. It may suggest that it is as easy to institute counter-cyclical measures in the education industry as in commerce and finance. We have no similar indices of prosperity and depression; and educa-

with any leeway should make it its business to imitate "life" or to be "realistic" in the Philistine sense of that term, but rather that it should make a good guess as to where "life" is leading, and then proceed to criticize and correct it. Since in most quarters the dangers of intellectual arrogance are fast passing, school officials might make it a matter of professional pride to be as unpopular (short of dismissal) with the community as they can. It would help educate parents as well as children if a few principals and super-intendents supported their teachers against any pressures for lowering of standards and insisted on high competence in subject matter in as many appointees as possible. This will occasionally involve them in defending and befriending someone like our drama teacher; eccentric as such teachers are apt to be in their devotion to a subject, they may not be quite the best "team players" in the teacher colleague-group.

Paradoxically, it is in a non-academic area that this is already standard practice. I refer to the sports coach, who is ordinarily expected to get his pupils to do their best (even, sometimes, at shocking cost to body and soul). In this field, "democracy" means a free way for talent and not, save in a few schools which are hostile to competition as such, that everyone must proceed at a medium pace, or be elected rather than selected for the team.[3] Many of us — forgetting that before the days of organized sports our schools and colleges were locales of barely controlled roistering — tend to look down on the coach, though he may today be a better teacher than many of his col-leagues by virtue of his more unequivocal aims: The excellence of his pupils is the answer to his prayers. Even while we moderate his zeal, we might use it as a model for teachers of painting and poetry, some of whom should un-questionably concern themselves with children's self-expression, but others with giving even the less gifted children the valuable sense that there are cultural continuities and standards of excellence.

---

tion is a lifelong, omnipresent affair, responsibility for which is neither centralized nor assigned. Even Keynesian balancing can conceal complex choices among general alterna-tives; thus, a Schumpeter might defend cycles as stimuli to innovation and creativity, and fear the equilibrium achieved by governmental stabilizers and shock absorbers. The choices in the case of the schools are even less concealed.

I realize that counter-cyclical action inevitably defends a good deal in the status quo that has little on its face to recommend it (although it is at the same time an experiment on behalf of an indeterminate future). These difficulties in the policy are so great that, let me repeat, I am not adding to teachers' burdens the further one of judging society and the school in order to make profound counter-cyclical judgments. Rather, I am asking that school officials, critics, and controllers make such judgments at the very outset when they set curricula and select personnel. However, teachers themselves may take comfort from counter-cyclical thinking in the many instances where they feel uneasy about their pre-occupation with subject matter, or less than fully committed to classroom group dynamics. Counter-cyclical considerations can be for them a protection against certain fashions, and a defense for views which, in other contexts, might properly be attacked as out of date or unduly rigid.

[3] Since writing the foregoing, I have come across an instance in a private school where the girls' basketball team was elected — to the dismay of new girls not popular enough to be chosen and of those who preferred spending the scarce time in the gym actually playing rather than voting.

Bad Angel: . . . *and then what* were *the studies
in Donne's mind, in Kant's two worlds
established, in Iago's learned deceit, in
the teacher's love still pocketed as diligence?*

Dr. Fold: *Well, not knowing their peer-matrix
I can't be sure what they studied. But
in relation to motivational factors
they'd perhaps score high in terms of
achievement.*

Bad Angel: *I see.* (Pointing with his umbrella.)
*And those still good men now staring
into shop windows . . . their studies?*

Dr. Fold: *Ah, yes. I'm pleased to tell you of
our symposium on the disadvantaged
learner, to be held tentatively next
spring. In Denver I believe.**

PART FOUR

The Curricular Debate

A NOT SO HUMOROUS IRONY of language is found in a Latin meaning for
the word *curriculum*. To the citizens of Rome a *curriculum* was a
race-course, not a mild term of pedagogy, and it could be wryly
argued that this ancient meaning still lives in current usage. Today
it is not difficult to find students and parents who view formal education as a race, the prize for its completion being not a wreath of
laurel but a sheepskin of volatile merit. Without stretching the
analogy it becomes obvious, too, that some educators tacitly interpret a school curriculum as a trial to be endured rather than as an
instrument for intellectual, moral, and emotional enrichment. The col-
loquial phrase "getting through school," used by educators and lay-

* From "In Praise of Arrogance," a dialogue by the editor.

259

men alike, connotes not a joyful anticipation of learning but a resignation to grueling competition.

Perhaps the analogy between chariot racing and education (accurate and grotesque as it is) is merely symptomatic of a greater analogy which plagues our culture — the implicit comparison between a desperate race and the life of man. A voracious appetite for facile accomplishment, for painless victory infects our daily movements. Even the children are contaminated.

The youngster in elementary school is frequently cautioned to develop study skills, not for the intrinsic rewards of knowledge, but as preparation for high school — the next lap of his race. In turn, the high school student learns to view his school experience as a tedious and unavoidable prelude to college. And the college freshman respectfully inquires of his biology professor, "What must I do to get through your course?" The freshman already anticipates his vocational race, for which the college curriculum is, to him, inchoate training. The race wears on, lap after dutiful lap, the yawning graves well hidden behind the flags and bunting of victories too vapid to be cherished. In the classrooms of American schools we find poignant justification for Thoreau's observation that the mass of men lead lives of quiet desperation. Educators, too, are prey to a quality of desperation; grimacing with their contortions of logic and sentiment, they are besieged by aggressive demands from industry for technicians, by the burgeoning number of new professions requiring trained practitioners, and by a growing fragmentation of experience resulting from rampant specialization in commerce and the sciences.

The enigmas of curriculum development are numerous and varied; but the sources of our bewilderment may be described by posing three questions, the first of which is: To what extent should liberal education govern curricula in elementary, secondary, and university education? Some men reply that liberal education is a dead institution, one that passed from our culture when universal public education became not only a fact but a responsibility. Curiously, this brand of critic never questions whether the "passing" of liberal education (an absurd assumption in the first place) was good or bad. He simply argues that in a society which no longer tolerates a traditional aristocracy an educational curriculum designed for aristocracy is obsolete. He fails to consider the possibility that any knowledge we presume to have about our past, our present, and our future is essentially that knowledge which constitutes the core of liberal studies. Although men may not always agree on a precise definition of liberal education, it *is* that body of wisdom whereby humanity remembers, interprets, and anticipates its realities of experience.

A second question often posed in debate over curricula is: How important a role should specialization play in elementary, secondary, and college curricula? It is an ambitious question, and one that has been carelessly answered by the assertion that modern demands in industry, the professions, and scientific technology may be met only by a school curriculum thoroughly specialized in content and teaching method. This answer ignores the absolute difference between education and training, and by so doing supports the cult of the robot, the tyranny by which the specialist is enslaved by his specialty. Still, the need for trained workers and technicians is obvious; and the schools must be responsive to that need. But how responsive must they be?

Inevitably circulating through any argument about curricula is a third query: What forces have caused the gigantic hiatus between the sciences and the humanities, the twin sources of civilization? Although Aristotle was responsible for an initial categorization of human knowledge (he defined the fields of botany, anatomy, zoology, psychology, etc.), his divisions of scholarship were developed to facilitate research, not to segment man's understanding of nature. Today, we still follow, for better or for worse, the Aristotelian method of classification, not only in industrial and technological research, but in academic fields as well. Tragically, we neglect to assemble into an organic vision of reality the specific findings of industrial, scientific, and humanistic research. Our researchers spin out from a center of common human endeavor to perfect their independent orbits. Rarely do they return to the human center. A fear of interdisciplinary study permeates the modern university. A self-conscious snobbery injects a climate of distrust into the outwardly respectable community of scholars. Moreover, what must be described as a disdain for versatility pervades the academic environment. Teachers, artists, scientists, and scholars who attempt to experiment with interdisciplinary content and method are frequently accused of dilettantism. To exploit one's versatility is sometimes to invite censure. Aristotle, though versatile, was evidently spared this humiliation.

If American students, on all levels of education, are to profit from rich and challenging curricula, from programs containing an appropriate balance of liberal and specialized education — each content relevant to the other — it remains for teachers and administrators to affirm that interdisciplinary education is a genuine end of learning, not an eccentric hobby for intellectual dilettantes. Life is lived *whole*. An interpretation of life must aspire to *wholeness*, must be that essential sum of experience, that wisdom, greater than its parts.

The essays in Part Four are divided into three groups, each group specifically relevant to one of the central questions in curricular debate. Aristotle, Gaetano Salvemini, and Stringfellow Barr investigate the potentialities of liberal education. The Harvard Committee, Herbert Spencer, and Bertrand Russell develop arguments and conclusions about the quality and quantity of specialization appropriate to a healthy curriculum. T. H. Huxley and Matthew Arnold reflect in their debate the intellectual isolation still hindering cooperation between scientists and humanists; in the final selection I. I. Rabi attempts a conciliation.

The tripartite structure of Part Four is for convenience, not for truth: the three basic questions are clarified but not resolved by such separation. To answer successfully one question is to answer them all. To ignore two questions in a stumbling pursuit of one is to ignore all questions. And until the seminal relationships *between* the queries are known, even modest hope for curricular improvement is a futile anticipation.

I. LIBERAL EDUCATION

Aristotle

Aristotle (384–322 B.C.) was born in Stagira but spent most of his childhood at Pella, the capital of Macedonia, where his father was court physician. At the age of seventeen Aristotle journeyed to Athens where he studied philosophy under Plato, remaining at the Academy until his teacher died in 347 B.C. Aristotle founded his own school, the Lyceum, in 366 B.C. and continued to study and teach until the death of Alexander the Great led to a growth of Athenian hostility against the Macedonians. Aristotle was accused of impiety, the same charge leveled against Socrates seventy-six years earlier. Fearing that his life was in danger, he fled Athens and settled in the island of Euboea, where he died soon after.

To comprehend adequately Aristotle's philosophy of liberal education it is first necessary to examine his idea of virtue as set forth in the Nicomachean Ethics. Unlike Plato, Aristotle believed that virtue is divisible into two realities, the intellectual state and the moral state. Liberal education, in coordination with the family and the political state, is responsible for the cultivation of both virtues. The following excerpt from the Ethics serves, therefore, as an introduction to the specific description of liberal education presented in Book VIII of the Politics.

Before the seventeenth century, scarcely a teacher failed to utilize Aristotelian educational theory. Today, when critics (some of whom it seems have never read Aristotle) decry the classical interpretation of liberal education, it is necessary to re-examine the sources of the movement. Ironically, the "learning-by-doing" principle advocated by modernists like John Dewey is directly anticipated by Aristotle in, for example, his discussion of musical education. To their own embarrassment critics of Aristotle sometimes overlook the highly empirical, even pragmatic, spirit that pervades the admittedly traditional structure of his arguments and the conclusions reached therein.

The selection from Book II of the Ethics is translated by James E. C. Welldon, with notes by Louise Ropes Loomis. The extract from Book VIII of the Politics is taken from Bohn's Classical Library.

26

From BOOK II OF THE
NICOMACHEAN ETHICS*

1. Virtue then is twofold, partly intellectual and partly moral, and intellectual virtue is originated and fostered mainly by teaching; it demands therefore experience and time. Moral[1] virtue on the other hand is the outcome of habit, and accordingly its name, *ethike*, is derived by a slight variation from *ethos*, habit. From this fact it is clear that moral virtue is not implanted in us by nature; for nothing that exists by nature can be transformed by habit. Thus a stone, that naturally tends to fall downwards, cannot be habituated or trained to rise upwards, even if we tried to train it by throwing it up ten thousand times. Nor again can fire be trained to sink downwards, nor anything else that follows one natural law be habituated or trained to follow another. It is neither by nature then nor in defiance of nature that virtues grow in us. Nature gives us the capacity to receive them, and that capacity is perfected by habit.

Again, if we take the various natural powers which belong to us, we first possess the proper faculties and afterwards display the activities. It is obviously so with the senses. Not by seeing frequently or hearing frequently do we acquire the sense of seeing or hearing; on the contrary, because we have the senses we make use of them; we do not get them by making use of them. But the virtues we get by first practicing them, as we do in the arts. For it is by doing what we ought to do when we study the arts that we learn the arts themselves; we become builders by building and harpists by playing the harp. Similarly, it is by doing just acts that we become just, by doing temperate acts that we become temperate, by doing brave acts that we become brave. The experience of states confirms this statement, for it is by training in good habits that lawmakers make the citizens good. This is the object all lawmakers have at heart; if they do not succeed in it, they fail of their purpose; and it makes the distinction between a good constitution and a bad one.

Again, the causes and means by which any virtue is produced and destroyed

---

[1] A student of Aristotle must familiarize himself with the conception of intellectual as well as of moral virtues, although it is not the rule in modern philosophy to speak of "virtues" of the intellect.

* From *On Man in the Universe*, edited by Louise Ropes Loomis (Roslyn, N.Y.: Walter J. Black, Inc., 1943), pp. 101–113. Used by permission of Walter J. Black, Inc.

are the same; and equally so in any art. For it is by playing the harp that both good and bad harpists are produced; and the case of builders and others is similar, for it is by building well that they become good builders and by building badly that they become bad builders. If it were not so, there would be no need of anybody to teach them; they would all be born good or bad in their several crafts. The case of the virtues is the same. It is by our actions in dealings between man and man that we become either just or unjust. It is by our actions in the face of danger and by our training ourselves to fear or to courage that we become either cowardly or courageous. It is much the same with our appetites and angry passions. People become temperate and gentle, others licentious and passionate, by behaving in one or the other way in particular circumstances. In a word, moral states are the results of activities like the states themselves. It is our duty therefore to keep a certain character in our activities, since our moral states depend on the differences in our activities. So the difference between one and another training in habits in our childhood is not a light matter, but important, or rather, all-important.

2. Our present study is not, like other studies,[2] purely theoretical in intention; for the object of our inquiry is not to know what virtue is but how to become good, and that is the sole benefit of it. We must, therefore, consider the right way of performing actions, for it is acts, as we have said, that determine the character of the resulting moral states.

That we should act in accordance with right reason is a common general principle, which may here be taken for granted. The nature of right reason, and its relation to the virtues generally, will be discussed later. But first of all it must be admitted that all reasoning on matters of conduct must be like a sketch in outline; it cannot be scientifically exact. We began by laying down the principle that the kind of reasoning demanded in any subject must be such as the subject matter itself allows; and questions of conduct and expediency no more admit of hard and fast rules than questions of health.

If this is true of general reasoning on ethics, still more true is it that scientific exactitude is impossible in treating of particular ethical cases. They do not fall under any art or law, but the actors themselves have always to take account of circumstances, as much as in medicine or navigation. Still, although such is the nature of our present argument, we must try to make the best of it.

The first point to be observed is that in the matters we are now considering deficiency and excess are both fatal. It is so, we see, in questions of health and strength. (We must judge of what we cannot see by the evidence of what we do see.) Too much or too little gymnastic exercise is fatal to strength. Similarly, too much or too little meat and drink is fatal to health, whereas a suitable amount produces, increases, and sustains it. It is the same with temperance, courage, and other moral virtues. A person who avoids and is afraid of everything and faces nothing becomes a coward; a person who is not afraid of anything but is ready to face everything becomes foolhardy.

---

[2] Such studies as generally occupied the attention of the Aristotelian school.

Similarly, he who enjoys every pleasure and abstains from none is licentious; he who refuses all pleasures, like a boor, is an insensible sort of person. For temperance and courage are destroyed by excess and deficiency but preserved by the mean.

Again, not only are the causes and agencies of production, increase, and destruction in moral states the same, but the field of their activity is the same also. It is so in other more obvious instances, as, for example, strength; for strength is produced by taking a great deal of food and undergoing a great deal of exertion, and it is the strong man who is able to take most food and undergo most exertion. So too with the virtues. By abstaining from pleasures we become temperate, and, when we have become temperate, we are best able to abstain from them. So again with courage; it is by training ourselves to despise and face terrifying things that we become brave, and when we have become brave, we shall be best able to face them.

The pleasure or pain which accompanies actions may be regarded as a test of a person's moral state. He who abstains from physical pleasures and feels pleasure in so doing is temperate; but he who feels pain at so doing is licentious. He who faces dangers with pleasure, or at least without pain, is brave; but he who feels pain at facing them is a coward. For moral virtue is concerned with pleasures and pains. It is pleasure which makes us do what is base, and pain which makes us abstain from doing what is noble. Hence the importance of having a certain training from very early days, as Plato[3] says, so that we may feel pleasure and pain at the right objects; for this is true education. . . .

3. But we may be asked what we mean by saying that people must become just by doing what is just and temperate by doing what is temperate. For, it will be said, if they do what is just and temperate they are already just and temperate themselves, in the same way as, if they practice grammar and music, they are grammarians and musicians.

But is this true even in the case of the arts? For a person may speak grammatically either by chance or at the suggestion of somebody else; hence he will not be a grammarian unless he not only speaks grammatically but does so in a grammatical manner, that is, because of the grammatical knowledge which he possesses.

There is a point of difference too between the arts and the virtues. The productions of art have their excellence in themselves. It is enough then that, when they are produced, they themselves should possess a certain character. But acts in accordance with virtue are not justly or temperately performed simply because they are in themselves just or temperate. The doer at the time of performing them must satisfy certain conditions; in the first place, he must know what he is doing; secondly, he must deliberately choose to do it and do it for its own sake; and thirdly, he must do it as part of his own firm and immutable character. If it be a question of art, these conditions, except only the condition of knowledge, are not raised; but if it be a question of virtue,

[3] *Laws*, II, 653.

mere knowledge is of little or no avail; it is the other conditions, which are the results of frequently performing just and temperate acts, that are not slightly but all-important. Accordingly, deeds are called just and temperate when they are such as a just and temperate person would do; and a just and temperate person is not merely one who does these deeds but one who does them in the spirit of the just and the temperate.

It may fairly be said then that a just man becomes just by doing what is just, and a temperate man becomes temperate by doing what is temperate, and if a man did not so act, he would not have much chance of becoming good. But most people, instead of acting, take refuge in theorizing; they imagine that they are philosophers and that philosophy will make them virtuous; in fact, they behave like people who listen attentively to their doctors but never do anything that their doctors tell them. But a healthy state of the soul will no more be produced by this kind of philosophizing than a healthy state of the body by this kind of medical treatment.

4. We have next to consider the nature of virtue.

Now, as the properties of the soul are three, namely, emotions, faculties, and moral states, it follows that virtue must be one of the three. By emotions I mean desire, anger, fear, pride, envy, joy, love, hatred, regret, ambition, pity — in a word, whatever feeling is attended by pleasure or pain. I call those faculties through which we are said to be capable of experiencing these emotions, for instance, capable of getting angry or being pained or feeling pity. And I call those moral states through which we are well or ill disposed in our emotions, ill disposed, for instance, in anger, if our anger be too violent or too feeble, and well disposed, if it be rightly moderate; and similarly in our other emotions.

Now neither the virtues nor the vices are emotions; for we are not called good or bad for our emotions but for our virtues or vices. We are not praised or blamed simply for being angry, but only for being angry in a certain way; but we are praised or blamed for our virtues or vices. Again, whereas we are angry or afraid without deliberate purpose, the virtues are matters of deliberate purpose, or require deliberate purpose. Moreover, we are said to be moved by our emotions, but by our virtues or vices we are not said to be moved but to have a certain disposition.

For these reasons the virtues are not faculties. For we are not called either good or bad, nor are we praised or blamed for having simple capacity for emotion. Also while Nature gives us our faculties, it is not Nature that makes us good or bad; but this point we have already discussed. If then the virtues are neither emotions nor faculties, all that remains is that they must be moral states.

5. The nature of virtue has been now described in kind. But it is not enough to say merely that virtue is a moral state; we must also describe the character of that moral state.

We may assert then that every virtue or excellence puts into good condition that of which it is a virtue or excellence, and enables it to perform its work well. Thus excellence in the eye makes the eye good and its function good, for by excellence in the eye we see well. Similarly, excellence of the horse makes a horse excellent himself and good at racing, as carrying its rider, and at facing the enemy. If then this rule is universally true, the virtue or excellence of a man will be such a moral state as makes a man good and able to perform his proper function well. How this will be the case we have already explained, but another way of making it clear will be to study the nature or character of virtue.

Now of everything, whether it be continuous or divisible, it is possible to take a greater, a smaller, or an equal amount, and this either in terms of the thing itself or in relation to ourselves, the equal being a mean between too much and too little. By the mean in terms of the thing itself, I understand that which is equally distinct from both its extremes, which is one and the same for every man. By the mean relatively to ourselves, I understand that which is neither too much nor too little for us; but this is not one nor the same for everybody. Thus if 10 be too much and 2 too little, we take 6 as a mean in terms of the thing itself; for 6 is as much greater than 2 as it is less than 10, and this is a mean in arithmetical proportion. But the mean considered relatively to ourselves may not be ascertained in that way. It does not follow that if 10 pounds of meat is too much and 2 too little for a man to eat, the trainer will order him 6 pounds, since this also may be too much or too little for him who is to take it; it will be too little, for example, for Milo[4] but too much for a beginner in gymnastics. The same with running and wrestling; the right amount will vary with the individual. This being so, the skillful in any art avoids alike excess and deficiency; he seeks and chooses the mean, not the absolute mean, but the mean considered relatively to himself.

Every art then does its work well, if it regards the mean and judges the works it produces by the mean. For this reason we often say of successful works of art that it is impossible to take anything from them or to add anything to them, which implies that excess or deficiency is fatal to excellence but that the mean state ensures it. Good artists too, as we say, have an eye to the mean in their works. Now virtue, like Nature herself, is more accurate and better than any art; virtue, therefore, will aim at the mean. I speak of moral virtue, since it is moral virtue which is concerned with emotions and actions, and it is in these we have excess and deficiency and the mean. Thus it is possible to go too far, or not far enough in fear, pride, desire, anger, pity, and pleasure and pain generally, and the excess and the deficiency are alike wrong; but to feel these emotions at the right times, for the right objects, towards the right persons, for the right motives, and in the right manner, is the mean or the best good, which signifies virtue. Similarly, there may be excess, deficiency, or the mean, in acts. Virtue is concerned with both emotions and actions, wherein excess is an error and deficiency a fault, while the mean is successful and praised, and success and praise are both characteristics of virtue.

4 The famous wrestler, Milo of Croton.

It appears then that virtue is a kind of mean because it aims at the mean.

On the other hand, there are many different ways of going wrong; for evil is in its nature infinite, to use the Pythagorean[5] phrase, but good is finite and there is only one possible way of going right. So the former is easy and the latter is difficult; it is easy to miss the mark but difficult to hit it. And so by our reasoning excess and deficiency are characteristics of vice and the mean is a characteristic of virtue.

> For good is simple, evil manifold.[6]

6. Virtue then is a state of deliberate moral purpose, consisting in a mean relative to ourselves, the mean being determined by reason, or as a prudent man would determine it. It is a mean, firstly, as lying between two vices, the vice of excess on the one hand, and the vice of deficiency on the other, and, secondly, because, whereas the vices either fall short of or go beyond what is right in emotion and action, virtue discovers and chooses the mean. Accordingly, virtue, if regarded in its essence or theoretical definition, is a mean, though, if regarded from the point of view of what is best and most excellent, it is an extreme.

But not every action or every emotion admits of a mean. There are some whose very name implies wickedness, as, for example, malice, shamelessness, and envy among the emotions, and adultery, theft, and murder among the actions. All these and others like them are marked as intrinsically wicked, not merely the excesses or deficiencies of them. It is never possible then to be right in them; they are always sinful. Right or wrong in such acts as adultery does not depend on our committing it with the right woman, at the right time, or in the right manner; on the contrary, it is wrong to do it at all. It would be equally false to suppose that there can be a mean or an excess or deficiency in unjust, cowardly, or licentious conduct; for, if that were so, it would be a mean of excess and deficiency, an excess of excess and a deficiency of deficiency. But as in temperance and courage there can be no excess or deficiency, because the mean there is in a sense an extreme, so too in these other cases there cannot be a mean or an excess or a deficiency, but however the acts are done, they are wrong. For in general an excess or deficiency does not have a mean, nor a mean an excess or deficiency. . . .

*   *   *

8. There are then three dispositions, two being vices, namely, excess and deficiency, and one virtue, which is the mean between them; and they are all in a sense mutually opposed. The extremes are opposed both to the mean and to each other, and the mean is opposed to the extremes. For as the equal

---

[5] The Pythagoreans, who saw a mystical and moral significance in numbers, took the opposite principles of "the finite" and "the infinite" to represent respectively good and evil.
[6] A line — perhaps Pythagorean — of unknown authorship.

if compared with the less is greater, but if compared with the greater is less, so the mean state, whether in emotion or action, if compared with deficiency is excessive, but if compared with excess is deficient. Thus the brave man appears foolhardy compared with the coward, but cowardly compared with the foolhardy. Similarly, the temperate man appears licentious compared with the insensible man but insensible compared with the licentious; and the liberal man appears extravagant compared with the stingy man but stingy compared with the spendthrift. The result is that the extremes each denounce the mean as belonging to the other extreme; the coward calls the brave man foolhardy, and the foolhardy man calls him cowardly; and so on in other cases.

But while there is mutual opposition between the extremes and the mean, there is greater opposition between the two extremes than between extreme and the mean; for they are further removed from each other than from the mean, as the great is further from the small and the small from the great than either from the equal. Again, while some extremes show some likeness to the mean, as foolhardiness to courage and extravagance to liberality, there is the greatest possible dissimilarity between extremes. But things furthest removed from each other are called opposites; hence the further things are removed, the greater is the opposition between them.

In some cases it is deficiency and in others excess which is more opposed to the mean. Thus it is not foolhardiness, an excess, but cowardice, a deficiency, which is more opposed to courage, nor is it insensibility, a deficiency, but licentiousness, an excess, which is more opposed to temperance. There are two reasons why this should be so. One lies in the nature of the matter itself; for when one of two extremes is nearer and more like the mean, it is not this extreme but its opposite that we chiefly contrast with the mean. For instance, as foolhardiness seems more like and nearer to courage than cowardice, it is cowardice that we chiefly contrast with courage; for things further removed from the mean seem to be more opposite to it. This reason lies in the nature of the matter itself; there is a second which lies in our own nature. The things to which we ourselves are naturally more inclined we think more opposed to the mean. Thus we are ourselves naturally more inclined to pleasures than to their opposites, and are more prone therefore to self-indulgence than to moderation. Accordingly we speak of those things in which we are more likely to run to great lengths as more opposed to the mean. Hence licentiousness, which is an excess, seems more opposed to temperance than insensibility.

9. We have now sufficiently shown that moral virtue is a mean, and in what sense it is so; that it is a mean as lying between two vices, a vice of excess on the one side and a vice of deficiency on the other, and as aiming at the mean in emotion and action.

That is why it is so hard to be good; for it is always hard to find the mean in anything; it is not everyone but only a man of science who can find the mean or center of a circle. So too anybody can get angry — that is easy —

and anybody can give or spend money, but to give it to the right person, to give the right amount of it, at the right time, for the right cause and in the right way, this is not what anybody can do, nor is it easy. That is why goodness is rare and praiseworthy and noble. One then who aims at a mean must begin by departing from the extreme that is more contrary to the mean; he must act in the spirit of Calypso's advice,

> Far from this spray and swell hold thou thy ship,[7]

for of the two extremes one is more wrong than the other. As it is difficult to hit the mean exactly, we should take the second best course,[8] as the saying is, and choose the lesser of two evils. This we shall best do in the way described, that is, steering clear of the evil which is further from the mean. We must also note the weaknesses to which we are ourselves particularly prone, since different natures tend in different ways; and we may ascertain what our tendency is by observing our feelings of pleasure and pain. Then we must drag ourselves away towards the opposite extreme; for by pulling ourselves as far as possible from what is wrong we shall arrive at the mean, as we do when we pull a crooked stick straight.

In all cases we must especially be on our guard against the pleasant, or pleasure, for we are not impartial judges of pleasure. Hence our attitude towards pleasure must be like that of the elders of the people in the *Iliad* towards Helen, and we must constantly apply the words they use;[9] for if we dismiss pleasure as they dismissed Helen, we shall be less likely to go wrong. By action of this kind, to put it summarily, we shall best succeed in hitting the mean.

Undoubtedly this is a difficult task, especially in individual cases. It is not easy to determine the right manner, objects, occasion, and duration of anger. Sometimes we praise people who are deficient in anger, and call them gentle, and at other times we praise people who exhibit a fierce temper as high spirited. It is not however a man who deviates a little from goodness, but one who deviates a great deal, whether on the side of excess or of deficiency, that is blamed; for he is sure to call attention to himself. It is not easy to decide in theory how far and to what extent a man may go before he becomes blameworthy, but neither is it easy to define in theory anything else in the region of the senses; such things depend on circumstances, and our judgment of them depends on our perception.

---

[7] *Odyssey* XII, 219, 220; but it is Odysseus who speaks there, and the advice has been given him not by Calypso but by Circe.

[8] The Greek proverb means properly "we must take to the oars, if sailing is impossible."

[9]   "No marvel that the Trojans and shining-greaved Achaeans
    For such a woman year on year do suffer toil and woe;
    Since fearfully is she in face like the deathless goddesses —
    E'en so, in all her splendor, let the ships take her home,
    Let her not stay, a curse to us and to our babes hereafter."
                                        Iliad, III.

So much then is plain, that the mean is everywhere praiseworthy, but that we ought to aim at one time towards an excess and at another towards a deficiency; for thus we shall most easily hit the mean, or in other words reach excellence.

27

From BOOK VIII of the POLITICS

1. No one will doubt that the legislator should direct his attention above all to the education of youth, or that the neglect of education does harm to states. The citizen should be molded to suit the form of government under which he lives. For each government has a peculiar character which originally formed and which continues to preserve it. The character of democracy creates democracy, and the character of oligarchy creates oligarchy; and always the better the character, the better the government.

Now for the exercise of any faculty or art a previous training and habituation are required; clearly therefore for the practice of virtue. And since the whole city has one end, it is manifest that education should be one and the same for all, and that it should be public, and not private, — not as at present, when every one looks after his own children separately, and gives them separate instruction of the sort which he thinks best; the training in things which are of common interest should be the same for all. Neither must we suppose that any one of the citizens belongs to himself, for they all belong to the state, and are each of them a part of the state, and the care of each part is inseparable from the care of the whole. In this particular the Lacedaemonians are to be praised, for they take the greatest pains about their children, and make education the business of the state.

2. That education should be regulated by law and should be an affair of state is not to be denied, but what should be the character of this public education, and how young persons should be educated, are questions which remain to be considered. For mankind are by no means agreed about the things to be taught, whether we look to virtue or the best life.

Neither is it clear whether education is more concerned with intellectual or with moral virtue. The existing practice is perplexing; no one knows on what principle we should proceed — should the useful in life, or should virtue, or should the higher knowledge, be the aim of our training; all three opinions have been entertained. Again, about the means there is no agreement; for different persons, starting with different ideas about the nature of virtue, naturally disagree about the practice of it.

There can be no doubt that children should be taught those useful things which are really necessary, but not all things; for occupations are divided into liberal and illiberal; and to young children should be imparted only such kinds of knowledge as will be useful to them without vulgarizing them. And any occupation, art, or science, which makes the body or soul or mind of the freeman less fit for the practice or exercise of virtue, is vulgar; wherefore we call those arts vulgar which tend to deform the body, and likewise all paid employments, for they absorb and degrade the mind.

There are also some liberal arts quite proper for a freeman to acquire, but only in a certain degree, and if he attend to them too closely, in order to attain perfection in them, the same evil effects will follow. The object also which a man sets before him makes a great difference; if he does or learns anything for his own sake or for the sake of his friends, or with a view to excellence, the action will not appear illiberal; but if done for the sake of others, the very same action will be thought menial and servile. The received subjects of instruction, as I have already remarked, are partly of a liberal and partly of an illiberal character.

3. The customary branches of education are in number four; they are — (1) reading and writing, (2) gymnastic exercises, (3) music, to which is sometimes added (4) drawing. Of these, reading and writing and drawing are regarded as useful for the purposes of life in a variety of ways, and gymnastic exercises are thought to infuse courage. Concerning music a doubt may be raised — in our own day most men cultivate it for the sake of pleasure, but originally it was included in education, because Nature herself, as has often been said, requires that we should be able, not only to work well, but to use leisure well; for, as I must repeat once and again, the first principle of all action is leisure. Both are required, but leisure is better than occupation; and therefore the question must be asked in good earnest, what ought we to do when at leisure? Clearly we ought not to be amusing ourselves, for then amusement would be the end of life. But if this is inconceivable, and yet amid serious occupations amusement is needed more than at other times (for he who is hard at work has need of relaxation, and amusement gives relaxation, whereas occupation is always accompanied with exertion and effort), at suitable times we should introduce amusements, and they should be our medicines, for the emotion which they create in the soul is a relaxation, and from the pleasure we obtain rest. Leisure of itself gives pleasure and happiness and enjoyment of life, which are experienced, not by the busy man, but by those who have leisure. For he who is occupied has in view some end which he has not attained; but happiness is an end which all men deem to be accompanied with pleasure and not with pain. This pleasure, however, is regarded differently by different persons, and varies according to the habit of individuals; the pleasure of the best man is the best, and springs from the noblest sources.

It is clear then that there are branches of learning and education which we must study with a view to the enjoyment of leisure, and these are to be valued for their own sake; whereas those kinds of knowledge which are useful in business are to be deemed necessary, and exist for the sake of other things. And therefore our fathers admitted music into education, not on the ground either of its necessity or utility, for it is not necessary, nor indeed useful in the same manner as reading and writing, which are useful in money-making, in the management of a household, in the acquisition of knowledge, and in political life, nor like drawing, useful for a more correct judgment of the works of artists, nor again like gymnastic, which gives health and strength; for neither of these is to be gained from music. There remains, then, the use of music for intellectual enjoyment in leisure; which appears to have been the reason of its introduction, this being one of the ways in which it is thought that a freeman should pass his leisure; as Homer says —

> How good it is to invite men to the pleasant feast,

and afterwards he speaks of others whom he describes as inviting

> The bard who would delight them all.[1]

And in another place Odysseus says there is no better way of passing life than when

> Men's hearts are merry and the banqueters in the hall, sitting in order, hear the voice of the minstrel.[2]

It is evident, then, that there is a sort of education in which parents should train their sons, not as being useful or necessary, but because it is liberal or noble. Whether this is of one kind only, or of more than one, and if so, what they are, and how they are to be imparted, must hereafter be determined. Thus much we are now in a position to say that the ancients witness to us; for their opinion may be gathered from the fact that music is one of the received and traditional branches of education. Further, it is clear that children should be instructed in some useful things, — for example, in reading and writing, — not only for their usefulness, but also because many other sorts of knowledge are acquired through them. With a like view they may be taught drawing, not to prevent their making mistakes in their own purchases, or in order that they may not be imposed upon in the buying or selling of articles, but rather because it makes them judges of the beauty of the human form. To be seeking always after the useful does not become free and exalted souls. Now it is clear that in education habit must go before reason, and the body before the mind; and therefore boys should be handed over to the trainer, who creates in them the proper habit of body, and to the wrestling-master, who teaches them their exercises.

[1] *Odyssey*, XVII. 385.   [2] *Odyssey*, IX. 7.

4. Of these states which in our own day seem to take the greatest care of children, some aim at producing in them an athletic habit, but they only injure their forms and stunt their growth. Although the Lacedaemonians have not fallen into this mistake, yet they brutalize their children by laborious exercises which they think will make them courageous. But in truth, as we have often repeated, education should not be exclusively directed to this or to any other single end. And even if we suppose the Lacedaemonians to be right in their end, they do not attain it. For among barbarians and among animals courage is found associated, not with the greatest ferocity, but with a gentle and lionlike temper. There are many races who are ready enough to kill and eat men, such as the Achaeans and Heniochi, who both live about the Black Sea; and there are other inland tribes, as bad or worse, who all live by plunder, but have no courage. It is notorious that the Lacedaemonians, while they were themselves assiduous in their laborious drill, were superior to others, but now they are beaten both in war and gymnastic exercises. For their ancient superiority did not depend on their mode of training their youth, but only on the circumstance that they trained them at a time when others did not. Hence we may infer that what is noble, not what is brutal, should have the first place; no wolf or other wild animal will face a really noble danger; such dangers are for the brave man. And parents who devote their children to gymnastics while they neglect their necessary education, in reality vulgarize them; for they make them useful to the state in one quality only, and even in this argument proves them to be inferior to others. We should judge the Lacedaemonians not from what they have been but from what they are; for now they have rivals who compete with their education; formerly they had none.

It is an admitted principle that gymnastic exercises should be employed in education and that for children they should be of a lighter kind, avoiding severe regimen or painful toil, lest the growth of the body be impaired. The evil of excessive training in early years is strikingly proved by the example of the Olympic victors; for not more than two or three of them have gained a prize both as boys and as men; their early training and severe gymnastic exercises exhausted their constitutions. When boyhood is over, three years should be spent in other studies; the period of life which follows may then be devoted to hard exercise and strict regimen. Men ought not to labor at the same time with their minds and with their bodies; for the two kinds of labor are opposed to one another, the labor of the body impedes the mind, and the labor of the mind the body.

5. Concerning music there are some questions which we have already raised; these we may now resume and carry further; and our remarks will serve as a prelude to this or any other discussion of the subject. It is not easy to determine the nature of music, or why any one should have a knowledge of it. Shall we say, for the sake of amusement and relaxation, like sleep or drinking, which are not good in themselves, but are pleasant, and at the same time "make care to cease," as Euripides[3] says? And there-

[3] *Bacchae*, 380.

fore men rank them with music, and make use of all three, — sleep, drinking, music, — to which some add dancing. Or shall we argue that music conduces to virtue, on the ground that it can form our minds and habituate us to true pleasures as our bodies are made by gymnastic to be of a certain character? Or shall we say that it contributes to the enjoyment of leisure and mental cultivation, which is a third alternative? Now obviously youth are not to be instructed with a view to their amusement, for learning is no pleasure, but is accompanied with pain. Neither is intellectual enjoyment suitable to boys of that age, for it is the end, and that which is imperfect cannot attain the perfect or end. But perhaps it may be said that boys learn music for the sake of the amusement which they will have when they are grown up. If so, why should they learn themselves, and not, like the Persian and Median kings, enjoy the pleasure and instruction which is derived from hearing others? (for surely skilled persons who have made music the business and profession of their lives will be better performers than those who practice only to learn). If they must learn music, on the same principle they should learn cookery, which is absurd. And even granting that music may form the character, the objection still holds: why should we learn ourselves? Why cannot we attain true pleasure and form a correct judgment from hearing others, like the Lacedaemonians? For they, without learning music, nevertheless can correctly judge, as they say, of good and bad melodies. Or again, if music should be used to promote cheerfulness and refined intellectual enjoyment, the objection still remains — why should we learn ourselves instead of enjoying the performance of others? We may illustrate what we are saying by our conception of the Gods; for in the poets Zeus does not himself sing or play on the lyre. Nay, we call professional performers vulgar; no freeman would play or sing unless he were intoxicated or in jest. But these matters may be left for the present.

The first question is whether music is or is not to be a part of education. Of the three things mentioned in our discussion, which is it? — Education or amusement or intellectual enjoyment, for it may be reckoned under all three, and seems to share in the nature of all of them. Amusement is for the sake of relaxation, and relaxation is of necessity sweet, for it is the remedy of pain caused by toil, and intellectual enjoyment is universally acknowledged to contain an element not only of the noble but of the pleasant, for happiness is made up of both. All men agree that music is one of the pleasantest things, whether with or without song; as Musaeus says,

Song is to mortals of all things the sweetest.

Hence and with good reason it is introduced into social gatherings and entertainments, because it makes the hearts of men glad: so that on this ground alone we may assume that the young ought to be trained in it. For innocent pleasures are not only in harmony with the perfect end of life, but they also provide relaxation. And whereas men rarely attain the end, but often rest by the way and amuse themselves, not only with a view to some good, but also for the pleasure's sake, it may be well for them at times to find a refreshment in music. It sometimes happens that men make amusement the end, for the end probably contains some element of pleasure, though not any ordinary or lower pleasure; but they mistake the lower for the higher, and in seeking for the one find the other, since every pleasure has a likeness to the end of action. For the end is not eligible, nor do the pleasures which we have described exist, for the sake of any future good but of the past, that is to say, they are the alleviation of past toils and pains. And we may infer this to be the reason why men seek happiness from common pleasures. But music is pursued, not only as an alleviation of past toil, but also as providing recreation. And who can say whether, having this use, it may not also have a nobler one? In addition to this common pleasure, felt and shared in by all (for the pleasure given by music is natural, and therefore adapted to all ages and characters), may it not have also some influence over the character and the soul? It must have such an influence if characters are affected by it. And that they are so affected is proved by the power which the songs of Olympus and of many others exercise; for beyond question they inspire enthusiasm, and enthusiasm is an emotion of the ethical part of the soul. Besides, when men hear imitations, even unaccompanied by melody or rhythm, their feelings move in sympathy. Since then music is a pleasure, and virtue consists in rejoicing and loving and hating aright, there is clearly nothing which we are so much concerned to acquire and to cultivate as the power of forming right judgments, and of taking delight in good dispositions and noble actions.

Gaetano Salvemini

Responses to the question "What is culture?" differ, of course, depending upon the historical time of inquiry. Gaetano Salvemini, Emeritus Professor of History at Harvard University, asked the question in the bleak climate of 1939. His answer reflects the view of the modern teacher who, in an age of specialization, still champions the cause of liberal education as envisioned in classical antiquity. Salvemini defines human culture as that comprehensive phenomenon embracing physical, intellectual, aesthetic, and moral attributes; and his program for its enrichment reads like a modern version of Greek and Roman educational doctrine.

Particularly intriguing is Salvemini's notion of the "right to be igno-rant," an idea which runs contrary to the progressive urge to train the student in as many skills as the school budget can bear.

Salvemini has taught at the University of Florence and at Yale. His books include Under the Axe of Fascism *(1936),* The French Revolu-tion *(1954), and* Prelude to World War II *(1954). In his writing, teach-ing, and research Salvemini has fulfilled the dual occupation of historical scholar and philosopher of current history.*

28

WHAT IS CULTURE?*

I. Professional Culture and General Culture

There is great truth in that definition of culture according to which culture consists in "knowing something of everything and everything of something."

The man who knows everything about something, without knowing any-thing about all the rest, restricts his intellectual activities. He quenches in himself all curiosity outside the narrow circle of his specialty. He secludes himself from the world. He is the man of a single book, as our forefathers said. He cannot in any way be considered a man of culture. The specialist has killed the man. Our forefathers were wont to say *Mathematicus purus asinus purus:* The mathematician who knows nothing beyond his mathe-matics is a thorough ass.

Specialization is usually regarded as a professional malady peculiar to those who dedicate themselves to science, and particularly to university professors. But the banker, too, suffers from the same psychological deformity when he lives absorbed in the one preoccupation of growing rich, looking neither right nor left, piling up transaction upon transaction and wealth upon wealth, and completely stifling his inner life. So also does the judge who fits the whole human spirit into the code of legal procedure, and turns a cold eye upon the infinite welter of human miseries which life brings before him, intent only on classifying them according to the framework of the law. So

---

* Reprinted by permission of the publishers from Gaetano Salvemini, *Historian and Scientist: An Essay on the Nature of History and the Social Sciences.* Cambridge, Mass.: Harvard University Press, copyright, 1939, by The President and Fellows of Harvard College.

does the engineer who seeks around him nothing but machines to construct, formulas to apply, and refractory materials to conquer, and forgets that behind the machines there are men who feel and think and suffer, and that men are not made for the machines but the machines to serve men. So does the military chief who in his barrack life regards the whole world as a barrack, and carries the habit of undisputed command and the need for immediate obedience into spheres where that habit and that need are out of place and even dangerous. These men, too, are one-sided specialists. A psychological deformation has taken place in them similar to that which as a rule is attributed to scientists alone.

To avoid the bad results produced on the inner life by excessive limitation of the intellectual range, we need, besides specialized and professional knowledge, a wide and varied stock of information of all kinds. In other words we must know something of everything, besides knowing everything of something. This nonprofessional culture we are led to acquire not by the desire to earn money but by a free and disinterested desire to cultivate our mind, to extend the field of our knowledge, and to live in addition to our own life the life of our fellows. We usually give the name of "general culture" to this not strictly professional knowledge, which is not intended to be turned into hard cash. Sometimes we call it "culture" pure and simple, as if to show that true culture does not consist in the knowledge we need in a special profession but begins precisely where professional utility ends.

For a day laborer the ability to read and write is culture. For the intellectual the ability to read and write is nothing: culture begins for him far beyond that. Knowledge which in a doctor is professional and thus not a part of culture, becomes culture when it is found in the intellectual store of a lawyer. Vice versa, legal knowledge, which is culture for a doctor, does not imply in the lawyer any intellectual superiority or strength outside his profession. A friend of mine, a professor completely absorbed in the study of his special subject, was wont to say: "Culture is the luxury which my wife can afford herself."

Culture therefore is the sum of all knowledge which serves no practical purpose but which one must possess if one wants to be a human being and not a specialized machine. Culture is the indispensable superfluity.

This stock of nonprofessional information which presumably serves no practical purpose needs to be organically arranged round that more solid nucleus of professional learning which is, so to speak, the personal property of the specialist. The man who has a smattering of everything and never concentrates his intellectual activities on a fixed point may perhaps score easy conversational triumphs; he succeeds better than the specialist in "cutting a good figure in society," as the expression is; but in the world of thought and the world of action he is utterly useless. He is not a man of culture; he is a parasite on the culture of others.

This is why we need not only to know something of everything but also everything of something.

II. The Right to Be Ignorant

On the other hand, the definition that culture consists in "knowing everything of something and something of everything" must be taken with many reservations.

In 1933 the professors of Princeton University, who so many times had subjected their pupils to intelligence tests, were in their turn subjected by their pupils to a test of the same nature. A questionnaire of forty-one statements drawn from all fields of knowledge — architecture, art and archeology, astronomy, biology, chemistry, the classics, economics, engineering, English, geology, history, mathematics, military science, modern languages, Oriental languages, philosophy, physics, politics, psychology, geography, music, and "library" — was submitted to twenty-five professors, who were asked to mark each question "true" or "false." The result of the test was disastrous for the professors. It showed "the inability of most modern scholars to answer comparatively simple questions outside their own fields. . . . Some of Princeton's most distinguished teachers made lamentable scores."[1]

If I had been one of the guinea pigs in that experiment, I should have made a very low score. I should have been able to answer only twelve questions, most of them relating to historical, economic, political, or artistic matters. To the other twenty-nine questions I should have been unable to give any answer. In many cases I should have been unable even to understand the question. Sentences like the following: "Recent developments in the manufacture of steel wire have emphasized the economy of cantilever as compared with suspension bridges," or "The roots of a general polynomial of a degree higher than four are not complete numbers," or "The four-dimensional analogue of a cube has twelve corners," or "One gram of methyl alcohol added to one kilogram of water is more effective in lowering the freezing point than one gram of ethyl alcohol," were wholly above or below my understanding. Words might have slipped from one of these sentences into another, and I should not even have been aware of the confusion.

Yet I am not ashamed of my ignorance. A man cannot know everything. I am an historian by profession, and I have been a teacher of history for about fifty years; yet I am far from knowing everything about history. I possess a reasonably wide knowledge concerning about half a dozen groups of historical facts, which I have studied in the sources. Even of these facts, however, I cannot be said to know "everything." My colleagues say that I am an expert in these subjects, because I know more about them than the majority of historians and have brought to light facts which were formerly unknown, but even on these subjects there are facts immeasurably more numerous than those which I have succeeded in acquiring. Those who have carried on research after me in the same field have not found too great difficulty in surpassing my knowledge. This holds good only of the half dozen groups of historical facts which I have studied directly. Of most events of history I

[1] *Princeton Alumni Weekly*, April 7, 1933.

only know what is said in certain textbooks, and I shall never have either the opportunity or the time to go beyond the textbooks. Of many facts, again, I know nothing, or almost nothing. If I had to pass an examination in the history of the United States, I should certainly fail.

We shall never succeed in "knowing everything" even in the field of our professional culture, however hard we work, however great our powers of assimilation, and however narrow the limits which we lay down for our activities.

If it is beyond human powers to know everything about one thing, it is appalling to think what an immense burden of fatigue would be shouldered by the man who adopted the program of "knowing something about everything." The gaps in our culture, both general and professional, will always remain enormous. What one succeeds in learning and what one will never know stand in the proportions of a finite quantity to infinity: that is to say, our finite knowledge in relation to our infinite ignorance will always be equal to zero.

We are reluctant to recognize, in ourselves and in others, the necessity of being ignorant about an infinite number of things. We torment others and ourselves because we have neither the courage nor the humility to admit that our capacity to learn is and always will be limited, and that in these circumstances others as well as ourselves have the right of being and remaining ignorant of an infinite number of things. We think it "strange" that others do not know what we know, even if, on their part, they know a great many other things of which we are ignorant. We are a little like a certain lady I used to know, who read one novel a year, talked for the whole year about this novel, and regarded as ignorant those people who had not read her novel.

Our educational system often fails to recognize the right of youth to be ignorant about an infinite number of things.

If we examine one by one the different ways in which we have gathered the concrete facts of which our personal culture is today built up, we realize that very few of them came to us from school; and, vice versa, that we have forgotten in the course of our life much of the knowledge once imparted to us at school. The facts which we possess today have been acquired by us since our school days, in our daily experience of life, in reading books and reviews, listening to public lectures, conversing and discussing various subjects with friends, going to the theater or cinema, looking at advertisements and reading the papers — especially in reading the daily papers, which, with all their inaccuracies and shortcomings, are today the most effective and economical disseminators of varied knowledge.

Look into yourselves for a moment and think of all the information about hygiene, legal procedure, international history, art, science, etc., you absorb every day, without any effort, by reading a good newspaper. Even if your only object is to answer a crossword puzzle, you are obliged to search out a wide mass of information: you must consult dictionaries and encyclopedias; you must call upon the culture of your friends to help you in interpreting metaphors and allusions. These are many new materials which increase your knowledge.

No school can impart all the knowledge which may be necessary, useful, or pleasant in life. What the school can give is a small number of clear and well-coördinated facts and ideas, capable of serving as a framework into which to fit the further experiences of life. After we leave school unexpected information reaches us day by day throughout the whole course of our life. This unexpected information acquires meaning and value only as it fits into the framework of the knowledge gained at school. The school gives us keys to open locks and compasses to guide us on the sea of life. It teaches us to be on our guard against unlikely or false statements. It gives us a sense of proportion and perspective. It prepares our thought to receive, little by little, the seeds which will afterwards bear fruit. It instills into us the taste for learning and the discipline of study. It teaches us how to learn for ourselves whenever the need or the opportunity arises. Had our schools not given us this intellectual discipline, the heterogeneous notions we pick up day by day in after life would remain so much indigestible material, never to be assimilated. They would be not culture but scattered and useless breadcrumbs.

Unfortunately, education is too often based on the prejudice that the pupil will never learn anything in his life after he has left school, and that therefore he must learn at school everything which may be in some way necessary, or indeed merely useful, to him in life. The newspapers are full of complaints about the inefficiency of the schools. One day some well-intentioned person mourns that in the schools of a given city the history of that city is not part of the curriculum. Another day some educator proposes that on the senior high school level the boys and girls shall be instructed in social finance, family budgeting, installment planning, taxation, and government. On still another day someone despairs because the "nation's children are unable to carry on government," and therefore suggests that they shall be obliged to study sociology, social psychology, and current events. On another day we are told that boys and girls should be taken at the age of ten and instructed in aviation until they are eighteen. Another day cries of despair because twenty-seven per cent of the pupils do not know "the number of churches," forty-three per cent do not know "how many newspapers" there are, and only about a fifth know "the local death rate and the average annual rainfall" in their community. Besides being instructed in these indispensable matters, high school students should be versed also in "questions involving nationalism, internationalism, race, and politics" and should be informed on "the total breadth of various social sciences."[2] The students themselves are convinced that it is their right to be taught everything in school and that after leaving school they will no longer learn anything. While I am taking a last glance at these pages, I read that two hundred Harvard students have signed a petition asking for a "special practical guidance course" in marriage. Evidently they do not expect any practical knowledge from their personal

[2] *New York Times*, Jan. 24, 1939.

experience after leaving school, when it comes to choosing their wives. At the same time everybody complains that the colleges are sending out many graduates who cannot write their mother tongue.

I have no quarrel either with aviation or with the science of government or of marriage, and even less with writing one's mother tongue. I only ask, "What are the other subjects that the high school student will be allowed to ignore in order to find time to study aviation, marriage, the total breadth of various social sciences, and the rest?" There are only twenty-four hours in a day. How many hours a day must the high school student devote to study? Everything cannot be crowded into these hours, whatever they may be. You cannot expect a boy or girl to know aviation, government, the science of marriage, the history of his own town, etc., and at the same time expect him to know how to write correct and forceful English. There is not time for everything. One has to choose. If boys and girls are to acquire a thorough knowledge of English, the science of marriage, aviation, and the rest must be postponed to a more appropriate time. On the other hand, why should boys and girls devote their youth to learning to carry on government? How many university professors reach the age of eighty without knowing anything about family budgeting and installment planning?

The result of the fatal misconception that education consists in encyclopedic knowledge crammed in at school is that the pupils are overburdened, bewildered, and suffocated by an incoherent mass of facts, which are often at loggerheads among themselves, and which the pupils must have at the tips of their tongues, ready to repeat them parrot-wise. The soul, as Plutarch said, is not a vessel to be filled but a fire to be kindled. This fire is not kindled by crushing the spirit under the dead weight of material facts and stuffing it with an unassimilated medley of encyclopedic knowledge. No wonder, therefore, if more than a third of the pupils in the seventh grade answer that "habeas corpus" is a disease — an answer that would put them at the top of their class in Nazi Germany or Fascist Italy; if one out of ten defines "habeas corpus" as a lawyer — which in truth is not far from the mark; and if one out of every ten defines poverty as "the boyhood of great men," while five per cent of the seniors, having become better acquainted with the realities of life, answer that poverty is an "unhappy state."[3] They have had no time to think, reflect, or assimilate. They have acquired neither a solid groundwork of facts nor soundness of judgment. They are incapable of analyzing, abstracting, associating, and coördinating ideas. Of this kind of education Oscar Wilde was thinking, probably, when he stated that "people are made by stupid education." They have studied every conceivable thing; but the result of all this labor is that nothing remains in their minds except a violent dislike of study. They graduate in order to have done with studying, as some men take a wife in order to do away with love.

The evil is in this, not in the fact that young people do not know how many churches there are and what the rainfall is in their respective com-

[3] *New York Times*, Jan. 24, 1939.

munities. If I were a meteorologist or a farmer, the knowledge of the average annual rainfall in my community would form a necessary element in my professional equipment, and I should be a fool if I were ignorant of such an important piece of information. But since I am an historian by trade I may without great disadvantage remain in ignorance concerning that phenomenon, so important for meteorologists and farmers. Of course I should not feel ashamed if I knew not only the average annual rainfall but also the death rate, the birth rate, the number of churches, newspapers, motorcars, deaf-mutes, and telegraph poles, and many other numbers not only in my community but in all communities of the world. I should like to know everything about everything. But this is impossible; I have to give up many things. I start with giving up the rainfall. The only thing about rainfall I need to know is that when it rains I must take an umbrella — and this I did not learn at school.

To achieve good results, the school must not attempt to teach either everything on something or something on everything; it must not overburden and weary the brain with encyclopedic knowledge: it must recognize the right of the young to be ignorant.

III. Intellectual Culture

What then is culture?

To answer this question, let us observe how a man with a highly specialized training, say a physician, behaves if he is at the same time a man of culture.

However great may be his medical knowledge, he does not know medicine in the sense of having always present in his memory all the innumerable possible maladies which may torment the human race. He recognizes at first sight and knows how to treat immediately only those diseases which occur most commonly in the practice of his profession. In addition he knows that there exist diseases which present different symptoms from those about which he has most experience. When he is confronted with one of such cases, he reserves his opinion before giving a definite verdict. He returns to his books. He returns again to observe the patient. When he is sure of what he says, he gives his opinion. The difference between the great physician and the mediocre or incompetent practitioner does not lie in the former's knowing everything and the latter's knowing very little. The former also knows very little in the face of the infinite number of facts which constitute the doctrine and practice of medicine, but he is capable of facing new problems whenever the necessity or the desire arises, and despite the gaps in his learning; whereas the second not only knows very little but is incapable of dealing with unexpected difficulties. A further difference between the cultured physician and the practitioner who cares about nothing beyond his professional round is that the former, with his wide range of outside interests, remains intellectually fresh and vigorous long after his colleague has fallen victim to professional somnambulism and lost all human contact with his fellows.

If knowledge of history means the ability to repeat the whole of history by heart, nobody, not even the greatest historian, knows history. But he knows that he does not know the whole of history, and this is already a great deal. Moreover, he is capable of studying and understanding historical facts whenever the desire or the necessity arises. This is what is really important. In addition, he knows that reality is something infinitely more vast and complex than the field of his own profession, and he tries to keep the doors and windows of his mind open towards the unforeseen contingencies of life. This is more important than his professional and nonprofessional knowledge.

To put the matter in a nutshell, culture consists not in the mass of raw material stored in memory but in the capacity of the mind to be always on the alert, to be rich in curiosity about varied fields, and to be able, when necessary, to acquire new knowledge. Culture is the habit of clear and logical thinking, is the courage of independent judgment. "Culture is what remains in our mind after we have forgotten everything we have learned."

Although culture consists not so much in concrete knowledge as in a capacity to master facts and organize them in our minds, we must not conclude that there is a contradiction between knowledge and culture, between learning and understanding. Understanding cannot be achieved without acquiring at the same time a wide knowledge of concrete facts, both professional and nonprofessional. A well-formed brain is always a well-stocked brain. Every new bit of information, on entering the mind which has habits of order and clarity, is at once illumined, vivified, and enriched by associating itself with already acquired notions which the well-stocked and agile mind brings into play. No idea is ever formulated without immediately becoming a nucleus around which are coördinated other ideas and experiences. Thus, abundance of information is the natural result of true "culture."

But anybody who aims at this result must give up the illusion of being able to learn everything. If one studies history with the sole purpose of hurriedly wiping out the disgrace of one's ignorance, one will read the first book as quickly as possible so as to acquire the greatest possible mass of information; but behind the first book there is another book waiting to be read; and behind that, another awaits reproachfully. Never a moment's rest or relaxation. The result is that the mind wears itself out and exhausts itself with a burden of indigested knowledge. The delicate mechanism of the mind threatens to break down without even increasing its store of concrete facts.

Knowledge acquired in frantic haste soon fades from the memory, because memory, as a rule, retains facts and ideas only when they are logically coördinated. Even if memory is so tenacious that it never forgets a thing once acquired, these hurried and haphazard acquisitions do not constitute culture; they add nothing to the strength, beauty, or refinement of the mind. At the most, they turn the brain into a secondhand shop.

A history book is to be studied not with the aim of stuffing the memory with facts but with that of training the mind to observe the complexity of the social structure, the continuity of historical processes, the relativity of institutions and ideas, and the relations of cause and effect which bind together social phenomena, whether past or contemporary.

To read a book properly, one must take time over it and meditate on it at leisure. Meanwhile one must give up the idea of studying many other books. In this way one's culture will rest on a comparatively small number of facts. But these facts will be a lasting possession, because they are not scattered and inorganic fragments. They form a compact system, firmly joined by intimate logical ties to all the other elements of one's culture. One will never be able to recall to one's mind a single part of the knowledge so well mastered without immediately witnessing the effortless revival of all the other parts. After a year, or five, or ten, the concrete facts thus acquired will drop from one's memory as the autumn leaves fall one by one from the tree. Other facts will take their place and will in their turn fall into oblivion and make way for others. But they will leave the mind with a greater intellectual agility, a more vigorous, plastic, and widely ranging thought. This will be the permanent gain to culture.

Study is for the intelligence what gymnastics are for the body. In gymnastic exercises the immediate results have a practical value only for the professional who has specialized in a definite branch of athletics with the purpose of earning money in matches. The great majority of those who play games do not seek financial profit from them but only physical culture pure and simple. You row for the sheer pleasure of the exercise and also because afterwards your body is better balanced and your muscles more fully developed.

Study is not so delightful as rowing. But even the learning to row is not all pleasure in the beginning. It is only when the beginner has got over the first ache of his unaccustomed muscles that rowing becomes a pleasure. Study, too, once the habit is formed, becomes a source of delight. And, besides its immediate results, it enriches us with a further gain which is still more precious: it makes the mind stronger and renders it capable of new efforts and conquests.

Imagine a boy struggling with a foreign text which he does not understand. Before being able to translate it, he has to put forth all the faculties of his mind to grasp the thought of the author. Memories of grammar and vocabulary alone are not enough. Reason must supply the guiding thread. Where memory and reason fall short, imagination must step into the breach with hypotheses, as in scientific research. Results known to be certain must become starting points or checks for new hypotheses. In laying bare the thoughts of others, the boy learns to probe his own thoughts; when he comes to the work of translation he must summon to his aid all the subtleties of his own mother tongue, in order to reproduce as closely as possible ideas which are nearly always expressed in a manner foreign to his native idiom. At the end of all this toil he has nothing to show but one poor wretched page of translation. The uneducated and superficial observer, seeing nothing beyond this meager return, regards the hours spent in wrestling with these difficulties as sheer waste of the boy's time, and thinks to himself how much better this time might have been spent in learning to set up a wireless apparatus or in organizing an advertising campaign which should induce millions of men and women to masticate a new brand of chewing-gum. From the point of view of an immediate financial return, it is obvious that the boy has been wasting his time. But in making this apparently useless effort he awakes and refines his critical acumen. He grows used to observing methodically, thinking clearly and logically, and expressing himself with order and precision. He becomes a man of heightened reasoning powers.

IV. Aesthetic and Moral Culture

Intellectual culture is not the only aspect of culture. Every human being is a bundle of possibilities not only intellectual but also aesthetic and moral. Alongside of intellectual culture there also exist an aesthetic culture and a moral culture.

When we listen to a symphony by Beethoven, or gaze at Botticelli's "Venus Rising from the Sea," or read Shelley's *Prometheus Unbound*, we are doing nothing to increase our balance at the bank, supposing we have one. No doubt these are opportunities for us to increase our stock of knowledge by learning that there once existed a certain Beethoven who was a composer of music, that Venus was a fair goddess of ancient Greece, and that Prometheus came to a bad end because he wanted to know too much. But, if that is all, we should have done better to turn to an encyclopedia. The work of art is not made to increase our erudition. It is there to give us joy, to refine our taste, to heighten our vital energy, to enrich our experience. This explains why we return again and again to the same work of art without ever growing tired of it, without ever feeling that it is a waste of time. This is aesthetic culture.

Let us now read that short poem of Kipling's entitled "If." After reading it, we are none the wiser about the way the Britishers founded their empire or how many inhabitants it contains. But we do feel that our own energies, our courage to face new problems of thought and action, and our powers of rapid decision and firm purposes have been heightened. This is moral culture. Tolstoy's *Resurrection* does not give us one single item of information which is of the slightest practical utility. Even from the point of view of aesthetic value, *Resurrection* is far from being the finest of Tolstoy's works. And yet, when we read it, something most profound and unforgettable enters our souls. We become conscious of all our own moral ugliness, of all those failings which we have never confessed to anyone else, and hardly acknowledge to ourselves; but at the same time we are lifted to moral heights of which before we had never dreamed. Our spirit is swept along by a magnificent wave of desire for goodness. Alas, we cannot maintain ourselves always on that level. We lack the heroism of the great. But, for having even once touched those heights, we are never quite the same again after we return to our everyday life. Something remains in our innermost selves which will never be entirely lost. This is moral culture.

Most boys would prefer a jolly walk in the company of friends to attending school. Yet they have to go to school; and by doing so they accustom themselves to realize that life is not made up only of pleasure, and that there are pleasures which one must give up in order to do work which one should like to escape. To wake up at a given hour, to arrive on time at school to obey the rules which regulate conduct in school, all this is not pleasant, may even be regarded as a burden at moments. But through the sacrifices which are needed in the daily life at school the boy acquires habits of order and discipline indispensable in after life. This is moral culture. The dogged effort to which our school years accustom us, besides giving us invaluable intellectual habits, also forms in us certain moral habits of industry, tenacity, self-control, which are infinitely more essential in after life than any acquisition of concrete knowledge and any degree of intellectual refinement.

The difficulties of certain studies are simply a foretaste of the far greater difficulties of life. A certain number of failures at school are all to the good if the experience of failure teaches the young person to avoid more disastrous and irreparable failures in after life. Life after all is but a series of examinations which cannot be taken a second time.

We have the right to be ignorant. We have no right to be lazy. Our ignorance must be a conscious ignorance, eager to conquer itself, and not a complacent, resigned ignorance. We must not passively accept it, like oxen chewing the cud. But the capacity to overcome our ignorance whenever necessity arises is not acquired without strenuous effort. "In the sweat of thy brow shalt thou earn thy bread." Culture is the bread of the soul. It is not found readymade in the cradle. We must toil and suffer to acquire and preserve it.

This means that the foundation of a solid intellectual culture is to be found in a strong moral character. However fine an intellect may be, it will never produce its fruit unless coupled with sufficient strength of character; and, conversely, a powerful will can achieve great things with an intelligence of only mediocre quality.

The human spirit cannot be cut up in slices. We can never say: "Now by this exercise we are going to educate the mind, and by this other exercise we are going to train the character." Every intellectual effort is at the same time a training of character. And, conversely, we cannot conceive of any moral endeavor unaccompanied by an effort of intelligence.

Even the physical culture attained by games, when not carried to such excess that it leaves no room for intellectual culture, is of indirect benefit to the mind, in that it brings rest and a respite from books and gives the mind time to recover freshness and vigor for further labors. When it does not degenerate into brutality, as in boxing or bullfighting, sport is a most valuable factor in the formation of character in so far as it teaches self-control, coöperation, subordination of self to the good of the team, fair play towards the adversary, modesty in success, courage and good humor in defeat.

Physical culture, intellectual culture, aesthetic culture, and moral culture are the different aspects of human culture. The ideal human personality is attained by the balanced development of all four. What human society needs is that its members should have healthy bodies, well-stocked and alert minds, refined tastes, and well-disciplined characters. But in the long run what the community most needs is moral culture. If one aspect is to be stressed at the expense of the others, then it should be that of moral culture.

A French novelist, Jean Aicard, in his novel *Maurin des Maures*, tells the story of an unlettered man of the people who takes his eleven-year-old son to a pensioned naval surgeon with the request to give the lad a bit of schooling. "What do you want me to teach him?" asks the surgeon. "I don't know. But I want him not to be like me, hardly able to read. I am nothing better than a savage." "I see. Does the boy know how to read?" "Yes, he has learnt the three R's." "Well, what do you want to turn him to?" The father could not find a reply. "But surely you have some plan or other for the lad's future. Do you want him to be a farmer, or a soldier, or a sailor, or a hunter, or a gardener? According as you decide, I will try to adapt my teaching." After a long hesitation the father finally found what he wanted: "Teach him justice." The common sense of this man of the people, ignorant but intelligent and morally sound, realized that it was futile to decide what a boy of eleven was to do when he grew up. The boy would get his specialized training by himself later on when he was old enough to know his own mind. But one thing he would need, more essential than an intellectual culture extending beyond the three R's. That was a moral training that would make him grow up an honest man.

So let us conclude with the words of this unlettered man, who, though he thought himself nothing better than a savage, was more civilized than most of the men who pass for such. Develop your intellectual, aesthetic, and physical culture, but above all learn "justice."

Stringfellow Barr

At present a professor of humanities at Rutgers University, String-fellow Barr is a recipient of the Lindback Award for distinguished teaching. Before his appointment to the Rutgers faculty, Barr served as an

*advisory editor for the Britannica Edition of the Great Books. From
1937 to 1946 he was President of St. John's College, where he instituted
a four-year required course of study in the liberal arts which emphasized
both scientific and humanistic contributions to civilization.*

*Barr has resorted to fiction as well as to expository writing in his
attempts to expose the eccentricities, virtues, and stupidities alive in
education today. In "Liberal Education: A Common Adventure" he
asks the question ". . . are there any intellectual skills that every member
of a free society should acquire up to the extent of his native ability?"
It is an old question, and one that must ever be asked by each new generation if culture is to survive the fads and indolence of the educational
huckster.*

29

LIBERAL EDUCATION:

A COMMON ADVENTURE*

There is a specter which haunts American education and all our discussion
of it. It is a question that we almost never make explicit, a question most of
us have never consciously formulated: are there any intellectual skills that
every member of a free society should acquire up to the extent of his native
ability? Because we generally refuse to permit the question to become a
conscious one, it remains spectral, and therefore confusingly haunts our discussions. If there are indeed some things that every free man should be able
to do, then those things should be central to our schools and colleges.

The nearest we have come to an answer is, I imagine, our professed desire
to abolish illiteracy. It is true that, while the American people are not only the
richest people on earth but the richest people history records, we are not the
most literate people. Nevertheless, we were the first people to make a serious
attempt at universal schooling, an attempt not unconnected with our dogma,
which I find many Americans now doubting, that all men are born free and
equal. And I suppose that this dogma reflects an even older belief that all
men are the children of God. Again, it is true that our press abounds in
almost daily complaints that even those of us who are technically classed as

* From *The Antioch Review*, Vol. 15, No. 3 (September, 1955), pp. 300–312. Used
by permission of The Antioch Press, owners of the copyright.

literates, do not read very correctly and that those who might teach us to do so are being forced into other occupations because we decline to pay our teachers enough to afford them even a modestly decent living. Even if we did read correctly, it might remain true that we do not read very attentively, or imaginatively, and it certainly might remain true that difficult but important books that can be published in many countries and sold at a profit cannot be safely published here without subsidy. Millions of our college graduates are simply not well enough educated to be able to read them, or to want to read them. A very large number of them are now reading the comics instead, on the erroneous assumption that if a book is important but difficult, its reading had best be left to specialists, or at least to people who "took a course" in the subject matter the book represents.

I suggest that any people which wishes to be a free community must be able to communicate, and communicate better than animals appear to do, better even than adolescent boys do. There are many grades of communication and therefore many grades of literacy. When I was in India last year, I discovered what the reader may already know: that those citizens are classed by the census as literate who can sign their own names or — perhaps more precisely — draw a recognizable picture of their name in one of the scripts now used in India. But there is another sense of "literate" than the literal sense of being able to read and write. There are Indian peasants who cannot do either, but who can recite hundreds or even thousands of lines of great poetry and who can frame their own thoughts with accuracy and even with nobility. While I am sure that we Americans, living in a highly technological society, must learn to read and write, beyond our own signatures, I must say I frankly envied the Indians for their great oral tradition.

Maybe we should think of literacy as an indefinitely expansible process. Maybe our ideal for each free man should be that he become as literate as possible. That ideal would involve his learning to handle the two great sets of symbols which men have used for millennia when they have sought to communicate: words and numbers. If so, language and mathematics must be the common property of a free community. Its members must be able to speak better, listen better, read better, write better, and think better than we Americans now can. How well? I know of no limit to how well it is desirable for human beings to do these things. Most of us still fall so far short of William Shakespeare that there is still room for improvement. As for the mock modesty of saying that we are not geniuses and cannot hope to communicate better than we already do, I wonder whether we can make this claim with any greater truth than we could make another: that we cannot learn to use our body more skillfully than we already do? Art is long. We are here talking about art — about what were traditionally called the liberal arts.

How are these arts of communication acquired? If we would drop our educational jargon and watch a young child learn to talk, I suspect we should have the key. Little children learn to talk by listening to people do it who already know how, and then imitating them. They can keep on learning to talk better and better by listening frequently to talkers who bear the same relation to them that grownups bear to children, and by imitating these superlative talkers. Again, I myself find Shakespeare one of the best talkers I get a chance to listen to — much better than any talker now alive in the town I live in, and much better than nearly any other talker whose "talk" I can listen to only in printed words across the centuries that separate us.

This, I would suppose, is why over many long centuries men have turned to books: in order to tune in on the Great Conversation that we call civilization. This is what it means to be the child of a great civilization and not a cultural bastard. But, in doing this, we should show some of the humility and some of the daring that little children habitually show. We should dare to listen attentively and humbly even to conversation that is out of our depth, provided it is good. After all, every person who ever learned to speak English learned by listening, at least so long as he was a small child, to conversation that was out of his depth. It is when the child stretches his mind to follow what seems at first like gibberish that his own command of language steadily expands. Those who want, even when they are adults, to increase their own powers to communicate, and even to commune, with other men can scarcely do better than listen to great talk out of their depth, trusting in the same unbelievable miracle that enables a child to learn to talk.

Over the centuries and throughout many lands a few men have talked magnificently, and a few of these few have transmitted to us in books what they said. We commonly call such books classics. They are so called, I believe, because they communicate with great skill ideas about matters that human experience has taught us are important, just as a painting, a statue, a sonata, or indeed a football game may achieve the rank of classic through the pre-eminent skill with which it was painted, sculpted, or played. The reasons for having even young children, and certainly college students, read such books and look at such paintings and listen to such music are that life is short; that these things are the best of their kind that civilization has salvaged; and that the best is none too good for a man.

Thousands of other books and paintings and sonatas may be ever so worth reading or hearing or seeing; but of the making of such things there is no end. Any attempt at coverage would be folly. And the second best will always be second. There may be a difference of opinion about which of man's creations belong to this top rank. Somebody has to decide; and the professional obligation to decide falls on the teacher. If he cannot make a better rough choice than his pupil, then there is a lot to be said for their changing places and for reallocating the salary accordingly — such as it now is. Patients who distrust their doctors are well advised to seek doctors they trust. Writing one's own prescription is at best inefficient and at worst dangerous. Those patients who develop allergies for certain medicines can always speak to their doctors about it.

For those of us who glorify "individual differences" at the expense of whatever may be the common property of educated men, there is always the student who simply doesn't "like" Shakespeare. Some men there are who cannot abide a harmless, necessary cat. But I am by no means sure that Shakespeare is quite that special: he has so often been called universal that there really may be something in it. And I should think that, while no student may be required to love Shakespeare, all students may properly be invited to listen to him. This is precisely our point of second abdication. We teachers, having first asked the student which of several subjects, none of which he knows, he thinks he would prefer, next let him drop whatever subject seems to present difficulties. I suppose these practices are akin to our practice of letting children decide which foods they will eat before they have tasted them, or at least after the first mouthful.

If our schools and colleges were now teaching all the members of the American community how to read, in the sense in which I have been using "read," I would happily exempt them from the multitude of other responsibilities they have assumed in place of that one. The information they now try to dispense can be readily found and acquired by an educated man — that is, by one who has learned to read, to use his mind imaginatively and rigorously. I have suggested that the quickest way I know of from my own teaching experience to teach people to read, and to read well, is to help them read those things most worth reading. The traditional name for such things is "the classics."

But the classics, though traditionally used for this purpose, were over the centuries used almost exclusively by a select few. Can classics be read for this purpose by everybody? Aren't some young men and women too stupid to read them, or too uninterested, or too ill prepared? I can only answer that I have myself used them with undergraduates whose previous school training branded them as stupid, uninterested, and unprepared, and I am convinced that what they gained from the classics was more than they would have gained from more trivial books. Some of these undergraduates had reached college in some sense able to read, but only in some very vague sense. Some of them arrived in college so uninterested that their eyes wore a kind of glaze. Some of them seemed to have very little ability, although in their stupefied condition it was impossible to know what their bad grades in high school meant. They had clearly never been awakened from a sort of intellectual somnambulism, and there was no earthly way of knowing what their powers were if they should ever be brought into anything like full use.

The difference between what such undergraduates got out of the classics and what their abler, or more interested, or better prepared classmates got was a wider gap than one sees in most classrooms, precisely because one of the most magical properties of a true classic is that it can be read on many levels. When I was eight, my father gave me for my birthday a copy of *Macbeth* and told me he would give me other plays of Shakespeare as fast as I could read them. That is exactly fifty years ago, and I cannot reconstruct precisely what I got out of that first reading of *Macbeth*. But I infer that it was very little, since my favorite character was King Duncan and since I muttered his lines while striding across the floor with my dressing-gown trailing behind me as I had reason to believe his kingly robes must have trailed. When I was eleven, I witnessed my first performance of a Shakespearean play — and it was *Macbeth*. I was amazed by meanings I saw in the play which had evaded me in my King Duncan period. I was sixteen the next time I read the play, and I was surprised by how little I had understood the play when I had seen it performed five years before. Every time I have seen it performed since, or even read it, this surprise has been repeated. But I loved the play when I was eight, as many children have; and at eleven I was mad about it. Not, of course, for precisely the same reasons that I read it now. In between each reading, I have been experiencing my own life — partly in the light of my last previous reading — and it is not surprising that I see things in *Macbeth* that I had no real way of seeing the time before.

I ask the reader's pardon for this autobiographical note, but sometimes a homely illustration can jar us "educators" out of our jargon and our self-imposed mystification about matters every good teacher knows. One of these matters is that thousands of young boys have taken their Homer straight and reveled in him. Those who read him without reveling often get the point from discussing what happened on the plain of Troy with those who have managed to be transported there. As for those who prefer other types of reading, this is a matter of taste, and fortunately for mankind tastes change, sometimes for the better, but only by further tasting of things we at first do not much like. The teacher's job is not to discover the restricted and transient tastes of an immature mind nor to protect it from other tastes, but to help it acquire other tastes.

The true classic is, I believe, highly communicable, and can be read on many levels, by the stupid and the brilliant alike. It is written about important matters, matters that remain important in their essence, so that the classics which treat of them retain the flavor of the contemporary book, with its immediacy and relevance, for successive generations of men: in short, they endure. But, even so, the author's way of treating important matters varies from time to time and from place to place. There is high discipline in experiencing these "translations" of a basic problem from country to country and from century to century. I think, therefore, there is every reason for a faculty to choose first-rate books from many times and places. A choice I was myself once involved in ran from Homer to contemporary authors. It is true that the list of books we used, a list that grew out of a famous list the American Library Association had once published, included only Western classics, and there are strong arguments both for and against including the classics of the Oriental tradition.

But just as there are good reasons for not confining one's choice of the best and greatest products of the human mind to one country or one century, so there are, I believe, equally compelling reasons for not confining oneself to one, or to a few, "fields." Graduate work properly concentrates on a field of knowledge which it has deliberately abstracted out of man's intellectual experience as a whole. But in the last analysis fields are for cattle, not for the human mind. "That is not in my field" never exonerates a human mind from inquiry. The atomic bomb has dramatized, as it had never before been so dazzlingly dramatized in my lifetime, what happens when we cultivate one field hard and leave others to lie fallow. It is a postwar cliché that mankind simply cannot afford to know so much more about nuclear physics than it does about the moral and political problems which the atom raises.

One suspects therefore that the most profitable use of classics involves the reading of classics in all the major areas that man's mind has entered. The last lecture that Sir William Osler gave before his death deplored the fact that Oxford's famous Literae Humaniores included such things as the great Greek and Latin monuments in philosophy, in history, in poetry, but not the imposing monuments the Greeks and Romans left in mathematics and the natural sciences. What that brilliant scientist then said should be pondered afresh. What he did not say about Greek treatises was: "*Nous avons changé tout cela.*"

If an educated faculty selects a list of books it thinks worthwhile for students to chew on, instead of leaving it to the students who have come to college for help in getting educated to choose the books for themselves, the same faculty has to retain the right and duty to revise the list whenever it changes its mind or finds that a given book releases its students' powers even more than another and slightly "better" book. The faculty of St. John's College in Annapolis was shocked to find that, when the college catalogue included "A List of a Hundred Great Books," newspapers tended to translate the caption into "The Hundred Best Books." It is an important shift.

The books really are "to chew on," not to master. The idea that a schoolboy or even a college undergraduate is going to "master" Plato's *Republic* seems to me to be lacking in a sense of humor. Let us pass over in courteous silence any claim his professor may make that he himself really has mastered Plato. The reason students have for many centuries read books of this sort as a means of practicing the liberal arts on worthwhile material was not to master the books. The reason a puppy may wisely be given a large bone to gnaw on is not so that he can chew it up and swallow it but so that he can sharpen his teeth trying to. A well-read man is one who has sharpened his intellectual teeth on many such books. But the bones will not be serviceable tooth-sharpeners unless they exemplify an author in the act of practicing the liberal arts, the arts of communication, of "readin' an' writin,' " in an eminent degree. And the author is unlikely to do that on trivial subject matter. At this point our bone metaphor creaks pretty badly. For the fact is that our undergraduate, when he lives for several years with the classics, trying to comprehend them to the limit of his developing powers, not only learns to practice the liberal arts himself but he lives among the ennobling images and deals with the great and permanent ideas that the great poets' imaginations have caught and the great philosophers have identified and grasped. He becomes familiar with the great questions, including those which perhaps no man has answered. They tell the story that when Gertrude Stein lay dying, with the faithful Alice B. Toklas at her bedside, Miss Stein asked: "Alice, what is the answer?" Miss Toklas reported to have answered: "Gertrude, there is no answer." Whereupon, the great Gertrude parried with: "Alice, what is the question?" and turned over and died. If an undergraduate can learn from the great classics always to seek the problem before offering a pat solution, he will have learned more than have most of his contemporaries.

If over the centuries "the classics" have nurtured and disciplined and rendered supple and subtle the minds of men, if even in our pioneering, scrambling young republic they nourished many of our leaders and formed the basis of college studies until less than a century ago, why did we abandon them — since they really have been all but abandoned? We cannot, I believe, safely infer that we abandoned them because we found they did not really nourish or that what we teach now has been demonstrated to nourish more. I believe the historical evidence points to two principal reasons for our current suspicion of them. First, the way the classics were taught had robbed them of their function; and the most nourishing food can be ruined by a cook until it is both unpalatable and indigestible. So the classics were thrown out. Secondly, the failure of the college of liberal arts to assimilate to its intellectual tradition the brilliant achievements of natural science doomed the very phrase "liberal arts" to mean useless but ornamental learning. Whereupon science, technology, and the industrial culture which they have created, swept the classics aside. These two causes for the decline of liberal education in America will bear closer scrutiny.

By the time my generation reached school and college, "the classics" had turned into courses in Latin and Greek: Caesar-Cicero-Virgil and perhaps Xenophon-Herodotus-Homer. There was a pronounced tendency to "take" sixty lines a day. We did not read and discuss such authors; we studied and recited on them. Not William Shakespeare himself, not even King Duncan, can survive the sixty-lines-a-day treatment. And although I am more grateful for the Greek I learned as an undergraduate than for anything else I learned at the time, I must confess that I did not really "read" the Greeks and the Romans until I was a grown man and read them in English translation. As a matter of fact, many of the Greek and Roman classics that I would want an undergraduate to read today did not exist in English when I was young or existed only in very expensive editions. Today cheap and good translations abound, and at paperbound prices.

There are few more powerful exercises in the liberal arts than putting into the best English one can muster the best things written in Greek or Latin. And there are few better ways of learning how to write English. But, when all this his been granted, the fact remains that he who reads the classics at the rate of sixty lines a day is doing a dreadful thing, and he will eventually die of boredom, or revolt. Our scholars and undergraduates revolted; Greek has largely died out in our colleges, and in most places Latin is busy dying. The books which a few of our forefathers read (knowing enough Greek or

Latin) and found inspiring are shrinking now to excerpts or appear as subjects of discussion in textbooks or are studied in some "fields" out of their total context and as specialized knowledge. Whether the classics — Greek, Roman, or those written in later tongues — play a vital role again will depend, I suspect, on whether we read them in English and read them straight through in the way we read, or ought to read, other books worth reading. Many people are beginning to do this, especially those who have finished college and are still hungry for something they feel they somehow missed.

We owe a great deal to the followers of John Dewey, and to "progressive education" in general, for backing up the revolt against the sixty lines a day, the sadistic grammatical drill, the mnemonic doggerel verses, the pedantry, the false claims that Hellenist and Latinist resorted to when they had lost their purpose and redoubled their effort. Greek and Latin studies had lost their liberal arts content: now they were not merely difficult, but dull and irrelevant. A curricular revolution all but liquidated them — instead of rediscovering their proper use as media peculiarly adapted to the practice of the liberal arts. Revolutions have a way of throwing out the baby with the bath. But the guilt for depriving generations of students of the classics rests more on the head of the confused classicist than on the head of his unconvinced colleagues. The time has come to recover the bruised baby without bothering about the bath-water.

If and when we recover the liberal arts, we ought to do so with the mature knowledge that, being human arts, they are always subject to decay and misuse. That is one reason historians talk of civilization and barbarism, of Renaissances and Dark Ages. The liberal arts, the arts of "reading," have often been revived and we could revive them again.

I have tried to suggest that the classics, or some of them, can be read with joy and profit by children, but at some point they should be read as a sort of final inoculation for the long educational process called Life, an inoculation that Europe tried to give a few youngsters in its British "public school," its French *lycée*, its German *Gymnasium;* and America gave in its "academies." And for this inoculation, for this "general education," which a modern democracy needs to give to as many of its citizen-rulers as possible, it is not necessary to wait until what we call "college age."

I would certainly plump for fifteen rather than the seventeen at which the average American matriculates today, remembering always that while a fifteen-year-old will "get less out of" such books than his elder brother, the problem is not primarily to get stuff out of the books and into the human head but to initiate a certain kind of intellectual growth in the student as early as that sort of process can be initiated. Then he will have both the ability and the desire to "get something out of the books" during the period that extends from his graduation until his death. They are worth that much of a man's time. Graduation should certify merely to a successful inoculation and to the formation of certain habits of mind. I know of few college curricula today that can certify to so much.

If my guess is correct — and it is at least based on some direct personal teaching experience — four-year liberal arts colleges could be graduating people at nineteen instead of twenty-one, more able than our present college graduates are to study law or medicine or to enter practical affairs. I find an amazing proportion of business executives and teachers in graduate and professional schools who agree with these judgments, but few teachers in schools or undergraduate colleges willing to consider so drastic a shift. Anything less drastic will, I suggest, prove less than enough. But if we cannot face reorganizing our colleges for a different age level, at least let us try to achieve basic education by twenty-one.

In addition to reading and discussing the classics under competent guidance, the undergraduate ought to translate portions of them too if he is to learn how to use his mother tongue well. Nearly any language that contains a classic will do for this purpose. For that matter, "translating" an English writer like Gibbon into contemporary English, or even into current slang will help. But, at the risk of appearing blindly conservative, I would plump for Greek or Latin. My reason is simple: Greek and Latin are highly inflected tongues, which force attention on the precise meaning of a sentence. Their inner structure is such that the bones show more clearly than in French or German, and they do not breed the contempt and inattention that our own familiar English breeds. What they say has to be dug out, and the digging process poses neatly some basic problems of language in general, English included. Even sixty-lines-a-day can be tolerated if backed up by an exciting program on reading in English translation.

In addition to translating into English what some man like Sophocles said so well in Greek, the student of the liberal arts ought to translate what Euclid said about quadratic equations in geometrical form into what can be said about them in modern algebra. The growing fear of mathematics in our schools and colleges would be frightening in any sort of society. In a society based on a complicated technology, it is completely terrifying. It poses the problem of whether a community of button-pushers, who do not know what happens when they push buttons except for the final result, can hope to retain both the community's economic base and its freedom of political and moral choice. In terms of its daily problems, it is today quite simply too ignorant to retain both.

Mathematics leads us naturally into the second reason I posited for our surrender of the classics in the college of liberal arts: the refusal of our grandfathers and our fathers to incorporate into the liberal arts the intellectual process we call modern science. Modern science has had its revenge of Academe. After having been considered in the late nineteenth century the intellectual kitchen of the campus which young gentlemen trod, it created a new material environment that left the humanities stranded in their own snobbery and preciosity, until at last the "social sciences" and even the philological course in language began to ape the scientist's methods which he had evolved for the specific purposes for which he used them — the investigation of the behavior of matter. The results have often been grotesque, and nobody has been more horrified by those results than the leading natural scientists.

The protection against this ironical comedy, this typical idolatry, this minor blasphemy lay in admitting to start with that the laboratory experiment can be a classic too. It lay also in doing what no second-rate scientist wants to tolerate: the study of the great classics of scientific thought, regardless of whether later experimentation and improved instruments have forced a revision of the hypothesis. The average scientist today would not know any more than the average scholar in "the humanities," why Osler thought Greek scientific masterpieces were worth reading and understanding.

It would presumably be perverse to study the great crucial experiments in natural science merely out of books, no matter how wonderful these books may be as products of the human intellect, while not bothering to set up the experiments the books are based on in a college laboratory. The art, as well as the science, incorporated in those experiments is precisely the art our immediate ancestors so grudgingly admitted to sacred Academe. Nor had we better stop at laboratories: workshops can play a role too. The manual arts support the liberal arts. The liberal arts, when seriously pursued in all the areas where man's mind has roamed, can put machine oil on a man's hands and grease in his hair. There has never been anything dandyesque or upper-class about the liberal arts, although a leisure class has often tried to make them so.

And who will teach the classics in the sort of context I have just described? Ah, there's the rub. Most professors are suffering acutely from intellectual agoraphobia, and the special aspect of a specialized subject matter has been their protection against being caught out intellectually, as it has been their best hope of promotion and recognition. Moreover, we professors did not ourselves receive the sort of education I have been describing, except where we have picked it up as best we could. Frequently, we are not even very much interested in teaching, certainly not in teaching undergraduates, and most certainly not in helping to prepare people for college. We are interested in "publishing," although only the most hopeful of us can attach much importance to the bulk of what we are publishing. To teach the liberal arts in the manner I have tried to describe would involve entering again into our mother's womb or at least studying things we long ago decided never to look at again — such, let us say, as mathematics. Or, according to the particular case, language. We have lost our amateur standing, and we prefer to think that this sort of teaching, as against the sort we do daily, would be intellectual charlatanry.

Yet the classics are still there. We even pay them lip service. With their exuberant intellectual vitality they could bring us back to life, rid us of our academic false modesty and our ill-concealed anti-intellectualism, and revive our people's vision of the common good. If such things happened, there might be what men call a revival of learning.

II. SPECIALIZATION

Harvard Committee

In his Introduction to General Education in a Free Society *James Bryant Conant, in reference to the study made by the Harvard Committee, states that ". . . it is an inquiry into the problems of general education in both school and college by a committee largely composed of members of the Faculty of Arts and Sciences — in short, men of distinction in special fields of learning. . . . That a group of men whose lives had hitherto been devoted to university affairs should take great pains and spend much time investigating the current educational situation in the United States is, I believe, without precedent. That they were joined in the enterprise by colleagues from the Faculty of Education who know schools from long experience makes the case no less exceptional. . . ."*

The following excerpt from the Committee's study is a brief and lucid definition of general and special education, one that has been lauded and damned since its publication in 1945. Rarely, however, does a group endeavor result in expression as succinct as that embodied in the Harvard report.

30

GENERAL AND SPECIAL EDUCATION*

Education is broadly divided into general and special education; our topic now is the difference and the relationship between the two. The term, general education, is somewhat vague and colorless; it does not mean some airy

* Reprinted by permission of the publishers from *General Education in a Free Society: Report of the Harvard Committee.* Cambridge, Mass.: Harvard University Press. Copyright, 1945, by The President and Fellows of Harvard College.

education in knowledge in general (if there be such knowledge), nor does it mean education for all in the sense of universal education. It is used to indicate that part of a student's whole education which looks first of all to his life as a responsible human being and citizen; while the term, special education, indicates that part which looks to the student's competence in some occupation. These two sides of life are not entirely separable, and it would be false to imagine education for the one as quite distinct from education for the other — more will be said on this point presently. Clearly, general education has somewhat the meaning of liberal education, except that, by applying to high school as well as to college, it envisages immensely greater numbers of students and thus escapes the invidium which, rightly or wrongly, attaches to liberal education in the minds of some people. But if one cling to the root meaning of liberal as that which befits or helps to make free men, then general and liberal education have identical goals. The one may be thought of as an earlier stage of the other, similar in nature but less advanced in degree.

The opposition to liberal education — both to the phrase and to the fact — stems largely from historical causes. The concept of liberal education first appeared in a slave-owning society, like that of Athens, in which the community was divided into freemen and slaves, rulers and subjects. While the slaves carried on the specialized occupations of menial work, the freemen were primarily concerned with the rights and duties of citizenship. The training of the former was purely vocational; but as the freemen were not only a ruling but also a leisure class, their education was exclusively in the liberal arts, without any utilitarian tinge. The freemen were trained in the reflective pursuit of the good life; their education was unspecialized as well as unvocational; its aim was to produce a rounded person with a full understanding of himself and of his place in society and in the cosmos.

Modern democratic society clearly does not regard labor as odious or disgraceful; on the contrary, in this country at least, it regards leisure with suspicion and expects its "gentlemen" to engage in work. Thus we attach no odium to vocational instruction. Moreover, in so far as we surely reject the idea of freemen who are free in so far as they have slaves or subjects, we are apt strongly to deprecate the liberal education which went with the structure of the aristocratic ideal. Herein our society runs the risk of committing a serious fallacy. Democracy is the view that not only the few but that all are free, in that everyone governs his own life and shares in the responsibility for the management of the community. This being the case, it follows that all human beings stand in need of an ampler and rounded education. The task of modern democracy is to preserve the ancient ideal of liberal education and to extend it as far as possible to all the members of the community. In short, we have been apt to confuse accidental with fundamental factors, in our suspicion of the classical idea. To believe in the equality of human beings is to believe that the good life, and the education which trains the citizen for the good life, are equally the privilege of all. And these are the touchstones of the liberated man: first, is he free; that is to say, is he able to judge and plan for himself, so that he can truly govern himself? In order to do this, his must be a mind capable of self-criticism; he must lead that self-examined life which according to Socrates is alone worthy of a free man. Thus he will possess inner freedom, as well as social freedom. Second, is he universal in his motives and sympathies? For the civilized man is a citizen of the entire universe; he has overcome provincialism, he is objective, and is a "spectator of all time and all existence." Surely these two are the very aims of democracy itself.

But the opposition to general education does not stem from causes located in the past alone. We are living in an age of specialism, in which the avenue to success for the student often lies in his choice of a specialized career, whether as a chemist, or an engineer, or a doctor, or a specialist in some form of business or of manual or technical work. Each of these specialties makes an increasing demand on the time and on the interest of the student. Specialism is the means for advancement in our mobile structure; yet we must envisage the fact that a society controlled wholly by specialists is not a wisely ordered society. We cannot, however, turn away from specialism. The problem is how to save general education and its values within a system where specialism is necessary.

The very prevalence and power of the demand for special training makes doubly clear the need for a concurrent, balancing force in general education. Specialism enhances the centrifugal forces in society. The business of providing for the needs of society breeds a great diversity of special occupations; and a given specialist does not speak the language of the other specialists. In order to discharge his duties as a citizen adequately, a person must somehow be able to grasp the complexities of life as a whole. Even from the point of view of economic success, specialism has its peculiar limitations. Specializing in a vocation makes for inflexibility in a world of fluid possibilities. Business demands minds capable of adjusting themselves to varying situations and of managing complex human institutions. Given the pace of economic progress, techniques alter speedily; and even the work in which the student has been trained may no longer be useful when he is ready to earn a living or soon after. Our conclusion, then, is that the aim of education should be to prepare an individual to become an expert both in some particular vocation or art and in the general art of the free man and the citizen. Thus the two kinds of education once given separately to different social classes must be given together to all alike.

In this epoch in which almost all of us must be experts in some field in order to make a living, general education therefore assumes a peculiar importance. Since no one can become an expert in all fields, everyone is compelled to trust the judgment of other people pretty thoroughly in most areas of activity. I must trust the advice of my doctor, my plumber, my lawyer, my radio repairman, and so on. Therefore I am in peculiar need of a kind of sagacity by which to distinguish the expert from the quack, and the better from the worse expert. From this point of view, the aim of general education may be defined as that of providing the broad critical sense by which to recognize competence in any field. William James said that an educated person knows a good man when he sees one. There are standards and a style for every type of activity — manual, athletic, intellectual, or artistic; and the educated man should be one who can tell sound from shoddy work in a field outside his own. General education is especially required in a democracy where the public elects its leaders and officials; the ordinary citizen must be discerning enough so that he will not be deceived by appearances and will elect the candidate who is wise in his field.

Both kinds of education — special as well as general — contribute to the task of implementing the pervasive forces of our culture. Two complementary forces are at the root of our culture: on the one hand, an ideal of man and society distilled from the past but at the same time transcending the past as a standard of judgment valid in itself, and, on the other hand, the belief that no existent expressions of this ideal are final but that all alike call for perpetual scrutiny and change in the light of new knowledge. Specialism is usually the vehicle of this second force. It fosters the open-mindedness and love of investigation which are the wellspring of change, and it devotes itself to the means by which change is brought about. The fact may not always be obvious. There is a sterile specialism which hugs accepted knowledge and ends in the bleakest conservatism. Modern life also calls for many skills which, though specialized, are repetitive and certainly do not conduce to inquiry. These minister to change but unconsciously. Nevertheless, the previous statement is true in the sense that specialism is concerned primarily with knowledge in action, as it advances into new fields and into further applications.

Special education comprises a wider field than vocationalism; and correspondingly, general education extends beyond the limits of merely literary preoccupation. An example will make our point clearer. A scholar — let us say a scientist (whether student or teacher) — will, in the laudable aim of saving himself from narrowness, take a course in English literature, or perhaps read poetry and novels, or perhaps listen to good music and generally occupy himself with the fine arts. All this, while eminently fine and good, reveals a misapprehension. In his altogether unjustified humility, the scientist wrongly interprets the distinction between liberal and illiberal in terms of the distinction between the humanities and the sciences. Plato and Cicero would have been very much surprised to hear that geometry, astronomy, and the sciences of nature in general, are excluded from the humanities. There is also implied a more serious contempt for the liberal arts, harking back to the fallacy which identifies liberal education with the aristocratic ideal. The implication is that liberal education is something only genteel. A similar error is evident in the student's attitude toward his required courses outside his major field as something to "get over with," so that he may engage in the business of serious education, identified in his mind with the field of concentration.

Now, a general education is distinguished from special education, not by subject matter, but in terms of method and outlook, no matter what the field. Literature, when studied in a technical fashion, gives rise to the special science of philology; there is also the highly specialized historical approach to painting. Specialism is interchangeable, not with natural science, but with the method of science, the method which abstracts material from its context and handles it in complete isolation. The reward of scientific method is the utmost degree of precision and exactness. But, as we have seen, specialism as an educational force has its own limitations; it does not usually provide an insight into general relationships.

A further point is worth noting. The impact of specialism has been felt not only in those phases of education which are necessarily and rightly specialistic; it has affected also the whole structure of higher and even of secondary education. Teachers, themselves products of highly technical disciplines, tend to reproduce their knowledge in class. The result is that each subject, being taught by an expert, tends to be so presented as to attract potential experts. This complaint is perhaps more keenly felt in colleges and universities, which naturally look to scholarship. The undergraduate in a college receives his teaching from professors who, in their turn, have been trained in graduate schools. And the latter are dominated by the ideal of specialization. Learning now is diversified and parceled into a myriad of specialties. Correspondingly, colleges and universities are divided into large numbers of departments, with further specialization within the departments. As a result, a student in search of a general course is commonly frustrated. Even an elementary course is devised as an introduction to a specialism within a department; it is significant only as the beginning of a series of courses of advancing complexity. In short, such introductory courses are planned for the specialist, not for the student seeking a general education. The young chemist in the course in literature and the young writer in the course in chemistry find themselves in thoroughly uncomfortable positions so long as the purpose of these courses is primarily to train experts who will go on to higher courses rather than to give some basic understanding of science as it is revealed in chemistry or of the arts as they are revealed in literature.

It is most unfortunate if we envisage general education as something formless — that is to say, the taking of one course after another; and as something negative, namely, the study of what is not in a field of concentration. Just as we regard the courses in concentration as having definite relations to one another, so should we envisage general education as an organic whole whose parts join in expounding a ruling idea and in serving a common aim. And to do so means to abandon the view that all fields and all departments are equally valuable vehicles of general education. It also implies some prescription. At the least it means abandoning the usual attitude of regarding "distribution" as a sphere in which the student exercises a virtually untrammeled freedom of choice. It may be objected that we are proposing to limit the liberty of the student in the very name of liberal education. Such an objection would only indicate an ambiguity in the conception of liberal education. We must distinguish between liberalism in education and education in liberalism. The former, based as it is on the doctrine of individualism, expresses the view that the student should be free in his choice of courses. But education in liberalism is an altogether different matter; it is education which has a pattern of its own, namely, the pattern associated with the liberal outlook. In this view, there are truths which none can be free to ignore, if one is to have that wisdom through which life can become useful. These are the truths concerning the structure of the good life and concerning the factual conditions by which it may be achieved, truths comprising the goals of the free society.

Finally, the problem of general education is one of combining fixity of aim with diversity in application. It is not a question of providing a general education which will be uniform through the same classes of all schools and colleges all over the country, even were such a thing possible in our decentralized system. It is rather to adapt general education to the needs and intentions of different groups and, so far as possible, to carry its spirit into special education. The effectiveness of teaching has always largely depended on this willingness to adapt a central unvarying purpose to varying outlooks. Such adaptation is as much in the interest of the quick as of the slow, of the bookish as of the unbookish, and is the necessary protection of each. What is wanted, then, is a general education capable at once of taking on many different forms and yet of representing in all its forms the common knowledge and the common values on which a free society depends.

Herbert Spencer

Representing the high optimism of nineteenth-century science, Herbert Spencer (1820–1903) attempted to construct a systematic philosophy based on the theory of evolution. The following selection is, with a few minor omissions, the first chapter of Education: Intellectual, Moral, and Physical, *a book which exudes Spencer's concern for order, completeness, and utilitarian logic.*

Spencer's main argument is that education must be "useful" to be worthy, and of all worthy pursuits science is the most sublime. Partly rejecting the lofty ideals of Comenius and Rousseau, Spencer asserts that the most important educational question is not "How can we help the individual child?" but "What knowledge is most necessary for

children to learn?" Spencer answers his own question by claiming that
a scientific education is most necessary, and therein lies his commitment
to a specialized curriculum.
    An astute rebuttal to the Spencerian point of view is found in
Bertrand Russell's essay " 'Useless' Knowledge."

31

WHAT KNOWLEDGE IS OF MOST WORTH?

It has been truly remarked that, in order of time, decoration precedes dress. Among people who submit to great physical suffering that they may have themselves handsomely tattooed, extremes of temperature are borne with but little attempt at mitigation. Humboldt tells us that an Orinoco Indian, though quite regardless of bodily comfort, will yet labor for a fortnight to purchase pigment wherewith to make himself admired; and that the same woman who would not hesitate to leave her hut without a fragment of clothing on, would not dare to commit such a breach of decorum as to go out unpainted. Voyagers uniformly find that colored beads and trinkets are much more prized by wild tribes than are calicoes or broadcloths. And the anecdotes we have of the ways in which, when shirts and coats are given, they turn them to some ludicrous display, show how completely the idea of ornament predominates over that of use. Nay, there are still more extreme illustrations: witness the fact narrated by Captain Speke of his African attendants, who strutted about in their goat-skin mantles when the weather was fine, but when it was wet, took them off, folded them up, and went about naked, shivering in the rain! Indeed, the facts of aboriginal life seem to indicate that dress is developed out of decorations. And when we remember that even among ourselves most think more about the fineness of the fabric than its warmth, and more about the cut than the convenience — when we see that the function is still in great measure subordinated to the appearance — we have further reason for inferring such an origin.

It is not a little curious that the like relations hold with the mind. Among mental as among bodily acquisitions, the ornamental comes before the useful. Not only in times past, but almost as much in our own era, that knowledge which conduces to personal well-being has been postponed to that which brings applause. In the Greek schools, music, poetry, rhetoric, and a philosophy which, until Socrates taught, had but little bearing upon action, were the dominant subjects; while knowledge aiding the arts of life had a very subordinate place. And in our own universities and schools at the present moment the like antithesis holds. We are guilty of something like a platitude when we say that throughout his after-career a boy, in nine cases out of ten, applies his Latin and Greek to no practical purposes. The remark is trite that in his shop, or his office, in managing his estate or his family, in playing his part as director of a bank or a railway, he is very little aided by this knowledge he took so many years to acquire — so little, that generally the greater part of it drops out of his memory; and if he occasionally vents a Latin quotation or alludes to some Greek myth, it is less to throw light on the topic in hand than for the sake of effect. If we inquire what is the real motive for giving boys a classical education, we find it to be simply conformity to public opinion. Men dress their children's minds as they do their bodies, in the prevailing fashion. As the Orinoco Indian puts on his paint before leaving his hut, not with a view to any direct benefit, but because he would be ashamed to be seen without it; so a boy's drilling in Latin and Greek is insisted on, not because of their intrinsic value, but that he may not be disgraced by being found ignorant of them — that he may have "the education of a gentleman" — the badge marking a certain social position, and bringing a consequent respect.

This parallel is still more clearly displayed in the case of the other sex. In the treatment of both mind and body, the decorative element has continued to predominate in a greater degree among women than among men. Originally personal adornment occupied the attention of both sexes equally. In these latter days of civilization, however, we see that in the dress of men the regard for appearance has, in a considerable degree, yielded to the regard for comfort; while in their education the useful has of late been trenching on the ornamental. In neither direction has this change gone so far with women. The wearing of ear-rings, finger-rings, bracelets; the elaborate dressings of the hair; the still occasional use of paint; the immense labor bestowed in making habiliments sufficiently attractive; and the great discomfort that will be submitted to for the sake of conformity, show how greatly, in the attiring of women, the desire of approbation overrides the desire for warmth and convenience. And similarly in their education, the immense preponderance of "accomplishments" proves how here, too, use is subordinated to display. Dancing, deportment, the piano, singing, drawing — what a large space do these occupy! If you ask why Italian and German are learned, you will find that, under all the sham reasons given, the real reason is, that a knowledge of those tongues is thought ladylike. It is not that the books written in them may be utilized, which they scarcely ever are; but that Italian and German songs may be sung, and that the extent of attainment may bring whispered admiration. The births, deaths, and marriages of kings, and other like historic trivialities, are committed to memory, not because of any direct benefits that can possibly result from knowing them, but because society considers them parts of a good education — because the absence of such knowledge may bring the contempt of others. When we have named reading, writing, spelling, grammar, arithmetic, and sewing, we have named about all the things a girl is taught with a view to their direct uses in life; and even some of these have more reference to the good opinion of others than to immediate personal welfare.

Thoroughly to realize the truth that with the mind as with the body the ornamental precedes the useful, it is needful to glance at its rationale. This lies in the fact that, from the far past down even to the present, social needs have subordinated individual needs, and that the chief social need has been the control of individuals. It is not, as we commonly suppose, that there are no governments but those of monarchs, and parliaments, and constituted authorities. These acknowledged governments are supplemented by other unacknowledged ones, that grow up in all circles, in which every man or woman strives to be king or queen or lesser dignitary. To get above some and be reverenced by them, and to propitiate those who are above us, is the universal struggle in which the chief energies of life are expended. By the accumulation of wealth, by style of living, by beauty of dress, by display of knowledge or intellect, each tries to subjugate others, and so aids in weaving that ramified network of restraints by which society is kept in order. It is not the savage chief only who, in formidable warpaint, with scalps at his belt, aims to strike awe into his inferiors; it is not only the belle who, by elaborate toilet, polished manners, and numerous accomplishments, strives to "make conquests," but the scholar, the historian, the philosopher, use their acquirements to the same end. We are none of us content with quietly unfolding our own individualities to the full in all directions, but have a restless craving to impress our individualities upon others, and in some way subordinate them. And this it is which determines the character of our education. Not what knowledge is of most real worth is the consideration, but what will bring most applause, honor, respect — what will most conduce to social position and influence — what will be most imposing. As throughout life not what we are, but what we shall be thought, is the question; so in education, the question is, not the intrinsic value of knowledge, so much as its extrinsic effects on others. And this being one dominant idea, direct utility is scarcely more regarded than by the barbarian when filing his teeth and staining his nails.

If there needs any further evidence of the rude, undeveloped character of our education, we have it in the fact that the comparative worths of different kinds of knowledge have been as yet scarcely even discussed — much less discussed in a methodic way with definite results. Not only is it that no standard of relative values has yet been agreed upon, but the existence of any such standard has not been conceived in any clear manner. And not only is it that the existence of any such standard has not been clearly conceived, but the need for it seems to have been scarcely even felt. Men read books on this topic, and attend lectures on that; decide that their children shall be instructed in these branches of knowledge, and shall not be instructed in those; and all under the guidance of mere custom, or liking, or prejudice, without ever considering the enormous importance of determining in some rational way what things are really most worth learning. It is true that in all circles we have occasional remarks on the importance of this or the other order of information. But whether the degree of its importance justifies the expenditure of the time needed to acquire it, and whether there are not things of more importance to which the time might be better devoted, are queries which, if raised at all, are disposed of quite summarily, according to personal predilections. It is true, also, that from time to time we hear revived the standing controversy respecting the comparative merits of classics and mathematics. Not only, however, is this controversy carried on in an empirical manner, with no reference to an ascertained criterion, but the question at issue is totally insignificant when compared with the general question of which it is part. To suppose that deciding whether a mathematical or a classical education is the best, is deciding what is the proper *curriculum*, is much the same thing as to suppose that the whole of dietetics lies in determining whether or not bread is more nutritive than potatoes.

The question which we contend is of such transcendent moment, is, not whether such or such knowledge is of worth, but what is its *relative* worth? When they have named certain advantages which a given course of study has secured them, persons are apt to assume that they have justified themselves; quite forgetting that the adequateness of the advantages is the point to be judged. There is, perhaps, not a subject to which men devote attention that has not *some* value. A year diligently spent in getting up heraldry would very possibly give a little further insight into ancient manners and morals, and into the origin of names. Any one who should learn the distances between all the towns in England might, in the course of his life, find one or two of the thousand facts he had acquired of some slight service when arranging a journey. Gathering together all the small gossip of a county, profitless occupation as it would be, might yet occasionally help to establish some useful fact — say, a good example of hereditary transmission. But in these cases every one would admit that there was no proportion between the required labor and the probable benefits. No one would tolerate the proposal to devote some years of a boy's time to getting such information, at the cost of much more valuable information which he might else have got.

And if here the test of relative value is appealed to and held conclusive, then should it be appealed to and held conclusive throughout. Had we time to master all subjects we need not be particular. To quote the old song:

> Could a man be secure
> That his days would endure
> As of old, for a thousand long years,
> What things might he know!
> What deeds might he do!
> And all without hurry or care.

"But we that have but span-long lives" must ever bear in mind our limited time for acquisition. And remembering how narrowly this time is limited, not only by the shortness of life but also still more by the business of life, we ought to be especially solicitous to employ what time we have to the greatest advantage. Before devoting years to some subject which fashion or fancy suggests, it is surely wise to weigh with great care the worth of various alternative results which the same years might bring if otherwise applied.

In education, then, this is the question of questions, which it is high time we discussed in some methodic way. The first in importance, though the last to be considered, is the problem how to decide among the conflicting claims of various subjects on our attention. Before there can be a rational *curriculum*, we must settle which things it most concerns us to know; or, to use a word of Bacon's, now unfortunately obsolete, we must determine the relative values of knowledges.

To this end a measure of value is the first requisite. And happily, respecting the true measure of value, as expressed in general terms, there can be no dispute. Every one in contending for the worth of any particular order of information, does so by showing its bearing upon some part of life. In reply to the question, "Of what use is it?" the mathematician, linguist, naturalist, or philosopher explains the way in which his learning beneficially influences action — saves from evil or secures good — conduces to happiness. When the teacher of writing has pointed out how great an aid writing is to success in business — that is, to the obtaining of sustenance — that is, to satisfactory living — he is held to have proved his case. And when the collector of dead facts (say a numismatist) fails to make clear any appreciable effects which these facts can produce on human welfare, he is obliged to admit that they are comparatively valueless. All then, either directly or by implication, appeal to this as the ultimate test.

How to live? — that is the essential question for us. Not how to live in the mere material sense only, but in the widest sense. The general problem which comprehends every special problem is the right ruling of conduct in all directions under all circumstances. In what way to treat the body; in what way to treat the mind; in what way to manage our affairs; in what way to bring up a family; in what way to behave as a citizen; in what way to utilize all those sources of happiness which nature supplies — how to use our faculties to the greatest advantage of ourselves and others — now to live completely? And this being the great thing needful for us to learn, is, by consequence, the great thing which education has to teach. To prepare us for complete living is the function which education has to discharge; and the only rational mode of judging of any educational course is to judge in what degree it discharges such function.

This test, never used in its entirety, but rarely even partially used, and used then in a vague, half-conscious way, has to be applied consciously, methodically, and throughout all cases. It behooves us to set before ourselves, and ever to keep clearly in view, complete living as the end to be achieved; so that in bringing up our children we may choose subjects and methods of instruction with deliberate reference to this end. Not only ought we to cease from the mere unthinking adoption of the current fashion in education, which has no better warrant than any other fashion, but we must also rise above that rude, empirical style of judging displayed by those more intelligent people who do bestow some care in overseeing the cultivation of their children's minds. It must not suffice simply to *think* that such or such information will be useful in after life, or that this kind of knowledge is of more practical value than that; but we must seek out some process of estimating their respective values, so that as far as possible we may positively *know* which are most deserving of attention.

Doubtless the task is difficult — perhaps never to be more than approximately achieved. But considering the vastness of the interests at stake, its difficulty is no reason for pusillanimously passing it by, but rather for devoting every energy to its mastery. And if we only proceed systematically, we may very soon get at results of no small moment.

Our first step must obviously be to classify, in the order of their importance, the leading kinds of activity which constitute human life. They may naturally be arranged into, 1. Those activities which directly minister to self-preservation; 2. Those activities which, by securing the necessaries of life, indirectly minister to self-preservation; 3. Those activities which have for their end the rearing and discipline of offspring; 4. Those activities which are involved in the maintenance of proper social and political relations; 5. Those miscellaneous activities which make up the leisure part of life, devoted to the gratification of the tastes and feelings.

That these stand in something like their true order of subordination, it needs no long consideration to show. The actions and precautions by which, from moment to moment, we secure personal safety must clearly take precedence of all others. Could there be a man, ignorant as an infant of all surrounding objects and movements, or how to guide himself among them, he would pretty certainly lose his life the first time he went into the street, notwithstanding any amount of learning he might have on other matters. And as entire ignorance in all other directions would be less promptly fatal than entire ignorance in this direction, it must be admitted that knowledge immediately conducive to self-preservation is of primary importance.

That next after direct self-preservation comes the indirect self-preservation, which consists in acquiring the means of living, none will question. That a man's industrial functions must be considered before his parental ones is manifest from the fact that, speaking generally, the discharge of the parental functions is made possible only by the previous discharge of the industrial ones. The power of self-maintenance necessarily preceding the power of maintaining offspring, it follows that knowledge needful for self-maintenance has stronger claims than knowledge for family welfare — is second in value to none save knowledge needful for immediate self-preservation.

As the family comes before the state in order of time — as the bringing up of children is possible before the state exists, or when it has ceased to be, whereas the state is rendered possible only by the bringing up of children —

it follows that the duties of the parent demand closer attention than those of the citizen. Or, to use a further argument, since the goodness of a society ultimately depends on the nature of its citizens, and since the nature of its citizens is more modifiable by early training than by anything else, we must conclude that the welfare of the family underlies the welfare of society. And hence knowledge directly conducing to the first must take precedence of knowledge directly conducing to the last.

Those various forms of pleasurable occupation which fill up the leisure left by graver occupations — the enjoyments of music, poetry, painting, etc. — manifestly imply a pre-existing society. Not only is a considerable development of them impossible without a long-established social union, but their very subject-matter consists in great part of social sentiments and sympathies. Not only does society supply the conditions to their growth, but also the ideas and sentiments they express. And consequently that part of human conduct which constitutes good citizenship is of more moment than that which goes out in accomplishments or exercise of the tastes; and, in education, preparation for the one rank before preparation for the other.

Such then, we repeat, is something like the rational order of subordination: That education which prepares for direct self-preservation; that which prepares for indirect self-preservation; that which prepares for parenthood; that which prepares for citizenship; that which prepares for the miscellaneous refinements of life. We do not mean to say that these divisions are definitely separable. We do not deny that they are intricately entangled with each other in such way that there can be no training for any that is not in some measure a training for all. Nor do we question that of each division there are portions more important than certain portions of the preceding divisions: that, for instance, a man of much skill in business, but little other faculty, may fall farther below the standard of complete living than one of but moderate power of acquiring money but great judgment as a parent; or that exhaustive information bearing on right social action, joined with entire want of general culture in literature and the fine arts, is less desirable than a more moderate share of the one joined with some of the other. But after making all qualifications, there still remain these broadly-marked divisions: and it still continues substantially true that these divisions subordinate one another in the foregoing order, because the corresponding divisions of life make one another *possible* in that order.

Of course the ideal of education is complete preparation in all these divisions. But failing this ideal, as in our phase of civilization every one must do more or less, the aim should be to maintain *a due proportion* between the degrees of preparation in each. Not exhaustive cultivation in any one, supremely important though it may be — not even an exclusive attention to the two, three, or four divisions of greatest importance; but an attention to all — greatest where the value is greatest, less where the value is less, least where the value is least. For the average man (not to forget the cases in which peculiar aptitude for some one department of knowledge rightly makes that one the bread-winning occupation) — for the average man, we say, the desideratum is a training that approaches nearest to perfection in the things which most subserve complete living, and falls more and more below perfection in the things that have more and more remote bearings on complete living.

In regulating education by this standard there are some general considerations that should be ever present to us. The worth of any kind of culture, as aiding complete living, may be either necessary or more or less contingent. There is knowledge of intrinsic value, knowledge of quasi-intrinsic value, and knowledge of conventional value. Such facts as that sensations of numbness and tingling commonly precede paralysis, that the resistance of water to a body moving through it varies as the square of the velocity, that chlorine is a disinfectant — these, and the truths of science in general, are of intrinsic value: they will bear on human conduct ten thousand years hence as they do now. The extra knowledge of our own language, which is given by an acquaintance with Latin and Greek, may be considered to have a value that is quasi-intrinsic; it must exist for us and for other races whose languages owe much to these sources, but will last only as long as our languages last. While that kind of information which, in our schools, usurps the name History — the mere tissue of names and dates and dead unmeaning events — has a conventional value only, it has not the remotest bearing upon any of our actions, and it is of use only for the avoidance of those unpleasant criticisms which current opinion passes upon its absence. Of course, as those facts which concern all mankind throughout all time must be held of greater moment than those which concern only a portion of them during a limited era, and of far greater moment than those which concern only a portion of them during the continuance of a fashion, it follows that in a rational estimate, knowledge of intrinsic worth must, other things equal, take precedence of knowledge that is of quasi-intrinsic or conventional worth.

One further preliminary. Acquirement of every kind has two values — value as *knowledge* and value as *discipline*. Besides its use for guidance in conduct, the acquisition of each order of facts has also its use as mental exercise; and its effects as a preparative for complete living have to be considered under both these heads.

These, then, are the general ideas with which we must set out in discussing a *curriculum*: Life as divided into several kinds of activity of successively decreasing importance; the worth of each order of facts as regulating these several kinds of activity, intrinsically, quasi-intrinsically, and conventionally; and their regulative influences estimated both as knowledge and discipline.

*   *   *

And now we come to that remaining division of human life which includes the relaxations, pleasures, and amusements filling leisure hours. After considering what training best fits for self-preservation, for the obtaining of sustenance, for the discharge of parental duties, and for the regulation of social and political conduct, we have now to consider what training best fits for the miscellaneous ends not included in these — for the enjoyments of nature, of literature, and of the fine arts, in all their forms. Postponing them as we do to things that bear more vitally upon human welfare, and bringing everything, as we have, to the list of actual value, it will perhaps be inferred that we are inclined to slight these less essential things. No greater mistake could be made, however. We yield to none in the value we attach to aesthetic culture and its pleasures. Without painting, sculpture, music, poetry, and the emotions produced by natural beauty of every kind, life would lose half its charm. So far from thinking that the training and gratification of the tastes are unimportant, we believe that the time will come when they will occupy a much larger share of human life than now. When the forces of nature have been fully conquered to man's use — when the means of production have been brought to perfection — when labor has been economized to the highest degree — when education has been so systematized that a preparation for the more essential activities may be made with comparative rapidity — and when, consequently, there is a great increase of spare time, then will the poetry, both of art and nature, rightly fill a large space in the minds of all.

But it is one thing to admit that aesthetic culture is in a high degree conducive to human happiness, and another thing to admit that it is a fundamental requisite to human happiness. However important it may be, it must yield precedence to those kinds of culture which bear more directly upon the duties of life. As before hinted, literature and the fine arts are made possible by those activities which make individual and social life possible; and manifestly, that which is made possible must be postponed to that which makes it possible. A florist cultivates a plant for the sake of its flower, and regards the roots and leaves as of value chiefly because they are instrumental in producing the flower. But while, as an ultimate product, the flower is the thing to which everything else is subordinate, the florist very well knows that the root and leaves are intrinsically of greater importance, because on them the evolution of the flower depends. He bestows every care in rearing a healthy plant, and knows it would be folly if, in his anxiety to obtain the flower, he were to neglect the plant. Similarly in the case before us. Architecture, sculpture, painting, music, poetry, etc., may be truly called the efflorescence of civilized life. But even supposing them to be of such transcendent worth as to subordinate the civilized life out of which they grow (which can hardly be asserted), it will still be admitted that the production of a healthy civilized life must be the first consideration, and that the knowledge conducing to this must occupy the highest place.

And here we see most distinctly the vice of our educational system. It neglects the plant for the sake of the flower. In anxiety for elegance it forgets substance. While it gives no knowledge conducive to self-preservation — while of knowledge that facilitates gaining a livelihood it gives but the rudiments, and leaves the greater part to be picked up anyhow in after life — while for the discharge of parental functions it makes not the slightest provision — and while for the duties of citizenship it prepares by imparting a mass of facts, most of which are irrelevant, and the rest without a key, it is diligent in teaching everything that adds to refinement, polish, eclat. However fully we may admit that extensive acquaintance with modern languages is a valuable accomplishment, which, through reading, conversation, and travel, aids in giving a certain finish, it by no means follows that this result is rightly purchased at the cost of that vitally important knowledge sacrificed to it. Supposing it true that classical education conduces to elegance and correctness of style, it can not be said that elegance and correctness of style are comparable in importance to a familiarity with the principles that should guide the rearing of children. Grant that the taste may be greatly improved by reading all the poetry written in extinct languages, yet it is not to be inferred that such improvement of taste is equivalent in value to an acquaintance with the laws of health. Accomplishments, the fine arts, *belles-lettres*, and all those things which, as we say, constitute the efflorescence of civilization, should be wholly subordinate to that knowledge and discipline in which civilization rests. *As they occupy the leisure part of life, so should they occupy the leisure part of education.*

*   *   *

Thus far our question has been the worth of knowledge of this or that kind for purposes of guidance. We have now to judge the relative values of different kinds of knowledge for purposes of discipline. This division of our subject we are obliged to treat with comparative brevity; and happily no very lengthened treatment of it is needed. Having found what is best for the one end, we have by implication found what is best for the other. We may be quite sure that the acquirement of those classes of facts which are most useful for regulating conduct involves a mental exercise best fitted for strengthening the faculties. It would be utterly contrary to the beautiful economy of nature if one kind of culture were needed for the gaining of information and another kind were needed as a mental gymnastic. Everywhere throughout creation we find faculties developed through the performance of those functions which it is their office to perform, not through the performance of artificial exercises devised to fit them for these functions. The red Indian acquires the swiftness and agility which make him a successful hunter by the actual pursuit of animals; and by the miscellaneous activities of his life he gains a better balance of physical powers than gymnastics ever give. That skill in tracking enemies and prey which he has reached by long practice implies a subtlety of perception far exceeding anything produced by artificial training. And similarly throughout. From the Bushman, whose eye, which being habitually employed in identifying distant objects that are to be pursued or fled from, has acquired a quite telescopic range, to the accountant whose daily practice enables him to add up several columns of figures simultaneously, we find that the highest power of a faculty results from the discharge of those duties which the conditions of life require it to discharge. And we may be certain, *a priori*, that the same law holds throughout education. The education of most value for guidance must at the same time be the education of most value for discipline.

*   *   *

We conclude, then, that for discipline as well as for guidance, science is of chiefest value. In all its effects, learning the meaning of things is better than learning the meaning of words. Whether for intellectual, moral, or religious training, the study of surrounding phenomena is immensely superior to the study of grammars and lexicons.

Thus to the question with which we set out, What knowledge is of most worth? the uniform reply is — science. This is the verdict on all the counts. For direct self-preservation, or the maintenance of life and health, the all-important knowledge is — science. For that indirect self-preservation which we call gaining a livelihood, the knowledge of greatest value is — science. For the due discharge of parental functions, the proper guidance is to be found only in — science. For that interpretation of national life, past and present, without which the citizen can not rightly regulate his conduct, the indispensable key is — science. Alike for the most perfect production and highest enjoyment of art in all its forms, the needful preparation is still — science. And for purposes of discipline — intellectual, moral, religious — the most efficient study is, once more — science. The question which at first seemed so perplexed has become, in the course of our inquiry, comparatively simple. We have not to estimate the degrees of importance of different orders of human activity, and different studies as severally fitting us for them, since we find that the study of science, in its most comprehensive meaning, is the best preparation for all these orders of activity. We have not to decide between the claims of knowledge of great though conventional value, and knowledge of less though intrinsic value, seeing that the knowledge which we find to be of most value in all other respects is intrinsically most valuable: its worth is not dependent upon opinion, but is as fixed as is the relation of man to the surrounding world. Necessary and eternal as are its truths, all science concerns all mankind for all time. Equally at present and in the remotest future must it be of incalculable importance for the regulation of their conduct that men should understand the science of life, physical, mental, and social, and that they should understand all other science as a key to the science of life.

And yet the knowledge which is of such transcendent value is that which, in our age of boasted education, receives the least attention. While this which we call civilization could never have arisen had it not been for science, science forms scarcely an appreciable element in what men consider civilized training. Though to the progress of science we owe it that millions find support where once there was food only for thousands, yet of these millions but a few thousand pay any respect to that which has made their existence possible. Though this increasing knowledge of the properties and relations of things has not only enabled wandering tribes to grow into populous nations, but has given to the countless members of those populous nations comforts and pleasures which their few naked ancestors never even conceived, or could have believed, yet is this kind of knowledge only now receiving a grudging recognition in our highest educational institutions. To the slowly growing acquaintance with the uniform coexistences and sequences of phenomena — to the establishment of invariable laws — we owe our emancipation from the grossest superstitions. But for science we should be still worshipping fetishes, or, with hecatombs of victims, propitiating diabolical deities.

Paraphrasing an Eastern fable, we may say that in the family of knowledges, science is the household drudge, who, in obscurity, hides unrecognized perfections. To her has been committed all the work; by her skill, intelligence, and devotion have all the conveniences and gratifications been obtained; and while ceaselessly occupied ministering to the rest, she has been kept in the background, that her haughty sisters might flaunt their fripperies in the eyes of the world. This parallel holds yet further. For we are fast coming to the *dénouement*, when the positions will be changed; and while these haughty sisters sink into merited neglect, science, proclaimed as highest alike in worth and beauty, will reign supreme.

Bertrand Russell

Bertrand Russell, an English philosopher, social critic, and mathematician, has taught at many schools, notably the University of California, Harvard, and the University of Peking. Of his many books, those of general interest to the student of education are Education and the Good Life (1926), Education and the Social Order (1932), Impact of Science on Society (1953), and My Philosophical Development (1959).

In " 'Useless' Knowledge" Russell examines the non-utilitarian rewards of learning, affirming that a merely useful education is indeed a dangerous and narrow acquisition. Like Spencer an advocate of scientific method, Russell nevertheless objects to the notion that a technical education is superior to a liberal arts program.

32

"USELESS" KNOWLEDGE*

Francis Bacon, a man who rose to eminence by betraying his friends, asserted, no doubt as one of the ripe lessons of experience, that "knowledge is power." But this is not true of *all* knowledge. Sir Thomas Browne wished to know what song the sirens sang, but if he had ascertained this it would not have enabled him to rise from being a magistrate to being High Sheriff of his county. The sort of knowledge that Bacon had in mind was that which we call scientific. In emphasizing the importance of science, he was belatedly carrying on the tradition of the Arabs and the early Middle Ages, according to which knowledge consisted mainly of astrology, alchemy, and pharmacology, all of which were branches of science. A learned man was one who, having mastered these studies, had acquired magical powers. In the early eleventh century, Pope Silvester II, for no reason except that he read books, was universally believed to be a magician in league with the devil. Prospero, who in Shakespeare's time was a mere phantasy, represented what had been for centuries the generally received conception of a learned man, so far at least as his powers of sorcery were concerned. Bacon believed — rightly, as we now know — that science could provide a more powerful magician's wand than any that had been dreamed of by the necromancers of former ages.

The Renaissance, which was at its height in England at the time of Bacon, involved a revolt against the utilitarian conception of knowledge. The Greeks had acquired a familiarity with Homer, as we do with music-hall songs, because they enjoyed him, and without feeling that they were engaged in the pursuit of learning. But the men of the sixteenth century could not begin to understand him without first absorbing a very considerable amount of linguistic erudition. They admired the Greeks, and did not wish to be shut out from their pleasures; they therefore copied them, both in reading the classics and in other less avowable ways. Learning, in the Renaissance, was part of the *joie de vivre*, just as much as drinking or love-making. And this was true not only of literature, but also of sterner studies. Every one knows the story of Hobbes's first contact with Euclid: opening the book, by chance, at the theorem of Pythagoras, he exclaimed, "By God, this is impossible," and proceeded to read the proofs backwards until, reaching the axioms, he became convinced. No one can doubt that this was for him a voluptuous

* From *In Praise of Idleness and Other Essays* by Bertrand Russell (London: George Allen & Unwin Ltd., 1935). Used by permission of George Allen & Unwin Ltd., London.

moment, unsullied by the thought of the utility of geometry in measuring fields.

It is true that the Renaissance found a practical use for the ancient languages in connection with theology. One of the earliest results of the new feeling for classical Latin was the discrediting of the forged decretals and the donation of Constantine. The inaccuracies which were discovered in the Vulgate and the Septuagint made Greek and Hebrew a necessary part of the controversial equipment of Protestant divines. The republican maxims of Greece and Rome were invoked to justify the resistance of Puritans to the Stuarts and of Jesuits to monarchs who had thrown off allegiance to the Pope. But all this was an effect, rather than a cause, of the revival of classical learning, which had been in full swing in Italy for nearly a century before Luther. The main motive of the Renaissance was mental delight, the restoration of a certain richness and freedom in art and speculation which had been lost while ignorance and superstition kept the mind's eye in blinkers.

The Greeks, it was found, had devoted a part of their attention to matters not purely literary or artistic, such as philosophy, geometry, and astronomy. These studies, therefore, were respectable, but other sciences were more open to question. Medicine, it was true, was dignified by the names of Hippocrates and Galen; but in the intervening period it had become almost confined to Arabs and Jews, and inextricably intertwined with magic. Hence the dubious reputation of such men as Paracelsus. Chemistry was in even worse odor, and hardly became respectable until the eighteenth century.

In this way it was brought about that knowledge of Greek and Latin, with a smattering of geometry and perhaps astronomy, came to be considered the intellectual equipment of a gentleman. The Greeks disdained the practical applications of geometry, and it was only in their decadence that they found a use for astronomy in the guise of astrology. The sixteenth and seventeenth centuries, in the main, studied mathematics with Hellenic disinterestedness, and tended to ignore the sciences which had been degraded by their connection with sorcery. A gradual change towards a wider and more practical conception of knowledge, which was going on throughout the eighteenth century, was suddenly accelerated at the end of that period by the French Revolution and the growth of machinery, of which the former gave a blow to gentlemanly culture while the latter offered new and astonishing scope for the exercise of ungentlemanly skill. Throughout the last hundred and fifty years, men have questioned more and more vigorously the value of "useless" knowledge, and have come increasingly to believe that the only knowledge worth having is that which is applicable to some part of the economic life of the community.

In countries such as France and England, which have a traditional educational system, the utilitarian view of knowledge has only partially prevailed. There are still, for example, professors of Chinese in the universities who read the Chinese classics but are unacquainted with the works of Sun Yat-sen, which created modern China. There are still men who know ancient history in so far as it was related by authors whose style was pure, that is to say, up to Alexander in Greece and Nero in Rome, but refuse to know the much more important later history because of the literary inferiority of the historians who related it. Even in France and England, however, the old tradition is dying, and in more up-to-date countries, such as Russia and the United States, it is utterly extinct. In America, for example, educational commissions point out that fifteen hundred words are all that most people employ in business correspondence, and therefore suggest that all others should be avoided in the school curriculum. Basic English, a British invention, goes still further, and reduces the necessary vocabulary to eight hundred words. The conception of speech as something capable of aesthetic value is dying out, and it is coming to be thought that the sole purpose of words is to convey practical information. In Russia the pursuit of practical aims is even more whole-hearted than in America: all that is taught in educational institutions is intended to serve some obvious purpose in education or government. The only escape is afforded by theology: the sacred Scriptures must be studied by some in the original German, and a few professors must learn philosophy in order to defend dialectical materialism against the criticisms of bourgeois metaphysicians. But as orthodoxy becomes more firmly established, even this tiny loophole will be closed.

Knowledge, everywhere, is coming to be regarded not as a good in itself, or as a means of creating a broad and humane outlook on life in general, but as merely an ingredient in technical skill. This is part of the greater integration of society which has been brought about by scientific technique and military necessity. There is more economic and political interdependence than there was in former times, and therefore there is more social pressure to compel a man to live in a way that his neighbors think useful. Educational establishments, except those for the very rich, or (in England) such as have become invulnerable through antiquity, are not allowed to spend their money as they like, but must satisfy the State that they are serving a useful purpose by imparting skill and instilling loyalty. This is part and parcel of the same movement which has led to compulsory military service, boy scouts, the organization of political parties, and the dissemination of political passion by the Press. We are all more aware of our fellow-citizens than we used to be, more anxious, if we are virtuous, to do them good, and in any case to make them do us good. We do not like to think of any one lazily enjoying life, however refined may be the quality of his enjoyment. We feel that everybody ought to be doing something to help on the great cause (whatever it may be), the more so as so many bad men are working against it and ought to be stopped. We have not leisure of mind, therefore, to acquire any knowledge except such as will help us in the fight for whatever it may happen to be that we think important.

There is much to be said for the narrowly utilitarian view of education. There is not time to learn everything before beginning to make a living, and undoubtedly "useful" knowledge is *very* useful. It has made the modern world. Without it, we should not have machines or motor cars or railways or aeroplanes; it should be added that we should not have modern advertising or modern propaganda. Modern knowledge has brought about an immense improvement in average health, and at the same time has discovered how to exterminate large cities by poison gas. Whatever is distinctive of our world, as compared with former times, has its source in "useful" knowledge. No community as yet has enough of it, and undoubtedly education must continue to promote it.

It must also be admitted that a great deal of the traditional cultural education was foolish. Boys spent many years acquiring Latin and Greek grammar, without being, at the end, either capable or desirous (except in a small percentage of cases) of reading a Greek or Latin author. Modern languages and history are preferable, from every point of view, to Latin and Greek. They are not only more useful, but they give much more culture in much less time. For an Italian of the fifteenth century, since practically everything worth reading, if not in his own language, was in Greek or Latin, these languages were the indispensable keys to culture. But since that time great literatures have grown up in various modern languages, and the development of civilization has been so rapid that knowledge of antiquity has become much less useful in understanding our problems than knowledge of modern nations and their comparatively recent history. The traditional schoolmaster's point of view, which was admirable at the time of the Revival of Learning, became gradually unduly narrow, since it ignored what the world has done since the fifteenth century. And not only history and modern languages, but science also, when properly taught, contributes to culture. It is therefore possible to maintain that education should have other aims than direct utility, without defending the traditional curriculum. Utility and culture, when both are conceived broadly, are found to be less incompatible than they appear to the fanatical advocates of either.

Apart, however, from the cases in which culture and direct utility can be combined, there is indirect utility, of various different kinds, in the possession of knowledge which does not contribute to technical efficiency. I think some of the worst features of the modern world could be improved by a greater encouragement of such knowledge and a less ruthless pursuit of mere professional competence.

When conscious activity is wholly concentrated on some one definite purpose, the ultimate result, for most people, is lack of balance accompanied by some form of nervous disorder. The men who directed German policy during the War made mistakes, for example, as regards the submarine campaign which brought America on to the side of the Allies, which any person coming fresh to the subject could have seen to be unwise, but which they could not judge sanely owing to mental concentration and lack of holidays. The same sort of thing may be seen wherever bodies of men attempt tasks which put a prolonged strain upon spontaneous impulses. Japanese Imperialists, Russian Communists, and German Nazis all have a kind of tense fanaticism which comes of living too exclusively in the mental world of certain tasks to be accomplished. When the tasks are as important and as feasible as the fanatics suppose, the result may be magnificent; but in most cases narrowness of outlook has caused oblivion of some powerful counteracting force, or has made all such forces seem the work of the devil, to be met by punishment and terror. Men as well as children have need of play, that is to say, of periods of activity having no purpose beyond present enjoyment. But if play is to serve its purpose, it must be possible to find pleasure and interest in matters not connected with work.

The amusements of modern urban populations tend more and more to be passive and collective, and to consist of inactive observation of the skilled activities of others. Undoubtedly such amusements are much better than none, but they are not as good as would be those of a population which had, through education, a wider range of intelligent interests not connected with work. Better economic organization, allowing mankind to benefit by the productivity of machines, should lead to a very great increase of leisure, and much leisure is apt to be tedious except to those who have considerable intelligent activities and interests. If a leisured population is to be happy, it must be an educated population, and must be educated with a view to mental enjoyment as well as to the direct usefulness of technical knowledge.

The cultural element in the acquisition of knowledge, when it is successfully assimilated, forms the character of a man's thoughts and desires, making them concern themselves, in part at least, with large impersonal objects, not only with matters of immediate importance to himself. It has been too readily assumed that, when a man has acquired certain capacities by means of knowledge, he will use them in ways that are socially beneficial. The narrowly utilitarian conception of education ignores the necessity of training a man's purposes as well as his skill. There is in untrained human nature a very considerable element of cruelty, which shows itself in many ways, great and small. Boys at school tend to be unkind to a new boy, or to one whose clothes are not quite conventional. Many women (and not a few men) inflict as much pain as they can by means of malicious gossip. The Spaniards enjoy bullfights; the British enjoy hunting and shooting. The same cruel impulses take more serious forms in the hunting of Jews in Germany and kulaks in Russia. All imperialism affords scope for them, and in war they become sanctified as the highest form of public duty.

Now while it must be admitted that highly educated people are sometimes cruel, I think there can be no doubt that they are less often so than people whose minds have lain fallow. The bully in a school is seldom a boy whose proficiency in learning is up to the average. When a lynching takes place, the ringleaders are almost invariably very ignorant men. This is not because mental cultivation produces positive humanitarian feelings, though it may do so; it is rather because it gives other interests than the ill-treatment of neighbors, and other sources of self-respect than the assertion of domination. The two things most universally desired are power and admiration. Ignorant men can, as a rule, only achieve either by brutal means, involving the acquisition of physical mastery. Culture gives a man less harmful forms of power and more deserving ways of making himself admired. Galileo did more than any monarch has done to change the world, and his power immeasurably exceeded that of his persecutors. He had therefore no need to aim at becoming a persecutor in his turn.

Perhaps the most important advantage of "useless" knowledge is that it promotes a contemplative habit of mind. There is in the world much too much readiness, not only for action without adequate previous reflection, but also for some sort of action on occasions on which wisdom would counsel inaction. People show their bias on this matter in various curious ways. Mephistopheles tells the young student that theory is gray but the tree of life is green, and every one quotes this as if it were Goethe's opinion, instead of what he supposes the devil would be likely to say to an undergraduate. Hamlet is held up as an awful warning against thought without action, but no one holds up Othello as a warning against action without thought. Professors such as Bergson, from a kind of snobbery towards the practical man, decry philosophy, and say that life at its best should resemble a cavalry charge. For my part, I think action is best when it emerges from a profound apprehension of the universe and human destiny, not from some wildly passionate impulse of romantic but disproportioned self-assertion. A habit of finding pleasure in thought rather than in action is a safeguard against unwisdom and excessive love of power, a means of preserving serenity in misfortune and peace of mind among worries. A life confined to what is personal is likely, sooner or later, to become unbearably painful; it is only by windows into a larger and less fretful cosmos that the more tragic parts of life become endurable.

A contemplative habit of mind has advantages ranging from the most trivial to the most profound. To begin with minor vexations, such as fleas, missing trains, or cantankerous business associates. Such troubles seem hardly worthy to be met by reflections on the excellence of heroism or the transitoriness of all human ills, and yet the irritation to which they give rise destroys many people's good temper and enjoyment of life. On such occasions, there is much consolation to be found in out-of-the-way bits of knowledge which have some real or fancied connection with the trouble of the moment; or even if they have none, they serve to obliterate the present from one's thoughts. When assailed by people who are white with fury, it is pleasant to remember the chapter in Descartes' *Treatise on the Passions* entitled "Why those who grow pale with rage are more to be feared than those who grow red." When one feels impatient over the difficulty of securing international cooperation, one's impatience is diminished if one happens to think of the sainted King Louis IX, before embarking on his crusade, allying himself with the Old Man of the Mountain, who appears in the Arabian Nights as the dark source of half the wickedness in the world. When the rapacity of capitalists grows oppressive, one may be suddenly consoled by the recollection that Brutus, that exemplar of republican virtue, lent money to a city at 40 per cent, and hired a private army to besiege it when it failed to pay the interest.

Curious learning not only makes unpleasant things less unpleasant, but also makes pleasant things more pleasant. I have enjoyed peaches and apricots more since I have known that they were first cultivated in China in the early days of the Han dynasty; that Chinese hostages held by the great King Kaniska introduced them into India, whence they spread to Persia, reaching the Roman Empire in the first century of our era; that the word "apricot" is derived from the same Latin source as the word "precocious," because the apricot ripens early; and that the A at the beginning was added by mistake, owing to a false etymology. All this makes the fruit taste much sweeter.

About a hundred years ago, a number of well-meaning philanthropists started societies "for the diffusion of useful knowledge," with the result that people have ceased to appreciate the delicious savor of "useless" knowledge. Opening Burton's *Anatomy of Melancholy* at haphazard on a day when I was threatened by that mood, I learnt that there is a "melancholy matter," but that, while some think it may be engendered of all four humors, "Galen holds that it may be engendered of three alone, excluding phlegm or pituita, whose true assertion Valerius and Menardus stiffly maintain, and so doth Fuscius, Montaltus, Montanus. How (say they) can white become black?" In spite of this unanswerable argument, Hercules de Saxonia and Cardan, Guianerius and Laurentius, are (so Burton tells us) of the opposite opinion. Soothed by these historical reflections, my melancholy, whether due to three humors or to four, was dissipated. As a cure for too much zeal, I can imagine few measures more effective than a course of such ancient controversies.

But while the trivial pleasures of culture have their place as a relief from the trivial worries of practical life, the more important merits of contemplation are in relation to the greater evils of life, death and pain and cruelty, and the blind march of nations into unnecessary disaster. For those to whom dogmatic religion can no longer bring comfort, there is need of some substitute, if life is not to become dusty and harsh and filled with trivial self-assertion. The world at present is full of angry self-centered groups, each incapable of viewing human life as a whole, each willing to destroy civilization rather than yield an inch. To this narrowness no amount of technical instruction will provide an antidote. The antidote, in so far as it is a matter of individual psychology, is to be found in history, biology, astronomy, and all those studies which, without destroying self-respect, enable the individual to see himself in his proper perspective. What is needed is not this or that specific piece of information, but such knowledge as inspires a conception of the ends of human life as a whole: art and history, acquaintance with the lives of heroic individuals, and some understanding of the strangely accidental and ephemeral position of man in the cosmos — all this touched with an emotion of pride in what is distinctly human, the power to see and to know, to feel magnanimously and to think with understanding. It is from large perceptions combined with impersonal emotion that wisdom most readily springs.

Life, at all times full of pain, is more painful in our time than in the two centuries that preceded it. The attempt to escape from pain drives men to triviality, to self-deception, to the invention of vast collective myths. But these momentary alleviations do but increase the sources of suffering in the long run. Both private and public misfortune can only be mastered by a process in which will and intelligence interact: the part of will is to refuse to shirk the evil or accept an unreal solution, while the part of intelligence is to understand it, to find a cure if it is curable, and, if not, to make it bearable by seeing it in its relations, accepting it as unavoidable, and remembering what lies outside it in other regions, other ages, and the abysses of interstellar space.

III. HUMANITIES AND SCIENCES:
THE SCHOLASTIC SCHISM

T. H. Huxley and Matthew Arnold

Toward the end of the nineteenth century, T. H. Huxley (1825–1895), a distinguished scientist, provoked a tremendous controversy by his attack on classical education and the world of English letters. His assault took the form of an address delivered in 1880, and repercussions to it were not long in forming.

Huxley develops his position methodically, ordering his entire exposition around two assumptions: ". . . The first is, that neither the discipline nor the subject-matter of classical education is of such direct value to the student of physical science as to justify the expenditure of valuable time upon either; and the second is, that for the purpose of attaining real culture, an exclusively scientific education is at least as effectual as an exclusively literary education."

Matthew Arnold (1822–1888), a brilliant representative of English letters, accepted the challenge implicit in Huxley's speech. In 1882 Arnold launched his counterattack, and the enlarging gulf between letters and science not only became discernible but seemed almost to be welcomed by the two factions.

The Huxley-Arnold debate is significant in that it develops in depth the major levels of hostility operative in the late nineteenth century and foretells the catastrophic alienation of intellect that has come to pass in our time. The tragedy of this isolation is not that it has occurred, for its occurrence is merely a disaster vulnerable to corrective reform, but that it was encouraged by two of the most gifted men of the Victorian era. Still, the Huxley-Arnold debate did serve to identify eloquently the terms of combat, though it did little to circumvent the war.

33

SCIENCE AND CULTURE*
by Thomas Henry Huxley

I hold very strongly by two convictions: — The first is, that neither the discipline nor the subject-matter of classical education is of such direct value to the student of physical science as to justify the expenditure of valuable time upon either; and the second is, that for the purpose of attaining real culture, an exclusively scientific education is at least as effectual as an exclusively literary education.

I need hardly point out to you that these opinions, especially the latter, are diametrically opposed to those of the great majority of educated Englishmen, influenced as they are by school and university traditions. In their belief, culture is obtainable only by a liberal education; and a liberal education is synonymous, not merely with education and instruction in literature, but in one particular form of literature, namely, that of Greek and Roman antiquity. They hold that the man who has learned Latin and Greek, however little, is educated; while he who is versed in other branches of knowledge, however deeply, is a more or less respectable specialist, not admissible into the cultured caste. The stamp of the educated man, the University degree, is not for him.

I am too well acquainted with the generous catholicity of spirit, the true sympathy with scientific thought, which pervades the writings of our chief apostle of culture, to identify him with these opinions; and yet one may cull from one and another of those epistles to the Philistines, which so much delight all who do not answer to that name, sentences which lend them some support.

Mr. Arnold tells us that the meaning of culture is "to know the best that has been thought and said in the world." It is the criticism of life contained in literature. That criticism regards "Europe as being, for intellectual and spiritual purposes, one great confederation, bound to a joint action and working to a common result; and whose members have, for their common outfit, a knowledge of Greek, Roman, and Eastern antiquity, and of one another. Special, local, and temporary advantages being put out of account, that modern nation will in the intellectual and spiritual sphere make most progress, which most thoroughly carries out this programme. And what is that

* From an address delivered in 1880.

but saying that we too, all of us, as individuals, the more thoroughly we carry it out, shall make the more progress?"

We have here to deal with two distinct propositions. The first, that a criticism of life is the essence of culture; the second, that literature contains the materials which suffice for the construction of such a criticism.

I think that we must all assent to the first proposition. For culture certainly means something quite different from learning or technical skill. It implies the possession of an ideal, and the habit of critically estimating the value of things by comparison with a theoretic standard. Perfect culture should supply a complete theory of life, based upon a clear knowledge alike of its possibilities and of its limitations.

But we may agree to all this, and yet strongly dissent from the assumption that literature alone is competent to supply this knowledge. After having learnt all that Greek, Roman, and Eastern antiquity have thought and said, and all that modern literatures have to tell us, it is not self-evident that we have laid a sufficiently broad and deep foundation for that criticism of life which constitutes culture.

Indeed, to any one acquainted with the scope of physical science, it is not at all evident. Considering progress only in the "intellectual and spiritual sphere," I find myself wholly unable to admit that either nations or individuals will really advance, if their common outfit draws nothing from the stores of physical science. I should say that an army, without weapons of precision and with no particular base of operations, might more hopefully enter upon a campaign on the Rhine, than a man, devoid of a knowledge of what physical science has done in the last century, upon a criticism of life.

When a biologist meets with an anomaly, he instinctively turns to the study of development to clear it up. The rationale of contradictory opinions may with equal confidence be sought in history.

It is, happily, no new thing that Englishmen should employ their wealth in building and endowing institutions for educational purposes. But, five or six hundred years ago, deeds of foundation expressed or implied conditions as nearly as possible contrary to those which have been thought expedient by Sir Josiah Mason. That is to say, physical science was practically ignored, while a certain literary training was enjoined as a means to the acquirement of knowledge which was essentially theological.

The reason of this singular contradiction between the actions of men alike animated by a strong and disinterested desire to promote the welfare of their fellows, is easily discovered.

At that time, in fact, if any one desired knowledge beyond such as could be obtained by his own observation, or by common conversation, his first necessity was to learn the Latin language, inasmuch as all the higher knowledge of the western world was contained in works written in that language. Hence, Latin grammar, with logic and rhetoric, studied through Latin, were the fundamentals of education. With respect to the substance of the knowledge imparted through this channel, the Jewish and Christian Scriptures, as interpreted and supplemented by the Romish Church, were held to contain a complete and infallibly true body of information.

Theological dicta were, to the thinkers of those days, that which the axioms and definitions of Euclid are to the geometers of these. The business of the philosophers of the middle ages was to deduce, from the data furnished by the theologians, conclusions in accordance with ecclesiastical decrees. They were allowed the high privilege of showing, by logical process, how and why that which the Church said was true, must be true. And if their demonstrations fell short of or exceeded this limit, the Church was maternally ready to check their aberrations — if need were, by the help of the secular arm.

Between the two, our ancestors were furnished with a compact and complete criticism of life. They were told how the world began and how it would end; they learned that all material existence was but a base and insignificant blot upon the fair face of the spiritual world, and that nature was, to all intents and purposes, the playground of the devil; they learned that the earth is the centre of the visible universe, and that man is the cynosure of things terrestrial; and more especially was it inculcated that the course of nature had no fixed order, but that it could be, and constantly was, altered by the agency of innumerable spiritual beings, good and bad, according as they were moved by the deeds and prayers of men. The sum and substance of the whole doctrine was to produce the conviction that the only thing really worth knowing in this world was how to secure that place in a better which, under certain conditions, the Church promised.

Our ancestors had a living belief in this theory of life, and acted upon it in their dealings with education, as in all other matters. Culture meant saintliness — after the fashion of the saints of those days; the education that led to it was, of necessity, theological; and the way to theology lay through Latin.

That the study of nature — further than was requisite for the satisfaction of everyday wants — should have any bearing on human life was far from the thoughts of men thus trained. Indeed, as nature had been cursed for man's sake, it was an obvious conclusion that those who meddled with nature were likely to come into pretty close contact with Satan. And, if any born scientific investigator followed his instincts, he might safely reckon upon earning the reputation, and probably upon suffering the fate, of a sorcerer.

Had the western world been left to itself in Chinese isolation, there is no saying how long this state of things might have endured. But, happily, it was not left to itself. Even earlier than the thirteenth century, the development of Moorish civilization in Spain and the great movement of the Crusades had introduced the leaven which, from that day to this, has never ceased to work. At first, through the intermediation of Arabic translations, afterwards by the study of the originals, the western nations of Europe became acquainted with the writings of the ancient philosophers and poets, and, in time, with the whole of the vast literature of antiquity.

Whatever there was of high intellectual aspiration or dominant capacity in

Italy, France, Germany, and England, spent itself for centuries in taking possession of the rich inheritance left by the dead civilizations of Greece and Rome. Marvelously aided by the invention of printing, classical learning spread and flourished. Those who possessed it prided themselves on having attained the highest culture then within the reach of mankind.

And justly. For, saving Dante on his solitary pinnacle, there was no figure in modern literature, at the time of the Renascence, to compare with the men of antiquity; there was no art to compete with their sculpture; there was no physical science but that which Greece had created. Above all, there was no other example of perfect intellectual freedom — of the unhesitating acceptance of reason as the sole guide to truth and the supreme arbiter of conduct.

The new learning necessarily soon exerted a profound influence upon education. The language of the monks and schoolmen seemed little better than gibberish to scholars fresh from Vergil and Cicero, and the study of Latin was placed upon a new foundation. Moreover, Latin itself ceased to afford the sole key to knowledge. The student who sought the highest thought of antiquity found only a second-hand reflection of it in Roman literature, and turned his face to the full light of the Greeks. And after a battle, not altogether dissimilar to that which is at present being fought over the teaching of physical science, the study of Greek was recognized as an essential element of all higher education.

Thus the Humanists, as they were called, won the day; and the great reform which they effected was of incalculable service to mankind. But the Nemesis of all reformers is finality; and the reformers of education, like those of religion, fell into the profound, however common, error of mistaking the beginning for the end of the work of reformation.

The representatives of the Humanists, in the nineteenth century, take their stand upon classical education as the sole avenue to culture, as firmly as if we were still in the age of Renascence. Yet, surely, the present intellectual relations of the modern and the ancient worlds are profoundly different from those which obtained three centuries ago. Leaving aside the existence of a great and characteristically modern literature, of modern painting, and, especially, of modern music, there is one feature of the present state of the civilized world which separates it more widely from the Renascence than the Renascence was separated from the middle ages.

This distinctive character of our own times lies in the vast and constantly increasing part which is played by natural knowledge. Not only is our daily life shaped by it, not only does the prosperity of millions of men depend upon it, but our whole theory of life has long been influenced, consciously or unconsciously, by the general conceptions of the universe which have been forced upon us by physical science.

In fact, the most elementary acquaintance with the results of scientific investigation shows us that they offer a broad and striking contradiction to the opinion so implicitly credited and taught in the middle ages.

The notions of the beginning and the end of the world entertained by our forefathers are no longer credible. It is very certain that the earth is not the chief body in the material universe, and that the world is not subordinated to man's use. It is even more certain that nature is the expression of a definite order with which nothing interferes, and that the chief business of mankind is to learn that order and to govern themselves accordingly. Moreover this scientific "criticism of life" presents itself to us with different credentials from any other. It appeals not to authority, not to what anybody may have thought or said, but to nature. It admits that all our interpretations of natural fact are more or less imperfect and symbolic, and bids the learner seek for truth not among words but among things. It warns us that the assertion which outstrips evidence is not only a blunder but a crime.

The purely classical education advocated by the representatives of the Humanists in our day gives no inkling of all this. A man may be a better scholar than Erasmus, and know no more of the chief causes of the present intellectual fermentation than Erasmus did. Scholarly and pious persons, worthy of all respect, favour us with allocutions upon the sadness of the antagonism of science to their mediaeval way of thinking, which betray an ignorance of the first principles of scientific investigation, an incapacity for understanding what a man of science means by veracity, and an unconsciousness of the weight of established scientific truths, which is almost comical.

There is no great force in the *tu quoque* argument, or else the advocates of scientific education might fairly enough retort upon the modern Humanists that they may be learned specialists, but that they possess no such sound foundation for a criticism of life as deserves the name of culture. And, indeed, if we were disposed to be cruel, we might urge that the Humanists have brought this reproach upon themselves, not because they are too full of the spirit of the ancient Greek, but because they lack it.

The period of the Renascence is commonly called that of the "Revival of Letters," as if the influences then brought to bear upon the mind of Western Europe had been wholly exhausted in the field of literature. I think it is very commonly forgotten that the revival of science, effected by the same agency, although less conspicuous, was not less momentous.

In fact, the few and scattered students of nature of that day picked up the clue to her secrets exactly as it fell from the hands of the Greeks a thousand years before. The foundations of mathematics were so well laid by them that our children learn their geometry from a book written for the schools of Alexandria two thousand years ago. Modern astronomy is the natural continuation and development of the work of Hipparchus and of Ptolemy; modern physics of that of Democritus and of Archimedes; it was long before modern biological science outgrew the knowledge bequeathed to us by Aristotle, by Theophrastus, and by Galen.

We cannot know all the best thoughts and sayings of the Greeks unless we know what they thought about natural phenomena. We cannot fully apprehend their criticism of life unless we understand the extent to which that criticism was affected by scientific conceptions. We falsely pretend to be the inheritors of their culture unless we are penetrated, as the best minds among them were, with an unhesitating faith that the free employment of reason, in accordance with scientific method, is the sole method of reaching truth.

Thus I venture to think that the pretensions of our modern Humanists to the possession of the monopoly of culture and to the exclusive inheritance of the spirit of antiquity must be abated, if not abandoned. But I should be very sorry that anything I have said should be taken to imply a desire on my part to depreciate the value of a classical education, as it might be and as it sometimes is. The native capacities of mankind vary no less than their opportunities; and while culture is one, the road by which one man may best reach it is widely different from that which is most advantageous to another. Again, while scientific education is yet inchoate and tentative, classical education is thoroughly well organized upon the practical experience of generations of teachers. So that, given ample time for learning and destination for ordinary life, or for a literary career, I do not think that a young Englishman in search of culture can do better than follow the course usually marked out for him, supplementing its deficiencies by his own efforts.

But for those who mean to make science their serious occupation, or who intend to follow the profession of medicine, or who have to enter early upon the business of life — for all these, in my opinion, classical education is a mistake; and it is for this reason that I am glad to see "mere literary education and instruction" shut out from the curriculum of Sir Josiah Mason's College, seeing that its inclusion would probably lead to the introduction of the ordinary smattering of Latin and Greek.

Nevertheless, I am the last person to question the importance of genuine literary education, or to suppose that intellectual culture can be complete without it. An exclusively scientific training will bring about a mental twist as surely as an exclusively literary training. The value of the cargo does not compensate for a ship's being out of trim; and I should be very sorry to think that the Scientific College would turn out none but lop-sided men.

There is no need, however, that such a catastrophe should happen. Instruction in English, French, and German is provided, and thus the three greatest literatures of the modern world are made accessible to the student. French and German, and especially the latter language, are absolutely indispensable to those who desire full knowledge in any department of science. But even supposing that the knowledge of these languages acquired is not more than sufficient for purely scientific purposes, every Englishman has, in his native tongue, an almost perfect instrument of literary expression; and, in his own literature, models of every kind of literary excellence. If an Englishman cannot get literary culture out of his Bible, his Shakespeare, his Milton, neither, in my belief, will the profoundest study of Homer and Sophocles, Vergil and Horace, give it to him.

Thus, since the constitution of the College makes sufficient provision for literary as well as for scientific education, and since artistic instruction is also contemplated, it seems to me that a fairly complete culture is offered to all who are willing to take advantage of it.

But I am not sure that at this point the "practical" man, scotched but not slain, may ask what all this talk about culture has to do with an Institution, the object of which is defined to be "to promote the prosperity of the manufactures and the industry of the country." He may suggest that what is wanted for this end is not culture, not even a purely scientific discipline, but simply a knowledge of applied science.

I often wish that this phrase, "applied science," had never been invented. For it suggests that there is a sort of scientific knowledge of direct practical use, which can be studied apart from another sort of scientific knowledge, which is of no practical utility, and which is termed "pure science." But there is no more complete fallacy than this. What people call applied science is nothing but the application of pure science to particular classes of problems. It consists of deductions from those general principles, established by reasoning and observation, which constitute pure science. No one can safely make these deductions until he has a firm grasp of the principles; and he can obtain that grasp only by personal experience of the operations of observation and of reasoning on which they are founded.

Almost all the processes employed in the arts and manufactures fall within the range either of physics or of chemistry. In order to improve them, one must thoroughly understand them; and no one has a chance of really understanding them unless he has obtained that mastery of principles and that habit of dealing with facts, which is given by long-continued and well-directed purely scientific training in the physical and the chemical laboratory. So that there really is no question as to the necessity of purely scientific discipline, even if the work of the College were limited by the narrowest interpretation of its stated aims.

And, as to the desirableness of a wider culture than that yielded by science alone, it is to be recollected that the improvement of manufacturing processes is only one of the conditions which contribute to the prosperity of industry. Industry is a means and not an end; and mankind work only to get something which they want. What that something is depends partly on their innate, and partly on their acquired, desires.

If the wealth resulting from prosperous industry is to be spent upon the gratification of unworthy desires, if the increasing perfection of manufacturing processes is to be accompanied by an increasing debasement of those who carry them on, I do not see the good of industry and prosperity.

Now it is perfectly true that men's views of what is desirable depend upon their characters, and that the innate proclivities to which we give that name are not touched by any amount of instruction. But it does not follow that even mere intellectual education may not, to an indefinite extent, modify the practical manifestation of the characters of men in their actions, by supplying them with motives unknown to the ignorant. A pleasure-loving character will have pleasure of some sort; but, if you give him the choice, he may prefer pleasures which do not degrade him to those which do. And this choice is offered to every man who possesses in literary or artistic culture a never-failing source of pleasures, which are neither withered by age, nor staled by custom, nor embittered in the recollection by the pangs of self-reproach. . . .

34

LITERATURE AND SCIENCE*
by Matthew Arnold

I am going to ask whether the present movement for ousting letters from their old predominance in education, and for transferring the predominance in education to the natural sciences — whether this brisk and flourishing movement ought to prevail, and whether it is likely that in the end it really will prevail. An objection may be raised which I will anticipate. My own studies have been almost wholly in letters, and my visits to the field of the natural sciences have been very slight and inadequate, although those sciences have always strongly moved my curiosity. A man of letters, it will perhaps be said, is not competent to discuss the comparative merits of letters and natural science as means of education. To this objection I reply, first of all, that his incompetence, if he attempts the discussion but is really incompetent for it, will be abundantly visible; nobody will be taken in; he will have plenty of sharp observers and critics to save mankind from that danger. But the line I am going to follow is, as you will soon discover, so extremely simple, that perhaps it may be followed without failure even by one who for a more ambitious line of discussion would be quite incompetent.

Some of you may possibly remember a phrase of mine which has been the object of a good deal of comment; an observation to the effect that in our culture, the aim being *to know ourselves and the world*, we have, as the means to this end, *to know the best which has been thought and said in the world.* A man of science, who is also an excellent writer and the very prince of debaters, Professor Huxley, in a discourse at the opening of Sir Josiah Mason's college at Birmingham, laying hold of this phrase, expanded it by quoting some more words of mine, which are these: "The civilized world is to be regarded as now being, for intellectual and spiritual purposes, one great confederation, bound to a joint action and working to a common result; and whose members have for their proper outfit a knowledge of Greek, Roman,

* From a lecture delivered in 1882.

and Eastern antiquity, and of one another. Special local and temporary advantages being put out of account, that modern nation will in the intellectual and spiritual sphere make most progress, which most thoroughly carries out this programme."

Now on my phrase, thus enlarged, Professor Huxley remarks that when I speak of the above-mentioned knowledge as enabling us to know ourselves and the world, I assert *literature* to contain the materials which suffice for thus making us know ourselves and the world. But it is not by any means clear, says he, that after having learnt all which ancient and modern literatures have to tell us, we have laid a sufficiently broad and deep foundation for that criticism of life, that knowledge of ourselves and the world, which constitutes culture. On the contrary, Professor Huxley declares that he finds himself "wholly unable to admit that either nations or individuals will really advance, if their outfit draws nothing from the stores of physical science. An army without weapons of precision, and with no particular base of operations, might more hopefully enter upon a campaign on the Rhine, than a man, devoid of a knowledge of what physical science has done in the last century, upon a criticism of life."

This shows how needful it is for those who are to discuss any matters together to have a common understanding as to the sense of the terms they employ — how needful, and how difficult. What Professor Huxley says, implies just the reproach which is so often brought against the study of *belles lettres*, as they are called: that the study is an elegant one, but slight and ineffectual; a smattering of Greek and Latin and other ornamental things, of little use for any one whose object is to get at truth, and to be a practical man. So, too, M. Renan talks of the "superficial humanism" of a school-course which treats us as if we were all going to be poets, writers, preachers, orators, and he opposes this humanism to positive science, or the critical search after truth. And there is always a tendency in those who are remonstrating against the predominance of letters in education to understand by letters *belles lettres*, and by *belles lettres* a superficial humanism, the opposite of science or true knowledge.

But when we talk of knowing Greek and Roman antiquity, for instance, which is the knowledge people have called the humanities, I for my part mean a knowledge which is something more than a superficial humanism, mainly decorative. "I call all teaching *scientific*," says Wolf, the critic of Homer, "which is systematically laid out and followed up to its original sources. For example: a knowledge of classical antiquity is scientific when the remains of classical antiquity are correctly studied in the original languages." There can be no doubt that Wolf is perfectly right; that all learning is scientific which is systematically laid out and followed up to its original sources, and that a genuine humanism is scientific.

When I speak of knowing Greek and Roman antiquity, therefore, as a help to knowing ourselves and the world, I mean more than a knowledge of so much vocabulary, so much grammar, so many portions of authors in the

Greek and Latin languages — I mean knowing the Greeks and Romans, and their life and genius, and what they were and did in the world; what we get from them, and what is its value. That, at least, is the ideal; and when we talk of endeavouring to know Greek and Roman antiquity, as a help to knowing ourselves and the world, we mean endeavouring so to know them as to satisfy this ideal, however much we may still fall short of it.

The same also as to knowing our own and other modern nations, with the like aim of getting to understand ourselves and the world. To know the best that has been thought and said by the modern nations, is to know, says Professor Huxley, "only what modern *literatures* have to tell us; it is the criticism of life contained in modern literature." And yet "the distinctive character of our times," he urges, "lies in the vast and constantly increasing part which is played by natural knowledge." And how, therefore, can a man, devoid of knowledge of what physical science has done in the last century, enter hopefully upon a criticism of modern life?

Let us, I say, be agreed about the meaning of the terms we are using. I talk of knowing the best which has been thought and uttered in the world; Professor Huxley says this means knowing *literature*. Literature is a large word; it may mean everything written with letters or printed in a book. Euclid's *Elements* and Newton's *Principia* are thus literature. All knowledge that reaches us through books is literature. But by literature Professor Huxley means *belles lettres*. He means to make me say, that knowing the best which has been thought and said by the modern nations is knowing their *belles lettres* and no more. And this is no sufficient equipment, he argues, for a criticism of modern life. But as I do not mean, by knowing ancient Rome, knowing merely more or less of Latin *belles lettres*, and taking no account of Rome's military, and political, and legal, and administrative work in the world; and as, by knowing ancient Greece, I understand knowing her as the giver of Greek art, and the guide to a free and right use of reason and to scientific method, and the founder of our mathematics and physics and astronomy and biology — I understand knowing her as all this, and not merely knowing certain Greek poems, and histories, and treatises, and speeches — so as to the knowledge of modern nations also. By knowing modern nations, I mean not merely knowing their *belles lettres*, but knowing also what has been done by such men as Copernicus, Galileo, Newton, Darwin. "Our ancestors learned," says Professor Huxley, "that the earth is the centre of the visible universe, and that man is the cynosure of things terrestrial; and more especially was it inculcated that the course of nature had no fixed order, but that it could be, and constantly was, altered." But for us now, continues Professor Huxley, "the notions of the beginning and the end of the world entertained by our forefathers are no longer credible. It is very certain that the earth is not the chief body in the material universe and that the world is not subordinated to man's use. It is even more certain that nature is the expression of a definite order, with which nothing interferes." "And yet," he cries, "the purely classical education advocated by the representatives of the humanists in our day gives no inkling of all this!"

In due place and time I will just touch upon that vexed question of classical education; but at present the question is as to what is meant by knowing the best which modern nations have thought and said. It is not knowing their *belles lettres* merely which is meant. To know Italian *belles lettres* is not to know Italy, and to know English *belles lettres* is not to know England. Into knowing Italy and England there comes a great deal more, Galileo and Newton amongst it. The reproach of being a superficial humanism, a tincture of *belles lettres*, may attach rightly enough to some other disciplines; but to the particular discipline recommended when I proposed knowing the best that has been thought and said in the world, it does not apply. In that best I certainly include what in modern times has been thought and said by the great observers and knowers of nature.

There is, therefore, really no question between Professor Huxley and me as to whether knowing the great results of the modern scientific study of nature is not required as a part of our culture, as well as knowing the products of literature and art. But to follow the processes by which those results are reached, ought, say the friends of physical science, to be made the staple of education for the bulk of mankind. And here there does arise a question between those whom Professor Huxley calls with playful sarcasm "the Levites of culture," and those whom the poor humanist is sometimes apt to regard as its Nebuchadnezzars.

The great results of the scientific investigation of nature we are agreed upon knowing, but how much of our study are we bound to give to the processes by which those results are reached? The results have their visible bearing on human life. But all the processes, too, all the items of fact, by which those results are reached and established, are interesting. All knowledge is interesting to a wise man, and the knowledge of nature is interesting to all men. It is very interesting to know that from the albuminous white of the egg the chick in the egg gets the materials for its flesh, bones, blood, and feathers, while from the fatty yolk of the egg it gets the heat and energy which enable it at length to break its shell and begin the world. It is less interesting, perhaps, but still it is interesting, to know that when a taper burns, the wax is converted into carbonic acid and water. Moreover, it is quite true that the habit of dealing with facts, which is given by the study of nature, is, as the friends of physical science praise it for being, an excellent discipline. The appeal, in the study of nature, is constantly to observation and experiment; not only is it said that the thing is so, but we can be made to see that it is so. Not only does a man tell us that when a taper burns the wax is converted into carbonic acid and water, as a man may tell us, if he likes, that Charon is punting his ferry-boat on the river Styx, or that Victor Hugo is a sublime poet, or Mr. Gladstone the most admirable of statesmen; but we are made to see that the conversion into carbonic acid and water does actually happen. This reality of natural knowledge it is, which makes the friends of physical science contrast it, as a knowledge of things, with the humanist's knowledge, which is, say they, a knowledge of words. And hence Professor Huxley is moved to lay it down that, "for the purpose of attaining real culture, an exclusively scientific education is at least as effectual as an exclusively literary education." And a certain President of the Section for Mechanical Science in the British Association is, in Scripture phrase, "very bold," and declares that if a man, in his mental training, "has substituted literature and history for natural science, he has chosen the less useful alternative." But whether we go these lengths or not, we must all admit that in natural science the habit gained of dealing with facts is a most valuable discipline, and that every one should have some experience of it.

More than this, however, is demanded by the reformers. It is proposed to make the training in natural science the main part of education, for the great majority of mankind at any rate. And here, I confess, I part company with the friends of physical science, with whom up to this point I have been agreeing. In differing from them, however, I wish to proceed with the utmost caution and diffidence. The smallness of my own acquaintance with the disciplines of natural science is ever before my mind, and I am fearful of doing these disciplines an injustice. The ability and pugnacity of the partisans of natural science make them formidable persons to contradict. The tone of tentative inquiry, which befits a being of dim faculties and bounded knowledge, is the tone I would wish to take and not to depart from. At present it seems to me that those who are for giving to natural knowledge, as they call it, the chief place in the education of the majority of mankind, leave one important thing out of their account: the constitution of human nature. But I put this forward on the strength of some facts not at all recondite, very far from it; facts capable of being stated in the simplest fashion, and to which, if I so state them, the man of science will, I am sure, be willing to allow their due weight.

Deny the facts altogether, I think, he hardly can. He can hardly deny that when we set ourselves to enumerate the powers which go to the building up of human life, and say that they are the power of conduct, the power of intellect and knowledge, the power of beauty, and the power of social life and manners — he can hardly deny that this scheme, though drawn in rough and plain lines enough, and not pretending to scientific exactness, does yet give a fairly true representation of the matter. Human nature is built up by these powers; we have the need for them all. When we have rightly met and adjusted the claims of them all, we shall then be in a fair way for getting soberness and righteousness with wisdom. This is evident enough, and the friends of physical science would admit it.

But perhaps they may not have sufficiently observed another thing: namely, that the several powers just mentioned are not isolated, but there is, in the generality of mankind, a perpetual tendency to relate them one to another in divers ways. With one such way of relating them I am particularly concerned now. Following our instinct for intellect and knowledge, we acquire pieces of knowledge; and presently, in the generality of men, there arises the desire to relate these pieces of knowledge to our sense for conduct, to our sense for beauty — and there is weariness and dissatisfaction if the desire is balked.

Now in this desire lies, I think, the strength of that hold which letters have upon us.

All knowledge is, as I said just now, interesting; and even items of knowledge which from the nature of the case cannot well be related, but must stand isolated in our thoughts, have their interest. Even lists of exceptions have their interest. If we are studying Greek accents, it is interesting to know that *pais* and *pas*, and some other monosyllables of the same form of declension, do not take the circumflex upon the last syllable of the genitive plural, but vary, in this respect, from the common rule. If we are studying physiology, it is interesting to know that the pulmonary artery carries dark blood and the pulmonary vein carries bright blood, departing in this respect from the common rule for the division of labour between the veins and the arteries. But every one knows how we seek naturally to combine the pieces of our knowledge together, to bring them under general rules, to relate them to principles; and how unsatisfactory and tiresome it would be to go on forever learning lists of exceptions, or accumulating items of fact which must stand isolated.

Well, that same need of relating our knowledge, which operates here within the sphere of our knowledge itself, we shall find operating, also, outside that sphere. We experience, as we go on learning and knowing — the vast majority of us experience — the need of relating what we have learnt and known to the sense which we have in us for conduct, to the sense which we have in us for beauty.

A certain Greek prophetess of Mantineia in Arcadia, Diotima by name, once explained to the philosopher Socrates that love, and impulse, and bent of all kinds, is, in fact, nothing else but the desire in men that good should forever be present to them. This desire for good, Diotima assured Socrates, is our fundamental desire, of which fundamental desire every impulse in us is only some one particular form. And therefore this fundamental desire it is, I suppose — this desire in men that good should be forever present to them — which acts in us when we feel the impulse for relating our knowledge to our sense for conduct and to our sense for beauty. At any rate, with men in general the instinct exists. Such is human nature. And the instinct, it will be admitted, is innocent, and human nature is preserved by our following the lead of its innocent instincts. Therefore, in seeking to gratify this instinct in question, we are following the instinct of self-preservation in humanity.

But, no doubt, some kinds of knowledge cannot be made to directly serve the instinct in question, cannot be directly related to the sense for beauty, to the sense for conduct. These are instrument-knowledges; they lead on to other knowledges, which can. A man who passes his life in instrument-knowledges is a specialist. They may be invaluable as instruments to do something beyond, for those who have the gift thus to employ them; and they may be disciplines in themselves wherein it is useful for every one to have some schooling. But it is inconceivable that the generality of men should pass all their mental life with Greek accents or with formal logic. My friend

Professor Sylvester, who is one of the first mathematicians in the world, holds transcendental doctrines as to the virtue of mathematics, but those doctrines are not for common men. In the very Senate House and heart of our English Cambridge I once ventured, though not without an apology for my profaneness, to hazard the opinion that for the majority of mankind a little of mathematics, even, goes a long way. Of course this is quite consistent with their being of immense importance as an instrument to something else; but it is the few who have the aptitude for using them, not the bulk of mankind.

The natural sciences do not, however, stand on the same footing with these instrument-knowledges. Experience shows us that the generality of men will find more interest in learning that, when a taper burns, the wax is converted into carbonic acid and water, or in learning the explanation of the phenomenon of dew, or in learning how the circulation of the blood is carried on, than they find in learning that the genitive plural of *pais* and *pas* does not take the circumflex on the termination. And one piece of natural knowledge is added to another, and others are added to that, and at last we come to propositions so interesting as Mr. Darwin's famous proposition that "our ancestor was a hairy quadruped furnished with a tail and pointed ears, probably arboreal in his habits." Or we come to propositions of such reach and magnitude as those which Professor Huxley delivers, when he says that the notions of our forefathers about the beginning and the end of the world were all wrong, and that nature is the expression of a definite order with which nothing interferes.

Interesting, indeed, these results of science are, important they are, and we should all of us be acquainted with them. But what I now wish you to mark is, that we are still, when they are propounded to us and we receive them, we are still in the sphere of intellect and knowledge. And for the generality of men there will be found, I say, to arise, when they have duly taken in the proposition that their ancestor was "a hairy quadruped furnished with a tail and pointed ears, probably arboreal in his habits," there will be found to arise an invincible desire to relate this proposition to the sense in us for conduct, and to the sense in us for beauty. But this the men of science will not do for us, and will hardly even profess to do. They will give us other pieces of knowledge, other facts, about other animals and their ancestors, or about plants, or about stones, or about stars; and they may finally bring us to those great "general conceptions of the universe, which are forced upon us all," says Professor Huxley, "by the progress of physical science." But still it will be *knowledge* only which they give us; knowledge not put for us into relation with our sense for conduct, our sense for beauty, and touched with emotion by being so put; not thus put for us, and therefore, to the majority of mankind, after a certain while, unsatisfying, wearying.

Not to the born naturalist, I admit. But what do we mean by a born naturalist? We mean a man in whom the zeal for observing nature is so uncommonly strong and eminent, that it marks him off from the bulk of mankind. Such a man will pass his life happily in collecting natural knowledge and reasoning upon it, and will ask for nothing, or hardly anything, more. I have heard it said that the sagacious and admirable naturalist whom we lost not very long ago, Mr. Darwin, once owned to a friend that for his part he did not experience the necessity for two things which most men find so necessary to them — religion and poetry; science and the domestic affections, he thought, were enough. To a born naturalist, I can well understand that this should seem so. So absorbing is his occupation with nature, so strong his love for his occupation, that he goes on acquiring natural knowledge and reasoning upon it, and has little time or inclination for thinking about getting it related to the desire in man for conduct, the desire in man for beauty. He relates it to them for himself as he goes along, so far as he feels the need; and he draws from the domestic affections all the additional solace necessary. But then Darwins are extremely rare. Another great and admirable master of natural knowledge, Faraday, was a Sandemanian. That is to say, he related his knowledge to his instinct for conduct and to his instinct for beauty, by the aid of that respectable Scottish sectary, Robert Sandeman. And so strong, in general, is the demand of religion and poetry to have their share in a man, to associate themselves with his knowing, and to relieve and rejoice it, that, probably, for one man amongst us with the disposition to do as Darwin did in this respect, there are at least fifty with the disposition to do as Faraday.

Education lays hold upon us, in fact, by satisfying this demand. Professor Huxley holds up to scorn mediaeval education with its neglect of the knowledge of nature, its poverty even of literary studies, its formal logic devoted to "showing how and why that which the Church said was true must be true." But the great mediaeval Universities were not brought into being, we may be sure, by the zeal for giving a jejune and contemptible education. Kings have been their nursing fathers, and queens have been their nursing mothers, but not for this. The mediaeval Universities came into being, because the supposed knowledge, delivered by Scripture and the Church, so deeply engaged men's hearts, by so simply, easily, and powerfully relating itself to their desire for conduct, their desire for beauty. All other knowledge was dominated by this supposed knowledge and was subordinated to it, because of the surpassing strength of the hold which it gained upon the affections of men, by allying itself profoundly with their sense for conduct, their sense for beauty.

But now, says Professor Huxley, conceptions of the universe fatal to the notions held by our forefathers have been forced upon us by physical science. Grant to him that they are thus fatal, that the new conceptions must and will soon become current everywhere, and that every one will finally perceive them to be fatal to the beliefs of our forefathers. The need of humane letters, as they are truly called, because they serve the paramount desire in men that good should be forever present to them — the need of humane letters, to establish a relation between the new conceptions, and our instinct for beauty, our instinct for conduct, is only the more visible. The Middle Age could do without humane letters, as it could do without the study of nature, because its supposed knowledge was made to engage its emotions so powerfully. Grant that the supposed knowledge disappears, its power of being made to engage the emotions will of course disappear along with it — but the emotions themselves, and their claim to be engaged and satisfied, will remain. Now if we find by experience that humane letters have an undeniable power of engaging the emotions, the importance of humane letters in a man's training becomes not less, but greater, in proportion to the success of modern science in extirpating what it calls "mediaeval thinking."

Have humane letters, then, have poetry and eloquence, the power here attributed to them of engaging the emotions, and do they exercise it? And if they have it and exercise it, *how* do they exercise it, so as to exert an influence upon man's sense for conduct, his sense for beauty? Finally, even if they both can and do exert an influence upon the senses in question, how are they to relate to them the results — the modern results — of natural science? All these questions may be asked. First, have poetry and eloquence the power of calling out the emotions? The appeal is to experience. Experience shows that for the vast majority of men, for mankind in general, they have the power. Next, do they exercise it? They do. But then, *how* do they exercise it so as to affect man's sense for conduct, his sense for beauty? And this is perhaps a case for applying the Preacher's words: "Though a man labour to seek it out, yet he shall not find it; yea, farther, though a wise man think to know it, yet shall he not be able to find it." Why should it be one thing, in its effect upon the emotions, to say, "Patience is a virtue," and quite another thing, in its effect upon the emotions, to say with Homer,

τλητὸν γὰρ Μοῖραι θυμὸν θέσαν ἀνθρώποισιν —

"for an enduring heart have the destinies appointed to the children of men"? Why should it be one thing, in its effect upon the emotions, to say with the philosopher Spinoza, *Felicitas in ea consistit quod homo suum esse conservare potest* — "Man's happiness consists in his being able to preserve his own essence," and quite another thing, in its effect upon the emotions, to say with the Gospel, "What is a man advantaged, if he gain the whole world, and lose himself, forfeit himself?" How does this difference of effect arise? I cannot tell, and I am not much concerned to know; the important thing is that it does arise, and that we can profit by it. But how, finally, are poetry and eloquence to exercise the power of relating the modern results of natural science to man's instinct for conduct, his instinct for beauty? And here again I answer that I do not know *how* they will exercise it, but that they can and will exercise it I am sure. I do not mean that modern philosophical poets and modern philosophical moralists are to come and relate for us, in express terms, the results of modern scientific research to our instinct for conduct, our instinct for beauty. But I mean that we shall find, as a matter of experience, if we know the best that has been thought and uttered in the world — we shall find that the art and poetry and eloquence of men who lived, perhaps, long ago, who had the most limited natural knowledge, who had the most erroneous conceptions about many important matters — we shall find that this art, and poetry, and eloquence, have in fact not only the power of refreshing and delighting us; they have also the power — such is the strength and worth, in essentials, of their authors' criticism of life — they have a fortifying, and elevating, and quickening, and suggestive power, capable of wonderfully helping us to relate the results of modern science to our need for conduct, our need for beauty. Homer's conceptions of the physical universe were, I imagine, grotesque; but really, under the shock of hearing from modern science that "the world is not subordinated to man's use, and that man is not the cynosure of things terrestrial," I could, for my own part, desire no better comfort than Homer's line which I quoted just now,

$$\tau\lambda\eta\tau\grave{o}\nu\ \gamma\grave{a}\rho\ \text{M}o\hat{\iota}\rho\alpha\iota\ \theta\upsilon\mu\grave{o}\nu\ \theta\acute{\epsilon}\sigma\alpha\nu\ \grave{a}\nu\theta\rho\acute{\omega}\pi o\iota\sigma\iota\nu -$$

"for an enduring heart have the destinies appointed to the children of men"!

And the more that men's minds are cleared, the more that the results of science are frankly accepted, the more that poetry and eloquence come to be received and studied as what in truth they really are — the criticism of life by gifted men, alive and active with extraordinary power at an unusual number of points — so much the more will the value of humane letters, and of art also, which is an utterance having a like kind of power with theirs, be felt and acknowledged, and their place in education be secured.

Let us, therefore, all of us, avoid indeed as much as possible any invidious comparison between the merits of humane letters, as means of education, and the merits of the natural sciences. But when some President of a Section for Mechanical Science insists on making the comparison, and tells us that "he who in his training has substituted literature and history for natural science has chosen the less useful alternative," let us make answer to him that the student of humane letters only, will, at least, know also the great general conceptions brought in by modern physical science; for science, as Professor Huxley says, forces them upon us all. But the student of the natural sciences only, will, by our very hypothesis, know nothing of humane letters; not to mention that in setting himself to be perpetually accumulating natural knowledge, he sets himself to do what only specialists have in general the gift for doing genially. And so he will probably be unsatisfied, or at any rate incomplete, and even more incomplete than the student of humane letters only.

I once mentioned in a school-report, how a young man in one of our English training colleges having to paraphrase the passage in *Macbeth* beginning,

Can'st thou not minister to a mind diseased?

turned this line into, "Can you not wait upon the lunatic?" And I remarked what a curious state of things it would be, if every pupil of our national schools knew, let us say, that the moon is two thousand one hundred and sixty miles in diameter, and thought at the same time that a good paraphrase for

> Can'st thou not minister to a mind diseased?

was, "Can you not wait upon the lunatic?" If one is driven to choose, I think I would rather have a young person ignorant about the moon's diameter, but aware that "Can you not wait upon the lunatic?" is bad, than a young person whose education had been such as to manage things the other way.

Or to go higher than the pupils of our national schools. I have in my mind's eye a member of our British Parliament who comes to travel here in America, who afterwards relates his travels, and who shows a really masterly knowledge of the geology of this great country and of its mining capabilities, but who ends by gravely suggesting that the United States should borrow a prince from our Royal Family, and should make him their king, and should create a House of Lords of great landed proprietors after the pattern of ours; and then America, he thinks, would have her future happily and perfectly secured. Surely, in this case, the President of the Section for Mechanical Science would himself hardly say that our member of Parliament, by concentrating himself upon geology and mineralogy, and so on, and not attending to literature and history, had "chosen the more useful alternative."

If then there is to be separation and option between humane letters on the one hand, and the natural sciences on the other, the great majority of mankind, all who have not exceptional and overpowering aptitudes for the study of nature, would do well, I cannot but think, to choose to be educated in humane letters rather than in the natural sciences. Letters will call out their being at more points, will make them live more. . . .

I. I. Rabi

"Scientist and Humanist: Can the Minds Meet?" is, first, an acknowledgment of the historical shifts in prestige endured by the humanities and sciences and, second, a definition of the qualitative difference between knowledge and wisdom. Significantly, the author's views, al-

though debauched by oversimplifications, suggest an encouraging trend: Rabi, a professor of physics, recognizes the unexpendable values of the humanities as, in another instance, C. P. Snow, a man of letters by vocation, supports the beauties and accomplishments of modern science in his book The Two Cultures and the Scientific Revolution.

An astute example of an earlier attempt at conciliation is discovered in "Science and Literature" from Indoor Studies, *a delightful book by the American naturalist John Burroughs, a contemporary of Arnold and Huxley.*

35

SCIENTIST AND HUMANIST: CAN THE MINDS MEET?*

I

For more than half a century, from the period of the Darwinian controversy till the end of the 1930s, science remained almost unchallenged as the source of enlightment, understanding, and hope for a better, healthier, and safer world. The benefits brought by science were and are still visible everywhere one looks. Human ills are being overcome; food supplies are becoming more abundant; travel and communication are quick and easy, and the comforts of life, especially for the common man, are vastly increased. In the person of Albert Einstein science enjoyed a world-wide respect almost akin to reverence and hardly equaled since the time of Isaac Newton.

In the last decade or so we have begun to detect signs of significant change. The knowledge and techniques developed through science for the illumination of the mind and the elevation of the spirit, for the prolongation and the amelioration of life, have been used for the destruction of life and the degradation of the human spirit. Technological warfare, biological warfare, psychological warfare, brainwashing, all make use of science with frightening results.

I do not suggest that warfare and its attendant horror is a result of modern science. Ancient Greece, at the zenith of that remarkable civilization, in a

* From the *Atlantic Monthly*, January, 1956, pp. 64–67. Used by permission of I. I. Rabi and the *Atlantic Monthly*.

land united by a common culture and a common religion, destroyed itself in a bitter and useless war more thoroughly than Europe has done in the present century even with the aid of electronics, aviation, and high explosives. What I mean is that our epoch in history, which has produced one of the greatest achievements of the human race, may be passing into a twilight that does not precede the dawn.

Science, the triumph of the intellect and the rational faculties, has resulted in the hydrogen bomb. The glib conclusion is that science and the intellect are therefore false guides. We must seek elsewhere, some people say, for hope and salvation; but, say the same people, while doing so we must keep ahead of the Russians in technology and in the armaments race. Keep the fearsome fruits but reject the spirit of science. Such is the growing mood of some people at the present time. It is a mood of anti-intellectualism which can only hasten the destruction which these people fear. Anti-intellectualism has always been endemic in every society, perhaps in the heart of every human being. In times of stress this attitude is stimulated and people tend to become impatient and yield to prejudice and emotion just when coolness, subtlety, and reason are most needed.

We are told, and most of us believe, that we are living in a period of crisis unequaled in history. To be cheerful and proud of our accomplishment and optimistic of the future is almost akin to subversion. To be considered objective and realistic, one must view with alarm. Yet we are not living in a period of hard times and unemployment! We have, I cannot say enjoyed but, rather, bemoaned, a period of prosperity and world-wide influence for good unequaled in history. Nevertheless, despite all, we seem to be acquiring a complacency of despair. In this mood, unable to adjust to new values, we hark back to a past which now looks so bright in retrospect, and we raise the banner of "Back to the Humanities."

What is meant by the slogan "Back to the Humanities"? What are people really looking for? What knowledge, what guidance, what hope for salvation, what inspiration, or what relief from anxiety does a practical-minded people like ours expect from a knowledge of the humanities? They do not wish to re-establish the study of the Greek and Roman classics in their original tongues, or to re-create the Greek city-state in Metropolitan Boston.

I venture to suggest that what they mean is something quite different from what is meant by the humanities. The progress of civilization in the modern age, especially in our own century, has brought with it an immense increase of knowledge of every kind, from archaeology to zoology. More is known of the history of antiquity than was known to Herodotus. We have penetrated farther into the heavens and into the innermost secrets of the structure of matter than anyone could have dreamt of in previous generations. We have run through the satisfactions of representational art to the puzzling outlines of abstract art. The increase in physical comfort and in communication has brought with it a whole set of new problems. The great increase in population necessarily means further crowding and additional social and cultural adjustment. Under these circumstances, it is natural for people to look for guidance toward a balanced adjustment.

II

What people are really looking for is wisdom. To our great store of knowledge we need the added quality of wisdom.

Wisdom is inseparable from knowledge; it is knowledge plus a quality which is within the human being. Without it knowledge is dry, almost unfit for human consumption, and dangerous in application. The absence of wisdom is clearly noticeable; the learned fool and the educated bore have been with us since the beginnings of recorded history. Wisdom adds flavor, order, and measure to knowledge. Wisdom makes itself most manifest in the application of knowledge to human needs.

Every generation of mankind has to remake its culture, its values, and its goals. Changing circumstances make older habits and customs valueless or obsolete. New knowledge exposes the limitations and the contingent nature of older philosophies and of previously accepted guides to action. Wisdom does not come in formulas, proverbs, or wise saws, but out of the living actuality. The past is important for understanding the present, but it is not the present. It is in a real sense created in the present, and changes from the point of view of every generation.

When change is slow, the new is gradually assimilated, and only after a number of generations is it noticeable that the world is really different. In our century enormous changes in the circumstances of our lives and in our knowledge have occurred rapidly — in every decade. It is therefore not at all surprising that our intellectual, our social, and our political processes have failed to keep abreast of contemporary problems. It is not surprising that we become confused in the choice of our goals and the paths which we must take to reach them.

Clearly a study of the Greek and Roman classics in their original tongues or even in a good translation is a most rewarding venture in itself. This literature has never been surpassed in any age. And in reading this literature one is struck by how applicable the situations are to the present day. The fact that we can still be moved strongly by this literature is an illustration not merely of the constancy of structure of the human nervous system but also of the fact that great art and profound insights have a character which is independent of any age.

The humanities preserve and create values; even more they express the symbolic, poetic, and prophetic qualities of the human spirit. Without the humanities we would not be conscious of our history; we would lose many of our aspirations and the graces of expression that move men's hearts. Withal the humanities discern but a part of the life of man — true, a vital part but only a part.

It has often been claimed that the chief justification for the study of the humanities is that it teaches us values. In fact some people go even further and claim that the humanities, in which literature, parts of philosophy, and the history and appreciation of the fine arts are included, are the *only* sources of values other than the more spiritual values of religion.

This claim cannot pass without challenge. It cannot be said that it is absurd, but rather that it is a symptom of our failure in the present age to achieve a unity and balance of knowledge which is imbued with wisdom. It is a symptom of both ignorance and a certain anti-rational attitude which has been the curse of our century. It betrays a lack of self-confidence and faith in the greatness of the human spirit in contemporary man. It is the expression of a form of self-hatred which is rationally unjustifiable although deeply rooted.

Man is made of dust and to dust returneth; he lives in a universe of which he is also a part. He is free only in a symbolic sense; his nature is conditioned by the dust out of which he is made. To learn to understand himself he must learn to understand the universe in which he lives. There is more than enough in this enterprise to engage the boldest, the most imaginative, and the keenest minds and spirits of every generation. The universe is not given to us in the form of a map or guide. It is made by human minds and imaginations out of slight hints which come from acute observation and from the profound stratagems of experiments.

How can we hope to obtain wisdom, the wisdom which is meaningful in our own time? We certainly cannot attain it as long as the two great branches of human knowledge, the sciences and the humanities, remain separate and even warring disciplines.

Why is science, even more than the humanities, as a living component of our society so misunderstood? A glance at a current dictionary definition may give us a clue.

Science: "A branch of knowledge dealing with facts or truths systematically arranged and showing the operation of general law."

This definition brings to my mind a solitaire player or head bookkeeper for a mail-order concern. It is a partial truth which is also a caricature. It is out of harmony with the picture of Archimedes jumping out of his bath crying Eureka! or Galileo in misery and degradation during his trial and recantation, or Einstein creating the universe out of one or two deductions from observation and a profound aesthetic feeling for symmetry. Nor does this definition account for the violence of the opposition to scientific discovery which still exists in the same quarters in our own age.

It is often argued that physical science is inherently simple, whereas the study of man is inherently complicated. Yet a great deal is known of man's nature. Wise laws for government and personal conduct were known in remotest antiquity. The literature of antiquity shows a profound understanding of human natures and emotions. Not man but the external world was bewildering. The world of nature instead of seeming simple was infinitely complex and possessed of spirits and demons. Nature had to be worshiped and propitiated by offerings, ceremonies, and prayers. Fundamentally nature was unpredictable, antagonistic to human aspiration, full of significance and purpose, and generally evil. Knowledge of nature was suspect because of the power which it brought, a power which was somehow allied with evil. There were of course always men who had insights far beyond these seemingly naïve notions, but they did not prevail over what seemed to be the evidence of the senses and of practical experience.

It was therefore not until late in the history of mankind, not until a few seconds ago so to speak, that it was recognized that nature is understandable and that a knowledge of nature is good and can be used with benefit; that it does not involve witchcraft or a compact with the devil. What is more, any person of intelligence can understand the ideas involved and with sufficient skill learn the necessary techniques, intellectual and manual.

This idea which is now so commonplace represents an almost complete break with the past. To revere and trust the rational faculty of the mind — to allow no taboo to interfere in its operation, to have nothing immune from its examination — is a new value which has been introduced into the world. The progress of science has been the chief agent in demonstrating its importance and riveting it into the consciousness of mankind. This value does not yet have universal acceptance in this country or in any other country. But in spite of all obstacles it will become one of the most treasured possessions of all mankind because we can no longer live without it. We have gone too far along the direction which it implies ever to turn back without unimaginable disaster.

The last world war was started in an attempt to turn back to dark reaction against the rational faculty and to introduce a new demonology into the world. It failed as will every other such attempt. Once the mind is free it will be destroyed rather than be put back in chains.

III

To my mind the value content of science or literary scholarship lies not in the subject matter alone; it lies chiefly in the spirit and living tradition in which these disciplines are pursued. The spirit is almost always conditioned by the subject. Science and the humanities are not the same thing; the subject matter is different and the spirit and tradition are different. Our problem in our search for wisdom is to blend these two traditions in the minds of individual men and women.

Many colleges and universities are trying to do just this, but there is one serious defect in the method. We pour a little of this and a little of that into the student's mind in proportions which result from mediation between the departments and from the particular predilections of the deans and the president. We then hope that these ingredients will combine through some mysterious alchemy and the result will be a man educated, well-rounded, and wise. Most often, however, these ingredients remain well separated in the compartmentalized mind, or they may form an indigestible precipitate which is not only useless but positively harmful, until time the healer washes it all away.

Wisdom is by its nature an interdisciplinary quality and not the product of a collection of specialists. Although the colleges do indeed try to mold the student toward a certain ideal of the educated man of the twentieth century, it is too often a broad education administered by specialists. The approximate counterpart to this ideal of the educated man, embodied in a real living person, is a rare being on any college faculty. Indeed, in most colleges and universities the student is the only really active connecting link between the different departments. In a certain paradoxical sense the students are the only broadly educated body in the university community, at least in principle.

The affairs of this country — indeed of almost every country — whether in government, education, industry, or business, are controlled by people of broad experience. However, this broad experience rarely includes the field of science. How can our leaders make wise decisions now in the middle of the twentieth century without a deep understanding of scientific thought and feeling for scientific traditions? The answer is clear in the sad course that events have taken.

This anguished thought has impelled many scientists, often to their own personal peril, to concern themselves with matters which in the past were the exclusive domain of statesmen and military leaders. They have tried to advise, importune, and even cajole our leaders to include the scientific factor in our fateful policy decisions. They have been successful, but only in special instances.

I am not making a plea for the scientist statesman comparable to the philosopher king. The scientist rarely has this kind of ambition. The study of nature in its profundity, beauty, and subtlety is too attractive for him to wish to forsake his own creative and rewarding activity. The scientist away from his science is like an exile who longs for the sights and sounds of his native land. What the scientist really desires is for his science to be understood, to become an integral part of our general culture, to be given proper weight in the cultural and practical affairs of the world.

The greatest difficulty which stands in the way of a meeting of the minds of the scientist and the non-scientist is the difficulty of communication, a difficulty which stems from some of the defects of education to which I have alluded. The mature scientist, if he has any taste in these directions, can listen with pleasure to the philosopher, the historian, the literary man, or even to the art critic. There is little difficulty from that side because the scientist has been educated in our general culture and lives in it on a day-to-day basis. He reads newspapers, magazines, books, listens to music, debates politics, and participates in the general activities of an educated citizen.

Unfortunately this channel of communication is often a one-way street. The non-scientist cannot listen to the scientist with pleasure and understanding. Despite its universal outlook and its unifying principle, its splendid tradition, science seems to be no longer communicable to the great majority of educated laymen. They simply do not possess the background of the science of today and the intellectual tool necessary for them to understand what effects science will have on them and on the world. Instead of understanding, they have only a naïve awe mixed with fear and scorn. To his colleagues in the university the scientist tends to seem more and more like a man from another planet, a creature scattering antibiotics with one hand and atomic bombs with the other.

The problems to which I have addressed myself are not particularly American. The same condition exists in England, France, and indeed in all other countries. From my observation we are perhaps better off than most. Our American colleges and universities, since they are fairly recent and are rapidly expanding, have not settled into complacency. They are quite ready to experiment to achieve desired ends. Our experimental methods have taught us how to impart the most diverse forms of knowledge. Although wisdom is more elusive, once the objective is clear that the ultimate end of education is knowledge imbedded in wisdom we shall find ways to move toward that ideal. The ideal of the well-rounded man is a meaningless ideal unless this sphericity means a fusion of knowledge to achieve balanced judgment and understanding, which are qualities of wisdom.

The problems are, of course, depressingly difficult. In the secondary schools — with their overcrowding, their teachers overworked and inadequately trained, the school boards, and, not least, the powerful clique of professional educators who form a society within our society — all that is unique and characteristic of science and mathematics is being crowded out of the curriculum and replaced by a fairy tale known as general science. The colleges and universities are in much better shape, although the great population increase is about to hit them with masses of inadequately prepared students. Most people would be quite content with a holding operation in which we could maintain the quality that is already possessed.

However, it seems to me that something could be done even now with the faculty members of the colleges and the universities. Wisdom can achieve a hybrid vigor by crossing the scientist and the humanist through a more extensive and intensive interaction within the faculty. Why should not the professor of physics be expected to refresh himself periodically by taking a course in aesthetics or comparative literature or in the Greek drama? Why shouldn't the professor of medieval philosophy or the professor of ancient history take a course in modern physics and become acquainted with the profound thoughts underlying relativity and quantum mechanics? It would let in some fresh air, or at least different air, to blow away some of the cobwebs which grow in the unventilated ivory towers.

Somewhere a beginning has to be made to achieve a more architectural quality in our culture, a quality of proportion and of organic unity, and it is reasonable to start with the members of the faculties of our institutions of higher learning. Here are all the strands of the tapestry which is to represent our culture, living in close proximity but separate, adding up to nothing more than the sum of the parts. The scientists must learn to teach science in the spirit of wisdom and in the light of the history of human thought and human effort, rather than as the geography of a universe uninhabited by mankind. Our colleagues in the non-scientific faculties must understand that if their teachings ignore the great scientific tradition and its accomplishments, their words, however eloquent and elegant, will lose meaning for this generation and be barren of fruit.

Only with a united effort of science and the humanities can we hope to succeed in discovering a community of thought which can lead us out of the darkness and the confusion which oppress all mankind.

In every child who is born, under no matter what circumstances, and of no matter what parents, the potentiality of the human race is born again. . . .
JAMES AGEE

PART FIVE

Education and the Autonomous Ideal

WE LIVE IN THE AGE of the committee. A nation decides to go to war, a women's club conspires to serve Chablis at its social — it makes no difference: the rights of action emanate from the committee room. As in so many areas of modern life, the distillation of school policy is an act of the often tedious and usually necessary routine of the committee meeting. Perhaps time served in conference rooms counts as one of the more modest sacrifices made in the name of democracy. For all its apparent virtue, the group assembly takes on an impersonal tone, inducing its members to act and speak as *members* rather than as men confronting each other with their ideals unsheathed and their minds aggressively engaged. It happens all the time: the stifling benignity of the group inhibiting the play of imagination and the articulation of ideal. Compromise and sloppy consensus are the habitual results of such an atmosphere, and this side of despotism it is almost impossible to escape. Small wonder someone was encouraged to quip, "A committee is a group of the unable appointed by the unwilling to do the impossible." Assuredly, the institution of group "problem solving" remains one of the sacred acts of secular man in the twentieth century. With the ink scarcely dry on his credential, the young teacher learns not only the names of his first students but also (and much to his shock) his duties on various committees, some of them vital, some of them useless, all of them *cooperative.* He is thereby introduced to that fitful competition

353

between individual idealism, if he possesses it, and the good-natured tyranny of collective realism.

The submergence of the individual beneath a decorous surface of cooperation is but one sign among many of the well-chronicled conformity of our times. To strive with independence, thereby risking a clean failure, requires a courage that may invite our public adulation and our private disdain. So easy it is to try amiably for competence, eschewing excellence. So flippantly our lives, professional and private, dwell lazily within that time christened by Herbert Gold "the age of happy problems." Our unhappy problems, the genuine dilemmas, are masked with the tints and pastels of lesser, insulating trials. The nerve to risk failure is today a clandestine virtue.

Once, during a lull at an educational conference when knots of teachers and administrators had formed in the foyer of a banquet hall, a youthful high school science teacher remarked casually that, to him, the official philosophy for the dedicated teacher was Functional Defeatism. Those within hearing distance answered this judgment with smiles and chuckles. Even a guffaw or two was heard. But the teacher was serious. He went on to explain that, in essence, the function of a teacher is to inspire, cajole, trick, and excite students to surpass the merely *realistic* goals for intellectual growth set by the school district, the state, and the nation. But this function is inevitably pursued within a context of defeat, for the world in its stolid imperfection conspires against the hopes of the teacher. The conspiracy insures a desired failure, for an easily achieved dream suggests a suspiciously feeble idealism. In conclusion, the young teacher confessed that he *knew* his aspirations were beyond fulfillment in his time. Hence his self-styled philosophy of Functional Defeatism.

What is important about the preceding anecdote is not the specific dimensions of the teacher's philosophy but the fact that he had ideals and was unafraid to admit that they might never be translated into action. In a sense, an ideal is irrelevant to success. It thrives when loved, not when fulfilled. Educational ideals linger with a stamina, pressing their believers — while under the normal threats of disillusionment — to progress within the limitations of the actual world. But progress in education may continue to be unconscionably slowed by several forms of cowardice: by the tawdry fear which grasps a teacher who denies his ideals at the first sign of administrational hostility; by the almost official fear that reduces an administrator to sycophancy before the despotism born of ignorance so characteristic of some school boards; by the fear parading as discretion which allows board members to be intimidated by a small, though strident, clique of taxpayers; by the fear of community indifference which constrains parents from publicly demanding that their schools adopt curricula worthy of a child's mind, curricula taught by inspired teachers gifted in serving ends beyond the parochial demands of the community.

The authors included in Part Five present their private visions of the ideal, their arguments based upon *ought* rather than *is*. If these men are to be accused of wanting too much, so be it. Their greed for improving education is the prerogative of the visionary whose ideals are, after all, uncompromised forms of the imagination. The visions of such men as Emerson, Stevenson, and Whitehead are needed far more than the penuries of the bovine educator who, inflated with condescension, finds his fashion in disparaging the naked dream.

When one pauses to recollect his childhood, he recalls with gratitude those teachers who enabled him to examine new versions of experience. He may remember, too, the tired drudge, the pedagogue who lumbered through the semester befouling the atmosphere with an arduous lassitude. The teacher may have had dyspepsia, or gout. Or maybe he was simply underpaid, or unloved. Or maybe he was just a bad teacher. But maybe, too, he had lost all aspiration for an ideal. If so, he had lost the needed sense of tragedy implicit in the defeat of an ideal, lost all energy to function in defeat, lost therefore all hope of victory over the internal and external enemies of education.

Robert Louis Stevenson

Robert Louis Stevenson (1850–1894), author of romantic works such as Treasure Island *and* Doctor Jekyll and Mr. Hyde, *is also noted for his revelations of social hypocrisy and provincialism. Always a busy man, he nevertheless chose his pursuits carefully so that his cherished states of "idleness" would not be slighted.*

Although "An Apology for Idlers" may be read as a quaint salute to the tranquil existence, lurking within its spirited tone is a serious tribute to the life which flowers beyond the tyrannies of obligation.

Regarding education, the author's message is brusque and timely. Stevenson's disgust with the merely trained, impoverished student is contrasted with his "idle" man, the student who respects his life as it is lived and employs his mind in a continually rich interpretation of experience.

36

AN APOLOGY FOR IDLERS

BOSWELL: We grow weary when idle.

JOHNSON: That is, sir, because others being busy, we want company; but if we were all idle, there would be no growing weary; we should all entertain one another.

Just now, when everyone is bound, under pain of a decree in absence convicting them of *lèse*-respectability, to enter on some lucrative profession, and labor therein with something not far short of enthusiasm, a cry from the opposite party, who are content when they have enough, and like to look on and enjoy in the meanwhile, savors a little of bravado and gasconade. And yet this should not be. Idleness so called, which does not consist in doing nothing, but in doing a great deal not recognized in the dogmatic formularies of the ruling class, has as good a right to state its position as industry itself.

356

It is admitted that the presence of people who refuse to enter in the great handicap race for sixpenny pieces, is at once an insult and a disenchantment for those who do. A fine fellow (as we see so many) takes his determination, votes for sixpences, and in the emphatic Americanism "goes for" them. And while such a one is ploughing distressfully up the road, it is not hard to understand his resentment, when he perceives cool persons in the meadows by the wayside, lying with a handkerchief over their ears and a glass at their elbow. Alexander is touched in a very delicate place by the disregard of Diogenes. Where was the glory of having taken Rome for those tumultuous barbarians, who poured into the Senate-house, and found the Fathers sitting silent and unmoved by their success? It is a sore thing to have labored along and scaled the arduous hilltops, and when all is done find humanity indifferent to your achievement. Hence physicists condemn the unphysical; financiers have only a superficial toleration for those who know little of stocks; literary persons despise the unlettered; and people of all pursuits combine to disparage those who have none.

But though this is one difficulty of the subject, it is not the greatest. You could not be put in prison for speaking against industry, but you can be sent to Coventry for speaking like a fool. The greatest difficulty with most subjects is to do them well; therefore, please to remember this is an apology. It is certain that much may be judiciously argued in favor of diligence; only there is something to be said against it, and that is what, on the present occasion, I have to say. To state one argument is not necessarily to be deaf to all others, and that a man has written a book of travels in Montenegro, is no reason why he should never have been to Richmond.

It is surely beyond a doubt that people should be a good deal idle in youth. For though here and there a Lord Macaulay may escape from school honors with all his wits about him, most boys pay so dear for their medals that they never afterwards have a shot in their locker, and begin the world bankrupt. And the same holds true during all the time a lad is educating himself, or suffering others to educate him. It must have been a very foolish old gentleman who addressed Johnson at Oxford in these words: "Young man, ply your book diligently now, and acquire a stock of knowledge; for when years come upon you, you will find that poring upon books will be but an irksome task." The old gentleman seems to have been unaware that many other things besides reading grow irksome, and not a few become impossible, by the time a man has to use spectacles and cannot walk without a stick. Books are good enough in their own way, but they are a mighty bloodless substitute for life. It seems a pity to sit like the Lady of Shalott, peering into a mirror with your back turned on all the bustle and glamor of reality. And if a man reads very hard, as the old anecdote reminds us, he will have little time for thought.

If you look back on your own education, I am sure it will not be the full, vivid, instructive hours of truantry that you regret; you would rather cancel some lack-luster periods between sleep and waking in the class. For my own part, I have attended a good many lectures in my time. I still remember that the spinning of a top is a case of Kinetic Stability. I still remember that Emphyteusis is not a disease, nor Stillicide a crime. But though I would not willingly part with such scraps of science, I do not set the same store by them as by certain other odds and ends that I came by in the open street while I was playing truant. This is not the moment to dilate on that mighty place of education, which was the favorite school of Dickens and of Balzac, and turns out yearly many inglorious masters in the Science of the Aspects of Life. Suffice it to say this: if a lad does not learn in the streets, it is because he has no faculty of learning. Nor is the truant always in the streets, for if he prefers, he may go out by the gardened suburbs into the country. He may pitch on some tuft of lilacs over a burn, and smoke innumerable pipes to the tune of the water on the stones. A bird will sing in the thicket. And there he may fall into a vein of kindly thought, and see things in a new perspective. Why, if this be not education, what is? We may conceive Mr. Worldly Wiseman accosting such a one, and the conversation that should thereupon ensue:

"How now, young fellow, what dost thou here?"

"Truly, sir, I take mine ease."

"Is not this the hour of the class? and should'st thou not be plying thy Book with diligence, to the end thou mayest obtain knowledge?"

"Nay, but thus also I follow after Learning, by your leave."

"Learning, quotha! After what fashion, I pray thee? Is it mathematics?"

"No, to be sure."

"Is it metaphysics?"

"Nor that."

"Is it some language?"

"Nay, it is no language."

"Is it a trade?"

"Nor a trade neither."

"Why, then, what is't?"

"Indeed, sir, as time may soon come for me to go upon Pilgrimage, I am desirous to note what is commonly done by persons in my case, and where are the ugliest Sloughs and Thickets on the Road; as also, what manner of staff is of the best service. Moreover, I lie here, by this water, to learn by root-of-heart a lesson which my master teaches me to call Peace, or Contentment."

Hereupon Mr. Worldly Wiseman was much commoved with passion, and shaking his cane with a very threatful countenance, broke forth upon this wise: "Learning, quotha!" said he: "I would have all such rogues scourged by the Hangman!"

And so he would go his way, ruffling out his cravat with a crackle of starch, like a turkey when it spreads its feathers.

Now this, of Mr. Wiseman's, is the common opinion. A fact is not called a fact, but a piece of gossip, if it does not fall into one of your scholastic categories. An inquiry must be in some acknowledged direction, with a name to go by; or else you are not inquiring at all, only lounging; and the workhouse is too good for you. It is supposed that all knowledge is at the bottom of a well, or the far end of a telescope. Sainte-Beuve, as he grew older, came to regard all experience as a single great book, in which to study for a few years ere we go hence; and it seemed all one to him whether you should read in chapter xx, which is the differential calculus, or in chapter xxxix, which is hearing the band play in the gardens. As a matter of fact, an intelligent person, looking out of his eyes and hearkening in his ears, with a smile on his face all the time, will get more true education than many another in a life of heroic vigils. There is certainly some chill and arid knowledge to be found upon the summits of formal and laborious science; but it is all round about you, and for the trouble of looking, that you will acquire the warm and palpitating facts of life. While others are filling their memory with a lumber of words, one-half of which they will forget before the week be out, your truant may learn some really useful art: to play the fiddle, to know a good cigar, or to speak with ease and opportunity to all varieties of men. Many who have "plied their book diligently," and know all about some one branch or another of accepted lore, come out of the study with an ancient and owl-like demeanor, and prove dry, stockish, and dyspeptic in all the better and brighter parts of life. Many make a large fortune, who remain underbred and pathetically stupid to the last. And meanwhile there goes the idler, who began life along with them — by your leave, a different picture. He has had time to take care of his health and his spirits; he has been a great deal in the open air, which is the most salutary of all things for both body and mind; and if he has never read the great Book in very recondite places, he has dipped into it and skimmed it over to excellent purpose. Might not the student afford some Hebrew roots, and the business man some of his half-crowns, for a share of the idler's knowledge of life at large, and Art of Living? Nay, and the idler has another and more important quality than these. I mean his wisdom. He who has much looked on at the childish satisfaction of other people in their hobbies will regard his own with only a very ironical indulgence. He will not be heard among the dogmatists. He will have a great and cool allowance for all sorts of people and opinions. If he finds no out-of-the-way truths, he will identify himself with no very burning falsehood. His way takes him along a by-road, not much frequented, but very even and pleasant, which is called Common-place Lane and leads to the Belvedere of Common-sense. Thence he shall command an agreeable, if not very noble prospect; and while others behold the East and West, the Devil and the Sunrise, he will be contentedly aware of a sort of morning hour upon all sublunary things, with an army of shadows running speedily and in many different directions into the great daylight of Eternity. The shadows and the generations, the shrill doctors and the plangent wars, go by into ultimate silence and emptiness; but underneath all this, a man may see, out of the Belvedere windows, much green and peaceful landscape; many firelit parlors; good people laughing, drinking, and making love as they did before the Flood or the French Revolution; and the old shepherd telling his tale under the hawthorn.

Extreme *busyness*, whether at school or college, kirk or market, is a symptom of deficient vitality; and a faculty for idleness implies a catholic appetite and a strong sense of personal identity. There is a sort of dead-alive, hackneyed people about, who are scarcely conscious of living except in the exercise of some conventional occupation. Bring these fellows into the country or set them aboard ship, and you will see how they pine for their desk or their study. They have no curiosity; they cannot give themselves over to random provocations; they do not take pleasure in the exercise of their faculties for its own sake; and unless Necessity lays about them with a stick, they will even stand still. It is no good speaking to such folk: they *cannot* be idle, their nature is not generous enough: and they pass those hours in a sort of coma, which are not dedicated to furious moiling in the gold-mill. When they do not require to go to office, when they are not hungry and have no mind to drink, the whole breathing world is a blank to them. If they have to wait an hour or so for a train, they fall into a stupid trance with their eyes open. To see them, you would suppose there was nothing to look at and no one to speak with; you would imagine they were paralyzed or alienated: and yet very possibly they are hard workers in their own way, and have good eyesight for a flaw in a deed or a turn of the market. They have been to school and college, but all the time they had their eye on the medal; they have gone about in the world and mixed with clever people, but all the time they were thinking of their own affairs. As if a man's soul were not too small to begin with, they have dwarfed and narrowed theirs by a life of all work and no play; until here they are at forty, with a listless attention, a mind vacant of all material of amusement, and not one thought to rub against another, while they wait for the train. Before he was breeched, he might have clambered on the boxes; when he was twenty, he would have stared at the girls; but now the pipe is smoked out, the snuff-box empty, and my gentleman sits bolt upright upon a bench, with lamentable eyes. This does not appeal to me as being Success in Life.

But it is not only the person himself who suffers from his busy habits, but his wife and children, his friends and relations, and down to the very people he sits with in a railway-carriage or an omnibus. Perpetual devotion to what a man calls his business is only to be sustained by perpetual neglect of many other things. And it is not by any means certain that a man's business is the most important thing he has to do. To an impartial estimate it will seem clear that many of the wisest, most virtuous, and most beneficent parts that are to be played upon the Theatre of Life are filled by gratuitous performers, and pass, among the world at large, as phases of idleness. For in that Theatre, not only the walking gentlemen, singing chambermaids, and diligent fiddlers in the orchestra, but those who look on and clap their hands from the benches do really play a part and fulfil important offices towards the general result.

You are no doubt very dependent on the care of your lawyer and stockbroker, of the guards and signalmen who convey you rapidly from place to place, and the policemen who walk the streets for your protection; but is there not a thought of gratitude in your heart for certain other benefactors who set you smiling when they fall in your way, or season your dinner with good company? . . . Though Falstaff was neither sober nor very honest, I think I could name one or two long-faced Barabbases whom the world could better have done without. Hazlitt mentions that he was more sensible of obligation to Northcote, who had never done him anything he could call a service, than to his whole circle of ostentatious friends; for he thought a good companion emphatically the greatest benefactor. I know there are people in the world who cannot feel grateful unless the favor has been done them at the cost of pain and difficulty. But this is a churlish disposition. A man may send you six sheets of letter-paper covered with the most entertaining gossip, or you may pass half an hour pleasantly, perhaps profitably, over an article of his; do you think the service would be greater if he had made the manuscript in his heart's blood, like a compact with the devil? Do you really fancy you should be more beholden to your correspondent if he had been damning you all the while for your importunity? Pleasures are more beneficial than duties because, like the quality of mercy, they are not strained, and they are twice blest. There must always be two to a kiss, and there may be a score in a jest; but wherever there is an element of sacrifice, the favor is conferred with pain, and, among generous people, received with confusion.

There is no duty we so much underrate as the duty of being happy. By being happy we sow anonymous benefits upon the world, which remain unknown even to ourselves, or, when they are disclosed, surprise nobody so much as the benefactor. The other day, a ragged, barefoot boy ran down the street after a marble, with so jolly an air that he set everyone he passed into a good humor; one of these persons, who had been delivered from more than usually black thoughts, stopped the little fellow and gave him some money with this remark: "You see what sometimes comes of looking pleased." If he had looked pleased before, he had now to look both pleased and mystified. For my part, I justify this encouragement of smiling rather than tearful children; I do not wish to pay for tears anywhere but upon the stage; but I am prepared to deal largely in the opposite commodity. A happy man or woman is a better thing to find than a five-pound note. He or she is a radiating focus of good will; and their entrance into a room is as though another candle had been lighted. We need not care whether they could prove the forty-seventh proposition; they do a better thing than that, they practically demonstrate the great Theorem of the Liveableness of Life. Consequently, if a person cannot be happy without remaining idle, idle he should remain. It is a revolutionary precept; but, thanks to hunger and the workhouse, one not easily to be abused; and within practical limits, it is one of the most incontestable truths in the whole Body of Morality. Look at one of your industrious fellows for a moment, I beseech you. He sows hurry and reaps indigestion; he puts a vast deal of activity out to interest, and receives a large measure of nervous derangement in return. Either he absents himself entirely from all fellowship, and lives a recluse in a garret, with carpet slippers and a leaden inkpot; or he comes among people swiftly and bitterly, in a contraction of his

whole nervous system, to discharge some temper before he returns to work. I
do not care how much or how well he works, this fellow is an evil feature in
other people's lives. They would be happier if he were dead. They could
easier do without his services in the Circumlocution Office than they can
tolerate his fractious spirits. He poisons life at the well-head. It is better to
be beggared out of hand by a scapegrace nephew, than daily hag-ridden by a
peevish uncle.

And what, in God's name, is all this pother about? For what cause do they
embitter their own and other people's lives? That a man should publish three
or thirty articles a year, that he should finish or not finish his great allegorical
picture, are questions of little interest to the world. The ranks of life are full;
and although a thousand fall, there are always some to go into the breach.
When they told Joan of Arc she should be at home minding women's work,
she answered there were plenty to spin and wash. And so, even with your
own rare gifts! When nature is "so careless of the single life," why should
we coddle ourselves into the fancy that our own is of exceptional importance?
Suppose Shakespeare had been knocked on the head some dark night in Sir
Thomas Lucy's preserves, the world would have wagged on better or worse,
the pitcher gone to the well, the scythe to the corn, and the student to his
book; and no one been any the wiser of the loss. There are not many works
extant, if you look the alternative all over, which are worth the price of a
pound of tobacco to a man of limited means. This is a sobering reflexion for
the proudest of our earthly vanities. Even a tobacconist may, upon consideration, find no great cause for personal vainglory in the phrase; for although tobacco is an admirable sedative, the qualities necessary for retailing
it are neither rare nor precious in themselves. Alas and alas! you may take it
how you will, but the services of no single individual are indispensable. Atlas
was just a gentleman with a protracted nightmare! And yet you see merchants
who go and labor themselves into a great fortune, and thence into the bank-
ruptcy court; scribblers who keep scribbling at little articles until their temper
is a cross to all who come about them, as though Pharaoh should set the
Israelites to make a pin instead of a pyramid; and fine young men who work
themselves into a decline, and are driven off in a hearse with white plumes
upon it. Would you not suppose these persons had been whispered, by the
Master of the Ceremonies, the promise of some momentous destiny? and that
this lukewarm bullet on which they play their farces was the bull's-eye and
center-point of all the universe? And yet it is not so. The ends for which they
gave away their priceless youth, for all they know, may be chimerical or
hurtful; the glory and riches they expect may never come, or may find them
indifferent; and they and the world they inhabit are so inconsiderable that the
mind freezes at the thought.

Ralph Waldo Emerson

Ralph Waldo Emerson (1803–1882), essayist, poet, lecturer, and philosopher of the New England Renaissance, taught school for about four years before devoting his time to writing and to extensive lecturing. In this essay Emerson describes his vision of enlightened educational practice, exposing as much of his inner life as one may expect in a piece of exposition. Never to be characterized as an "educator" in the narrow sense, Emerson is nevertheless always educating, enlivening a potentially turgid didacticism with epigrammatic jabs, vivacious prose rhythms, and opulent uses of allusion and personification. Clearly, his life threatened to fulfill the renaissance ideal of the versatile man, for his writings are imbued with an extraordinary blend of practical wisdom and scholarly knowledge, of life sensed and life reasoned.

Other works by Emerson of general interest are The American Scholar *(an address delivered in 1837),* Essays, First Series *(1841),* Essays, Second Series *(1844), and his collected poems.*

37

EDUCATION

A new degree of intellectual power seems cheap at any price. The use of the world is that man may learn its laws. And the human race have wisely signified their sense of this, by calling wealth, means — Man being the end. Language is always wise.

Therefore I praise New England because it is the country in the world where is the freest expenditure for education. We have already taken, at the planting of the Colonies, (for aught I know for the first time in the world,) the initial step, which for its importance might have been resisted as the most radical of revolutions, thus deciding at the start the destiny of this country — this, namely, that the poor man, whom the law does not allow to take an ear of corn when starving, nor a pair of shoes for his freezing feet, is allowed to put his hand into the pocket of the rich, and say, You shall educate me, not as you will, but as I will: not alone in the elements, but, by further provision, in the languages, in sciences, in the useful and in elegant arts. The child shall be taken up by the State, and taught, at the public cost, the rudiments of knowledge, and, at last, the ripest results of art and science.

Humanly speaking, the school, the college, society, make the difference between men. All the fairy tales of Aladdin or the invisible Gyges or the talisman that opens kings' palaces or the enchanted halls underground or in the sea, are only fictions to indicate the one miracle of intellectual enlargement. When a man stupid becomes a man inspired, when one and the same man passes out of the torpid into the perceiving state, leaves the din of trifles, the stupor of the senses, to enter into the quasi-omniscience of high thought — up and down, around, all limits disappear. No horizon shuts down. He sees things in their causes, all facts in their connection.

One of the problems of history is the beginning of civilization. The animals that accompany and serve man make no progress as races. Those called domestic are capable of learning of man a few tricks of utility or amusement, but they cannot communicate the skill to their race. Each individual must be taught anew. The trained dog cannot train another dog. And Man himself in many races retains almost the unteachableness of the beast. For a thousand years the islands and forests of a great part of the world have been filled with savages who made no steps of advances in art or skill beyond the necessity of being fed and warmed. Certain nations with a better brain and usually in more temperate climates, have made such progress as to compare with these as these compare with the bear and the wolf.

Victory over things is the office of Man. Of course, until it is accomplished, it is the war and insult of things over him. His continual tendency, his great danger, is to overlook the fact that the world is only his teacher, and the nature of sun and moon, plant and animal only means of arousing his interior activity. Enamored of their beauty, comforted by their convenience, he seeks them as ends, and fast loses sight of the fact that they have worse than no values, that they become noxious, when he becomes their slave.

This apparatus of wants and faculties, this craving body, whose organs ask all the elements and all the functions of Nature for their satisfaction, educate the wondrous creature which they satisfy with light, with heat, with water, with wood, with bread, with wool. The necessities imposed by this most irritable and all-related texture have taught Man hunting, pasturage, agriculture, commerce, weaving, joining, masonry, geometry, astronomy. Here is a world pierced and belted with natural laws, and fenced and planted with civil partitions and properties, which all put new restraints on the young inhabitant. He too must come into this magic circle of relations, and know health and sickness, the fear of injury, the desire of external good, the charm of riches, the charm of power. The household is a school of power. There, within the door, learn the tragi-comedy of human life. Here is the sincere thing, the wondrous composition for which day and night go round. In that routine are the sacred relations, the passions that bind and sever. Here is poverty and all the wisdom its hated necessities can teach, here labor drudges, here affections glow, here the secrets of character are told, the guards of man, the guards of woman, the compensations which, like angels of justice, pay every debt: the opium of custom, whereof all drink and many go mad. Here is Economy and Glee and Hospitality and Ceremony and Frankness and Calamity and Death and Hope.

Every one has a trust of power — every man, every boy a jurisdiction, whether it be over a cow or a rood of a potato-field, or a fleet of ships, or the laws of a state. And what activity the desire of power inspires! What toils it sustains! How it sharpens the perceptions and stores the memory with facts. Thus a man may well spend many years of life in trade. It is a constant teaching of the laws of matter and of mind. No dollar of property can be created without some direct communication with Nature, and of course some acquisition of knowledge and practical force. It is a constant contest with the active faculties of men, a study of the issues of one and another course of action, an accumulation of power, and, if the higher faculties of the individual be from time to time quickened, he will gain wisdom and virtue from his business.

As every wind draws music out of the Aeolian harp, so doth every object in Nature draw music out of his mind. Is it not true that every landscape I behold, every friend I meet, every act I perform, every pain I suffer, leaves me a different being from that they found me? That poverty, love, authority, anger, sickness, sorrow, success, all work actively upon our being and unlock for us the concealed faculties of the mind? Whatever private or petty ends are frustrated, this end is always answered. Whatever the man does, or whatever befalls him, opens another chamber in his soul — that is, he has got a new feeling, a new thought, a new organ. Do we not see how amazingly for this end Man is fitted to the world?

What leads him to science? Why does he track in the midnight heaven a pure spark, a luminous patch wandering from age to age, but because he acquires thereby a majestic sense of power; learning that in his own constitution he can set the shining maze in order, and finding and carrying their law in his mind, can, as it were, see his simple idea realized up yonder in giddy distances and frightful periods of duration. If Newton come and first of men perceive that not alone certain bodies fall to the ground at a certain rate, but that all bodies in the Universe, the universe of bodies, fall always, and at one rate; that every atom in Nature draws to every other atom — he extends the power of his mind not only over every cubic atom of his native planet, but he reports the condition of millions of worlds which his eye never saw. And what is the charm which every ore, every new plant, every new fact touching winds, clouds, ocean currents, the secrets of chemical composition and decomposition possess for Humboldt? What but that much revolving of similar facts in his mind has shown him that always the mind contains in its transparent chambers the means of classifying the most refractory phenomena, of depriving them of all casual and chaotic aspect, and subordinating them to a bright reason of its own, and so giving to man a sort of property — yea, the very highest property in every district and particle of the globe.

By the permanence of Nature, minds are trained alike, and made intelligible to each other. In our condition are the roots of language and communication, and these instructions we never exhaust.

In some sort the end of life is that the man should take up the universe into himself, or out of that quarry leave nothing unrepresented. Yonder mountain must migrate into his mind. Yonder magnificent astronomy he is at last to import, fetching away moon, and planet, solstice, period, comet and binal star, by comprehending their relation and law. Instead of the timid stripling he was, he is to be the stalwart Archimedes, Pythagoras, Columbus, Newton, of the physic, metaphysic and ethics of the design of the world.

For truly the population of the globe has its origin in the aims which their existence is to serve; and so with every portion of them. The truth takes flesh in forms that can express it; and thus in history an idea always overhangs, like the moon, and rules the tide which rises simultaneously in all the souls of a generation.

Whilst thus the world exists for the mind; whilst thus the man is ever invited inward into shining realms of knowledge and power by the shows of the world, which interpret to him the infinitude of his own consciousness, — it becomes the office of a just education to awaken him to a knowledge of this fact.

We learn nothing rightly until we learn the symbolical character of life. Day creeps after day, each full of facts, dull, strange, despised things, that we cannot enough despise — call heavy, prosaic and desert. The time we seek to kill: the attention it is elegant to divert from things around us. And presently the aroused intellect finds gold and gems in one of these scorned facts — then finds that the day of facts is a rock of diamonds; that a fact is an Epiphany of God.

We have our theory of life, our religion, our philosophy; and the event of each moment, the shower, the steamboat disaster, the passing of a beautiful face, the apoplexy of our neighbor, are all tests to try our theory, the approximate result we call truth, and reveal its defects. If I have renounced the search of truth, if I have come into the port of some pretending dogmatism, some new church or old church, some Schelling or Cousin, I have died to all use of these new events that are born out of prolific time into multitude of life every hour. I am as a bankrupt to whom brilliant opportunities offer in vain. He has just foreclosed his freedom, tied his hands, locked himself up and given the key to another to keep.

When I see the doors by which God enters into the mind; that there is no sot or fop, ruffian or pedant into whom thoughts do not enter by passages which the individual never left open, I can expect any revolution in character. "I have hope," said the great Leibnitz, "that society may be reformed, when I see how much education may be reformed."

It is ominous, a presumption of crime, that this word Education has so cold, so hopeless a sound. A treatise on education, a convention for education, a lecture, a system, affects us with slight paralysis and a certain yawning of the jaws. We are not encouraged when the law touches it with its fingers. Education should be as broad as man. Whatever elements are in him that should foster and demonstrate. If he be dexterous, his tuition should make it appear; if he be capable of dividing men by the trenchant sword of his thought, education should unsheathe and sharpen it; if he is one to cement society by his all-reconciling affinities, oh! hasten their action! If he is jovial, if he is mercurial, if he is great-hearted, a cunning artificer, a strong commander, a potent ally, ingenious, useful, elegant, witty, prophet, diviner — society has need of all these. The imagination must be addressed. Why always coast on the surface and never open the interior of nature, not by science, which is surface still, but by poetry? Is not the Vast an element of the mind? Yet what teaching, what book of this day appeals to the Vast?

Our culture has truckled to the times — to the senses. It is not manworthy. If the vast and the spiritual are omitted, so are the practical and the moral. It does not make us brave or free. We teach boys to be such men as we are. We do not teach them to aspire to be all they can. We do not give them a training as if we believed in their noble nature. We scarce educate their bodies. We do not train the eye and the hand. We exercise their understandings to the apprehension and comparison of some facts, to a skill in numbers, in words; we aim to make accountants, attorneys, engineers; but not to make able, earnest, great-hearted men. The great object of Education should be commensurate with the object of life. It should be a moral one; to teach self-trust: to inspire the youthful man with an interest in himself; with a curiosity touching his own nature; to acquaint him with the resources of his mind, and to teach him that there is all his strength, and to inflame him with a piety towards the Grand Mind in which he lives. Thus would education conspire with the Divine Providence. A man is a little thing whilst he works by and for himself, but, when he gives voice to the rules of love and justice, is godlike, his word is current in all countries; and all men, though his enemies, are made his friends and obey it as their own.

In affirming that the moral nature of man is the predominant element and should therefore be mainly consulted in the arrangements of a school, I am very far from wishing that it should swallow up all the other instincts and faculties of man. It should be enthroned in his mind, but if it monopolize the man he is not yet sound, he does not yet know his wealth. He is in danger of becoming merely devout, and wearisome through the monotony of his thought. It is not less necessary that the intellectual and the active faculties should be nourished and matured. Let us apply to this subject the light of the same torch by which we have looked at all the phenomena of the time; the infinitude, namely, of every man. Everything teaches that.

One fact constitutes all my satisfaction, inspires all my trust, viz., this perpetual youth, which, as long as there is any good in us, we cannot get rid of. It is very certain that the coming age and the departing age seldom understand each other. The old man thinks the young man has no distinct purpose, for he could never get anything intelligible and earnest out of him. Perhaps the young man does not think it worth his while to explain himself to so hard and inapprehensive a confessor. Let him be led up with a long-sighted forbearance, and let not the sallies of his petulance or folly be checked with disgust or indignation or despair.

I call our system a system of despair, and I find all the correction, all the revolution that is needed and that the best spirits of this age promise, in one word, in Hope. Nature, when she sends a new mind into the world, fills it beforehand with a desire for that which she wishes it to know and do. Let us wait and see what is this new creation, of what new organ the great Spirit had need when it incarnated this new Will. A new Adam in the garden, he is to name all the beasts in the field, all the gods in the sky. And jealous provision seems to have been made in his constitution that you shall not invade and contaminate him with the worn weeds of your language and opinions. The charm of life is this variety of genius, these contrasts and flavors by which Heaven has modulated the identity of truth, and there is a perpetual hankering to violate this individuality, to warp his ways of thinking and behavior to resemble or reflect their thinking and behavior. A low self-love in the parent desires that his child should repeat his character and fortune; an expectation which the child, if justice is done him, will nobly disappoint. By working on the theory that this resemblance exists, we shall do what in us lies to defeat his proper promise and produce the ordinary and mediocre. I suffer whenever I see that common sight of a parent or senior imposing his opinion and way of thinking and being on a young soul to which they are totally unfit. Cannot we let people be themselves, and enjoy life in their own way? You are trying to make that man another *you*. One's enough.

Or we sacrifice the genius of the pupil, the unknown possibilities of his nature, to a neat and safe uniformity, as the Turks whitewash the costly mosaics of ancient art which the Greeks left on their temple walls. Rather let us have men whose manhood is only the continuation of their boyhood, natural characters still; such are able and fertile for heroic action; and not that sad spectacle with which we are too familiar, educated eyes in uneducated bodies.

I like boys, the masters of the playground and of the street — boys, who have the same liberal ticket of admission to all shops, factories armories, town-meetings, caucuses, mobs, target-shootings, as flies have; quite unsuspected, coming in as naturally as the janitor — known to have no money in their pockets, and themselves not suspecting the value of this poverty; putting nobody on his guard, but seeing the inside of the show — hearing all the asides. There are no secrets from them, they know everything that befalls in the fire company, the merits of every engine and of every man at the brakes, how to work it, and are swift to try their hand at every part; so too the merits of every locomotive on the rails, and will coax the engineer to let them ride with him and pull the handles when it goes to the engine-house. They are there only for fun, and not knowing that they are at school, in the court-house, or the cattle-show, quite as much and more than they were, an hour ago, in the arithmetic class.

They know truth from counterfeit as quick as the chemist does. They detect weakness in your eye and behavior a week before you open your mouth, and have given you the benefit of their opinion quick as a wink. They make no mistakes, have no pedantry, but entire belief on experience. Their elections at base-ball or cricket are founded on merit, and are right. They don't pass for swimmers until they can swim, nor for stroke-oar until they can row: and I desire to be saved from their contempt. If I can pass with them, I can manage well enough with their fathers.

Everybody delights in the energy with which boys deal and talk with each other; the mixture of fun and earnest, reproach and coaxing, love and wrath, with which the game is played; — the good-natured yet defiant independence of a leading boy's behavior in the school-yard: How we envy in later life the happy youths to whom their boisterous games and rough exercise furnish the precise element which frames and sets off their school and college tasks, and teaches them, when least they think it, the use and meaning of these. In their fun and extreme freak they hit on the topmost sense of Horace. The young giant, brown from his hunting-tramp, tells his story well, interlarded with lucky allusions to Homer, to Virgil, to college-songs, to Walter Scott; and Jove and Achilles, partridge and trout, opera and binomial theorem, Caesar in Gaul, Sherman in Savannah, and hazing in Holworthy, dance through the narrative in merry confusion, yet the logic is good. If he can turn his books to such picturesque account in his fishing and hunting, it is easy to see how his reading and experience, as he has more of both, will inter-penetrate each other. And every one desires that this pure vigor of action and wealth of narrative, cheered with so much humor and street rhetoric, should be carried into the habit of the young man, purged of its uproar and rudeness, but with all its vivacity entire. His hunting and campings-out have given him an indispensable base: I wish to add a taste for good company through his impatience of bad. That stormy genius of his needs a little direction to games, charades, verses of society, song, and a correspondence year by year with his wisest and best friends. Friendship is an order of nobility; from its revelations we come more worthily into nature. Society he must have or he is poor indeed; he gladly enters a school which forbids conceit, affectation, emphasis and dulness, and requires of each only the flower of his nature and experience; requires good-will, beauty, wit, and select information; teaches by practice the law of conversation, namely, to hear as well as to speak.

Meantime, if circumstances do not permit the high social advantages, solitude has also its lessons. The obscure youth learns there the practice instead of the literature of his virtues; and, because of the disturbing effect of passion and sense, which by a multitude of trifles impede the mind's eye from the quiet search of that fine horizon-line which truth keeps — the way to knowledge and power has ever been an escape from too much engagement with affairs and possessions; a way, not through plenty and superfluity, but by denial and renunciation, into solitude and privation; and, the more is taken away, the more real and inevitable wealth of being is made known to us. The solitary knows the essence of the thought, the scholar in society only its fair face. There is no want of example of great men, great benefactors, who have been monks and hermits in habit. The bias of mind is sometimes irresistible in that direction. The man is, as it were, born deaf and dumb, and dedicated to a narrow and lonely life. Let him study the art of solitude, yield as gracefully as he can to his destiny. Why cannot he get the good of his doom, and if it is from eternity a settled fact that he and society shall be nothing to each other, why need he blush so, and make wry faces to keep up a freshman's seat in the fine world? Heaven often protects valuable souls charged with great secrets, great ideas, by long shutting them up with their own thoughts. And the most genial and amiable of men must alternate society with solitude, and learn its severe lessons.

There comes the period of the imagination to each, a later youth; the power of beauty, the power of books, of poetry. Culture makes his books realities to him, their characters more brilliant, more effective on his mind, than his actual mates. Do not spare to put novels into the hands of young people as an occasional holiday and experiment; but, above all, good poetry in all kinds, epic, tragedy, lyric. If we can touch the imagination, we serve them, they will never forget it. Let him read *Tom Brown at Rugby*, read *Tom Brown at Oxford* — better yet, read *Hodson's Life* — Hodson who took prisoner the king of Delhi. They teach the same truth — a trust, against all appearances, against all privations, in your own worth, and not in tricks, plotting, or patronage.

I believe that our own experience instructs us that the secret of Education lies in respecting the pupil. It is not for you to choose what he shall know, what he shall do. It is chosen and foreordained, and he only holds the key to his own secret. By your tampering and thwarting and too much governing he may be hindered from his end and kept out of his own. Respect the child. Wait and see the new product of Nature. Nature loves analogies, but not repetitions. Respect the child. Be not too much his parent. Trespass not on his solitude.

But I hear the outcry which replies to this suggestion: — Would you verily throw up the reins of public and private discipline; would you leave the young child to the mad career of his own passions and whimsies, and call this anarchy a respect for the child's nature? I answer — Respect the child, respect him to the end, but also respect yourself. Be the companion of his thought, the friend of his friendship, the lover of his virtue — but no kinsman of his sin. Let him find you so true to yourself that you are the irreconcilable hater of his vice and the imperturbable slighter of his trifling.

The two points in a boy's training are, to keep his *naturel* and train off all but that: — to keep his *naturel*, but stop off his uproar, fooling and horse-play; keep his nature and arm it with knowledge in the very direction in which it points. Here are the two capital facts, Genius and Drill. The first is the inspiration in the well-born healthy child, the new perception he has of Nature. Somewhat he sees in forms or hears in music or apprehends in mathematics, or believes practicable in mechanics or possible in political society, which no one else sees or hears or believes. This is the perpetual romance of new life, the invasion of God into the old dead world, when he sends into quiet houses a young soul with a thought which is not met, looking for something which is not there, but which ought to be there: the thought is dim, but it is sure, and he casts about restless for means and masters to verify it; he makes wild attempts to explain himself and invoke the aid and consent of bystanders. Baffled for want of language and methods to convey his meaning, not yet clear to himself, he conceives that though not in this house or town, yet in some other house or town is the wise master who can put him in possession of the rules and instruments to execute his will. Happy this child with a bias, with a thought which entrances him, leads him, now into deserts, now into cities, the fool of an idea. Let him follow it in good and in evil report, in good or bad company; it will justify itself; it will lead him at last into the illustrious society of the lovers of truth.

In London, in a private company, I became acquainted with a gentleman, Sir Charles Fellowes, who, being at Xanthus, in the Aegean Sea, had seen a Turk point with his staff to some carved work on the corner of a stone almost buried in the soil. Fellowes scraped away the dirt, was struck with the beauty of the sculptured ornaments, and, looking about him, observed more blocks and fragments like this. He returned to the spot, procured laborers and uncovered many blocks. He went back to England, bought a Greek grammar and learned the language; he read history and studied ancient art to explain his stones; he interested Gibson the sculptor; he invoked the assistance of the English Government; he called in the succor of Sir Humphry Davy to analyze the pigments; of experts in coins, of scholars and connoisseurs; and at last in his third visit brought home to England such statues and marble reliefs and such careful plans that he was able to reconstruct, in the British Museum where it now stands, the perfect model of the Ionic trophy-monument, fifty years older than the Parthenon of Athens, and which has been destroyed by earthquakes, then by iconoclast Christians, then by savage Turks. But mark that in the task he had achieved an excellent education, and become associated with distinguished scholars whom he had interested in his pursuit; in short, had formed a college for himself; the enthusiast had found the master, the masters, whom he sought. Always genius seeks genius, desires nothing so much as to be a pupil and to find those who can lend it aid to perfect itself.

Nor are the two elements, enthusiasm and drill, incompatible. Accuracy is essential to beauty. The very definition of the intellect is Aristotle's: "that by which we know terms or boundaries." Give a boy accurate perceptions. Teach him the difference between the similar and the same. Make him call things by their right names. Pardon in him no blunder. Then he will give you solid satisfaction as long as he lives. It is better to teach the child arithmetic and Latin grammar than rhetoric or moral philosophy, because they require exactitude of performance; it is made certain that the lesson is mastered, and that power of performance is worth more than the knowledge. He can learn anything which is important to him now that the power to learn is secured: as mechanics say, when one has learned the use of tools, it is easy to work at a new craft.

Letter by letter, syllable by syllable, the child learns to read, and in good time can convey to all the domestic circle the sense of Shakespeare. By many steps each just as short, the stammering boy and the hesitating collegian, in the school debate, in college clubs, in mock court, comes at last to full, secure, triumphant unfolding of his thought in the popular assembly, with a fulness of power that makes all the steps forgotten.

But this function of opening and feeding the human mind is not to be fulfilled by any mechanical or military method; is not to be trusted to any skill less large than Nature itself. You must not neglect the form, but you must secure the essentials. It is curious how perverse and intermeddling we are, and what vast pains and cost we incur to do wrong. Whilst we all know in our own experience and apply natural methods in our own business — in education our common sense fails us, and we are continually trying costly machinery against Nature, in patent schools and academies and in great colleges and universities.

The natural method forever confutes our experiments, and we must still come back to it. The whole theory of the school is on the nurse's or mother's knee. The child is as hot to learn as the other is to impart. There is mutual delight. The joy of our childhood in hearing beautiful stories from some skilful aunt who loves to tell them, must be repeated in youth. The boy wishes to learn to skate, to coast, to catch a fish in the brook, to hit a mark with a snowball or a stone; and a boy a little older is just as well pleased to teach him these sciences. Not less delightful is the mutual pleasure of teaching and learning the secret of algebra, or of chemistry, or of good reading and good recitation of poetry or of prose, or of chosen facts in history or in biography.

Nature provided for the communication of thought, by planting with it in the receiving mind a fury to impart it. 'T is so in every art, in every science. One burns to tell the new fact, the other burns to hear it. See how far a young doctor will ride or walk to witness a new surgical operation. I have seen a carriage-maker's shop emptied of all its workmen into the street, to scrutinize a new pattern from New York. So in literature, the young man who has taste for poetry, for fine images, for noble thoughts, is insatiable for this nourishment, and forgets all the world for the more learned friend — who finds equal joy in dealing out his treasures.

Happy the natural college thus self-instituted around every natural teacher: the young men of Athens around Socrates; of Alexandria around Plotinus; of

Paris around Abelard; of Germany around Fichte, or Niebuhr, or Goethe: in short the natural sphere of every leading mind. But the moment this is organized, difficulties begin. The college was to be the nurse and home of genius; but, though every young man is born with some determination in his nature, and is a potential genius; is at last to be one; it is, in the most, obstructed and delayed, and, whatever they may hereafter be, their senses are now opened in advance of their minds. They are more sensual than intellectual. Appetite and indolence they have, but no enthusiasm. These come in numbers to the college: few geniuses: and the teaching comes to be arranged for these many, and not for those few. Hence the instruction seems to require skilful tutors, of accurate and systematic mind, rather than ardent and inventive masters. Besides, the youth of genius are eccentric, won't drill, are irritable, uncertain, explosive, solitary, not men of the world, not good for every-day association. You have to work for large classes instead of individuals; you must lower your flag and reef your sails to wait for the dull sailors; you grow departmental, routinary, military almost with your discipline and college police. But what doth such a school to form a great and heroic character? What abiding Hope can it inspire? What Reformer will it nurse? What poet will it breed to sing to the human race? What discoverer of Nature's laws will it prompt to enrich us by disclosing in the mind the statute which all matter must obey? What fiery soul will it send out to warm a nation with his charity? What tranquil mind will it have fortified to walk with meekness in private and obscure duties, to wait and to suffer? Is it not manifest that our academic institutions should have a wider scope; that they should not be timid and keep the ruts of the last generation, but that wise men thinking for themselves and heartily seeking the good of mankind, and counting the cost of innovation, should dare to arouse the young to a just and heroic life; that the moral nature should be addressed in the school-room, and children should be treated as the high-born candidates of truth and virtue?

So to regard the young child, the young man, requires, no doubt, rare patience: a patience that nothing but faith in the remedial forces of the soul can give. You see his sensualism; you see his want of those tastes and perceptions which make the power and safety of your character. Very likely. But he has something else. If he has his own vice, he has its correlative virtue. Every mind should be allowed to make its own statement in action, and its balance will appear. In these judgments one needs that foresight which was attributed to an eminent reformer, of whom it was said "his patience could see in the bud of the aloe the blossom at the end of a hundred years." Alas for the cripple Practice when it seeks to come up with the bird Theory, which flies before it. Try your design on the best school. The scholars are of all ages and temperaments and capacities. It is difficult to class them — some are too young, some are slow, some perverse. Each requires so much consideration, that the morning hope of the teacher, of a day of love and progress, is often closed at evening by despair. Each single case, the more it is considered, shows more to be done; and the strict conditions of the hours, on one side, and the number of tasks, on the other. Whatever becomes of our method, the conditions stand fast — six hours, and thirty, fifty, or a hundred and fifty pupils. Something must be done, and done speedily, and in this distress the wisest are tempted to adopt violent means, to proclaim martial law, corporal punishment, mechanical arrangement, bribes, spies, wrath, main strength and ignorance, in lieu of that wise genial providential influence they had hoped, and yet hope at some future day to adopt. Of course the devotion to details reacts injuriously on the teacher. He cannot indulge his genius, he cannot delight in personal relations with young friends, when his eye is always on the clock, and twenty classes are to be dealt with before the day is done. Besides, how can he please himself with genius, and foster modest virtue? A sure proportion of rogue and dunce finds its way into every school and requires a cruel share of time, and the gentle teacher, who wished to be a Providence to youth, is grown a martinet, sore with suspicions; knows as much vice as the judge of a police court, and this love of learning is lost in the routine of grammars and books of elements.

A rule is so easy that it does not need a man to apply it; an automaton, a machine, can be made to keep a school so. It facilitates labor and thought so much that there is always the temptation in large schools to omit the endless task of meeting the wants of each single mind, and to govern by steam. But it is at frightful cost. Our modes of Education aim to expedite, to save labor; to do for masses what cannot be done for masses, what must be done reverently, one by one: say rather, the whole world is needed for the tuition of each pupil. The advantages of this system of emulation and display are so prompt and obvious, it is such a time-saver, it is so energetic on slow and on bad natures, and is of so easy application, needing no sage or poet, but any tutor or schoolmaster in his first term can apply it — that it is not strange that this calomel of culture should be a popular medicine. On the other hand, total abstinence from this drug, and the adoption of simple discipline and the following of nature, involves at once immense claims on the time, the thoughts, on the life of the teacher. It requires time, use, insight, event, all the great lessons and assistances of God; and only to think of using it implies character and profoundness; to enter on this course of discipline is to be good and great. It is precisely analogous to the difference between the use of corporal punishment and the methods of love. It is so easy to bestow on a bad boy a blow, overpower him, and get obedience without words, that in this world of hurry and distraction, who can wait for the returns of reason and the conquest of self; in the uncertainty too whether that will ever come? And yet the familiar observation of the universal compensations might suggest the fear that so summary a stop of a bad humor was more jeopardous than its continuance.

Now the correction of this quack practice is to import into Education the wisdom of life. Leave this military hurry and adopt the pace of Nature. Her secret is patience. Do you know how the naturalist learns all the secrets of the forest, of plants, of birds, of beasts, of reptiles, of fishes, of the rivers and the sea? When he goes into the woods the birds fly before him and he finds none; when he goes to the river bank, the fish and reptile swim away and leave him alone. His secret is patience; he sits down, and sits still; he is a statue; he is a log. These creatures have no value for their time, and he must put as low a rate on his. By dint of obstinate sitting still, reptile, fish, bird and beast, which all wish to return to their haunts, begin to return. He sits still; if they approach, he remains passive as the stone he sits upon. They lose their fear. They have curiosity too about him. By and by the curiosity masters the fear, and they come swimming, creeping and flying towards him; and as he is still immovable, they not only resume their haunts and their ordinary labors and manners, show themselves to him in their work-day trim, but also volunteer some degree of advances towards fellowship and good understanding with a biped who behaves so civilly and well. Can you not baffle the impatience and passion of the child by your tranquillity? Can you not wait for him, as Nature and Providence do? Can you not keep for his mind and ways, for his secret, the same curiosity you give to the squirrel, snake, rabbit, and the sheldrake and the deer? He has a secret; wonderful methods in him; he is — every child — a new style of man; give him time and opportunity. Talk of Columbus and Newton! I tell you the child just born in yonder hovel is the beginning of a revolution as great as theirs. But you must have the believing and prophetic eye. Have the self-command you wish to inspire. Your teaching and discipline must have the reserve and taciturnity of Nature. Teach them to hold their tongues by holding your own. Say little; do not snarl; do not chide; but govern by the eye. See what they need, and that the right thing is done.

I confess myself utterly at a loss in suggesting particular reforms in our ways of teaching. No discretion than can be lodged with a school-committee, with the overseers or visitors of an academy, of a college, can at all avail to reach these difficulties and perplexities, but they solve themselves when we leave institutions and address individuals. The will, the male power, organizes, imposes its own thought and wish on others, and makes that military eye which controls boys as it controls men; admirable in its results, a fortune to him who has it, and only dangerous when it leads the workman to overvalue and overuse it and precludes him from finer means. Sympathy, the female force — which they must use who have not the first — deficient in instant control and the breaking down of resistance, is more subtle and lasting and creative. I advise teachers to cherish mother-wit. I assume that you will keep the grammar, reading, writing, and arithmetic in order; 't is easy, and of course you will. But smuggle in a little contraband wit, fancy, imagination, thought. If you have a taste which you have suppressed because it is not shared by those about you, tell them that. Set this law up, whatever becomes of the rules of the school: they must not whisper, much less talk; but if one of the young people says a wise thing, greet it, and let all the children clap their hands. They shall have no book but school-books in the room; but if one has brought in a Plutarch or Shakespeare or Don Quixote or Goldsmith or any other good book, and understands what he reads, put him at once at the head of the class. Nobody shall be disorderly, or leave his desk without permission, but if a boy runs from his bench, or a girl, because the fire falls, or to check some injury that a little dastard is inflicting behind his desk on some helpless sufferer, take away the medal from the head of the class and give it on the instant to the brave rescuer. If a child happens to show that he knows any fact about astronomy, or plants, or birds, or rocks, or history, that interests him and you, hush all the classes and encourage him to tell it so that all may hear. Then you have made your school-room like the world. Of course you will insist on modesty in the children, and respect to their teachers, but if the boy stops you in your speech, cries out that you are wrong and sets you right, hug him!

To whatever upright mind, to whatsoever beating heart I speak, to you it is committed to educate men. By simple living, by an illimitable soul, you inspire, you correct, you instruct, you raise, you embellish all. By your own act you teach the beholder how to do the practicable. According to the depth from which you draw your life, such is the depth not only of your strenuous effort, but of your manners and presence.

The beautiful nature of the world has here blended your happiness with your power. Work straight on in absolute duty, and you lend an arm and an encouragement to all the youth of the universe. Consent yourself to be an organ of your highest thought, and lo! suddenly you put all men in your debt, and are the fountain of an energy that goes pulsing on with waves of benefit to the borders of society, to the circumference of things.

Horace Mann

Horace Mann (1796–1859), an outstanding American educator, began his career as a student of law after graduating with honors from Brown University. In 1823 he was admitted to the bar and four years later was elected to the legislature of Massachusetts. In 1835 the legislature created a Board of Education, and Mann, much to his surprise, was named to be its secretary, a position which carried the virtual responsibility of a state superintendent of education. Mann ignored his other interests and devoted his energies to improving conditions in public education. He was elected to Congress in 1848, filling the vacancy created by the death of John Quincy Adams. In 1853 he became Pres-

ident of Antioch College, and but for his death six years later would undoubtedly have exerted an influence on higher education comparable to his impact on elementary and secondary education.

During his tenure as secretary to the Board of Education, Mann issued a series of "Annual Reports" in which he discussed the problems, advances, and failures of public schools. The Twelfth Annual Report, *from which the following excerpts are taken, is Mann's last and most comprehensive statement on education, a document which reiterates major themes sounded in earlier writings. Throughout the entire report Mann's dream of equal, disciplined, and inspired public education is constantly before the reader.*

38

PHYSICAL, INTELLECTUAL, MORAL, AND RELIGIOUS EDUCATION

Without undervaluing any other human agency, it may be safely affirmed that the common school, improved and energized as it can easily be, may become the most effective and benignant of all the forces of civilization. Two reasons sustain this position. In the first place, there is a universality in its operation, which can be affirmed of no other institution whatever. If administered in the spirit of justice and conciliation, all the rising generation may be brought within the circle of its reformatory and elevating influences. And, in the second place, the materials upon which it operates are so pliant and ductile as to be susceptible of assuming a greater variety of forms than any other earthly work of the Creator. The inflexibility and ruggedness of the oak, when compared with the lithe sapling or the tender germ, are but feeble emblems to typify the docility of childhood when contrasted with the obduracy and intractableness of man. It is these inherent advantages of the common school, which, in our own state, have produced results so striking, from a system so imperfect, and an administration so feeble. In teaching the blind and the deaf and dumb, in kindling the latent spark of intelligence that lurks in an idiot's mind, and in the more holy work of reforming abandoned and outcast children, education has proved what it can do by glorious experiments. These wonders it has done in its infancy, and with the lights of a limited experience; but when its faculties shall be fully developed, when it shall be trained to wield its mighty energies for the protection of society against the giant vices which now invade and torment it — against intemperance, avarice, war, slavery, bigotry, the woes of want, and the wickedness of waste — then there will not be a height to which these enemies of the race can escape which it will not scale, nor a Titan among them all whom it will not slay.

I proceed, then, in endeavoring to show how the true business of the schoolroom connects itself, and becomes identical, with the great interests of society. The former is the infant, immature state of those interests; the latter their developed adult state. As "the child is father to the man," so may the training of the schoolroom expand into the institutions and fortunes of the state. . . .

PHYSICAL EDUCATION

My general conclusion, then, under this head is that it is the duty of all the governing minds in society — whether in office or out of it — to diffuse a knowledge of these beautiful and beneficent laws of health and life throughout the length and breadth of the state; to popularize them; to make them, in the first place, the common acquisition of all, and through education and custom the common inheritance of all, so that the healthful habits naturally growing out of their observance shall be inbred in the people, exemplified in the personal regime of each individual, incorporated into the economy of every household, observable in all private dwellings, and in all public edifices, especially in those buildings which are erected by capitalists for the residence of their work-people, or for renting to the poorer classes; obeyed by supplying cities with pure water; by providing public baths, public walks, and public squares; by rural cemeteries; by the drainage and sewerage of populous towns, and by whatever else may promote the general salubrity of the atmosphere: in fine, by a religious observance of all those sanitary regulations with which modern science has blessed the world.

For this thorough diffusion of sanitary intelligence, the common school is the only agency. It is, however, an adequate agency. Let human physiology be introduced as an indispensable branch of study into our public schools; let no teacher be approved who is not master of its leading principles, and of their applications to the varying circumstances of life; let all the older classes in the schools be regularly and rigidly examined upon this study by the school-committees — and a speedy change would come over our personal habits, over our domestic usages, and over the public arrangements of society. Temperance and moderation would not be such strangers at the table. Fashion, like European sovereigns, if not compelled to abdicate and fly, would be forced to compromise for the continual possession of her throne by the surrender to her subjects of many of their natural rights. A sixth order of architecture would be invented — the hygienic — which, without subtracting at all from the beauty of any other order, would add a new element of utility to them all. The "health regulations" of cities would be issued in a revised code, — a code that would bear the scrutiny of science. And, as the result and reward of all, a race of men and women, loftier in stature, firmer in structure, fairer in form, and better able to perform the duties and bear the burdens of life, would revisit the earth. The minikin specimens of the race, who now go on dwindling and tapering from parent to child, would reascend to manhood and womanhood. Just in proportion as the laws of health and life were discovered and obeyed, would pain, disease, insanity, and untimely death, cease from among men. Consumption would remain; but it would be consumption in the active sense.

Intellectual Education

Another cardinal object which the government of Massachusetts, and all the influential men in the state, should propose to themselves, is the physical well-being of all the people — the sufficiency, comfort, competence, of every individual in regard to food, raiment, and shelter. And these necessaries and conveniences of life should be obtained by each individual for himself, or by each family for themselves, rather than accepted from the hand of charity or extorted by poor laws. It is not averred that this most desirable result can, in all instances, be obtained; but it is, nevertheless, the end to be aimed at.

True statesmanship and true political economy, not less than true philanthropy, present this perfect theory as the goal, to be more and more closely approximated by our imperfect practice. The desire to achieve such a result cannot be regarded as an unreasonable ambition; for, though all mankind were well fed, well clothed, and well housed, they might still be but half civilized.

Our ambition as a state should trace itself to a different origin, and propose to itself a different object. Its flame should be lighted at the skies. Its radiance and its warmth should reach the darkest and the coldest abodes of men. It should seek the solution of such problems as these: To what extent can competence displace pauperism? How nearly can we free ourselves from the low-minded and the vicious, not by their expatriation, but by their elevation? To what extent can the resources and powers of nature be converted into human welfare, the peaceful arts of life be advanced, and the vast treasures of human talent and genius be developed? How much of suffering, in all its forms, can be relieved? or, what is better than relief, how much can be prevented? Cannot the classes of crimes be lessened and the number of criminals in each class be diminished? Our exemplars, both for public and for private imitation, should be the parables of the lost sheep and of the lost piece of silver.

When we have spread competence through all the abodes of poverty, when we have substituted knowledge for ignorance in the minds of the whole people, when we have reformed the vicious and reclaimed the criminal, then may we invite all neighboring nations to behold the spectacle, and say to them, in the conscious elation of virtue, "Rejoice with me," for I have found that which was lost. Until that day shall arrive, our duties will not be wholly fulfilled, and our ambition will have new honors to win. . . .

Surely nothing but universal education can counterwork this tendency to the domination of capital and the servility of labor. If one class possesses all the wealth and education, while the residue of society is ignorant and poor, it matters not by what name the relation between them may be called; the latter, in fact and in truth, will be the servile dependants and subjects of the former. But, if education be equally diffused, it will draw property after it by the strongest of all attractions; for such a thing never did happen, and never can happen, as that an intelligent and practical body of men should be permanently poor. Property and labor in different classes are essentially antagonistic; but property and labor in the same class are essentially fraternal. The people of Massachusetts have, in some degree, appreciated the truth, that the unexampled prosperity of the state — its comfort, its competence, its general intelligence and virtue — is attributable to the education, more or less perfect, which all its people have received; but are they sensible of a fact equally important, namely, that it is to this same education that two-thirds of the people are indebted for not being to-day the vassals of as severe a tyranny, in the form of capital, as the lower classes of Europe are bound to in the form of brute force?

Education, then, beyond all other devices of human origin, is the greater equalizer of the conditions of men — the balance-wheel of the social machinery. I do not here mean that it so elevates the moral nature as to make men disdain and abhor the oppression of their fellow-men. This idea pertains to another of its attributes. But I mean that it gives each man the independence and the means by which he can resist the selfishness of other men. It does better than to disarm the poor of their hostility towards the rich: it prevents being poor. Agrarianism is the revenge of poverty against wealth. The wanton destruction of the property of others — the burning of hay-ricks and corn-ricks, the demolition of machinery because it supersedes hand-labor, the sprinkling of vitriol on rich dresses — is only agrarianism run mad. Education prevents both the revenge and the madness. On the other hand, a fellow-feeling for one's class or caste is the common instinct of hearts not wholly sunk in selfish regards for person or family. The spread of education, by enlarging the cultivated class or caste, will open a wider area over which the social feelings will expand; and, if this education should be universal and complete, it would do more than all things else to obliterate factitious distinctions in society. . . .

I hold all past achievements of the human mind to be rather in the nature of prophecy than of fulfillment — the first-fruits of the beneficence of God in endowing us with the faculties of perception, comparison, calculation, and causality, rather than the full harvest of their eventual development. For look at the magnificent creation into which we have been brought, and at the adaptation of our faculties to understand, admire, and use it. All around us are works worthy of an infinite God; and we are led, by irresistible evidence, to believe that, just so far as we acquire this knowledge, we shall be endued with his power. From history and from consciousness, we find ourselves capable of ever-onward improvement: and therefore it seems to be a denial of first principles — it seems no better than impiety — to suppose that we shall ever become such finished scholars, that the works of the All-wise will have no new problem for our solution, and will, therefore, be able to teach us no longer.

Nor is it any less than impiety to suppose that we shall ever so completely enlist the powers of Nature in our service, that exhausted Omnipotence can reward our industry with no further bounties. This would be to suppose that we shall arrive at a period when our active and progressive natures will become passive and stationary; when we shall have nothing to do but to sit in indolent and inglorious contemplation of past achievements; and when, all aspirations having been lost in fruition, we shall have outlived the joys of hope and the rewards of effort, and no new glories will beckon us onward to new felicities.

Moral Education

Moral education is a primal necessity of social existence. The unrestrained passions of men are not only homicidal, but suicidal; and a community without a conscience would soon extinguish itself. Even with a natural conscience, how often has evil triumphed over good! From the beginning of time, wrong has followed right, as the shadow, the substance. As the relations of men become more complex, and the business of the world more extended, new opportunities and new temptations for wrong-doing have been created. With the endearing relations of parent and child came also the possibility of infanticide and parricide; and the first domestic altar that brothers ever reared was stained with fratricidal blood. Following close upon the obligations to truth came falsehood and perjury, and closer still upon the duty of obedience to the divine law came disobedience. With the existence of private relations between men came fraud; and with the existence of public relations between nations came aggression, war, and slavery. And so, just in proportion as the relations of life became more numerous, and the interests of society more various and manifold, the range of possible and of actual offenses has been continually enlarging. As for every new substance there may be a new shadow, so for every new law there may be a new transgression. . . .

The race has existed long enough to try many experiments for the solution of this greatest problem ever submitted to its hands; and the race has experimented, without stint of time or circumscription of space to mar or modify legitimate results. Mankind have tried despotisms, monarchies, and republican forms of government. They have tried the extremes of anarchy and of autocracy. They have tried Draconian codes of law, and for the lightest offenses have extinguished the life of the offender. They have established theological standards, claiming for them the sanction of divine authority, and the attributes of a perfect and infallible law; and then they have imprisoned, burnt, massacred, not individuals only, but whole communities at a time, for not bowing down to idols which ecclesiastical authority had set up. These and other great systems of measures have been adopted as barriers against error and guilt: they have been extended over empires, prolonged through centuries, and administered with terrible energy; and yet the great ocean of vice and crime overleaps every embankment, pours down upon our heads, saps the foundations under our feet, and sweeps away the securities of social order, of property, liberty, and life. . . .

But to all doubters, disbelievers, or despairers in human progress, it may still be said, there is one experiment which has never yet been tried. It is an experiment which, even before its inception, offers the highest authority for its ultimate success. Its formula is intelligible to all; and it is as legible as though written in starry letters on an azure sky. It is expressed in these few simple words: *"Train up a child in the way he should go; and when he is old, he will not depart from it."* This declaration is positive. If the conditions are complied with, it makes no provision for a failure. Though pertaining to morals, yet, if the terms of the direction are observed, there is no more reason to doubt the result than there would be in an optical or a chemical experiment.

But this experiment has never yet been tried. Education has never yet been brought to bear with one-hundredth part of its potential force upon the natures of children, and through them upon the character of men and of the race. In all the attempts to reform mankind which have hitherto been made, whether by changing the frame of government, by aggravating or softening the severity of the penal code, or by substituting a government — created for a God-created religion — in all these attempts, the infantile and youthful mind, its amenability to influences, and the enduring and self-operating character of the influences it receives, have been almost wholly unrecognized. Here, then, is a new agency, whose powers are but just beginning to be understood, and whose mighty energies hitherto have been but feebly invoked; and yet, from our experience, limited and imperfect as it is, we do know that, far beyond any other earthly instrumentality, it is comprehensive and decisive. . . .

Is any high-minded, exemplary, and conscientious man disposed to believe that this substantial extirpation of social vices and crimes is a Utopian idea, is more than we have any reason to expect while human nature remains as it is, let me use the *ad hominem* argument to refute him. Let me refer him to himself, and ask him why the same influences which have saved him from gaming, intemperance, dissoluteness, falsehood, dishonesty, violence, and their kindred offenses, and have made him a man of sobriety, frugality, and probity, why the same influences which have saved him from ruin, might not, if brought to bear upon others, save them also. So far as human instrumentalities are concerned, we have abundant means for surrounding every child in the state with preservative and moral influences as extensive and as efficient as those under which the present industrious, worthy, and virtuous members of the community were reared. And as to all those things in regard to which we are directly dependent upon the divine favor, have we not the promise, explicit and unconditional, that the men *shall not* depart from the way in which they should go, if the children are trained up in it? It has been overlooked that this promise is not restricted to parents, but seems to be addressed indiscriminately to all, whether parents, communities, states, or mankind.

RELIGIOUS EDUCATION

. . . On this subject, I propose to speak with freedom and plainness, and more at length than I should feel required to do, but for the peculiar circumstances in which I have been placed. It is matter of notoriety, that the views of the Board of Education — and my own, perhaps still more than those of the Board — on the subject of religious instruction in our Public Schools, have been subjected to animadversion. Grave charges have been made against us, that our purpose was to exclude religion; and to exclude that, too, which is the common exponent of religion — the Bible — from the Common Schools of the State; or, at least, to derogate from its authority, and destroy its influence in them. Whatever prevalence a suspicion of the truth of these imputations may have heretofore had, I have reason to believe that further inquiry and examination have done much to disabuse the too credulous recipients of so groundless a charge. Still, amongst a people so commendably sensitive on the subject of religion, as are the people of Massachusetts, any suspicion of irreligious tendencies, will greatly prejudice any cause, and, so far as any cause may otherwise have the power of doing good, will greatly impair that power.

It is known, too, that our noble system of Free Schools for the whole people, is strenuously opposed; — by a few persons in our own State, and by no inconsiderable numbers in some of the other states of this Union; — and that a rival system of "Parochial" or "Sectarian Schools," is now urged upon the public by a numerous, a powerful, and a well-organized body of men. It has pleased the advocates of this rival system, in various public addresses, in reports, and through periodicals devoted to their cause, to denounce our system as irreligious and anti-Christian. They do not trouble themselves to describe what our system is, but adopt a more summary way to forestall public opinion against it, by using general epithets of reproach, and signals of alarm.

In this age of the world, it seems to me that no student of history, or observer of mankind, can be hostile to the precepts and the doctrines of the Christian religion, or opposed to any institutions which expound and exemplify them; and no man who thinks, as I cannot but think, respecting the enduring elements of character, whether public or private, can be willing to have his name mentioned while he is living, or remembered when he is dead, as opposed to religious instruction, and Bible instruction for the young. In making this final Report, therefore, I desire to vindicate my conduct from the charges that have been made against it; and, so far as the Board has been implicated in these charges, to leave my testimony on record for their exculpation. Indeed, on this point, the Board and myself must be justified or condemned together; for I do not believe they would have enabled me, by their annual reëlections, to carry forward any plan for excluding either the Bible or religious instruction from the schools; and had the Board required me to execute such a purpose, I certainly should have given them the earliest opportunity to appoint my successor. I desire, also, to vindicate the system with which I have been so long and so intimately connected, not only from the aspersion, but from the suspicion, of being an irreligious, or anti-Christian, or an un-Christian system. I know, full well, that it is unlike the systems which prevail in Great Britain, and in many of the continental nations of Europe, where the Established Church controls the education of the young, in order to keep itself established. But this is presumptive in its favor, rather than against it.

All the schemes ever devised by governments, to secure the prevalence and permanence of religion among the people, however variant in form they may have been, are substantially resolvable into two systems. One of these systems holds the regulation and control of the religious belief of the people to be one of the functions of government, like the command of the army or the navy, or the establishment of courts, or the collection of revenues. According to the other system, religious belief is a matter of individual and parental concern; and, while the government furnishes all practicable facilities for the independent formation of that belief, it exercises no authority to prescribe, or coercion to enforce it. The former is the system, which, with very few exceptions, has prevailed throughout Christendom, for fifteen hundred years. Our own government is almost a solitary example among the nations of the earth, where freedom of opinion, and the inviolability of conscience, have been even theoretically recognized by the law. . . .

The very terms, *Public School*, and *Common School*, bear upon their face, that they are schools which the children of the entire community may attend. Every man, not on the pauper list, is taxed for their support. But he is not taxed to support them as special religious institutions; if he were, it would satisfy, at once, the largest definitions of a Religious Establishment. But he is taxed to support them, as a *preventive* means against dishonesty, against fraud, and against violence; on the same principle that he is taxed to support criminal courts as a *punitive* means against the same offences. He is taxed to support schools, on the same principle that he is taxed to support paupers; because a child without education is poorer and more wretched than a man without bread. He is taxed to support schools, on the same principle that he would be taxed to defend the nation against foreign invasion, or against rapine committed by a foreign foe; because the general prevalence of ignorance, superstition, and vice, will breed Goth and Vandal at home, more fatal to the public well-being, than any Goth or Vandal from abroad. And, finally, he is taxed to support schools, because they are the most effective means of developing and training those powers and faculties in a child, by which, when he becomes a man, he may understand what his highest interests and his highest duties are; and may be, in fact, and not in name only, a free agent. The elements of a political education are not bestowed upon any school child, for the purpose of making him vote with this or that political party, when he becomes of age; but for the purpose of enabling him to choose for himself, with which party he will vote. So the religious education which a child receives at school, is not imparted to him, for the purpose of making him join this or that denomination, when he arrives at years of discretion, but for the purpose of enabling him to judge for himself, according to the dictates of his own reason and conscience, what his religious obligations are, and whither they lead. But if a man is taxed to support a school, where religious doctrines are inculcated which he believes to be false, and which he believes that God condemns; then he is excluded from the school by the Divine law, at the same time that he is compelled to support it by the human law. This is a double wrong. It is politically wrong, because, if such a man educates his children at all, he must educate them elsewhere, and thus pay two taxes, while some of his neighbors pay less than their due proportion of one; and it is religiously wrong, because he is constrained, by human power, to promote what he believes the Divine Power forbids. The principle involved in such a course is pregnant with all tyrannical consequences. It is broad enough to sustain any claim of ecclesiastical domination, ever made in the darkest ages of the world. Every religious persecution, since the time of Constantine, may find its warrant in it, and can be legitimately defended upon it. If a man's estate may be taken from him to pay for teaching a creed which he believes to be false, his children can be taken from him to be taught the same creed; and he, too, may be punished to any extent, for not voluntarily surrendering both his estate and his offspring. If his children can be compulsorily taken and taught to believe a creed which the parent disbelieves, then the parent can be compulsorily taken and made to subscribe the same creed. And, in regard to the extent of the penalties which may be invoked to compel conformity, there is no stopping-place between taking a penny and inflicting perdition. It is only necessary to call a man's reason and conscience and religious faith, by the name of recusancy, or contumacy, or heresy, and so to inscribe them on the statute book; and then the nonconformist or dissenter may be subdued by steel, or cord, or fire; by anathema and excommunication in this life, and the terrors of endless perdition in the next. Surely, that system cannot be an irreligious, an anti-Christian, or an un-Christian one, whose first and cardinal principle it is, to recognize and protect the highest and dearest of all human interests, and of all human rights. . . .

It is still easier to prove that the Massachusetts school system is not anti-Christian nor un-Christian. The Bible is the acknowledged expositor of Christianity. In strictness, Christianity has no other authoritative expounder. This Bible is in our Common Schools, by common consent. Twelve years ago, it was not in all the schools. Contrary to the genius of our government, if not contrary to the express letter of the law, it had been used for sectarian purposes — to prove one sect to be right, and others to be wrong. Hence, it had been excluded from the schools of some towns, by an express vote. But since the law and the reasons on which it is founded, have been more fully explained and better understood; and since sectarian instruction has, to a great extent, ceased to be given, the Bible has been restored. I am not aware of the existence of a single town in the State, in whose schools it is not now introduced, either by a direct vote of the school committee, or by such general desire and acquiescence, as supersede the necessity of a vote. In all my intercourse, for twelve years, whether personal or by letter, with all the school officers in the State, and with tens of thousands of individuals in it, I have never heard an objection made to the use of the Bible in school, except in one or two instances; and, in those cases, the objection was put upon the ground, that daily familiarity with the book, in school, would tend to impair a reverence for it.

If the Bible, then, is the exponent of Christianity; if the Bible contains the communications, precepts, and doctrines, which make up the religious system, called and known as Christianity; if the Bible makes known those truths, which, according to the faith of Christians, are able to make men wise unto salvation; and if this Bible is in the schools, how can it be said that Christianity is excluded from the schools; or how can it be said that the school system, which adopts and uses the Bible, is an anti-Christian, or an un-Christian system? If that which is the acknowledged exponent and basis of Christianity is in the schools, by what tergiversation in language, or paralogism in logic, can Christianity be said to be shut out from the schools? If the Old Testament were in the schools, could a Jew complain, that Judaism was excluded from them? If the Koran were read regularly and reverently in the schools, could a Mahommedan say that Mahommedanism was excluded? Or, if the Mormon Bible were in the schools, could it be said that Mormonism was excluded from them?

Is it not, indeed, too plain, to require the formality of a syllogism, that if any man's creed is to be found in the Bible, and the Bible is in the schools, then that man's creed is in the schools? This seems even plainer than the proposition, that two and two make four; — that is, we can conceive of a creature so low down in the scale of intelligence, that he could not see what sum would be produced by adding two and two together, who still could not fail to see, that, if a certain system, called Christianity, were contained in, and inseparable from, a certain book called the Bible, then wherever the Bible might go, there the system of Christianity must be. . . .

And further; our law explicity and solemnly enjoins it upon all teachers, without any exception, "to exert their best endeavors, to impress on the minds of children and youth committed to their care and instruction, the principles of piety, justice, and a sacred regard to truth, love to their country, humanity and universal benevolence, sobriety, industry, and frugality, chastity, moderation, and temperance, and those other virtues which are the ornament of human society, and the basis upon which a republican constitution is founded." Are not these virtues and graces part and parcel of Christianity? In other words, can there be Christianity without them? While these virtues and these duties towards God and man, are inculcated in our schools, any one who says that the schools are anti-Christian or un-Christian, expressly affirms that his own system of Christianity does not embrace any one of this radiant catalogue; that it rejects them all; that it embraces their opposites!

And further still; our system makes it the express duty of all the "resident ministers of the Gospel" to bring all the children within the moral and Christian inculcations above enumerated; so that he who avers that our system is an anti-Christian or an un-Christian one, avers that it is both anti-Christian and un-Christian for a "minister of the Gospel" to promote, or labor to diffuse, the moral attributes and excellences, which the statute so earnestly enjoins.

So far, the argument has been of an affirmative character. Its scope and purpose show, or, at least, tend to show, *by direct proof*, that the school system of Massachusetts is not an anti-Christian, nor an un-Christian system. But there is still another mode of proof. The truth of a proposition may be established, by showing the falsity or absurdity of all conflicting propositions. So far as this method can be applied to moral questions, its aid may safely be invoked here.

What are the other courses, which the State of Massachusetts might adopt or sanction, in relation to the education of its youth? They are these four: —

1. It might establish schools, but expressly exclude all religious instruction from them — making them merely schools for secular instruction.

2. It might adopt a course, directly the reverse of this. It might define and prescribe a system of religion for the schools, and appoint the teachers and officers, whose duty it should be to carry out that system.

3. It might establish schools by law, and empower each religious sect, whenever and wherever it could get a majority, to determine what religious faith should be taught in them. And,

4. It might expressly disclam and refuse all interference with the education of the young, and abandon the whole work to the hazards of private enterprise, or to parental will, ability, or caprice.

1. A system of schools from which all religious instruction should be excluded, might properly be called un-Christian, or, rather, non-Christian, in the same sense in which it could be called non-Jewish, or non-Mahommedan; that is, as having no connection with either. I do not suppose a man can be found in Massachusetts, who would declare such a system to be his first choice.

2. Were the State to establish schools, and prescribe a system of religion to be taught in them, and appoint the teachers and officers to superintend it, could there be any better definition or exemplification of an Ecclesiastical Establishment? . . .

For any human government, then, to attempt to coerce and predetermine the religious opinions of children, by law, and contrary to the will of their parents, is unspeakably more criminal than the usurpation of such control over the opinions of men. The latter is treason against truth; but the former is sacrilege. As the worst of all crimes against chastity are those which debauch the infant victim before she knows what chastity is; so the worst of all crimes against religious truth, are those which forcibly close up the avenues, and bar the doors, that lead to the forum of reason and conscience. The spirit of ecclesiastical domination, in modern times, finding that the principles of men are too strong for it, is attempting the seduction of children. Fearing the opinions that may be developed by mature reflection, it anticipates and forestalls those opinions; and seeks to imprint, upon the ignorance and receptiveness of childhood, the convictions which it could never fasten upon the minds of men in their maturity. . . .

3. As a third method, the government might establish schools by law, and empower each religious sect, whenever and wherever it could get a majority, to determine what religious faith should be taught in them.

Under such a system, each sect would demand that its own faith should be inculcated in all the schools; — and this, on the clear and simple ground that such faith is the only true one. Each differing faith, believed in by all the other sects, must, of course, be excluded from the schools; — and this, on the equally clear and simple ground, that there can be but one true faith; and which that is, has already been determined, and is no longer an open question. Under such a system, it will not suffice to have the Bible in the schools, to speak for itself. Each sect will rise up and virtually say, "Although the Bible from Genesis to Revelation is in the schools, yet its true meaning and doctrines are not there; Christianity is not there, unless our commentary, our creed, or our catechism, is there also. A revelation from God is not sufficient. Our commentary, or our teacher, must go with it, to reveal what the revelation means. . . . Your schools may be like the noble Bereans, searching the Scriptures daily, but unless the result of those searchings have our countersign and endorsement, those schools are un-Christian and anti-Christian."

Now, it is almost too obvious to be mentioned, that such a claim as the above, reduces society at once to this dilemma: If one religious sect is authorized to advance it, for itself, then all other sects are equally authorized to do the same thing, for themselves. The right being equal among all the sects, and each sect being equally certain and equally determined; what shall be done? Will not each sect, acting under religious impulses — which are the strongest impulses that ever animate the breast of man — will not each sect do its utmost to establish its supremacy in all the schools? Will not the heats and animosities engendered in families, and among neighbors, burst forth with a devouring fire, in the primary, or district school meetings; and when the inflammable materials of all the district meetings are gathered together in the town meeting, what can quell or quench the flames, till the zealots, themselves, are consumed in the conflagration they have kindled?

Why would not all those machinations and oppressions be resorted to, in order to obtain the ascendancy, if religious proselytism should be legalized in the schools, which would be resorted to, as I have endeavored, in a preceding part of this report, to explain, if political proselytism were permitted in the schools? . . .

4. One other system — if it may be so called — is supposable; and this exhausts the number of those which stand in direct conflict with ours. It is this: Government might expressly disclaim and refuse all interference with the education of the young, abandoning the whole work to the hazards of private enterprise, or to parental will, ability, or caprice. . . .

*   *   *

If, then, a government would recognize and protect the rights of religious freedom, it must abstain from subjugating the capacities of its children to any legal standard of religious faith, with as great fidelity as it abstains from controlling the opinions of men. It must meet the unquestionable fact, that the old spirit of religious domination is adopting new measures to accomplish its work — measures, which, if successful, will be as fatal to the liberties of mankind, as those which were practiced in by-gone days of violence and terror. These new measures are aimed at children instead of men. They propose to supersede the necessity of subduing free thought, *in the mind of the adult, by forestalling* the development of any capacity of free thought, *in the mind of the child.* They expect to find it easier to subdue the free agency of children, by binding them in fetters of bigotry, than to subdue the free agency of men, by binding them in fetters of iron. For this purpose, some are attempting to deprive children of their right to labor, and, of course, of their daily bread, unless they will attend a government school, and receive its sectarian instruction. Some are attempting to withhold all means, even of secular education, from the poor, and thus punish them with ignorance, unless, with the secular knowledge which they desire, they will accept theological knowledge which they condemn. Others, still, are striving to break down all free Public School systems, where they exist, and to prevent their establishment, where they do not exist, in the hope, that on the downfall of these, their system will succeed. The sovereign antidote against these machinations is Free Schools for all, and the right of every parent to determine the religious education of his children.

This topic invites far more extended exposition; but this must suffice. In bidding an official Farewell to a system, with which I have been so long connected, to which I have devoted my means, my strength, my health, twelve years of time, and doubtless, twice that number of years from what might otherwise have been my term of life, I have felt bound to submit these brief views in its defense. In justice to my own name and memory; in justice to the Board of which I was originally a member, and from which I have always sought counsel and guidance; and in justice to thousands of the most wise, upright, and religious-minded men in Massachusetts, who have been my fellow-laborers in advancing the great cause of Popular Education, under the auspices of this system, I have felt bound to vindicate it from the aspersions cast upon it, and to show its consonance with the eternal principles of equity and justice. I have felt bound to show, that, so far from its being an irreligious, an anti-Christian, or an un-Christian system, it is a system which recognizes religious obligations in their fullest extent; that it is a system which invokes a religious spirit, and can never be fitly administered without such a spirit; that it inculcates the great commands, upon which hang all the law and the prophets; that it welcomes the Bible, and therefore welcomes all the doctrines which the Bible really contains, and that it listens to these doctrines so reverently, that, for the time being, it will not suffer any rash mortal to thrust in his interpolations of their meaning, or overlay the text with any of the "many inventions" which the heart of man has sought out. It is a system, however, which leaves open all other means of instruction — the pulpits, the Sunday schools, the Bible classes, the catechisms, of all denominations, — to be employed according to the preferences of individual parents. It is a system which restrains itself from teaching, that what it does teach is all that needs to be taught, or that should be taught; but leaves this to be decided by each man for himself, according to the light of his reason and conscience; and on his responsibility to that Great Being, who, in holding him to an account for the things done in the body, will hold him to the strictest account for the manner in which he has "trained up" his children.

Such, then, in a religious point of view, is the Massachusetts system of Common Schools. Reverently, it recognizes and affirms the sovereign rights of the Creator; sedulously and sacredly it guards the religious rights of the creature; while it seeks to remove all hindrances, and to supply all furtherances to a filial and paternal communion between man and his Maker. In a social and political sense, it is a *Free* school system. It knows no distinction of rich and poor, of bond and free, or between those who, in the imperfect light of this world, are seeking, through different avenues, to reach the gate of heaven. Without money and without price, it throws open its doors, and spreads the table of its bounty, for all the children of the State. Like the sun, it shines, not only upon the good, but upon the evil, that they may become good; and, like the rain, its blessings descend, not only upon the just, but upon the unjust, that their injustice may depart from them and be known no more.

Alfred North Whitehead

An internationally known philosopher, mathematician, and educator, Alfred North Whitehead (1861–1947) defines in this essay, among other desired ends of learning, the cultivation of Style — that "ultimate morality of mind." In his concrete demands for educational reform, Whitehead preserves a rare continuity between the lures of contemplation and the necessities of action.

Concerning Whitehead's talent for teaching, Justice Felix Frankfurter was moved to write: "Professor Whitehead had a benign and beautiful presence, a voice and diction that made music of English speech, humor that lighted up dark places, humility that made the foolish wiser and evoked the wisdom of the taciturn. For twenty years Professor Whitehead exercised this great and radiating influence. He did so at Harvard because he was there. He did so beyond because he was what he was."

"The Aims of Education" is the first chapter of his book bearing the same title, which was published in 1929.

39

THE AIMS OF EDUCATION*

Culture is activity of thought, and receptiveness to beauty and humane feeling. Scraps of information have nothing to do with it. A merely well-informed man is the most useless bore on God's earth. What we should aim at producing is men who possess both culture and expert knowledge in some special direction. Their expert knowledge will give them the ground to start from, and their culture will lead them as deep as philosophy and as high as art. We have to remember that the valuable intellectual development is self-development, and that it mostly takes place between the ages of sixteen

* Reprinted with permission of the publisher from *The Aims of Education* by Alfred North Whitehead. Copyright 1929 by The Macmillan Company. Renewed 1957 by Evelyn Whitehead.

and thirty. As to training, the most important part is given by mothers before the age of twelve. A saying due to Archbishop Temple illustrates my meaning. Surprise was expressed at the success in after-life of a man, who as a boy at Rugby had been somewhat undistinguished. He answered, "It is not what they are at eighteen, it is what they become afterwards that matters."

In training a child to activity of thought, above all things we must beware of what I will call "inert ideas" — that is to say, ideas that are merely received into the mind without being utilised, or tested, or thrown into fresh combinations.

In the history of education, the most striking phenomenon is that schools of learning, which at one epoch are alive with a ferment of genius, in a succeeding generation exhibit merely pedantry and routine. The reason is that they are overladen with inert ideas. Education with inert ideas is not only useless: it is, above all things, harmful — *Corruptio optimi, pessima.* Except at rare intervals of intellectual ferment, education in the past has been radically infected with inert ideas. That is the reason why uneducated clever women, who have seen much of the world, are in middle life so much the most cultured part of the community. They have been saved from this horrible burden of inert ideas. Every intellectual revolution which has ever stirred humanity into greatness has been a passionate protest against inert ideas. Then, alas, with pathetic ignorance of human psychology, it has proceeded by some educational scheme to bind humanity afresh with inert ideas of its own fashioning.

Let us now ask how in our system of education we are to guard against this mental dryrot. We enunciate two educational commandments, "Do not teach too many subjects," and again, "What you teach, teach thoroughly."

The result of teaching small parts of a large number of subjects is the passive reception of disconnected ideas, not illumined with any spark of vitality. Let the main ideas which are introduced into a child's education be few and important, and let them be thrown into every combination possible. The child should make them his own, and should understand their application here and now in the circumstances of his actual life. From the very beginning of his education, the child should experience the joy of discovery. The discovery which he has to make is that general ideas give an understanding of that stream of events which pours through his life, which is his life. By understanding I mean more than a mere logical analysis, though that is included. I mean "understanding" in the sense in which it is used in the French proverb, "To understand all is to forgive all." Pedants sneer at an education which is useful. But if education is not useful, what is it? Is it a talent to be hidden away in a napkin? Of course, education should be useful, whatever your aim in life. It was useful to Saint Augustine and it was useful to Napoleon. It is useful, because understanding is useful.

I pass lightly over that understanding which should be given by the literary side of education. Nor do I wish to be supposed to pronounce on the relative merits of a classical or a modern curriculum. I would only remark that the understanding which we want is an understanding of an insistent present. The only use of a knowledge of the past is to equip us for the present. No more deadly harm can be done to young minds than by depreciation of the present. The present contains all that there is. It is holy ground; for it is the past, and it is the future. At the same time it must be observed that an age is no less past if it existed two hundred years ago than if it existed two thousand years ago. Do not be deceived by the pedantry of dates. The ages of Shakespeare and of Molière are no less past than are the ages of Sophocles and of Virgil. The communion of saints is a great and inspiring assemblage, but it has only one possible hall of meeting, and that is the present; and the mere lapse of time through which any particular group of saints must travel to reach that meeting-place makes very little difference.

Passing now to the scientific and logical side of education, we remember that here also ideas which are not utilised are positively harmful. By utilising an idea, I mean relating it to that stream, compounded of sense perceptions, feelings, hopes, desires, and of mental activities adjusting thought to thought, which forms our life. I can imagine a set of beings which might fortify their souls by passively reviewing disconnected ideas. Humanity is not built that way — except perhaps some editors of newspapers.

In scientific training, the first thing to do with an idea is to prove it. But allow me for one moment to extend the meaning of "prove"; I mean — to prove its worth. Now an idea is not worth much unless the propositions in which it is embodied are true. Accordingly an essential part of the proof of an idea is the proof, either by experiment or by logic, of the truth of the propositions. But it is not essential that this proof of the truth should constitute the first introduction to the idea. After all, its assertion by the authority of respectable teachers is sufficient evidence to begin with. In our first contact with a set of propositions, we commence by appreciating their importance. That is what we all do in after-life. We do not attempt, in the strict sense, to prove or to disprove anything, unless its importance makes it worthy of that honour. These two processes of proof, in the narrow sense, and of appreciation, do not require a rigid separation in time. Both can be proceeded with nearly concurrently. But in so far as either process must have the priority, it should be that of appreciation by use.

Furthermore, we should not endeavour to use propositions in isolation. Emphatically I do not mean, a neat little set of experiments to illustrate Proposition I and then the proof of Proposition I, a neat little set of experiments to illustrate Proposition II and then the proof of Proposition II, and so on to the end of the book. Nothing could be more boring. Interrelated truths are utilised *en bloc,* and the various propositions are employed in any order, and with any reiteration. Choose some important applications of your theoretical subject; and study them concurrently with the systematic theoretical exposition. Keep the theoretical exposition short and simple, but let it be strict and rigid so far as it goes. It should not be too long for it to be easily known with thoroughness and accuracy. The consequences of a plethora of half-digested theoretical knowledge are deplorable. Also the theory should not be muddled up with the practice. The child should have no doubt when it is proving and when it is utilising. My point is that what is proved should be utilised, and that what is utilised should — so far as is practicable — be proved. I am far from asserting that proof and utilisation are the same thing.

At this point of my discourse, I can most directly carry forward my argument in the outward form of a digression. We are only just realising that the art and science of education require a genius and a study of their own; and that this genius and this science are more than a bare knowledge of some branch of science or of literature. This truth was partially perceived in the past generation; and headmasters, somewhat crudely, were apt to supersede learning in their colleagues by requiring left-hand bowling and a taste for football. But culture is more than cricket, and more than football, and more than extent of knowledge.

Education is the acquisition of the art of the utilisation of knowledge. This is an art very difficult to impart. Whenever a text-book is written of real educational worth, you may be quite certain that some reviewer will say that it will be difficult to teach from it. Of course it will be difficult to teach from it. If it were easy, the book ought to be burned; for it cannot be educational. In education, as elsewhere, the broad primrose path leads to a nasty place. This evil path is represented by a book or a set of lectures which will practically enable the student to learn by heart all the questions likely to be asked at the next external examination. And I may say in passing that no educational system is possible unless every question directly asked of a pupil at any examination is either framed or modified by the actual teacher of that pupil in that subject. The external assessor may report on the curriculum or on the performance of the pupils, but never should be allowed to ask the pupil a question which has not been strictly supervised by the actual teacher, or at least inspired by a long conference with him. There are a few exceptions to this rule, but they are exceptions, and could easily be allowed for under the general rule.

We now return to my previous point, that theoretical ideas should always find important applications within the pupil's curriculum. This is not an easy doctrine to apply, but a very hard one. It contains within itself the problem of keeping knowledge alive, of preventing it from becoming inert, which is the central problem of all education.

The best procedure will depend on several factors, none of which can be neglected, namely, the genius of the teacher, the intellectual type of the pupils, their prospects in life, the opportunities offered by the immediate surroundings of the school, and allied factors of this sort. It is for this reason that the uniform external examination is so deadly. We do not denounce it because we are cranks, and like denouncing established things. We are not so childish. Also, of course, such examinations have their use in testing slackness. Our reason of dislike is very definite and very practical. It kills the best part of culture. When you analyse in the light of experience the central task of education, you find that its successful accomplishment depends on a delicate adjustment of many variable factors. The reason is that we are dealing with human minds, and not with dead matter. The evocation of curiosity, of judgment, of the power of mastering a complicated tangle of circumstances, the use of theory in giving foresight in special cases — all these powers are not to be imparted by a set rule embodied in one schedule of examination subjects.

I appeal to you, as practical teachers. With good discipline, it is always possible to pump into the minds of a class a certain quantity of inert knowledge. You take a text-book and make them learn it. So far, so good. The child then knows how to solve a quadratic equation. But what is the point of teaching a child to solve a quadratic equation? There is a traditional answer to this question. It runs thus: The mind is an instrument, you first sharpen it, and then use it; the acquisition of the power of solving a quadratic equation is part of the process of sharpening the mind. Now there is just enough truth in this answer to have made it live through the ages. But for all its half-truth, it embodies a radical error which bids fair to stifle the genius of the modern world. I do not know who was first responsible for this analogy of the mind to a dead instrument. For aught I know, it may have been one of the seven wise men of Greece, or a committee of the whole lot of them. Whoever was the originator, there can be no doubt of the authority which it has acquired by the continuous approval bestowed upon it by eminent persons. But whatever its weight of authority, whatever the high approval which it can quote, I have no hesitation in denouncing it as one of the most fatal, erroneous, and dangerous conceptions ever introduced into the theory of education. The mind is never passive; it is a perpetual activity, delicate, receptive, responsive to stimulus. You cannot postpone its life until you have sharpened it. Whatever interest attaches to your subject-matter must be evoked here and now; whatever powers you are strengthening in the pupil must be exercised here and now; whatever possibilities of mental life your teaching should impart must be exhibited here and now. That is the golden rule of education, and a very difficult rule to follow.

The difficulty is just this: the apprehension of general ideas, intellectual habits of mind, and pleasurable interest in mental achievement can be evoked by no form of words, however accurately adjusted. All practical teachers know that education is a patient process of the mastery of details, minute by minute, hour by hour, day by day. There is no royal road to learning through an airy path of brilliant generalisations. There is a proverb about the difficulty of seeing the wood because of the trees. That difficulty is exactly the point which I am enforcing. The problem of education is to make the pupil see the wood by means of the trees.

The solution which I am urging is to eradicate the fatal disconnection of subjects which kills the vitality of our modern curriculum. There is only one subject-matter for education, and that is Life in all its manifestations. Instead of this single unity, we offer children — Algebra, from which nothing follows; Geometry, from which nothing follows; Science, from which nothing follows; History, from which nothing follows; a Couple of Languages, never mastered; and lastly, most dreary of all, Literature, represented by plays of Shakespeare, with philological notes and short analyses of plot and character to be in substance committed to memory. Can such a list be said to represent Life, as it is known in the midst of the living of it? The best that can be said of it is that it is a rapid table of contents which a deity might run over in his mind while he was thinking of creating a world, and had not yet determined how to put it together.

Let us now return to quadratic equations. We still have on hand the unanswered question. Why should children be taught their solution? Unless quadratic equations fit into a connected curriculum, of course there is no reason to teach anything about them. Furthermore, extensive as should be the place of mathematics in a complete culture, I am a little doubtful whether for many types of boys algebraic solutions of quadratic equations do not lie on the specialist side of mathematics. I may here remind you that as yet I have not said anything of the psychology or the content of the specialism which is so necessary a part of an ideal education. But all that is an evasion of our real question, and I merely state it in order to avoid being misunderstood in my answer.

Quadratic equations are part of algebra, and algebra is the intellectual instrument which has been created for rendering clear the quantitative aspects of the world. There is no getting out of it. Through and through the world is infected with quantity. To talk sense, is to talk in quantities. It is no use saying that the nation is large, — How large? It is no use saying that radium is scarce, — How scarce? You cannot evade quantity. You may fly to poetry and to music, and quantity and number will face you in your rhythms and your octaves. Elegant intellects which despise the theory of quantity are but half developed. They are more to be pitied than blamed. The scraps of gibberish, which in their school-days were taught to them in the name of algebra, deserve some contempt.

This question of the degeneration of algebra into gibberish, both in word and in fact, affords a pathetic instance of the usefulness of reforming educational schedules without a clear conception of the attributes which you wish to evoke in the living minds of the children. A few years ago there was an outcry that school algebra was in need of reform, but there was a general agreement that graphs would put everything right. So all sorts of things were extruded, and graphs were introduced. So far as I can see, with no sort of idea behind them, but just graphs. Now every examination paper has one or two questions on graphs. Personally, I am an enthusiastic adherent of graphs. But I wonder whether as yet we have gained very much. You cannot put life into any schedule of general education unless you succeed in exhibiting its relation to some essential characteristic of all intelligent or emotional perception. It is a hard saying, but it is true; and I do not see how to make it any easier. In making these little formal alterations you are beaten by the very nature of things. You are pitted against too skilful an adversary, who will see to it that the pea is always under the other thimble.

Reformation must begin at the other end. First, you must make up your mind as to those quantitative aspects of the world which are simple enough to be introduced into general education; then a schedule of algebra should be framed which will about find its exemplification in these applications. We need not fear for our pet graphs, they will be there in plenty when we once begin to treat algebra as a serious means of studying the world. Some of the simplest applications will be found in the quantities which occur in the simplest study of society. The curves of history are more vivid and more informing than the dry catalogues of names and dates which comprise the greater part of that arid school study. What purpose is effected by a catalogue of undistingushed kings and queens? Tom, Dick, or Harry, they are all dead. General resurrections are failures, and are better postponed. The quantitative flux of the forces of modern society is capable of very simple exhibition. Meanwhile, the ideas of the variable, of the function, of rate of change, of equations and their solution, of elimination, are being studied as an abstract science for their own sake. Not, of course, in the pompous phrases with which I am alluding to them here, but with that iteration of simple special cases proper to teaching.

If this course be followed, the route from Chaucer to the Black Death, from the Black Death to modern Labour troubles, will connect the tales of the mediaeval pilgrims with the abstract science of algebra, both yielding diverse aspects of that single theme, Life. I know what most of you are thinking at this point. It is that the exact course which I have sketched out is not the particular one which you would have chosen, or even see how to work. I quite agree. I am not claiming that I could do it myself. But your objection is the precise reason why a common external examination system is fatal to education. The process of exhibiting the applications of knowledge must, for its success, essentially depend on the character of the pupils and the genius of the teacher. Of course I have left out the easiest applications with which most of us are more at home. I mean the quantitative sides of sciences, such as mechanics and physics.

Again, in the same connection we plot the statistics of social phenomena against the time. We then eliminate the time between suitable pairs. We can speculate how far we have exhibited a real causal connection, or how far a mere temporal coincidence. We notice that we might have plotted against the time one set of statistics for one country and another set for another country, and thus, with suitable choice of subjects, have obtained graphs which certainly exhibited mere coincidence. Also other graphs exhibit obvious causal connections. We wonder how to discriminate. And so are drawn on as far as we will.

But in considering this description, I must beg you to remember what I have been insisting on above. In the first place, one train of thought will not suit all groups of children. For example, I should expect that artisan children will want something more concrete and, in a sense, swifter than I have set down here. Perhaps I am wrong, but that is what I should guess. In the second place, I am not contemplating one beautiful lecture stimulating, once and for all, an admiring class. That is not the way in which education proceeds. No; all the time the pupils are hard at work solving examples, drawing graphs, and making experiments, until they have a thorough hold on the whole subject. I am describing the interspersed explanations, the directions which should be given to their thoughts. The pupils have got to be made to feel that they are studying something, and are not merely executing intellectual minuets.

Finally, if you are teaching pupils for some general examination, the problem of sound teaching is greatly complicated. Have you ever noticed the zig-zag moulding round a Norman arch? The ancient work is beautiful, the modern work is hideous. The reason is that the modern work is done to exact measure, the ancient work is varied according to the idiosyncrasy of the workman. Here it is crowded, and there it is expanded. Now the essence of getting pupils through examinations is to give equal weight to all parts of the schedule. But mankind is naturally specialist. One man sees a whole subject, where another can find only a few detached examples. I know that it seems contradictory to allow for specialism in a curriculum especially designed for a broad culture. Without contradictions the world would be simpler, and perhaps duller. But I am certain that in education wherever you exclude specialism you destroy life.

We now come to the other great branch of a general mathematical education, namely Geometry. The same principles apply. The theoretical part should be clear-cut, rigid, short, and important. Every proposition not absolutely necessary to exhibit the main connection of ideas should be cut out, but the great fundamental ideas should be all there. No omission of concepts, such as those of Similarity and Proportion. We must remember that, owing to the aid rendered by the visual presence of a figure, Geometry is a field of unequalled excellence for the exercise of the deductive faculties of reasoning. Then, of course, there follows Geometrical Drawing, with its training for the hand and eye.

But, like Algebra, Geometry and Geometrical Drawing must be extended beyond the mere circle of geometrical ideas. In an industrial neighbourhood, machinery and workshop practice form the appropriate extension. For example, in the London Polytechnics this has been achieved with conspicuous success. For many secondary schools I suggest that surveying and maps are the natural applications. In particular, plane-table surveying should lead pupils to a vivid apprehension of the immediate application of geometric truths. Simple drawing apparatus, a surveyor's chain, and a surveyor's compass, should enable the pupils to rise from the survey and mensuration of a field to the construction of the map of a small district. The best education is to be found in gaining the utmost information from the simplest apparatus.

The provision of elaborate instruments is greatly to be deprecated. To have constructed the map of a small district, to have considered its roads, its contours, its geology, its climate, its relation to other districts, the effects on the status of its inhabitants, will teach more history and geography than any knowledge of Perkin Warback or of Behren's Straits. I mean not a nebulous lecture on the subject, but a serious investigation in which the real facts are definitely ascertained by the aid of accurate theoretical knowledge. A typical mathematical problem should be: Survey such and such a field, draw a plan of it to such and such a scale, and find the area. It would be quite a good procedure to impart the necessary geometrical propositions without their proofs. Then, concurrently in the same term, the proofs of the propositions would be learnt while the survey was being made.

Fortunately, the specialist side of education presents an easier problem than does the provision of a general culture. For this there are many reasons. One is that many of the principles of procedure to be observed are the same in both cases, and it is unnecessary to recapitulate. Another reason is that specialist training takes place — or should take place — at a more advanced stage of the pupil's course, and thus there is easier material to work upon. But undoubtedly the chief reason is that the specialist study is normally a study of peculiar interest to the student. He is studying it because, for some reason, he wants to know it. This makes all the difference. The general culture is designed to foster an activity of mind; the specialist course utilises this activity. But it does not do to lay too much stress on these neat antitheses. As we have already seen, in the general course foci of special interest will arise; and similarly in the special study, the external connections of the subject drag thought outwards.

Again, there is not one course of study which merely gives general culture, and another which gives special knowledge. The subjects pursued for the sake of a general education are special subjects specially studied; and, on the other hand, one of the ways of encouraging general mental activity is to foster a special devotion. You may not divide the seamless coat of learning. What education has to impart is an intimate sense for the power of ideas, for the beauty of ideas, and for the structure of ideas, together with a particular body of knowledge which has peculiar reference to the life of the being possessing it.

The appreciation of the structure of ideas is that side of a cultured mind which can only grow under the influence of a special study. I mean that eye for the whole chessboard, for the bearing of one set of ideas on another. Nothing but a special study can give any appreciation for the exact formulation of general ideas, for their relations when formulated, for their service in the comprehension of life. A mind so disciplined should be both more abstract and more concrete. It has been trained in the comprehension of abstract thought and in the analysis of facts.

Finally, there should grow the most austere of all mental qualities; I mean the sense for style. It is an aesthetic sense, based on admiration for the direct attainment of a foreseen end, simply and without waste. Style in art, style in literature, style in science, style in logic, style in practical execution have fundamentally the same aesthetic qualities, namely, attainment and restraint. The love of a subject in itself and for itself, where it is not the sleepy pleasure of pacing a mental quarter-deck, is the love of style as manifested in that study.

Here we are brought back to the position from which we started, the utility of education. Style, in its finest sense, is the last acquirement of the educated mind; it is also the most useful. It pervades the whole being. The administrator with a sense for style hates waste; the engineer with a sense for style economises his material; the artisan with a sense for style prefers good work. Style is the ultimate morality of mind.

But above style, and above knowledge, there is something, a vague shape like fate above the Greek gods. That something is Power. Style is the fashioning of power, the restraining of power. But, after all, the power of attainment of the desired end is fundamental. The first thing is to get there. Do not bother about your style, but solve your problem, justify the ways of God to man, administer your province, or do whatever else is set before you.

Where, then, does style help? In this, with style the end is attained without side issues, without raising undesirable inflammations. With style you attain your end and nothing but your end. With style the effect of your activity is calculable, and foresight is the last gift of gods to men. With style your power is increased, for your mind is not distracted with irrelevancies, and you are more likely to attain your object. Now style is the exclusive privilege of the expert. Whoever heard of the style of an amateur painter, of the style of an amateur poet? Style is always the product of specialist study, the peculiar contribution of specialism to culture.

English education in its present phase suffers from a lack of definite aim, and from an external machinery which kills its vitality. Hitherto in this address I have been considering the aims which should govern education. In this respect England halts between two opinions. It has not decided whether to produce amateurs or experts. The profound change in the world which the nineteenth century has produced is that the growth of knowledge has given foresight. The amateur is essentially a man with appreciation and with immense versatility in mastering a given routine. But he lacks the foresight which comes from special knowledge. The object of this address is to suggest how to produce the expert without loss of the essential virtues of the amateur. The machinery of our secondary education is rigid where it should be yielding, and lax where it should be rigid. Every school is bound on pain of extinction to train its boys for a small set of definite examinations. No headmaster has a free hand to develop his general education or his specialist studies in accordance with the opportunities of his school, which are created by its staff, its environment, its class of boys, and its endowments. I suggest that no system of external tests which aims primarily at examining individual scholars can result in anything but educational waste.

Primarily it is the schools and not the scholars which should be inspected. Each school should grant its own leaving certificates, based on its own curriculum. The standards of these schools should be sampled and corrected. But the first requisite for educational reform is the school as a unit, with its approved curriculum based on its own needs, and evolved by its own staff. If we fail to secure that, we simply fall from one formalism into another, from one dung-hill of inert ideas into another.

In stating that the school is the true educational unit in any national system for the safeguarding of efficiency, I have conceived the alternative system as being the external examination of the individual scholar. But every Scylla is faced by its Charybdis — or, in more homely language, there is a ditch on both sides of the road. It will be equally fatal to education if we fall into the hands of a supervising department which is under the impression that it can divide all schools into two or three rigid categories, each type being forced to adopt a rigid curriculum. When I say that the school is the educational unit, I mean exactly what I say, no larger unit, no smaller unit. Each school must have the claim to be considered in relation to its special circumstances. The classifying of schools for some purposes is necessary. But no absolutely rigid curriculum, not modified by its own staff, should be permissible. Exactly the same principles apply, with the proper modifications, to universities and to technical colleges.

When one considers in its length and in its breadth the importance of this question of the education of a nation's young, the broken lives, the defeated hopes, the national failures, which result from the frivolous inertia with which it is treated, it is difficult to restrain within oneself a savage rage. In the conditions of modern life the rule is absolute, the race which does not value trained intelligence is doomed. Not all your heroism, not all your social charm, not all your wit, not all your victories on land or at sea, can move back the finger of fate. Today we maintain ourselves. Tomorrow science will have moved forward yet one more step, and there will be no appeal from the judgement which will then be pronounced on the uneducated.

We can be content with no less than the old summary of educational ideal which has been current at any time from the dawn of our civilisation. The essence of education is that it be religious.

Pray, what is religious education?

A religious education is an education which inculcates duty and reverence. Duty arises from our potential control over the course of events. Where attainable knowledge could have changed the issue, ignorance has the guilt of vice. And the foundation of reverence is this perception, that the present holds within itself the complete sum of existence, backwards and forwards, that whole amplitude of time, which is eternity.

Marten ten Hoor

"Education for Privacy" is a refreshing criticism of a very alive and rather sacred cow in education today. Dr. ten Hoor, Emeritus Professor of Philosophy at the University of Alabama, begins his complaint with a proposition: "Never in the history of the world have there been so many people occupied with the improvement of so few." He develops his ideal of education for privacy by defending the necessity for individual struggle, suffering, and commitment. To ten Hoor an educational system that fails to prepare the student for an independent life does little for the cause of democracy, less for the happiness of man. Parallels to the author's argument are found in sources as disparate as the Socratic dictum "know thyself" and modern expressions by Dostoevsky, Kierkegaard, Nietzsche, Sartre, Camus, and Buber — writers usually identified with the diffusive energies of existentialism.

40

EDUCATION FOR PRIVACY *

In view of the hundreds of conferences which have been held on liberal education, it would seem to be impossible to say anything new on the subject. Since there seems to be nothing new to say, one must, in order to be original, be contrary, eccentric or partisan. I have chosen to be partisan. The proposition to be defended is, frankly, a half-truth. If it can be established, there will be some cause for satisfaction; for the establishment of a half-truth is not a bad average in this complex and confused world. There is the justification, moreover, that the other, and possibly the better, half has in our day had practically all the attention.

Stated concretely, the proposition is this: Never in the history of the world

* From *The American Scholar*, Winter, 1953–54. Used by permission of Marten ten Hoor.

have there been so many people occupied with the improvement of so few. To sharpen the point by a specific example: Never have there been so many people making a good living by showing the other fellow how to make a better one. If you are skeptical, I recommend that you try this exercise — add up, as of the current date, the social workers, planners and reformers; the college presidents, deans and professors; the editors of magazines, journals and newspapers (not forgetting college newspapers); almost everybody in Washington, D.C., during recent years; and the tens of thousands of miscellaneous social-minded folks who attend conferences, workshops and institutes organized for the improvement of the human race. Subtract that figure from the total population of this country, and compare this figure with a corresponding figure for, say, the year 1900. You will then see what I mean when I say that this is the era of undiscriminating allegiance to good causes. To come nearer home, compute the sum of all college and university presidents, deans and professors who have in the last five years attended meetings devoted to the improvement of education. Compare that figure with the number of those who remained on the campus working and you will find proof even *in academia.*

As further evidence, and as a striking symptom, there is the recent popularity of educational surveys. Most states and many institutions have experienced several. I have lived through eleven, without noticeable improvement in myself or my neighbors. Note the procedure and the technique, for there you will find the moral. The surveyors are always from another state or another institution. This is in accordance with the well-known principle that an expert is an ordinary person who is away from home. These outsiders are brought in because of their objectivity, objectivity being the capacity for discovering faults abroad which you cannot recognize at home. To be a good educational surveyor — or any kind of social analyst, for that matter — you must have a sharp eye for foreign motes but a dull one for domestic beams. You must be a contented extrovert, so that, after diagnosing the faults of others, you can continue to live in perfect comfort with your own.

I must confess that I view all this indiscriminate altruism with a jaundiced eye. It does seem to me that these days there are too many leaders and too few followers; too many preachers and too few sinners — self-conscious sinners, that is. If this were an illustrated article, I would insert at this point a wonderful cartoon I saw not long ago. A little boy was asking an obviously astounded and embarrassed father, "But if we're here to help others, what are the others here for?" Nobody has time these days to improve himself, so busy is he with attempts to improve his neighbor. There is something wrong with that equation. It seems to me that it is time to try to balance it. I suggest that this can be done by shifting some weight from one side to the other, by shifting the emphasis from social improvement to self-improvement. I suggest that over the door of every academic cubicle there should hang the sign which Thoreau had over the door of his hut: "*My* destiny mended here, not yours." In short, I propose to make a plea for *education for privacy.*

Before undertaking to identify some of the elements of this type of education, I should like to offer some justification of my skepticism concerning the present emphasis on social-mindedness in education. To begin with, it is so easy to assume that your neighbor is much worse off than yourself. The universality of this tendency is undoubtedly accounted for psychologically by its attractive by-products. The assumption produces a feeling of comfort. If there is some slight suspicion that all is not well within, it is compensating to concentrate on the plight of one's neighbor. Since attention to him is distracting, it keeps the individual from worrying about himself. To do something about a neighbor's ignorance also makes one feel virtuous. This absorbing concern for the improvement of one's neighbor is undoubtedly a product of civilization. It is doubtful if primitive man worried much about it. The cannibal, in fact, represents the other extreme: he uses his neighbor solely for his own improvement.

In the second place, I doubt if the reformer always has the wisdom necessary to direct the lives of so many people — but this is certainly assumed. How many people are there who have demonstrated the capacity to prescribe for others? If an individual makes a mistake in trying to improve himself, this is not so serious; but consider the consequences if he has induced all his neighbors to do the same thing. History is filled with examples of self-confident leaders who led their followers straight to a common catastrophe. The fact is that we still know so little about human personality in the concrete. To be sure, there are excellent textbook pictures, with revealing analytical tables and graphs. But this is personality in the abstract. Any physician will tell you that he rarely finds a textbook picture in a patient. Not only is every human being a complex with variations, but there are the environment in which that complex functions and the accidental circumstances which confuse the vision and disrupt life.

Nor has the reformer too much reason for assuming that he has discerned the good life for his neighbors. Let us take as a familiar example the characteristic projection by parents into the lives of their children. This is something we can readily understand and, because it is suffused with parental affection, forgive. But how many parents are there who realize that each child is to some extent a new complex of elements and who can bring themselves to substitute that confounding reality for the fond subjective creation? Too often the recommendation of a way of life is nothing more than the advocacy of a personal preference.

From subjectivism in this sense of the term there is no complete escape. Even leadership is personalized in an individual. Hitler was an individual: he spun his fantastic and criminal notions out of his own warped private personality. It is therefore terribly important that everything shall be right in the reformer before he undertakes to reform others. "Nobody," says a character in Norman Douglas' *South Wind*, "has the right to call himself well disposed towards society until he has grasped the elementary fact that the only way to improve society is to improve oneself." And may I suggest in this connection that a major in the social sciences does not automatically qualify a student for social leadership?

Further reason for doubt is to be found in the characteristic reactions of the hypersocial-minded. They become so indignant when people resist their ministrations. They are so determinedly selfish in their unselfishness. Ideas, particularly ideas designed for the improvement of others, so quickly become inflated. In extreme cases, they devour themselves. How antagonistic even educators become over professional differences as to how the ignorant should be rendered less so! Note the bitterness between rival reform groups. Let us not forget that human beings have killed one another in the mass even on the authority of their religions. Note how political leaders fall out, quarrel, conspire, injure one another in their unselfish efforts to save the country. In the absence of sophistication and modesty, reform notions grow into delusions; their advocates become more and more autocratic; leadership becomes pathological; the desire to help one's fellow-men is transformed into fanaticism and tyranny — and societies become authoritarian.

Here lies the explanation of the tendency of hypersocial-mindedness to suppress individualism and to produce too much uniformity. There are good reasons for doubting the wisdom of this lack of interest in the individual as a unique personality. There is, to begin with, the obvious and inescapable fact that everybody is an individual. The higher the scale of life, the more individuals differ and the greater their potentialities for differing. Society must make provision for individual differences. Authoritarianisms of the type of national socialism and communism are primitivistic, for they propose to turn back the course of social change and to establish societies in which individuals shall have a status more closely resembling that of ants, bees, or even of atoms or electrons than of human personalities. They have forgotten, or propose to ignore, the incontrovertible fact that the great works of art, literature, music, philosophy, religion and science — that is, the world's great manifestations of excellence and leadership — were the products of intensely individual persons. Indeed, some of the world's great geniuses have been self-centered, unsocial and iconoclastic, with little or no interest in the improvement of their fellow-men.

But society can well afford that. A regimented society will not only suppress and possibly ultimately breed out these "exaggerated" individuals, but will generally discourage the manifestations of the adventurous and original spirit. Government and education designed to do this will bring about a tragic cultural impoverishment in human life; for individual differences enrich life, they stimulate the intelligence and the imagination, and they invite comparison and criticism. They keep the individual alive *as an individual,* and not merely as a bearer of the racial genius or a servant of the state.

It is true that modern life requires a certain amount of regimentation. Individuals obviously cannot be permitted to run amuck. At least the great majority of persons must adapt themselves to other persons. Mechanical contrivances, such as traffic lights, must replace individual judgment; laws are to some extent substitutes for individual choice. But let us not forget that it is not the basic purpose of these substitutes to repress individuality, but rather to make possible a more general and richer realization of individuality. It is not the purpose of social organization to reduce man to the subhuman, but to create more favorable opportunities for the realization of what is uniquely human.

The need of complex societies for a high degree of organization is one reason why so much attention is focused on the improvement of the other fellow. Especially in a democracy, where everyone is more or less free to advocate schemes for the improvement of society, lively and self-confident minds are inclined to expend their intellectual and emotional potential on reform movements. The attention of the reformer is consequently drawn away from contemplation of the state of his own soul. Since he is so happily exercised in improving others, the habit of self-examination gradually atrophies. How then can he be sure that he is the right person to prescribe for his neighbors? Should he not stop now and then to take an inventory of his resources? Does he in fact have these resources? It is because I have serious doubts of this sort, and because of the increasing neglect in education of attention to the accumulation of these resources, that I feel it time to make a plea for education for privacy.

What now are the essential elements of this education for privacy? In speaking of elements it is of course implied that the ideal construct of these elements constitutes an organized whole, a personality. It is this ideal at which we aim, though we know full well that in any concrete individual, no matter how well educated after the formula which we shall propose, one or the other desirable characteristic is certain to be under- or overemphasized.

The first requirement, clearly, is to learn how to think — not out loud or in print, but privately. The thinker himself, not his neighbor, is to be the beneficiary. To think does not mean to spend hours in idle daydreaming or in vagrant imaginings, or to make occasional impulsive sallies at ideas which happen to appear before the attention. The reference is certainly not to the semi-somnolent and comfortable ruminations which go on in the wandering mind of an inattentive student in the classroom. What is meant is systematic reflection, the constant purpose of which is to bring order out of the multiplicity and variety of things in which the human being is immersed.

To be sure, many people go through life with their senses alert, observing and savoring in generous measure the richness of the world about them. But what they experience they retain only in the form of materials for recollection. The mind gradually accumulates a rich inventory of goods, which can be brought out on display when there is social opportunity for it. But the relationship of these resources in the mind is one of mere contiguity, like that of goods in a department store. Experience has not resulted in an over-all understanding because it has not been systematically thought about. Such individuals

> . . . see all sights from pole to pole,
> And glance, and nod, and bustle by,
> And never once possess [their] soul
> Before [they] die.

To possess one's soul in an intellectual sense means to have found some answer, or partial answer, to the questions: What is the nature of this world in which I find myself, what is my place in it, and what must be my attitude toward it? The problem is one of intellectual and spiritual orientation.

The benefits of such intellectual and spiritual adaptation have been extolled by the wise men of all ages and all countries. A "view of life" prepares us for what life brings us, for what happens to us in our physical environment, and most important of all, for what people turn out to be and for what they do. To be spiritually and intellectually lost in the world, on the contrary, is to be unarmed and helpless. A disorganized mind is unprepared for reality and easily frustrated. The fate that awaits the individual so afflicted is to be always a stranger and a wanderer in the world. The "lost soul" of literature, the ultimate in tragic creation, suffers from this great spiritual illness.

It may be unfortunate, but it is a fact that the sharper and livelier the intelligence and the more sensitive the spirit, the more serious the danger of disorientation. The simple-minded find life simple. Plants find themselves easy to live with, no doubt; for it cannot be difficult to vegetate successfully. It is not likely that the cow's ruminations are philosophical. Man, for better or worse, is a rational animal. The more he thinks, the greater the need of organization among his ideas. The more subjects a student studies in college, the more extensive the potential disorder of his mind. It is not surprising that the scholarly mind, lost in a Babel of learning, seeks escape into a clearly defined specialty, and the practical mind, as soon as its owner has permission, into the comforts of a business, a profession, or domesticity. To be sure, we must integrate the curriculum. But what good is this if the professor's mind remains perched on its gaunt pinnacle or secluded in the laboratory?

The systematic way to the attainment of the organization of ideas is through philosophy and religion. It is true that the great intellectual constructions of the metaphysicians are not available to all men, and that even to the initiated they sometimes offer but poor comfort. Moreover, all of us have known individuals of great simplicity and humbleness of mind, quite untutored in dialectic, who somehow and in the simplest terms have securely located themselves in the cosmos. Especially in the realm of religious experience do we find examples of this. The spirit seems to have found peace in terms of some all-embracing conviction or great renunciation. But this is not often possible for the inquisitive and analytical mind. To cast all burdens upon the Lord in one grand resolve sometimes implies ignorance of the nature of those burdens. There is only consciousness of their oppressive weight, but no understanding of their nature or causes. To be sure, the critical intelligence may also come ultimately to make this renunciation, but it will not feel justified in doing so until it has reflected upon causes and relationships and seen the problem of human trouble and sorrow *whole*. The solution must be a conquest, not an escape.

For this, the mind certainly needs philosophy, sacred or secular. No learned profession, however, can offer the inquiring mind an official formula which every man need only apply in order to be permanently on understanding terms with the world. To be sure, there are systems of metaphysics, sacred and secular, from which the troubled spirit can choose a ready-made synthesis. But this does not make the chosen system of ideas an integral part of the inner personality. Intellectual orientation to the world must be something more than an acquisition; it must be an organic growth. The student should by all means seek out the great religious and philosophical thinkers, study their systems, and add their insights to his own. But in the last analysis he must work out his own solution, for such a solution must be the end product of his *own* reflection in the context of his *own* experience. Only through the alchemy of private reflection do philosophical ideas become private resources. Only then will they be available in time of crisis. When the normal course of existence is interrupted by conflict and frustration, it is a bit late to begin developing fundamental guiding ideas; that is the time to apply them.

A dramatic example of the saving grace of such resources is related by Admiral Byrd in his book on his expedition to the South Pole, entitled *Alone*. He had been left behind by the expedition in a dugout located several feet below the surface of the icecap. From this he periodically emerged through a vertical tunnel to make scientific observations. It happened that the heater in his subterranean shelter developed a leak of which he was not aware. Before he realized it, he had been dangerously poisoned and he became seriously ill. During his convalescence he found himself struggling to overcome not only the physical damage done to his body, but also a deep spiritual depression, an obstinate conviction of the meaninglessness of life, which threatened to overwhelm him. There was no physician or psychoanalyst or cleric available. His fellow-explorers would not return for months. He was absolutely *alone*. He had to guide himself out of this slough of despair. This he did, after many agonizing days, by steady thinking, by "digging down into" his intellectual resources. And it was then, to use his own homely but vivid phrase, that he "uncovered the pay-dirt of philosophy." He did not then collect the materials of his readjustment; he used them to recover his sanity. In this crisis, what would he have done without these resources?

But periods of crisis are not the only time when man needs an orderly mind. If a ship is to hold its course it needs a steady helm in good weather as well as in bad. I hasten to remark that this figure of speech has serious limitations, for a navigator has his chart prepared when he begins his voyage.

Man, on the contrary, is faced with the problem of making a chart as he goes along. As a matter of fact, the plan of life is for every man to some extent an unconscious precipitate of his experience. We are not completely free agents: compulsion and fate, in the form of the physical world, our fellow-men and social institutions, push the individual this way and that. What happens to him and what he becomes are clearly the result of a complex of inner and outer compulsions, over many of which he has no control.

We are not here primarily concerned with action, however, but with interpretation. In philosophical reflection, the individual to some extent plays the part of the Greek chorus. He observes himself as actor in a cosmic setting. If he does so systematically, he will gradually discern not only his own role, but the direction of the whole drama. Only when he understands the meaning of the play can he orient himself in it. Such an understanding, vague and incomplete though it may be, will enable him to achieve his own view of life. If he is so fortunate as to see (what seems to him) the truth and to see it whole, he will thenceforth have a vision of the future as well as an understanding of the present and the past. If a rational man does not do that, why should he consider himself the crown of creation? If he does accomplish this, he can exult with the poet Dyer:

> My mind to me a kingdom is;
> Such present joys therein I find
> As far exceeds all earthly bliss
>
> . . . .
>
> Look, what I lack my mind supplies
> Lo, thus I triumph like a king,
> Content with that my mind doth bring.

In education for privacy, however, more is involved than philosophical orientation to the cosmos. There is equally urgent need for education in the establishment and maintenance of moral harmony. From the days of primitive religion, through Greek tragedy, the Christian epic of sin and salvation, and modern psychology, Freudian and non-Freudian, to contemporary existentialism, there runs the theme of the uneasy conscience. The dramatic specter of moral guilt is the principal character in many of the greatest creations of literary genius. No matter what the learned explanation, the psychological state is one of inner moral disharmony. Though it may have outer causes, it is a private affliction and must be cured privately. In moments of despair or periods of cynicism we may doubt the existence or discernibility of moral meaning in the universe; but such a conclusion does not relieve the individual of the necessity for solving his personal moral problem. Even complete moral negativism, if not itself a moral philosophy, leaves the individual no recourse but to establish a private moral order in his life of action and reflection.

Here again, the more sensitive the individual, the greater the potentiality for disorganization. It is the sensitive who are the most deeply wounded by moral indifference, disorder and brutality. The predisposing causes of moral disorganization may be in the people and the things we love, in the institutions which demand that we conform to their customs and taboos, in the great world which so often mocks our need for moral significance and order. But a vision of the good life, the spirit must have; for devoid of it, the imagination is without moral perspective, conduct without guiding principles, and action without trustworthy habits. For an individual so unprepared for life, confusion will efface meaning and create frustration, with the onset in the case of the unusually sensitive spirit of pathological disturbances which may for a period or for a lifetime destroy happiness. Education for privacy must therefore include the education of the moral personality, the gradual acquisition by the self of moral resources. Here, too, there are available to the student in generous measure the works of the great philosophical and religious thinkers, for probably no one of the persistent problems of life has had more of their systematic and concentrated attention. It is relevant here to note that the previously discussed philosophical orientation to the world is sometimes the foundation for moral orientation.

A third requirement in the education of the personality is the development of emotional stability. Of all the immediate causes of unhappiness, emotional disorder is unquestionably the most serious and the most common. Currently there is a feeling that under the pressures of modern life its incidence is steadily increasing. Unfortunately, emotions are the component of the personality about which we know the least, as modern science has come to realize. Our ignorance is largely a consequence of the fact that traditionally the emotions have been considered to be effects rather than causes. Preoccupation with the flattering conviction that man is a rational animal has been attended with the assumption that therefore our emotions are under the domination of the reason. This assumption has been one of the basic tenets of formal education, though puzzled parents and self-conscious adults no doubt have all along had their suspicions. In our day, educators are being enlightened by psychology and the medical sciences on the subject of the devastating power of the emotions. Moreover, the modern conception of the integrated personality has redirected our approach to this subject, so that now we hypothesize and investigate in terms of interrelations and interactions. The simple classical vision of the reason enthroned in the psyche, making judgments, issuing commands, and directing the conscious life of the individual, is difficult to maintain in the face of the past record and the current spectacle of human behavior.

Let us grant that the contemporary individual lives in an age in which, as Goethe put it, "humanity twists and turns like a person on a sickbed trying to find a comfortable position." To offset this, however, he has the advantage of a better understanding of the compulsive and disruptive power of the emotions. He is aware of their insidious tendency to direct his thinking and affect his judgment. He knows that they feed on themselves and that, if they are of the destructive kind, they can bring him to the verge of despair. He knows that they can completely disorient him, isolating him from the friendship and sympathy of his fellow-men and estranging him from the beauty and utility of the world. He must learn that there is little he can do to remove the external causes, the irritants in his social and physical environment. In order to maintain or restore emotional stability *within* himself, he must learn to control the effects of these irritants *on* himself. Education of the emotions is education in self-control, in equanimity and serenity.

To these three objectives of education for privacy — the attainment of a philosophical point of view, a steady vision of the good life, and serenity of spirit — I should like to add one more: the individual should be able to live entertainingly with himself. He should accumulate resources on which he can draw when he is at leisure. The universal symptom of the absence of such resources is the homely but hapless state of boredom. It is an anomalous condition of the spirit, a state of indifference lying between pain and pleasure. Neither the mind nor the hands can find anything interesting to do. In contrast with the other troubles of the spirit which have been mentioned, there is little excuse for this great emptiness. For there is a marvelous cure for boredom, universally available, readily tapped and virtually inexhaustible: the fine arts.

This claim hardly needs defense. Nor is it necessary to enumerate the arts and to identify their respective potentialities for beguiling the mind and the heart. For illustrative purposes, however, let us consider one form of art enjoyment which is available to virtually every normal human being, young or old, learned or simple, saint or sinner — reading. Its great virtue for education for privacy is that it is a strictly private experience. No other human being is necessary to the reader at the moment of reading. He can take his book with him to the jungle or the desert, on the ocean or the mountain top. He can select his company at will, and rid himself of it by a turn of the hand. It is potentially an inexhaustible resource: all ages of history; all countries; all varieties of human beings, and even of animals and plants and physical things; the entire range of human thoughts and feelings, hopes and fears, conquests and failures, victories and defeats; the real and the ideal — all are available at the turn of a page for the reader's contemplation and understanding.

When we measure the impoverishment of him to whom this world is literally and figuratively a closed book, whose ear is deaf to music and whose eye blind to the glories of painting and sculpture, we come to realize the responsibility of liberal education for instruction in the arts. I say instruction purposely, because I believe that the presentation of opportunities for enjoyment and training in appreciation are not enough: there should also be instruction and encouragement in the production of art. As even the bungling amateur knows, there is no greater source of pleasure than creative activity. The training of the most modest talent is an enrichment of a personality and develops another private resource for leisure hours. Even the unsuccessful attempt to create art, moreover, clarifies the understanding of art. To be sure, just as it is not necessary to trouble our friends with our thoughts, so it is not necessary to bore our friends with our productions. It is, after all, not the improvement of the neighbor but the improvement of oneself that is the immediate object of education for privacy.

An understanding of the world, a vision of the good life, serenity of spirit, appreciation and practice of the fine arts — these, then, are the elements of the integrated personality, the development of which is the immediate object of liberal education. These are the resources which are accumulated in the course of education for privacy. Why, now, is it so important for every individual to possess these resources? In the first place, simply because he is going to need them. We never know when we are going to lose our external resources, our public possessions. Without private resources the individual has nothing to turn to when disappointment, frustration, or misfortune become his lot. In the great depression which is still vivid in our memories, there were many individuals who possessed only external resources. When they lost these, life was over for them. They could not go on living with themselves because of their intellectual, moral, emotional, and artistic poverty. He who possessed these resources, however, could exclaim with Thoreau: "Oh, how I laugh when I think of my vague, indefinite riches! No run on the bank can drain it, for my wealth is not possession but enjoyment."

Resources of the spirit are like savings: they must be accumulated before they are needed. When they are needed, there is no substitute for them. Sooner or later, the individual faces the world alone, and that moment may overwhelm him if he has no resources within himself. Distraction helps but little and betrays us when we least expect it. We can escape our physical environment and our neighbors, but we cannot escape ourselves. Everyone with any maturity of experience and self-knowledge knows that the loneliest moments are sometimes experienced in the midst of the greatest crowds and the most elaborate entertainments. . . .

And now, in conclusion, I wish again to pay my respects to the other half-truth, the improvement of others, which was so cavalierly dismissed in the beginning of this essay. That objective together with the other objective, self-improvement, compose the whole truth, which is the grand objective of liberal education. Education for privacy and education for public service constitute education of the whole personality. He who is not educated for privacy is hardly fit to educate others. The blind cannot lead the blind. The man who is not at peace with himself cannot be trusted to lead his fellow-men in the ways of peace. The unbalanced leader is certain to unbalance the society in which he functions. Even the leader who is intent on the side of the good but who is a fanatic will stimulate fanaticism in his followers, arouse dogmatism and bigotry, and induce oppression and cruelty. When he is on the side of evil, he will lead his followers into such excesses and wickedness as will shame all humanity, and which even the innocent will wish to forget as soon as possible. Social pathology must in the last analysis be focused on the sickness of the individuals who compose the society. It is pure imagination, if not nonsense, to ascribe the ignorance, unbalance and wickedness of a collection of human beings to a mysterious social entity such as the group mind or the social organism. We might as well divorce the concept of an epidemic from the notion of the individuals who are ill, or ascribe hunger to a societal stomach. People mislead one another exactly as they infect one another. The psychopathic leader is potentially as dangerous as the carrier of an infectious disease.

The safe leader, in terms of the elements of education for privacy, is one who understands his place in the world and can thus envisage the place of his fellow-men; who can morally respect himself and can thus be respected by others; who has learned to control his emotions and can thus be trusted to exert control over others; who has learned to live in peace and contentment with himself and can thus with propriety urge others to do likewise.

We are living in a world and in a time when powerful leaders with millions of fanatical followers are committed to the forcible regimentation of their fellow-men, according to formulas which have no initial authority but that of their own private dogmatism. They not only refuse to recognize the right of private thought and personal conscience to be considered in the management of public affairs, but they have abolished the concept of the individual as a private personality and have reduced him to the level of the bee in the hive. To restore the individual to his former dignity as a a human being is the urgent need of the day. This, in my opinion, should be the special objective of contemporary education.

But liberal education must so educate the individual that he is manifestly worthy of having his dignity recognized. If he wishes to lead his fellows, he must first learn to lead himself. Without education for privacy he will neither merit leadership nor learn to recognize it in others. He will strive in vain for happiness and success in private or public life until he has achieved understanding, goodness, serenity, and contentment within himself. That, according to my exegesis, is in this connection the meaning of the Biblical text: "For what is a man profited, if he shall gain the whole world, and lose his own soul?" It is surely what Thomas Hardy meant when he wrote:

> He who is with himself dissatisfied,
> Though all the world find satisfaction in him,
> Is like a rainbow-coloured bird gone blind,
> That gives delight it shares not.

Bernard Iddings Bell

In the Preface to his book Crisis in Education, *Bernard Iddings Bell, an Episcopal clergyman, author, and educator, sets the focus for his attack on certain practices in modern education in these words: "The intention is to disturb a pseudopatriotic complacency; to recall with alarm the cultural childishness revealed by current trends in journalism, by the radio, by our magazines of large circulation and by our best-selling books, by the substitution of purchased amusement for recreation actively pursued, by the caliber of our drama and cinema, by mass response to emotionalized propaganda, by advertising which appeals chiefly to greed or to vanity, by the patent decay in good manners . . . by all the various aspects of behavior which indicate to a dispassionate student of human affairs the incompetence of a people and the insecurity of a civilization; to ask to what extent our educational theory and practice are responsible for the unsatisfactory state of our life and culture."*

Although Bell's statistics are obviously dated, his specific proposals for educational reform are very much under debate. "First Steps in Reformation" *is the final chapter of* Crisis in Education.

41

FIRST STEPS IN REFORMATION*

. . . Education is something which develops not *in vacuo* but in a society, in a culture into which the schools and colleges and universities are caught up. Sometimes observers of education do not remember this. They suppose that administrators and teachers can mold a civilization to their will. The opposite is far more true: that the desires of the citizens generally bring almost irresistible pressure on school people to train children — and adults

* From *Crisis in Education* by Bernard Iddings Bell (New York: Whittlesey House, 1949), pp. 200–230. Used by permission of Mrs. Bernard Iddings Bell and Whittlesey House, New York.

— toward the fulfillment of those ends which are vulgarly esteemed valuable, to do little more than that. If the commonly valued ends are inadequate, if they are subhuman or worse, it is little the schools can do to save society. When the wise man sets out to restore through the schools life lived in terms of really human pursuits, he does well to realize that he can succeed only to a limited degree, that he can succeed at all only if he is willing to pay the price that society exacts from those who oppose the expectations of the customers: the taxpayers, the parents, the children themselves. It is hard to see how any improvement worth mentioning can come to our society as long as educators are wholly obedient servants of the Common Man. But to an extent there can be at least some betterment of the American pattern through the agency of the schools. With no notion that by way of the simple and immediate reforms which I am about to suggest any radical improvement will come about and yet with a feeling that something might thus be better done, even though only in a preliminary way, I set down a few things which seem to me to deserve immediate attention.

I

. . . The teaching profession must be organized more widely and more definitely than it now is, to see to it that the public is aroused, first of all, to insist on adequate financial support of education and, secondly, to resist all political control, all attempts to transform the schools, colleges, and universities into agencies for the spreading of government-devised propaganda.

At present we spend a pitiable amount on education, less than 1 per cent of national income. One per cent is spent by our people for reading matter: books, magazines, newspapers, which may be regarded by the optimistic as money used for education. Add the two items together, and we get, at the very outside, 2 per cent of national income expended on things of the mind plus academic training. We spend far more on luxuries. A survey made in 1941 showed that the average family had then an income of $1,905. The average family expenditure for automobiles was $171, for recreation, $69; for tobacco, $35; for reading material, $16; for education, $15. Professor S. E. Harris, who cites these figures, sensibly concludes that "in the light of large increases in luxury expenditures generally and the small rise in expenditures for education over these years, it is difficult to take at its face value the statement frequently made that Americans cannot afford to pay more for education."[1]

They can pay more, but they will pay more only when it is taxed out of them. It is a curious characteristic of the usual contemporary American that he will contribute little or nothing voluntarily toward the support of social services: for health, for safety, for education; that he prefers to waste his

[1] Seymour E. Harris, *How Shall We Pay for Education?*, Harper & Brothers, New York, 1948.

substance not in riotous living but in fripperies and amusements; that because he has been taught it, he assumes that government will provide and pay for the social services. To that extent almost all our people, including some of the most Tory Republicans, are Socialists. Governments politically chosen and seeking reelection usually give to the social services according to the intensity of popular pressures, not according to surveyed need. If education is to get the money it must have (or else continue to be the anemic thing it is), the educators must shout long and lustily and get as many other people as possible, especially parents, to shout with them long and lustily until their voices are heard in every town meeting, city or county council, state legislature, the Congress in Washington.

But at the very same time that it cries for money enough to do its important job, the profession, again with the secured backing of enlightened parents, must resist firmly all attempts on the part of political persons and boards to control its policies and personnel. Otherwise, . . . education will soon become only an agency for the entrenchment in privilege of whatever class happens to dominate the State.

. . . Thus to insist upon support and freedom, both at the same time, will sound like heresy to the usual American statesman; but for all that, the thing is a necessity, quite as much a necessity in the United States as in Great Britain, where the battle for support and freedom at the same time has largely been won.

II

We need to recognize that there is an inexcusable waste of student time involved in our system of schooling as now organized. Formal education takes entirely too long.

The waste injures, first of all, those who are going on to the professions: medicine, the law, business administration, diplomacy and consular service, education, forestry, agriculture, research in science, and the rest. Consider for example the young American of today who desires to become a medical doctor. After leaving high school at eighteen years of age, he must go four years to college, then four years to a medical school (if it is a good one), then two years to an internship. By the time he is through with all this and ready to begin work, he is twenty-eight years old. Then — and probably not until then — he can get busy, settle down, marry. About the same amount of time should be required in the other professions.

The waste also hurts those who are going into business, industry, finance. These should have, and the best of them demand, four years in college, after which they must get jobs and learn how to handle themselves in terms of their jobs. This takes four or five years more. They too are well on toward thirty before they can function competently. Even young men and women who desire to learn a trade, if they are to have anything of a general education, are in their twenties before they are ready for apprenticeship.

This is obviously too long a time to spend on education apart from self-support and self-expression; and it is unduly extravagant for the country as a whole to support out of labor so many people for so many years. In consequence, the tendency has been to telescope the college and technical or professional training, with resulting restriction in the amount and adequacy of general education for citizenship and for a rich and rational enjoyment of living. When we bemoan the too utilitarian nature of our colleges and to is largely forced on them by sheer pressure to get the students out and about some extent of our high schools, we might have grace to remember that this their business at a reasonable age. If we are to have both general education and vocational training — and obviously we need them both — we must avoid all possible waste and duplication from the beginning to the end of our system.

Most observers are sure that the major waste is in the elementary schools and high schools. How to remedy this will require a great deal of study on the part of experts who are not hindered by the inertia of things as they are. It would even now seem possible and worth while to divide our schools somewhat differently from the way they are traditionally divided in the United States. The usual method is:

a. Eight years of grammar school, ages six through fourteen
b. Four years of high school, ages fifteen through eighteen
c. Four years of college, ages nineteen through twenty-two
d. Three or four years of professional training, ages twenty-three through twenty-five or twenty-six.

Instead of this it is suggested that we set up:

a. Six years of grammar school, ages six through twelve
b. Four years of intermediate school, ages thirteen through sixteen
c. Three years of college, ages seventeen through nineteen
d. Four years of professional- and technical-school training, ages twenty through twenty-three

The new grammar school should be required to teach in six years all that the grammar school now takes eight years to give. No other nation encourages its teachers and pupils to fool around the way ours do "in the grades."

The four-year intermediate school (call it "high school" if you will, but the term has gained an aroma of undisciplined adolescence, of ridiculous pretension to social prematurity, which makes it an unfortunate name for anything that wishes to be regarded as a real school) should complete the training, begun lower down, in the skills necessary for reading, writing, arithmetic, accuracy in sensory observation; should enable pupils to go into algebra, geometry, history, the study of nature; should expose them to contact with the best in arts and letters.

At the end of the intermediate school, at about sixteen, those who cannot or will not profit further by intellectual disciplines should be directed into special schools which can develop them on manual lines plus civilize them by more but very much simplified study of literature, of history, of scientific principles and techniques.

The rest of the pupils should go on through the college for three years, years devoted to dialectical and humanistic studies plus first steps in acquiring the techniques (laboratory and otherwise) which will be used in later professional training. Even if these techniques are never used in the years to come, they are worth while because they have distinct disciplinary value.

Then *the professional or technical schools* should take over for four years.

About three years would be saved by the redistribution suggested; two in grammar and one later on. Equally important, *everyone who has the ability could afford time to get both general and vocational education.* The present scandalous (one is tempted to say "criminal" and would except that the fault is caused by incompetence rather than malice) throwing away of precious time and cultivation of lazy habits in thought and action would exist no more.

A radical redistribution of school time — this or some other — is imperative, and quickly.[2]

[2] One institution of learning in the United States more than others has recognized and tried to deal with the necessity for a new and more realistic arrangement in the successive stages of education — the University of Chicago, with its "College" and "Divisions."

The College at Chicago is entered normally at age sixteen, on graduation from a junior high school or after two years in an old-line high school. Only highly competent candidates are admitted; others are expected to stay at home and go on through the usual senior high school, maybe through the conventional and, Chicago thinks, pedestrian junior college, or even the almost equally jog-trot senior college common in America. After four years of rigorous training in dialectic and in the basic substance of the humanities, the social sciences, mathematics and the natural sciences, the bachelors' degree is conferred, normally at about age twenty, on such as can pass rigorous comprehensive examinations in the three fields; and college days are over. Only those are encouraged to go farther who have definite and specialized objectives. Up to this point the student has followed a rigid, inflexible, and difficult discipline in thinking and in general knowledge. Now he enters the Divisions, the University proper, where his specialization at once begins. After three years, normally at age twenty-three, he receives the M.A. degree and, if he wishes, after two years more, the Ph.D. degree at about age twenty-five.

Much as one who observes the Chicago situation may admire the general result, there is a certain inevitable trepidation at the thought of boys and girls of sixteen and seventeen being plunged into university life and left to sink or swim on their own in almost entire freedom from other than intellectual supervision. The results, social and personal, are often pathetically ludicrous, more than occasionally tragic, almost always an unnecessary burden to the student. Unless there is a revision of the College in this respect the whole experiment may come a cropper; those in midadolescence are not adults and cannot with justice to themselves be treated as adults. A good many people in charge at Chicago recognize this but not all; for some it is hard to admit that boys and girls are not made into men and women merely by following a sound curriculum.

Nor, to be sure, does the Chicago arrangement save much time. It does insure, however, that by age twenty-five the student has had an opportunity, much larger than is usual in this country, to get rigorous training in how to think, a sound general education, and competent graduate-school training.

If the College can be in some way better controlled socially, perhaps geographically segregated, and if the scheme can be preceded by more rapid, more sound work in elementary school and junior high school, the University of Chicago arrangement will be even more valuable than it is, though *only for competent students.*

III

We must make it possible for highly competent students of low income or from low-income families to go on with their education through high school, college, graduate or professional school at public expense, and this without expectation that they take time off from their studies to support or partially support themselves by gainful employment.

In this respect England is more realistic, at least above the secondary-school level, more "democratic," than we in the United States. For years England has had a system of county scholarships — the counties more or less correspond to our states. Anyone about to be graduated from a secondary school may take the carefully devised examination for a scholarship. If he shows considerable intellectual promise he receives an annual grant sufficient to cover, at the university or professional school of his choice, all fees, lodging and board expenses, clothing, even a reasonable amount of fun. He gets a lump sum ranging from about a thousand to sixteen hundred dollars or so a year and can spend it as he desires. The only requirement is that he shall continue to do first-rate work in his university or other higher school.

"Do you expect the recipients of these sums to repay them later on?" I asked an examiner for Hampshire.

"Of course not," he replied. "The grants are an investment for the nation's future leadership and effectiveness."

"And how many scholarships are awarded annually?"

"As many as there are young men and women who can show us that they have the necessary brains."

Oxford and Cambridge are commonly regarded in America as attended by the sons and daughters either of the nobility or of the economically privileged; as a matter of fact, a large proportion of those studying on the Cam and the Cher are poor men's children, supported by county scholarships. The same is true of the younger universities.

Of late Great Britain has come to recognize more and more that a similar arrangement ought to be made for bright but poor children in secondary schools; that there should be grants sufficient to pay, when needed, a child's share of family living expenses as well as his fees, so that he may go on with his studies and give his whole time to them. Take, for instance, the following recommendation to the (national) Board of Education: "We recommend that the Board of Education should ensure and secure maintenance allowances and other aids to pupils in grant-in-aid secondary schools sufficient to prevent children from being withdrawn prematurely solely on economic

---

The suggestion offered in the text is not by any means the only one which, if followed, might do the trick; there are those who think it has merit. At all events the 8-4-4-3 division which now prevails in the United States is wasteful, ineffective, perpetuated chiefly by inertia and timidity.

[Editor's note: The University of Chicago has since returned to the standard four-year, 18–22 age pattern. In recent years early entrants have comprised only about five per cent of entering College classes.]

grounds; and that when fees in secondary schools are abolished and when families' or children's allowances are in operation, the Board should ensure some supplement to these aids if experience shows such to be necessary."[3] This recommendation is being followed in postwar educational reorganization.

We are not yet so wise. Often our state or municipal universities do, it is true, provide free or nearly free tuition, and almost all our secondary schools are of the free-tuition type; but tuition fees are a small part of the cost of education to pupils and their families. We still handicap the poor man's sons and daughters. It is conservatively estimated that going on beyond the high school is financially possible only for one in three really bright children of parents whose family income is less than twenty-five hundred dollars; for one in two whose family income is between three and five thousand dollars; for one in one whose family income is over seven thousand dollars. They do not all go, of course, from the higher income group, but it can be wangled when desired.

Moreover, those who matriculate in higher education are often forced to drop out for financial reasons. Just before the war this was true of 12 per cent of students who entered our colleges. It is also true that many high-school students, often the brighter ones, must leave school because their parents cannot afford to keep them longer from gainful labors. Such cases are most frequent in states where wages are low but in which, thanks to the oneness of our national setup, the cost of living mounts at a rate almost equal to that in more affluent commonwealths.

Even when bright students do not have to drop out of high school and college, frequently they are forced to support or partly to support themselves while studying by all sorts of time-wasting and energy-consuming part-time labor: waiting on table, stoking furnaces, baby sitting, taxi driving, all kinds of jobs. So general is this practice that Americans have rationalized it and find, or pretend to find, great virtue in the business. As a matter of fact, it is at least 90 per cent vicious. Study in high school or beyond ought to demand full-time effort; if it does not, the standards need to be raised. The strain of self-support while studying is often inhuman. I know a graduate law student, for instance, in one of our foremost universities who last year, in order to make both ends meet, worked seven hours a night, seven nights a week, at a hotel desk. The double duty — this and his studies — broke his health, and he had to quit the university for a year in order to recover his nervous equilibrium. His is a not unheard-of case. Even those who do not break under strain often do inferior work and frequently injure their health so that they pay heavily later on, all their lives, with nervous indigestion or worse. Such nonsense is not only wasteful of brain power; it is a handicap to the leadership of tomorrow.

It is hard not to agree with S. E. Harris who, after study of the facts,

[3] *Teachers and Youth Leaders*, Board of Education, H.M. Stationery Office, London, 1944.

statistical and otherwise, concludes that ". . . the loss of talent is serious. . . . We need not only free schools for all and tuition subsidies for the talented in college; we also need aid to finance the upkeep of those who show talent or promise at all ages."[4] *We should, as a matter of investment for the public welfare, adequately support men and women who show evidence of superior brain power. Only thus can we really equalize and democratize educational opportunity.*

How high a standard of intelligence is it profitable to subsidize publicly? Professor Ralph W. Tyler of the University of Chicago thinks we should certainly look after at least the top 1 per cent, since from it will come the persons most capable of productive and creative research.[5] This is not enough. Excellent work is done, indispensable work, by those who are not supergeniuses. The British way is good: fix no percentage and do not place entire reliance on intelligence quotients; whenever a boy comes along who by examination shows high promise of achievement and who has need, provide him with money enough to cover tuition and upkeep on a modest but decent level; see to it that he continues to enjoy this assistance as long as he continues to do first-rate work; do the same for the bright girl; and see to it also that public money is not wasted on the higher education of those who are mediocre or worse.[6] *Refuse to finance those who are not competent, forbid students to "work their way through," adequately provide for those who are able scholastically, and the standards of achievement will rise overnight.*

IV

Forbid by law the assigning at any stage of schooling of more than twenty-five pupils to a teacher. It is impossible really to teach more pupils than that. This is an entirely proper demand made by the better educational associations. But if we satisfy it we must have, for the same number of pupils as at present, at least 25 per cent more teachers than now. Where do we get them? Whence do we pay them?

V

We must enlist, train, and sustain both more teachers and much more able teachers than we now have, and this at every level. The teaching profession is demanding more pay. Of the justice of this insistence, more in a moment or two. First let us ask if the teachers that we have at present,

---

[4] Seymour E. Harris, *How Shall We Pay for Education?*, Harper & Brothers, New York, 1948.

[5] *Ibid.*

[6] If the mediocre or worse have money of their own to waste or their parents and friends are foolish enough to furnish it, let them go to high school or college or beyond as long as the authorities of these various places of resort will tolerate their presence; but let them do it at their own charges.

taking them by and large, are worth more than we pay them. The answer is that for the most part they are not.[7] Many of them have not had an education, either general or professional, sufficient for effective teaching.

> The average four-year college course given in American colleges and universities does not encompass an impressive amount of "higher" education, measured by, say, British standards. But only fifteen American states out of the forty-eight require a college degree for teachers; and more than half of all the teachers in the country have none. Over 6 per cent of American public-school teachers have no training beyond high school; 35 per cent have had less than two years of post-high-school training; and over 14 per cent hold substandard certificates, indicating incapacity to meet even the minimum requirements of their states . . . and it is certainly no sign of progress that the average American teacher today has less college education than the average of five years ago.[8]

Even when we recognize these low-qualification standards, however, almost any unprejudiced observer will admit that our teachers are not paid enough to live on. They were underpaid before the war; they are worse underpaid today. Between 1939 and 1948 the general cost of living rose about 55 per cent; the pay of teachers, in spite of an estimated increase of three hundred fifty million dollars in 1947–1948 over 1946–1947, has gone up only about 25 per cent. Stipends will have to be raised at least a further billion dollars if we are to establish a wage for teachers of from twenty-five hundred to six thousand dollars a year, a reasonable and not extravagant remuneration.

The low pay now prevailing is the largest factor in preventing the enlistment of the proper kind of women in teaching, and it prevents most men from even thinking of teaching except in university positions; it also hinders the continuance of qualified persons in the profession. But there are other deterrents beside low pay.

There is also insecurity of tenure. In most parts of the country teachers in grammar schools and high schools are "hired" year by year, their competence judged and sentence rendered annually by local school boards made up for the most part of popularly elected persons inexperienced in pedagogy and subject to political pressure and to even less reputable forms of social prejudice. Even in higher education there is insecurity for those under the rank of associate professor, which means for the greater part of every college staff.

Another hindrance to our getting enough competent teachers is the common feeling that teaching is not a profession of dignity, not a learned profession, only a sort of hack trade which receives little public honor, honor such as might help make the low pay endurable.

---

[7] "The supply of well-qualified teachers has always been insufficient to meet the demands. Under such circumstances it has been difficult to maintain standards for certification of teachers, and thousands of persons have been certified, in many cases granted teachers' certificates for life, who are not at all well qualified for the positions they hold." Russell and Judd, *The American Educational System*, Houghton Mifflin Company, Boston, 1940.

[8] Dorothy Thompson, "Education and Civilization," *Ladies' Home Journal*, October, 1947, p. 11.

There is also the irksome difficulty, widely known, of a teacher's having to deal with undisciplined children. A schoolmistress whom I knew to be experienced and able, living in the Far West, a master of arts from a good university, once wrote me that at the age of thirty-five, after ten years' service in a public junior high school, she had abandoned the profession and taken a position selling blouses for a jobbing firm. I protested at the change and asked if she were doing it in the hope of more money. She replied, "Not at all. I lose my pension rights; besides, I am not sure I shall make more in the new work. The truth is that I could not stick it any longer. I could not face the thought of being insulted for another year, day after day, by a pack of impudent and unlicked cubs of fourteen or so, the males crude enough and the females worse, whose homes did not discipline them, discipline of whom was on principle ignored by the very 'progressive' and in my opinion wholly unrealistic school authorities, and whom I was forbidden by law in any way myself to punish. Life is too short and self-respect is too strong for me to go on."

I told this to a teacher in a school in the Bronx, one of the best esteemed teachers in the New York City school system. "Of course," she said. "Your acquaintance is quite right about it. The same thing is true in New York City. A woman must have the hide of a rhinoceros to teach in the public schools in our metropolis. It is a rare day that I am not insulted by some of the little beasts, cursed at, shoved and jostled, called a vile name or two. If I let myself notice, I should have to follow your friend's example. I have learned to ignore it."

In parts of the country that are more civilized than the monster cities, in smaller communities where the home has not collapsed, in places where administrators try to deal with real children instead of with the little angels imagined by a good many professors of education, teachers are not quite so trampled on by their charges; but, speaking generally, "the teacher's lot is not a happy one," and gentlemen and gentlewomen think twice before they contemplate teaching and often do not think twice about abandoning it later on for other vocations.

Coupled with this resentment against undiscipline, teachers often feel an irritation at being ordered about by theorists from schools of education who are put into posts of authority over them and who, though they have had small teaching experience themselves, continually want to change procedures to fit in with new ideas thought up in a study somewhere. Teachers think that before pedagogic changes are made, particularly changes which involve radical adjustment of philosophical approach, they who do the instructing should be consulted and persuaded and convinced of the necessity and wisdom thereof; that reforms should come not from the top down but from the bottom up. They are weary of change and rechange. They see their pupils regarded not as growing human beings but as guinea pigs for experimentation and themselves as unwilling laboratory technicians. Inner revolt drives thousands out of teaching every year and prevents other thousands from preparing for it, and these frequently the cream of the crop. Most teachers realize the facts of the case, but it is usually considered impolitic to say anything about them in public unless one first gets out of teaching. This curious silence is good evidence of "the sickness that destroyeth in the noonday."

To sum up, if we wish teachers in proper numbers and of the right sort, we should:

a. Pay them from twenty-five hundred to six thousand dollars a year and give them assurance of tenure unless incompetence can be proved, and proper pensions on retirement after service.

b. Raise the academic requirements for teachers as rapidly as possible so that teaching becomes a reputable profession. If pedagogues are paid a living wage, the public may thus be made at least a little more sure that it gets its money's worth.[9]

c. Subsidize secondary-school and college students who show potential competence for teaching so that they may prepare themselves for it. Give them if they have need an annual allowance of at least a thousand dollars from the public funds, to be used toward tuition and support in reputable places of training, with a requirement that if they do not enter the profession or leave it voluntarily after less than five years' service they shall pay back all sums advanced to them at the rate of $200 a year.[10]

d. Require that no one be given supervisory authority over teachers who has had less than five years of actual teaching experience.

e. Restore to the schools a discipline sufficiently effective to protect teachers from insult and intimidation at the hands of their pupils.

Other things are doubtless necessary for getting and holding competent instructors in sufficient numbers; but the steps just mentioned would seem almost indispensable.

VI

We need to combat the notion that the only attitude toward God which is legitimate in a tax-supported school is the attitude that ignores God as though He does not exist or, if He does exist, does not matter.

It is of course proper that atheists should be able to send their children to atheistic schools if they so desire; but it is hard to see why atheists, few in number as they are, should be allowed to force atheistic-by-negation educa-

---

[9] How fast should standards be raised? At least this much: that by 1955 it will be true that no one will be licensed to teach, in any school in the land, who has not had two years' general education beyond the high school plus one year's training in the theory and practice of education; that by 1960 no one will be licensed to teach in any school who has not had three years of general education beyond the high school plus one full year in professional subjects; that by 1960 no one will be licensed to teach in a secondary school who has not the master-of-arts degree, with at least one of the five years beyond the high school that are required for that degree devoted to a study of pedagogy. These would seem to be an almost irreducible minimum of requirement, that is if we are to stop playing around with education in the United States.

[10] It is far better to subsidize normal students than to subsidize normal schools. Subsidized schools are subject to political pressures; subsidized students are not so easily pliable.

tion on the children of the great majority of us who do pay at least theoretical attention to the Deity. As the American school system is now conducted, more and more conducted, there is no such thing as religious liberty in American education. There is liberty only to be unreligious. "In God we trust" we still put on our coins; we cannot entrust our children to Him. If the public schools must "leave religion out," then the only decent thing is to permit religious groups to run their own schools, which of course we now do, and to give them tax money to run them with, which we do not.[11] Such a step would not in the least violate the principle, embodied in the Constitution, that there must be no established Church in the United States. No one wishes to set up an exclusive *ecclesia*. Those who think that to give public funds to a religious body for schools in which religion matters is somehow tied up with reuniting Church and State, would seem to be just plain ignorant and illogical people, and this whether they sit on cracker barrels or on the Supreme Court of the United States.

If it be contended that multiple school systems divide the body politic, which to some extent they do, then in reply it may be pointed out that the only way to retain complete unity and at the same time give freedom to those who desire that their children shall recognize God is to see to it that time is given in the public schools to a common examination by the growing chil-

[11] 1. "Let no one say that in a nation where there are different religious beliefs it is impossible for public instruction otherwise than by neutral or mixed schools. In such a case it becomes the duty of the State, indeed it is the easier and more reasonable method of procedure, to leave free scope to the initiative of the Church and the Family, while giving them such assistance as justice demands." So wrote Pope Pius XI in 1929 in the encyclical on *The Education of Christian Youth*. I am not a Roman Catholic, but I do not see how this statement can be refuted except by an appeal to prejudice. What the Pope here says applies to all sorts of private schools. The State has the right, the duty, to see to it that they are pedagogically up to standard; if they are, they should be supported on the same per capita basis as those run by the State itself.

2. The Lambeth Conference of Anglican Bishops from all over the world, which met in London in July–August 1948, made perfectly plain in its Resolution 29 what one non-Roman Church with 35,000,000 members feels about parochial schools: "The Conference, while giving full support to state education, is convinced that there is a unique value for the community in the long tradition of church education. The Conference believes that the freedom of experiment which this tradition affords and the religious, moral, and social training which is its specific purpose are invaluable for the best interests of education and that everything possible should be done to open the benefits of such church education to all who desire them." (*The Lambeth Conference 1948*, London, S.P.C.K., p. 33.)

3. "The fundamental theory of liberty upon which all governments of this Union repose excludes any general power of the State to standardize its children by forcing them to accept instruction from public teachers only. The child is not the mere creature of the State; those who nurture him and direct his destiny have the right, coupled with the high duty, to recognize and prepare him for additional obligations." These were the words of the Supreme Court of the United States in decision of the "Oregon Case," in which the Court nullified, in 1922, a law passed by the state of Oregon which required that every child go to public school and so abolished all private schools. But, it may be asked, if only the public schools are state-supported, if to send children to a school not state-run is possible only at an extra cost beyond the means of most citizens, is the usual parent not in effect coerced to accept the public school even against his conscience? Where is the liberty guaranteed by the Constitution? It would seem to be liberty almost impossible for the poor and reserved for the financially better off.

dren of what are the basic religious and moral ideas, all this taught objectively
and with no desire to bring about conviction (which is the province of the
Church and the home), and also to furnish opportunity in school hours for
the various current faiths in a community to teach their own children what
they themselves believe. But this is unlawful according to the Supreme
Court (Scopes case, 1948). Is the price of national unity, then, the abandonment of all religion? This is the nub of the matter.[12]

VII

*The schools should refuse to assume burdens properly parental; they have
quite enough to do without that.* If the American parent is incompetent to
look after the physical, social, and ethical upbringing of his or her children,
which is certainly true of many parents, possibly true of most of them, then
those who have the national welfare at heart, instead of piling impossible
burdens on the schools, had better make homemaking and some education
itself a basic part of schooling from six years of age onward and had better
go in dead earnest at the education of parents who already are parents.

VIII

*Adult education generally is grossly neglected among us, though happily
less so with each passing year.* The time never comes when a human being
can justly be called an "educated person." The world is not divided into the
educated and the uneducated, but rather into the educable and the un-
educable. If a man were really to come to the place that he was educated,
that is to say if he were to come to the end of growing apprehension and
understanding, all that could rightly be done to that man would be to dig a
hole and bury him. Fortunately few reach such a sad estate. The educable
process should be made available for men and women of all ages from baby-
hood to death.

Nor should it be regarded as enough to assist adults to improve their
technical skills and so increase their incomes. There is real hunger for general
knowledge, liberal knowledge, among adult persons: witness the introduction
of courses in political theory for farmers in Kansas, under the joint direction
of the Farm Bureau and the Institute of Citizenship at Kansas State College;
witness the great success of the Peoples' High Schools in Denmark,[13] which

[12] A very fine treatment, almost indispensable, of this whole matter of religion in the
public schools is J. Paul Williams, *The New Education and Religion: A Challenge to
Secularism in Education,* Association Press, New York, 1945. This book traces the history
back of our present absurd but portentous situation and examines, penetratingly and in-
formedly, every suggestion that has been made or is now being made to deal with it. It was
of course written before the 1948 decision of the Supreme Court above referred to.

[13] These are described by Sir Richard Livingstone in *The Future in Education,* The
Macmillan Company, New York, 1941; republished in his *On Education,* The Macmillan
Company, New York, 1944. Livingstone's writings about education should be read by
everyone who is concerned with what may be taught adults.

do *not* teach technology but devote themselves to the teaching of history, bases of Danish culture, the literature of the country, the principles of political and social organization, which admit no pupil under eighteen years of age and none who is not engaged in industry or agriculture; witness the wide spread of the "Great-books Movement"; witness the growth of lecture courses, women's clubs, town halls. There are many things which cannot be studied to much advantage or otherwise than in an atmosphere of artificiality except by people who are grown-up and at work: political science, for instance, or how to handle loneliness and frustration. A community ought to be thoroughly ashamed of itself which does not devote as much thought, time, money, to the education of adults over twenty as it provides for the nurture of children under twenty.

IX

Thought needs to be given to what may be done in respect to teaching morals and manners.

The chief difficulty here is that our American civilization has no agreed-upon ethical standards, standards which can be assumed and taught to the oncoming generation as a matter of course. We are a people with no common world view, no generally accepted definition of the nature and purpose of man. Such being the case, it becomes a necessity for each school or college to determine the sort of moral theory to which it intends to commit itself, together with the brand of good manners which it will derive from that theory. If this is not done, the result will be the turning out of amoral graduates and unmannered boors. The ethical commitment of a college or school should be made clear to those who teach, to those who learn, to those to whom appeal is made for pupils and support.

But to whom or to what is a man responsible for his behavior? Only to himself? In spite of the dictum of Polonius, to be true to oneself does not necessarily result in being false to no other man, not unless the self to which one is true is a self devoted to more than self. Otherwise, for people to be true each to himself or herself is more apt to result in anarchy than in an ordered way of life. Is one to be responsible, for what one is and does, only to the will of majorities? This results in a conformist mediocrity. Is one to look to the total social group for standards of behavior, for sanctions? The end of this is a totalitarian setup manipulated by the ruthless and unscrupulous, a negation of just opportunity for freedom of expression and for voluntary self-investment. Is man's responsibility to mere tradition? This is deadly to creative and critical thinking, without which no society can long survive. Is it to negation of tradition? This way lies a deal of precious nonsense and preciosity. Is human responsibility to that which is beyond man? *If so, religion is involved, primarily involved, inescapably involved in education.*

We need a deeply concerned consideration of the basis of right conduct and decent manners, a consideration carried on not merely on the level of high philosophy but also on the pedagogic level of how to train for character and social cooperation. We need this immediately, demandingly; but our professors of education, our administrators, our teachers, are usually little concerned with inquiry about purpose — purpose in politics, purpose in labor, purpose in living, purpose in anything, including purpose in education itself. This neglect is almost too absurd to be imagined; yet it is a fact. It is obviously ridiculous to try to develop growing human beings without asking what a man is to aim at and why. *We might well have a moratorium on discussion of methods and organization of education until we come to some decision about the moral ends of education.*

Ideally decision about such matters should be reached by society as a whole and govern our education as a matter of course; but in a confused state of social disruption like ours in this midtwentieth century, general agreement about morals is next to impossible. In this lies national peril; we have no agreed-upon ethical ideology; there is nothing commonly held as imperative to be promoted or defended, nothing which compels the glad devotion of lives and fortunes unless we get returns in profits and praise. It will be a long time, possibly a fatally long time, before we again have a national morality unless it be a totalitarian and secularistic morality, which God forbid. Meanwhile each school or college or university is forced to define its own concept of the good life and then strive to impart it, unless that school or college or university is content, as most are in the United States today, to deal only with secondary matters while the commonwealth drifts toward dissolution. We might at least be informing our students about what the various ethical alternatives are. *Make moral philosophy once more the central consideration in education.* Of all the steps suggested or implied for the salvation of teaching and learning, . . . this is both the most immediately required and the most difficult.

Would the taking of the nine steps which have just been mentioned serve to rescue American thinking and action from incompetence, insure maturity among us, enable us to avoid alternations of ignorant conceit and of a panic fear, make out of education in America what it reasonably ought to be? Obviously not; but they would help a little, more than a little. In excuse for their obvious inadequacy as a program of reform, let it be remembered again that it is [my] purpose . . . not to prescribe but to diagnose; perhaps to get the patient, which is all of us, to know that in respect to our pedagogics we are a sick folk, that we have been too long fooled by doctrinaire pedagogues who ignore man as he is and children as they are. In short it is our thesis that education in these United States is in crisis, that it is being judged by the relentless impact of reality, that it is being judged and found wanting. Once we realize this, we shall soon have both wisdom and bravery to set about a radical and comprehensive reform.

INDEX

OF AUTHORS